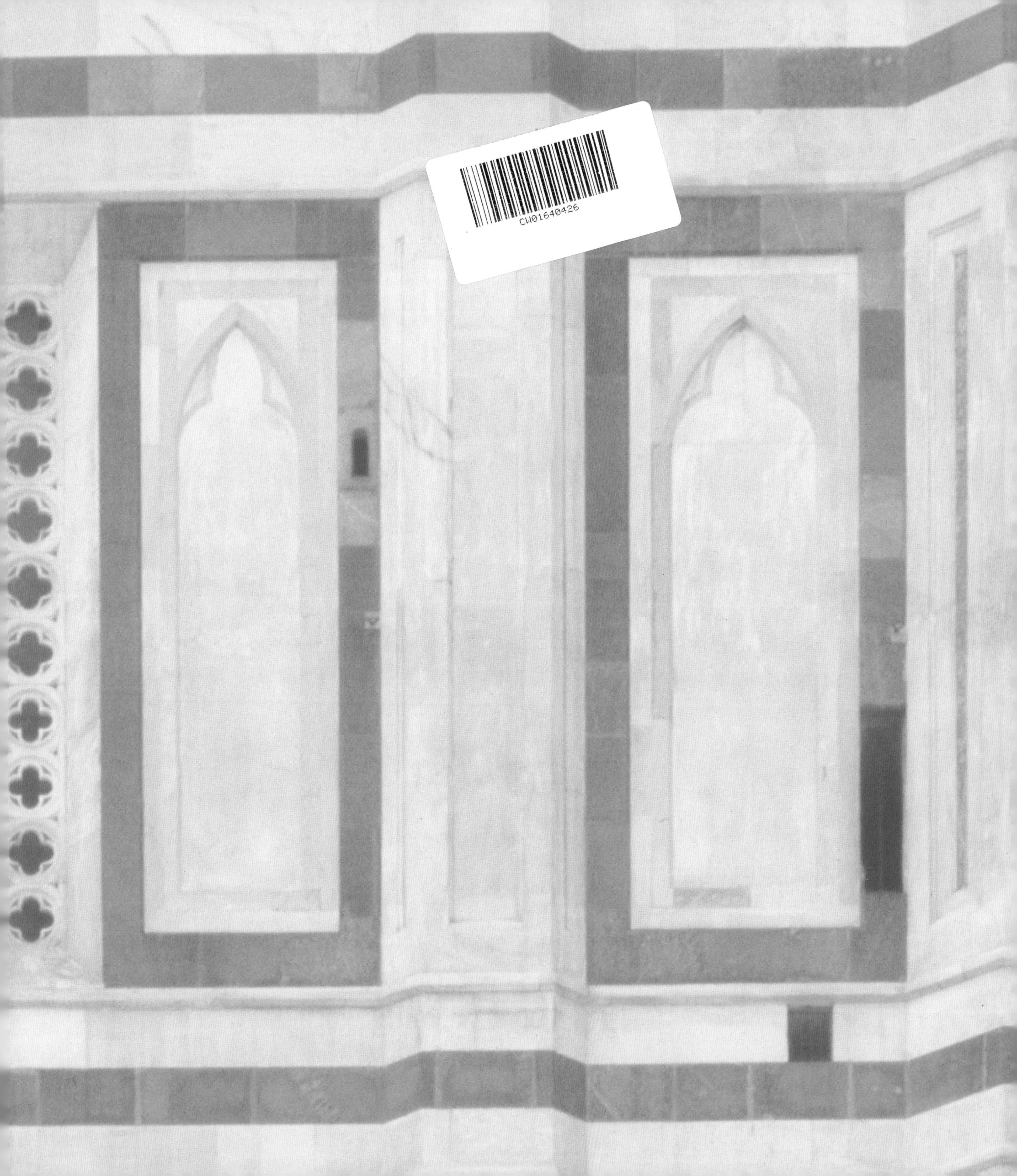

florence | the city and its architecture

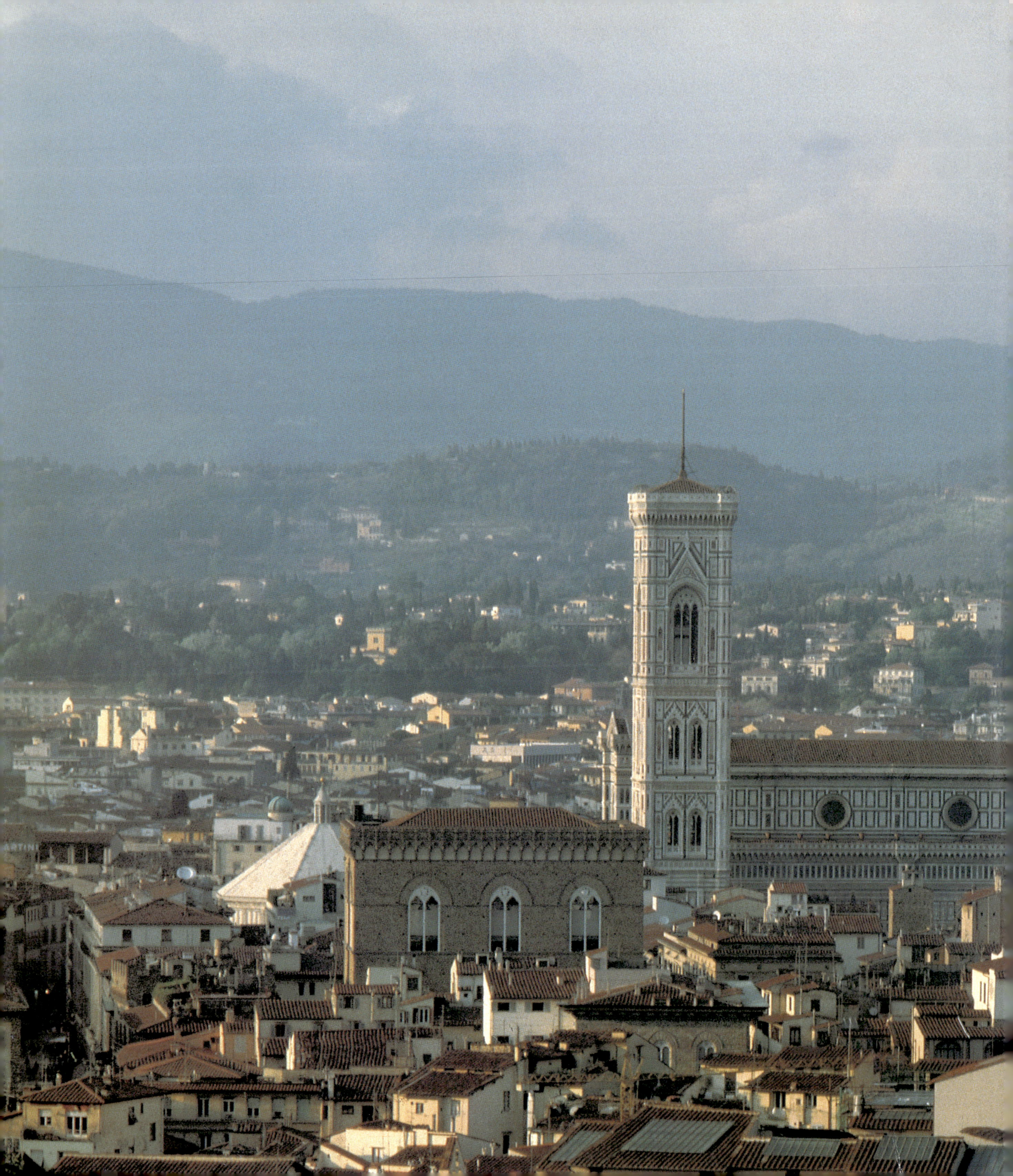

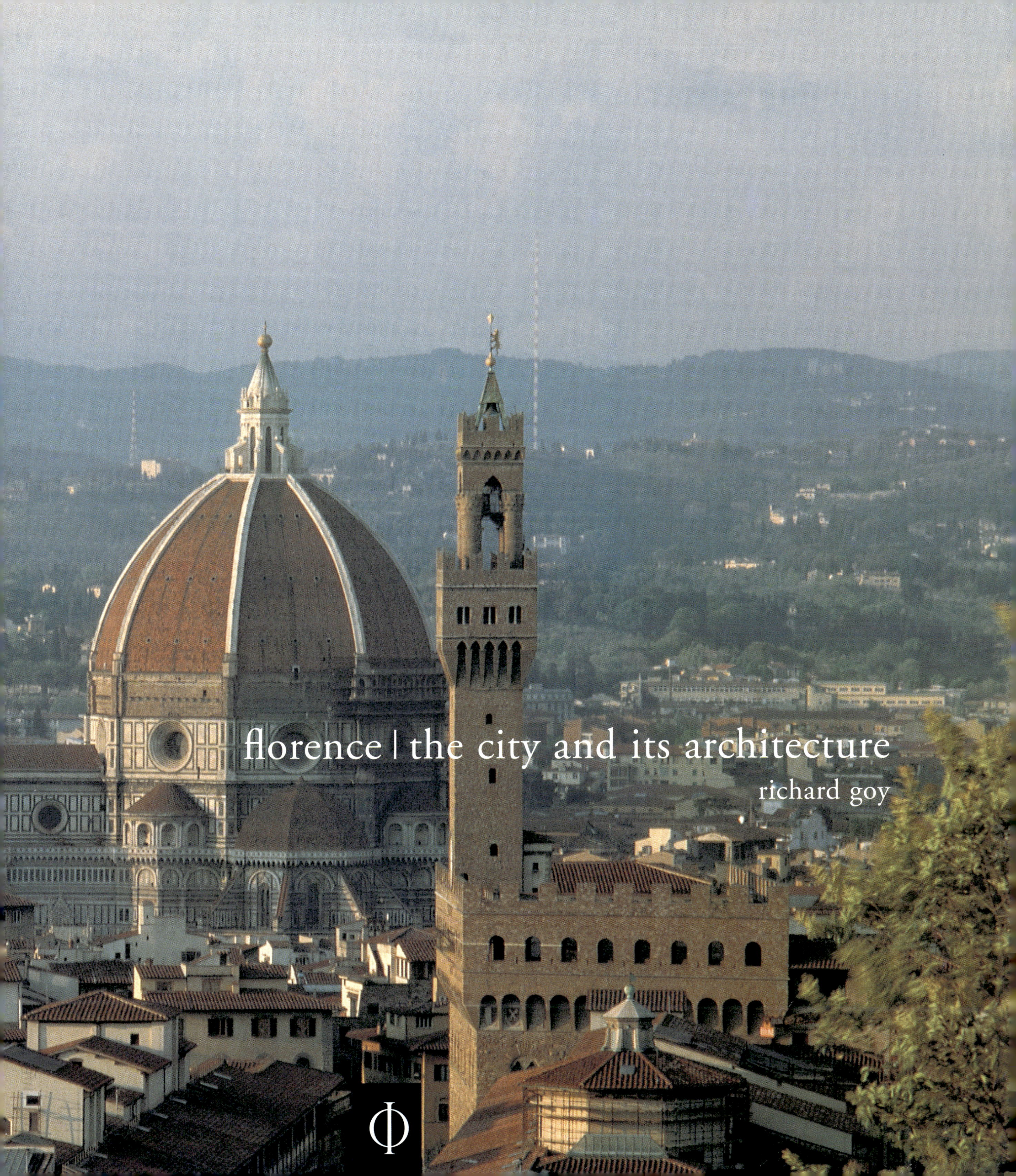
florence | the city and its architecture
richard goy

Contents

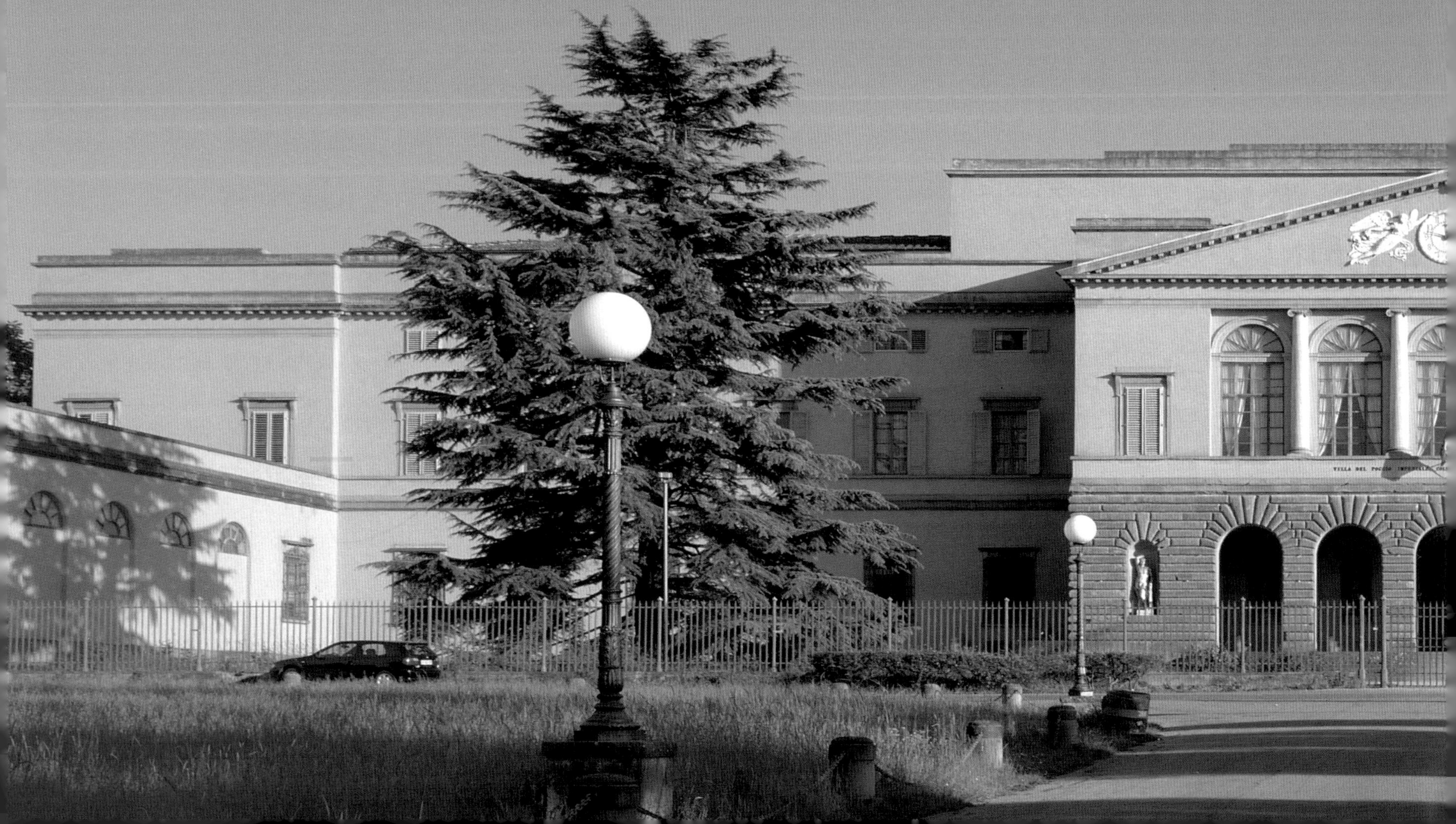

Part III | the architecture of florence

Part IV | florence since unification

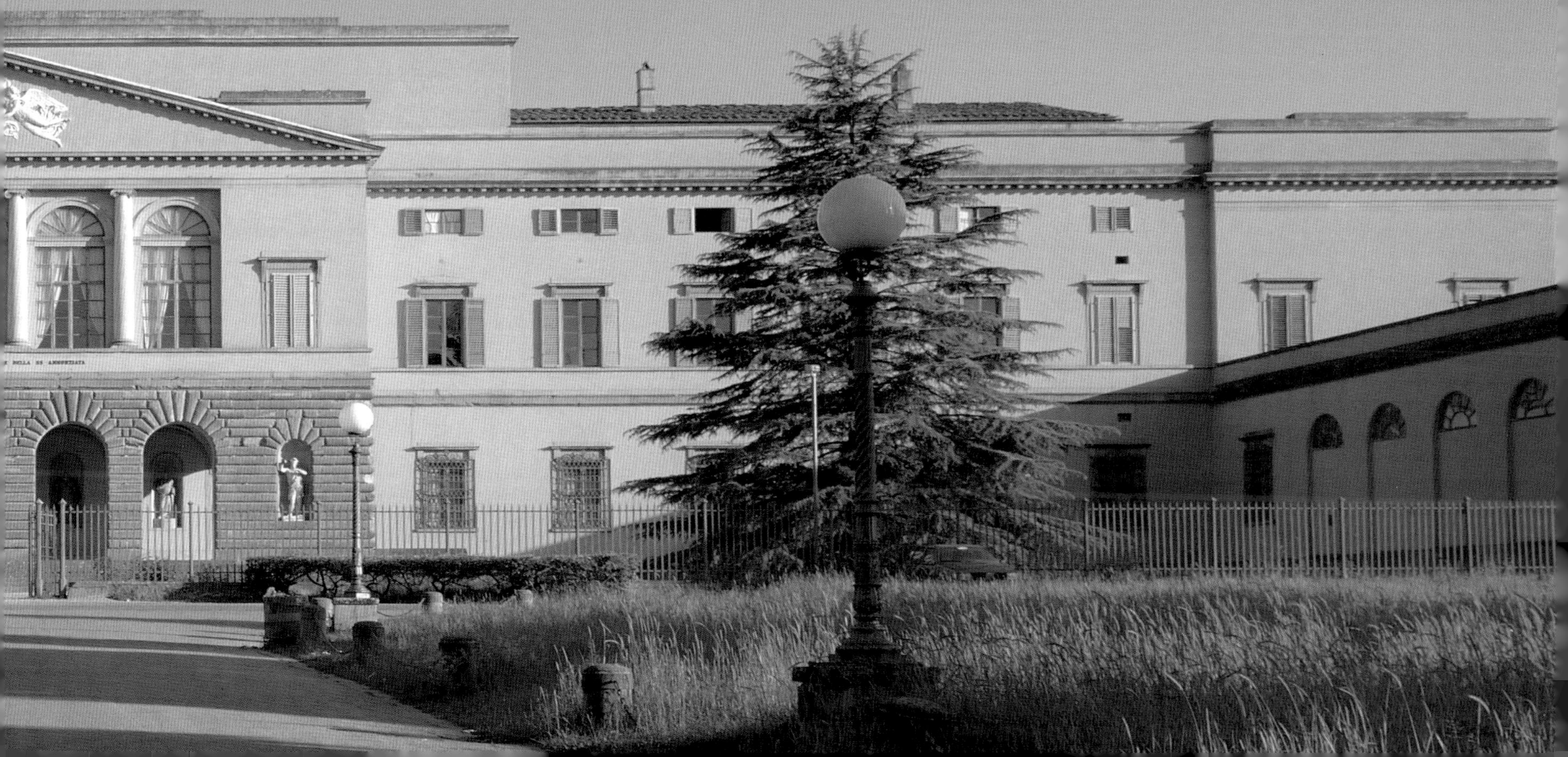

For Nubar and Pallina

Introduction

"See where it lies before us in a sun-lighted valley, bright with the winding Arno, and shut in by swelling hills; its domes, and towers, and palaces, rising from the rich country in a glittering heap, and shining in the sun like gold." **Charles Dickens**, *Pictures from Italy* (1844) [1]

Florence holds a truly unique role in the consciousness of the Western world as the city where in many ways our modern era is perceived to have begun. That extraordinary period of creativity in all the visual arts that began, arguably, with Cimabue and Giotto, and reached its precocious climax with the Mannerist genius of Michelangelo, is still popularly identified as the era in which the more distant medieval world, with its obscure rites and rituals, its arcane political structures, its social complexities and cultural ambiguities, finally gave way — so the myth tells us — to the clarity, reason, logic, and rationality of the Renaissance. Naturally, as with all popular myths, a kernel of objective truth has been wrapped in countless layers of simplification and interpretation. It is true, for example, that in Florence in the thirteenth and fourteenth centuries, a language developed that was to form the basis of modern Italian, largely through the threefold genius of Dante, Petrarch, and Boccaccio. It is also true that the inspired patronage of Cosimo and Lorenzo de' Medici, and Giovanni Rucellai and others, gave rise to the pivotal architectural works of Brunelleschi and Alberti. And it is equally the case that the broader patronage of the two Medici and their contemporaries, the Pitti, the Strozzi, and the Pazzi, gave rise, among many other events, to the renewed study of classical philosophers and to the establishment of cultural academies and public libraries from which this knowledge could be disseminated. For about two centuries, from the era of Dante to that of Michelangelo, the comparatively small but extremely wealthy city of Florence exerted an influence over the development of Western civilization that to this day remains the subject of research and debate, an influence unequaled in any other city within the Western tradition. The reasons for this extraordinary contribution are complex and must be considered in the social, cultural, and political context of the city in the later duecento and early trecento, the era of Dante — a period in which Florence was an exceptionally prosperous city, but also a city riven by often bloody factional strife.

Florence's political, economic, and social history must be examined in order to understand the foundations of these cultural achievements. In the early medieval period, Florence was simply one of the larger cities of Tuscany, not a great deal more populous or wealthy than, for example, Pisa or Siena. But it was very well located within the region, and the development of two economic activities, one productive, the other financial, formed the cornerstone for the development of the city's extraordinary wealth: the wool and textile industry, which came to employ thousands there, and banking. By the middle of the thirteenth century Florence was the foremost banking city in Europe, a position that was maintained unassailed until the financial crises of the 1340s. For a century, therefore, the great banking clans of the city, chiefly the Bardi, Peruzzi, and Frescobaldi, dominated international finance in Western Europe on an unprecedented scale. The greatest of the banking clans were members of the all-important *arte*, or guild, of the Calimala, as were almost all of the ancient mercantile dynasties of the city: the Acciaiuoli, Alberti, Capponi, Mozzi, Pazzi, Portinari, Spini, Strozzi, and so on, twenty-four of them in all. Not all were equally important as bankers, but collectively the banking power of the Calimala eventually surpassed that of neighboring Siena; the Calimala bankers acted for the kings of England, and were bankers to the papacy, to the kings of Naples and of Sicily, to the king of France, and to the Holy Roman emperor. Florence's bankers were not only by far the most powerful financiers in Europe, but they also either created or developed most of the banking techniques that we now take for granted: Bills of exchange, cheques, double-entry bookkeeping, and trading insurance were all introduced or developed in Florence during the thirteenth century, and despite the physical dangers of handling large sums of hard currency in this era, the gold florin became a universally accepted currency unit in Europe and beyond.

If the bankers of the Calimala represented one pole of Florentine wealth and power in the thirteenth and early fourteenth centuries, the other pole was represented by the Arte della Lana, the guild of the wool and textile industries. Although the bankers concentrated wealth in a comparatively small number of hands, by 1300 the Lana had overtaken the power and wealth of the Calimala largely as a result of the sheer size of the industry. The fourteenth-century chronicler Giovanni Villani reported that there were no fewer than three hundred workshops in the city during this period, which collectively employed around one-third of the entire population of Florence. Wool was imported from much of Europe — England, Flanders, Spain — and North Africa, and was then dyed and processed before being reexported, at greatly enhanced value. By the middle of the fourteenth century, when the Lana had already passed its peak in numbers and production, it is estimated that Florence still processed 10 percent of all the wool cloth in Europe.

Medieval Florence thus based its wealth on these two principal fields of activity, in both of which the city was unrivaled. This wealth was used not only for art patronage, but also to develop the city architecturally. The civic monuments of the Bargello and the Palazzo Vecchio both evince in stout, daunting stonework the city's pride in its government institutions, and at the very end of the thirteenth century, construction began on Florence's magnificent new cathedral, destined to become the symbol of the city's piety and spiritual strength, as well as an enduring monument to the skills and resources of its people. The extraordinary period of creativity under Cosimo de' Medici Il Vecchio and then Lorenzo Il Magnifico between around 1420 and 1500 was by no means a phenomenon without precedent in the history of the city. Indeed, the Renaissance as it is popularly conceived — that is, the Renaissance of Botticelli and Lorenzo, of Alberti and Ghiberti — was in fact the second stage of an urban, civic, and artistic renaissance that began in the era of Dante and the Comune, rather than under the Medici dynasty. Giotto and Dante were almost exact contemporaries, and if we accept the pivotal role of the former in the development of painting, and the fundamental role of the latter in literature, then the Florentine renaissance in its widest cultural sense began not with the famous patronage of Lorenzo (or even of Cosimo) but well over a century earlier, at the turn of the fourteenth century. The "second-stage" Renaissance made further, and broader, and in some spheres quite different, contributions to this cultural flowering, particularly in terms of the reevaluation of the classical heritage and its philosophy and architecture; but it is important to consider this more famous phase within a longer time-frame of cultural, and especially civic, renewal. The first stage can be said to have concluded in the middle of the fourteenth century with the human tragedy of the Black Death, the plague of 1348, and the almost contemporaneous financial crisis in which the great banking houses of the Bardi and Peruzzi both collapsed. In a similar fashion, the political and, to a large extent, the general cultural history of medieval and Renaissance Florence falls into two stages, or eras: that of the Comune, followed by that of the Medici. Communal Florence survived in various modified forms until Cosimo's triumphant return to the city in 1434, which began the Medici dynastic succession.

Despite Florence's frequently bloody and turbulent history, there was a great deal of which its citizens were very proud in their communal past, not least the establishment of many organs of state, of the *podestà*, or chief magistrate, and of the government by the priors of the guild system. These administrative bodies created a widespread identification with the city, a patriotism and sense of civic pride in both its institutions and its physical fabric. It was the result of urban improvement executed in the period of great communal prosperity in the later duecento and early trecento, from the paving of streets to the enforcement of building codes, all of them expressive of the concept of *civitas*, which many today believe to be an essentially Renaissance quality, but that was in fact widespread in the other city-states of this earlier era: Siena, Pisa, Lucca, and Pistoia, for example, in Tuscany alone. These qualities of urban enhancement, of civic and public works, the concept of good and bad government, were all strongly established long before Leon Battista Alberti codified and expressed them in his famous treatise on architecture, *De re aedificatoria* (1452). Alberti was therefore building on a powerful tradition that may have waxed and waned over time and with the vagaries of the economic and political situation, but that can still be identified today in the famous *campanilismo* — the strong local identity with one's own city — of the historic Italian city.

What is commonly perceived to be the "Florentine Renaissance" was thus less clearly defined, and contained many strong traits of an existing cultural tradition. One cannot deny the extraordinary artistic and cultural achievements that flowered in an unprecedented manner during the quattrocento, and whether one regards these developments as evolutionary or revolutionary remains a rather semantic issue, since, in a sense, they were bound to be both. The highly developed tradition of craftsmanship, for example, in many of the applied arts, and particularly sculpture, goldsmithing, and so on, already contained within it many of the skills necessary to transform visual perceptions. But it took Alberti to codify, for example, the laws of perspective and proportion; it took Brunelleschi not only to take structural engineering a great leap forward — at the cupola of the cathedral — but also to apply logical and rational principles of harmony and mathematical perfection to the entire fabric of his churches; and it took Ghiberti and Donatello to explore further the plastic and expressive qualities possible in the casting of bronze. Fundamental to much of this achievement was the "rediscovery" of the classical heritage, the renewed interest in the writings of Vitruvius, in the Greek and Roman philosophers, in the classical orders of architecture, the last diligently examined and recorded by almost all of the great masters of the Renaissance, from Alberti to Michelozzo. If the quattrocento remains the broadly perceived era of preeminence in the history of Florentine visual arts, as it still almost inevitably must, then one of the aims of this volume is to broaden this perception and, in particular, to try to clarify the background of this extraordinary period of creativity, and locate it within a much longer time-frame. This process involves examining the "prehistory" of the Renaissance in some detail, but also its "posthistory." Indeed, another result of the universal emphasis on the achievements of the quattrocento is the neglect of the later periods of Florence's cultural history.

Although by the seventeenth century decline was manifest, the sixteenth century was a period of great accomplishment in Florence: a century that began with the unique and charismatic genius of Michelangelo and concluded with the prodigious achievements of Giorgio Vasari, Bartolommeo Ammannati, and Bernardo Buontalenti, who collectively transformed large sectors of the city more comprehensively than any other group of architects, arguably even more than the previous famous triumvirate of Alberti, Michelozzo, and Brunelleschi a century earlier. The sixteenth century thus deserves considerable attention in both urban and architectural terms. It is undeniable, however, that the cultural preeminence of the city declined after the end of the sixteenth century, and despite the prodigious efforts of the later Medici to develop the Pitti as one of the largest and grandest ducal courts in Europe, Florence's underlying financial and economic resilience had long since withered away. Nevertheless, the city's urban and architectural history in later centuries has much to offer. Although the economic circumstances (and the polarization, and concentration, of patronage at the grand ducal court) resulted in very sparse representation of the higher baroque and rococo periods in Florence, with no works comparable, for example, to those in Rome, the rather less ostentatious Neoclassicism is well represented in the city. The succession of Lorraine grand dukes, though of varying ability and effectiveness, also considerably influenced the physical form of the city, and the reign of Pietro Leopoldo was in many ways a model of enlightened administration, civic responsibility, and urban improvement. The Lorraine era, which traditionally receives scant attention in general histories of Florence, thus deserves closer attention. At the end of the eighteenth century, Florence's history became inevitably entwined with, and subject to, that of the great powers of the time, and, like most former Italian city-states, was first subjugated to Napoleon's ambitions for domination of the peninsula. Buffeted by these external gales of fortune for some decades, both Florence and Tuscany finally joined the modern, unified state of Italy in 1861. The mid-nineteenth century was an era of unparalleled physical urban change, particularly under Giuseppe Poggi's radical visions for the city's modern transformation. Although Florence's role as capital of the nation was brief (1865–70), its effects were felt well beyond the nineteenth century. Despite the survival of much of the city's architectural past, Florence experienced enormous change to its fabric in the nineteenth and twentieth centuries, and one must attach due importance to these modern transformations; collectively they have resulted in the city of today, one that struggles, like many others, for a successful balance between the inestimable value of its cultural legacy and the practical functioning of a modern city.

This book has two specific aims, both identified in its title: one is to give a succinct but comprehensive account of the history of the urban fabric of Florence, from its Roman foundation to the transformations brought about in the modern era by the development of new methods of transport and communication; the other is to provide a survey of the architecture of the city, through the identification of its major urban nuclei and the stylistic development of the principal architectural typologies. Although a handful of (Italian) publications covers the first of these aims, and although countless studies have been made of the latter, I believe that a fusion of these two approaches in a single volume will shed light on the ways in which the city's urban development has influenced its architecture, and vice versa. A strong case can be made in claiming that the more traditional compartmentalization of such studies into "urban history" and "architectural history" are conventions that tend to hinder, more than they help, our appreciation of both.

The story of the city itself thus forms the first part of the book. Florence's historic center and great monuments are famous throughout the world, but to date few attempts have been made to provide a general, accessible account of the history of the fabric of the city in which these monuments are set. Without some knowledge of the broader influences and patterns of patronage, there is a strong tendency for such monuments to be considered and evaluated in a kind of spatial vacuum, devoid of urban — and social and political — context, and thereby largely devoid of important aspects of their meaning. The first part of the book is, therefore, a chronological urban history that draws on the principal political, social, and economic influences. It takes Florence's history up to the mid-nineteenth century, the decade of Italian unification, but does not continue the urban history of Florence uninterruptedly to the present because the city's modern history is so radically different — in terms of urban development, new building typologies, and the underlying political and economic background — that it needs to be approached in rather different terms.

Having established a solid foundation bearing on the subsoil of Florence's history, we are then in a position to begin to raise the walls of the city's principal monuments. There are two dominant hubs, or foci, in the city, which for centuries have been the most important elements in shaping and defining its physical form. So, the second part of the book draws from the first in identifying and analyzing in greater detail these two groups of monumental buildings: the Piazza del Duomo and the surrounding ecclesiastical monuments, and the urban axis from the great civic square, Piazza della Signoria, to Palazzo Pitti. For hundreds of years they have defined the two fundamental aspects of Florentine life, the spiritual and the political.

The third part of the book is essentially a typological discussion — according to both form and function — of the architecture of the city, preceded by a brief outline of the manner in which the city's craftsmen constructed these monuments, from obtaining stone to organizing the guild system.

The book ends with a discussion of the city's urban and architectural history in the century following Italian unification, and concludes with a commentary on contemporary architecture and the environmental and infrastructural issues that face the modern city of Florence.

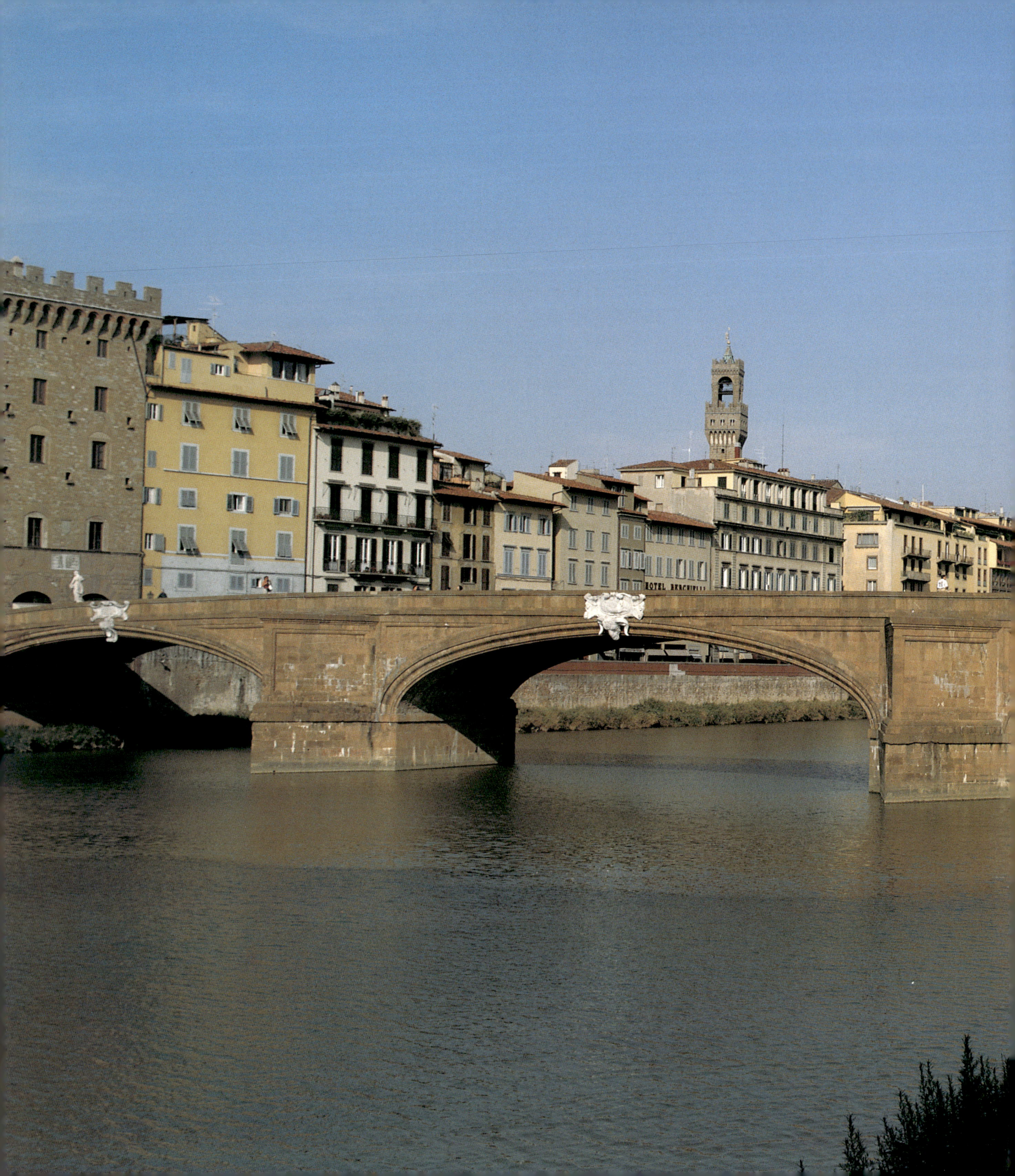

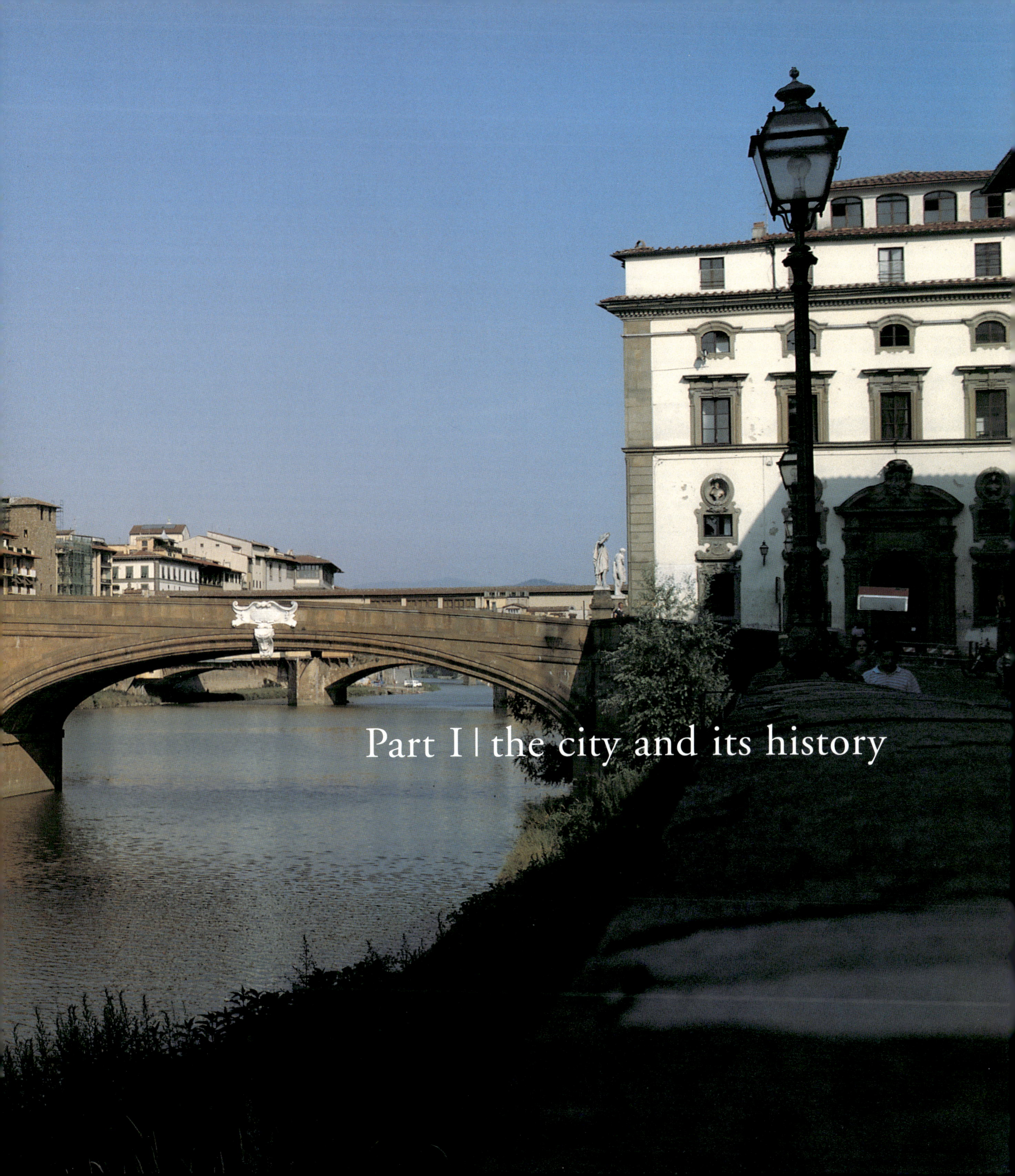

Part I | the city and its history

1 **The Origins of the City**

"Its Territory . . . shall be healthy, wide, pleasant, various, fruitful, secure, and abounding with plenty of Fruits, and great Quantities of Water. It must not want Rivers, Lakes, and an open passage to the Sea." **Leon Battista Alberti,** *De re aedificatoria* (1452) [1]

On a hillside just to the northeast of the city of Florence is the picturesque village of Fiesole. The Etruscans fortified this strategic spur overlooking the broad, shallow bowl of the Florentine amphitheater long before Florence was established. They were followed by a Roman settlement on the same site known as Faesulae, complete with a fine theater (which has survived), baths, and temples. Fiesole controlled the southwestern end of the important routes northward across the Apennines toward the great fertile plains of Romagna and the Adriatic coast. But in spring 59 BC, Fiesole was supplanted by Julius Caesar with a new Roman settlement on the plain below. This marked a decisive shift in the nature of settlements in this region: from a vantage point in the hills to a city on the plain controlling a bridgehead across the broad and sometimes torrential Arno River. Although recent excavations have identified traces of a much earlier, Copper Age settlement on the riverbank, the later two millennia of continuous settlement began with Caesar. Among several claimed derivations, the city's name is said to derive from the traditional spring games, *Ludi Florales*, held on the date of Florence's foundation.[2]

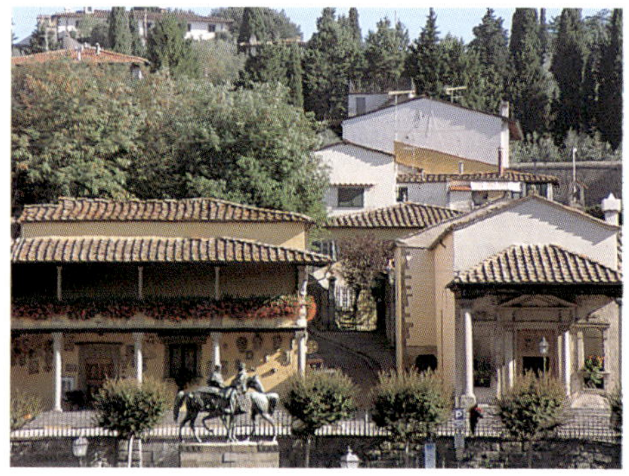

FIESOLE (above)

The Palazzo Pretorio (left) and the sixteenth-century church of Santa Maria Primerana (right), on the village square.

PONTE SANTA TRINITÀ (previous pages)

General view of one of the bridges that span the Arno.

The *campagna*, the countryside surrounding the site of the new city, had already been planned and romanized by the superimposition onto the landscape of the familiar territorial grid or *centuriazione*: a regular network of roads and tracks defining fields that is still traceable today, particularly to the west and northwest of the city, toward Prato. The rural *centuriazione* was based on a square grid with sides of 2,400 Roman feet (2,330 feet, or 710 meters). However, this was a planning system devised for taming and cultivating the land, not for the establishment of a new city; thus, when Florence was planned, not only was the street grid considerably smaller, but its orientation was shifted so that, although the *centuriazione* was aligned with the natural topography of the land, the city's grid was aligned in the usual Roman manner to the cardinal points of the compass. The point at which these two grids meet can easily be identified today in the angular alignment of streets just to the west of Palazzo Strozzi.[3]

Despite centuries of modifications, the heart of Florence remains a Roman city to this day, the regular layout of its street pattern clearly visible from the air, or from a glance at any modern street map. The city was planned with eight blocks running east–west, and six running north–south, forty-eight altogether. As in all such Roman planning, there were two principal axes within the city: the Cardo, the north–south axis (the present Via Roma and Via Calimala), and the Decumanus, orientated east–west, on the line of the present Via degli Strozzi, the Via del Corso, and its eastward continuation, Borgo degli Albizi. At the points where these axes met the surrounding defensive walls were four gates, one at the center of each face of the enclosing rectangle.[4] And at the junction of the two principal axes was the Forum, center of civic and commercial life, which now lies below the southern part of the great nineteenth-century clearance, the Piazza della Repubblica. The Forum was to retain its key role for centuries after the fall of the Roman Empire; its site became the Mercato Vecchio, hub of the city's market activities until it was obliterated in the most dramatic of the radical nineteenth-century "improvements."[5] Florence has thus in essence a regular, typical Roman foundation. The streets, gates, and ramparts were built first, together with a protective *fossa*, or ditch — permanent walls did not follow for some decades. Paving, sewerage, and water supply, those three touchstones of Roman urban civilization, also came early. Like the street grid, the Roman wells survived for a very long time; some were in almost continuous use until the nineteenth century. An aqueduct was also constructed to bring a more reliable source of water than the Arno, which generally reduced to a mere stream during the summer, and occasionally dried up entirely. A bridge was built across the river, the first permanent crossing of the Arno. The exact date of its construction is not known, but was probably around 50 BC. This northern bridgehead was to assume a vital importance, as it established Florence's role as a meeting place of trunk routes in the Roman road network.

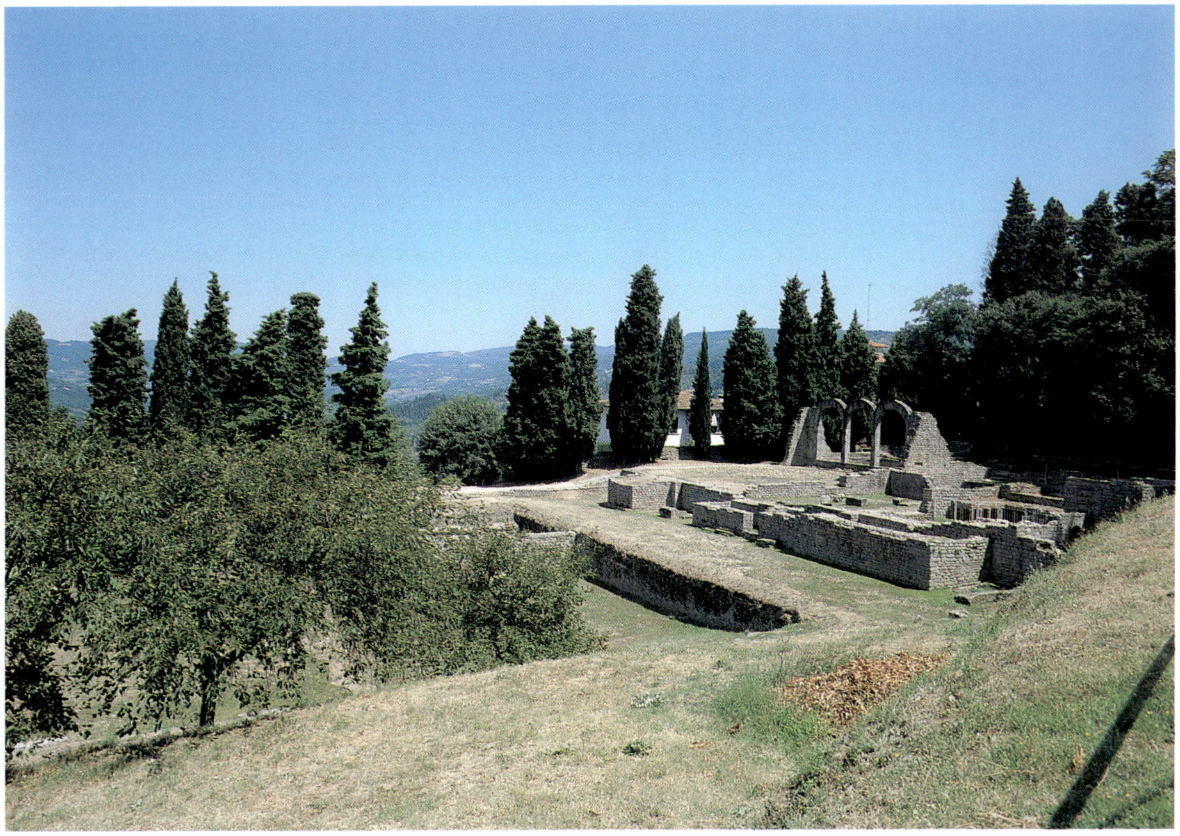

FIESOLE

Roman remains with the fragmentary arches of the baths. Massive sections of wall also attest to an Etruscan presence here before the definitive Roman settlement.

Florence grew over the following century or two to become one of the chief towns of northern Etruria. If not yet preeminent in the region, it was a sizeable town, with a population of perhaps 10,000 by the third century. As it grew, the city's original, rather narrow defensive confines became inadequate, and after the first century, Florence expanded beyond the walls to the east and southeast, where the theater and amphitheater were constructed. The site of the theater lies below the eastern part of the Palazzo Vecchio, while the plan of the amphitheater can be easily recognized today in the unusual elliptical configuration of the Via Torta, Via de' Bentaccordi, and Piazza de' Peruzzi, just west of the Piazza Santa Croce.[6] There was also a modest settlement across the river, in what was much later known as the district of Oltrarno, and whence the road ran south toward Rome. Westward expansion, however, was restricted by the existence of a muddy stream, the Mugnone, which entered the Arno just west of the walls, and on whose marshy banks settlement was difficult.

Probably during the reign of Diocletian (284–305), Florentia was designated capital of the region of Tuscia Annonaria, having established its superiority over the other Roman towns of the region: Pisa, Lucca, and Pistoia. This was primarily the result of its key role as a bridgehead and hub of trading routes in the region. From the southernmost bridgehead, the Via Cassia Nova (built by

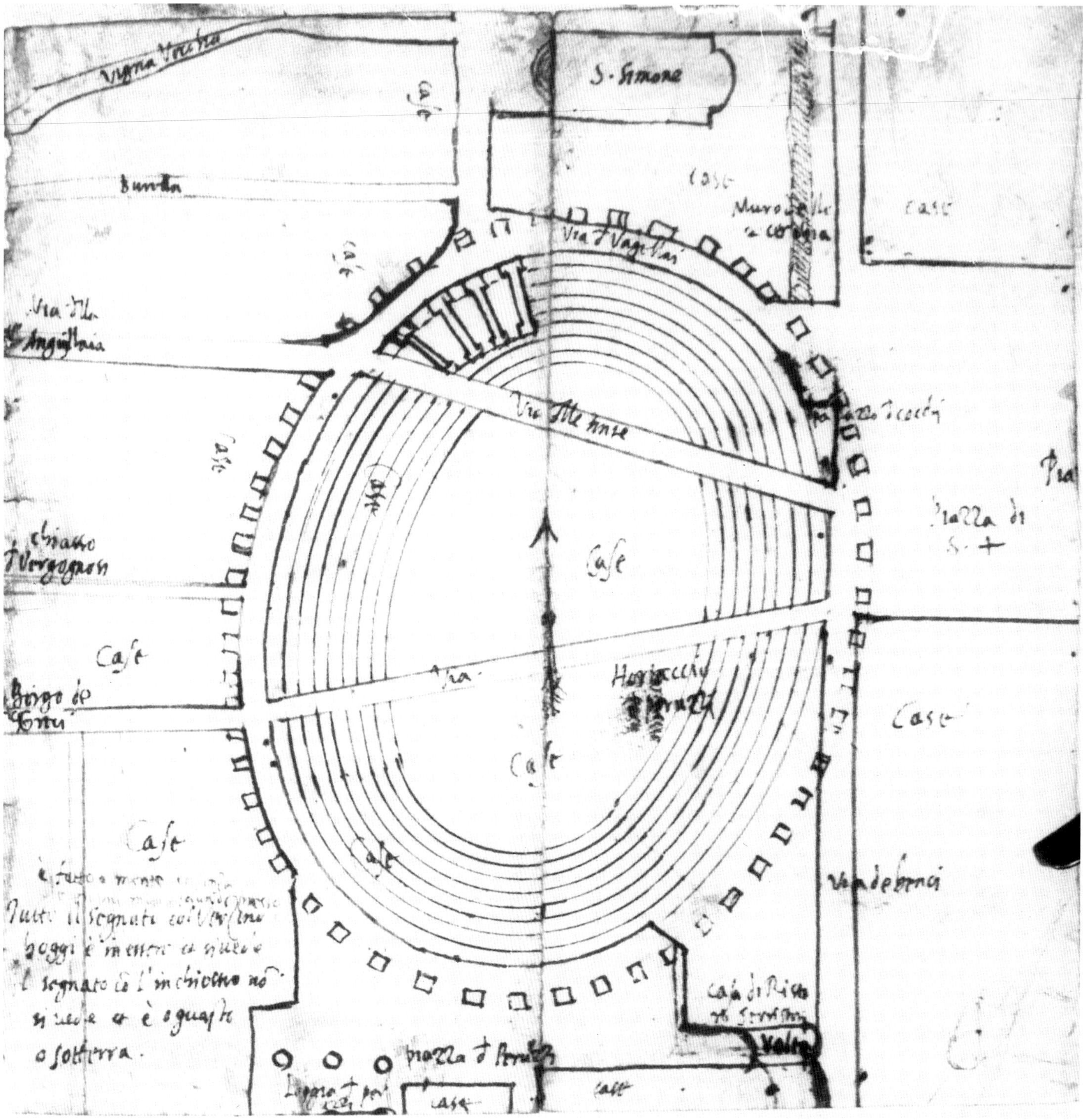
S. Simone
Vigna Vecchia
Case
Piazza di

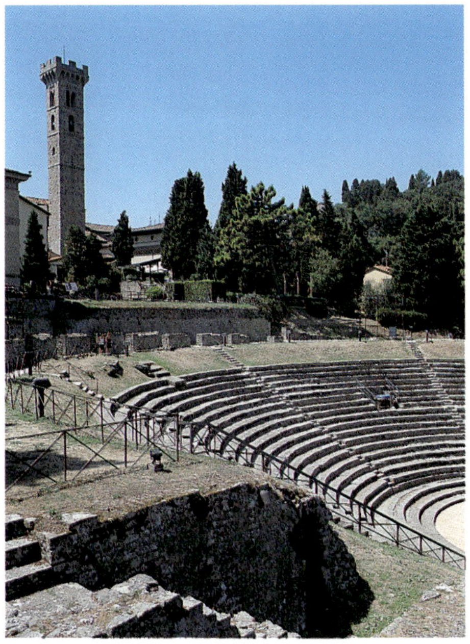

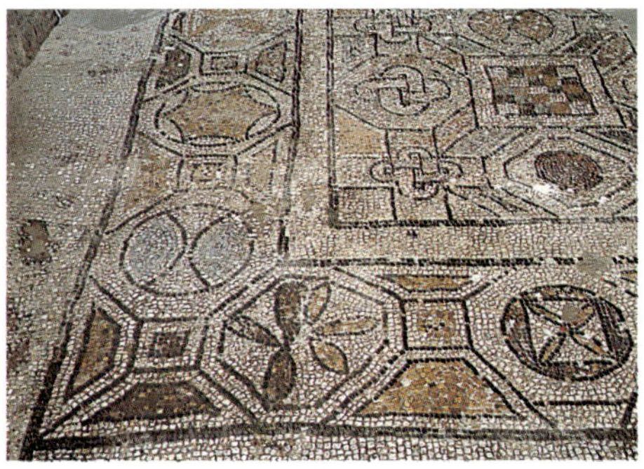

FIESOLE (top)

The Roman theater.

SANTA REPARATA (above)

Detail of floor mosaic from the ancient basilica, the remains of which now lie about 8 feet (2.5 meters) below the floor of the present cathedral.

VIA TORTA (opposite)

This eighteenth-century survey plan records the layout of the Roman amphitheater, the foundations of which lie beneath the elliptical pattern of streets just west of Santa Croce: Via Torta, Via Bentaccordi, and the Piazza de' Peruzzi.

Hadrian in AD 123) led south to Rome; the Via Pisana followed the south bank of the Arno to Pisa; the Via Senese to Siena via Poggibonsi; the Via Faventina, another trunk route, ran northward to the mountain passes toward Faenza and Bologna, thus giving access to the wealthy, fertile Po valley. The expansion of the Roman city probably reached its peak at the end of the second century, by which time there was significant development outside the walls, while the city was almost fully builtup within the walls.

The earliest Christian churches for which records have survived are Santa Felicità and San Lorenzo, the latter consecrated in 393 as the home of the new bishopric. Shortly thereafter, in 405, the Ostrogoths invaded the peninsula, and although they were repelled from the city, Roman Florentia never fully recovered from the widespread destruction.

Byzantines, Lombards, and Carolingians

In the early decades of the sixth century, the Goths from the north and the Byzantines of the East Roman Empire fought bitterly for possession of what remained of the city, and the latter refortified the site, but to a much more modest extent than the Romans. This so-called *cinta bizantina* (Byzantine belt) sheltered a population that was a mere fraction of that of the Roman city, perhaps as few as a thousand people.[7] However, with the brief stability of this Byzantine era (552–68) a handful of new churches was founded: Santa Maria in Campidoglio, San Ruffillo, Sant'Apollinare.[8] In 568 the Lombards invaded Italy from the Alps and established their capital at Pavia; they spread east and southward to conquer much of the Po valley, and crossed the Apennines to take Tuscany; by the end of the sixth century, Florence had become de facto a part of the Lombard kingdom of Italy. However, since the Byzantines remained in control of the present Romagna and the eastern seaboard, ruling from their capital at Ravenna, Florence was marginalized, reduced to being merely one of a number of small Tuscan towns. Lucca now established its position as the chief of these, while Pisa retained the great advantage of its seaport. But this marginality allowed for the slow emergence of a degree of independence, and the adoption of Christianity by the Lombards encouraged the foundation of a number of churches despite Florence's still very modest population. These included San Miniato al Monte and San Michele "*ad hortum*" (in the orchard), later known as Orsanmichele. The church of San Giovanni Battista, the baptistery that was to play a crucial role in Florence's ecclesiastical and cultural history, was also probably established at the beginning of the seventh century.[9] These new foundations, however, were all outside the original Roman city, as was San Lorenzo, seat of the bishopric. It is not known when the see was transferred to its second and permanent location, the patronal church of Santa Reparata, but this definitive move may have taken place toward the end of the seventh century.

In both the Byzantine and Lombard eras, Florence had been very small and compact in size, not much more than a substantial village; it was only with the Carolingian period of consolidation and stability in the ninth century that numbers increased significantly, and important urban works began to be undertaken. In 773–74 the Frankish emperor Charlemagne had conquered the Lombard capital of Pavia, and in the following years all of Lombard Italy was absorbed into the great Carolingian Empire, which incorporated the whole peninsula as far as Rome. It has been estimated that the population of Florence doubled — from 2,500 to 5,000 — during this period, and the city had reasserted sufficient influence to subject Fiesole to its jurisdiction. In 854 Lothario, the Carolingian king of Italy, declared Florence the capital of its own *contea*, or county, the largest and most important in Tuscany. During the ninth century, a new bridge was built across the Arno to belatedly replace the Roman bridge destroyed by the Goths; and what has been identified as a third circle of walls was built around the end of the century. They enclosed a compact rectangle, still smaller than the original Roman settlement, but larger than the Byzantine enclosure. However, the settlement was still so small that the northern boundary did not

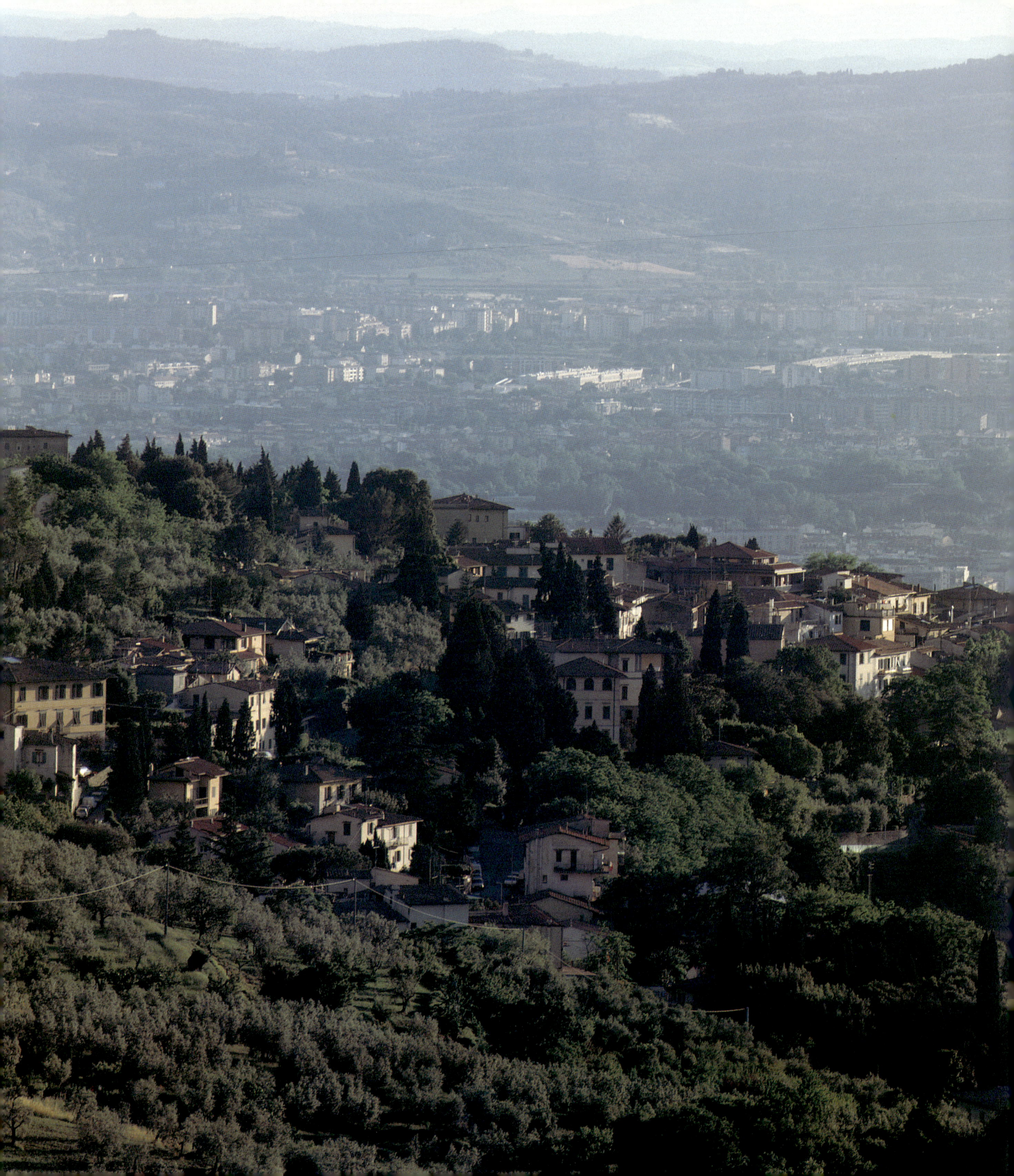

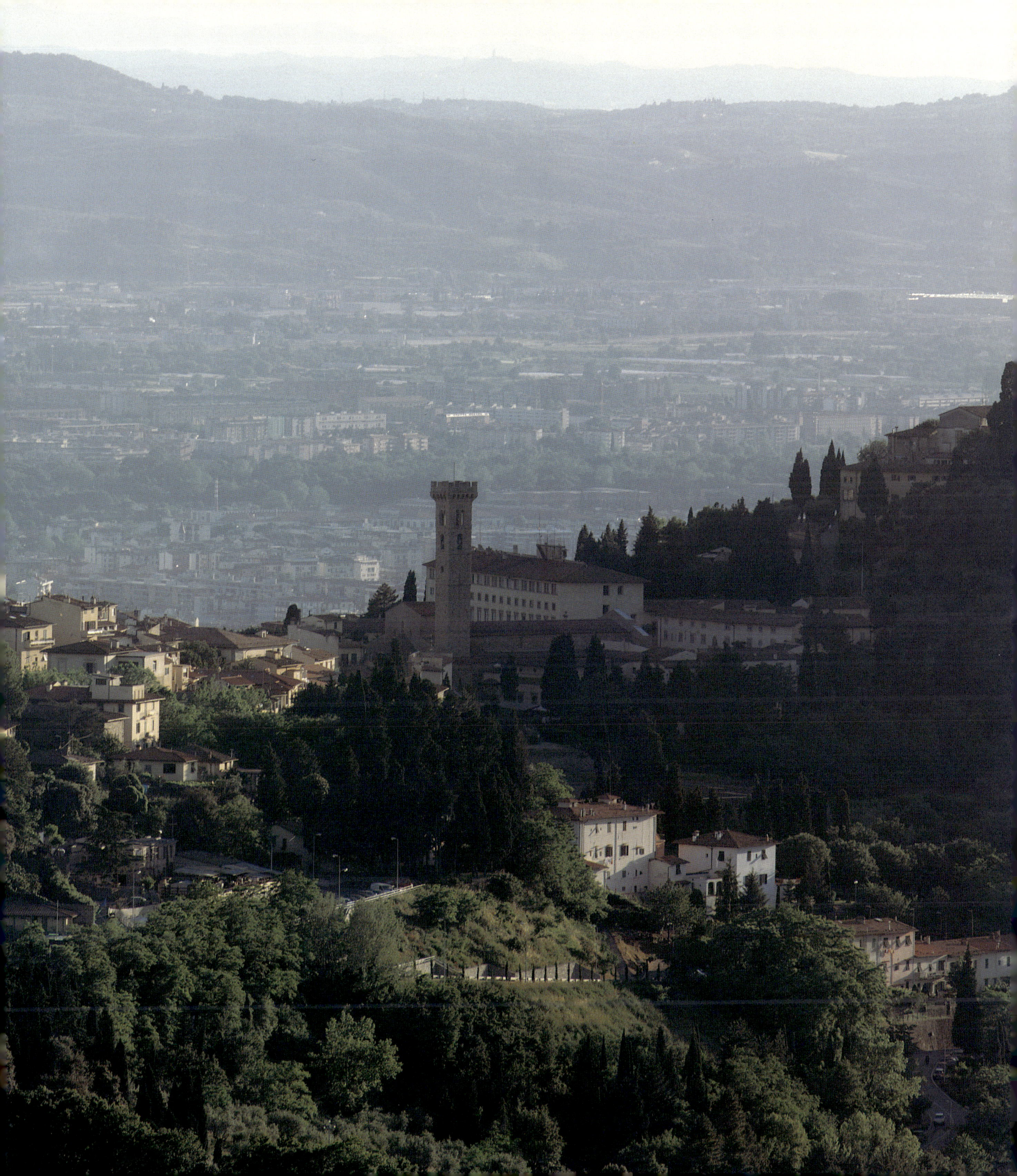

incorporate San Giovanni Battista or the adjacent church of Santa Reparata, which both remained outside its secure confines. Immediately adjacent to both churches stood the perhaps rather inaptly titled "palace" of the bishop, as well as that of the margrave or governor, thus forming a compact nucleus of both lay and ecclesiastical administrative power.[10]

In the late tenth and early eleventh centuries, important new religious houses were founded. The Benedictine Badia Fiorentina was founded in 978 by Willa, the widow of Uberto, marquis of Tuscany, whose title had been given to him by the emperor Otto I; it was a very wealthy foundation, with a generous endowment of land and property, and was to become the most highly favored nunnery for the daughters of Florence's nobility for centuries. A further series of Benedictine houses was established in Tuscany by Willa's son Ugo, among them the monastery at San Miniato, founded in 1018. Among the most significant events of this period was the definitive transfer of the seat of the marquisate of Tuscany by the formidable countess Matilda from Lucca to Florence in 1052, which restored the city's primacy over the region.

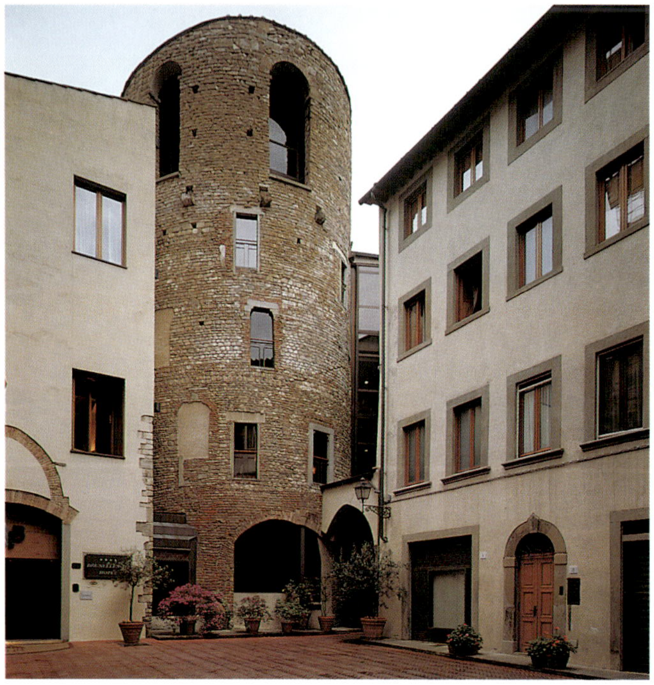

However, during the same period, a dispute developed between the papacy and the empire, which erupted into open conflict in 1075, when Pope Gregory VII condemned the right of lay investiture of bishops and abbots by the emperor. The real conflict regarded the question of the ascendancy of the two powers over the Church. It generated civil war in Germany and politically polarized northern Italy. Florence allied with Rome against the empire, and this gave the Tuscan city a greater role as a center of Christian spirituality and led to the foundation of a number of new monastic houses and the enlarging of existing monasteries, among them Santa Reparata and San Lorenzo. This partisanship also sowed the seeds of the bitter factional strife that would erupt a century later, when the city was torn between those who were in favor of papal sovereignty in Italy, the Guelfs, who had a powerful base in Florence in the city's merchant class, and those who continued to support the supreme role of the emperor, the Ghibellines.

Having taken the stand for Rome, Florence was vulnerable, and in 1078 Matilda ordered the construction of new defensive walls, the "fourth circle." On the east and west sides of the city, they followed the lines of the Roman walls, but in an important new extension to the north, they now also enclosed the administrative and ecclesiastical enclave of San Giovanni, Santa Reparata, and the palaces of both bishop and countess.[11] By this time, Florence's numbers had probably attained the levels that had been reached under Rome, with perhaps as many as 20,000 people. The administration of this very substantial town was further defined by its division into four *quartieri*, and by the tentative establishment of trade groups that were to develop into the all-important *arti* in the following centuries. A further indication of the city's maturity and preeminence in the region was the crushing of the ancient community of Fiesole in 1125, seen as a potential strategic base for the city's enemies. It did not cede without a bitter struggle, however; only after three successive sieges did Fiesole capitulate. Florence's retribution was ruthless: Fiesole was almost totally destroyed, with only the cathedral and the house of the bishop left standing.

FIESOLE

Previous pages: the village of Fiesole lies in a "saddle" some 980 feet (300 meters) above the bowl in which Florence was built.

Opposite: interior of the early-eleventh-century cathedral of San Romolo. The plan is basilican, with the raised choir typical of such churches; the same arrangement can also be seen at San Miniato.

TORRE DELLA PAGLIAZZA (left)

The oldest of the surviving fortified towers of Florence, and the only one to have a circular plan, the Byzantine *torre* was probably built in the sixth century, but altered on many occasions thereafter. Only in the 1970s was its structure cleared of later accretions.

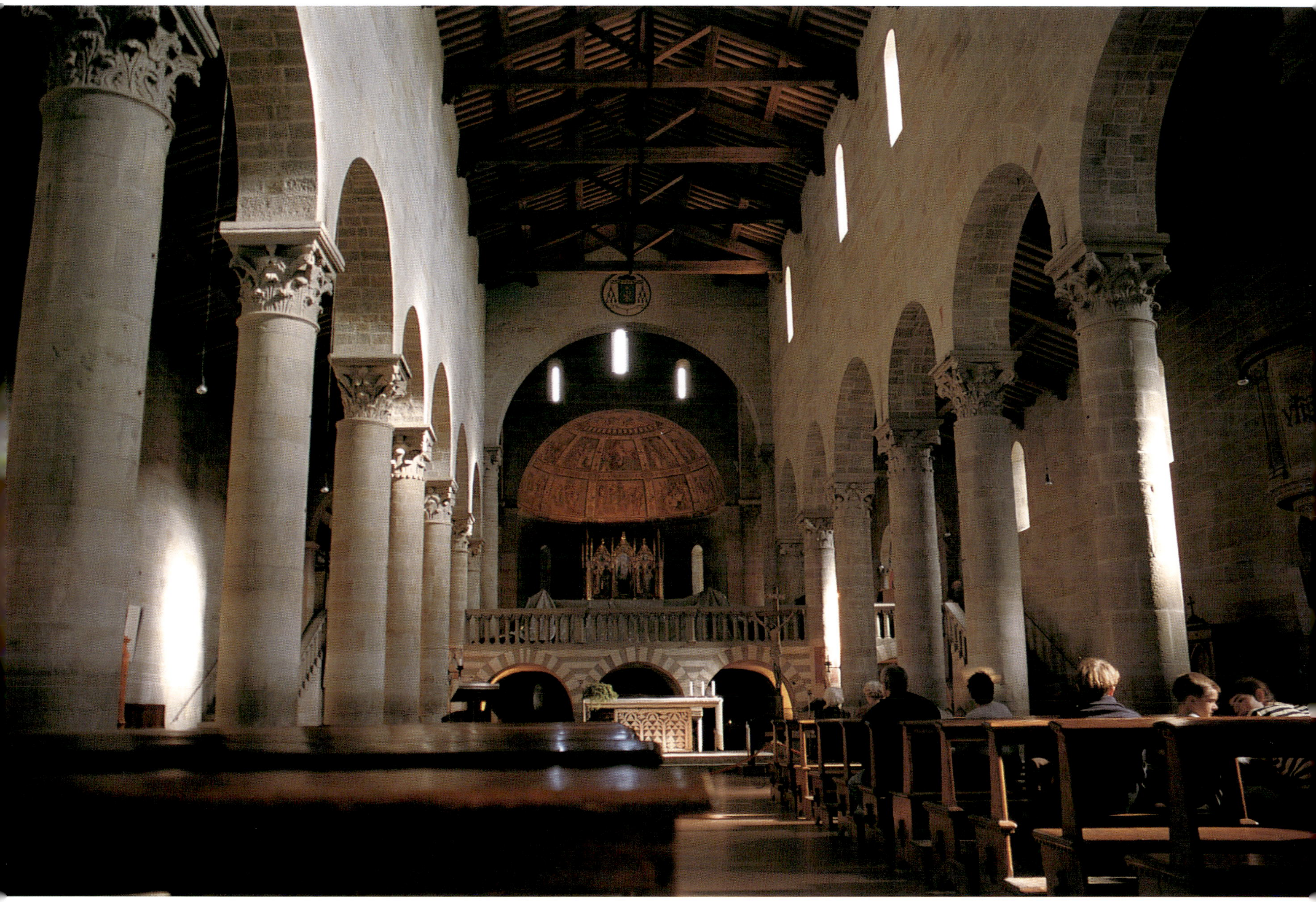

2 **The Maturing Medieval City**

"The Florentines then began to build the new city wall . . . from the eastern side at the Porta di San Pier Maggiore . . . enclosing the suburb and the church within the new walls . . . then toward the Borgo San Lorenzo, again so that the church now lay within the walls." **Giovanni Villani,** *Cronica fiorentina* (c. 1330) [1]

Florence was not formally recognized as a Comune, that is, as a largely self-governing city-state, by the emperor until 1183, although it had de facto been a Comune since the death of Countess Matilda in 1115. Much of the early twelfth century had been characterized by struggles between Florence and her neighbors for political supremacy over the region. Prato was extensively damaged before it succumbed to Florentine control, and the destruction of Fiesole in 1125 was followed by long disputes with Siena over territorial boundaries that continued for many decades.[2] Similar disputes characterized relations with Pistoia, Pisa, and Lucca; but Florence continued to grow in power, numbers, and influence. The city's government system was already complex: The Comune was administered by a general assembly, which, since there was no great hall suitable for such assemblies, met four times a year within the church of Santa Reparata. The governing class of the city's population was divided into nobles, knights, and merchants, but an increasingly important role in Florence's economy was now played by skilled groups of craftsmen, who were in the process of organizing themselves into what were to become the preeminently powerful *arti*. Among them, the most numerous and influential were the metalworkers (smiths, weapon makers, and so on), goldsmiths, workers in the leather industry, the food trades, and the building crafts; but the wool, silk, and textile industry was destined to become by far the largest and most powerful.[3]

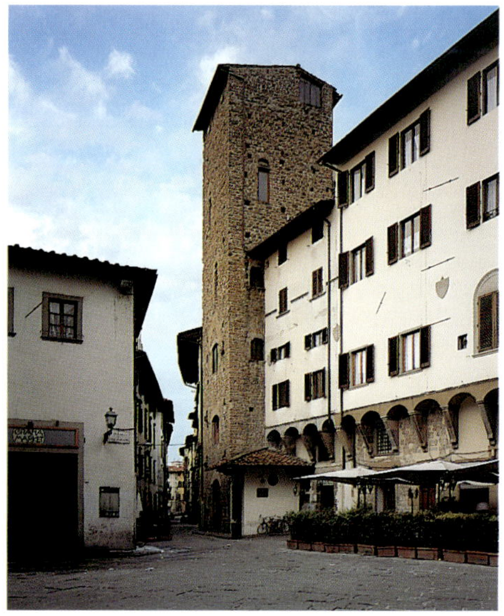

TORRE DEI CORBIZI

Once the property of the Donati, it is one of the most typical and best preserved of the surviving medieval towers, most of them from the thirteenth century.

During the twelfth century Florence grew more rapidly than any other city in Tuscany. Much of the city's expansion took place beyond the confines of the old walls, chiefly, at first, in the form of ribbon or cluster development outside the four principal gates, and later along the secondary radial roads and in annular growth just outside the shelter of the walls themselves. A ring of suburbs thus developed around the original nucleus, almost all of which can still be identified today: To the north was Borgo San Lorenzo, first recorded as such in 1117; a little to the east was Borgo di Balla (1120), then Borgo di San Pier Maggiore (Borgo Albizi, 1090). To the southeast were the *borghi* dei Greci and San Remigio, and at the southern end of the main axis, on the north bank of the Arno, was Borgo di Por Santa Maria. On the southern bank, Oltrarno, were the three clusters of Borgo di Piazza (centered on Via Guicciardini), San Jacopo, and Borgo Pidiglioso; an almost complete ring, therefore, of suburban nuclei, all of which developed further as the city's wealth and population grew.

By the later twelfth century Florence's population numbered approximately 30,000, making it a substantial city by the standards of the time, and in 1171 it was decided to build new walls, the so-called fifth circle, the first walls built by the Comune. Completed in barely two years, from 1173 to 1175, they enclosed an area roughly twice that of the previous enclosures, and brought within the city's confines the now sizeable suburb of Oltrarno.[4] The lines of these walls are still clearly traceable today: To the north they enclosed San Lorenzo, to the east they included Borgo Albizi, while to the west they extended as far as the present Piazza Goldoni on the north bank of the Arno. Their orientation was — for the first time — significantly different from the rectangular, gridded Roman plan, since it "twisted" toward the northwest and southeast; although still remaining the city's central nucleus, the innermost hub had become one element in a larger, more diffuse urban whole. The realization of the need to defend the Oltrarno as an intrinsic part of the city meant that the Arno itself was now fully integrated within the fabric of the city, rather than defining its southern edge with a borgo beyond. Equally important were two locations, upstream and downstream, where the city walls met the river's banks on both sides, and where twin "castles" or towers were constructed to fortify these key potential weaknesses in the city's defenses.

Until 1218 the only bridge across the Arno had been the one reconstructed on the site of the very first Roman bridge. In that year it was relocated and rebuilt in almost exactly the same location as the present Ponte Vecchio, with five stone arches. The role of the Arno in the medieval era was much more important than it is today, and the river was essential to the city's life in many different ways. It was navigable upstream roughly as far as the present Ponte alle Grazie, while downstream it joined the city with the important port of Pisa and the Mediterranean. The Arno provided water for numerous mills, it provided fish, it was essential for the all-important textile industry. Nevertheless, and despite the new fortifications of Oltrarno, the city never developed as much on the south bank as it did on the north. This is simply a matter of topography, well understood by the Romans when they set out the city's street grid: Oltrarno is closely circumscribed by hills — San Miniato, San Salvatore, San Giorgio, and Bellosguardo — such that there is less reasonably level land on which to build.

Although a large, flourishing town, Florence still possessed very few monumental buildings; among these few were the baptistery of San Giovanni and San Miniato al Monte, one on the northern edge of the city, the other on a hillside above Oltrarno, well beyond the builtup area. The city's form, basically disciplined by the Roman street grid, retained a general conformity of scale and space. There were as yet no major public squares, no civic foci, and the only spaces that could be identified as piazze were the markets. The most important, known as the *miluogo,* was located in what had been the Roman Forum, in the southeast corner of the present Piazza della Repubblica, but already by the eleventh century it seems that a second market had been established between this "Mercato Vecchio" and Por Santa Maria, the gate near the river, at the southern end of the old Roman north–south axis; weekly markets were held in both locations.[5] The second site is still known as the Mercato Nuovo today.

Many of Florence's houses remained very humble timber structures, but two major building typologies developed in this era that were to have a profound impact on the appearance of the mature medieval city: churches and tower houses. Among the city's churches, San Giovanni Battista remained by far the most prominent and symbolically important, the hub of the cluster of "public" buildings on the northern edge of the city. However, a number of other churches were founded or redeveloped in this period, among them Santi Apostoli in about 1050, Santo Stefano al Ponte begun after 1116, San Salvatore from 1032, and San Jacopo sopr'Arno from the twelfth century. The reconstruction of both Santa Reparata and San Lorenzo also began in midcentury, but San Miniato, particularly its beautiful, refined facade from about 1018 to 1063, remains the epitome of the rich but disciplined style identifiable as Florentine Romanesque.[6] Almost all of these projects acted as catalysts for more general urban developments that reflected the influence of the Church over the form of the developing city. Other church foundations outside the walls similarly acted as nuclei for further development, among them Santa Maria Novella, San Felice, and San Sepolcro, as well as charitable hospitals such as that attached to the Badia Fiorentina. Tower houses were a different typology entirely. They numbered only a handful in 1100, but the developing internal struggles resulted in such an increase in their number that more than a hundred were recorded by the end of the century, when the city bristled with their dramatic profiles.[7]

Between about 1175 and 1200, with the impetus provided by the construction of the new walls, development expanded rapidly in these newly enclosed districts. Nevertheless, the "ring" of church

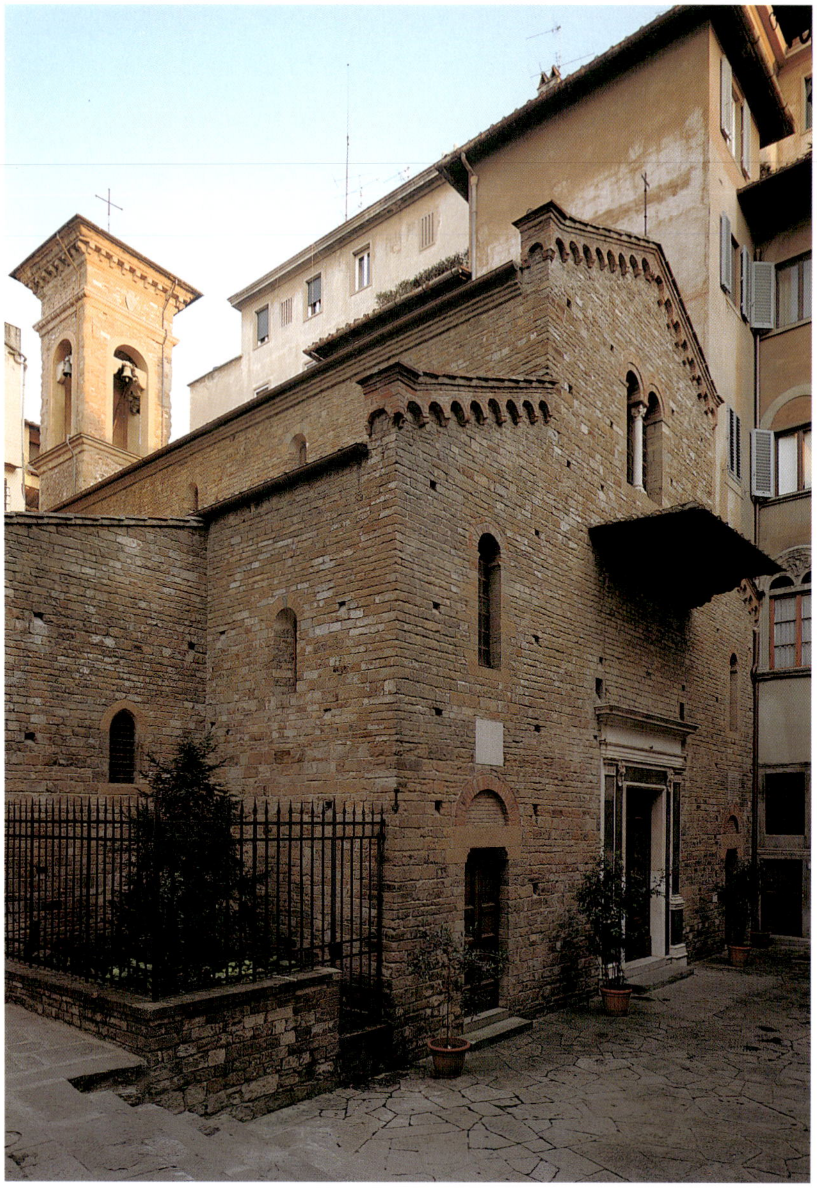

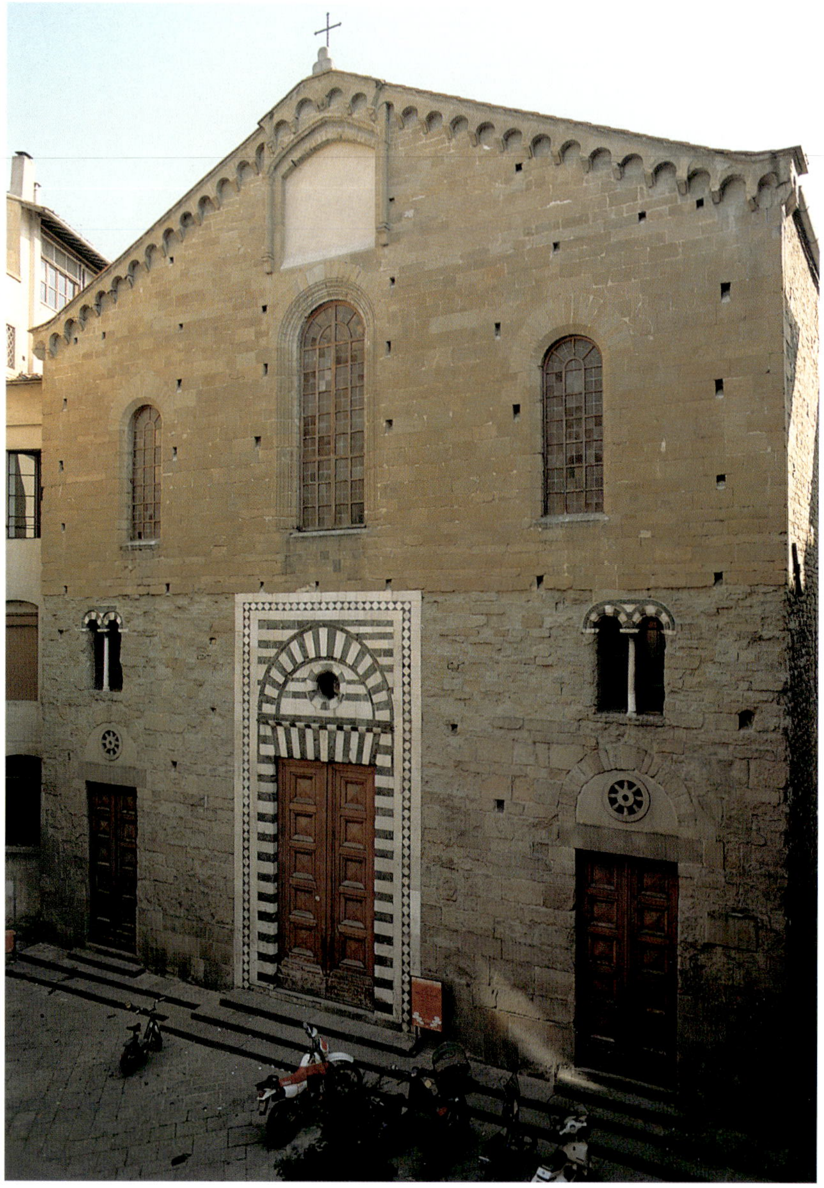

SANTI APOSTOLI (above, left)

The modest eleventh-century facade is a rare surviving example from this period; the portico was added in the fifteenth century.

SANTO STEFANO AL PONTE (above)

The simple stone Romanesque facade is enlivened by a polychrome marble portico, added in the fourteenth century.

SAN MINIATO AL MONTE (opposite)

Together with the baptistery, this refined, elegant work marks the pinnacle of the Florentine Romanesque style. The facade was probably built in the early years of the thirteenth century.

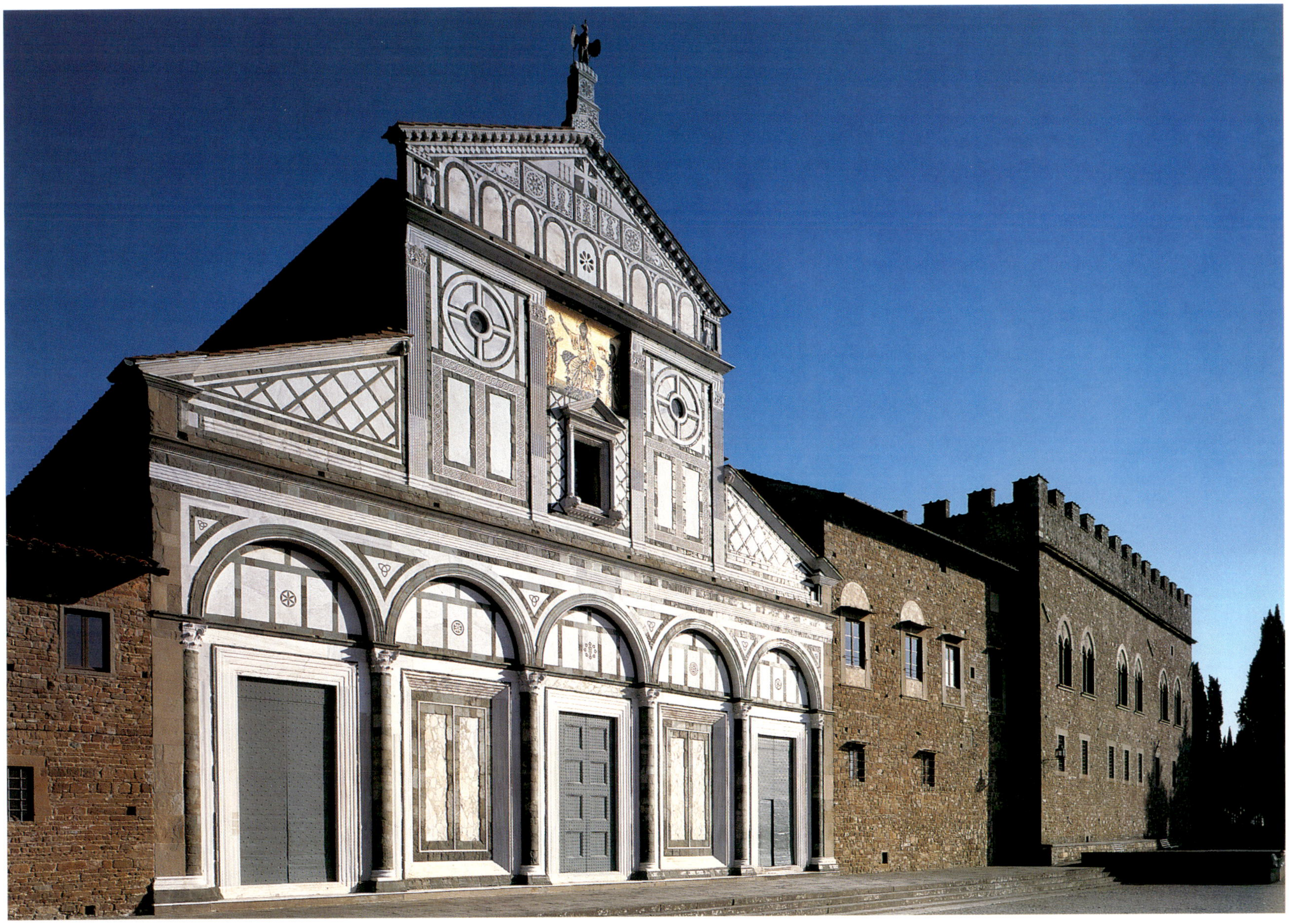

foundations in this interwall zone ensured that a large number of open spaces remained — cloisters, herb gardens, and so on — chiefly at San Lorenzo, Santa Maria Maggiore, Santa Trinità, and the Badia Fiorentina.[8] By the century's end, this brief but rapid expansion resulted in the total number of churches in the city, both monastic and parochial, increasing to around sixty.

The city's administration remained for a long time based on the division into four *quartieri*, subdivided into twenty-four parishes, but by the later twelfth century a new subdivision into six parts (*sestieri*) reflected its increase in size and complexity of administration. The establishment of the Oltrarno as one of these *sestiere* was a further recognition of its significance in the overall urban structure. Each *sestiere* had its own magistracies, with various rights and duties, while the parishes within these *sestieri* were governed like miniature states, with their own elected heads, or *capi*. Parish inhabitants held specific rights within their own parish that were not shared by the citizens of any other parish, and around these highly localized loyalties developed clusters of tower houses of the leading citizens, as well as shops, workshops, and, of course, the religious and social activities associated with the parish church itself. These tower houses represented one of the most remarkable but characteristic developments in the city after 1150, and continued to develop over much of the following century. There were perhaps as many as one hundred by 1200, and the sites of twice that number have been traced or identified today. These towers were always built of stone, and were contiguous with the houses of their owners; generally they were resorted to only in times of danger and civil unrest, and usually were reached by a small, defensible doorway on one of the upper floors of the house itself. The tower would contain sufficient emergency provisions for the family (or families) to remain there until the danger had passed. A further characteristic of these towers is that they were often built in clusters, by groups of families or clans sharing the same allegiance (Guelf or Ghibelline, "white" or "black"), thus forming a consolidated block, or *insula*, from whose various individual houses the towers could be reached directly without descending to the dangerous street below.[9]

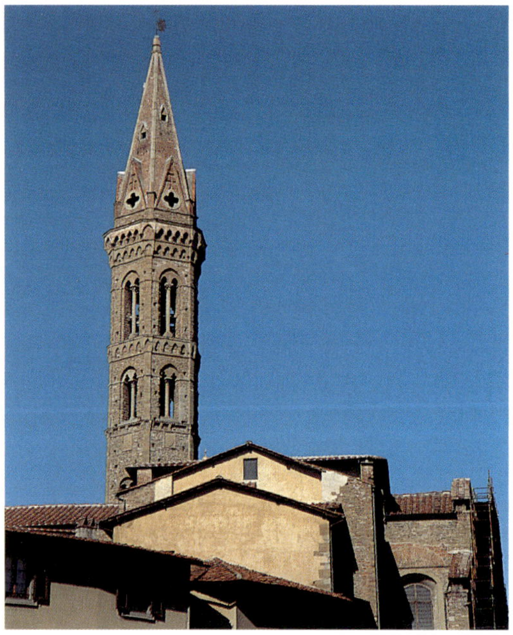

BADIA FIORENTINA

The elegant hexagonal campanile was built in c. 1330; the fabric of the church has a long, complex history of extension and adaptation.

The Duecento: Urban Consolidation

"In the year of Christ 1237 . . . all of the streets of Florence were begun to be paved, prior to which only very few had been paved, and as a result of this appropriate labor the city of Florence would now become cleaner, more beautiful and more healthy."

Giovanni Villani, *Cronica fiorentina* (c. 1330) [10]

Politically, the early duecento in Florence is characterized by internal conflicts as well as violent relations with neighboring cities. The year 1207 was particularly significant: It saw both the Florentine victory over Siena at the battle of Montalto, and for the first time the appointment of a foreign *podestà*, Gualfredotto da Milano, to govern the city. The first *podestà*, or chief magistrate, had in fact been nominated in 1193, but the appointment of a noble foreigner from another friendly state was intended to resolve the bitter fighting between factions within the city itself. The system had already been introduced elsewhere in Italy for most of the same reasons: The foreign governor would be an objective, impartial administrator with no vested partisan interests, and was to be supported by a Collegio Speciale as well as a Consiglio Generale, a general council containing the elected heads, or *priori*, of the chief guilds of the city.[11] A few years later a family quarrel between the Buondelmonti and the Amidei led, in 1216, to the assassination of Buondelmonte dei

PONTE RUBACONTE (PONTE ALLE GRAZIE) (below)

Photograph before the destruction of the bridge during World War II. It was rebuilt in a much simpler form, without the superstructures.

THE ARNO AND ITS BRIDGES (overleaf)

Panorama of the city from Piazzale Michelangelo, showing the Ponte Vecchio surmounted by its characteristic shops. Beyond are the Ponte Santa Trinità and the Ponte alla Carraia. The cupola of San Frediano in Cestello (left) dominates the Oltrarno.

Buondelmonti by a group of nobles — including the Uberti and Lamberti — precipitating the polarization of the Guelf and Ghibelline factions, which had a long-lasting and destructive effect on Florence's medieval history.

During this period, the city's most important guilds were founded, and their influence over Florence's cultural history would be equally profound. Among these principal *arti*, the oldest was that of the *mercanti*, founded in the twelfth century as the Societas Mercatorum but later more generally known as the Calimala. It was followed by the creation of the guild of the Cambiatori (bankers and money changers) in 1206, that of the Lana (wool workers) in 1212, and that of Por Santa Maria (silk workers) in 1218.

Urban consolidation was perhaps the most prominent feature of Florence's history in the duecento. The link between Oltrarno and the city center was reinforced by the building of two new bridges, to add to the hitherto solitary span over the Arno. The Ponte alla Carraia (downstream) was

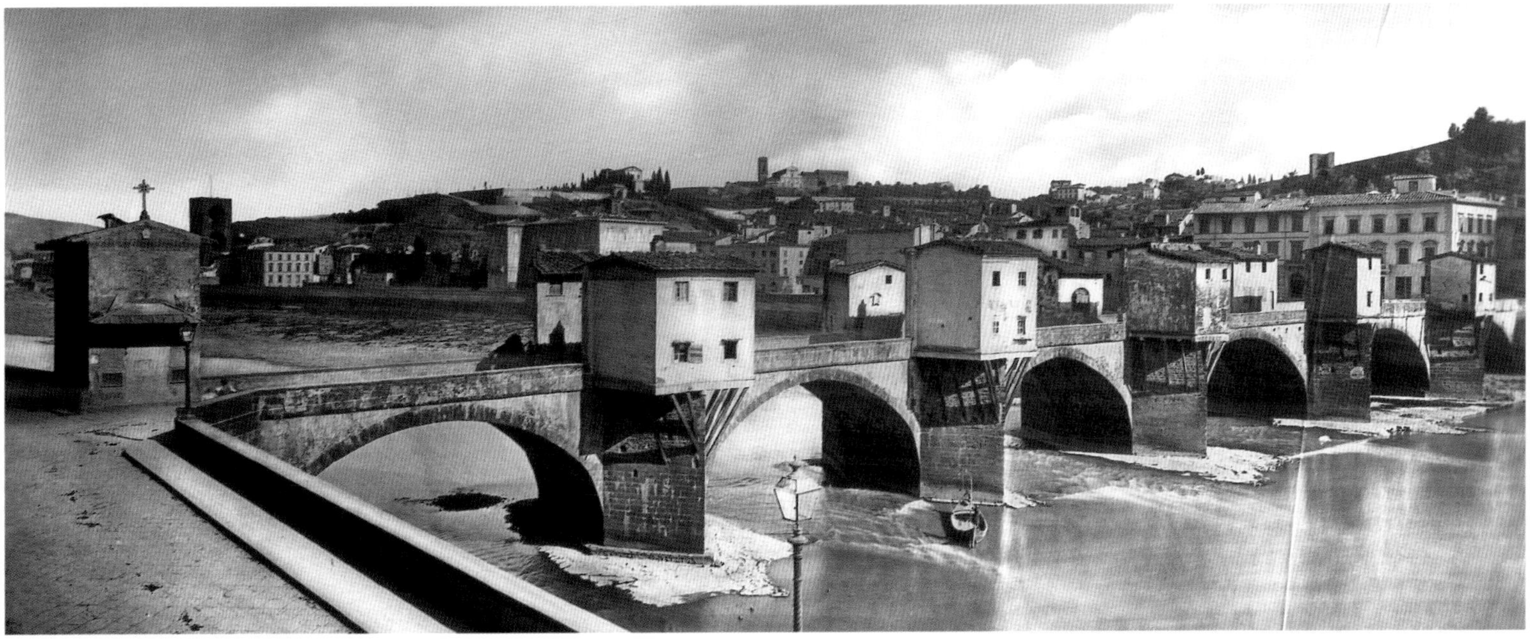

first built from 1218 to 1220, and was followed in 1237 by the Ponte Rubaconte, on the site of the present Ponte alle Grazie. Although both were outside the 1175 walls of the Comune, they considerably eased the congestion that had developed around the northern bridgehead of the original Ponte Vecchio. These two new bridges were followed by a fourth (which is the last surviving historic bridge), Ponte Santa Trinità, in 1252, within the walls midway between the Ponte Vecchio and the Ponte alla Carraia. The Ponte alla Carraia (originally simply known as the Ponte Nuovo) was of timber, built on stone piers, and formed an important connection to the riverborne trade with Pisa, 30 miles (48 km) downstream. The Ponte Rubaconte, named after the Milanese *podestà* of the time, was built entirely of stone, with nine arches. It later became known as the Ponte alle Grazie, after a chapel dedicated to Santa Maria delle Grazie was built on one of its piers in the fourteenth century.[12]

The Church effected fundamental changes to the fabric of the city in the duecento. In particular, the dynamic spread of the teachings of the two principal mendicant orders, the Dominicans and Franciscans (together with the establishments of the Servites, Carmelites, and Augustinians) resulted in the creation of important new nuclei that remain pivotal to the lives of the Florentines to this day — and that were translated into the city's fabric. These great new building projects

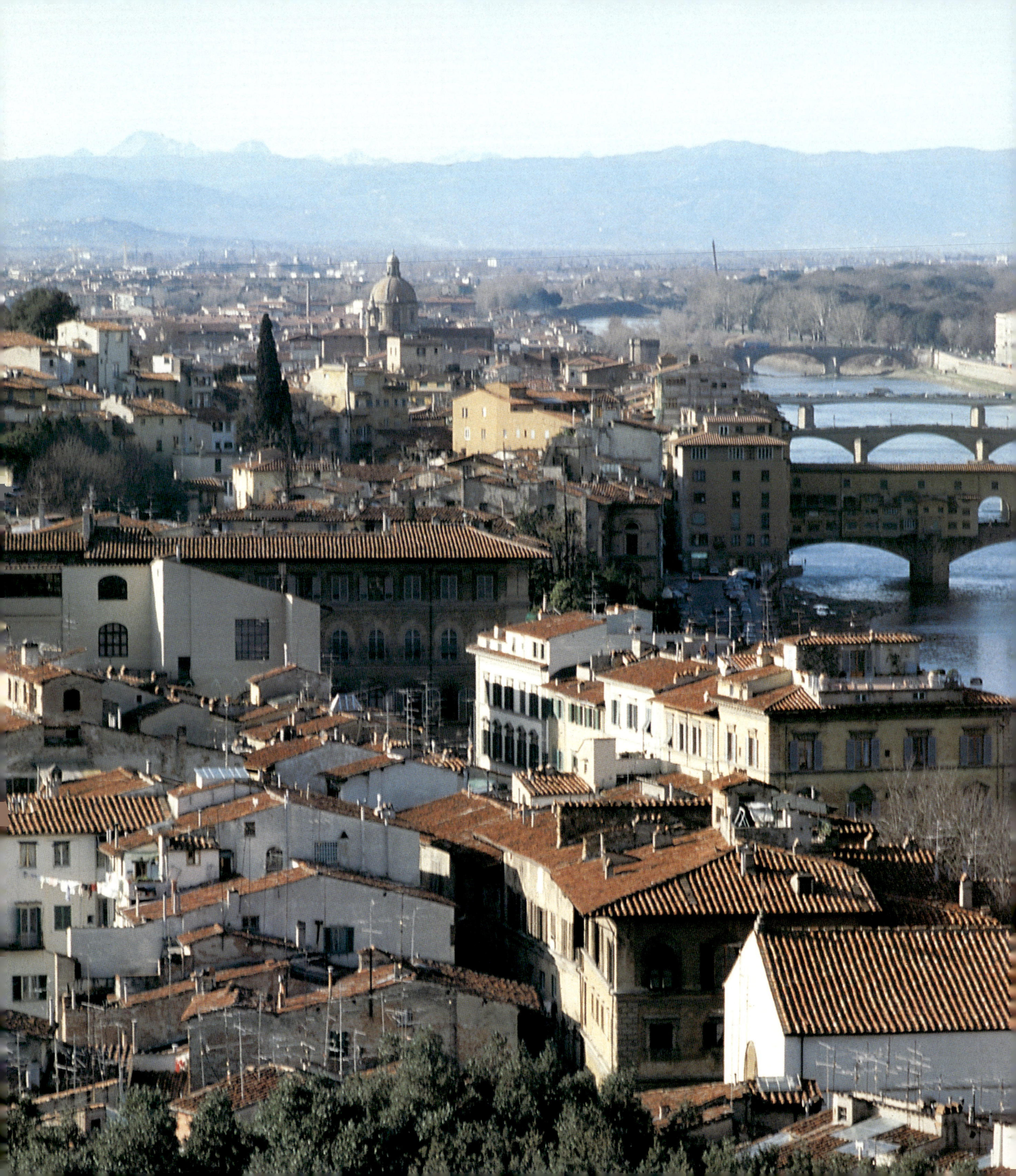

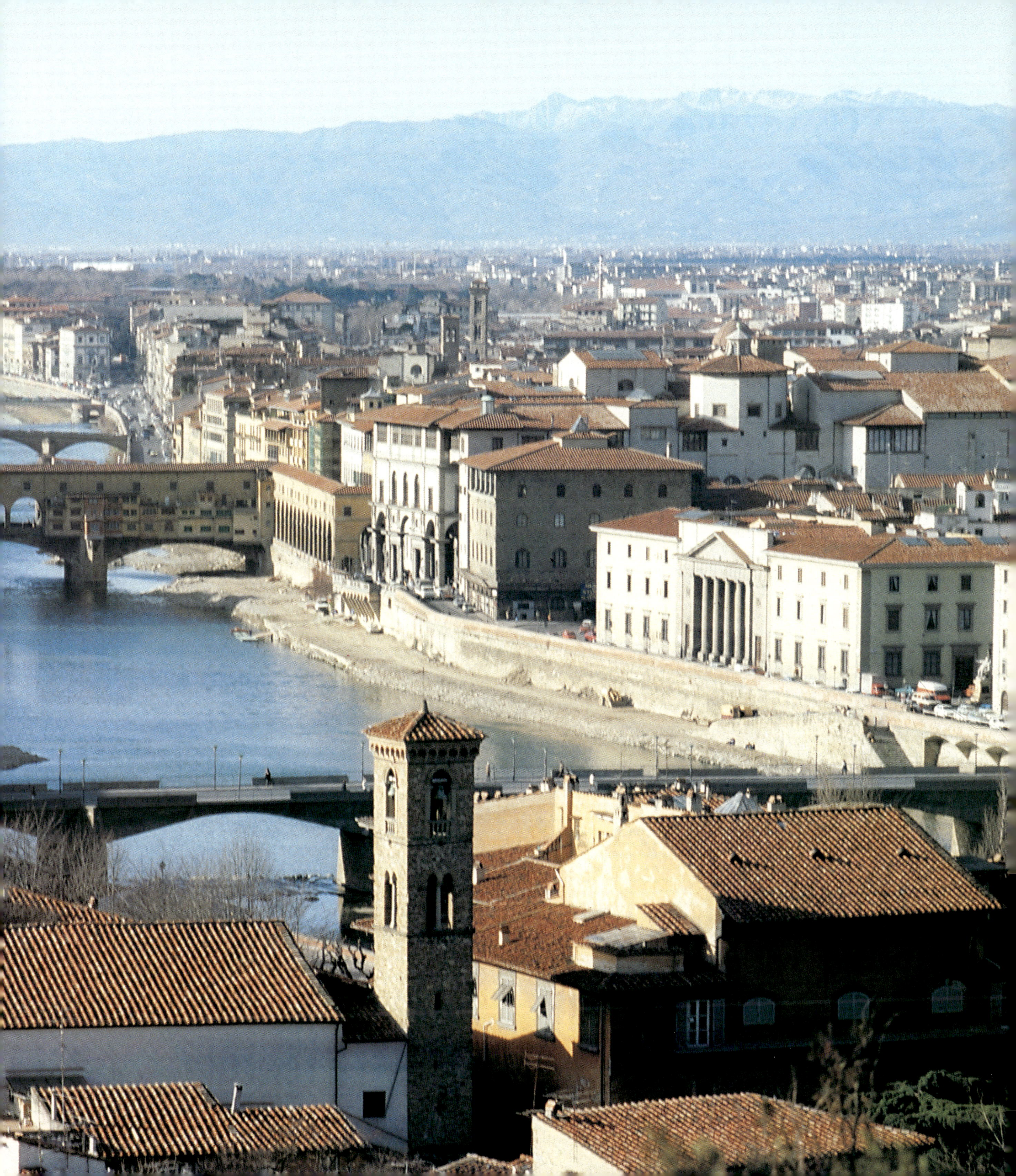

often took many decades to complete, and indeed, much of the duecento is characterized by the slow, steady spread of these extensive complexes — not simply the great new churches themselves, but also the large, sprawling ranges of monastic buildings, cloisters, refectories, kitchens, chapter houses, and so on. As in most Italian cities, by far the most dominant orders (both spiritually and in their effect on the urban fabric) were the Dominicans and Franciscans. In 1221 the former established their house, Santa Maria Novella, northwest of the city center, and only five years later the Franciscans settled their own monastery, Santa Croce, across the city to the east. By midcentury they had been joined by three other major orders: the Servites at the Santissima Annunziata in 1248, the Augustinians across the river at Santo Spirito in 1250, and that same year, the Carmelites on the south bank of the Arno. The Cistercians were also well represented, at Santa Trinità and Santa Maria Maggiore, both within the city, and at the Badia di Settimo, to the west of the city near the river.

THE FLORENTINE GUILDS (below, left)

Detail of the facade of the Palazzo del Tribunale di Mercatanzia showing some of the arms of the principal *arti*.

FIORINO D'ORO (below)

The gold florin, symbol of Florentine wealth and fiscal stability, was first struck in 1252. It became one of the great European coinages, accepted in all the major cities of the Continent.

VIA DE' SERVI (opposite)

One of the oldest and most important of the city's northern streets, although its southern end was demolished to build the vast new cathedral.

The foundations of Santa Croce and Santa Maria Novella were undoubtedly the most important new elements in the city's fabric. The latter edifice was built on land given by the cathedral, where

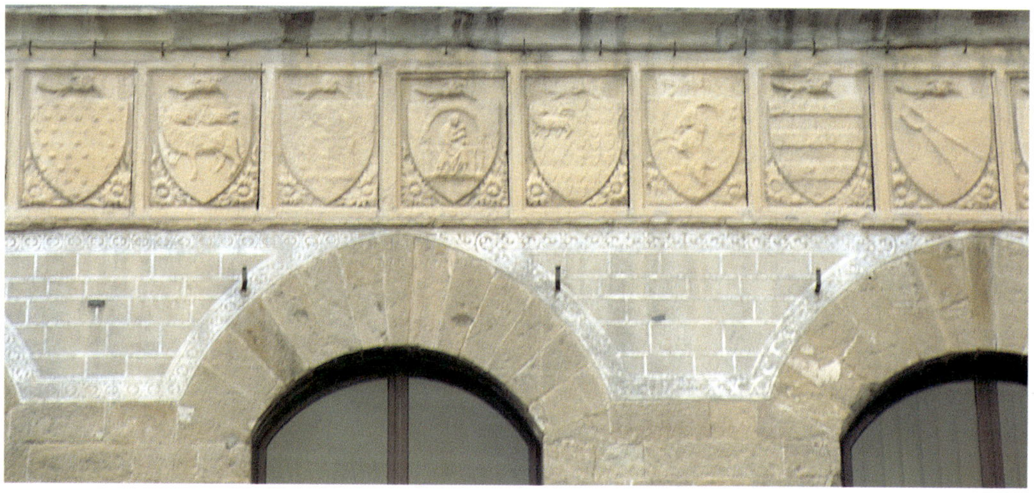

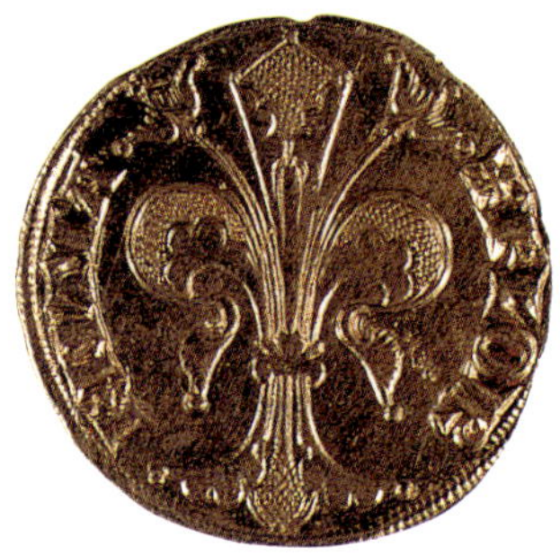

the church was begun in 1278; a few years later, the great square in front of the church was set out. A similar process was begun at Santa Croce, where the first church (founded in 1226) rapidly proved far too small and was replaced by the imposing structure, begun in 1295, that stands today. A great public square was also set out in front where people could assemble before hearing the preaching of the friars. Although there were significant philosophical differences between the two orders (the Dominicans were more intellectual, ascetic, rigorous, the Franciscans more practical and direct), both required broadly the same facilities that they did in all of the great Italian cities: a large, open nave to preach to crowds of up to several thousand people, who could, if necessary, overflow into the square at the front. Both orders also embraced a wide range of social, philanthropic, and educational activities, including the funding of hospitals, with lay confraternities associated with each of them. The two new foundations of the Oltrarno, the Carmini (Santa Maria del Carmine of the Carmelite order) and Santo Spirito (of the Augustinian order), also became foci for the social and spiritual lives of the citizens of the right bank. The latter church was rebuilt in 1269 after the original modest structure had become too small. Both churches were accompanied by the formation of a spacious piazza to create a religious and social focus.

Very closely linked to this rapid expansion of the monastic and preaching orders was the development of hospitals and other charitable institutions. Many had been established much earlier, such as the hospital attached to the Badia (1031) and that at San Pier Maggiore (in the eleventh century), but the Franciscans and Dominicans acted as catalysts for the creation of a number of new bodies, such as the hospital of San Gallo and those attached to Santa Trinità and

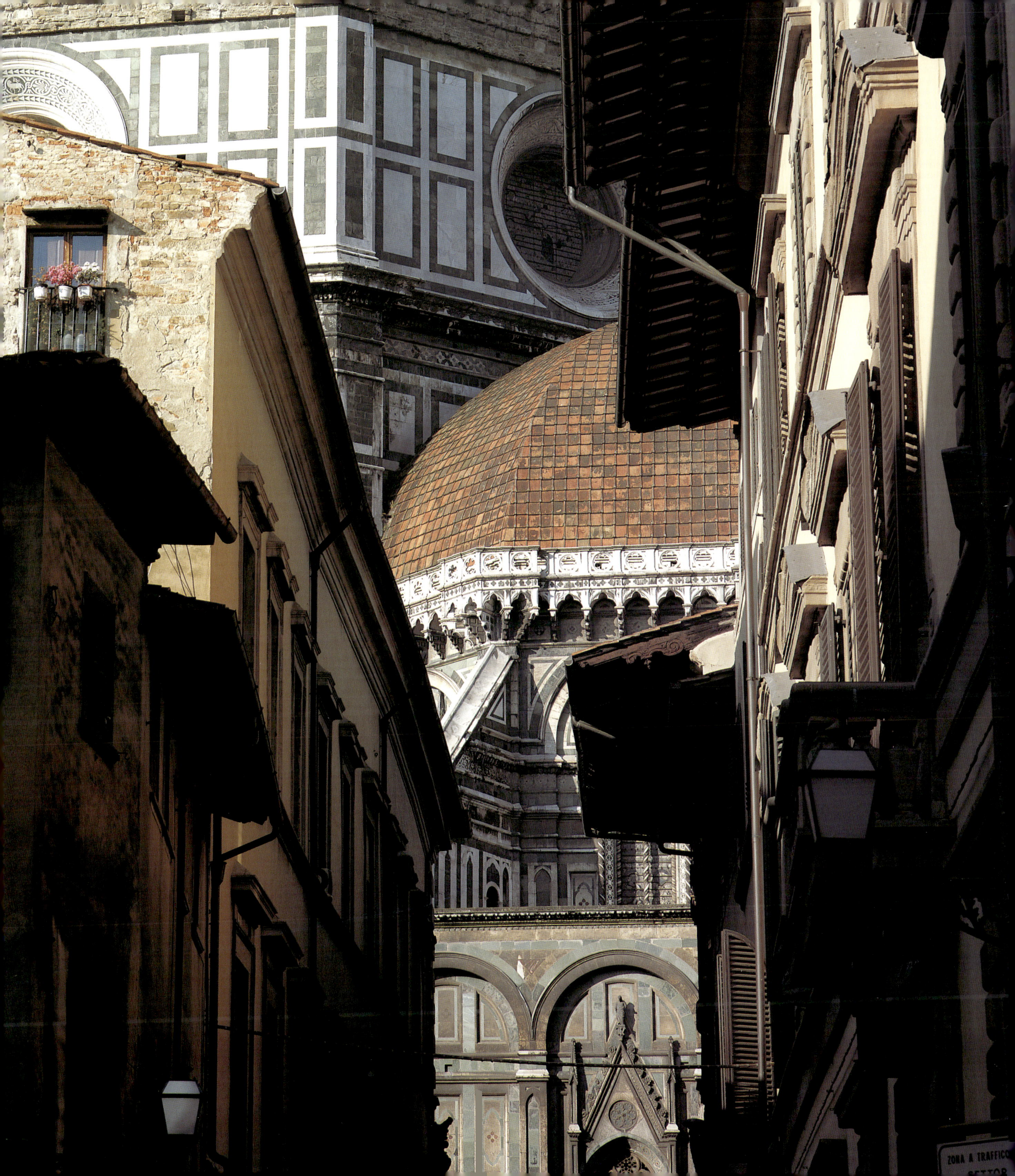
ZONA A TRAFFICO

the Santissima Annunziata. One such early foundation survives today: the Arcispedale di Santa Maria Nuova, founded in 1286, and enlarged in 1312. However, the present buildings date from a complete reconstruction in the seventeenth and eighteenth centuries. There were a number of others: the Compagnia Maggiore della Vergine Maria built two hospitals in Via de' Bardi, and another at Santa Maria Novella. According to the famous chronicler Giovanni Villani, by the early fourteenth century the city could boast of one thousand beds among all of these establishments.[13]

Despite these images of urban development, the Guelf–Ghibelline struggle erupted into larger-scale conflict repeatedly during the century. In 1248 the Ghibellines (supporters of the empire) rose against the Guelfs (loyal to the pope) and destroyed more than forty Guelf tower houses. The latter were exiled from the city for three years, until allowed to return in 1251. However, following Ghibelline attempts to consolidate their own power, in 1250 a popular insurrection of craftsmen and merchants against the Ghibelline nobility led to the establishment of the Primo Popolo, the first genuinely popular government — that is, government of the people by the people, rather than by the nobility.[14] It survived for a decade until the disastrous defeat of the Florentines and their Lucca allies by the Sienese at Montaperti in 1260. During these ten years of popular government the foundations were laid for the Palazzo del Capitano del Popolo (the Bargello). Finally the city was ruled by a "democratic" institution, which was to be housed in an appropriate new home.

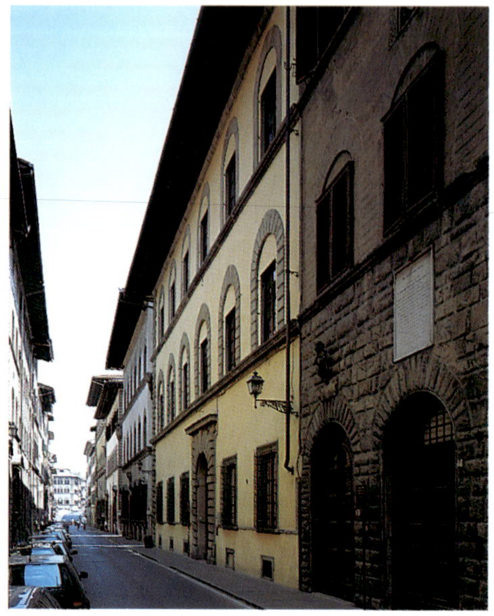

VIA MAGGIO (ORIGINALLY MAGGIORE)

One of the principal arteries leading south from the city center, the street was developed in the sixteenth century with a number of fine palazzi.

In 1258 the Ghibellines were evicted from Florence, and the houses of the famous Uberti clan destroyed, but the city continued to prosper. New public works were undertaken, such as the Santa Trinità bridge and a new street, the Via Maggiore (today's Via Maggio), which was cut through the congested alleys of Oltrarno to link this new bridge directly with the road south to Rome. And during this period the first golden florin, the *fiorino d'oro*, was struck at the mint, a potent symbol of the city's banking power and commercial wealth, despite the recent internal strife. The new coin rapidly became a pan-European recognition of Florentine financial expertise; symbolically it was decorated on one side with the city's patron saint, John the Baptist, and on the other with the lily, emblem of the city. Significantly, there were no representations of a power — neither pope nor emperor — to which the city owed allegiance.[15]

After the fiasco of Montaperti in 1260, a number of prominent Guelfs went into exile voluntarily, and the Ghibellines remained in the ascendancy until 1266. These were years of retribution, during which many towers and houses of the Guelf faction were destroyed; contemporary records show that some 103 palaces were demolished, as well as 85 towers and no fewer than 580 other houses. Despite this urban devastation, the effect of the political strife on Florence's commercial life was fairly modest, since most of the houses and workshops of the merchant bourgeoisie, the real backbone of the city's wealth, were unaffected. Thus, in 1282, two years after peace was made between the Guelfs and Ghibellines, the *arti maggiori*, the principal guilds that collectively represented the city's chief business and commercial activities, reformed the government. The new supreme governing body, known as the Priorato, was composed of elected members of these *arti*, themselves known as *priori*, later as *signori*. This new government was the Secondo Popolo, which ruled the city until the rise of the Medici. The original ruling *arti maggiori* had numbered only three, the Calimala, Cambio, and Lana, but were now joined by the other three principal *arti*, the Medici e Speziali (doctors and chemists), the Seta (silk workers), and the Vaiai e Pellicciai (leather workers). Later still, these six ruling guilds increased to twelve, and ultimately reorganized again into two groups: seven *arti maggiori* (the original six plus the Giudici e Notai, the justices and lawyers), and fourteen *arti minori*. In 1293 the pivotal Ordinamenti di Giustizia were published, marking the final consolidation of all political power in the hands of the mercantile *borghesia*. Henceforth the 147 clans of the nobility, both Guelf and Ghibelline, were decisively marginalized from the process of government.

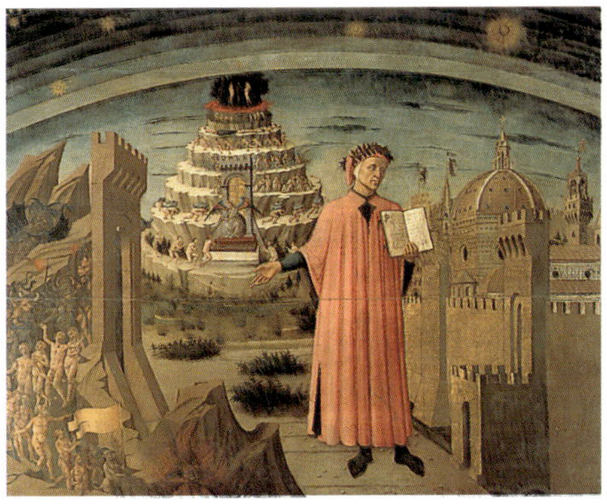

DOMENICO DI MICHELINO, *DANTE E I SUOI MONDI*, 1465

Detail of the fresco in the cathedral of Santa Maria del Fiore. In this famous painting, Dante stands with the cupola of the cathedral behind him on the right; in his hand, he holds the *Divine Comedy*, open at the famous first line: "*Nel mezzo del cammin di nostra vita . . .*" (Midway through the journey of our lives . . .)

Florence in the Time of Dante: The City in 1300

"*Fiorenza dentro dalla cerchia antica / Ond'ella toglie ancora e terza e nona / Si stava in pace, sobria e pudica . . .*" (Florence, within her ancient circled walls / Which calls her still to tierce and to nones / She lived in peace, was sober and was chaste.)

Dante Alighieri, *Paradiso* (c. 1319–20) [16]

Dante Alighieri was born in Florence in 1265, and his adult life coincided precisely with the city's peak of wealth and power.[17] The new, reforming government of the Secondo Popolo began a series of major public works in the period from 1280 to 1300 that permanently transformed the character and appearance of the city. Statutes of 1292 established bodies to control and maintain the condition of the Florence's walls, bridges, streets, paving, and so on. The aim behind these public ordinances was to impose discipline, order, and a measure of dignity onto the tightly packed, essentially organic (and in reality, fairly chaotic) form of the medieval city. Part of this campaign of reorganization included the means of government of the city itself, which was reordered into *quartieri* once again.

New streets were laid out, and others were cut through the existing urban fabric.[18] To the north of Santa Reparata, the Via de' Servi was laid out, as was the parallel Via de' Ricasoli; the Via de' Martelli formed the third of these new parallel routes, which, in time, established the character of this part of the city. This new, rational development pattern to the north of the city's nucleus was later extended and gave the entire zone a quite different character from that of the older districts to the south, with large, distinctive rectangular blocks of development (all orientated roughly north–south) separated by parallel streets. This rational pattern was continued by the construction of a new east–west cross axis through this district (the present Via Guelfa and Via Alfani). A similarly enlightened approach to planning was apparent on the western edge of the city center, with the enlargement of the Prato del Comune (the town meadow), next to Ognissanti church. The Prato was enlarged by the demolition of adjacent properties, and there was even a proposal to form an artificial lake, which, however, was not executed.[19] In the western part of the Oltrarno the improvement in communications offered by the Santa Trinità bridge and Via Maggio was also expanded upon by further large, rectangular blocks of development, analogous to those to the north.

Many other works of urban improvement were undertaken, among them the paving of streets. Paving had begun as early as 1237 but gathered considerable pace in the last two decades of the century. The Mercato Nuovo was paved in 1270, Piazza San Giovanni in 1288, and the Ponte Vecchio in 1294; by the century's end it was presupposed that all major new streets should be paved from the outset. The importance of paving as a process in "civilizing" the medieval city should not be underestimated, and was rightly considered a matter of great civic pride; much later, Alberti considered street paving a fundamental attribute of good *civitas*.[20] The definitive layout of Piazza Santa Maria Novella and Piazza Santo Spirito, as we see them today, was carried out in the same spirit of *civitas*. The former was defined in 1288, while the latter was enlarged in 1297 and in 1301, after demolitions. Both of these large squares, as well as that of Santa Croce, became major hubs in the urban network and important social centers.

But the most important planning decision of the era was, without doubt, the construction of a new city wall, the so-called sixth (and final) circle.[21] The initial impetus for its construction is said to have come from Arnolfo di Cambio, whose other pivotal contributions to the city's appearance will be discussed later; the fundamental reason for the wall's construction was simply the notable growth of the city's population. In 1260 Florence had around 75,000 inhabitants, a figure that increased to perhaps 85,000 in 1280, and as many as 100,000 by the end of the century. Florence was now one of the largest cities in Western Europe; only Paris and perhaps Milan, Venice, and

Naples were more populous. This remarkable increase in numbers was a direct reflection of the city's wealth and power, but it led to acute overcrowding, and there was great pressure to develop beyond the now highly constricting confines of the fifth circle of walls. The growth itself was due partly to internal demographic increase, and partly to migration from the *contado*, the surrounding countryside — the natural gravitational pull that such great and wealthy cities always exert over their dependent territories in times of prosperity.

Beyond the principal gates of the fifth circle was a necklace of extraurban clusters of development: the *borghi* of Pinti, Santa Croce, San Lorenzo, Porta Faenza, San Paolo, and Ognissanti. They were now all to be brought within the great sweep of the new walls, which were begun in 1284 but were so extensive that they were not finally completed until 1333, half a century later. It was the most dramatic expansion of the city's form in one single act since the Roman grid had been laid out a millennium earlier; the new walls multiplied by five the area contained within them. This new *intra muros* zone amounted to some 1,000 acres (430 hectares), and over 1,500 acres (600 hectares) including the Arno; the wall itself was approximately 5 miles long (8.5 km). Although most of the wall is now lost (significant sections can be seen today only in the Oltrarno), its course can be traced easily, and the location of all the principal gates, seven of which have survived, is also easily identifiable.[22] The wall effectively defined the city's limits until the modern era, and the new enclosed zone not only comfortably contained all of the aforementioned suburbs, but also embraced an extensive "green belt" of farms, orchards, and small land holdings, some of which survive until today.

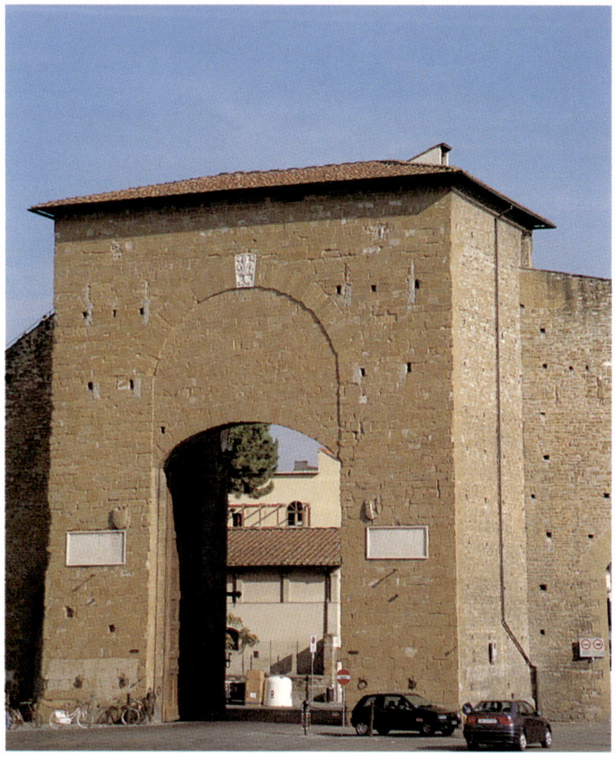

PORTA ROMANA (left)

The massive, simple form of the city's southern gate was built in the 1320s as the great new circle of walls was approaching completion.

PALAZZO DEL BARGELLO (opposite)

View of the upper story and the tower, with the campanile of the Badia Fiorentina to the left. Begun in 1255, the Bargello was the first structure purpose-built to house the city's administration.

Work started on the walls in February 1284. In the same year, the four principal gates were also begun: Ognissanti (to the west), Faenza (northwest), San Gallo (northeast), and the Porta alla Croce (east). This great project continued for decades, often interrupted by wars or other crises, but by 1290 nineteen gates had already been constructed. The comparatively short section of walls to the south of the Arno was completed by about 1294; these enclosed a roughly triangular area, with the river as its longest side and the other two sides running southward to meet at the Porta Romana. At their abutment with the riverbank, the gates of San Niccolò to the east and San Frediano to the west were built. The much longer principal sections of wall north of the river covered an irregular pentagonal plan, one side of which was formed by the river, while the others incorporated the chief gates, Ognissanti, San Gallo, and the Porta alla Croce. To construct the western section, the Mugnone stream, which had been diverted to allow for the building of the first communal walls, was diverted once again to run even farther west, just beyond the new wall, to discharge into the Arno west of Ognissanti, where the wall made a sharp turn toward the east, following Via Montebello until it met the Arno. In its completed form in the 1330s, the wall was defended by a total of 73 towers and had 15 gates. It was more than 36 feet (11 meters) high, while the towers generally rose as high as 115 feet (35 meters); only that of San Niccolò survives today to its original height. Immediately inside the circumference was a roadway for the rapid deployment of troops, and a similar open space provided a clear line of sight around the outside.[23]

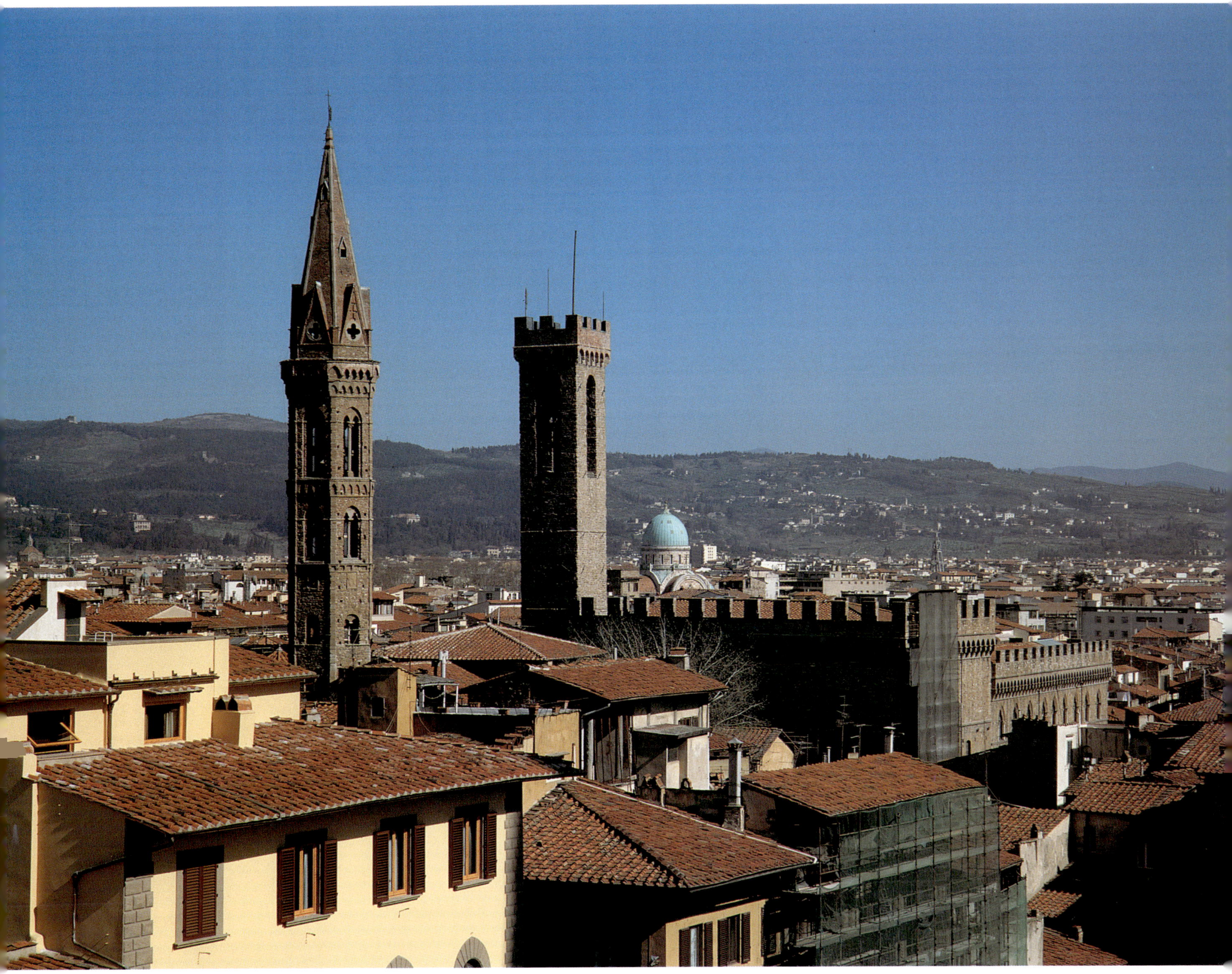

The architect of these great new walls is generally said to be Arnolfo di Cambio, who had an established reputation as a sculptor in Rome, Siena, and Orvieto. Arnolfo was to have a profound effect on the image of the city and its architectural history with the transformation of the old church of Santa Reparata, and the construction of the Palazzo Vecchio; and although there is still considerable debate regarding his level of involvement in at least some of the many buildings with which he is traditionally associated, there is little doubt that his influence was considerable. He recognized the importance of the key hubs and axes of the city, which is reflected not only in his development of the cathedral and the Palazzo Vecchio, but also in the enhancement of the principal axis, the Via dei Calzaiuoli, which linked them together. This recognition was reflected in the siting of a loggia on this axis, originally intended to house the grain market (and later to be replaced by Orsanmichele), and the beginning of the widening of the axis itself, a process, however, that was not completed until several centuries later. At the southern end of this axis, and only thirty years after the construction of the Bargello, the Comune decided to build a new palazzo *dei priori* to house the governing body of the Republic, that is, the heads of the principal *arti*. Although the government had been reorganized in 1282, it still had no appropriate building to accommodate it, and so, in 1298, sixteen years later, the Palazzo del Popolo was finally begun. The name is significant, representing a universal recognition of the popular nature of the government and its "democratic" basis. The nearby Bargello was to remain the seat of the *podestà*, so the two functions were clearly delineated and separated. The construction of the Palazzo del Popolo (or Palazzo Vecchio, as it is generally known today) took around thirty years; at its completion it represented the maturation of a building typology that had evolved slowly from the earlier, fortified castles, and was to form an exemplar for the last generation of palazzi such as those at Volterra and Montepulciano, albeit on a more modest scale. The piazza on which it stood was only slowly enlarged and improved to provide a worthy setting for this imposing structure, most symbolic of the city's great palaces. Until the construction of Brunelleschi's magnificent dome for the cathedral in the 1420s, the 312-foot (95 meter) tower of the palazzo was the most dominant structure in the city.[24]

The Palazzo del Popolo represents the final stage of the development of the communal seat of government as a building typology; at about the same time, the stylistic development of the Florentine individual family palazzo also reached a further stage of refinement. The wealth and strength of some of the great banking and mercantile families were expressed in the construction of imposing private palaces, some of which still exist today. These palaces were essentially more sophisticated and refined developments of the tower houses (or, more accurately, the houses with which these towers were associated) of the previous century, and are exemplified today by Palazzo Mozzi, Palazzo Spini Feroni, and Palazzo Gianfigliazzi. They are characterized by their rigorously disciplined, regular facades, usually impressively detailed stonework, and crowning crenellations; collectively they began to impose a new aesthetic order on the appearance of the city.

The last major project begun in this extraordinary building era was the new cathedral. Proposals originally had been made in 1285 to modernize the old, and still quite small, church of Santa Reparata, but these were quickly discarded as inappropriate for the patronal church of this great and wealthy city. The foundation for what was to become an immensely greater work was laid on 8 September 1296. The first record of the ubiquitous Arnolfo di Cambio as the *capomaestro*, or superintending master, appears shortly afterward, but he died probably only a few years later.[25] However, Arnolfo played a decisive — though debatable — role in establishing the plan and general dimensions of the new church. This immense project, which would take more than a century to complete, transformed the entire image and, indeed, the very identity of the city, and ultimately became Florence's greatest monument.

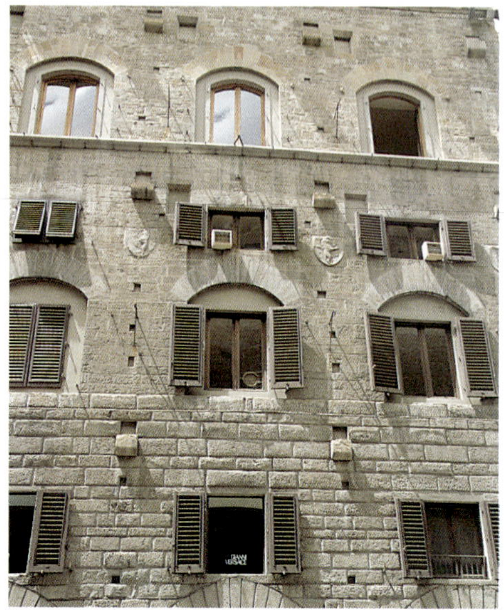

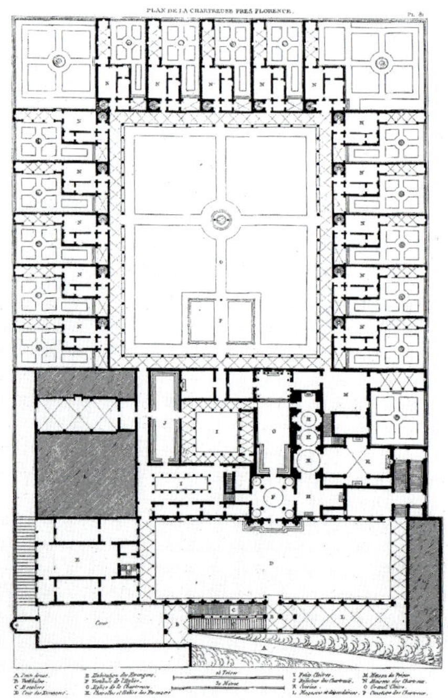

PALAZZO GIANFIGLIAZZI (top)

Detail of the facade; the palace stands diagonally opposite the even more imposing Palazzo Spini Feroni, both built in around 1290.

CERTOSA DI GALLUZZO (above)

Plan of the monastery of the charterhouse of Galluzzo, just south of Florence on the Via Cassia. The Certosa was a wealthy and influential monastic house and seat of learning, patronized by a number of noble clans, among them the Acciaiuoli and Visconti.

The Trecento: Crises and Triumphs

"At the top of the House (of the Ruler), there should be a high Watch-Tower, from whence you may at any Time see any Commotion in the City. . . . The Palace of a King should stand in the heart of a City; it should be easy of access, beautifully adorned." **Leon Battista Alberti,** *De re aedificatoria* (1452) [26]

The trecento was an era of violent contrasts in Florence's history: A series of disasters, both natural and of human origin, contrasted with the maturation of the city's form and the completion of some of its most outstanding works of architecture. Among the disasters that marred the century, the first was a catastrophic fire in 1304 that destroyed and seriously damaged about 1,700 buildings. The flames had been ignited by the disputes due to the factional division of the Guelfs into two rival subgroups. In 1300, following similar events in Pistoia, the Florentine Guelfs themselves divided into two factions, the *neri*, who favored a political alliance with the papacy, and the *bianchi*, who remained politically more independent. By 1301 the *neri* had succeeded in monopolizing the chief posts of the Republic's government, and in the following year, the *bianchi* — among them Dante Alighieri — were expelled from the city. (The city's famous literary figure was never to return, and died in exile in Ravenna.)[27] Another of the city's numerous fires was recorded in 1331 by Giovanni Villani in his famous chronicle. Famine struck Florence in 1315, and, in 1333, the city was devastated by one of the Arno's worst floods in its history. Finally in 1348 the plague — the Black Death — reached the city gates, eventually killing perhaps half of the population.

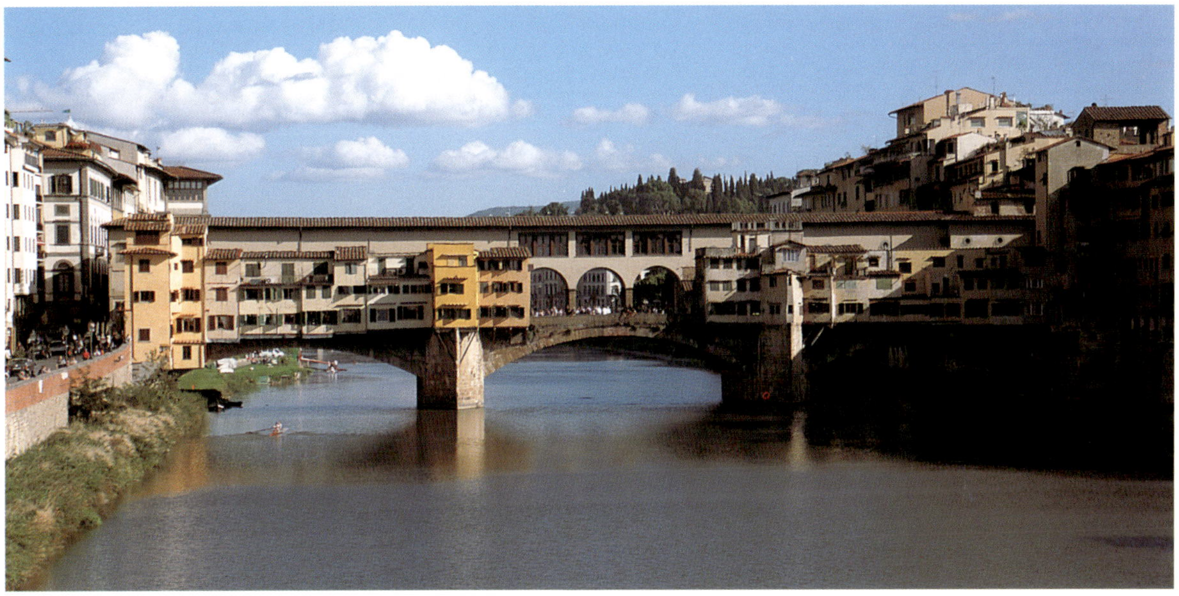

PONTE VECCHIO

Rebuilt in 1345 after its destruction in the floods of 1333, it remains one of the most characteristic and enduring images of the medieval city, surmounted by its jewelry shops.

As the century began, however, Florence was a flourishing city. Her coinage, the gold florin, was, like the Venetian ducat, an internationally recognized symbol of the city's wealth and financial stability. Politically, the early trecento was marked by the consolidation and enlargement of the Republic's territories; in 1306, Pistoia was taken after a long siege, and its lands divided between Florence and Lucca; in 1331, the whole Signoria, or lordship, of Pistoia became part of the Republic. Within the city the social and political structure had become more clearly polarized since the effective disenfranchisement of the old nobility. The population was now divided into two major classes, the *borghesia d'affari*, or the wealthy and influential business class represented by the *arti maggiori*, and the *minuto popolo*, the common people, principally engaged in the crafts and minor *arti* of the city. Since the former had complete command of the market economy, their hold over the latter steadily became stronger.

In the general urban development of the city, and despite the serious setbacks noted above, the century was characterized by the completion of many works begun toward the end of the previous century: works that further defined the urban form, but also individual buildings; the Bargello and the Palazzo del Popolo were both completed and extended. Fortunately, much of this activity is better documented than that of the earlier period; the invaluable accounts of Villani, for example, provide a great deal of precise information. The "formalization" of the city's form, which had begun with Arnolfo, was further codified in the trecento by a series of measures designed to control and regulate building works. This was a rather belated response to the very rapid and by no means fully planned growth in the decades prior to 1300, but it represented a twofold desire both to regulate and enhance the appearance and status of the city. A series of regulations controlled, for example, the width of new streets, paving, and attempted to eliminate the *sporti*, or overhanging jetties, that had proliferated in the crowded center as a rather desperate attempt to increase space on the upper stories of houses; external staircases were also to be phased out. Further regulations attempted to coordinate the alignment of new facades and impose a degree of unity on windows, cornices, and facing materials. Some of these measures were (arguably) purely practical — to reduce the risk of fire, for example — while others had a clearly more aesthetic premise. An example that embraced both categories is the 1325 measure that obliged a builder to construct the lowermost four *braccia*

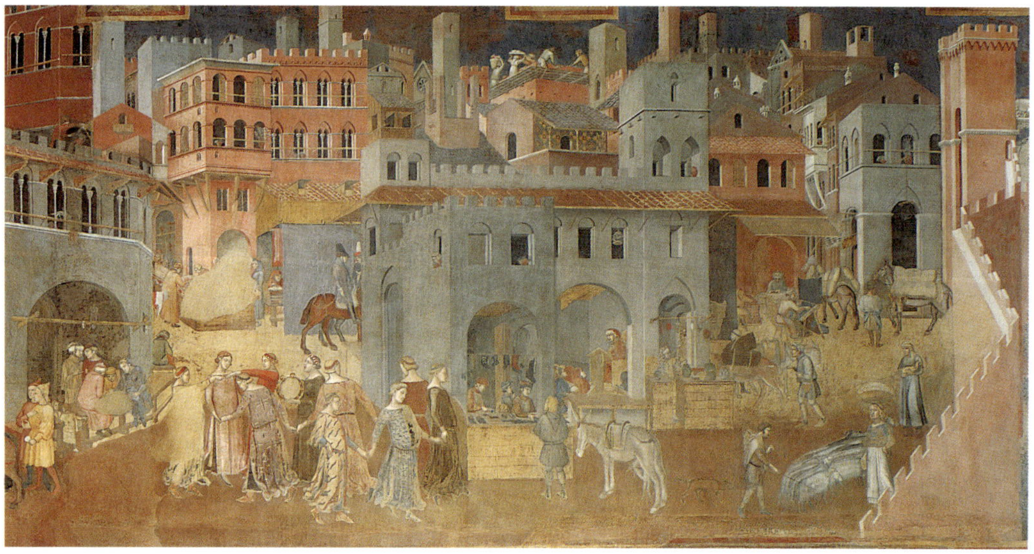

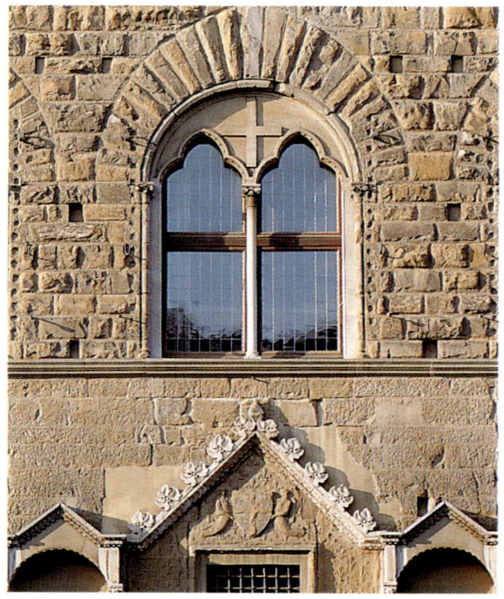

(about 8 feet; one *braccio* being equivalent to just under 2 feet, or 58.36 cm) of any new facade all in stone. Later, in the 1380s, all new facades on important piazze had to be of stone up to 16 *braccia* in height. New statutes, the Statuti del Comune, were published in 1325, which, among other requirements, imposed a form of window tax — an incentive to build new houses with fewer windows. More important in the longer term were the Ufficiali della Torre, founded in 1349, initially with the responsibility to maintain the city's defenses, but who accrued various other powers, such that they became a form of office of public works. Their name was changed to the Ufficiali delle Cinque Cosè, in reference to the five things for which they now took responsibility: mills, bridges, the city walls and gates, as well as the administration of goods and property confiscated from the "*ribelli*," that is, from the Ghibellines and other defeated factions.[28]

A number of works of urban improvement were undertaken in the early part of the new century. In particular, new streets were cut through the existing fabric while existing streets were widened in an effort to ease the congestion in the city center. These included a new street linking the Mercato Nuovo with the Bargello; the widening of the Via dell'Agnolo (for which Dante was the supervising officer), the Via del Palazzuolo, and Via Guicciardini; the first setting out of Piazza

AMBROGIO LORENZETTI, *THE ALLEGORIES OF GOOD AND BAD GOVERNMENT*, C. 1340 (Siena, Palazzo Pubblico) (below, left)

Detail of this famous fresco which represents the results of both good and bad government on the physical fabric of the city. The manner in which cities were best ruled was a widely debated issue in the city-states of medieval Italy.

PALAZZO VECCHIO (below)

Detail of the north facade with part of the original main entrance (at bottom); the original nucleus was built from 1299 to 1315, and was progressively enlarged toward the east.

ORSANMICHELE (opposite)

View of the facade toward the Via de' Calzaiuoli. This unique structure reached its final form after 1367, when the upper floors were completed; shortly afterward the ground floor was transformed into the present church.

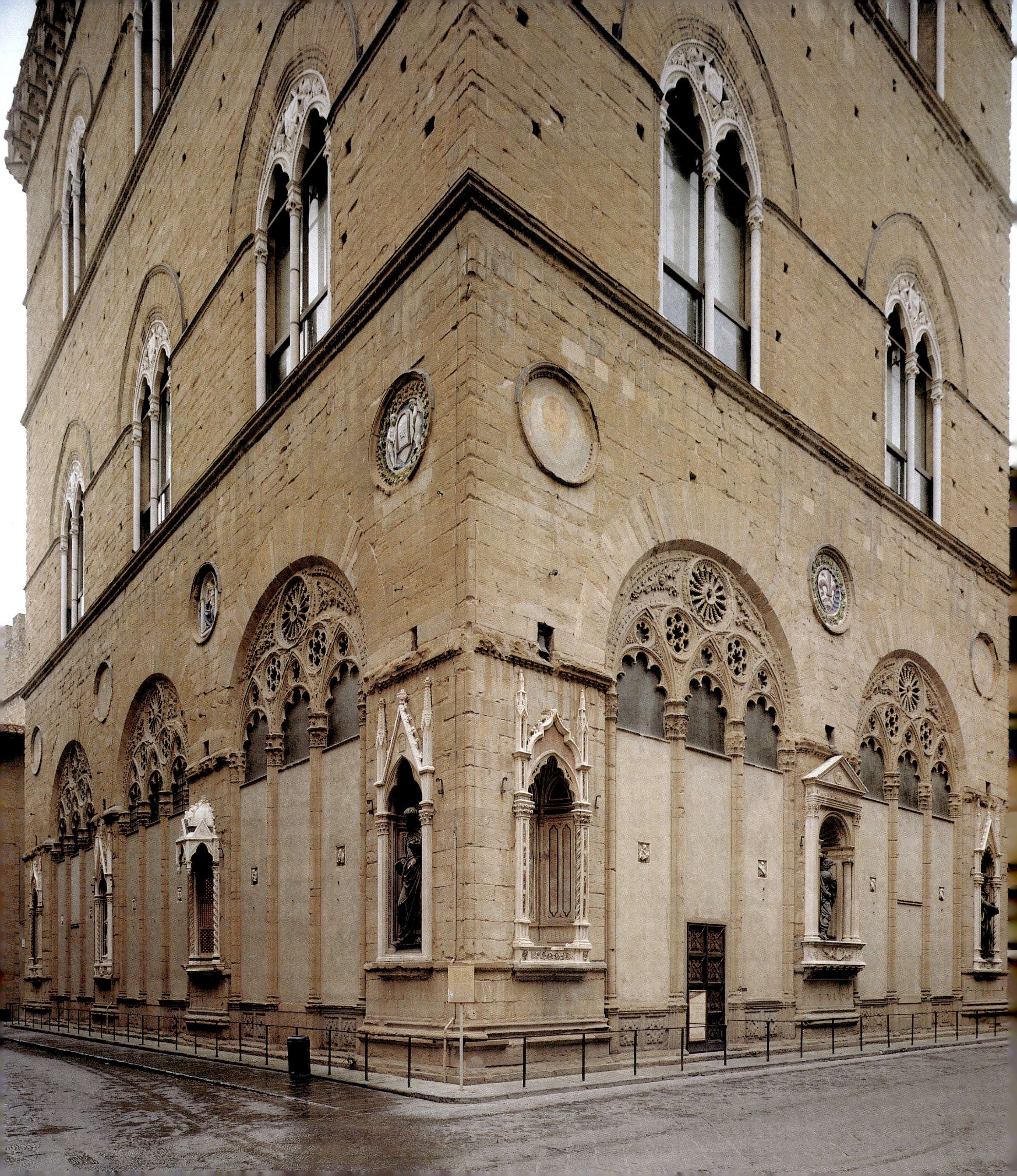

Pitti, and many others. All of these works indicate the activities of a commune attempting (as did many others) to impose order and discipline onto a city that, despite its rational underlying Roman street grid — by now much encroached upon and distorted — was as congested and chaotic as all other big medieval cities. But the most significant urban interventions of the trecento were those at the two principal nuclei of the city: the Piazza di San Giovanni and the Duomo, and the Piazza della Signoria in front of the new Palazzo del Popolo.

The formation of the Piazza della Signoria into an appropriate setting for the noble monumentality of the palazzo was a fragmented process, spread over many decades. Demolition to clear the square seems to have begun in 1307, with further clearances in 1318 and 1330. By the latter date its form was defined sufficiently clearly that it seemed appropriate to pave the square with brick and stone. Yet further demolitions took place in 1362. The palazzo itself was modified in 1342–43, when still further clearances were made to the south and west, thus creating a kind of cordon sanitaire around the building and rendering it easier to defend against insurrection.[29] The role of the piazza as the governmental and civic nucleus of the city developed in the course of the century, first with the construction of the Tribunale di Mercatanzia in 1359, then with the Loggia dei Pisani in 1364 (no longer extant), and finally with the grandiose Loggia della Signoria, begun in 1376.

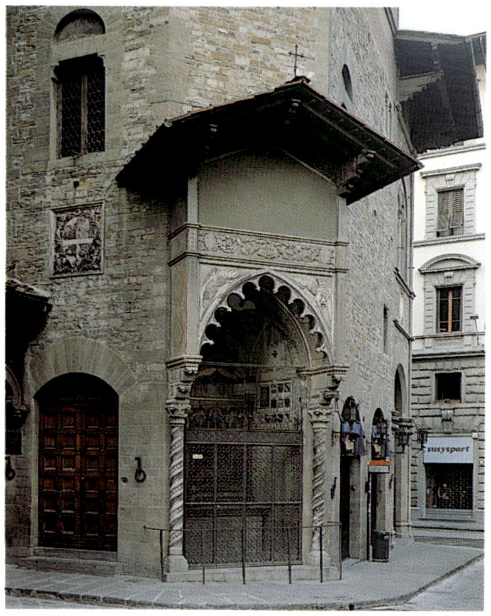

PALAZZO DELL'ARTE DELLA LANA (left)

Although built in the fourteenth century, the palazzo of the woolworker's guild acquired its present picturesque appearance as late as 1905, when the tabernacle of Santa Maria della Tromba was added onto the corner, following the clearances in the Mercato Vecchio.

ANDREA DI BUONAIUTO, *LA CHIESA MILITANTE E TRIONFANTE*, C. 1365 (opposite)

Fresco in the Spanish Chapel at Santa Maria Novella. The great new cathedral is depicted complete with a huge cupola (center left), although the structure of the cupola had not yet been begun.

The principal link between the seat of government and the cathedral was the axis of the Via de' Calzaiuoli. The importance of this axis was reinforced with the construction of Orsanmichele in 1336, to replace Arnolfo's loggia, which was destroyed in the fire of 1304. The new structure, by Francesco Talenti, Neri di Fioravanti, and Benci di Cione, offered a sharp contrast to the muscular stonework and essentially defensive character of the nearby palazzo. Orsanmichele was a very significant addition to the heart of the city, uniting the mercantile and spiritual worlds in a single structure.

The New Image of the City in the Trecento

With the written chronicles of Villani, painted images of the city from the mid-fourteenth century onward, the census details of 1352, and other records, one can re-create a detailed, comprehensive picture of Florence during the trecento. Villani provides us with some key data from the first quarter of the century. Florence's population in 1300 was probably on the order of 100,000, although this impressive number was drastically reduced by the tragedies of the century, above all the plague of 1348. According to Villani, 10,000 children in the city were learning to read, 1,000 students studied mathematics, and 500 studied grammar and logic. The great wool industry employed around one-third of the city's entire workforce, in about 200 workshops. There were no fewer than 80 banks and money-changing houses and an extraordinary 600 lawyers. The city contained 57 parishes (47 inside the walls, 10 without), while the 3,000 people in holy orders were accommodated in 5 *badie*, or abbeys, according to Villani (in fact there were 7), 24 other nunneries, and 10 friaries. Thirty hospitals of various kinds provided a total of more than 1,000 beds and employed 60 doctors and surgeons.[30] The census undertaken in 1352, in the immediate aftermath of the devastating plague, reflects the losses, but still records a total of 2,671 household heads engaged in industry. The overwhelming importance of wool production to the economy is apparent in the fact that half of this total worked in textiles, as many as those working in all of the other sectors together: food, metallurgy, leather, the construction industry, timber, luxury goods, chemicals, and so on. The Arte della Lana, the wool-workers' guild, had 9,000 members, out of a total population reduced by the Black Death to a mere 60,000.[31]

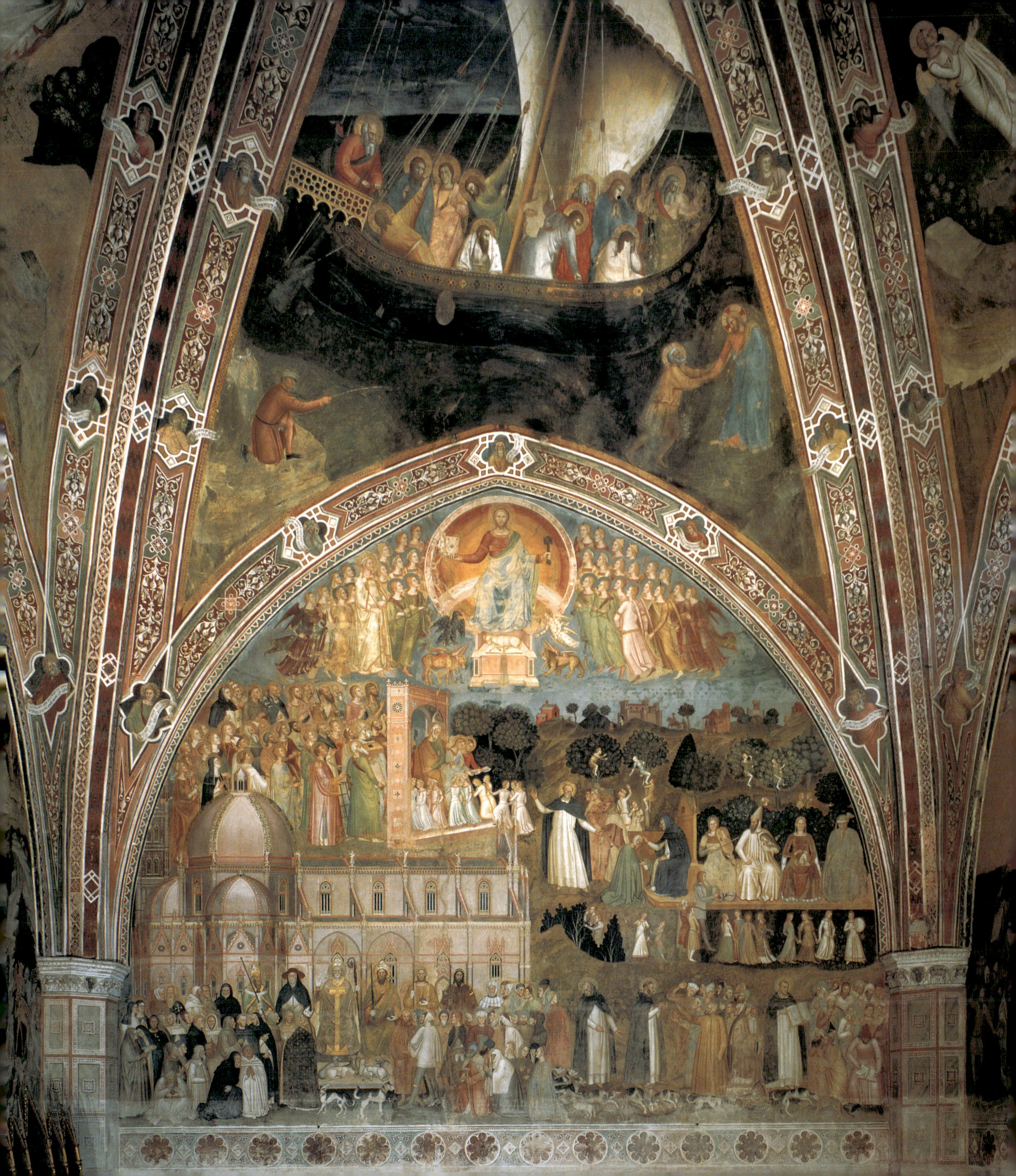

The oldest surviving visual images of the city date from the same period. The earliest recorded image is said to be the *Civitas Florentiae* by Antonio di Francesco da Barberino, painted perhaps in the 1330s. But rather more useful is a detail of the fresco of the Madonna della Misericordia from 1352, now in the Sala del Consiglio del Bigallo, where Florence is depicted as a densely packed, highly concentrated, homogeneous city, with many vertical features in the form of tower houses and campanili, and in which Santa Maria Novella and San Lorenzo can be clearly identified, as well as the baptistery and campanile, and the Palazzo del Popolo. A slightly later fresco in the audience chamber of the palazzo of the Arte dei Giudici e Notai (judges and lawyers) is a more symbolic depiction, with the city's structure and governance shown as a series of concentric circles: In the center are the emblems of the Comune, the Guelfs, and the Popolo; in the next ring are the arms of the city's *quartieri*, and *gonfaloni* (standards); in the next are the patron saints of the *arti*; in the

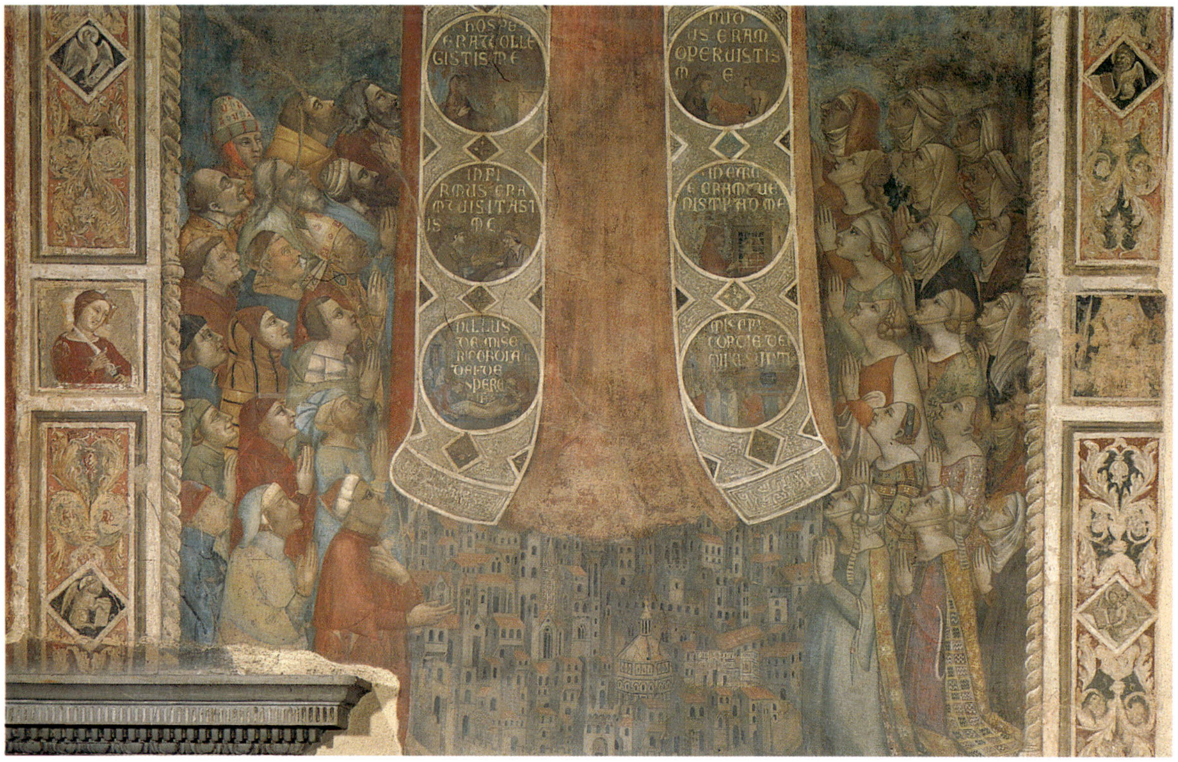

LA MADONNA DELLA MISERICORDIA, 1352

Detail of the fresco in the Sala del Consiglio del Bigallo. Below in the center is one of the earliest depictions of the city, surrounded by its stout new walls (the last circle), with the baptistery symbolically at the very center.

outermost are the coats of arms of the *arti* themselves, the whole finally surrounded by the city walls. Such symbolic representations were characteristic of the era. Leonardo Bruni, in *Laudatio florentinae urbis* (just after 1400), also depicted Florence as a hub with four concentric circles around it, but this time in slightly more literal terms: first, the city itself; then its defensive walls; then the outlying *borghi*; then the villas and farms of the immediate *contado*; and finally, the lands and castles of the territory of the state:

"The city is like the heart, positioned in the center of all [of its territories]; which, being first surrounded by its walls and by fine *borghi*, beyond these *borghi* in turn are the villas and similarly beyond these villas are the further lands and castles, all of which things are like a great outer circle bounding the whole region."[32]

All such manifestations sought to codify and, to some degree, mythicize the capital, its institutions of government, and its physical incarnation. The circular shape frequently used in such depictions reflects perfection, in much the same way that the circular format used in a depiction of Jerusalem portrays that city as the hub of Christianity, which spread throughout the world from this nucleus like ripples in a pond.

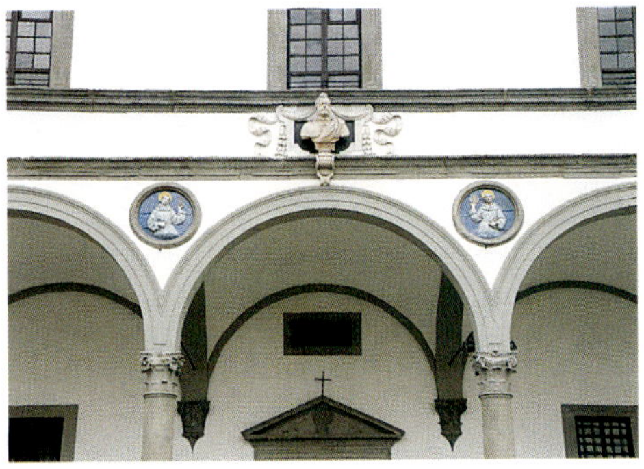

PIAZZA SANTA MARIA NOVELLA

Detail of the Loggia di San Paolo, built c. 1490. The loggia faces the church across the great open square, and although its architect is unknown, the design is clearly modeled on Brunelleschi's loggia for the Ospedale degli Innocenti, built a few decades earlier.

Florence in 1400: The Late Medieval Metropolis

"What city, not merely in Italy but in all the world, is more securely placed within its circle of walls, more proud in its palazzi, more bedecked with churches, more beautiful in its architecture, more imposing in its gates, richer in piazze, happier in its wide streets, greater in its people, more glorious in its citizenry, more inexhaustible in wealth, more fertile in its fields?" **Coluccio Salutati,** Chancellor of the Republic, Florence (1403) [33]

Although Florence did not expand to "fit" the Arnolfian walls for centuries, by the early trecento a degree of maturity and stability of urban structure had been achieved; there was only a handful of fairly clearly defined later developments. The first of these consisted of a large number of minor changes within the densely built-up fabric of the medieval core. The second was the expansion beyond this core, but still well within the walls of 1335. These walls had brought a large swath of previously vulnerable suburban land within the security of the new defenses, and was thus the most attractive zone for expansion. Much of this development was planned to some degree, and broadly followed the pattern of the earlier regular street grid to the north of San Lorenzo. Finally, there was a handful of individual works of architecture of great importance: those of Brunelleschi and, later, the many urban operations sponsored by the Medici. Most of these still affected limited zones of the city, though, and it was arguably only with the more grandiose plans of Cosimo I that the Medicean interventions became so widespread that they began to affect the very nature of the city as a whole.

In 1400 Florence was, within the walls, a fairly clearly structured city. It may be useful to summarize the chief zones of development before discussing how the city center itself functioned. The innermost rectangle, still based on the original Roman street grid, but now to some extent fragmented and distorted, remained at the city's core. It was very densely developed, and contained all of the central commercial activities — markets, banks, and so on — as well as the two principal hubs: the cathedral complex at the northern edge, and the Palazzo del Popolo in the south center. The zone immediately surrounding this core originally had been defined by the first circle of communal walls; it also was densely developed, although there remained a few patches of open land, chiefly in the form of gardens, small orchards, and cloisters attached to the monastic houses. The third zone was the very extensive tract enclosed by the last circle of walls. It incorporated a series of smaller nuclei, the *borghi* that formerly lay beyond the walls, but much of this belt was occupied by monastic houses, with their own gardens and orchards, and hospitals. There was ribbon development along the principal arteries radiating out from the city center, but a considerable amount of open land remained within the walls between these arterial developments. Beyond the walls, in the immediately surrounding *contado*, the land was extensively farmed, with semifortified farm-villas, some of which were already used by the wealthy for their *villeggiatura,* as country retreats to escape the heat of the city in the summer, as the setting of Boccaccio's famous stories testifies.

The commercial life of Florence was centered on the Mercato Vecchio, the Mercato Nuovo, and the adjacent Mercato del Grano, rebuilt after the 1304 fire. However, market activities spread to many of the surrounding streets; indeed, there were no fewer than eleven specialized piazze around the Mercato Vecchio, some little larger than courtyards, selling oil, wine, cheese, and other specialties. Street names from the nineteenth century — Via de' Pecori, Via delle Oche, Via dei Speziali — reflect these ancient specializations. In particular, the short tract between the Mercato Nuovo and the river, Por Santa Maria, was dense with mercantile activity, which continued northward up Via Calimala to the Mercato Vecchio and the present Via Roma.[34] The more important commercial activities were concentrated on Via Calimala, where many of the older banking and other trading families were also established, the Medici, Lamberti, and Tosinghi among them. The banks themselves were clustered around the nearby Mercato Nuovo, which was more extensive then than it is today; in 1421 no fewer than seventy-two banks were registered in

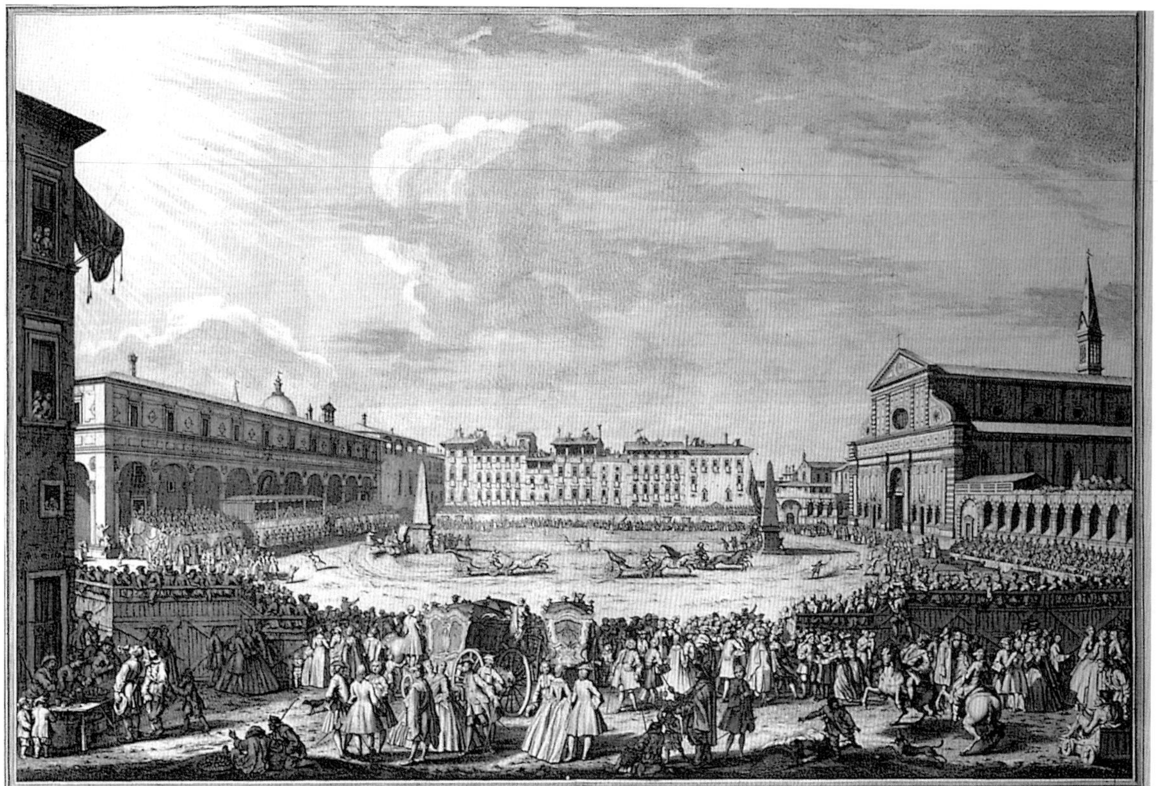

Veduta della Chiesa e Piazza di S. Maria Novella con la festa della Corsa de' Cocchi. T.XXII.

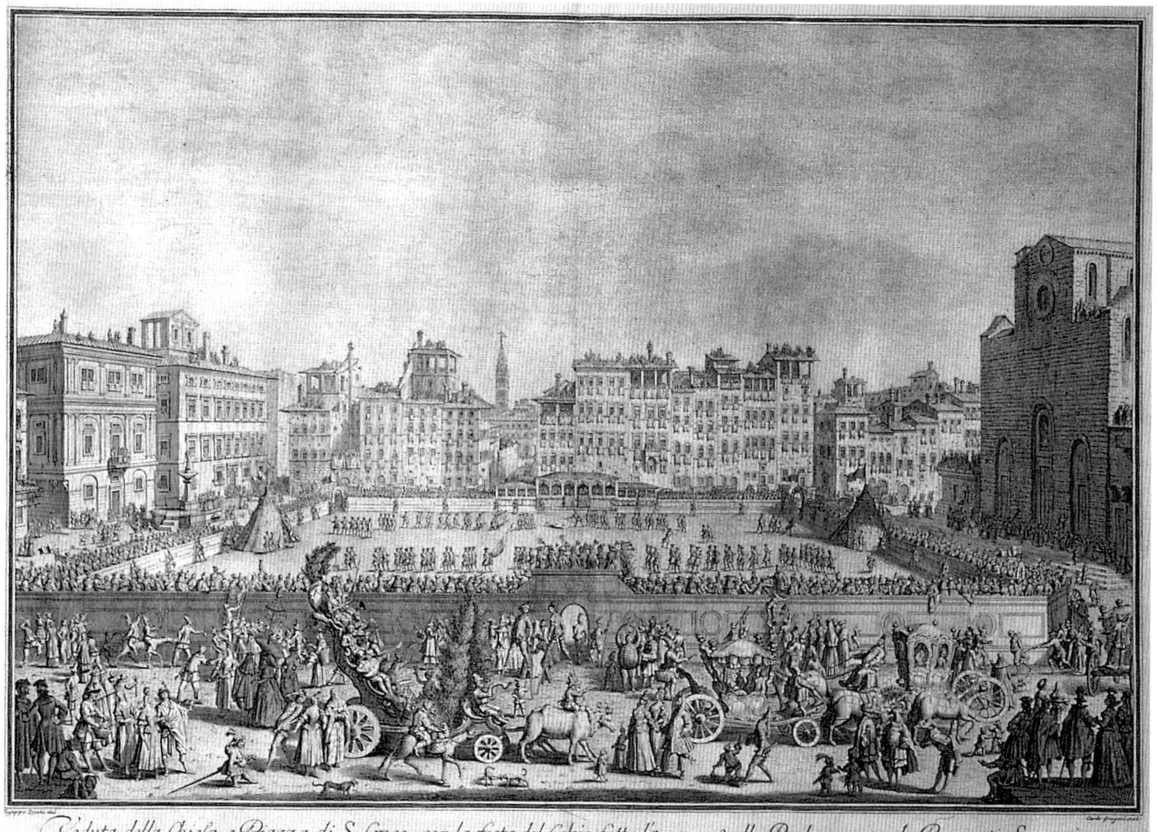

Veduta della Chiesa, e Piazza di S. Croce con la festa del Calcio fatta l'anno 1738 alla Real presenza de Regnanti Sovrani. XXIV

GIUSEPPE ZOCCHI, *VEDUTA DELLA CHIESA E PIAZZA DI SANTA MARIA NOVELLA CON LA FESTA DELLA CORSA DE'COCCHI*, 1744 (opposite top)

One of a series of popular views of the city published in 1744, the engraving depicts a carriage race in the Roman manner, around the square in front of Santa Maria Novella, reputedly instigated by Cosimo de' Medici in 1561; much of the piazza remains unchanged today.

GIUSEPPE ZOCCHI, *VEDUTA DELLA CHIESA E PIAZZA DI SANTA CROCE CON LA FESTA DEL CALCIO*, 1744 (opposite bottom)

From the same series as the above, this view illustrates a more popular sporting festival, the soccer game, which has been played in front of Santa Croce since the sixteenth century. Traditionally played between the districts of the city, this particular game was held in honor of the Royal family in 1738.

the city, many times more, for example, than there were in Venice at this time. The headquarters of the wealthiest of the *arti*, the Calimala, Por Santa Maria, Lana, and Cambiatori, were also concentrated on the Mercato Nuovo. The symbolic importance of the Mercato was further reinforced by a public proclamation stone, from which new laws were announced, as well as important political events and other news; a special chariot, or *carroccio*, was wheeled into the square to announce declarations of war.[35] On the south side of the market was the Palazzo di Parte Guelfa, the headquarters of the Capitano di Parte Guelfa, who was responsible for the maintenance of the city walls, fortresses, and other public buildings.

Trade flourished in all parts of the city center. However, there were in Florence (as in other great medieval cities) specific concentrations in certain streets and squares. For example, the *ortolani* traditionally sold their produce around the baptistery, the goldsmiths were grouped at Orsanmichele and the cathedral, butchers at Santi Apostoli, hatmakers at Santo Stefano al Ponte, and tailors and shoemakers around the Piazza dei Priori.[36] Goods were brought to market on carts or by asses or mules; wealthier merchants used horses; itinerant tinkers were everywhere. Almost all of the ground floors of buildings were occupied by shops and workshops; even the very wealthy leased the ground floors of their palaces to craftsmen. Public wells were generally located in smaller squares or courtyards, or set into niches in the walls of buildings, and they became focal points for social activity. There were fifty-seven of these in all, one for each parish. Public conveniences, on the other hand, were still probably nonexistent at this time; the Florentines had to make use of any quiet corner as the need arose.

By contrast to the extraordinary congestion of this innermost district, the area immediately around it was characterized by a string of substantial church complexes — San Lorenzo, Santa Trinità, Santo Spirito, the Carmini — that fragmented the urban pattern and contained more mixed development, with some older tower houses, humble timber cottages, and palaces built during the duecento, such as Palazzo Spini Feroni. The great monastic churches of Santa Maria Novella and Santa Croce, each with its own spacious piazza, became major secondary nuclei in this extensive outermost zone inside the new walls. Both churches became the hubs of their respective halves of the city.

The district of Santa Croce was characterized by craftsmen's workshops and a generally artisan population, with few palaces. Many dye-works (*tintorie*) were located here; the Corso dei Tintori has been thus named since 1313. They were not good neighbors, as the odors and effluent from the dye-works and tanneries undoubtedly served to ensure that these would remain working-class districts until modern times. The great piazza at Santa Croce was one of the major social hubs of the city, and because the Franciscans maintained a very close rapport with the people, the square was as much a part of the life of the church as it was of the daily secular lives of the inhabitants. The northern part of the city, beyond the cathedral and San Lorenzo, was known as Cafaggio. Its character was quite different from that of Santa Croce. Here the main axis was the Via San Gallo, and the urban scale, or grid, was much larger, with big rectangular blocks of development. Many of the streets were lined with hospitals and monastic institutions (a number of which are still there today), and the zone was largely residential, occupied by houses of the nobility and bourgeoisie, often with large gardens.[37] The area to the west was dominated by the sprawling monastic complex of Santa Maria Novella and the secondary complex of Ognissanti. The street plan of this zone was very simple, with routes radiating from the nucleus outward toward the gates, the Porta al Prato and Porta Faenza. As at Santa Croce, the proximity of the river meant that here, too, were wool workshops, dye-works, tanneries, and mills.

The district of Oltrarno had two principal foci: the churches of Santo Spirito and the Carmini. Like Santa Croce, it was a district chiefly of artisans, with many wool workshops but few noble palaces. It was only in the trecento that a few palazzi began to be built, chiefly along the Via Maggio, the main axis of the area. Almost all of the urban structure of the Oltrarno was focused on the bridgeheads toward the north bank, principally that of the Ponte Vecchio; building densities around this southern bridgehead were among the highest in the entire city. Some sections of the defensive wall that protected the Oltrarno were the last to be completed (and the southwestern part is one of the only two that survive today). It enclosed an area that, like the northern fringes, was by no means fully built-up. The western part of the Oltrarno, beyond the Via de' Serragli, developed in a rational manner, rather like Cafaggio, with an essentially rectangular street pattern focused on the Porta San Frediano. Much of the development here took the form of fairly modest terraces of housing, with orchards and small land holdings at the center of each block.

Florence's relationship with the Arno at the time was very different from that of today and, in several senses, much closer. For example, there were almost no public quays, or *lungarni*, along its

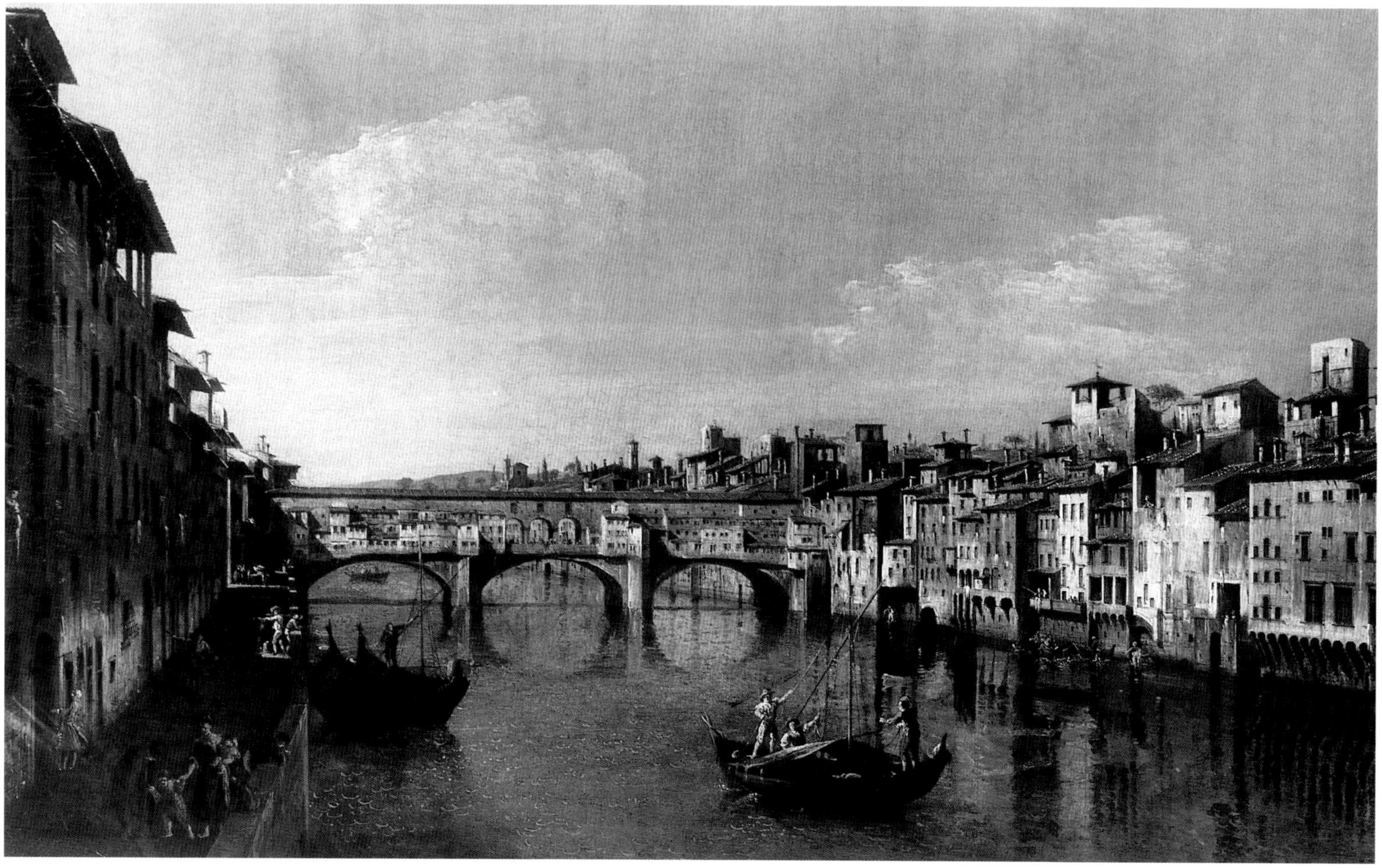

BERNARDO BELLOTTO, *VEDUTA DELL'ARNO DAL PONTE SANTA TRINITÀ*, C. 1740
(Fitzwilliam Museum, Cambridge, England)

Although the Ponte Vecchio itself remains unchanged, most of the buildings to the right, on the south bank, were destroyed in 1944 and rebuilt in a modern attempt to reinterpret these traditional forms.

banks in 1400, so locations where one could approach the riverbank directly were few. The first *lungarno*, between the Ponte alla Carraia and the Ponte Rubaconte, was built in 1300, but for a long time remained the only one. Elsewhere in the city center buildings encroached right to the water's edge, as can be seen today only on the south bank on either side of the Ponte Vecchio. The river was much more intensively used then than it is today; it was a truly working river, on which perhaps several thousand Florentines depended for fishing, milling, wool production, tanning, and dyeing, and as an artery for transport. Rafts of timber were floated down the Arno from the mountain forests in spring, much of it destined for the shipbuilding industries at Pisa. A small dock near the Ponte Rubaconte was used to unload goods for the city's needs. There was a great deal of river traffic between Florence and Pisa, which involved the transport of not only timber, but also exports of wool and imports of iron and other metals from Elba. As the river's level varied widely according to the seasons, and larger vessels could not reach the upper dock, a new quay was built on the south bank near San Frediano. Mills were concentrated on the north bank near Ognissanti, and there were many more upstream of the city in the Valdarno.

The Florentines had — quite rightly — great respect for the Arno and its unpredictable nature. The river's propensity for violent flash floods, particularly in the spring (when rains combined with melted snow from the mountains) and autumn, led, on many occasions, to appalling damage and widespread loss of life. The *alluvione* of November 1333, in which 300 were drowned, was one of the most destructive in Florence's history, and is vividly recorded in Villani's journal:

"[The waters] covered the whole plain of San Salvi to a depth of from ten to fifteen feet . . . the water washed away the city wall above the Corso dei Tintori . . . in the Baptistery of San Giovanni the water rose above the altar . . . and in the Bargello it rose in the courtyard to a height of ten feet. . . . The Ponte alla Carraia fell, with the exception of two arches. And immediately afterwards, the Trinità bridge, with the exception of one pier and one arch. . . . It was now the turn of the Ponte Vecchio. When it had become choked with the boughs of fallen trees brought down by the Arno, the water surged over the arches and, rushing upon the shops on the bridge, swept everything away except for the two central piers. And at the Ponte Rubaconte the water rushed over the top and destroyed the parapet."[38]

The Rubaconte bridge was the only one spared by the 1333 floods. The Ponte alla Carraia was the first to be rebuilt, from 1334 to 1337, followed by the reconstruction of the Ponte Vecchio in 1345.[39] (The Ponte Vecchio is the only Florentine bridge to have survived from that time to this day, while all of the others were destroyed during World War II and were later rebuilt.) The Ponte Vecchio was rebuilt with three arches instead of five, and is of more robust construction. The reduction in the number of piers meant that there would be far less resistance to the flow of the waters in future floods, but they had to be very soundly built. The cost of rebuilding the bridge was to be recouped by the income from the four groups of shops that were constructed on top of it. And as a conscious element of urban improvement, a substantial open space, or piazza, was left in the center, so that crowds could gather here to watch spectacles on the river below and appreciate the magnificent views of the surrounding hills.[40]

If the first half of the trecento was marked in political terms by a mixture of crisis and triumph in the city, much the same can be said of the latter part of the century. The terrible scourge of the plague returned several times after the devastating outbreak of 1348, and the recurring famines from 1365 to 1374 were accompanied by a further outbreak of the plague during the years 1373–75. The possibility of serious civil unrest in these difficult times was brought to a head in 1375. The initial seeds of this discontent were sown by the war that Florence declared against the papacy. The Florentines were themselves provoked to this action by the arrival on Tuscan territory of the mercenary troops of Sir John Hawkwood, an English soldier of fortune whose army, the "white company," had already conducted a campaign of terror in northern Italy, and who, the Florentines believed, was in the pay of the papacy; Rome replied to Florence's provocation by interdict. (Hawkwood was later given command of Florence's own army, and is for this reason commemorated in the famous portrait by Uccello in the cathedral.) The costs and sacrifices that arose from the war stirred considerable dissent within Florence and, together with the depressed economy and rising unemployment, finally led, in June 1378, to the revolt of the thousands of unskilled and dispossessed wool workers, the Ciompi. An initial attack on the palaces of the leading Guelf clans was followed by the assassination of the *podestà* and a direct assault on the Palazzo del Popolo. The Ciompi proclaimed one of their own as the new *gonfaloniere*, or standard-bearer, of the city, and established three new *arti* to represent their interests in the city's government.[41] But ultimately the rebellion did not succeed in its attempt to change the structure of government. The wealthier and more moderate *arti* did not support the radical Ciompi, and by 1382, after the *priori* had completed their term in office, the new guilds were dissolved. The oligarchy of the greater guilds was reestablished, and remained in power from this newly reinforced base until the Medici emerged early in the next century.

3 **Florence and the Medici**

"Now, if the cupola could be arched in a circular form, we might pursue the method adopted by the Romans in erecting the pantheon of Rome; that is, the Rotunda.
But here we must follow the eight sides of the building, dovetailing, and, so to speak, enchaining the stones, which will be a very difficult thing." **Giorgio Vasari,** *Lives of the Artists* (1568) [1]

JACOPO DA PONTORMO, *COSIMO DE' MEDICI IL VECCHIO,* 1519 (Florence, Uffizi)

During the early quattrocento, the emergence of a comparatively small coterie of wealthy and influential bankers and merchants slowly took a greater role in the city's government. Chief among them were Niccolò da Uzzano, Gino Capponi, and Maso degli Albizi; the last became the de facto ruler of this small, innermost group, and he was succeeded in power and influence by his son Rinaldo. Slowly the stage was being set for a fundamental shift in the manipulation and control of power in Florence. As the Albizi rule became less and less popular, the oligarchy looked to a member of another great banking family to replace them: Cosimo de' Medici.[2]

Cosimo's family had shown considerable sympathy for the Ciompi in the riots and disturbances of the 1370s, and his father, Giovanni di Bicci, was a highly respected figure with something of the common touch. He was an early patron of the arts: In 1402 he had paid for the north doors of the baptistery, designed by Lorenzo Ghiberti, as a votive offering against a further visitation of the plague. His son Cosimo was well educated in the humanist tradition and in the classics, and a flourishing intellectual culture would develop around him. Giovanni's bank had become the most successful in the city, partly as a result of his favor with the papacy, and upon his death, in 1429, Cosimo, age forty, became the head of the wealthiest and most widely diffused banking network in Europe, with branches all over Italy and in Bruges, Geneva, and London. But in 1433 Cosimo fell victim to the factional rivalry of the Albizi, and was imprisoned on charges of treason; he escaped, though, and went into exile in Venice. The Albizi fortunes in the city were turning, however, and during an absence of Rinaldo degli Albizi from Florence, a number of Cosimo's supporters arranged for him to return. In September 1434, Cosimo's exile was formally revoked, while at the same time the Albizi and many members of the clans that had supported them (including the Peruzzi, Strozzi, and Guicciardini) were exiled in turn. Cosimo effectively began to control the levers of power, although another wealthy industrialist, Luca Pitti, also retained considerable influence. But the extraordinary transformation in Florence's history that the Medici dynasty would bring about had already begun.

Cosimo, posthumously awarded the honorific title of "*pater patriae*," the father of the nation, effectively ruled the city until his death in 1464. He was succeeded for a few brief years by his son Piero "Il Gottoso" (the gouty), but Cosimo had laid the foundations for the remarkable rule of Piero's son Lorenzo, himself later awarded the honorific of "Il Magnifico" (the magnificent). During Cosimo's long period of power, and despite the fact that he, together with a powerful coalition of supporters, effectively controlled the government of the state, many earlier institutions survived. A new council, the Cento, or Council of One Hundred, was established to take responsibility for raising taxes and for issues of state security; here, too, the Medici "party" retained practical control. There were occasional voices of dissent and even of rebellion, however; in 1458 Luca Pitti, arguably the Medici's only serious challenger, raised a rebellion in the Piazza della Signoria and demanded the creation of a *parlamento*, or general assembly, but the rebels were rapidly countered by a Medici show of military strength, and they quickly dissipated.[3]

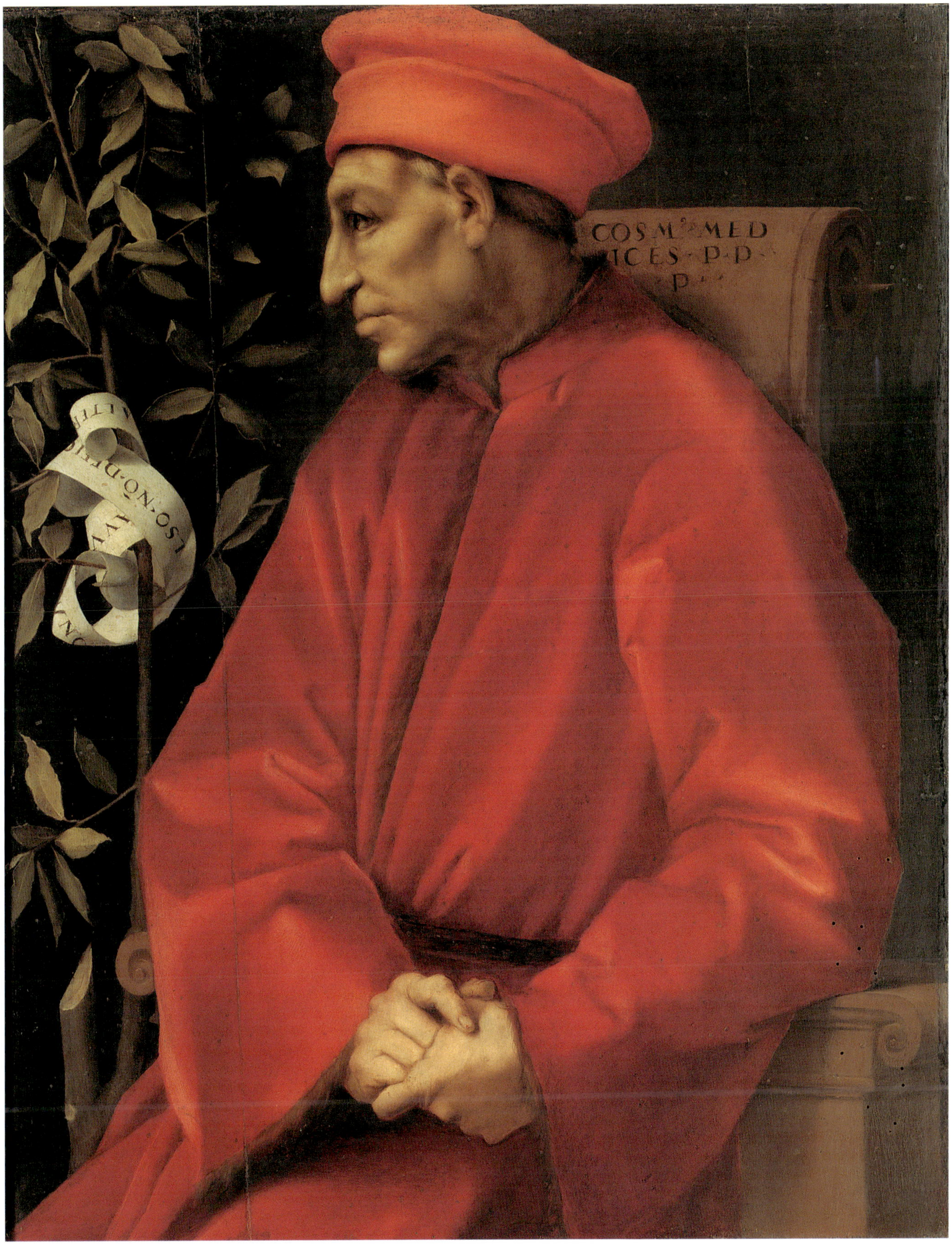
COS M MED
ICES P P
P

The picture of Florence in the early quattrocento is defined with considerable precision by the new *catasto*, or land registry, undertaken in 1427.[4] The registry, located at the surviving Palazzo Davanzati, is by no means comprehensive, but it allows further valuable insights into the social, occupational, and economic structure of the city. Of the 5,432 heads of household listed, two-thirds were engaged in industry, and 30 percent of all heads of family were working in the textile industry; this was still by far the largest single economic activity, and was complemented by a further 10 percent engaged in making clothes. Around 20 percent of those recorded were in the professions — law, theology, and medicine — among whom by far the most numerous were judges and lawyers, followed by employees of the Comune itself ("civil servants"), doctors and pharmacists, and spice dealers. Not identified, unfortunately, were the numerous banking dynasties that made Florence the financial hub of Italy.

PIAZZA DELLA SANTISSIMA ANNUNZIATA

Below, left: view from the south: Brunelleschi's loggia for the Ospedale degli Innocenti (right) was the first of three successive stages that were to transform this square into a classic formal urban set piece. The others were the matching portico of the Servite confraternity by Antonio da Sangallo in 1516 on the west side, and finally, the new colonnade and facade of the church of the Santissima Annunziata (center), by Giovanni Battista Caccini in the early 1600s. Below: plan of the piazza.

The city's urban development in the early quattrocento is marked, above all, by the interventions of Filippo Brunelleschi, whose influence was to be as profound and definitive as that of Arnolfo di Cambio a century earlier. But Brunelleschi was, of course, working in a city largely redefined by Arnolfo and characterized by its chief commercial axis, great monastic houses, bridges, and new

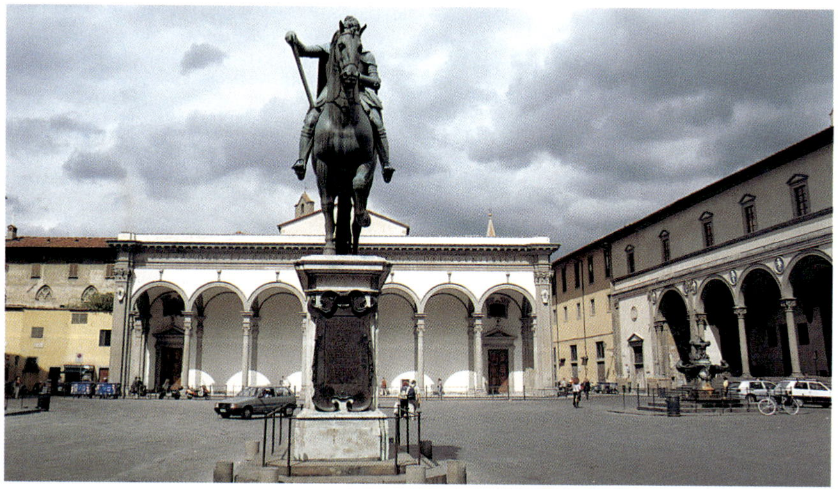

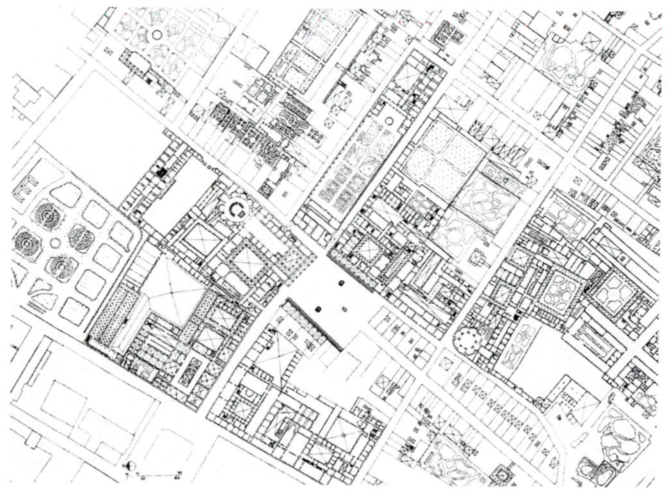

city wall and gates. Most significantly, the city was organized around two hubs of power, one spiritual and the other political — each signaled to the world at large by a tall tower. In this context, Brunelleschi's greatest achievement, the construction of the mighty cupola of the cathedral, was to stand alongside Giotto di Bondone's elegant campanile, a structure that would supersede all others as the defining image of the city: a fulcrum around which not only all Florence, but all of Tuscany was to revolve.

Brunelleschi's achievements are a fine example of the immense possibilities of a multifaceted genius in the right city at the right time. The humanistic culture in which his patrons themselves flourished was described by Manfredo Tafuri as "the earliest avant-garde culture of the modern era." Neither partner could have achieved their full potential without the other: Enlightened patrons needed Brunelleschi's skills, while he, in turn, required their open-minded patronage. Brunelleschi had a very particular vision: a vision of spatial organization, of the possibilities of the ways in which the city's buildings and spaces could be transformed and articulated in a new manner, one that was essentially formal and rational. The Renaissance city was to be built on the principles of order, symmetry, and harmony, and although it was clear that in a great, dense medieval fabric like that of Florence, any new interventions would be circumscribed by the limitations of the possible, works such as the Ospedale degli Innocenti and, above all, the cupola of the cathedral, imposed an order that extended far beyond their immediate urban site. Brunelleschi's influence extended long after his death, as can be seen in the long, phased

LA CITTÀ IDEALE, LATE FIFTEENTH CENTURY (Urbino, Gallerie Nazionale delle Marche)

One of three surviving panels painted anonymously, each similar in format, and representing variants of the Renaissance ideal of a rationally ordered and planned city. All three panels incorporate prominent use of one-point perspective to express the concepts of order and symmetry.

development of the Piazza della Santissima Annunziata, where his own key intervention at the Ospedale was followed in turn by Antonio da Sangallo's Loggia dei Serviti on the opposite side of the square in 1516, and the final completion of the composition by Giovanni Battista Caccini in 1601 with the new portico attached to the Santissima Annunziata itself.[5]

The portico or loggia as an urban element had already played an important role in the city's development: Porticoes for sheltering markets and logge attached to the palaces of the nobility were both well-established typologies, and in 1376 the grandest of them all, the Loggia della Signoria, had been begun. So Brunelleschi was working within a strong Florentine tradition when he developed the supremely elegant loggia for the Ospedale degli Innocenti. Here the loggia or colonnade is integrated with the structure behind it, forming an introductory element, a spacious zone of transition; but it also represents a powerful contribution toward the reordering of one of the city's major public spaces.[6]

Florence is a city surrounded by hills, in which the skyline plays a fundamental role in establishing the *imago urbis*. Before Brunelleschi, this skyline was punctuated solely by vertical elements, by the surviving towers of the noble houses, the various campanili of the churches

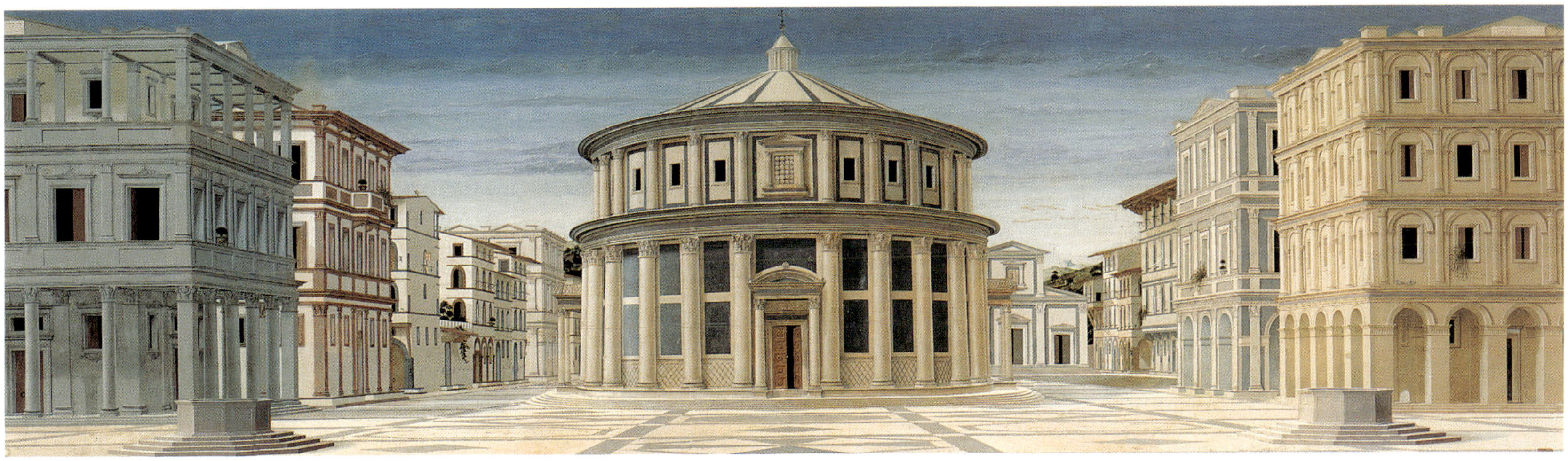

(above all, that of the cathedral itself), and by the two fortified towers of the Bargello and the Palazzo del Popolo. Now a new element, a massive, great vault identified the city: as a hub of the Christian faith; as the heart of the city's physical fabric; and above all, as a focus for Florentine and Tuscan cultural and spiritual identity, to which all of the state could look for guidance. There are few locations within the immediate environs from which the cupola can be seen in its entirety; its greater role, therefore, was to act as a beacon visible from almost every point in the surrounding *contado*.[7]

The tendency of clans to "adopt" a particular artist or architect is one of the more striking aspects of Florentine patronage in this important era. The Rucellai, for example, proved to be Alberti's most consistent and reliable patrons, while Michelozzo di Bartolommeo became almost exclusively the architect of the Medici clan, most importantly, perhaps, in the building of their new palace in the Via Larga, but also at San Marco and other centers of Medici patronage. Equally striking is the identification with, and subsequent development of, specific zones of the city by these individual clans. The Rucellai patronized the monastic church of Santa Maria Novella (of which Alberti completed the imposing facade), and which stands very close to the family palazzo; the clan also controlled much development in their own parish of San Pancrazio, including the family loggia built in the little piazza opposite their palazzo, and the family chapel of San Sepolcro, annexed to the parish church, which later housed Alberti's mausoleum for his longtime patron, Giovanni Rucellai.

The Medici, on the other hand, became the dominant patrons of the quarter of the city centered on their new palazzo — begun by Michelozzo in 1444 — and the family's own church, San Lorenzo, which was to be subject to a long series of interventions, enlargements, and elaborations over a period of more than two centuries. The Medici also spent large sums in the patronage of the monastery of San Marco (again in the northcentral part of the city, but a little farther out), as well as the enlargement of Santa Croce. A third and final example of such a concentration of patronage is given by the extremely wealthy Strozzi family, who built their own new palace toward the end of the quattrocento, and patronized the nearby church of Santa Trinità.

Arguably, however, no other pairing of patron and master had such a profound effect not only on the development of some of the city's key urban hubs or nuclei, but also on the development of Renaissance architecture itself, as the Medici support of Brunelleschi in the first half of the century. Brunelleschi's work at San Lorenzo began in about 1419 with the reconstruction of the nave, and although this imposing work was completed after his death, its commencement was followed shortly afterward by his Sagrestia Vecchia (the old sacristy, 1421–28), a small but highly significant work, the design of which became extremely influential. The sacristy was the first stage in the transformation of the church complex into the Medici family mausoleum, and was later joined by the Sagrestia Nuova and finally by Cosimo I's Cappella dei Principi. The first proposal to rebuild the Augustinian church of Santo Spirito dated from 1436, when Brunelleschi envisaged the complete reorientation of the building, so that it would face north instead of south; in front of its facade, a broad piazza was to extend to the banks of the Arno. His aim was to insert a powerful new element into the city's fabric, as well as tying the church to the center of Florence, and rendering it much more visible — indeed, making it perhaps the most prominent feature in the Oltrarno. However, the church as built retained the earlier, less urbanistically challenging orientation, although it remains an extremely important example of Brunelleschi's strongly disciplined approach, with its rhythmic and strictly modular system of bays, which inform the entire spatial hierarchy of the structure.[8]

The Medici and their allies were, of course, also active in their patronage of visual arts other than architecture. In particular, Cosimo nurtured the career of the young Donatello, for whom he provided accommodation within his own palace, and commissioned a number of important works, including *David* and *Judith and Holofernes*, and *St. George* for Orsanmichele. In later life, Donatello was given a pension by the Medici. Filippo Lippi, too, became a member of the Medici household, as did Fra Angelico, whose famous frescoes at San Marco were also the result of Cosimo's patronage.[9]

Cosimo's last years were marked by two great pan-Italian leagues or alliances. In 1450 he formed an alliance with Francesco Sforza, who, following the death of Filippo Maria Visconti, claimed the lordship of Milan, in which he was also supported by Genoa and by France. This new combined force, perceived as a serious threat to the balance of power in northern Italy, triggered a response from Venice, which formed a counteralliance with Alfonso, king of the Two Sicilies (who rejected Sforza's claim) and with Siena. However, the danger of all-out war in Italy was deflected by the fall of Constantinople to the Turks in 1453, and instead, in the summer of the following year, the various near-combatants formed a Holy League against the infidel at the Peace of Lodi. The last decade of Cosimo's rule, vindicated by these alliances, had brought a rare stability to the internal political situation in Florence, which brought back prosperity. In this period of increased wealth, the Florentine dynasties engaged in the characteristic behavior of the wealthy and powerful in such times: They built themselves great palaces.[10]

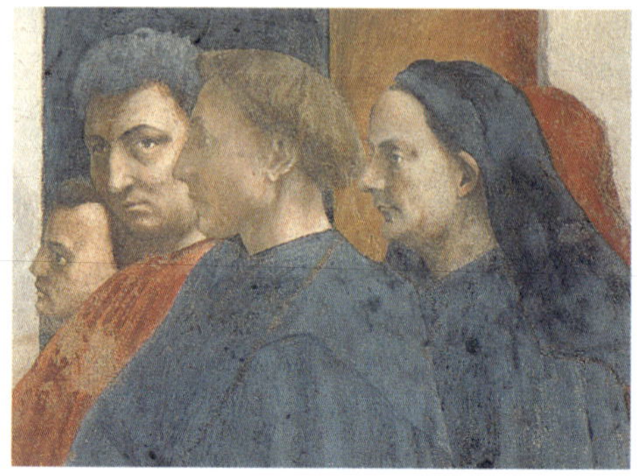

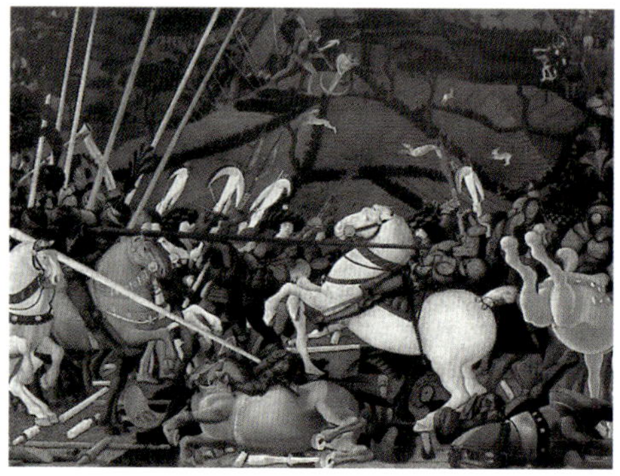

MASACCIO, *THE RESURRECTION OF THEOPHILUS'S SON*, 1424–27 (top)

Detail of a fresco in the Brancacci chapel at the Carmini; the figures are generally said to be portraits of Masolino, Alberti, and Brunelleschi, with Masaccio himself facing the spectator.

PAOLO UCCELLO, *THE BATTLE OF SAN ROMANO*, 1450s (Florence, Uffizi) (above)

Detail of one of three panels recording the battle between Florence and Lucca, which took place in 1432.

LOGGIA DEI RUCELLAI

The Rucellai family loggia stands just across the small triangular piazza from Alberti's palace and was built later, in the 1460s; little is known of its construction, but it was intended to display the products of the family's mercantile and industrial activities, as well as form a meeting place for the clan and its associates.

Piero di Cosimo and Lorenzo Il Magnifico

"... because the greatness of this man was of the highest order, and Florence never had a citizen equal to him, and his fame was very widespread both after his death and while he lived, [it seems] most suitable to give a detailed account of his habits and character. . . . There were in Lorenzo many and most excellent virtues; there were also in him some vices, due partly to nature, partly to necessity."

Francesco Guicciardini, *Storie fiorentine* (1509) [11]

Cosimo died on 1 August 1464; he was buried in the family church of San Lorenzo, his tomb marked by the simple inscription, decreed by the Florentines themselves, *pater patriae*. Despite this posthumous honor, the role of his son and heir, Piero, was by no means clearly defined, since he held no formal title or legal definition of his role. Piero survived for only five years, though, during which period he weathered a serious financial crisis in the city in 1464–65. War in the Levant between Venice and the Turks damaged trade and afflicted the stability of the banks in Florence, some of which (including that of the Medici) were severely exposed. Bankruptcies and unrest followed in the city, but Piero survived with his position strengthened. In 1465, however, attempts were made to usurp his power and a strong democracy movement swiftly developed.[12] Although it was quelled, Piero's constitutional position was still far from clear, and when he died, in 1469, his own heir, Lorenzo, was barely twenty years old. But Lorenzo was to preside over what historians have designated Florence's greatest period of artistic and cultural achievements, although the real extent of his role in many of these activities and creative works has recently been subject to scrutiny.

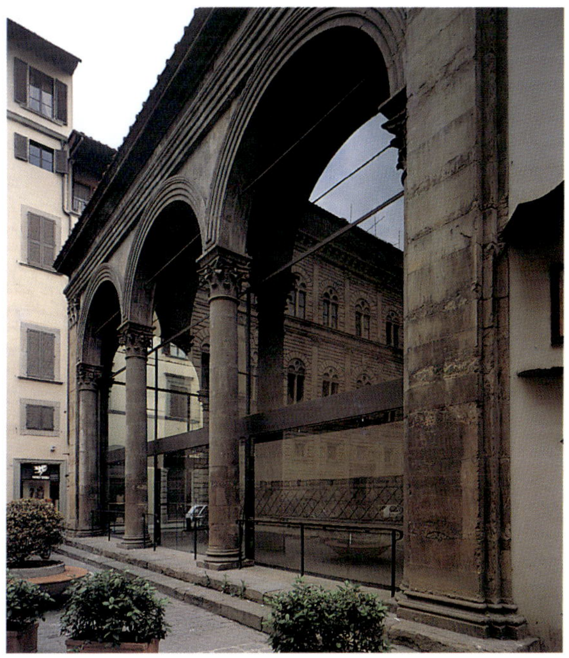

Lorenzo received an excellent humanistic education, including studies of Latin and the classics, as well as rhetoric, considered essential for his destined role in public life. He had traveled widely in Europe from the age of fifteen, and visited all the major courts and capitals of Italy. His mother, Lucrezia Tornabuoni, was also an important influence, a gifted writer and as financially astute as the Medici.[13] Only days after Lorenzo succeeded his father, the strength of the Medicean faction in the city's government, 700 men in all, voted to ensure the continuity of his political position; there were many in Florence who would benefit greatly from the stability and endurance of dynastic rule, even though Lorenzo's real character had not yet been ascertained. In fact, he showed comparatively little interest in the clan's great banking empire, and far more in the general encouragement of the arts and humanities, in writing poetry (for which he had great ability), and in the inevitable political affairs — particularly foreign policy — that his role would not permit him to ignore. But his unique position in the city's government led to resentment and conspiracy. Among those wealthy and influential clans that were not part of the Medicean network was the Pazzi family; relatively recently engaged in banking, they had lent money to pope Sixtus IV, and by 1477 were actively conspiring with other disaffected and alienated factions in the city. On Easter Sunday the following year, Lorenzo de' Medici and his brother Giuliano were attacked in the cathedral during High Mass. Giuliano was killed; Lorenzo escaped and took refuge in the sacristy. The Medicean reaction was swift and bloody; by the end of the day, three members of the Pazzi family as well as the archbishop of Pisa, who was an appointee of Sixtus and was implicated

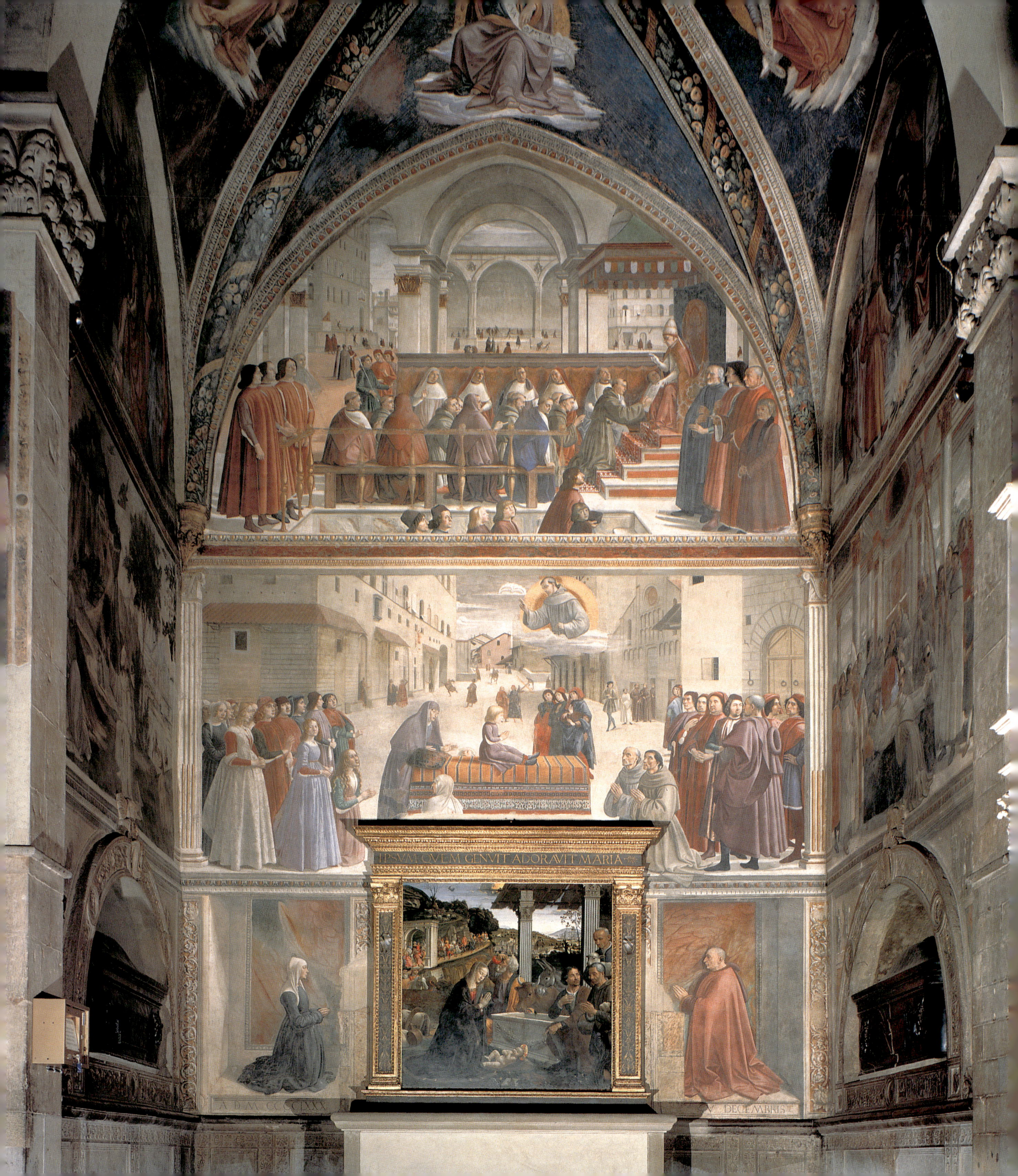
IPSVM QVEM GENVIT ADORAVIT MARIA
A D M CCCCLXXX
V DECEMBRIS

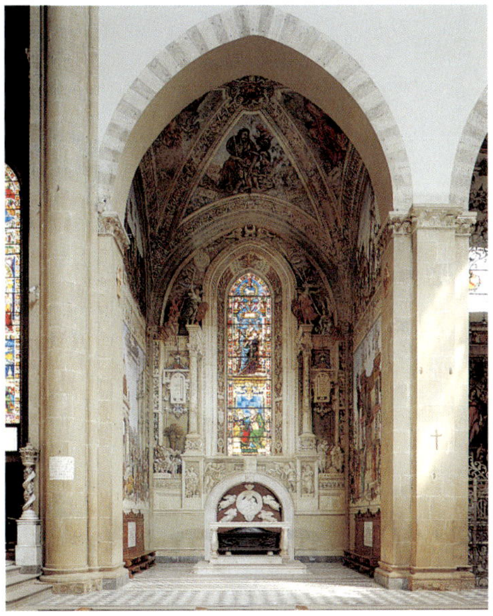

STROZZI CHAPEL, SANTA MARIA NOVELLA (above)

Built by Filippo Strozzi and decorated by Filippino Lippi and Benedetto da Maiano after 1489, the Strozzi chapel was one of a group of chapels patronized by the wealthiest and most influential Florentines, including the Rucellai, Bardi, and Tornabuoni.

SASSETTI CHAPEL, SANTA TRINITÀ, 1483–86 (opposite)

On the right side of the uppermost fresco panel, the murals by Domenico Ghirlandajo depict Lorenzo de' Medici with Francesco Sassetti standing on his left. Sassetti was the general manager of the Medici bank and the patron of the chapel.

in the plot, were all left hanging from the windows of the Palazzo del Popolo.[14] Over the next week, a further seventy conspirators were identified, tracked down, and assassinated. In retaliation Sixtus excommunicated Lorenzo, and the entire city was placed under papal interdict. Matching words with deeds, the papal armies approached Florence and defeated Lorenzo's forces at Poggibonsi, south of the city. But the war was concluded only after Lorenzo personally intervened in Naples to neutralize King Ferrante; shortly afterward, peace was signed with Rome.

The financial instability in Florence that these crises provoked led to further government reforms, including the establishment of a new council, the Seventy, who were to elect the Signoria, and whose members were elected for a five-year term, to ensure a high degree of stability. Only two years after the creation of the Seventy, though, in 1482, Florence became embroiled with the league of Italian states united against Venice's claims on Ferrara, this time with the combined forces of Naples and Milan. The military campaigns in northern Italy that followed throughout the early 1480s cost Lorenzo dearly in financial terms, although the city itself was not seriously threatened. Domestically still prosperous, Florence saw its economy suffer considerable losses in the fields of banking and international finance. The number of banks in the city fell from thirty-three in 1460 to only five by the 1490s, and the Medici bank itself suffered as much as the others; branches in London and Bruges were both closed by the early 1480s.[15]

Lorenzo's political role always remained somewhat ambiguous. In a sense (as he himself always claimed), he remained simply *primus inter pares*, and although a law was passed in 1481 stating that any conspiracy against Lorenzo was de facto a plot against the state itself, he held no official title other than the various offices he occupied at one time or another: member of the Seventy, of the Hundred, and so on — a public servant in theory no different from three hundred or so others. Nevertheless, his status and the strength of the Medicean faction gave him for twenty years more power and influence than any other man in Florence.[16]

The Image of the City in the Quattrocento

"Florence is more beautiful and five hundred and forty years older than your Venice. We spring from triply noble blood. We are one-third Roman, one-third Frankish and one third Fiesolan. . . . We have two trades greater than any four of yours in Venice put together — the trades of wool and silk . . . ask those who should know, as they go to fairs every year, whether they have seen the banks of the Medici, the Pazzi, the Capponi, the Buondelmonti, the Corsini, the Falconieri, the Portinari and the Ghini, and a hundred of others." **Benedetto Dei,** Letter to a Venetian, Florence (1472) [17]

Visual depictions of Florence became more and more numerous during the course of the century; the city appears frequently as a backdrop to the paintings of Sandro Botticelli, Masaccio, and Domenico Ghirlandajo. But the oldest existing documents that provide us with detailed information on the city's form date to the 1470s: the "*della catena*" view of about 1472, and the written description of Florence by Benedetto Dei from the same year.[18] The "*della catena*" view (so called because of the chain that surrounds the image), which is attributed to Francesco Rosselli, is a wood engraving on six panels; it has immense historical importance as the first detailed, reasonably accurate picture of the city, and because it is drawn from direct observation, according to the precepts of Alberti. Florence is seen from the southwest, from a point on or near the campanile on the hill of Monte Oliveto, but the viewpoint has been raised considerably higher to clarify many details within the city. Although the view gives undue prominence to the Oltrarno, it is centered precisely on the cupola of the cathedral, in a symbolic convention followed by almost all subsequent *vedutisti*, or views.

Many conclusions can be drawn from this comprehensive portrait. The city is girded by its daunting defensive walls, which are interrupted at frequent intervals by imposing towers. Beyond lie the gently rolling meadows of the immediate *contado*, scattered with farms and villas; the hills of Fiesole and San Francesco define the limits on the northeast side, while those of San Miniato define them to the southeast. Outside the walls, ribbon development beyond the Porta Faenza and Porta San Gallo is visible, as well as small clusters of housing outside the lesser gates. Immediately within the city walls is a large zone only partly built up, but ribbon development along the principal radial routes toward the city gates can be identified clearly. In the northern districts, the dominant features are the Santissima Annunziata church and the Ospedale degli Innocenti, together with their great piazza; closer to the viewer is the monastery of Santa Maria Novella. The heart of the city is extremely densely developed, and the chief features, with Brunelleschi's dome, are the baptistery, Giotto's campanile, and the cluster of civic structures: Orsanmichele, and the Palazzo del Popolo and the Bargello with their tall defensive towers. Palazzo Spini, later Feroni, dominates the bridgehead of Santa Trinità, while the other bridges are all clearly identifiable, particularly the Ponte Vecchio and Ponte Rubaconte, with their shops. The Oltrarno is circumscribed by its daunting wall, which rises around the back of Palazzo Pitti to enclose the future site of the Boboli gardens. The palazzo is the most dominant structure on this side of the river — followed by the two churches of the Carmini and Santo Spirito — although at this time Luca Pitti's new palace still consisted solely of the seven original central bays; its noble scale nevertheless clearly impressed Rosselli. Ribbon growth again can be seen on the south bank, particularly along the road toward Pisa.

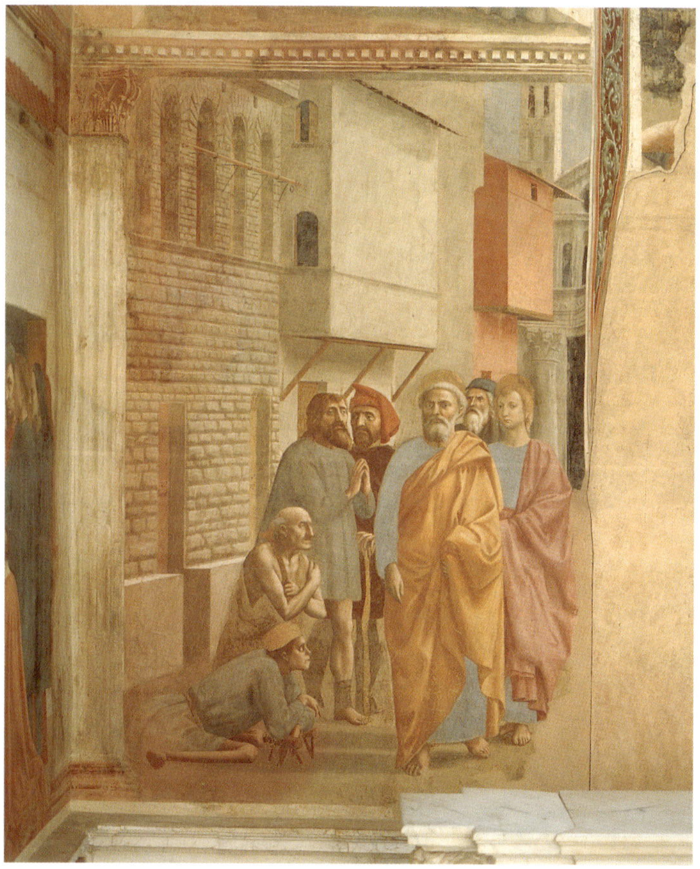

MASACCIO, *SAN PIETRO RISANA GLI INFERMI CON L'OMBRA* (left)

Detail of a fresco in the Brancacci chapel at the Carmini. Many painters of the period used the image of the city as a natural backdrop to the subjects of their paintings; here, the rusticated stone of a great palace contrasts with the simple stucco of the *sporti* of the ordinary houses.

FLORENTIA (Paris, Bibliotheque Nationale de France) (opposite)

Rendering to illustrate Ptolemy's *Geografia*, which was probably first drawn in about 1420, but was copied on more than one occasion later in the quattrocento. The city is represented by its principal monuments as a collection of urban landmarks rather than as a dense, crowded metropolis.

The "*della catena*" view was to be followed by many others, most of them using a very similar format in the mid-sixteenth century. For example, the "Nuremberg view" of 1493 (a woodcut forming part of Hartmann Schedel's *Liber chronicarum*) adopted an identical viewpoint and very similar representation.[19] A convention thus established proved remarkably durable. But the most important aspect was that all were built on a defined image: a unified city, a nucleus set within its beautiful natural context (rivers, hills, woods, olive groves, vineyards) over which it ruled, and with a clearly defined innermost core, at the very center of which always rises Brunelleschi's cupola, symbol of the city.

The "*della catena*" view was complemented by the written description of the city by Benedetto Dei in *Cronica fiorentina*. Dei was one of the Medici bank's agents, widely traveled in Europe, and his well-known *laudatio* forms one example of a widespread cultural phenomenon in the quattrocento: the praise of one's home city as being the greatest, wealthiest, best governed, and altogether most highly civilized place in the Western world, often also incorporating the denigration, sometimes subtle, sometimes direct, of other contenders for this honor. Thus, Dei begins every item in his painstaking list of factual data with the hypnotically repetitious phrase "*Florentia bella ha . . .*" (beautiful Florence has . . .).[20]

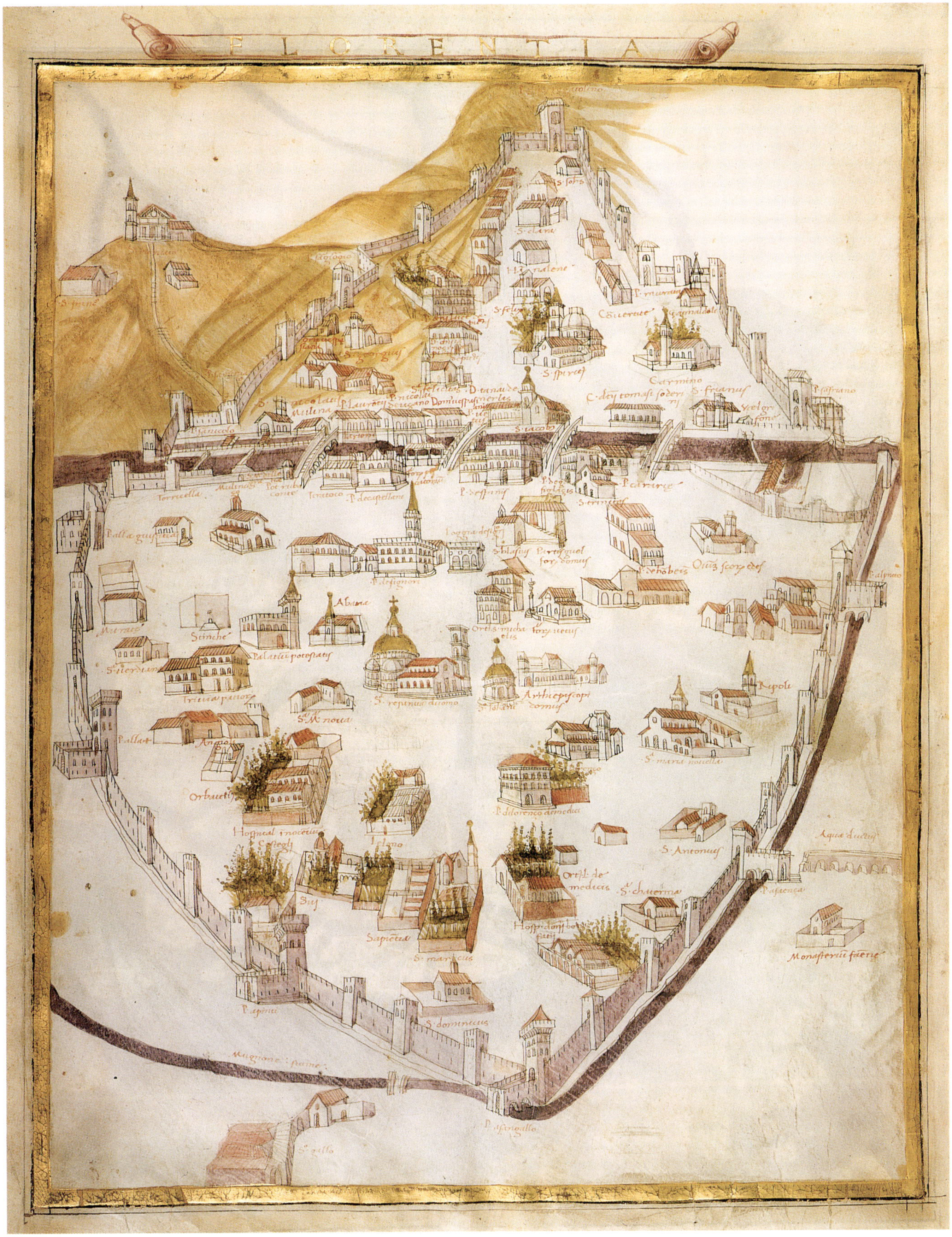
FLORENTIA

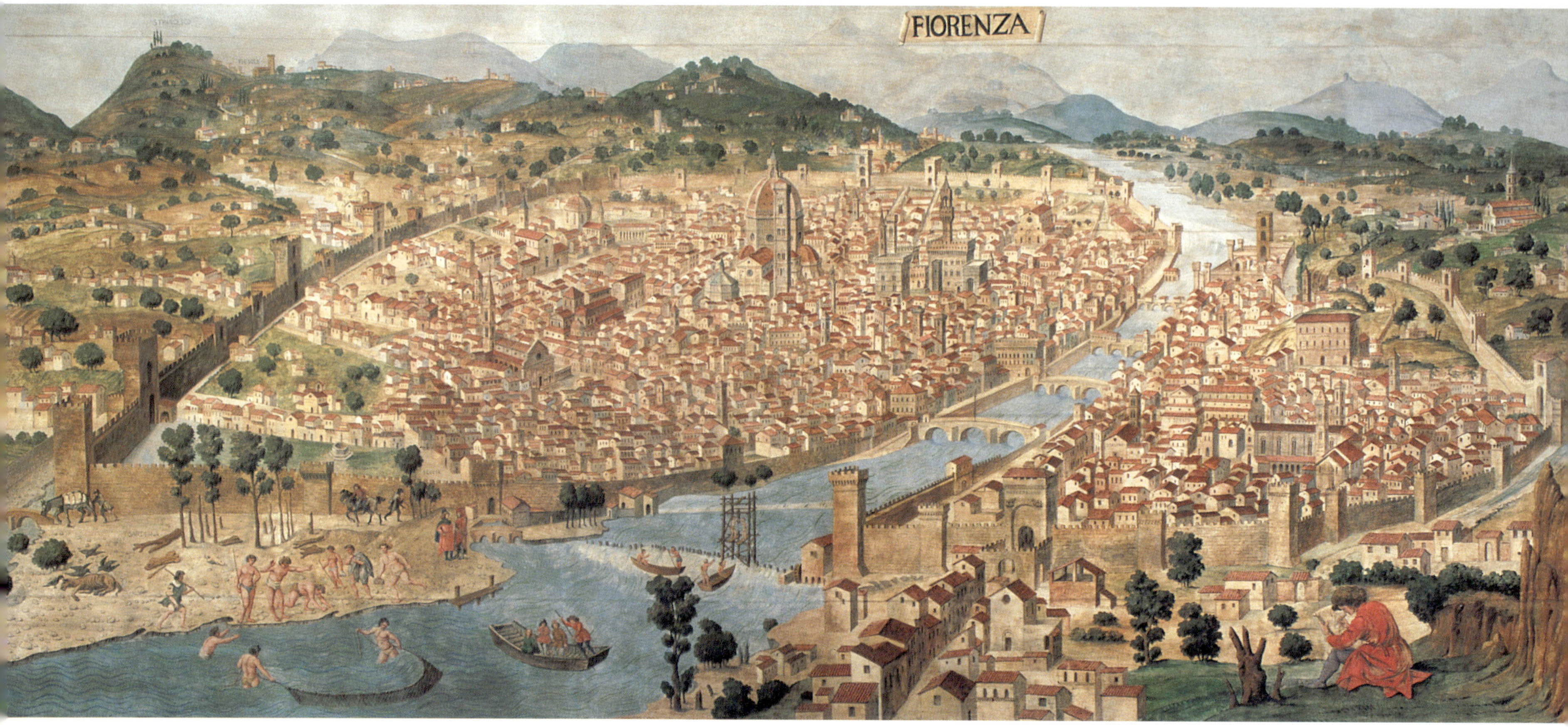
FIORENZA

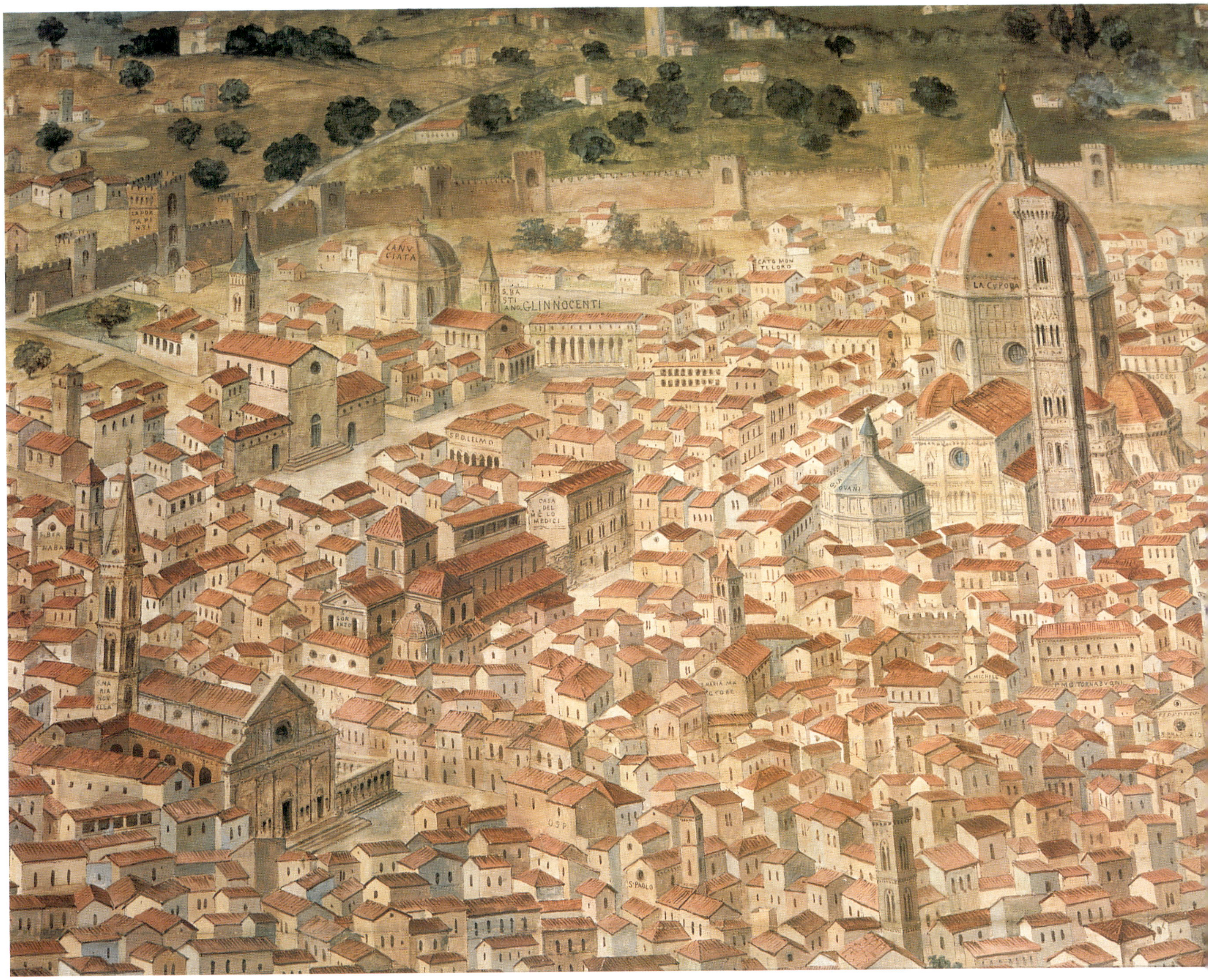

FRANCESCO ROSSELLI (ATTRIBUTED),
"*DELLA CATENA*" VIEW OF FLORENCE,
C. 1472

Opposite: the "*della catena*" view, so-called for the chain that frames the image, is the first accurate panoramic view of the city that has survived. This is a painted print of the original woodcut. Above: detail of the city center, with the cupola of the cathedral (top right) as the hub of the entire metropolis. In the foreground to the left is Santa Maria Novella.

Beautiful Florence had, among numerous other attributes, walls 7 miles (11.3 km) long, reinforced with 80 towers "*di prieta viva e a chalcina [*sic*]*" (all built of stone laid in mortar), and 4 bridges of ashlar stone and marble. In an interesting description of the *contado*, Dei recorded 3,600 palazzi (villas or substantial farms, not true palaces) within a distance of 5 miles (8 km) outside the walls, as well as 108 churches within the walls, and 23 palazzi representing each of the city's powerful *arti*. Dei identifies seven factors that made Florence the great city that it was when he wrote in 1472, without any one of which no city could be considered perfect: "complete liberty; second, a great and wealthy population; third, a river of sweet water in the center; fourth, the Signoria and the people; fifth, the university and the study of Greek; sixth, all of the *arti* and the crafts; and finally, the bankers and accountants who serve the whole world, with which none of the Venetians, Milanesi, Genovesi, Napolitani, and Senesi can compare."[21] Dei identifies 365 *chasade*, or clans, as well as 308 senior posts of government. He also enumerates most of the city's chief craft activities, among them the 270 workshops of the Arte della Lana, 83 of silk workers, 33 banks, 66 spice dealers, 30 goldbeaters and silver workers, as well as 44 shops selling gold, silver, and jewelry. Finally, Dei enumerates (or rather begins to, before losing himself) the twenty most notable sights in the city "which should be shown to foreign visitors. . . . First the campanile, second the cathedral, third the great cupola, fourth the beautiful palazzo [del Popolo], fifth the paved streets, sixth the "Nunziata" of Florence, seventh the hospital for the sick [probably Santa Maria Nova], eighth the river and wells of fresh water, ninth Santo Spirito, Santa Croce and Santa Maria Novella and their cloisters, and San Lorenzo and the city walls, and the chapel of the Pazzi and the tombs of the Medici and Rucellai and a thousand other notable things that make [Florence] another new Rome."

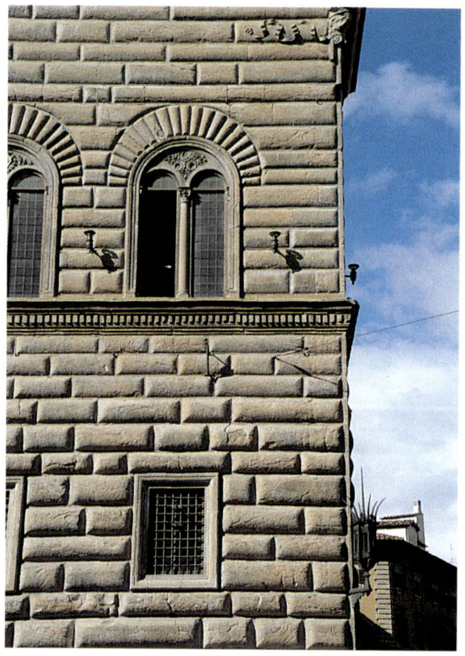

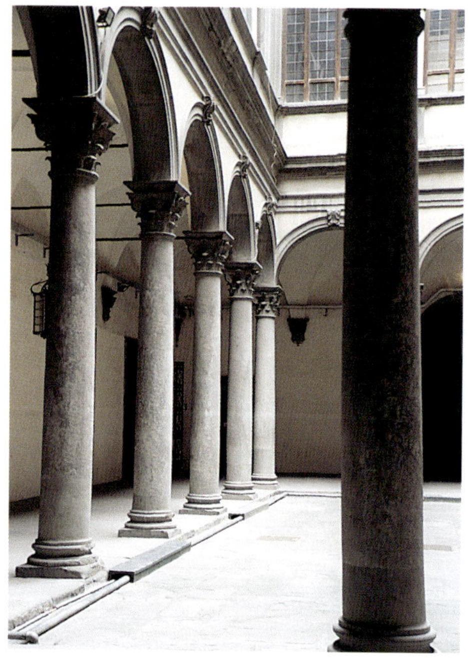

PALAZZO STROZZI

Below, left: facade detail. The immense palace built by Filippo Strozzi in the years after 1489 represents the pinnacle of the development of the Florentine Renaissance palazzo: rational, monumental, and rigorously disciplined. Below: *cortile*. The inner courtyard is in sharp contrast with the powerful modeling of the facade. This is a refined, private environment, where cultural life prevails over the external world of trade and finance.

The most dominant building typology of the quattrocento was undoubtedly the palazzo of the city's ruling class. As in Venice in the same era, these palaces reached their imposing maturity during this period, and although the styles in the two cities are quite different, in both cases they represent the culmination of a slow development that evolved not only aesthetically but also functionally over a period of perhaps three centuries.[22] Most of these new Florentine palaces (the chief of which were those of the Medici, Strozzi, Rucellai, Pitti, Pazzi, and Boni, which was later acquired by the Antinori) were built in the districts immediately surrounding the ancient core of the city, such that by the end of the century, a ring of palaces encircled the historic nucleus. They sometimes covered an entire city block, and were completely self-contained, usually with a courtyard in the center. The Medici and the other banking dynasties continued to run their banking operations from the traditional location around the Mercato Nuovo, however, and so, for the first time in Florence, a clear separation emerged between the palatial residence of the family or clan and the hub of its business activities. This separation was to have profound consequences for the urban development of Florence and the many other historic cities where this same duality occurred.

Among the new palaces noted above, that of Luca Pitti should be singled out, since it was built in the Oltrarno, on the "wrong" side of the river. Its original seven-bay design has often been attributed to Brunelleschi, although it was begun only in 1457, a decade after his death. One

FRA BARTOLOMEO, *SAVONAROLA*, UNDATED, PROBABLY C. 1496 (Florence, Museo di San Marco)

Savonarola's brief period of power instigated a number of political reforms and led to the urgent construction of the great Sala dei Cinquecento in the Palazzo Vecchio to house the new ruling body.

reason for the construction of such a grandiose structure on the left bank was a shortage of plots of sufficient size on the north side of the Arno; but in choosing to develop here, Pitti, one of the very few bankers who could rival the Medici in wealth and influence, gave a strong stimulus to development in the Oltrarno, and, with its spacious open square in front, the monumental palace immediately became one of the key urban foci on this side of the river.[23] Other imposing new palaces were more centrally located in the innermost ring around the ancient nucleus. Palazzo Strozzi is perhaps the most impressive, covering an entire rectangular city block, and offering two quite different impressions within and without. While the external facades remain among the most grandiose and monumental in the city, the inner courtyard in the center epitomizes the elegance and refinement of the privileged, sophisticated world inside.[24]

Crisis and Change: Savonarola and the New Republic

"... some writers distinguished three kinds of government, sic, the monarchical, the aristocratic and the democratic ... other authors, wiser according to the opinion of many, count six kinds. The three good ones are those which we have just named; the three bad ones result from the degradation of the other three, and each of them resembles its corresponding original." **Niccolò Machiavelli,** *The Discourses* (c. 1517) [25]

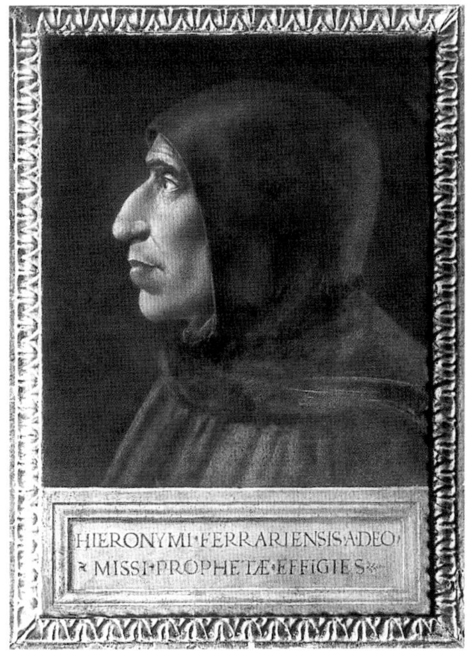

In 1492 Lorenzo de' Medici's health abruptly failed. He had inherited uricaemia from his father and grandfather and died on 8 April at Careggi, the family villa and estate a few miles north of the city walls where they, too, had died. Lorenzo was only forty-three years old, but his son Piero, now twenty years old, had long been groomed to take his place in the governance of the city. Like his father, Piero had been given a classical education and had been sent on diplomatic missions to broaden his education; he was also a poet and an avid collector of books and manuscripts. But Piero's rule was soon tested by the invasion of Italy in 1494 by Charles VII, king of France, intent on the conquest of Naples. This proved disastrous — at least in the short term — for the Medici dynasty. While Charles's army of 30,000 moved southward down the peninsula, Piero, concerned that the French might not perceive Tuscany as a wholehearted supporter of the cause, met Charles on the border and agreed to cede Pisa and Livorno, to aid the logistics of the French war campaign. The Florentines themselves were unaware of this alarmingly generous concession, and Piero was summoned to appear before the Signoria. When he replied to this demand by arming his own guards, a Florentine mob attacked and sacked his palace; Piero had barely enough time to flee to Bologna.

Four decades of upheaval and uncertainty in Florence's government ensued before the Medici were finally reinstated, this time as hereditary dukes. The first stage of this interregnum was the extraordinary and short-lived republic of Girolamo Savonarola (1452–1498). With Piero in exile, the Parlamento assembled to elect a new republican form of administration. A new constitution was drafted, heavily influenced by the views of the charismatic priest Savonarola, who had gained widespread support in the city for his popular reform proposals. The chief innovation was the Great Council, a body of men, all of whose fathers or grandfathers had held public office. Three thousand strong, the Great Council was to be housed in a vast new hall built alongside the original Palazzo del Popolo. Savonarola preached Counter-Reformation zealotry, a return to austerity and simplicity accompanied by the other familiar symbols of blinkered orthodoxy: book burnings and the destruction of symbols of luxury and decadence. But it was a brief moment of power and influence; Savonarola was summoned to Rome to face charges of heresy. He was found guilty, excommunicated, and, on his return to Florence, was burned at the stake in the Piazza della Signoria, just outside the palazzo where all of these recent constitutional reforms had taken place.[26]

The Republic, however, survived for a further ten years; in 1502 Piero Soderini was voted *gonfaloniere* of justice for life, a unique attempt to stabilize one of the vital posts of the Republic's government. However, the decade was marked by almost continuous warfare or preparation for war. Pisa was finally taken and brought back into the Republic's domains in 1509. Three years later, on 1 September 1512, after diplomatic pressure from France, Giuliano de' Medici rode back into the city; two weeks later, his brother Giovanni joined him. The two men were the surviving sons of Lorenzo Il Magnifico; their elder brother and heir apparent, Piero, had died in exile in 1503. In 1513 the election of Giovanni as pope, Leo X, formed the first of many close links between Rome and Tuscany over the following century; henceforth, the second reign of the Medici was to have both Florentine and Roman components.[27]

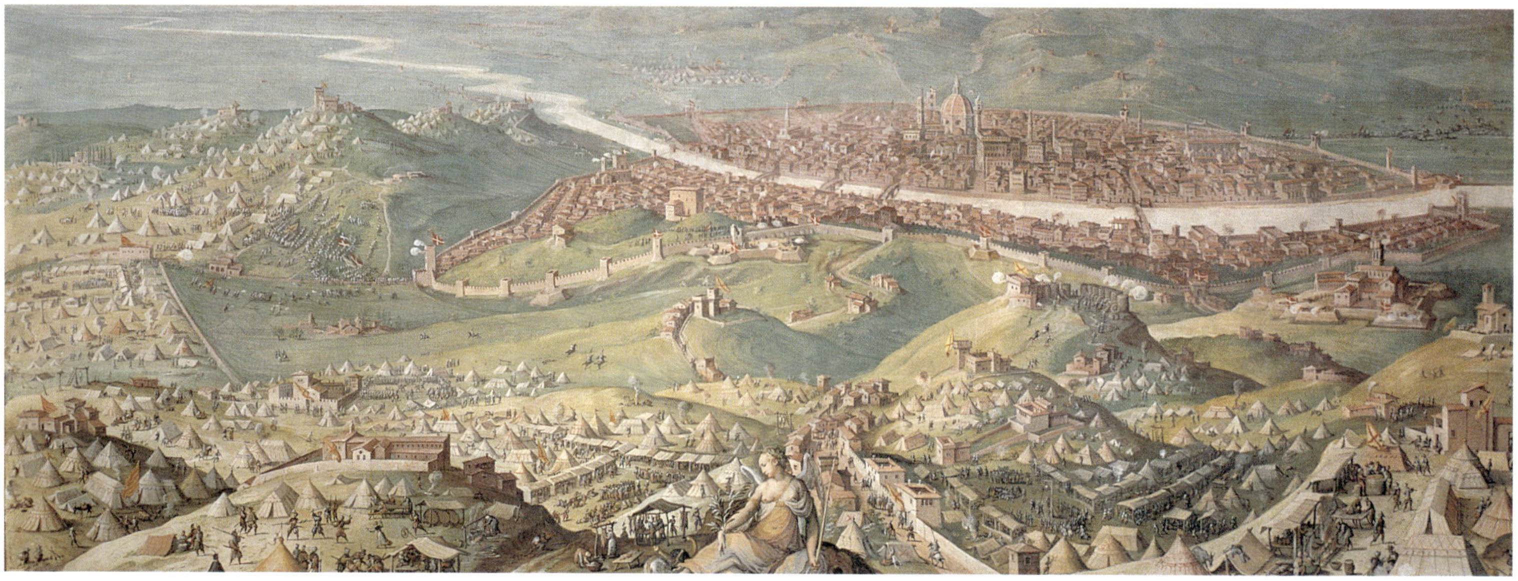

GIORGIO VASARI, *VEDUTA GENERALE DI FIRENZE*, C. 1561 (Florence, Palazzo Vecchio)

Although the siege of Florence had taken place thirty years earlier, Vasari's highly detailed depiction of the city at this time is an invaluable record.

In Florence the Great Council established by Savonarola was abolished while further reform was debated. In fact, the newly reformed government closely resembled that of Lorenzo, with the Medici effectively controlling the levers of power while still lacking a formal title or position. In 1522, a second Medici pope was elected, Giulio — the natural son of Lorenzo's murdered brother, Giuliano — who took the title of Clement VII. After the Sack of Rome in 1527 by Emperor Charles V, however, the Medici were again forced from Florence; a new republic was declared and the Great Council reinstated. Two years later, the city began to reinforce and prepare itself for a direct assault by the imperial forces, now allied with Pope Clement VII. Faced with such an overwhelming alliance, the Republic appointed Michelangelo as governor general and procurator of the city's fortifications. He organized the construction of new bastions in front of the medieval city gates, and began fortifying the hilltop of San Miniato with defensive works built of compressed earth and faced with brickwork. Before the anticipated assault, Clement VII had the city surveyed by Benvenuto della Volpaia, who built an accurate cork scale model of Florence and the surrounding hills; with this invaluable strategic information, Clement VII was able to direct and follow the entire course of the siege.

Florence withstood the siege for ten heroic months, but not without great physical damage. Many dozens of houses and villas in the *contado* were destroyed, and much of the territory needed to be recolonized after the war. One result is that very few surviving buildings in these surrounding

RAPHAEL, *POPE LEO X (GIOVANNI DE' MEDICI), WITH CARDINALS GIULIO DE' MEDICI AND LUIGI DE' ROSSI*, 1517 (Florence, Uffizi)

Giovanni was the second son of Lorenzo Il Magnifico.

territories predate the mid-sixteenth century. Florence finally capitulated on 12 August 1530. With the collapse of the resistance, the Republic also fell, and Alessandro de' Medici, grandson of Piero, was installed by Emperor Charles V as the city's new ruler. The government that resulted was a form of republic, but with Alessandro at the head of the chief deliberative and legislative bodies. One of his first acts was to embark on the construction of the Fortezza da Basso, or Fortezza San Giovanni, as a secure base for himself and his family: a fortress from which not only the adjacent, vulnerable *contado* to the northwest of the city could be covered, but — at least equally importantly — from which the city itself could be subdued in the event of future internal uprisings. This massive new fortress enclosed the medieval Porta Faenza, and within its walls lay a virtually self-contained town, incorporating quarters for infantry, captains, bombardiers, apartments for Alessandro and his family, a chapel, armories, stores, and munitions dumps. One of the handful of other urbanistic works undertaken by Alessandro was the restoration of the ancient family estate at Careggi and the acquisition and development of the Cascine, the Medici farm along the banks of the Arno to the west of the city.[28]

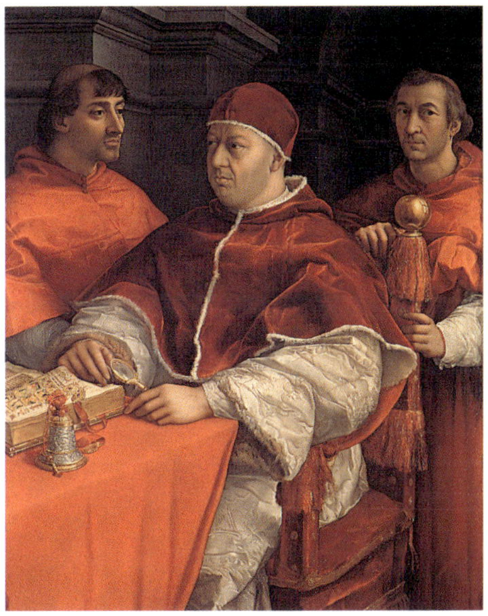

Two years after Alessandro's accession to power, a commission was set up at Pope Clement VII's insistence to instigate further reforms. On 27 April 1532 the Medici were written into the Florentine constitution as its hereditary rulers; a century after the rise to power of Cosimo, *pater patriae*, the Medici finally achieved the formal status they had sought for so long. Thereafter followed two centuries of Medici rule as dukes, and later grand dukes, of Tuscany.

Cosimo I: Duchy and Grand Duchy

"But if Giovanni Bologna has hitherto produced fine works, still finer may we expect from him in future, seeing that the Signor Prince . . . has lately commissioned him to execute a statue, of five braccia high, representing the Goddess of Victory . . . to be placed in the Hall, opposite to one by Michelagnolo [*sic*]." **Giorgio Vasari,** *Lives of the Artists* (1568) [29]

However, the succession was not so simply secured. In 1537 Alessandro was assassinated by his cousin Lorenzaccio and succeeded by the eighteen-year-old Cosimo, son of the famous *condottiere* Giovanni dalle Bande Nere.[30] Cosimo inherited a city in crisis, suffering from several decades of political upheaval and instability. After the disastrous siege, Florence was seriously depopulated; from a peak of perhaps 120,000 (including the immediate suburbs), its citizens now numbered barely 60,000, with all of the vulnerable *borghi* outside the walls effectively deserted. But the long rule of Cosimo marks a profound shift in the history of the city in many ways. He succeeded to the title of duke and, in 1569, acquired that of grand duke of Tuscany. These titles reflected the manner in which he was to regard his city; Florence became more and more a dynastic capital. The fundamental difference in how the city and the duchy were governed was gradually evinced in numerous ways, from the erection of commemorative monuments and columns to the setting out of new squares. The entire fabric of the city began to be used to express the dynasty; the *palle*, the family arms, universal symbol of Medici rule, could be seen everywhere.[31] In 1540, after only three years, Cosimo transferred his headquarters from the family palace in Via Larga to the Palazzo del Popolo, which became known as the Palazzo Ducale. The symbolic significance of this move cannot be overstated: Cosimo thus eliminated any residual meaning of the palazzo as physical expression of the political will of the Florentine people. Florence was a duchy, to be ruled from an appropriate ducal palace; the government of the people by the people had become a historical footnote.

Before considering Cosimo's numerous works in the city, it is important to record that his new title still had to be defended, as did the integrity of Florence itself against potential aggressors, and so he embarked on a great program of fortifications to strengthen the entire Tuscan state from its enemies. Important new or improved fortifications were instigated at Pisa, Arezzo, Pistoia, Siena, as well as smaller, though strategic, centers such as Volterra, Cortona, and Piombino. The port of Livorno was planned, and the first stages of its expansion and development put in hand. Cosimo also established new fortified settlements where he perceived weak links in the existing chain: Portoferraio on the island of Elba was transformed into Cosmopoli, while Terra del Sole became Eliopoli. A long line of new forts was built to defend the state's coastline, many of which survive today in whole or in part. Further new forts were built in the Mugello, the Medici's own homelands, to defend the northern boundaries from potential invasion across the mountains. Cosimo took a close personal interest in these works, most of which he visited under construction.[32] Wars with Siena during Cosimo's early reign convinced him that Florence's own defenses also had to be improved. In 1544 a new wall with bastions was built across the southern flank of the Oltrarno, within the earlier walls; it involved considerable demolitions, but was designed to the most modern defensive criteria. In the same period, most of the tall city gates in the medieval circle of walls were reduced in height so that their new flat roofs could be used more effectively for gun emplacements. The final major element in these improved fortifications was the completion of the works begun by Michelangelo in 1527 at San Miniato. These had initially been built hurriedly to withstand the siege, but were reconstructed in a more permanent, substantial form in the years prior to 1552.

GIORGIO VASARI, *COSIMO DE' MEDICI TRA I SUOI ARTISTI*, 1555–62 (Florence, Palazzo Vecchio)

The painting depicts the idea of enlightened cultural patronage that Cosimo I wished to promulgate.

Cosimo had inherited a depopulated and impoverished city in the 1530s, in which trade and industry languished. Here, too, he initiated a dynamic expansion of the textile industry, and in 1546 established a new tapestry industry by importing a company of weavers from Flanders to work in the city. Three years later the internal administration of the city was modernized by the overhauling of the Capitaniato di Parte Guelfa, which became a consolidated ministry of public works. Many projects were carried out under its auspices by Buontalenti, Ammannati, and a number of other versatile architects and engineers. The census ordered by Cosimo in 1552 provides a detailed picture of the social structure of the city at a time when it had still not fully recovered its numbers.[33] The city's population was 59,500, with 9,527 *fuochi*, literally fires or hearths, that is, households. The textile industry remained by far the largest employer, representing one-third of the household heads surveyed; it was still two and a half times the size of the next occupational group, that of the tailors, shoemakers, and clothiers. The next major groupings, in decreasing order of importance, were workers in the timber trades, the food trades, the construction industry, and the metalwork industries. Old patterns of distribution survived from much earlier periods: Most of the cloth dyers were still in the Santa Croce district, most of the textile workers in that of San Giovanni; Santo Spirito in the Oltrarno and Santa Croce remained, as they had been for two or three centuries, the poorest districts of the city.

Cosimo consolidated his pivotal role in the city arguably as much through his cultural achievements as by purely political means. Many, if not all, of his major acts of cultural patronage can be seen to have had the underlying purpose of extending his influence over the city's intellectual, social, and political life. He has been described as an enlightened despot, and certainly in the political sphere he enjoyed an unprecedented measure of power. Almost all of his urban proposals — some built, some unbuilt — are characterized not only by the prestige they brought to the dynasty, but also by their formality and regularity; in effect, by their attempt to further define and discipline the city's form.[34] This imposition of order can be seen clearly in the construction of the Uffizi and the rebuilding of the Santa Trinità bridge, in the Boboli gardens and in the improvements at Santa Maria Novella. If the quattrocento urban developments can be characterized as the enhancement of specific hubs of the city, then Cosimo's works can be seen as essentially dynamic; no clearer examples can be offered than the Uffizi, Vasari's corridor, and the expansion of Palazzo Pitti.[35]

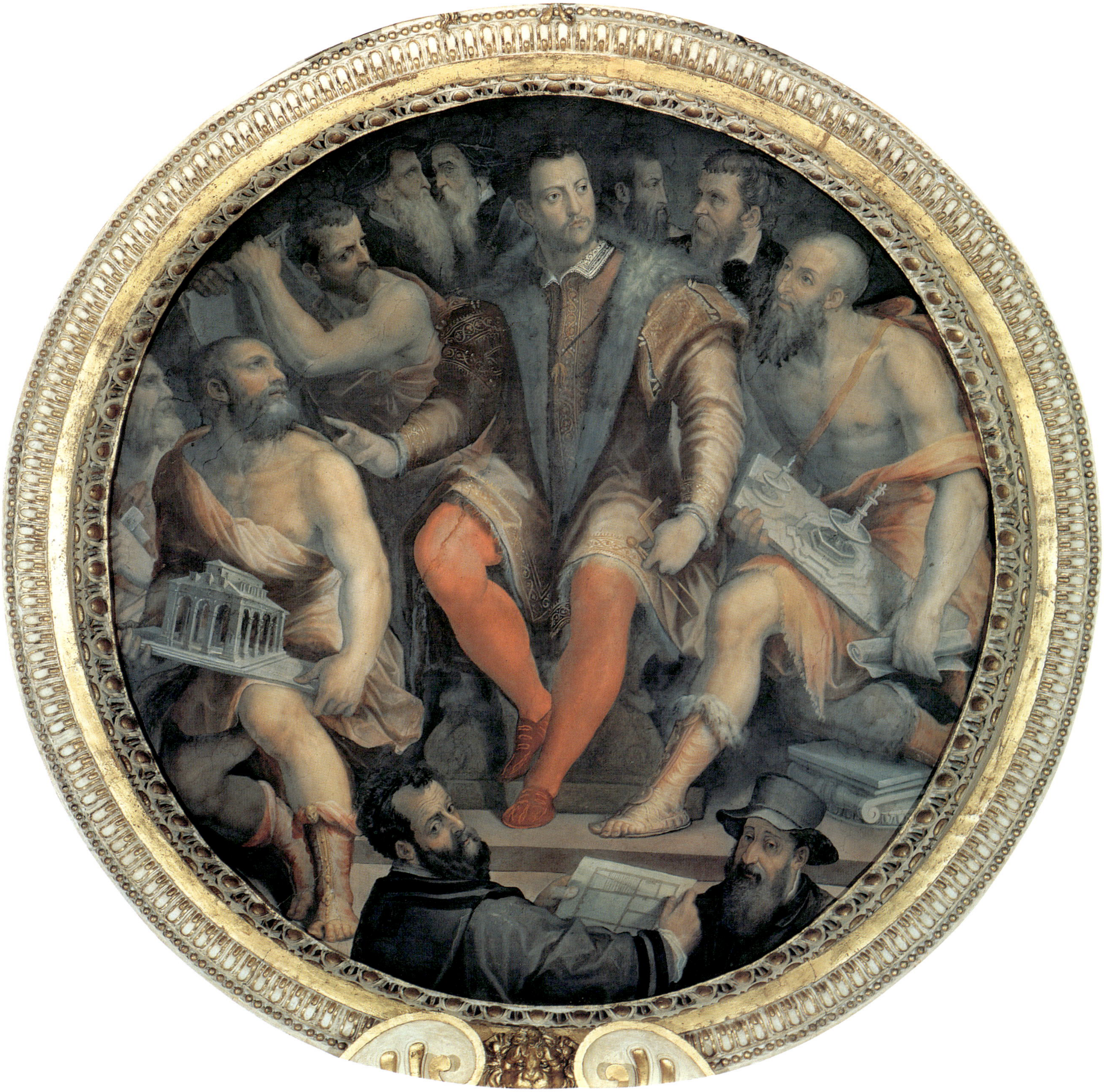

In 1549 Eleanora of Toledo, Cosimo's wife, acquired Palazzo Pitti, on the hillside just across the Arno. This purchase proved to be the catalyst for a series of important works that transformed the center of the city, and fundamentally shifted the center of gravity of the city's power base. The Medici considered Palazzo Pitti to be a palace from which Florence could be ruled, while at the same time, as a result of its location, remaining semidetached from the heart of the city. It afforded the possibility of light, fresh air, and green open space on the terraced hillside behind, which were difficult if not impossible to obtain on the north bank, and yet it still had the great advantage of remaining within the southern defensive walls. Almost immediately Eleanora began the process of taming the hillside behind the palace, which was to become the elaborate Boboli gardens. This first stage laid out the garden immediately behind the palace; later stages involved more complex works toward the south, on the site of one of the city's former stone quarries. In 1556 work had also begun under Ammannati to enlarge and transform Palazzo Pitti into a fittingly imposing palace for the dukes. The architect's chief contribution was the construction of two new wings that extended into the gardens at the rear, thus forming a monumental central courtyard, surrounded on three sides by the palace, and with the fourth side open to the terraced Boboli gardens.

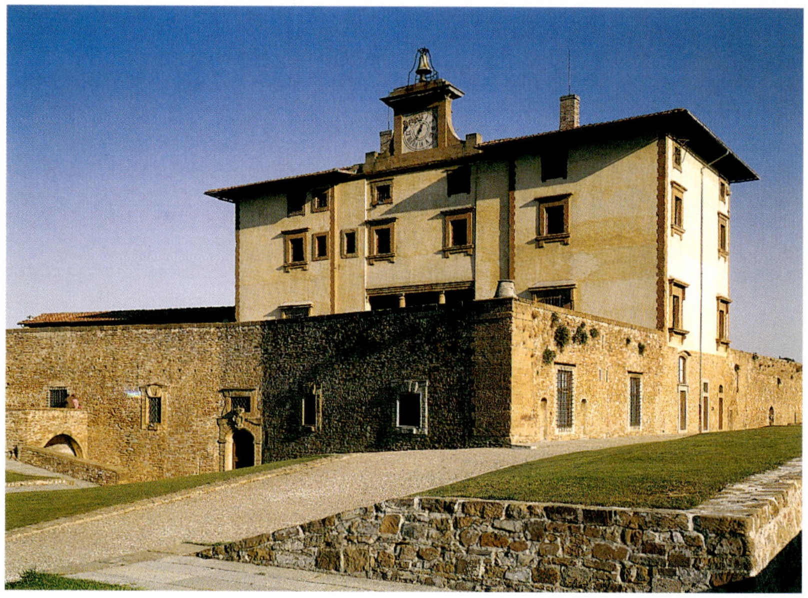

FORTEZZA BELVEDERE

The fortress was built by Bernardo Buontalenti in the 1590s, to the most advanced military specifications. The villa in the center housed the captain of the fort, and has much in common in its appearance with contemporary Medici villas elsewhere.

Within the constraints of Cosimo's autocratic form of government, cultural life flourished. One of the characteristic indications of this flowering was the establishment of new academies, in the spirit of Cosimo's predecessors. The Accademia Fiorentina was founded in 1541, along the lines of the Platonic academies of Cosimo Il Vecchio and Lorenzo, and in 1563 the Accademia delle Arti del Disegno was formed, the very first such establishment in Europe, with the ubiquitous and multitalented Giorgio Vasari as its first director.

Cosimo surrounded himself with courtiers, not simply the usual entourage of professional experts and advisors, but a kind of second court in the form of numerous architects and artists. Until the transfer to the Pitti, the Medici palace in Via Larga was for a time one of the great poles of political influence and patronage in the city; linked as it was directly with the cathedral, the Via de' Calzaiuoli, and the Piazza della Signoria, the whole ensemble formed a compact axis of power. The Medici also further consolidated their influence over their own quarter of the city. At its northernmost end, for example, the convent of San Marco became one of several hubs of Medicean urban strategy. The family was already closely associated with San Marco; Lorenzo had opened the *accademia* adjacent to the monastery, while libraries had been established both here and at the nearby Santissima Annunziata, and most of San Marco's monastic buildings had been remodeled by Michelozzo from Medici funds. The Santissima Annunziata also received generous Medici patronage. The Servite order that was housed there originated from the Mugello, as did the Medici, and the piazza had been enhanced by Sangallo's Loggia dei Serviti, built in 1516, to harmonize with Brunelleschi's loggia for the Ospedale degli Innocenti.

Perhaps even more significant in terms of direct cultural and artistic patronage (albeit less important in urban terms) were the later stages of work at San Lorenzo. The new sacristy had been begun in 1519 at the instigation of Pope Leo X to house the mortal remains of Lorenzo Il Magnifico, and most of the construction took place from 1520 to 1524. It remains one of Michelangelo's finest works, a perfect integration of architectonic structure with the more specific requirements of the monumental sculptures. The tumultuous political events of the time led to several interruptions in the execution of the works, as Michelangelo himself was entrusted with the improvement of the city's fortifications between 1527 and 1530 to withstand the imperial siege. The sacristy was therefore only completed during the duchy of Cosimo I, when Vasari and Ammannati finally installed Michelangelo's sculptures. The other great act of patronage at San Lorenzo was the construction of the Biblioteca Laurenziana, created to house the magnificent collection of books and manuscripts amassed by Cosimo Il Vecchio and augmented by Lorenzo. After various vicissitudes in the turbulent era prior to the establishment of the duchy, the collection was returned to Florence in 1523, when Michelangelo was commissioned by the Medici pope, Clement VII, to design a new library. Once again, though, it was incomplete upon Michelangelo's departure for Rome in 1534, and was continued and completed in the 1560s by Vasari and Ammannati, closely following Michelangelo's drawings. It contains the priceless collection of the Medici to this day. Like their other collections, the Biblioteca Laurenziana was organized on rational scientific principles and was carefully cataloged.

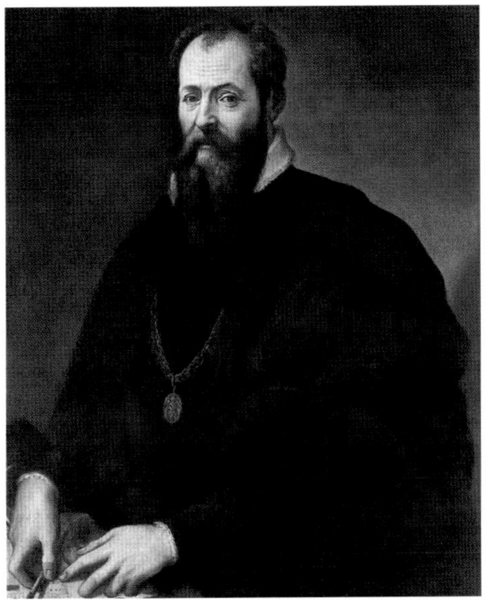

GIORGIO VASARI, *SELF-PORTRAIT*, probably 1550s (Florence, Uffizi)

The ubiquitous Vasari was one of the outstanding creative figures of the era; he was not only an architect, but also a prolific painter and writer.

In the decade after 1555 Cosimo undertook another outstanding series of works in the city. They required the services of skilled architects, the chief among whom were Ammannati and Vasari; both became official architects in the regular service of the duke.[36] One of the first works was the modernization of the ducal palace, the Palazzo del Popolo, by Vasari. The south side, on Via della Ninna, had already been enlarged, but Vasari's efforts were chiefly concentrated on the transformation of the interior. These works enhanced the image of the duchy with allegorical and classical imagery and extensive programs idealizing the Medici dynasty.

In 1555 Siena had been conquered and finally brought permanently within the confines of the state. One of the results of this conquest was the need to reorganize and rationalize the many departments of Cosimo's government to administer the newly enlarged territory. To this end, he decided to concentrate all thirteen of the principal magistracies into a new building, the Uffizi, or administrative offices.[37] Work began on Vasari's monumental structure in 1559, with the building of two long, parallel blocks, one of which was to be directly connected by a bridge to the south side of the Palazzo del Popolo, and both of which were to be joined together at their southern end by a loggia and colonnade facing the Arno. The complex was not completed until 1580, after Vasari's death. While the Uffizi were being built, the final link in this chain of construction activity and urban transformation was planned and executed by Vasari; the Corridoio Vasariano was built in the extremely short period of only a few months in 1565.[38] It played a crucial role, not only in the urban fabric, but also for Florence's government. Cosimo's court was now no longer based at the Palazzo del Popolo but at the Pitti, across the river, and the Corridoio was to be his lifeline, his own secure means of communication between his palace, his administrative headquarters — the Uffizi — and the Palazzo del Popolo.

The wider significance of all these transformations will be discussed more fully subsequently, but this summary of Cosimo's achievements should be concluded by a brief note on his other principal urban works. They, too, were to affect the fabric of the city. The erection of fountains, obelisks, and the appearance of the ubiquitous Medici arms throughout the city all gave more and more credence to the concept that this was "his" city, that Florence was now a Medici town.[39] A further example of this "Medicification" was Cosimo's construction of new logge. Logge had long been a prominent feature of the urban scene, but Cosimo gave considerable impetus to these urban incidents by building several new ones: the Loggia del Pesce, designed by Vasari, originally built to stand in the Mercato Vecchio; the loggia of the Mercato Nuovo, designed by Giovanni Battista del Tasso (1547–51); and the south loggia of the Uffizi. The Mercato Nuovo loggia was built specifically to concentrate the traders in gold, silk, and precious metals in one place, and could thus be seen as an indirect attempt to stimulate and encourage trade. Cosimo's rule was also marked by the modernization and refacing of older palace facades, particularly in the Via de' Tornabuoni and

Borgo degli Albizi. The improvement of Via Maggio, across the river, is significant, since it forms part of the shift of emphasis toward the Oltrarno instigated by the transfer of the court to Palazzo Pitti. The reconstruction of Ponte Santa Trinità by Ammannati following its partial collapse in 1557 could also be said to enhance the status of the left bank, since the new bridge was a particularly fine, elegant structure, all built of stone and unencumbered by shops.[40] Further works of urban improvement included the repaving of the Piazza della Signoria and the construction of the *lungarno* along the north bank, between the Ponte Vecchio and the Ponte alla Carraia.

Cosimo gathered around him a flourishing court, and with it a group of wealthy friends and associates. Each of them patronized an equally active court of creative professionals; many new private palaces were built, including a number designed by the prolific Ammannati. A fine representative example built for Cosimo's secretary, Ugolino Grifoni, is Palazzo Grifoni which, like others such as Palazzo Ramirez, Palazzo Larderel, and the so-called Palazzo Nonfinito, evince the spread of Roman Mannerism in palace design. This plethora of new or refaced palaces was accompanied by the trend, widespread in Tuscany but also elsewhere in Italy (particularly the Veneto), for city property owners, bankers and businessmen, to expand their property interests by the acquisition of large country estates, as well as the parallel development of urban land on a commercial basis. Rural investment had ancient origins in the *villeggiatura* and in the continuity of the historic pattern of rural ownership — like the Medici lands in the Mugello. As one can see in the *Decameron*, these patterns were already widespread and long established in Boccaccio's time, but had expanded by the sixteenth century, following the examples of Cosimo Il Vecchio and Lorenzo, whose country seats were important social and cultural hubs as well as working estates; the rural Medici estates eventually came to number as many as a dozen.[41] The contemporaries of Cosimo I not only expanded these estates but built houses and workers' cottages in the city, an example that was followed by several of the major *arti*, also important landowners. Examples of this speculative urban development can be seen today most notably in the Via de' Servi and Via Ricasoli.

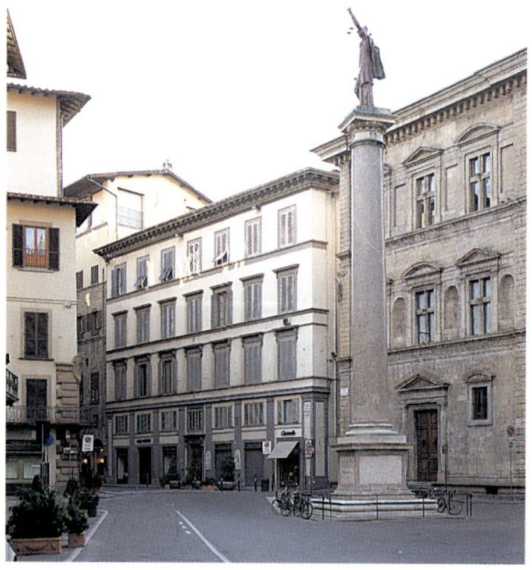

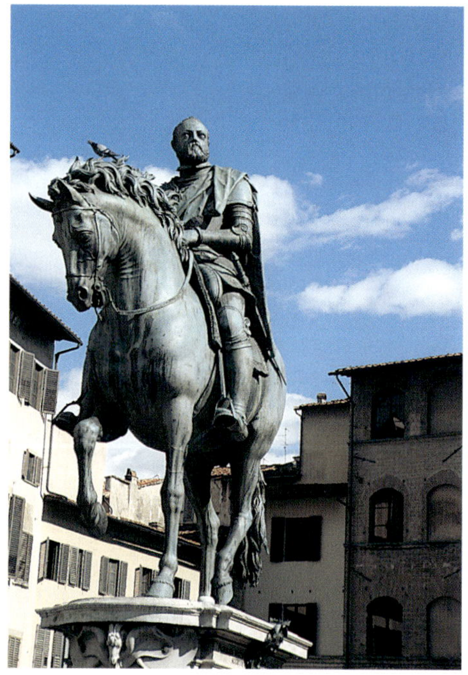

PIAZZA SANTA TRINITÀ (below, left)

The Colonna della Giustizia was erected by Cosimo I, another of his many interventions in the city's fabric; it was completed by the figure of Justice by Francesco del Tadda (1581). Immediately beyond the column is the sixteenth-century Palazzo Bartolini Salimbeni.

GIAMBOLOGNA, EQUESTRIAN STATUE OF COSIMO I, 1594–98 (below)

The bronze statue in the Piazza della Signoria was one of many works of adornment in the heart of the city that were effected by Cosimo I.

Despite Cosimo's largely successful attempts to stimulate trade and modernize industry, Florence ceded much of its cultural preeminence to Rome in the latter part of the sixteenth century, and it is characteristic that much of the greatest, later work of Michelangelo and others is to be found there. (Michelangelo settled in Rome permanently in 1534.) In Rome the patronage of the Church, together with the grandiose urban projects instigated, above all, by Sixtus V, proved to be an irresistible lure to many, and resulted in a number of outstanding works of Mannerist and early Baroque architecture on a scale Cosimo I and the later Medici could not emulate. Nevertheless, Florence in 1574 was broadly a stable, wealthy city; much of its industry had been revived, and banking flourished anew; the Medici bank itself prospered, with branches in Rome, Venice, and Lyon. But Cosimo was arguably the last of the truly great rulers of the dynasty, and although the decline was not as continuous or seamless as some histories suggest (Ferdinando's reign was by no means unsuccessful), a shift in the tide can already be detected with Cosimo's successor, Francesco.

GIUSTO UTENS, *VILLA MEDICI AT CASTELLO*, LATE SIXTEENTH CENTURY (Florence, Museo di Firenze com'era)

One of a series of fourteen lunettes painted by Utens at the end of the sixteenth century for Ferdinando I, to record the appearance of the various Medici villas and estates. They were intended to hang together in the villa at Artimino.

Cosimo's Successors: Francesco and Ferdinando I

"A very fine genius and extraordinary wealth of felicitous fancies, are likewise displayed by Bernardo Timante Buontalenti, who acquired the first principles of design, when in his childhood, from the works of Vasari, and has since made so much progress that he is now in the service of the most illustrious Signor, Don Francesco Medici, Prince of Florence, with whom he has been for some years, and who favors him greatly." **Giorgio Vasari**, *Lives of the Artists* (1568) [42]

The Medici succession passed seamlessly from Cosimo I to his son Francesco in 1574. Francesco had been waiting in the wings as regent for a full decade, and there was no voice of dissent in the capital. The long rule of Cosimo had personalized the appearance of Florence arguably more than any previous Medici, and enlightened despotism had also left the economy in a more prosperous

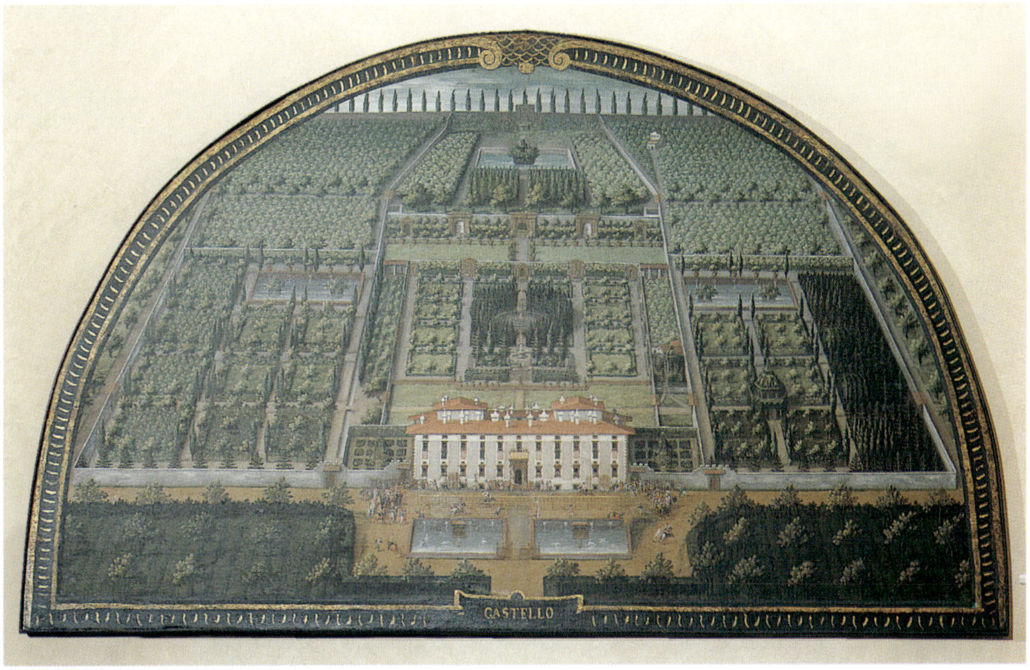

condition than it had been for many decades. Banking and international trade flourished, but this buoyant market was to witness a significant downturn during the reign of Francesco before his brother and successor, Ferdinando, ruled over a new period of expansion and prosperity. Thereafter the Medici succession took a markedly downward course.[43]

Francesco lacked the strong, forceful autocratic character of his father; indeed, he was a rather reluctant, lackluster successor. Nevertheless, he patronized a number of artistic and architectural initiatives. He encouraged the development of luxury crafts such as glassmaking, porcelain, and the famous *pietra dura*, and in 1570 commissioned Vasari, Giambologna, and others to build and decorate his own study in the Palazzo del Popolo, one of the finest late Renaissance interiors in the city.[44] It was also Francesco who pursued development of the new port town of Livorno to stimulate seaborne trade, after its foundation by Cosimo I. Pisa had long since declined as a major port as a result of the silting of the Arno, as in turn did Porto Pisano, and the expansion of Livorno (which took place in stages over many years) was to be one of the Medici grand dukes' last major legacies in Tuscany.

In this era of architectural Mannerism and caprice, two architects stand out for their prolific output: Ammannati and his follower Buontalenti. The former built the Neptune fountain in the Piazza della Signoria in the last decade of Cosimo I's rule, an apt symbol of his patronage, while Buontalenti was

Medici court architect for decades, from about 1570 to 1608; his name matched his many skills, not simply as an architect, but as an engineer, theater designer, and, arguably most important in this age of lavish spectacles, as the designer and choreographer of court festivals. Among his many permanent works are the Casino Medici in the Via Larga; the extension of the Boboli gardens and the fort-villa of Belvedere; and the rebuilding of the Medici country villa at Pratolino, where Francesco took up permanent residence with Bianca Cappello after the death of his first wife, Giovanna. Buontalenti also made a famous series of proposals for the facade of the cathedral.[45] This range of works is characteristic of the polymath himself, who in some ways was a typical product of his times, but also of the nature of Medici commissions, in particular, of course, the staged enhancement of the Pitti and its surroundings as the real heart of the dynastic succession and the hub of all effective political power. Equally characteristic is the Mannerist modernization of existing buildings and an increasing interest in nature, gardens, and artifices such as fountains and grottoes.

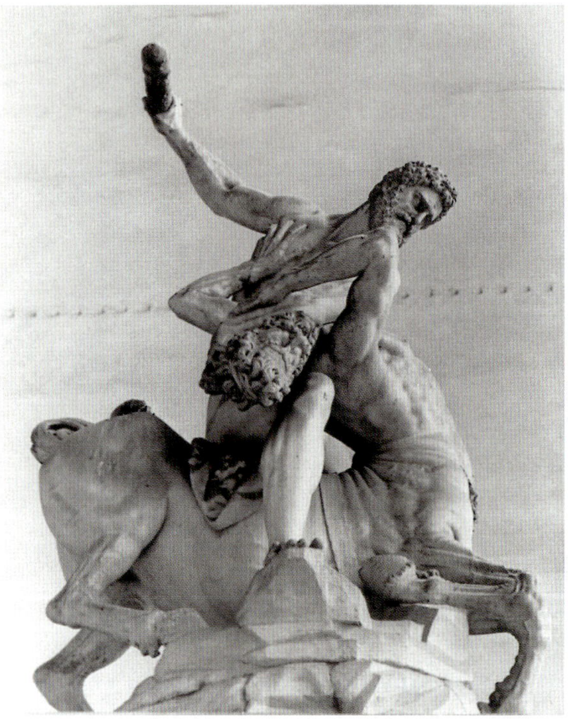

Francesco was succeeded in 1587 not by his son — none survived him — but by his brother, the cardinal Ferdinando. To a large degree, Ferdinando continued the policies, both cultural and political, of his brother, but took a more active, centralizing role in government than had the lax Francesco; in addition, the domestic economy, which had reflected a general European recession, began to recover. During Ferdinando's reign, Livorno expanded further and flourished; during this period, too, the Belvedere fort-villa was completed. His fascination with grandeur and villas reflected the tastes of the era, and he further embellished the city with public statuary: Giambologna's *Hercules and the Centaur* in the Loggia della Signoria, the equestrian statue of Cosimo I in the piazza nearby, and that of himself — again by Giambologna — in the Piazza della Santissima Annunziata. But the most significant act of Medici patronage was Ferdinando's commencement of the Cappella dei Principi at San Lorenzo. The idea of a great family mausoleum had first been proposed by Cosimo I, but the imposing structure was begun only in 1604, on an octagonal plan (in deference to the baptistery of San Giovanni) by Matteo Nigetti.[46] This rich ensemble, which would take more than forty years to complete, was crowned by a faceted cupola, a scaled-down homage to Brunelleschi's incomparable masterpiece. The Cappella dei Principi was the most expensive building project ever patronized by the Medici.

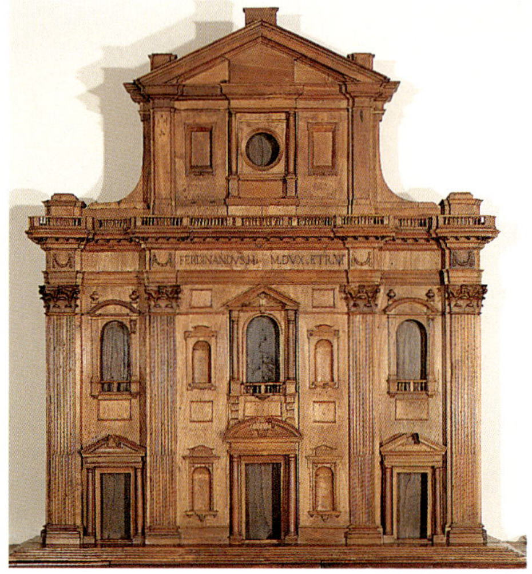

GIAMBOLOGNA, FACADE OF SANTA MARIA DEL FIORE (Florence, Museo dell'Opera) (above)

The Museo dell'Opera contains several superb models by a number of artists showing their proposals for the completion of the facade.

GIAMBOLOGNA, *HERCULES AND THE CENTAUR*, 1599 (left)

This is one of a group of notable sculptures that Cosimo I assembled and housed in the Loggia della Signoria, to form a kind of semipublic sculpture gallery.

Florence's appearance toward the end of the sixteenth century is recorded in a number of increasingly detailed representations. One of the first and most interesting is Vasari's view of the city in 1561 (in the Palazzo Vecchio), which illustrates the famous siege of 1529–30, showing Florence surrounded by the imperial armies.[47] Although there is undoubtedly a good deal of visual license in the depiction of the military detail, the topography certainly attempts to portray the city faithfully in its physical context, surrounded by an armature of hills. The view, from the south, was based on observation, although, as Vasari himself wrote, it was not possible to find a vantage point so high that one could see the whole city. Nevertheless, the detail is extremely accurate, a compact city nucleus dominated, as were all of these views, following the convention established by the "*della catena*" view, by the symbolic volume of the cathedral dome. The city's fortifications are also depicted — perhaps for propaganda reasons — as highly dominant, striding over the hills of Oltrarno in impressive fashion.

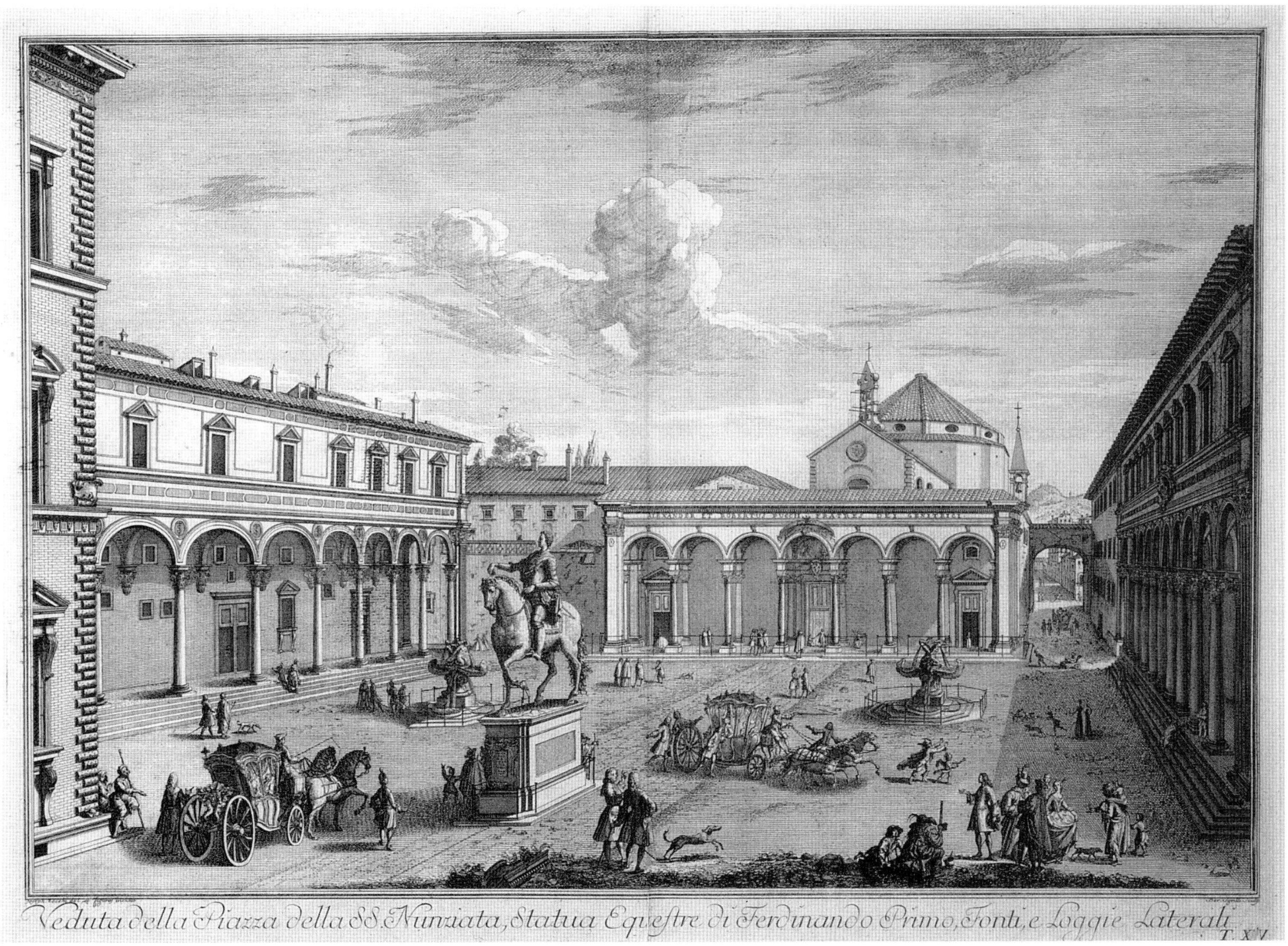

GIUSEPPE ZOCCHI, *VEDUTA DELLA PIAZZA DELLA SS NUNZIATA . . .*, 1744

Another view from the series of engravings published in 1744; the foreground is dominated by the equestrian statue of Ferdinando I, again by the prolific Giambologna.

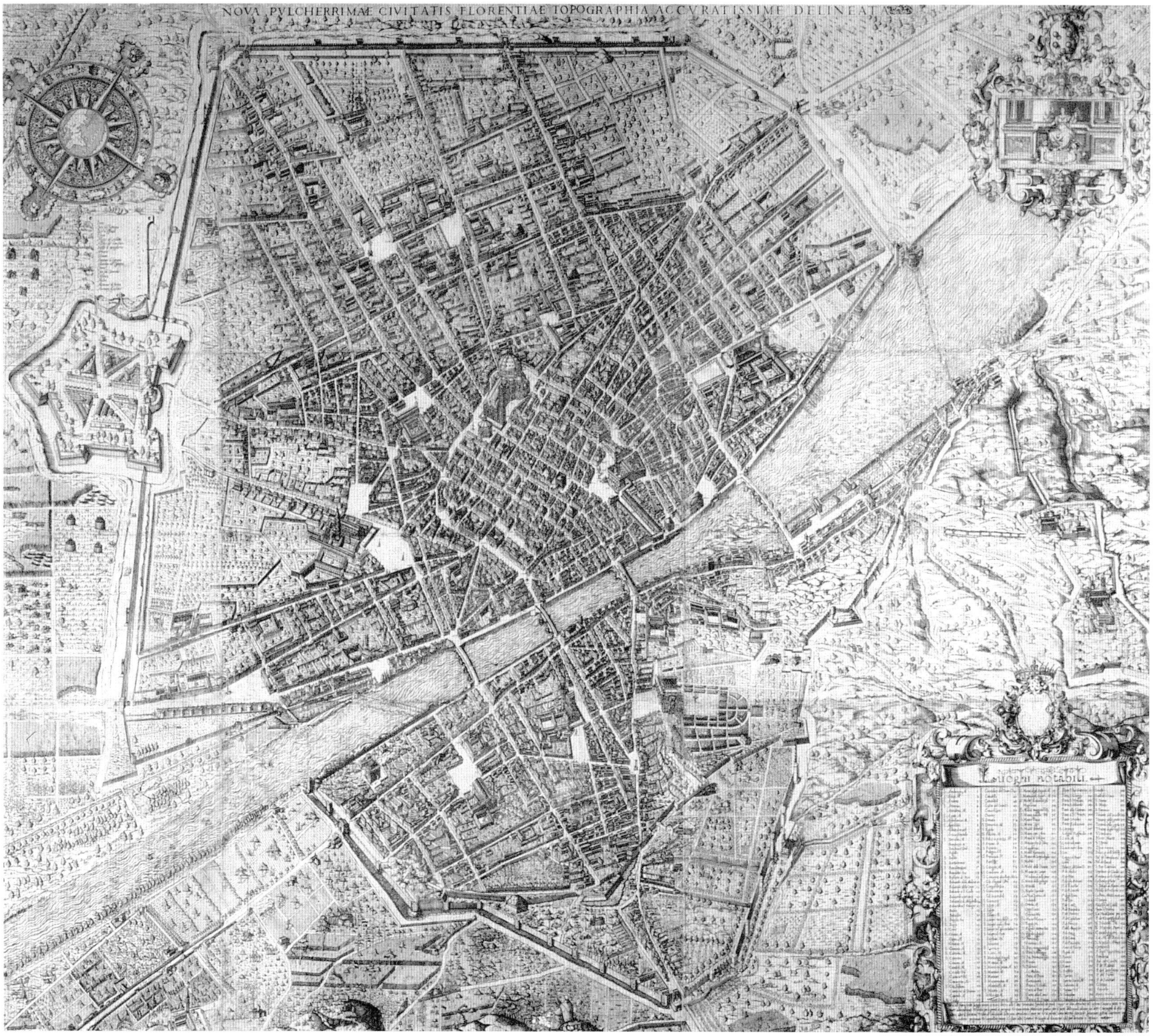

STEFANO BONSIGNORI, *NOVA PULCHERRIMAE CIVITAS FLORENTIAE*, 1584 (Florence, Museo di Firenze com'era)

Bonsignori's view of the city is invaluable for its unprecedented accuracy and detail.

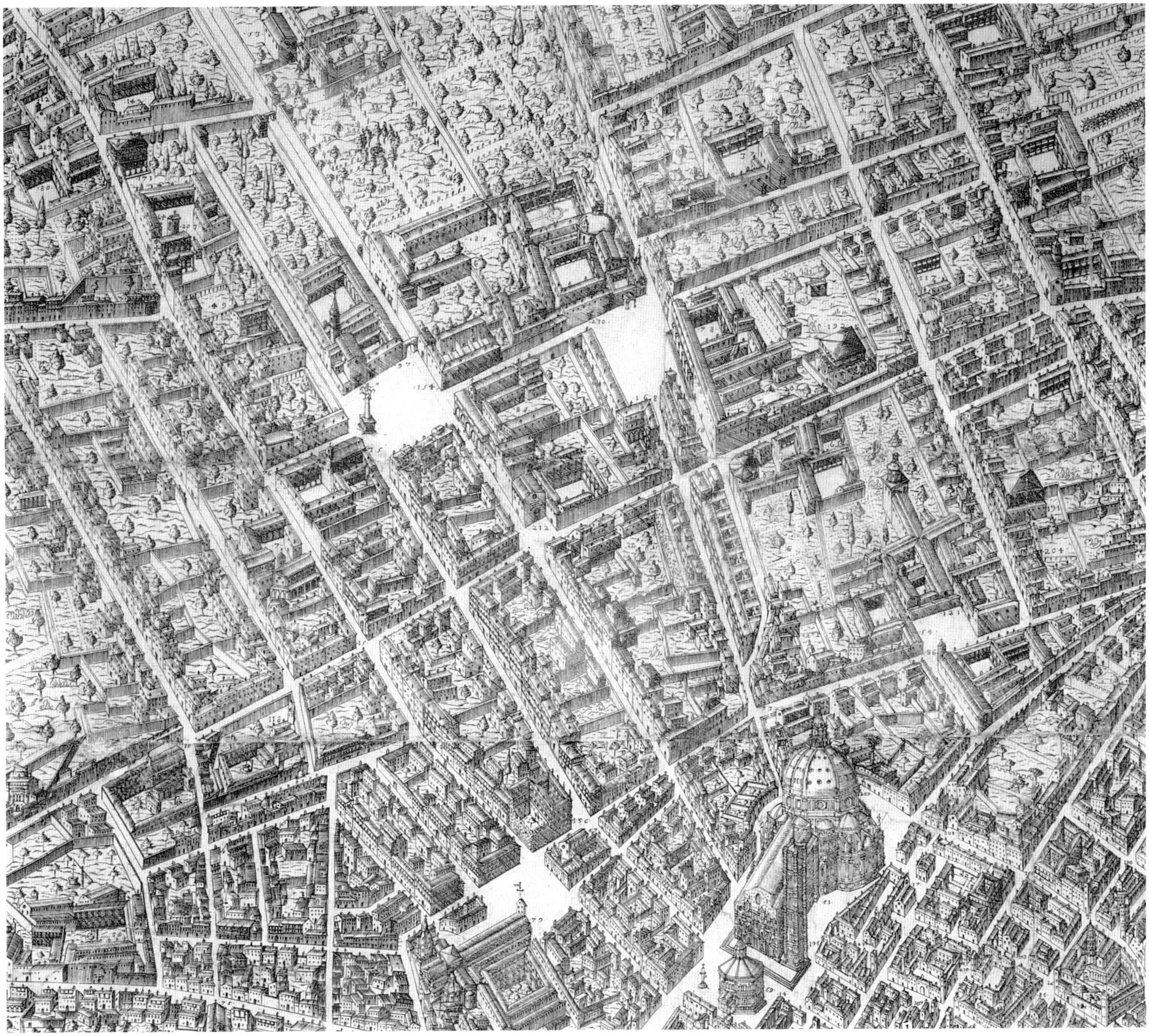

STEFANO BONSIGNORI, *NOVA PULCHERRIMAE CIVITAS FLORENTIAE*, 1584 (Florence, Museo di Firenze com'era)

Detail of the illustration opposite; the cathedral and San Lorenzo are near the bottom, with the two squares of San Marco and the Santissima Annunziata in the upper center. Beyond these built-up limits, the city's perimeter contained many gardens and orchards.

Several other later sixteenth-century views adopted more or less the same vantage point, which allowed a depiction somewhere between a natural image from one of the southern hills — usually Bellosguardo — and a bird's-eye view. Stefano Bonsignori's 1584 engraving, however, was markedly different from any depiction yet attempted; it was the first true bird's-eye view, from a considerable height: Florence seen directly from above and just south of the city center. The viewpoint is indeed so high that it approaches the fidelity of a true plan, and allows Bonsignori to illustrate the principal open spaces — Piazza della Signoria, the squares of Santa Croce, Santa Maria Novella, the Pitti — as well as the principal streets, with far more accuracy than any earlier representation. This was the product of a new era of scientific discovery and accurate information gathering.[48]

With this wealth of detail, some more specific observations can be made as to the city's appearance toward the end of the century. With a population of only approximately 60,000, Florence was by no means built up as far as the great circle of its walls, and with the exception of typical radial development along the main roads, most of the outermost zones remained completely undeveloped, a belt of orchards, vineyards, and private gardens. The northwestern districts were now dominated by the vast mass of the Fortezza da Basso, while the historic center was so densely developed that no green spaces survived at all. In the Oltrarno the extremely densely built-up zones around the bridgeheads contrasted both with the market gardens surrounding them and with the first development stage of the Boboli gardens. A degree of balance can thus be said to have been achieved between the city's nucleus and the "green belt" within the walls. Beyond, in the *contado*, a different kind of balance was achieved by the grand dukes with their collection of villas and estates encircling the city; these, too, were to be accurately recorded and depicted during this period, by a Flemish painter, Justus (Giusto) van Utens, who was commissioned by Ferdinando in 1598 to depict a series of fourteen lunettes for the Medici villa at Artimino.[49] Each lunette illustrates one of the Medici villas in its rural context, with its surrounding terraces, parterres, gardens, fishponds, woods, and orchards: another attempt to codify and record, with scientific objectivity.

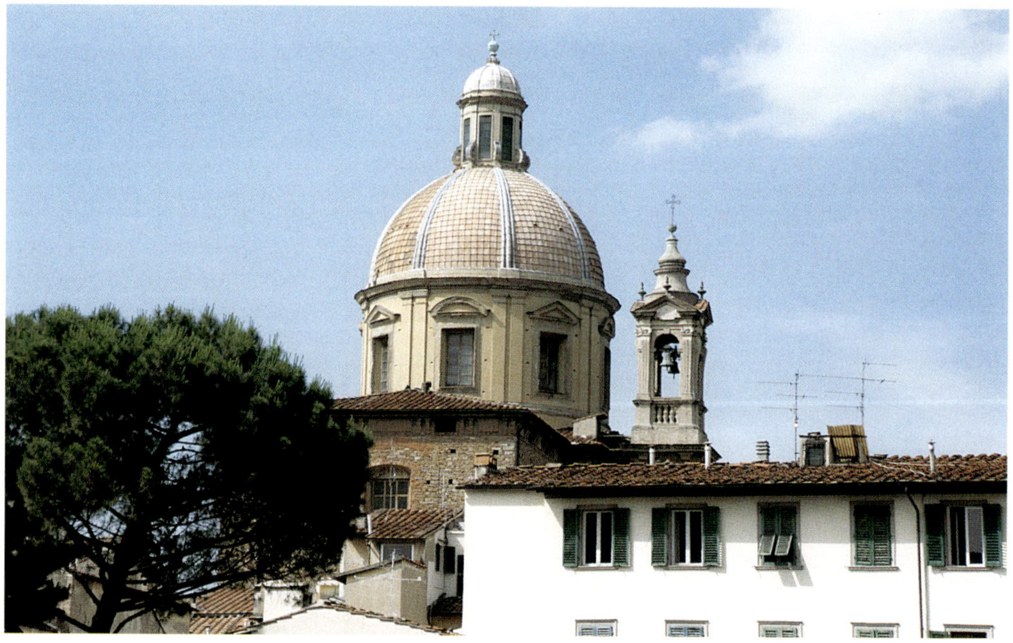

SAN FREDIANO IN CESTELLO

The cupola by Antonio Maria Ferri, built in the 1680s, dominates the Oltrarno.

The Later Medici

"The government of Tuscany . . . is monarchical, and more absolutely so than any other principality in Italy, the prince laying what taxes he pleases upon the people, and having always a good competent standing force to keep them in subjection."

Sir John Reresby, *Memoirs and Travels* (1657) [50]

Undeniably, with the rule of Cosimo II, first natural son of Ferdinando I, began the definitive decline of the house of the Medici and the city of Florence.[51] Ferdinando had considerably enhanced both Florence's general economic condition and the political independence that had suffered under Francesco. Cosimo II, only nineteen when he succeeded his father, ruled for eleven years, in extremely poor health; he died from tuberculosis at the age of thirty. Upon his death his own son Ferdinando was only eleven, so Cosimo's mother, Christine, and his widow, Maria Maddalena — sister of the Austrian emperor Ferdinando II — acted as regents until Ferdinando reached maturity.

Cosimo II was concerned chiefly with foreign policy. He had inherited the traditional Medici interests in the arts — music, poetry, and the court spectacles and festivities — but state coffers were far from overflowing, as farming had declined seriously under punitively high taxation, while the city's industries were threatened by foreign competition. Most of Cosimo's urban and architectural works were the continuation and completion of projects begun earlier by Ferdinando, among them the Cappella dei Principi, and the seemingly endless extension and elaboration of the palace and gardens at the Pitti. The enlargement of the palace was the result of a competition held in 1616, and the work, by Giulio Parigi, incorporated the definitive form of the piazza in front of this imposing facade. But the most characteristic event of the era was the spectacle organized for the entrance into the city of Cosimo and Maria Maddalena for their wedding in 1608. The festivities were among the most lavish ever staged in Florence, the centerpiece of which was the production of a pageant of Jason, the Argonauts, and the Golden Fleece on the Arno, complete with a fleet of galleys and extraordinary displays of fireworks. The statues of the four seasons added to the corners of the Santa Trinità bridge were a minor — though permanent — legacy of this spectacular event.

Another census undertaken in 1622 revealed that the city's population, just over 66,000, was still only slightly greater than it had been half a century earlier. It was further reduced, however, by the return of the plague in 1630, which, although by no means as devastating in Florence as it was elsewhere in Italy, nevertheless took up to 9,000 Florentine lives. Ferdinando II came of age in 1628 and ruled for a remarkable forty-two years. However, the dramatic shock of the plague masked a longer-term, general economic depression that had begun in about 1620 and would affect much of Western Europe. Tuscany, already weakened by falling demand for its principal exports, silk and wool fabrics, was further diminished by famine in 1621, and there were recurring outbreaks of the plague for some years after 1630. Ferdinando's reign thus began inauspiciously, and as the tax burden increased steadily, so did the polarization between the wealthy few, most of them centered on the court at the Pitti, and the far greater numbers of the poor and indigent. Farming crises and still more crippling taxes pushed many off the land and into the city, where there was no employment for them either; ever larger strains were placed on the extensive charitable networks of the capital.

With this polarization, the ostentatious wealth of the Pitti court became ever more prominent. Ferdinando patronized academic and cultural activity as well as festivities, and institutes such as the Accademia del Cimento and della Crusca, the Alterati, and the Nobili all flourished. So did the theater. Nor was the period devoid of significant works of architecture. Matteo Nigetti, Gherardo Silvani, and Giulio Parigi were the most prominent and prolific architects of this distinctly Baroque era, and with works such as San Frediano in Cestello and the facade of San Michele, palaces such as the Castelli, Strozzi del Poeta, and the Corsini (the most imposing of all), many parts of the city began to acquire a strongly Baroque flavor.[52] In 1659 the Medici sold the original family palace in the Via Larga to the Riccardi family. It had been the clan's base for more than two hundred years, and although over those centuries the Medici had progressed from being mere bankers to becoming the hereditary grand dukes of Tuscany — from the Palazzo del Popolo and thence to the Pitti — the disposal of the palace in the Via Larga was nevertheless an event of deep symbolic importance. The remaining dynasts lived in the overweening luxury of the Palazzo Pitti, an environment far removed from the austerity, prudence, and discipline of the world of Cosimo, *pater patriae*.

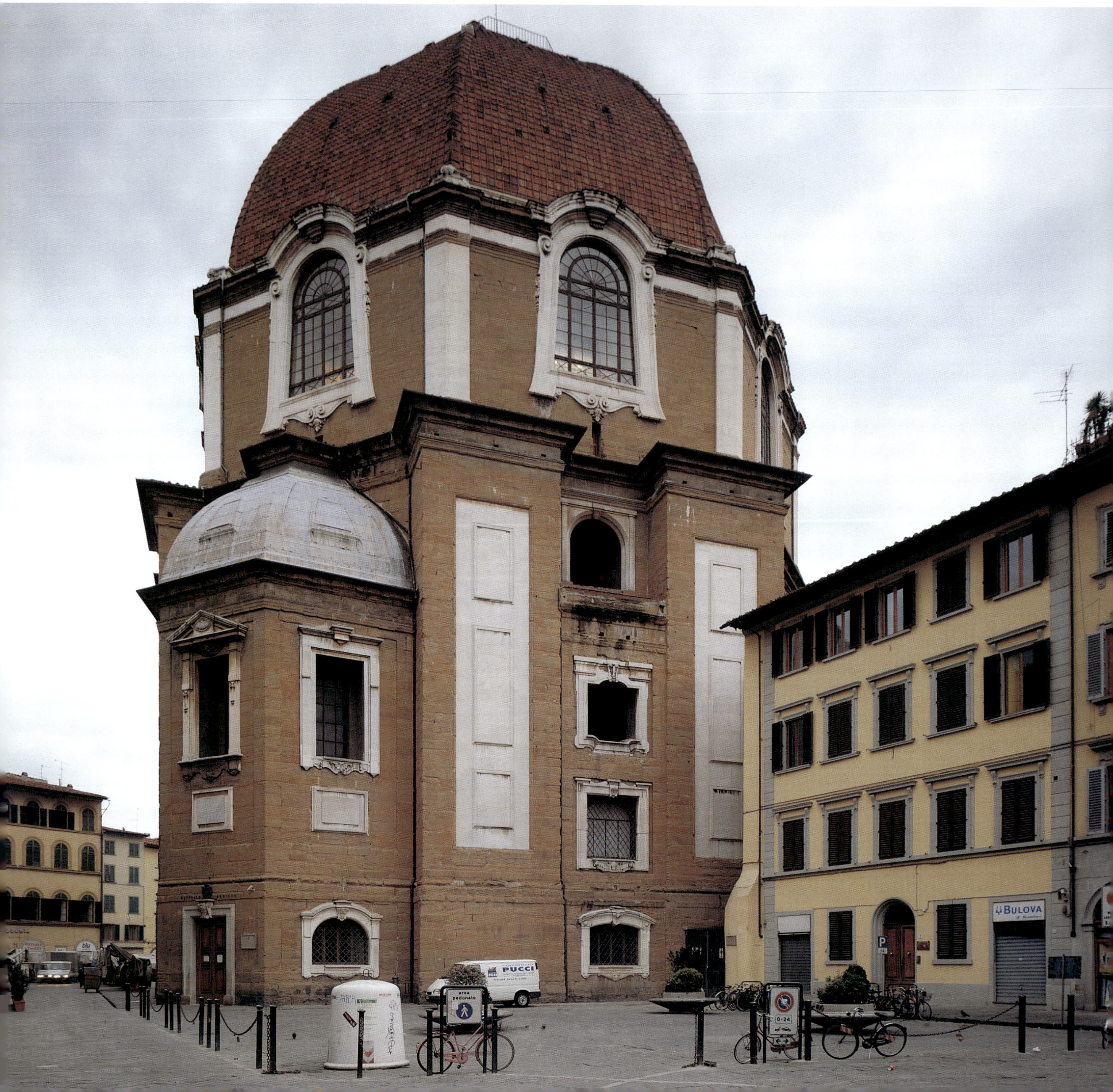
PUCCI
area pedonale
0-24
BULOVA

CAPPELLA DEI PRINCIPI (opposite)

The chapel at San Lorenzo, by Matteo Nigetti and others, was begun in 1604 and took decades to complete; its cupola is the largest in the city after that of the cathedral.

GAETANO VASCELLINI, *PIANTA DEL REALE GIARDINO DI BOBOLI*, 1789 (Florence, Museo di Firenze com'era) (below)

This plan of the Boboli gardens shows the layout of the gardens after the completion of the southern extensions, including the Isolotto.

Although Ferdinando, particularly in his later years, ruled with considerable ability and intelligence, supported by his vast private wealth, his son Cosimo III, who himself ruled for a record fifty-three years, did little to restore the economic wealth or political importance of Tuscany. His accumulation of titles reflects the vainglory and pretensions of what had become, in truth, an enfeebled "statelet" of very little European consequence. Ferdinando's new title of *serenissimo* (borrowed from the doges of Venice) was augmented by the bestowal upon Cosimo by the emperor of "His Royal Highness," a title as grandiloquent as it was hollow.

The city's chief industries, silk and wool, continued their apparently endless decline, while Cosimo's religious obsessions resulted in a dramatic expansion of the religious orders and monastic houses, the only growth industry of the era. By 1660 there were no fewer than 29 monasteries and friaries and 63 nunneries in the city, which approached 5,000 inhabitants in total, excluding all purely parochial offices. Accompanying this expansion was a parallel activity in the reconstruction of churches, new altars, and chapels all over the city. The Corsini chapel at the Carmini is representative of this Baroque activity, of which Giovanni Battista Foggini's San Giorgio alla Costa

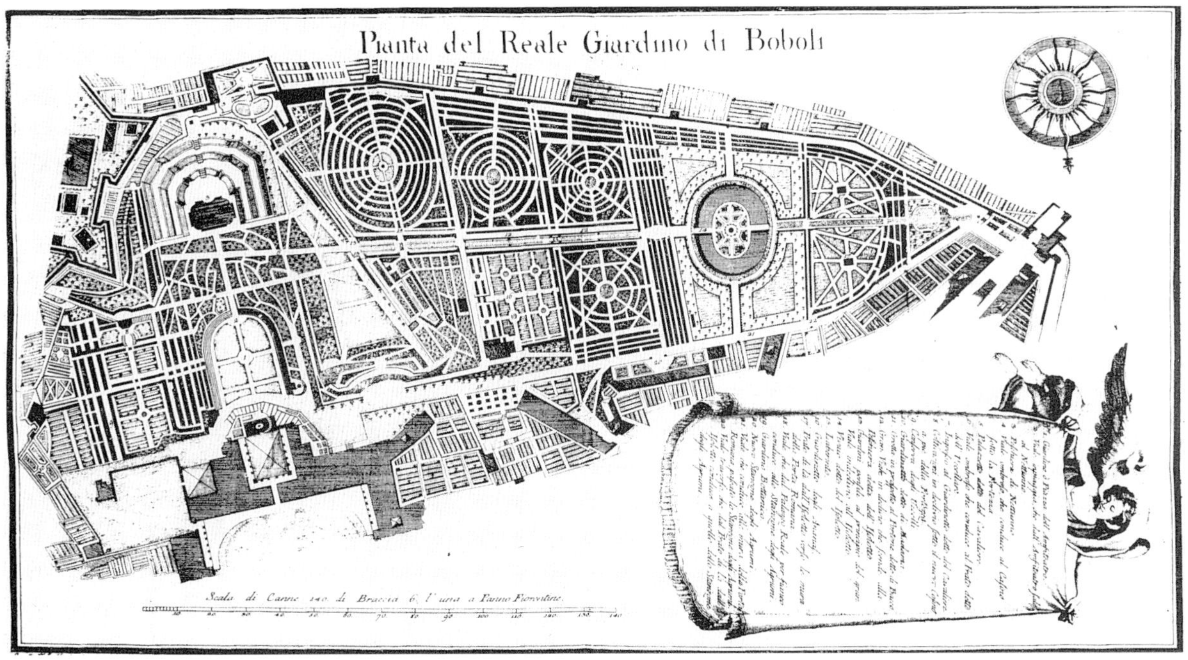

is another example. Religious festivals proliferated, the chief of which remained the national patronal feast of San Giovanni; so did the many forms of secular festivities — football at Santa Croce; the *gioco dell'anello* in the Via de' Tornabuoni; the Palio, its course crossing the city from Prato to San Pier Maggiore; displays of fireworks on the Arno; and other floating spectacles.

By 1710, Cosimo was concerned about the dynastic succession, since his son and heir, Ferdinando, married to Violante of Bavaria, had no offspring. Ferdinando did not rule, but he deserves mention as a remarkable patron of the arts and a shrewd collector; many of the finest works that can be seen today at the Pitti (by Raphael and Andrea del Sarto, for example) are his acquisitions, which also included contemporary Venetian works by the Ricci. Cosimo's daughter Anna Maria Luisa also produced no children who survived, and, after attempts to secure the line through his brother Francesco Maria had also failed, the only surviving Medici heir was Gian Gastone, younger brother of Ferdinando who had died in 1713. Cosimo died in 1723; Gian Gastone was by then fifty-three, an alcoholic and already senile. His reign of just ten years did achieve a little in the field of law reforms, in particular the nullification of the anti-Semitic laws of Cosimo III. Thus, not with triumph but with bathos, ended the dynasty that had shaped Florence's history for more than three hundred years.

4 **Florence under Foreign Rule**

"You cannot conceive what a scene of madness and distraction among all ranks of people reigns at this place during the carnival. . . . Every mortal masked, from a marquis to a shoe-black, traversing the streets from morning to night."

Robert Adam on the *Carnevale* in Florence (mid-eighteenth century) [1]

ARCO DI TRIONFO, PIAZZA DELLA LIBERTÀ

The arch was built by Jean-Nicholas Jadot from 1738 to 1740, to celebrate the entrance of Grand Duke Francesco of Lorraine into the city. Originally more simply Neoclassical, its crowning sculptures were added in 1744–55.

During much of Gian Gastone's brief reign, the great European powers had debated Florence's future among themselves. It was a destiny that he could affect in no way whatsoever, and in 1734 a congress decided that, after Gian Gastone's death, Tuscany would be ruled by Francis (Francesco Stefano) of the house of Lorraine.[2] Gian Gastone did obtain the concession that, although the new Lorraine grand duchy was to be hereditary, Tuscany would remain independent. Remarkably, this condition was upheld.

In 1739 Francesco Stefano made his formal entry into the city; his ceremonial arrival was marked by the hurried construction of the Arco di Trionfo in the Piazza della Libertà, which, despite heroic efforts, was still not quite complete on his arrival on 19 January.[3] Florence and Tuscany were weakened and chronically indebted, and before his fairly prompt return to Vienna (he never came back to Florence) Francesco Stefano left a regency charged with overhauling the tax system and boosting the enfeebled economy. A general — and long overdue — cleansing of the Florentine stables was thus begun that belatedly forced the Tuscan government into the eighteenth century. But Florence continued to be regarded as a minor resource of the Austrian empire, and many treasures were taken back to Vienna.

Little notable work took place in the city during this period. The fashion for the modernization of private palaces continued, and many more medieval stone facades were replaced by Baroque or Neoclassical elevations; the interiors were also frequently remodeled. One of the few sectors that did expand was the stage, with the building or rebuilding of theaters flourishing as never before during this period; the Pergola was the most famous among perhaps as many as seventeen in the city altogether.

In 1765 the absentee Francesco Stefano died and was succeeded by his son Pietro Leopoldo. If the distant reign of the former was characterized by the imposition of governmental and fiscal discipline after the decline and stagnation of the later Medici, his successor essentially built further on these reforms to bring Florence into the modern era. Pietro Leopoldo, who reigned from 1765 to 1792, began an ambitious program of economic, legal, and fiscal measures designed to turn Tuscany into a model modern state, albeit one of modest size and influence in the new Europe. Because Tuscany as a whole remained essentially a rural state, and to save the city's traditional wool and silk industries from almost terminal decline, agricultural reform was given a high priority. Within the city, Pietro Leopoldo set about to rationalize Florence's open spaces. A new garden (known as the Parterre, after the French fashion) was laid out just outside Porta San Gallo, and public walks or parks were created both inside and outside the walls, including the open spaces of San Salvatore, Monte Oliveto, the avenue to the villa of Poggio Imperiale, and the transformation of Le Cascine, formerly the Medici home farm, into a great public park and promenade along the north bank of the Arno.

One of Pietro Leopoldo's most far-reaching reforms concerned the religious orders. In sharp contrast to the remarkable expansion under the last Medici, many privileges were revoked, and

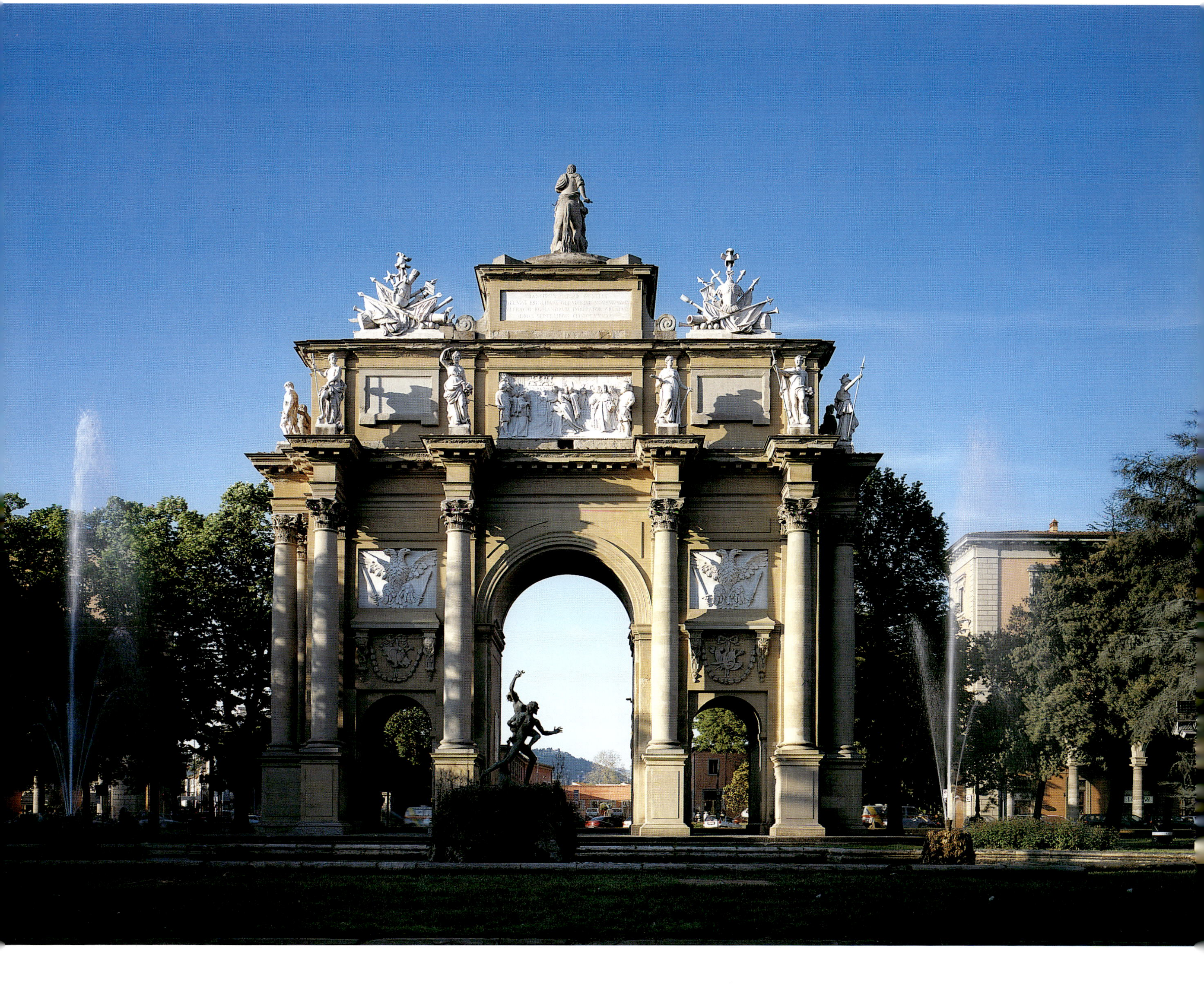

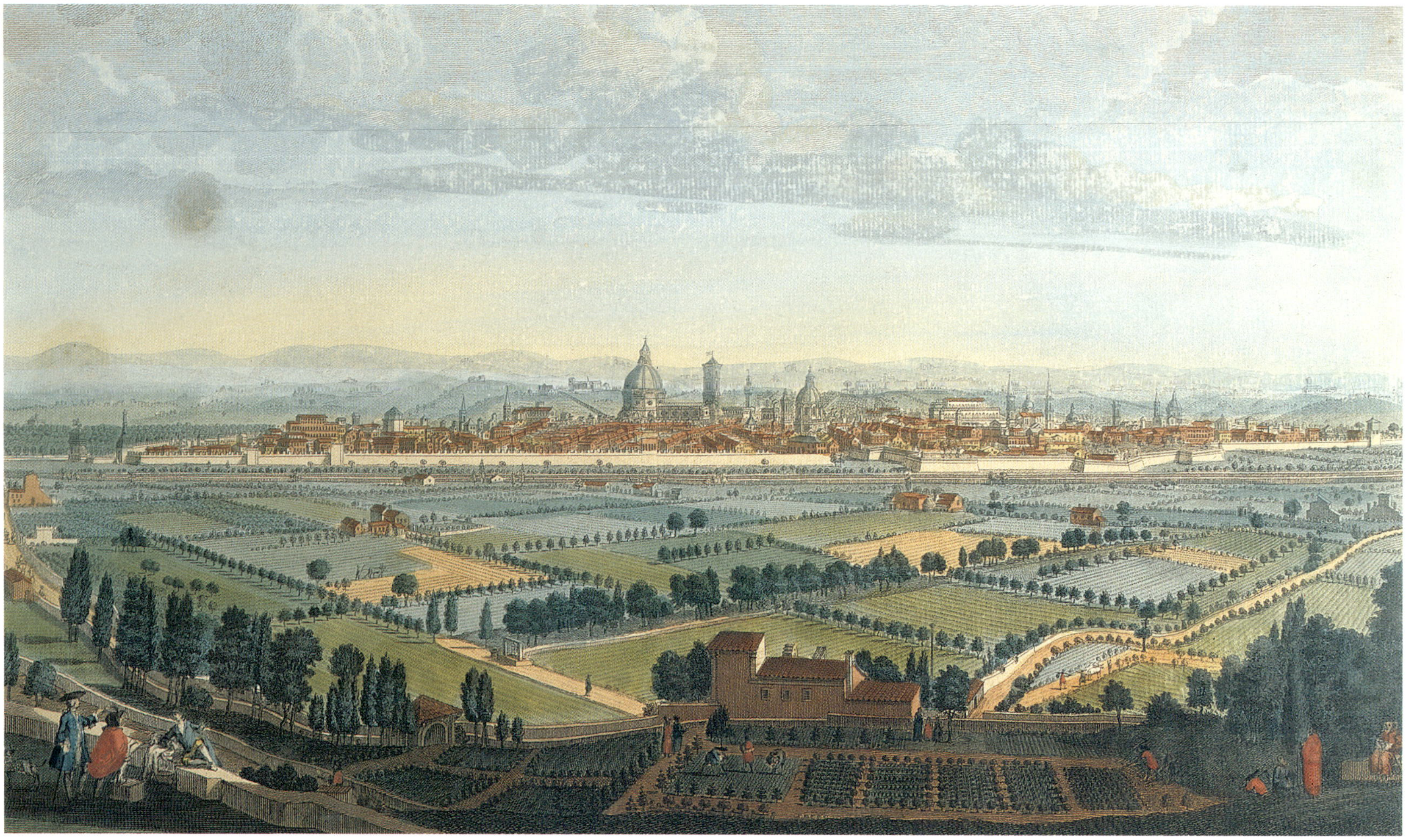

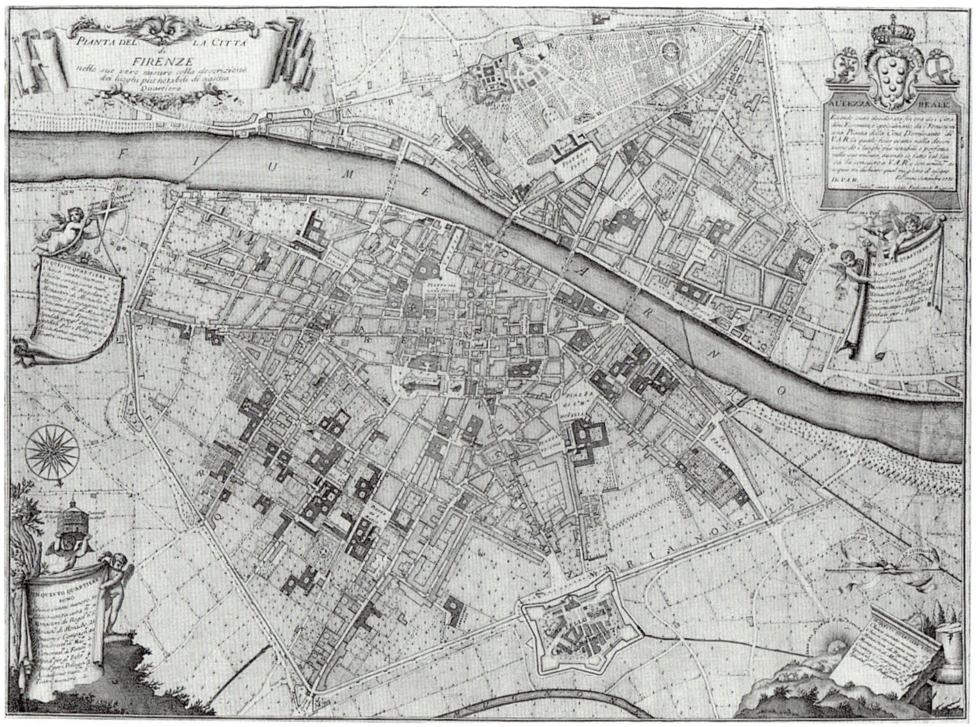

GIUSEPPE ZOCCHI, *VEDUTA DI FIRENZE DAL CONVENTO DEI PP CAPPUCCINI DI MONTUGHI*, 1744 (Florence, Museo di Firenze com'era) (above)

This well-known view is from the hill of Montughi, north of the Porta San Gallo, and depicts the intensively cultivated market gardens just outside Florence; the city itself is still confined within the walls.

FERDINANDO RUGGIERI, PLAN OF THE CITY OF FLORENCE, 1731 (Florence, Museo di Firenze com'era) (right)

The definitive record of Florence in the early eighteenth century, Ruggieri's detailed survey (which reversed the conventional orientation) was to form the basis of many other plans and views during the era of the Grand Tour.

many houses closed down entirely: around 150 in Florence alone, and more than 400 in Tuscany as a whole. Many of the properties thus abruptly vacated were adapted to become a network of hospitals and schools of all levels. Existing hospitals, such as Santa Maria Nova, were enlarged, while in 1784 the former hospital of San Matteo became the new seat of the Accademia delle Belle Arti. The education system was comprehensively overhauled and rationalized, with a new school in each of the four *quartieri* of the city, and new chairs were established in law and medicine. The library network was also radically modernized; the Magliabechiana and Laurenziana libraries were both enlarged, and the famous Uffizi galleries were first opened to the public in 1769. In the same spirit of education and enlightenment, a museum of natural history was opened in the Palazzo Torrigiani in 1775, in which were displayed the rich collections of the Medici.

The urban fabric of the city had suffered from decades of neglect: the paving of streets, sanitary conditions — particularly in the cottages of the poor — all were in need of fundamental modernization. So the city as a whole was given the responsibility of street paving and drainage and sewerage, replacing the ancient system whereby the maintenance of streets had been the responsibility solely of those properties adjoining the streets themselves. And in 1783 it was decided to install a street lighting system using oil lamps.

The Grand Tour: The Image of the City in the Eighteenth Century

In the settecento, the physical fabric of Florence was surveyed and published more frequently than ever before: Plans, maps, views, and guidebooks proliferated, many of them of great accuracy.[4] To some extent, this reflects the spirit of rational inquiry so characteristic of the era, an era of exploration, classification, and analysis, of the imposition of order and discipline, of structures. On another, more prosaic level, it responded to the characteristic phenomenon of the period: the spread of tourism and the Italian Grand Tour.

One of the first and most important was Ferdinando Ruggieri's survey, published in 1731, and it was followed by a notable outpouring of maps and plans of the city of unparalleled detail. Half a century later, Francesco Mangelli's 1783 engraving marks another milestone in the history of the mapping of the city. Both of these surveys reversed the conventional orientation, with north now at the bottom of the plan, but both are accurately plotted to scale (that of Mangelli at 1:2000) and both represent the maturation of this process of scientific recording. If we add to these many commercially produced guidebooks, maps, and views the paintings of *vedutisti* such as those of Bernardo Bellotto, Luigi Vanvitelli, and Giuseppe Zocchi, then we have in the eighteenth century the most comprehensively recorded picture of Florence's urban history.

During the first half of the century Florence remained something of a backwater as far as the Grand Tourists were concerned. The principal ports of call for these cultural visitors were Venice, Rome, and Naples, and although the route inevitably took most of them through Florence on their journey southward, it was not until the latter part of the century that the Medici dynasty and the artistic achievements under their patronage became the subject of serious examination and appreciation by foreign visitors. By the end of the century, well-researched biographies, particularly of Lorenzo Il Magnifico, were beginning to be published, and a reassessment not only of the principality, but also of the works of art the Medici had sponsored was well under way. And this appreciation increased greatly during the following century.

However, although they may have lacked the appreciation of the genius of Florence's Renaissance masters, the city did receive considerable praise from earlier settecento Grand Tourists.[5] The quality of accommodation in the form of inns or lodgings varied considerably, but Florence was generally considered to be one of the most attractive and civilized cities in Italy. It was certainly much more so than the other towns of Tuscany: Pisa was half deserted, with grass growing in the streets and virtually no lodgings for visitors, while both Lucca and Pistoia were dismissed as provincial, dowdy, and half abandoned. Florence, by contrast, enjoyed a delightful setting that was augmented by excellent food, famous monuments, and endless festivals, both lay and religious.

The Napoleonic Era and the Period to Unification

"We have had two revolutions here at Florence, Grand Duke out, Grand Duke in. The bells in the church opposite rang for both. The first planted a tree of liberty close to our door, then they pulled it down. The same tune, sung under the windows, did for 'Viva la republica' [sic] and 'Viva Leopoldo!'" **Elizabeth Barrett Browning,** letter to a friend, 30 April 1849 [6]

Tuscany was not spared by the invading armies of Napoleon, and on 27 March 1799 French troops occupied the city. Grand Duke Ferdinando III (Pietro Leopoldo's son) fled to Vienna and a provisional government was installed in Florence. This government survived, with various alterations, until 1814, when Ferdinando returned to Florence. In 1808, in the great wave of anticlericalism that swept throughout the Italian Napoleonic kingdom, the religious orders were suppressed in Tuscany; an extensive patrimony of public buildings thus became the property of the state and were converted into other uses or sold. The following year Tuscany formally became a part of the French Empire, and was ruled by Grand Duchess Elisa, sister of Napoleon. She reestablished the court at Palazzo Pitti and embarked on yet another program of sumptuous improvements. She also saved a number of religious foundations from the eradication proposed by her brother. As was characteristic of the Napoleonic treatment of Italian cities, ambitious programs of urban renewal and restructuring were initiated; and as elsewhere, some were executed while many were not. Among the architects who participated in this renewal of activity in the city, the most prominent was Giuseppe del Rosso, son of another architect, Zanobi, who proposed, among other grandiose works, a Foro Napoleonico, a great forum that was to occupy a huge block between San Marco and the city walls and that would have required the demolition of several monastic houses. The scheme, which was never executed, had as its centerpiece an immense monument to the emperor. Further works of clearance and reordering were proposed — but again not executed — in the Via de' Calzaiuoli and the Piazza San Giovanni. A series of public projects intended not only to improve the functioning and appearance of the city, but also to provide work for the large numbers of unemployed, were also begun during this decade. One such project was the formation of a new road around the inside of the city walls, ostensibly to create a public promenade, but also to facilitate the rapid deployment of troops should this prove necessary to maintain order.[7]

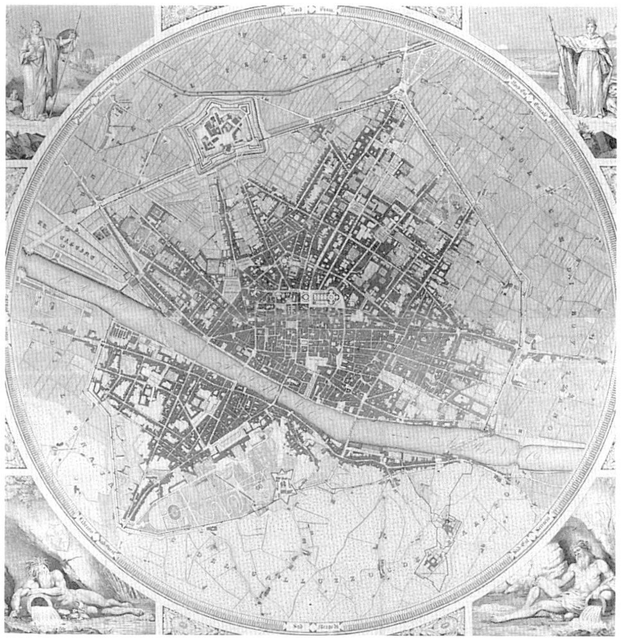

FEDERICO FANTOZZI, *PIANTA GEOMETRICA DI FIRENZE*, 1843 (Florence, Museo di Firenze com'era)

A century or so after Ruggieri, there is little change in the overall built-up extent of the city. With the exception of the nineteenth-century clearances around the Mercato Nuovo, the basic plan of the historic center has changed very little to this day.

In 1810 a new census was undertaken, and in 1817 a land registry survey was instigated, covering not only Florence but the whole of Tuscany.[8] This great project took more than ten years to compile but was finally published in 1831; in the following year a detailed land registry plan of the city center completed the impressive exercise. Both works remained the definitive record of land ownership until very recent times.

LUNGARNO AMERIGO VESPUCCI

These riverbanks and the adjacent developments of Le Cascine represent one of many mid-nineteenth-century works of reclamation and urban expansion.

After only five years, however, in 1814 Austrian pressures, together with the invading armies of Joachim Murat, king of Naples, from the south saw the return of Grand Duke Ferdinando III to the city, where he ruled as a highly regarded and enlightened *granduca* until his death ten years later. He was succeeded by his son Leopoldo II, who occupied the Pitti until 1859. It was during this era of general peace and stability that a number of urban works proposed by Napoleon were belatedly carried out. Indeed, the early-nineteenth-century impetus for urban improvement (a term that should perhaps be qualified, since some works involved considerable destruction) was to be continued for much of the century, during which time profound changes were made to the city's form and structure.

Among the physical works executed in this period was the extension of the Via Larga (today Via Cavour) northward toward the city walls to form a viable alternative route to the ancient Via San Gallo; at about the same time, the south side of the cathedral piazza was regularized and modernized. This side of the square had previously contained a fairly miscellaneous collection of structures with irregular alignments lacking the unity that characterized the east and northeast

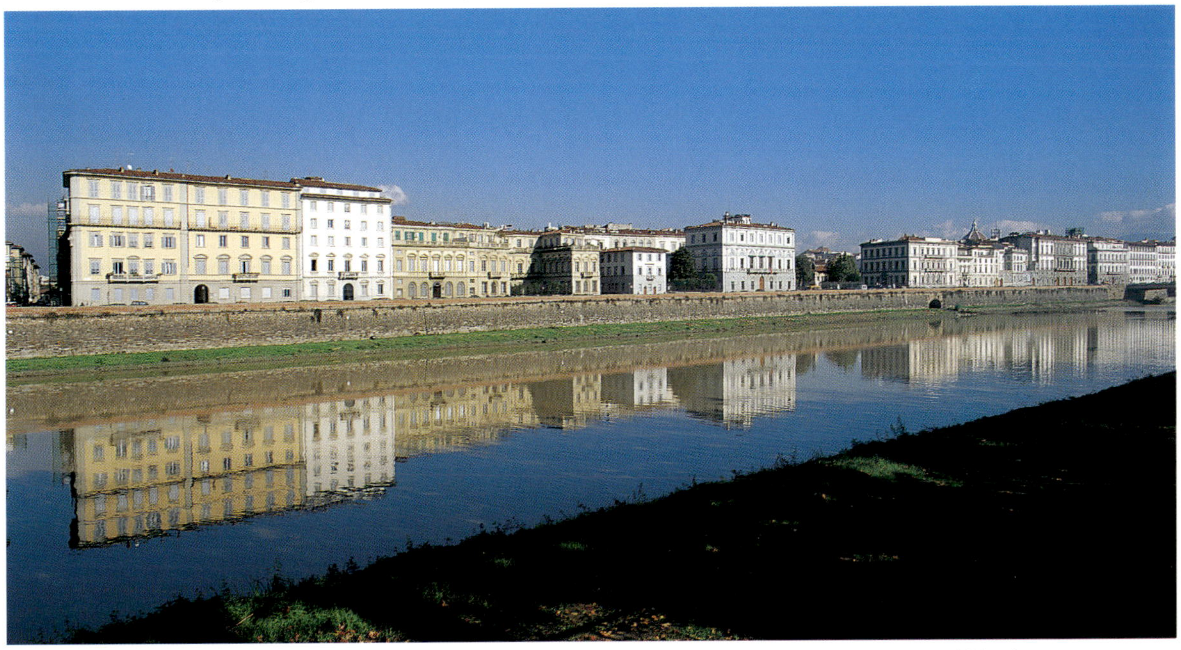

parts of the piazza; they were now replaced by the present regular, symmetrical Neoclassical blocks by Gaetano Baccani. The same architect, working in a very different manner, added the picturesque "medieval" campanile to Santa Croce during the same period.

If we look at the city as a whole in this era, we can identify distinct concentrations of functions and activities, some of them long established. For example, the north-central "Medicean" zone around Piazza San Marco had long been the focus for a number of monastic houses, cultural organizations, educational establishments, and hospitals. Across the river, on the other hand, the influence of the grand ducal court at Palazzo Pitti cast a broad shadow over the eastern part of the Oltrarno, in both literal and figurative senses. Not only were there clusters of fine palaces in the streets nearby, but the theater, too, was drawn to its environs; the Teatro Goldoni was built in 1817 by Giuseppe del Rosso and became the official court theater.

Many midcentury works of urban modernization were based on the premise of improving communications both within the city and between the historic center and the surrounding *contado*. Works that fulfilled both of these functions included the construction of two new bridges across the Arno to augment the old established four. Their locations are particularly significant: Ponte San Leopoldo (the present Ponte della Vittoria) was located downstream at the point where the city walls met the river, at the entrance to the Cascine and adjacent to the Porta al Prato. The other, Ponte San Ferdinando (the modern Ponte San Niccolò) occupied the equivalent location upstream, just above the Porta San Niccolò. These two new bridges thus made it possible to cross the river both upstream and downstream of the city center without having to enter the city at all.

V. SIMONCINI, *VIA DE' CALZAIUOLI*, C. 1845

Below, left: engraving of the street before its nineteenth-century widening. For centuries, the congestion in this principal artery connecting the cathedral with the Piazza della Signoria had been the subject of debate. Below: the same view after the widening in 1841–44.

Even more dramatic modernizations followed the completion of these bridges in 1837. In 1844 the widening of the Via de' Calzaiuoli was finally completed. This project had several centuries of history behind it; in the medieval period only the southernmost section had been widened, as far as Orsanmichele, to relieve congestion that had already been acute in the fourteenth century. The ancient spine of the city's commerce, the street was now widened by demolitions and faced with new blocks to present a uniform, regular, Neoclassical succession of facades — at the cost, of course, of considerable older fabric. The street today therefore has an almost entirely unified, nineteenth-century appearance.[9]

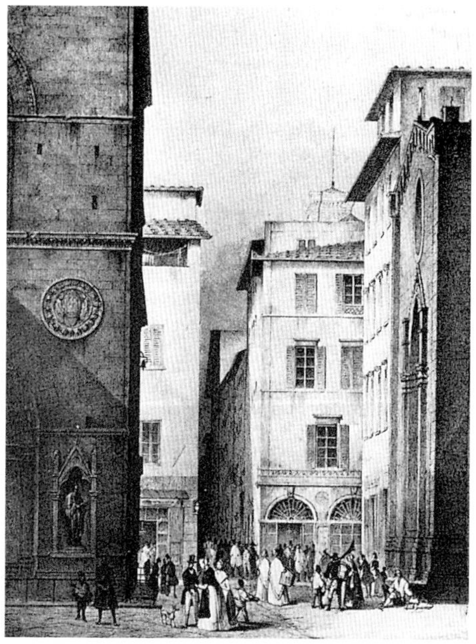

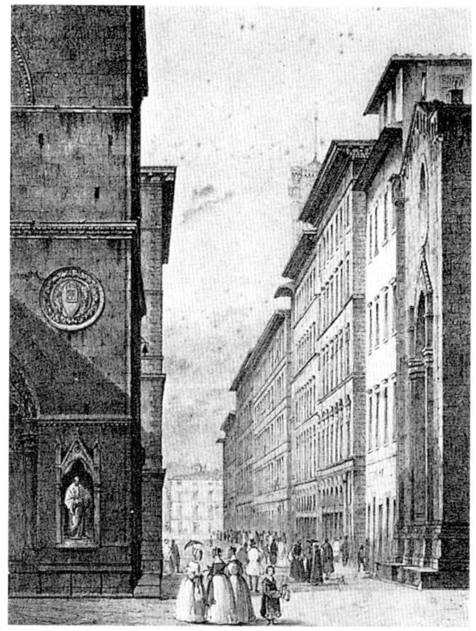

At the same time, a new railway line was constructed between Florence, Pisa, and Livorno, at the instigation of the great Scottish engineer Robert Stephenson. When completed in 1848, it was the first intercity line in Italy, and naturally required an appropriate terminus in Florence. The first station, just outside the Porta al Prato, was joined the following year by a second station nearby, originally dedicated to Maria Antonia, and built just behind Santa Maria Novella. In time this became Florence's principal station, as it served the national trunk line linking Florence with Rome and Naples to the south, and with Bologna and Milan to the north. Not only were the two stations built in close proximity in this northwestern part of the city, but in 1844, work began in laying out a new quarter known as Barbano, adjacent to the old Fortezza da Basso. It was a regularly planned district, centered on an extensive new square, the present Piazza dell'Indipendenza. Florence's population had been rising steadily over some decades (in 1844 it reached 81,000, and by 1859 was 113,000), and there was an acute lack of space in the congested center. Finally, therefore, five centuries after the construction of the city walls had enclosed a swath of greenbelt within its secure confines, the greenbelt was eroded by substantial new development. Within a few more decades, it disappeared almost entirely.[10] The development of Barbano was followed in 1850 by the layout of the Cascine district, a large, wedge-shaped zone between the Porta al Prato and the river, and the construction of the adjacent Lungarno Vespucci. Both developments were destined to be occupied by the middle and upper classes, and thus did little to relieve the acute pressures on housing for the poor. However, several larger-scale projects did address these social concerns, most of them built immediately after Unification. Collectively, they replaced the remains of the intramural greenbelt with a new belt of popular housing typologies not seen before in the city.

The construction of the station at Santa Maria Novella created a major new hub in the city's urban structure and led to an urgently perceived need for more direct communication with the city center; to this end, Via Panzani and Via de' Cerretani were both widened between 1859 and 1862, providing an important new axis between the station and the Piazza San Giovanni. The

THE RAILWAY STATION

The main railway station was built just behind Santa Maria Novella from 1846 to 1848. Its construction resulted in the demolition of some of the monastic buildings attached to the church.

second similar work in this part of the city was the cutting of Via Nazionale, which ran northeastward from the large modern square in front of the station toward the new quarter of Barbano. Both of these works addressed the need to superimpose new networks and links onto the ancient street plan to take account of recent and developing infrastructures. They were followed by several more after 1860.

The year 1848 was a pivotal one in the formation of the states of modern Europe, and the general ferment that affected many parts of the Continent was also felt in Tuscany. Uprisings in Pisa and Livorno led to unrest in Florence and provoked the grand duke to draft a more democratic constitution for Tuscany; he appointed Baron Ricasoli, a notable liberal reformer from an old, noble Florentine clan, as the city's *gonfaloniere*. Insurgency in Milan against the Austrian empire triggered a similar response in Florence, where thousands volunteered to fight with the *Piemontesi* to rid Italy of its Austrian overlords. Italian forces were no match for those of Austria's field marshal Joseph Radetsky, however, and decisive defeat came at Novara in March 1849. There were calls in Florence to replace the ineffective government of Leopoldo II; after several attempts to form an administration generally acceptable to the Florentines, Leopoldo fled south and a provisional government was established under Giuseppe Montanelli and Giuseppe Mazzini. After a few months, though, Leopoldo was asked to return, but he brought with him an Austrian army of occupation.

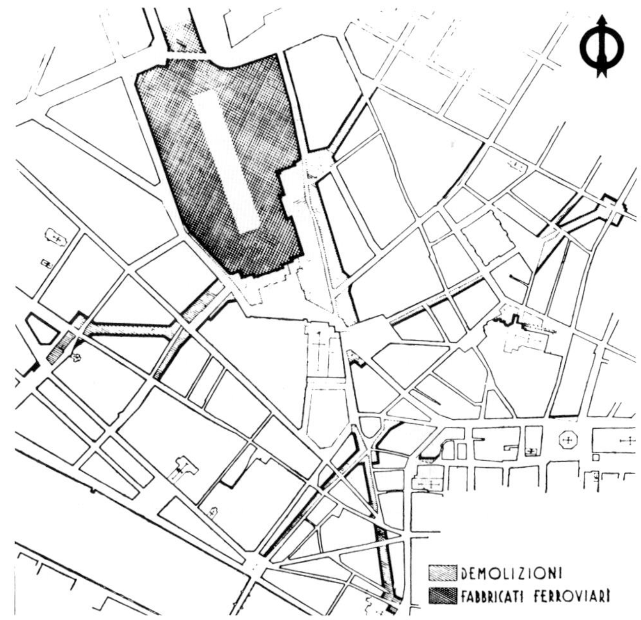

However, the political changes occurring elsewhere in the peninsula and the increasing pressures for unification ultimately could not be ignored. Ten years later Camillo Cavour, from his base in Sardinia, signed a pact with Napoleon III with the renewed intention of driving the Austrians from Italy; great victories followed at Magenta and Solferino in June 1859. Just before the triumph of Magenta, thousands took to the streets of Florence with the *tricolore*, demanding the end of Leopoldo's reign. His ministers at Palazzo Pitti resigned on 25 April, and two days later there was another massive public demonstration and a march through the city; Leopoldo was urged to abdicate but refused until, on the evening of 27 April, he conceded defeat and left the city with his family, never to return. A provisional government was formed immediately and ruled for nearly a year. On 15 March 1860 the people of Tuscany decided to unite with the kingdom of Piedmont under King Victor Emmanuel II. Cavour had conceded that his birthplace, Turin, could not realistically become the capital of a finally united Italy; it was not only far too "French," but also too remote from the geographical center of the peninsula. Rome also had difficult associations with the papacy, and was still comparatively poor and underdeveloped. And so, on 20 March 1860, the king arrived in Florence, the heart of Italy's cultural Renaissance, now chosen as the new capital of a united Italy.

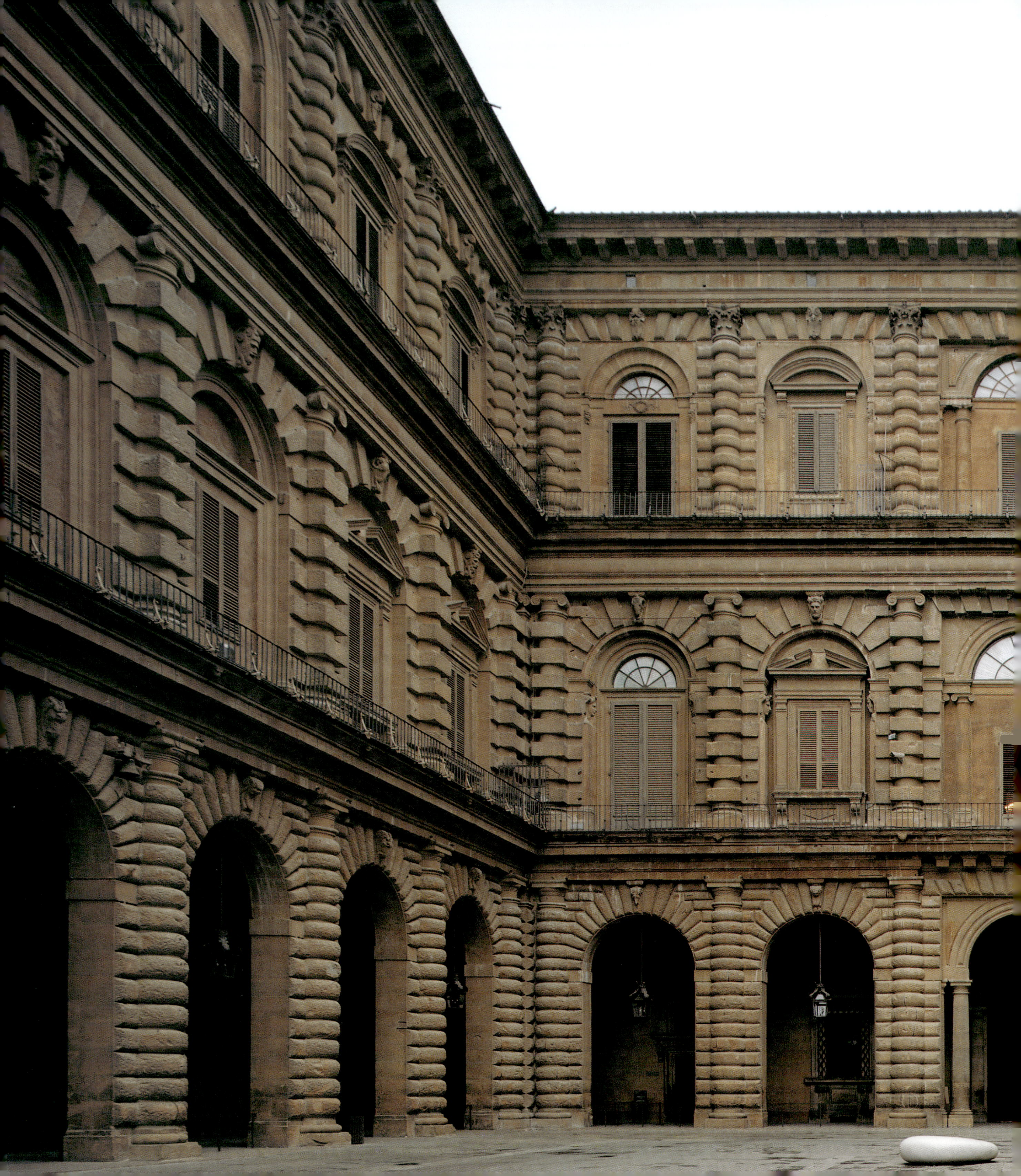

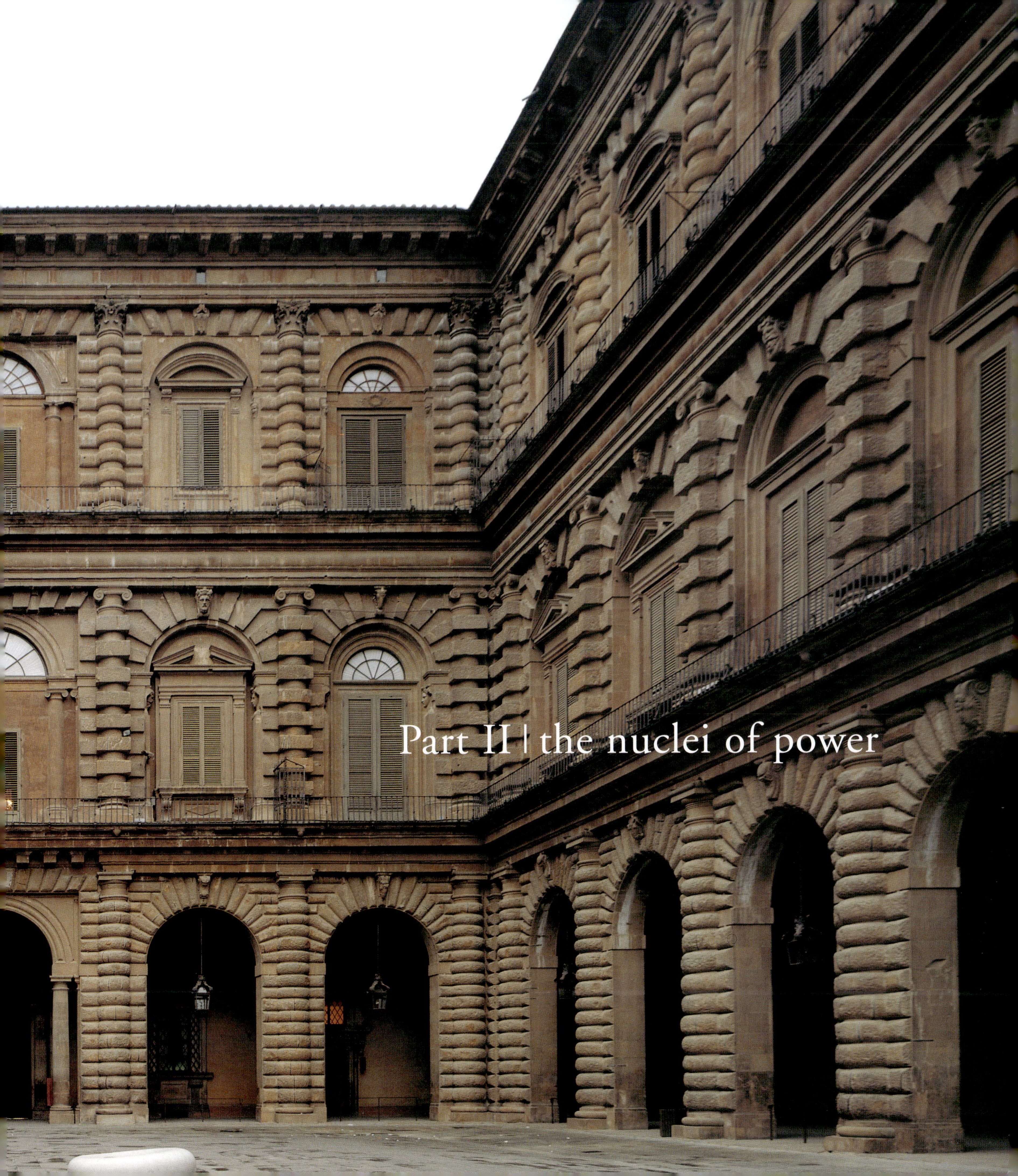

Part II | the nuclei of power

"For many people, who have travelled all over the world, say that this is the most beautiful temple, or rather, cathedral, of all that they have seen."

Giovanni Villani, *Cronica fiorentina* (c. 1330) [1]

Brunelleschi's magnificent cupola of the cathedral of Santa Maria del Fiore is the defining image of the spiritual nucleus of Florence. But it was not always so; the immense cathedral had taken more than a century to build, and the cupola, with its crowning lantern, was the last element to be completed. A hundred yards to the west of the great dome, the octagonal form of the baptistery of San Giovanni had represented the traditional core of Florentine faith for several centuries before Santa Maria del Fiore replaced the modest church of Santa Reparata. And while the cathedral was being built, the freestanding campanile was also rising adjacent to its southwestern corner. Thus the religious and spiritual heart of Florence is not represented by a single structure, and neither is it centered on a single public piazza; it is, rather, a group of buildings that, together with their surrounding spaces, developed over a long period of time. Although the detailed urban context is significantly different, the spiritual heart of Florence has more in common with that of Pisa than with the more widespread and simpler concept of "cathedral and piazza."

The story of the evolution of this complex of buildings begins with the baptistery of San Giovanni. The baptistery and the original church of Santa Reparata were beyond the walls of the early medieval city, a situation analogous to that of Pisa, where the Piazza del Duomo, or Piazza dei Miracoli, stands on the northernmost edge of the walled city. The seat of the Florentine bishopric was at San Lorenzo, just outside the northern wall, but the cathedra had been transferred to Santa Reparata probably in the seventh century. It was only with the construction of the so-called Matildine walls of 1078 that the church and baptistery were brought within the safety of the city's defensive confines.

The key relationship in this original grouping was that between the baptistery and the modest basilican form of Santa Reparata. The Florentine baptistery is massive, the largest that has survived. Recent archaeological investigations have established that the present facade of the cathedral stands about 20 feet (6 meters) farther to the east than that of the earlier, and smaller, basilica of Santa Reparata; even in its earliest configuration, therefore, the physical relationship between church and baptistery has always been extremely close.[2] The history of the baptistery is still unclear, and has been the source of endless debate and speculation through the centuries, but it is established that, characteristically, the baptistery stood a little distance to the west of the main facade of the church. In general, medieval baptisteries in Italy are located either directly to the west of the church, on its central axis, or to the west but to one side, usually toward the south. There was a widespread tradition of such freestanding structures in Italy. Their location at the west end was based on a liturgical principle; because baptism is the sacrament by which a person is accepted into the spiritual Church, the rite of baptism had to take place before the entry into the physical church. The act of baptism was thus literally as well as metaphorically one's reception into the Church. The spiritual and physical axial progression that began at the font in the center of the baptistery was continued into the church, down the nave, to culminate at the high altar, which was traditionally at the east end, toward Jerusalem.

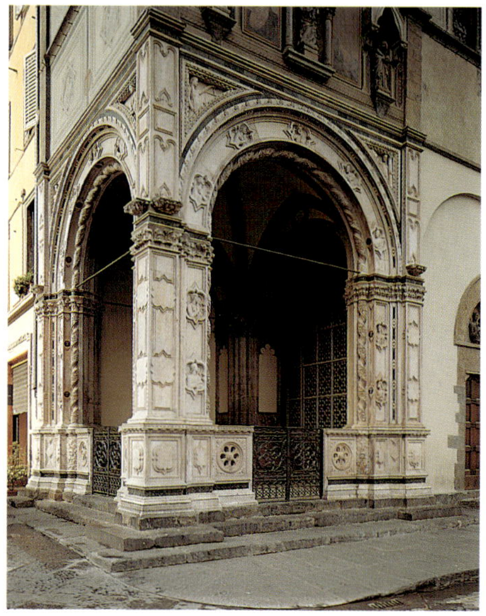

LOGGIA DEL BIGALLO (above)

Often attributed to Alberto Arnoldi, and built between 1352 and 1358, the richly carved loggia had been altered on several occasions, and has recently been comprehensively restored.

PIAZZA SAN GIOVANNI (opposite)

View from the west, with the baptistery, the cathedral, and the campanile. One of the most famous urban set pieces in Europe, the group did not achieve its final, present appearance until the facade of the cathedral itself was built in 1887.

PALAZZO PITTI (previous pages)

The cortile by Bartolommeo Ammannati, 1558–70.

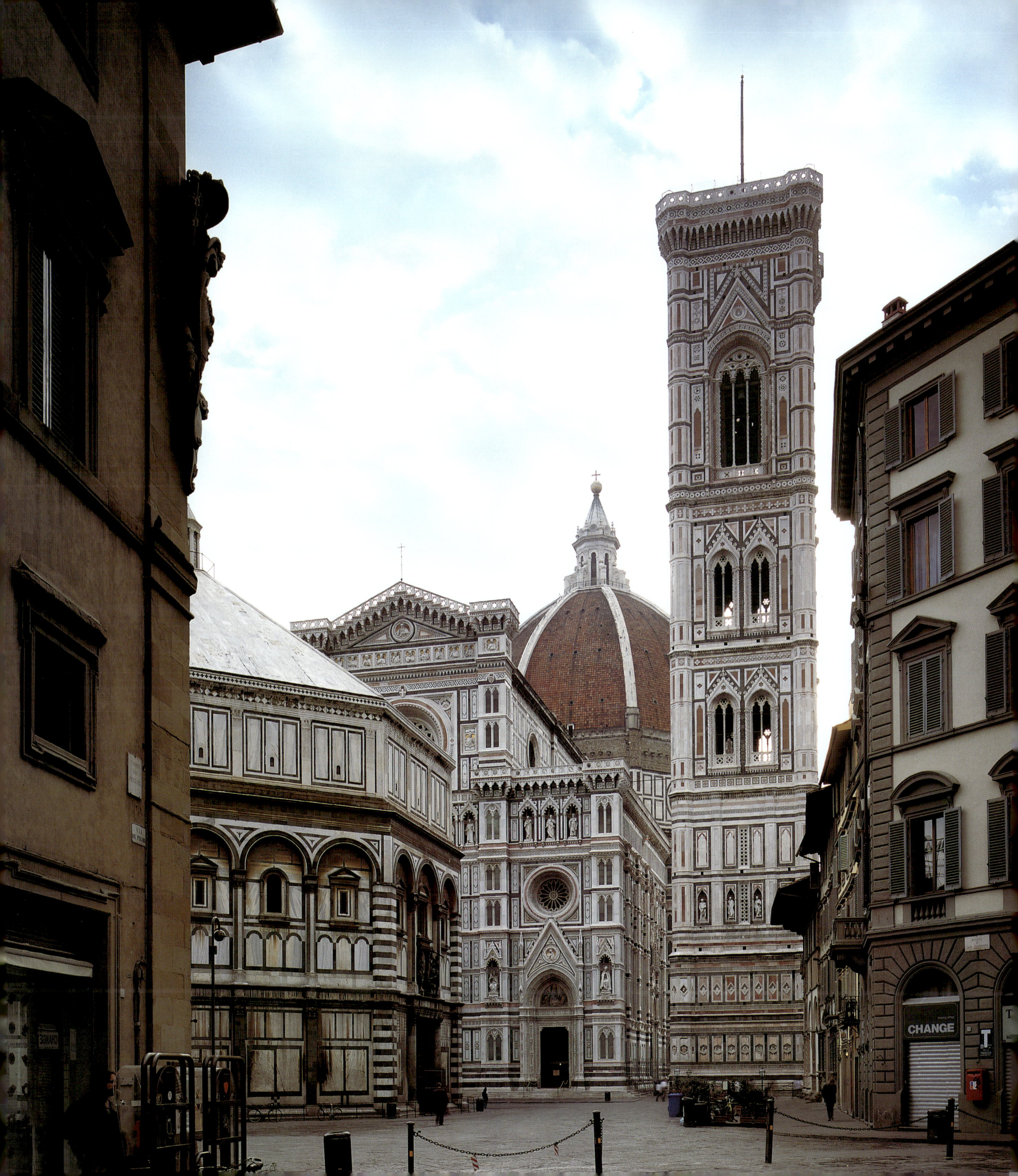
CHANGE

There is no great open space or parvis in front of the church, as in many medieval cities, but rather, a fairly constricted, almost intimate space between the two buildings. And the baptistery stands at the center of its own space, a breathing space, one might say, which wraps around it on all sides, rendering it clearly freestanding. The history of the squares and spaces surrounding Florence's monumental group is one of slow modification and expansion, a purposeful attempt both to enhance the dignity of the monuments' setting and to take account of the truly massive scale of the new cathedral. Toward the end of the duecento, during Florence's greatest period of wealth and communal prosperity, a number of works were begun to achieve these aims with respect to the baptistery and the new cathedral, for which the foundations had also been laid. In 1289 the Piazza di San Giovanni Battista was paved, and a few years later the adjacent Ospedale di San Giovanni was demolished to clear additional space. This was the first of many such clearances over the centuries. Most of the major works of urban improvement, however, took place in the trecento, as the massive form of the new cathedral, particularly the tribune — that is, the crossing and the eastern arms — was laid out. Indeed, widespread demolition became necessary all around the eastern end of the new church. In 1336 the Comune acquired and took down houses around the baptistery, which thus began to assert its presence within the tightly packed surrounding streets. Three years later, following requests from two guilds, the Arte della Lana and the Arte della Seta, it was decided to lower the levels of the streets immediately surrounding the Piazza San Giovanni. The church and baptistery both stood in one of the lowest parts of the city (and were, from time to time, badly affected by the flooding of the Arno), but the fact that the bases of the baptistery and the new campanile were lower than the surrounding streets was believed to seriously detract from the dignity of their setting, and so, despite the flood risk, street levels were lowered accordingly. The two guilds both retained close long-term responsibilities for the construction, maintenance, and decoration of the structures: the Arte della Seta for the baptistery and the Arte della Lana for the cathedral itself.

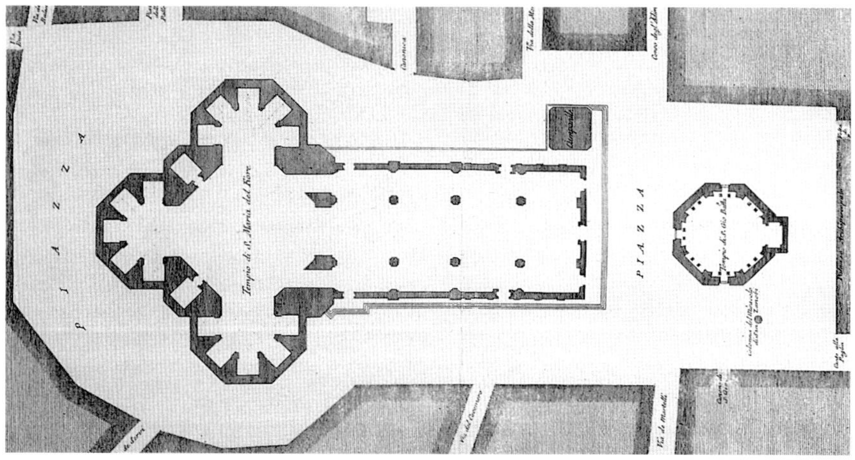

THE PIAZZA SAN GIOVANNI AND THE PIAZZA DEL DUOMO

This plan by Giovanni Battista Nelli (1733) shows the close, symbiotic relationship between the cathedral and the baptistery, as well as the layout of the Piazza del Duomo, wrapped around the cathedral's massive form.

Following these attempts to give import to the baptistery's setting, in 1352 the Loggia del Bigallo was built on the corner between the newly improved piazza and the Via de' Calzaiuoli, a key junction in the city's street pattern, as the street led directly to the Piazza della Signoria. By that time the building of the new campanile was fairly well advanced, and the loggia played a significant role in the articulation of spaces at this all-important corner. The design of the loggia is usually attributed to Alberto Arnoldi, a colleague of Francesco Talenti, and one of the *capomaestri* (chief masters) at the cathedral. It was built for a charitable confraternity, the Compagnia della Misericordia, but in 1425 the Compagnia del Bigallo was transferred to it. This body took responsibility for, among other things, the care of abandoned babies; after 1489 the Capitani del Bigallo administered the building, using the loggia as a place where these infants were "displayed" in an effort to find them adoptive homes.[3] The eastern bay of the loggia was very richly decorated in recognition of its key urban location, while the two adjacent bays, facing the baptistery's south wall, are by contrast much simpler. Above the north arch are three aedicules with statues by a follower of Nino Pisano. A decade after the loggia was begun, in 1363, the Arte di Calimala, the powerful merchants' guild, made a request to the Priorato, the city's supreme governing body, that all of the piazza's facades be rationalized, including the elimination of *sporti*, or overhanging jetties; the ordinance decreed that "all indecorous facades and irregular porticoes projecting onto the Piazza must be demolished and rebuilt." This was another clear indication of the government's will to ensure the aesthetic integrity and prestige of the square.[4]

The works of improvement to the setting of the baptistery, however, were still to continue. In 1376 another decree from the Priorato enforced the relocation of the straw market, the *mercato della paglia*, which had been held since ancient times around the column of San Zenobi, near San Giovanni. The market was now required to be relocated at least 100 *braccia* away from the church, and so it was moved a short distance to the northwest, to the Via de' Cerretani, a corner still known today as the Canto della Paglia. In this way the letter, if not the spirit, of the ordinance was followed. Nevertheless, such modest moves did much to further ameliorate the environment of this symbol of the city's long-standing Christian heritage, a symbol that, since the addition of its cladding of stone and marble in the twelfth century, had by then assumed its present appearance.

In the second half of the trecento, extensive demolitions were begun at the east end of the cathedral to make space for the church's massive crossing and eastern apses. (The final overall length of the church was to be more than three times that of the modest Santa Reparata it replaced.) In 1366 the nearby church of San Michele Visdomini fell victim to this program, but was rebuilt a few years later farther to the northeast, next to the Porta di Balla (one of the gates in the 1175 communal walls) in the Via de' Servi.

In order to set out the cathedral's apses, a space had to be carved out of the dense urban fabric on the northern, eastern, and southern sides. Demolitions began in 1370 on the north side, involving the loss of houses belonging to the Neri, Aliotti, and other prominent clans. In fact, the insertion of such a massive structure into the dense matrix of this part of the city necessitated not only such widespread demolition, but affected the whole street pattern of the neighborhood. The Via de' Servi, for example, had been an important route that ran northeast toward the hills of Fiesole, and, in the other direction, continued into the city center near the Via de' Calzaiuoli. This former key route was now completely blocked by the new cathedral, so that traffic had to be diverted around its great bulk, chiefly around the eastern end and along the south side, which thus became an important new route. The north side was also cleared to provide better circulation.

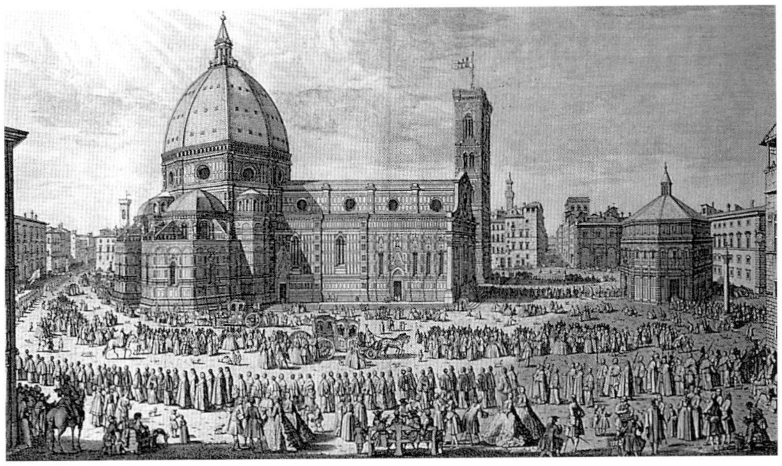

GIUSEPPE ZOCCHI, *VEDUTA DELLA METROPOLITANA FIORENTINA*, 1744

One of the best known of Zocchi's engravings of 1744, it illustrates the procession on the festival of Corpus Domini. The scale is considerably distorted to emphasize the participants, and Zocchi has given the cathedral a facade that never, in fact, existed.

As it developed, the Piazza del Duomo was not the square in front of the cathedral — that vital though modest space already existed — but the space in which the cathedral stood, a breathing space around its perimeter. There are from 1388 onward records of debates regarding the nature of the buildings that would be erected to face this newly cleared space, from the Via dell'Oriuolo as far as the Via de' Martelli — that is, the eastern and northern sides. Not surprisingly, a coordinated approach was considered essential; facades would be disciplined and ordered, unified by means of ground-floor colonnades of rusticated stonework, behind which would be shops and workshops. This colonnade became known as the "*fondamenta*," and above it, the upper facades were all to have regular fenestration to a design established by the Opera del Duomo, the department of works at the cathedral. The Opera itself was to be housed in part of this long development, occupying seven bays on the northern side between the Via Ricasoli and Via de' Servi. (The present Opera, however, is on the east side of the piazza.) The building was constructed in 1390 and incorporates on its facade the coat of arms of the Church and the Comune.[5]

The surroundings of the cathedral on the east and north sides generally retain their late medieval appearance and alignment, while the south and west sides have been altered significantly since the church was completed. To the west of the baptistery is the traditional site of the archbishops' palace; the palace itself was damaged by fire in 1533 and was consequently restored and partly rebuilt by Giovanni Antonio Dosio after 1573. However, further demolitions took place in 1895, when the entire front wing was taken down and rebuilt farther west, in order to provide still more space around the baptistery. The long, south side of the piazza was transformed in the nineteenth century. Prior to these clearances the apartments of

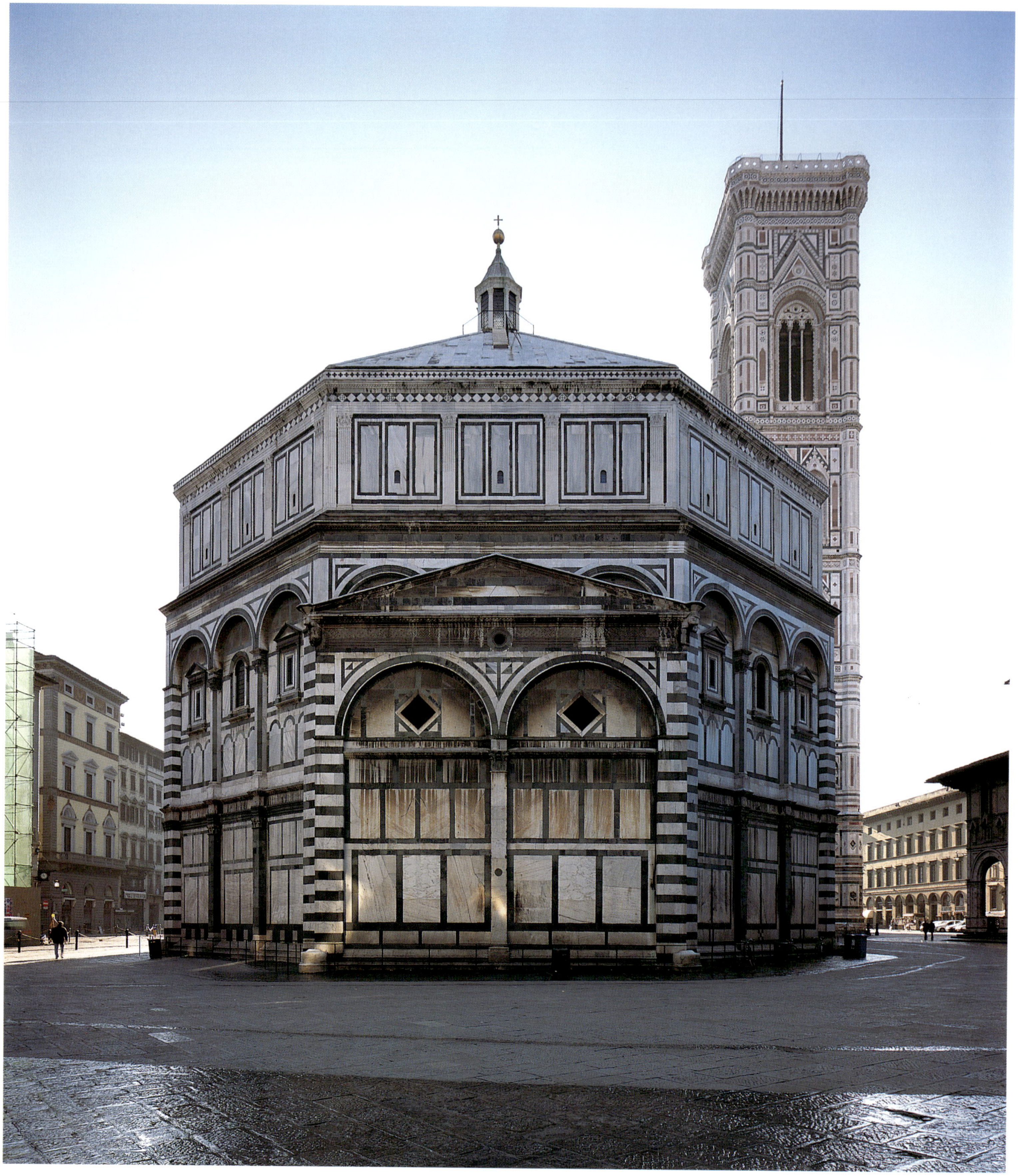

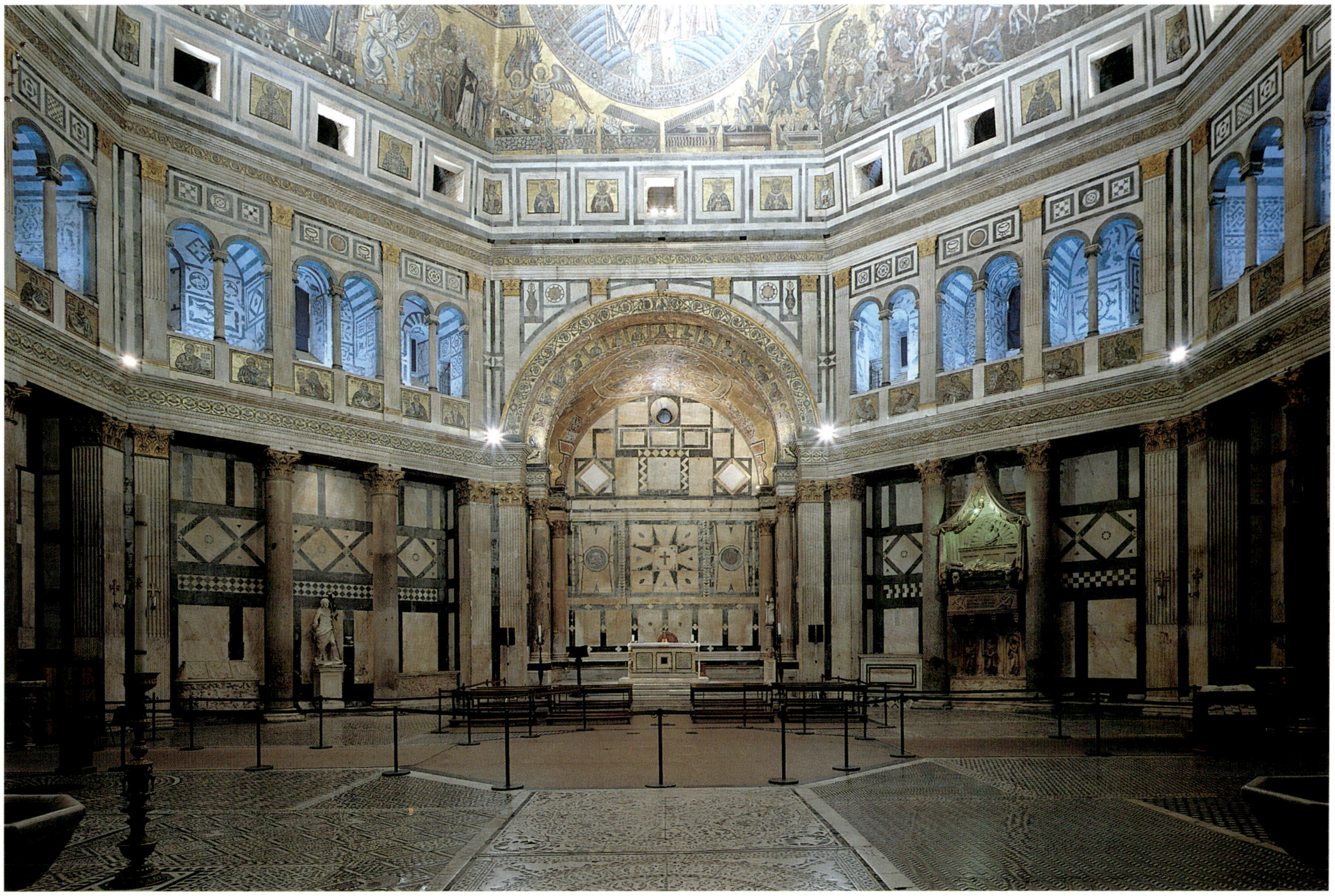

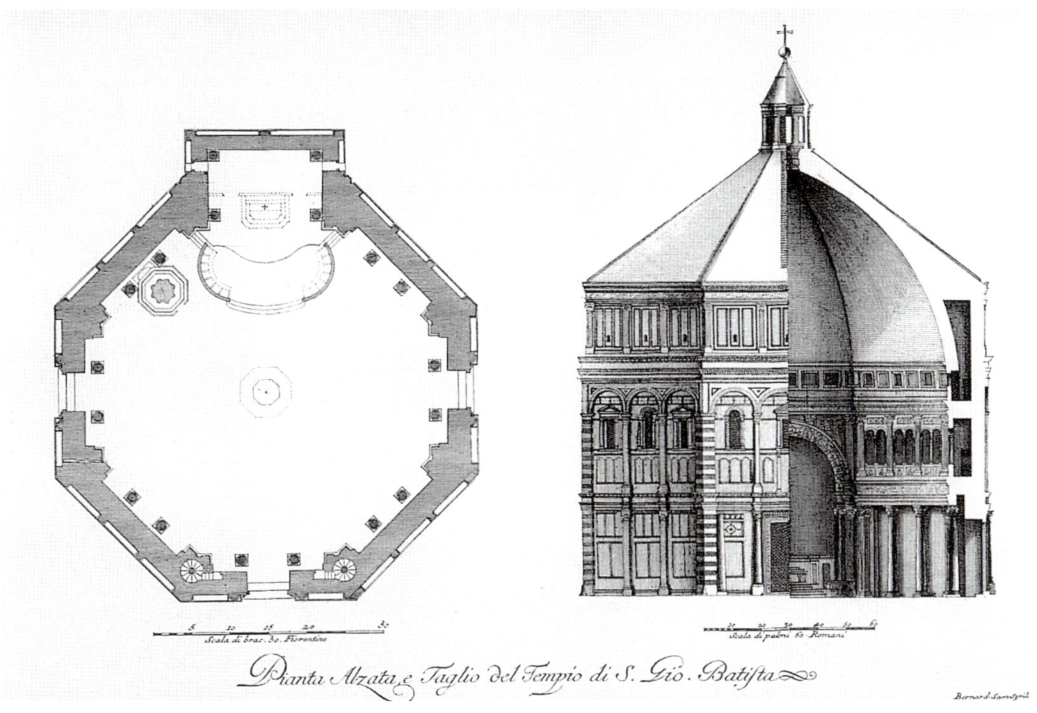

THE BAPTISTERY OF SAN GIOVANNI

Above: view of the interior toward the high altar. The interior is derived, in both its overall form and dimensions and in its architectural vocabulary, from the Roman Pantheon. Some of the columns and capitals are reused classical elements.
Left: plan and section by Giovanni Battista Nelli, 1733. The plan is a regular octagon, like that of many Italian baptisteries, with the addition of a small rectangular apse to house the altar.

Opposite: view of the exterior from the west. Although debate continues regarding the date of the original structure, its final external form is from 1202, when the projecting apse was built to house the high altar; the cladding was added in the eleventh to thirteenth centuries.

the canons of the cathedral, the Canonica, stood here, very close to the church itself. But in 1826 the old Canonica was demolished, and the present three regular blocks, built by Gaetano Baccani, were a final step in the imposition of order and regularity on the last remaining section of the old piazza.

As the religious hubs of the city, the piazze of the baptistery and the cathedral were naturally the focus of countless religious festivals. The chief of these was in celebration of the patron saint of Florence, John the Baptist, on 24 June. The feast, which lasted three days, was celebrated widely in Europe, often as a conflation with the pre-Christian summer solstice, and thus embraced a mixture of religious and lay or civic elements. In Florence the festival was centered on a great procession which began in the piazza between the cathedral and the baptistery before traversing the whole city; the procession itself also fused the worldly with the spiritual, since not only the clergy, but the lay bodies and institutions of the city, the *priori*, the Capitano del Popolo, representatives of all of the *arti,* participated — perhaps as many as ten thousand people altogether. Bells were rung throughout the city, while the procession was accompanied by music, with *trombe* and *pifferi* (trumpets and pipes), as well as choirs from the churches. The whole event thus mixed the civic with the spiritual in an inextricable manner. At the end of the procession, the participants returned to the cathedral, where a great canopy of blue cloth decorated with stars, representing the heavens, was suspended between the baptistery and the church facade. The celebrations were concluded with a solemn High Mass in the baptistery, for which occasion the silver-decorated high altar (now at the Museo dell'Opera) was repositioned at the center of the church. The three-day religious festival was paralleled by a famous market, at which all of the finest products of the city's artisanal workshops were proudly displayed.[6]

The Piazza di San Giovanni was also the setting for another characteristic religious festival, which still takes places today at Easter: the Scoppio del Carro. The origin of the *scoppio* ("blowing up," or explosion) is said to go back to the First Crusade, when Pazzino de' Pazzi, a Florentine who had participated in the taking of Jerusalem, returned in 1096 with stones from Christ's tomb. With the sparks from these holy stones a torch was ignited, which was then used to light lamps on Easter Sunday, as a symbol of Christ's resurrection. The festival, as it evolved, chiefly in the fifteenth century, used a cart, or *carro*, to transport the sacred torch around the city. In its most recent (and current) form, which originated in the seventeenth century, the cart, pulled by two oxen, is brought into the piazza between the cathedral and the baptistery on Easter morning. A mass is conducted inside the cathedral, and, at the moment of the Gloria, an artificial dove, carrying the sacred fire, is sent down a wire from the high altar out into the piazza, where the torch ignites the *carro* and initiates a deafening display of fireworks.[7]

The Baptistery "Il Bel San Giovanni"

"*E nell'antico vostro Batisteo / Insieme fui cristiano e Cacciaguida.*"
(And there, in your ancient Baptistery / both Cacciaguida and I were made Christian.) **Dante Alighieri,** *Paradiso* (c. 1319–20) [8]

Until the completion of the cathedral, the baptistery was the preeminent symbol of Florentine spiritual life, far more venerable and symbolic than the fairly modest Santa Reparata church nearby. Dante famously called it "il mio bel San Giovanni" and, like countless other Florentines, was himself baptized in the church. Until the urban improvements began in the era of Arnolfo di Cambio, the great mass of the baptistery formed an intrinsic part of the fabric of the city, despite the fact that it was the principal religious monument in Florence. Its regular octagonal form had a powerful geometrical simplicity, whose disciplined rhythm was reflected in a number of other Florentine churches of the Romanesque era: San Miniato, Santi Apostoli, San Salvatore, and others now lost.

The freestanding baptistery is an architectonic form that remains widespread in Italy. The earliest surviving examples can be dated with some certainty to the fifth, sixth, and seventh centuries; they are generally fairly modest brick structures, while the later baptisteries from the Romanesque era are much more imposing. By the Romanesque period they were also built to a considerable size, as baptisms generally took place on only two or three occasions each year, usually at Easter and Pentecost (occasionally also at Epiphany), when large numbers were baptized together. The other outstanding Tuscan examples are those at Pisa (c. 1152), which has a circular plan, and at Pistoia (c. 1300), with a more typical octagonal plan. Although plans do vary somewhat, they are always centralized, and the large majority are octagonal, with the font, itself often also octagonal, at the very center; the other fine examples at Cremona, Parma, and Asti all follow this form.

The story of San Giovanni in Florence remains to a large degree an enigma, its early history still confused and ambiguous. Indeed, it is arguable that more speculation and debate has surrounded its origin than that of any other major monument in Italy.[9] A long-established tradition claims that the basic structure of San Giovanni is very much older than its present appearance indicates, and that its origins should not be sought in early Christian baptisteries, but rather, in other centrally planned structures from the classical Roman era; indeed, it has often been claimed that the original structure was a Roman temple dedicated to Mars. This theory seems to have originated in the trecento, when such noble Roman associations were held in high esteem. Reference can be made to the famous example of the Pantheon, on which some of the internal detailing of San Giovanni is certainly modeled, as well as the so-called baptistery of Constantine, also in Rome. This latter structure, which was not built by Constantine but by Pope Sixtus III in about AD 430, is an octagonal structure that probably served as a model for many later baptisteries throughout Italy; the central part of this structure consists of two superimposed orders, together with an attic, as does San Giovanni in Florence. But the influence may also come from the Eastern Roman Empire, and from other octagonal structures such as San Vitale at Ravenna or the Dome of the Rock in Jerusalem, widely regarded as "perfect." A significant view remains that the basic structure dates from the fifth century. The original Roman structure would later have been converted into a Christian place of worship, after the Edict of Milan in 313 established religious freedom in the Roman Empire, thus rendering Christianity a lawful religion. Since the sixteenth century, however, this hypothesis has been regularly questioned. Excavations have indicated that the building does indeed stand on substantial Roman foundations of the first century, and Roman walls, floors, and mosaic pavement fragments can be seen below the present floor; these foundations do not, however, prove a date for the superstructure itself, and it is today believed by many to be a predominantly Romanesque construction of the eleventh century, perhaps incorporating earlier material from the fourth and fifth centuries. It is, however, universally acknowledged that it was clad externally in the medieval period.

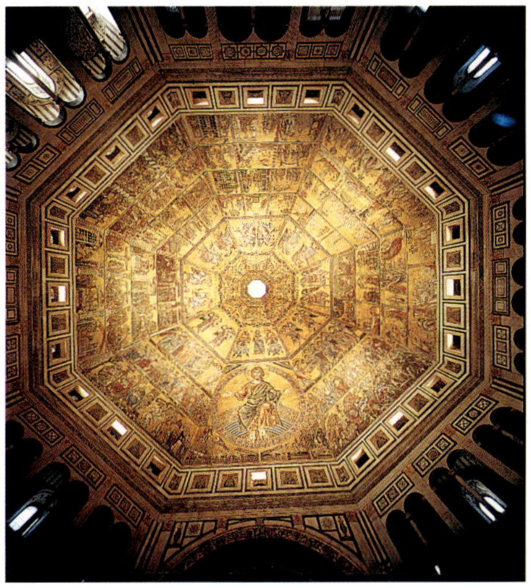

THE BAPTISTERY OF SAN GIOVANNI

View of the mosaics of the cupola. The mosaics were begun in c. 1270 and completed in the early fourteenth century. The complex iconographic program reads from the base toward the lantern in concentric rings, and depicts stories of the Old Testament as well as the life of Christ and John the Baptist. The three facets depicting the Universal Judgment dominate the zone facing the altar.

The earliest documentation dates from 897, when a baptistery undoubtedly stood on the site. Two years later, the baptistery is recorded again, as is the church of San Miniato, and there are two further references from the tenth century.[10] San Giovanni was reconsecrated in 1059 by Pope Niccolò II, and the present external cladding of white Luni marble and green marble from Prato was probably begun in the following decades.[11] It remained the seat of the see of Florence until 1128, when the bishop's cathedra was moved back to Santa Reparata, and San Giovanni was rededicated as the baptistery.

The majestic structure remained the chief religious symbol of the city throughout the medieval era. Its form is a regular octagon, modified only by the addition, in 1202, of the *scarsella*, the rectangular apse built onto the west side and incorporating the altar. The external appearance of the church was finally completed by the marble cladding and the addition of a small lantern on top of the pyramidal roof; this feature, added in 1174, is rich but disciplined, a characteristic example of what is today identified as Florentine Romanesque. In principle the external vocabulary consists of a giant order (or two superimposed orders) with a tall blind arcade containing three arched bays on each of the eight faces. Above this giant order is a much simpler attic, consisting of a virtually flat wall surface articulated with

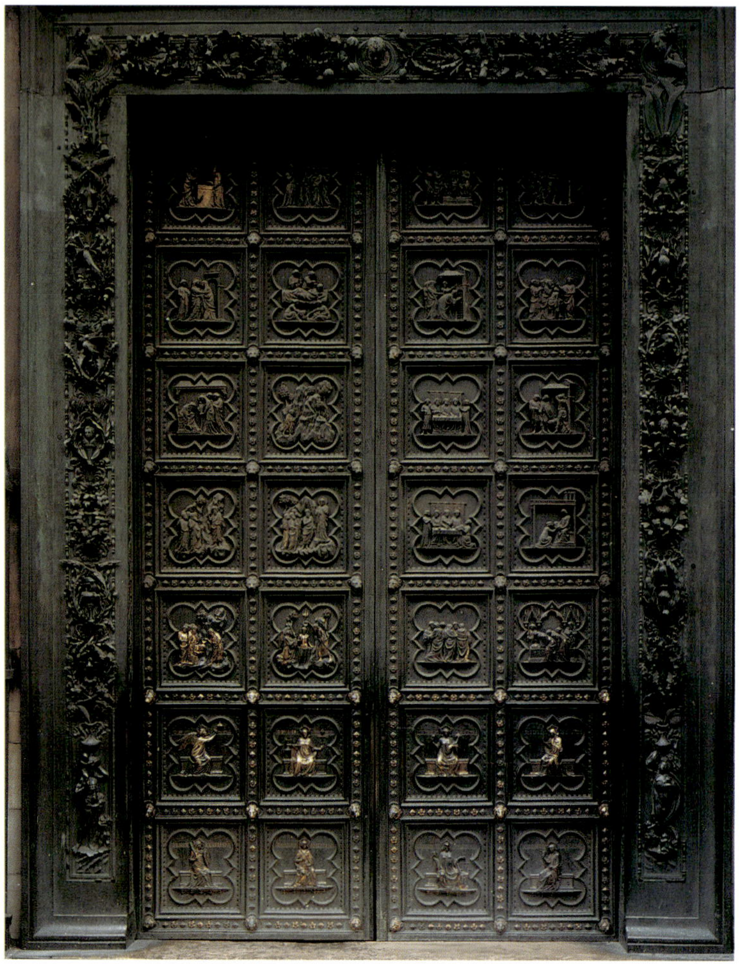

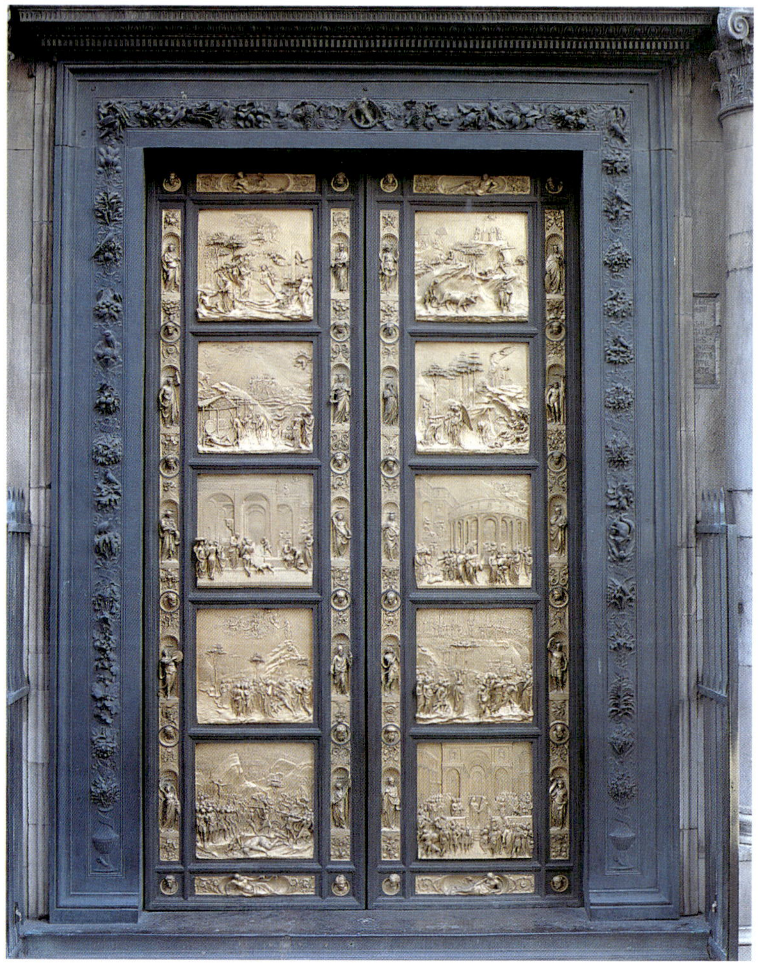

THE BAPTISTERY OF SAN GIOVANNI

Above, left: the south doors, gilded in bronze by Andrea Pisano in 1336, originally occupied the doorway facing the cathedral, but were repositioned in their present location in 1452. Above: the east doors, the "Porta del Paradiso," by Lorenzo Ghiberti, 1425–52. The original panels (some of which are on display in the Museo dell'Opera) were replaced by copies after the floods of 1966.

Opposite: detail of the east doors, showing Solomon receiving the Queen of Sheba.

simple rectangular panels of green and white marble. Directly above the attic rises the eight-sided pyramidal roof. The lower orders are more richly modeled, and the three principal doorways are inserted into the center of three of the cardinal faces: north, south, and east.

The interior of the church consists of a single volume, with two principal internal orders, of which the lower is the most Roman in appearance; indeed, it can be related directly to the Pantheon, and the materials here are undoubtedly reused classical columns, capitals, and architraves. The upper order is more Romanesque, with the exception of the richly fluted pilasters, which again appear classical. It incorporates a *matroneo*, or women's gallery, above which a low attic supports the springing of the cupola. Like that of the exterior, the internal wall cladding of geometric patterns, which was in place before 1113, consists of green and white marble. The marble mosaic pavement, very similar to that at San Miniato, dates from around the same time, that is, prior to 1200. At the very center of the space the plain section of floor indicates the former location of the baptismal font, which was destroyed in 1576. Above this solemn, imposing volume rises the eight-sided cupola. Although less daring than Brunelleschi's masterpiece nearby, it nevertheless remains a remarkable feat of construction, with a diameter of 85 feet (25.6 meters); it is often said, like the interior, to have been modeled on the Pantheon, but although the internal orders do derive directly from Rome, the inner cupola is not formed in the same manner as that of the Pantheon. The latter is a coffered dome structure, as can clearly be seen from the exposed interior, whereas the cupola of San Giovanni (which is not strictly a dome) consists of eight curved segments, a form that Brunelleschi adopted at the cathedral on an even more imposing scale several centuries later.

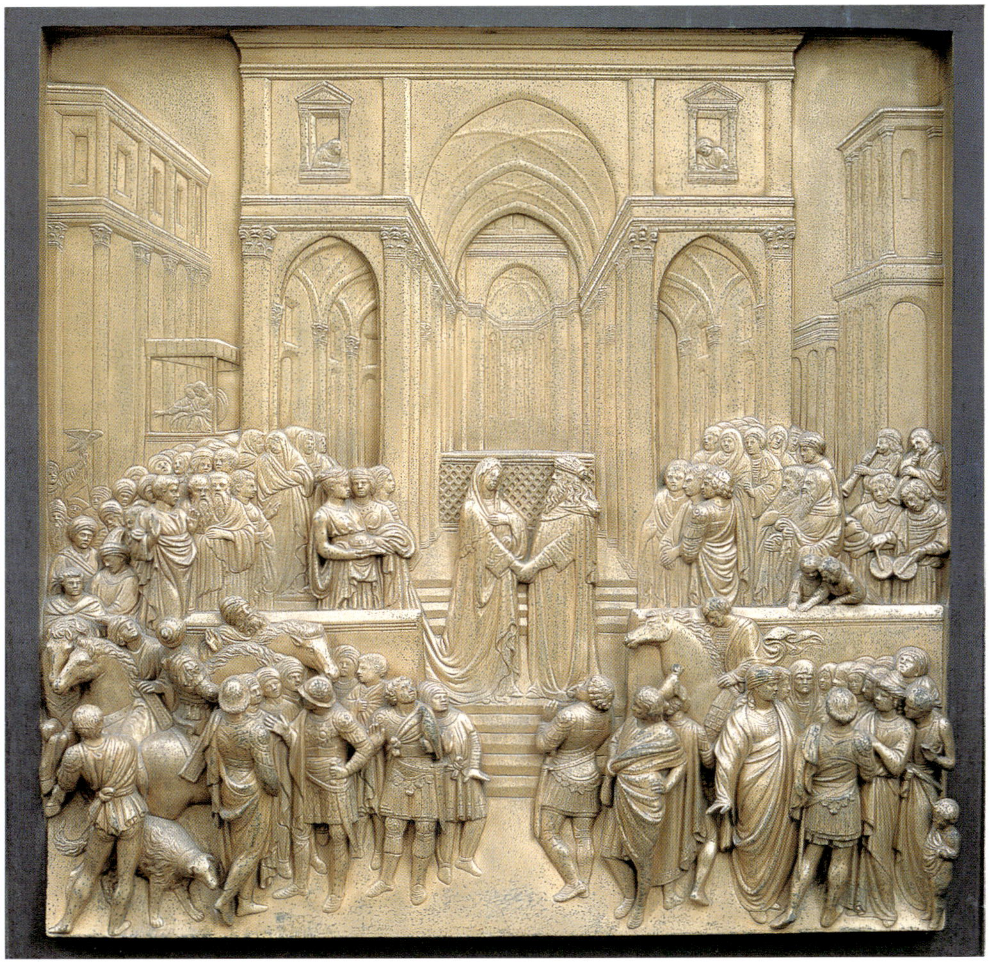

Just as the structure of San Giovanni derives from different sources and precedents, the mosaics of its cupola evince the influence of distant antecedents. The earliest mosaics are those on the soffit of the arch of the apse on the west side, the *scarsella*, begun in 1225 by Jacopo da Torrita. They were followed some decades later by the vast cycle of depictions on the cupola itself, whose entire inner surface is covered with mosaic, mostly from the period from about 1270 to 1300. Stylistically they show strong Venetian influence, and indeed it is highly likely that some of the masters from San Marco worked on them; the designs of the narrative cycles themselves, though, are believed to be the work of Cimabue and Gaddi. Like the famous cycles in the narthex at San Marco, they depict Old Testament stories from Genesis, as well as the lives of John the Baptist, Mary, and Christ. The dominant figure of Christ sitting in Universal Judgment, of strongly Venetian-Byzantine appearance, is the most powerful image among dozens of smaller scenes, which are arranged in concentric rows around the eight sides of the inner surface.[12]

The three rich portals on the north, east, and south facades are arguably the most famous features of the baptistery and have considerable symbolic importance, particularly that on the east side, directly facing the cathedral. They were the last major additions to the baptistery that can be seen today. The first, the present south door, was designed by Andrea Pisano in 1330, shortly before work started on Giotto's new campanile. Andrea's doors were originally located on the east facade, directly opposite the cathedral, and were thus the chief point of access into San Giovanni for more than a hundred years. They were displaced in 1452, when Lorenzo Ghiberti's second pair of doors was commissioned, and Andrea's were consequently "demoted" to the south porch. The decision to replace the old timber doors with doors of gilded bronze seems to have been inspired by the Porta di San Ranieri at Pisa cathedral, cast by Bonanno Pisano in 1180. Appropriate to their original location, the twenty uppermost panels on Andrea's two doors depict scenes from the life of John the Baptist, while the lowermost eight represent the Virtues. The whole ensemble is contained within a rigidly disciplined framework that is quintessentially Gothic, although the figures themselves are highly expressive, strongly and deeply molded.[13]

The second great portal was destined for the north side some seventy years later. The work was commissioned by the Arte di Calimala in 1401, and was launched in the form of a limited competition, with six participants. Ghiberti himself wrote the story of the competition, which he won against some daunting rivals, including Brunelleschi, Jacopo della Quercia, and Niccolò Lamberti. The doors, in gilded bronze like those of Andrea, cost a total of 22,000 florins, according to Ghiberti, and their general design and configuration closely followed the precedent that Andrea had established. There are twenty-eight panels, in four columns — two to each door leaf — but the themes of the uppermost twenty are scenes from the New Testament, while in the lowermost eight panels are the four Evangelists and the Fathers of the Church. Like those of Andrea, all of the panels, although richly and expressively formed, are unified within a strongly disciplined design framework.The entire project took twenty years to complete, during which time Ghiberti's notably flourishing studio became the training shop for a number of other masters, among them Donatello, Michelozzo, Paolo Uccello, and Masolino, at least some of whom may have made compositional contributions to the panels.

Ghiberti's second pair of doors, famously said to have been described by Michelangelo as the "Gates of Paradise," broke with the aesthetic precedent of his earlier work and that of Andrea. These doors were begun in 1425, and took twenty-seven years to complete. Instead of the regular, disciplined row of square panels set within an almost architectural framework, there are five large panels down the center of each door leaf, while long, narrow panels, which are returned across the topmost and lowermost edges, go down the edges of both leaves. In this case there was no competition; the overall program was initially drawn up by the writer and humanist scholar Leonardo Bruni, although it was somewhat altered in execution. The original intention, in fact, had been to maintain the strong rhythmic framework of the two earlier sets of doors, with twenty-eight square panels, but in about 1429 the work was redesigned so that the figures of the prophets were moved into the outer, narrower framework, and the ten large narrative panels became the dominant features. The original program of narrative scenes was retained, however, so the conflation of twenty scenes onto only ten large panels meant that each panel contained two distinct episodes from the Creation, the Fall, Cain and Abel, Noah, and Abraham. The result, with the assistance of Michelozzo, Benozzo Gozzoli, Bernardo Cennini, and Ghiberti's two sons, remains a triumph of pictorial art, of the imaginative re-creation of space and perspective, to say nothing of the technical ingenuity.

THE CAMPANILE

Below: view from the east. Begun to a design by Giotto in 1334, the tower was continued by Andrea Pisano and completed by Francesco Talenti in 1359.

Opposite: detail of the exterior.

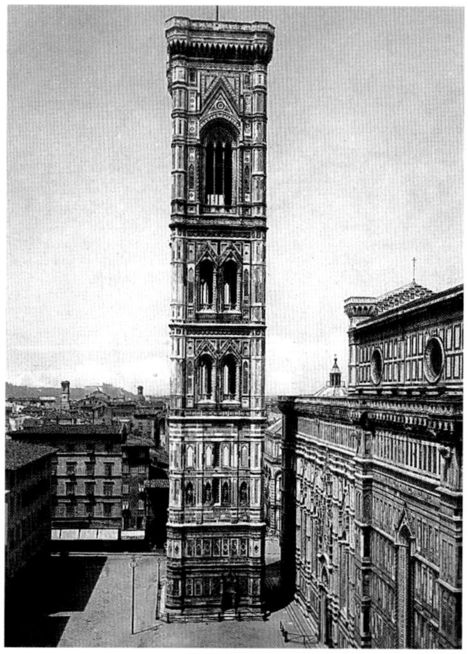

The Campanile

"... as superintendant of the works, the Comune appointed our fellow-citizen Giotto, the most skilful master of painting of our time. ... And he was given a salary by the Comune in recognition of his skills and excellence." **Giovanni Villani,** *Cronica fiorentina* (c. 1330) [14]

The tall, richly decorated campanile of the cathedral is frequently referred to as "Giotto's campanile," and is widely regarded as one of the most beautiful in Italy. Almost 280 feet (85 meters) tall, the tower is another characteristic monument of the city; from the surrounding

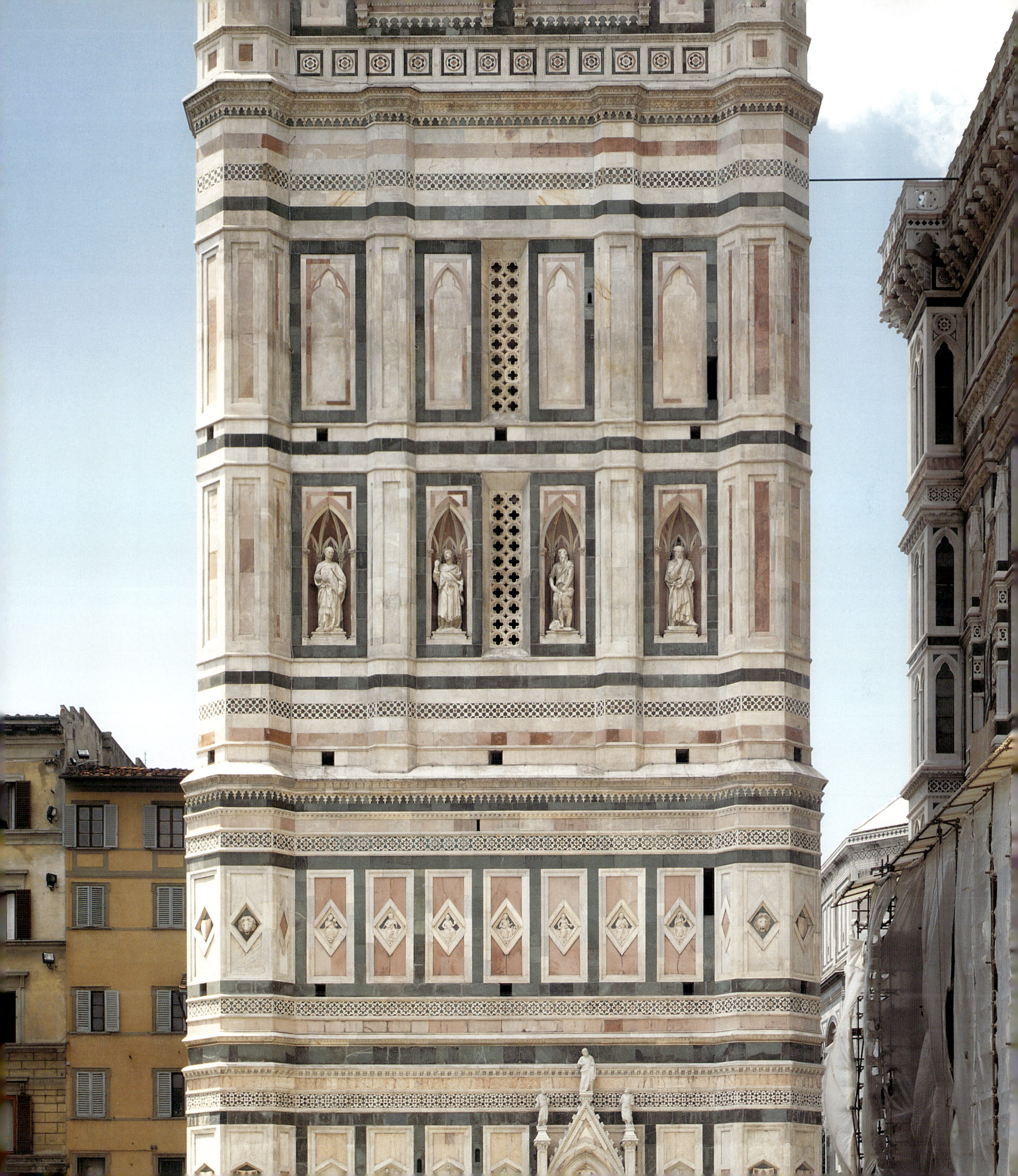

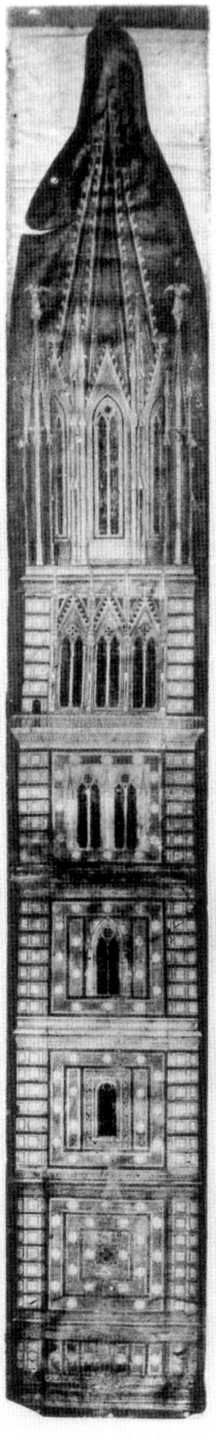

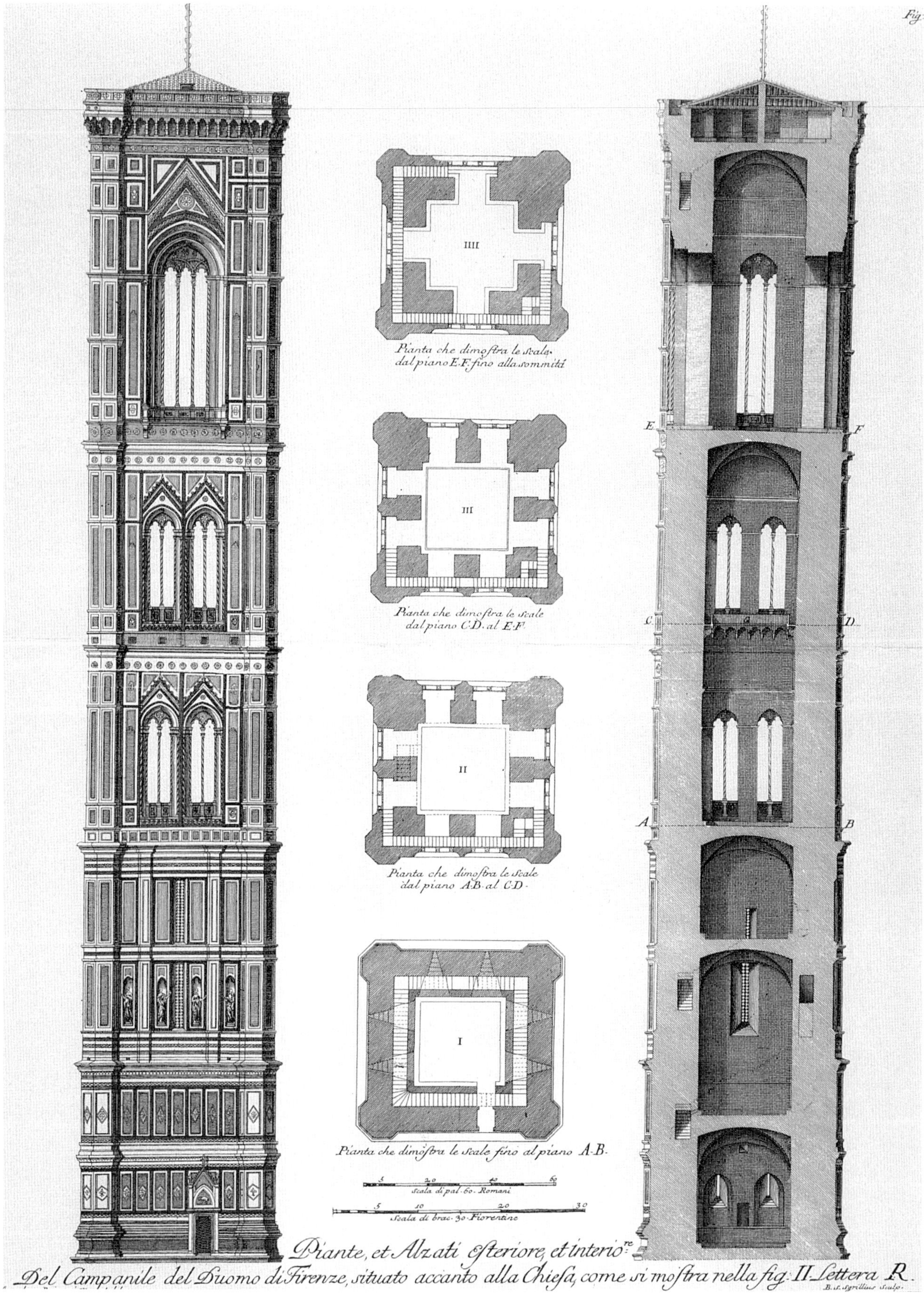
Fig.
Pianta che dimostra le scala dal piano E.F. fino alla sommità
Pianta che dimostra le scale dal piano C.D. al E.F.
Pianta che dimostra le scale dal piano A.B. al C.D.
Pianta che dimostra le scale fino al piano A.B.
Scala di pal. 60. Romani
Scala di brac. 30. Fiorentine
Piante, et Alzati esteriore, et interiore
Del Campanile del Duomo di Firenze, situato accanto alla Chiesa, come si mostra nella fig. II. Lettera R.
B. S. Sgrillius Sculp.

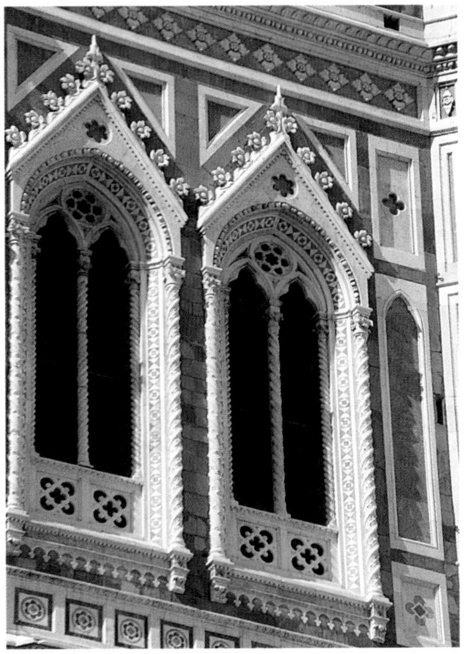

THE CAMPANILE

Above: detail of the windows, showing the rich cladding of Carrara and Prato marble.

Opposite, left: drawing of the original proposal for the elevation of the tower, generally accepted as the work of Giotto. Significant departures were made to this design in the execution of the upper levels, and the proposed crowning spire was never realized (Siena, Museo dell'Opera). Opposite, right: plans, section, and elevation by Giovanni Battista Nelli, 1733.

hills it forms a dramatic counterpoint both to the massive profile of Brunelleschi's cupola and the austere, equally vertical form of the tower of the Palazzo Vecchio. In fact, although Giotto di Bondone was chief master at the cathedral, his direct involvement with the building of the tower was limited. Construction started in July 1334 on the basis of a design that Giotto had submitted to the government — generally believed to be that shown on the famous drawing that survives today at Siena cathedral — but only the lowermost order had been completed by the time of Giotto's death in 1337.[15]

The work was continued by Andrea Pisano, whose first contribution was to repeat the first order with a second, almost identical one. The next two orders, however, departed significantly from the original proposal, and Andrea inserted a series of prominent statue niches, above which is a plain order of rectangular panels. In 1348 Andrea in turn departed, and after a period of two years during which no effective progress was made, Francesco Talenti was appointed, and he supervised the conclusion of the three tall upper stories until 1359. Talenti's three orders, with the uppermost very much taller than the two below, are graduated in the pattern of their window openings; the tall, elegant paired lights of the two lower orders are surmounted by the much taller and larger opening of the bell chamber. Talenti followed the original drawn design only in general terms, and his work differs considerably in detail; the major omission to the completed tower, though, was Giotto's proposed spire, which was intended to rise from an octagon at the top of the uppermost order, and would have added a further remarkable 165 feet (50 meters) to its already impressive height.

The campanile was clearly intended to be a richly decorated work from the outset, but it remains unclear how much (if any) of Arnolfo di Cambio's new cathedral was already clad in a similar, ornate way at the time work started on the campanile.[16] Work on the duomo had begun around forty years earlier, in 1296, but by the time of Arnolfo's death — probably in 1302 — comparatively little had been achieved. Nevertheless, the rich cladding of the exterior of the tower, in white, red, and green marble, clearly grows from the Florentine Romanesque tradition of both the adjacent baptistery and San Miniato. The baptistery, though, is clad solely with white and green marble, and in general retains a more geometric and disciplined appearance than the considerably richer tower; nor was the baptistery enlivened with sculpted forms or refined, traceried fenestration, as was the campanile.

The principle of the tower's design and its overall configuration, with its carefully graduated orders, owes a good deal to precedents elsewhere: The campanile of Siena cathedral from 1313, for example, although clad in the typical Sienese striped marble, has no fewer than six orders of windows, which gradually increase in size toward the top; and there were earlier precedents in other parts of Italy, for example, the famous Lombard tower of the abbey at Pomposa from 1063. Structurally, this graduation of the orders is logical, since the dead loads on the structure clearly reduce as one approaches the top where, traditionally, large openings were also necessary for the bell chamber, or *cella*, in order to carry the sound of the bells inside. Talenti's graduation of the heights of the stories themselves is also carefully contrived to counteract the strong optical effect of foreshortening on the spectator below, particularly that of the uppermost bell chamber. Credit for this optical correction cannot be given to Giotto, whose original drawing clearly indicates the principal orders with equal height.

The campanile remains unique in its elegance and richness. Its square plan is strengthened at the corners by four octagonal buttresses, while at the top, instead of the proposed spire, Talenti terminated the tower visually by a boldly projecting balcony, supported by rich bracketing, and capped by a low pyramidal roof, which cannot be seen from the streets below. The lowermost orders, as proposed by Giotto, consisted of two rows of relief panels, the lowest set within hexagonal frames and the upper rows in lozenge- or rhomboid-shaped frames. The sculptures (today replaced by

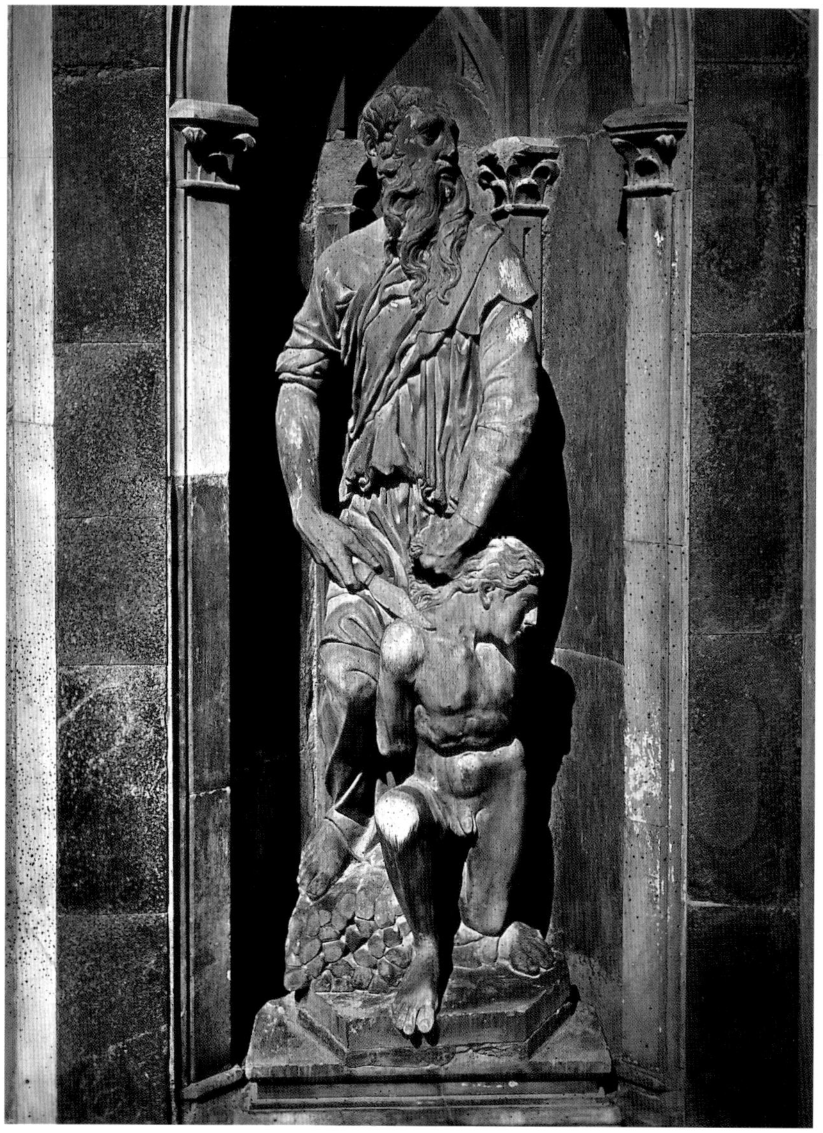

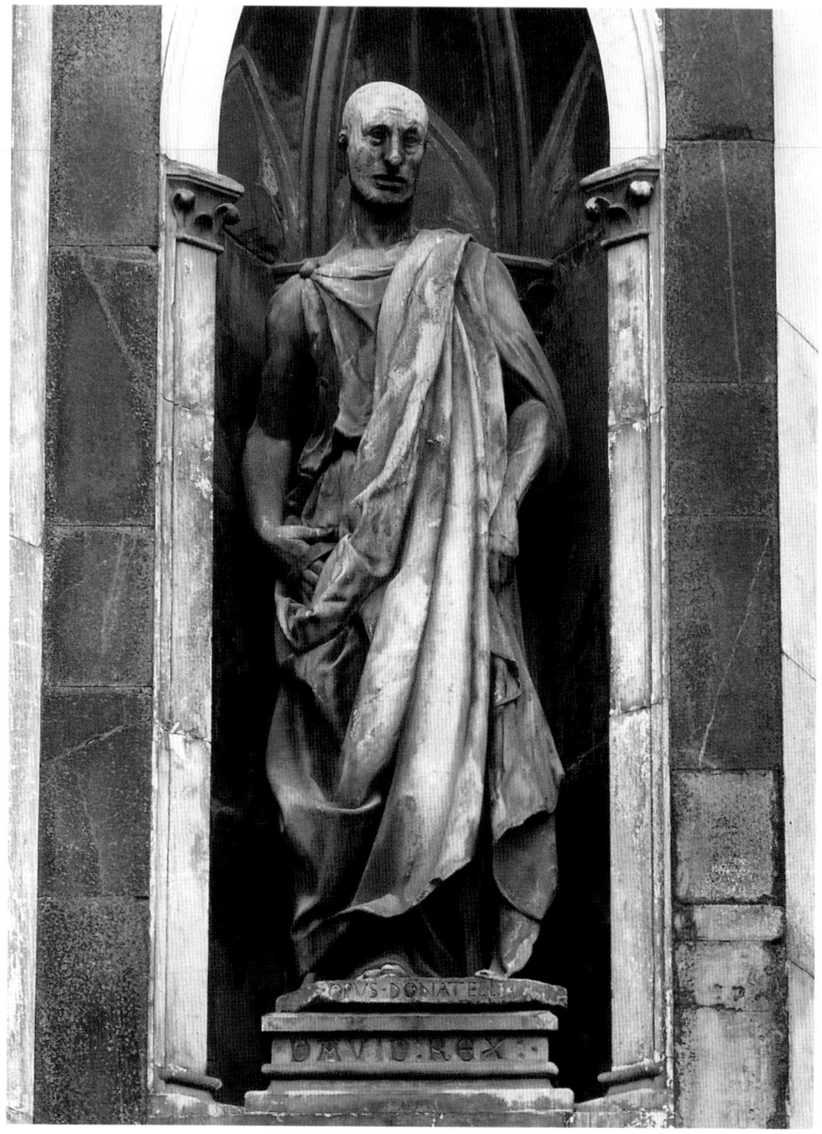

THE CAMPANILE

Above, left: Abraham sacrificing Isaac, by Donatello in collaboration with Nanni di Bartolo, c. 1421. Above: the figure of Habbakuk (Abacuc) by Donatello, c. 1421, formerly stood in one of the niches on the third order of the tower. The figures are now replaced by copies; the original works are held in the Museo dell'Opera.

copies) depict the skills of man building, hunting, and so on, and, above them, the planets, the Virtues, the sacraments, and the liberal arts; in all there are twenty-eight panels to each order. Given the lack of documentation, widespread divergence remains regarding the authorship of these panels; many of the lower ones are likely to be the work of Andrea Pisano rather than Giotto, while others, chiefly in the upper order, are probably by Nino, Andrea's son; others have been attributed to Alberto Arnoldi. (A few, later than the rest, are the work of Andrea della Robbia.)[17] The remaining significant sculptures are those in the niches of the third order. This section, designed by Andrea, departs significantly from Giotto's drawing, and the general program of these statues, four on each face, must be attributed to the former. They represent patriarchs, kings, prophets, and sibyls; the eight earliest survivors — all almost certainly designed, if not executed, by Andrea — are now in the Museo dell'Opera. In 1466 some of these earliest figures were already replaced by new works by Donatello and Nanni di Bartolo, the originals of which are now also in the Museo. The three upper orders rely essentially on architectonic detailing and the patterns of marble cladding.

Santa Reparata

The first cathedral was built in the early Christian era and was dedicated to Santa Reparata, a comparatively little known early martyr from Asia Minor. Excavations from 1966 to 1970 revealed the extent of this first church; the present floor of the duomo is just over 6 feet (2 meters) higher than the floor of the original basilica, the remains of which today form a kind of crypt below the west end of the nave.[18] The lowermost parts of the earliest walls are clearly identifiable and, in fact, reveal two earlier structures: The first was a simple early Christian basilican hall, with a central nave and two side aisles, of which sections of the perimeter wall and parts of floor mosaic have been excavated. In the eleventh century this church was enlarged and elaborated, with a raised choir at the eastern end terminating in a semicircular apse, in which the cathedra was located. In this period two side chapels were added to form transepts, each with apsidal east ends. A porch or narthex across the west facade may also have been added at this stage of the building's history. Santa Reparata was a fairly small church, the overall length of which is almost exactly contained within the first two bays of the present cathedral.[19]

By the latter part of the thirteenth century, Florence had become populous and wealthy, and it became evident that the existing church was inadequate not only for the prestige of the city, but also in purely practical terms. The last decades of the duecento saw the commencement of great urban projects, among them the construction of the city's new walls, and the same ambitious spirit informed the decision to rebuild the cathedral. In fact, the initial plan was to incorporate the earlier church, or parts of it, into the new structure, and Santa Reparata was to stand for some time longer while the immense edifice was slowly built around it. The old church was finally taken down only in 1374–75.

The New Cathedral, Santa Maria del Fiore

> "The foundation stone was laid with much solemnity on the day of St Mary [8 September 1296] by the Cardinal Legate of the pope, with many bishops. . . . And the church was consecrated to the honour of God and St Mary and given the name of Santa Maria del Fiore, although the people continued to call it by its former name of Santa Reparata." **Giovanni Villani,** *Cronica fiorentina* (c. 1330) [20]

Proposals for modernizing Santa Reparata were first discussed in 1285, and some works seem to have been begun around 1293. However, it became rapidly apparent that these were not satisfactory as a long-term solution, and that more drastic surgery was necessary. The new cathedral was to have a new dedication: Santa Maria del Fiore, the virgin of the lily, symbol of the city, although the dedication to Santa Reparata was still used as late as 1412, when the new name was finally imposed by public decree.[21] On 8 September 1296, the foundation stone was laid for what was intended to be a great new church, and a definitive record of Arnolfo di Cambio as the *capomaestro* of the works dates from four years later. However, Arnolfo died probably in 1302, and the debate continues to our day as to precisely how much he had managed to achieve in those six years or so, and how much of his original scheme was retained in the final structure, completed a century later. Excavations carried out between 1965 and 1974 support the conclusion that Arnolfo did intend an octagonal choir, and probably intended the three projecting eastern arms. The width of the nave of the church also corresponds to that which he originally envisaged, although the bay spacing is different: Arnolfo's nave was shorter than the present one, but it had five narrower bays.

It is generally agreed that Arnolfo began the new facade incorporating some of the fabric of Santa Reparata, as well as the lower parts of the flanking walls. After his death, no further work took place on this facade until after 1354, when Talenti became the new *capomaestro*. However, he, too, seems to have achieved comparatively little before work was halted once again. (Talenti was highly involved with the new campanile at this period, the completion of which seems to have taken priority.) The appearance of this facade, which was to remain unfinished for centuries, is preserved in a drawing by Bernardino Poccetti from 1587, and represents a complex, richly — in truth, rather fussily — modeled elevation, with three porticoes, and with the marble cladding completed up to the top of the porches, bare brickwork rising above.[22] The drawing is immensely valuable, since in the year after Poccetti's sketch, Arnolfo's fragmentary facade was dismantled. A number of the sculptures for this facade have survived, however, and are in the Museo dell'Opera. The most important is the *Virgin and Child*, an outstandingly naturalistic and technically accomplished work; at least some of the other survivors (including the figure of Santa Reparata) are from Arnolfo's hand, although attributions of other surviving pieces remain uncertain.

We know little of the state of the new cathedral between the death of Arnolfo and the appointment of Giotto as the new *capomaestro* in 1334; indeed, little progress seems to have been made. It seems clear, however, that in the three years before his death, in 1337, Giotto was primarily concerned with the campanile. Nevertheless, a new impetus began at the cathedral with his appointment, and this momentum was enhanced by the great outburst of religious fervor that accompanied the arrival of San Zanobi's body in the city. On the crest of this wave, the Signoria decided to make this project the definitive responsibility of the wealthy Arte della Lana. Giotto was in turn succeeded as *capomaestro* by Andrea Pisano, who for some time also concentrated on the next orders of the campanile, rather than the church itself. Andrea's activities between 1340 and his death in about 1348 are unclear, though, and he also worked on the cathedral at Orvieto, where he was succeeded by his son Nino.[23] Such divided loyalties hardly made for efficient progress at either of these monumental projects, and, after his death, Andrea was replaced by Francesco Talenti. Talenti is first recorded as *capomaestro* in 1351, and yet again seems to have concentrated first on completing the campanile; only after about 1356 did he turn his attention to the daunting challenge of the duomo.

However, a landmark in the development of the design of the church seems to have been reached the previous year, in August 1355, when Talenti was asked to make a model to show how the chapels at the rear (east end) should be completed. Talenti's proposal was to be judged by a commission of twelve men, including his fellow master craftsmen Neri di Fioravanti, Benci di Cione, and the artist Taddeo Gaddi. Two years later, in June 1357, the overall dimensions of the nave were finalized. It was to have just three bays, but of prodigious size, each one 34 *braccia* (almost 66 feet, or 20 meters) across, together with a tribune or crossing that was to be double the width of the nave, thus encompassing the widths of both of the side aisles; the overall length of the church was to be 164 *braccia* (313 feet, or 95 meters). The text of the surviving document recording this decision remains open to interpretation, however, and no single reading has found universal acceptance.[24] At this stage, the new fabric was still rising very slowly around the surviving

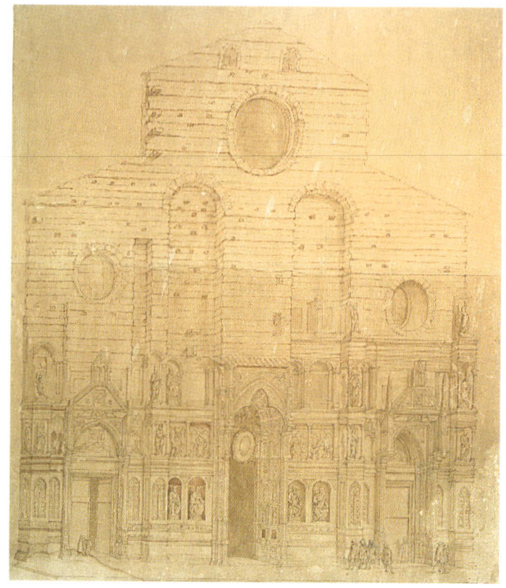

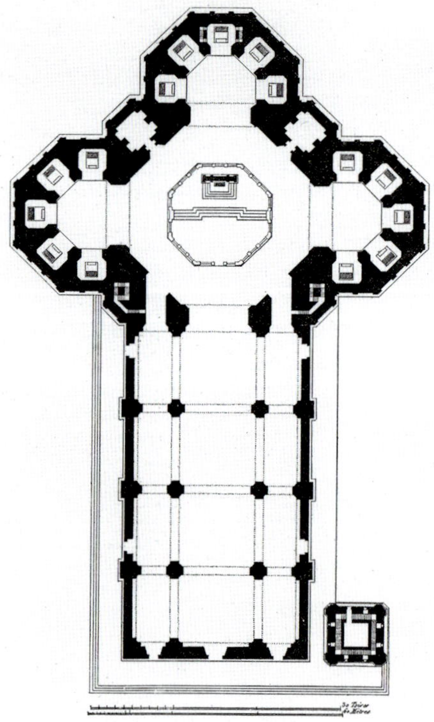

SANTA MARIA DEL FIORE

Top: drawing of the west facade of the cathedral by Bernardino Poccetti, 1587. This invaluable record depicts the extent of the facade that had been completed by Arnolfo di Cambio at the end of the thirteenth century, shortly before it was dismantled. (A number of the original sculptures survive today in the Museo dell'Opera.) Above: plan by Giovanni Battista Nelli, 1733, showing the four large bays of the nave, and the three equal arms of the eastern end radiating from the central octagon.

SANTA MARIA DEL FIORE

Right: long section through the nave and cupola, by Giovanni Battista Nelli, 1733. Nelli's fine engravings, made over 250 years ago, remain among the best and most accurate surveys of the cathedral. Bottom: north elevation by Nelli, 1733. The proximity of the adjacent buildings render it impossible to see this facade in its entirety.

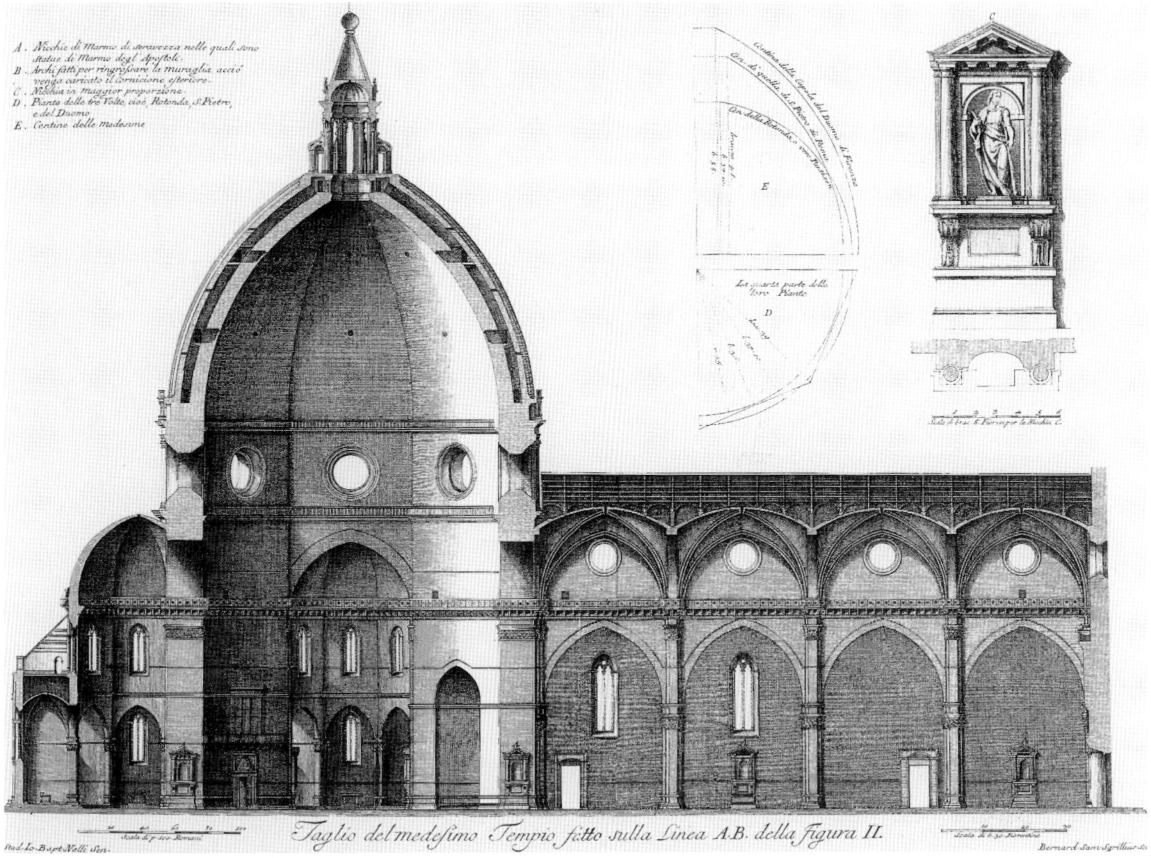

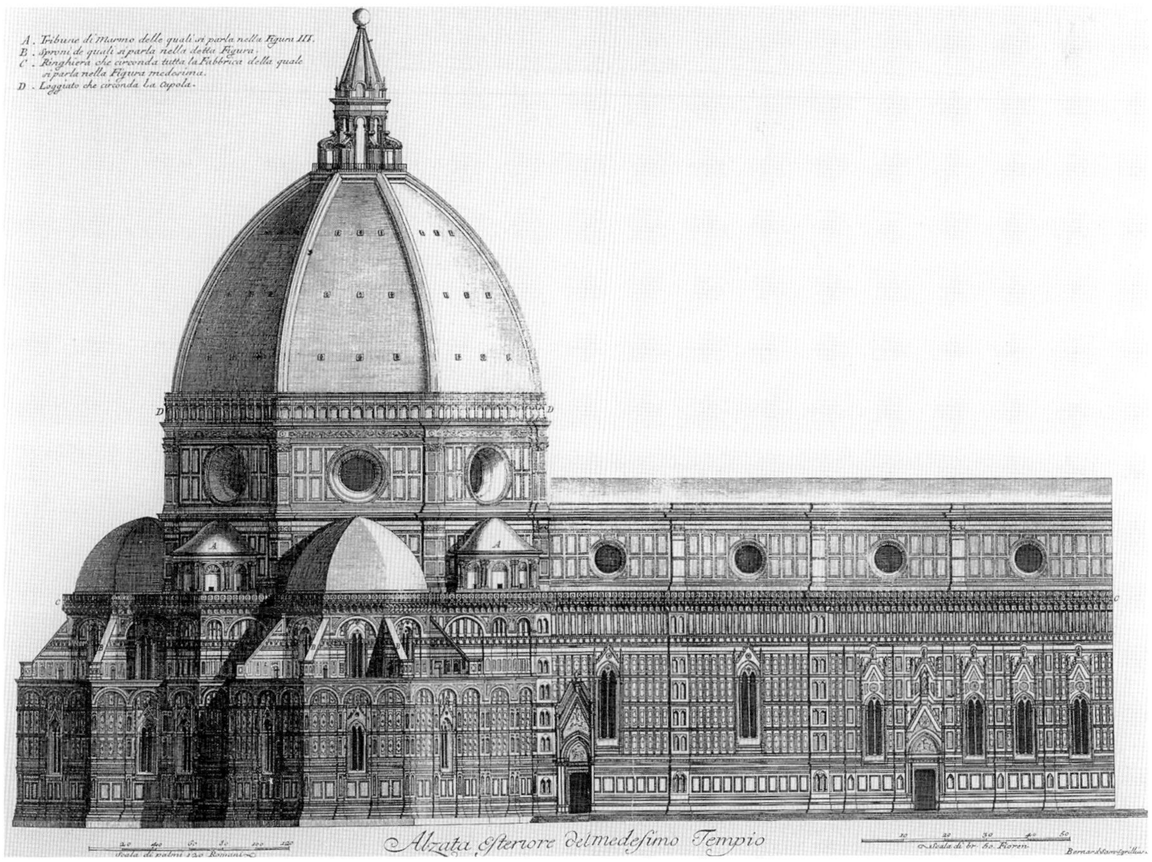

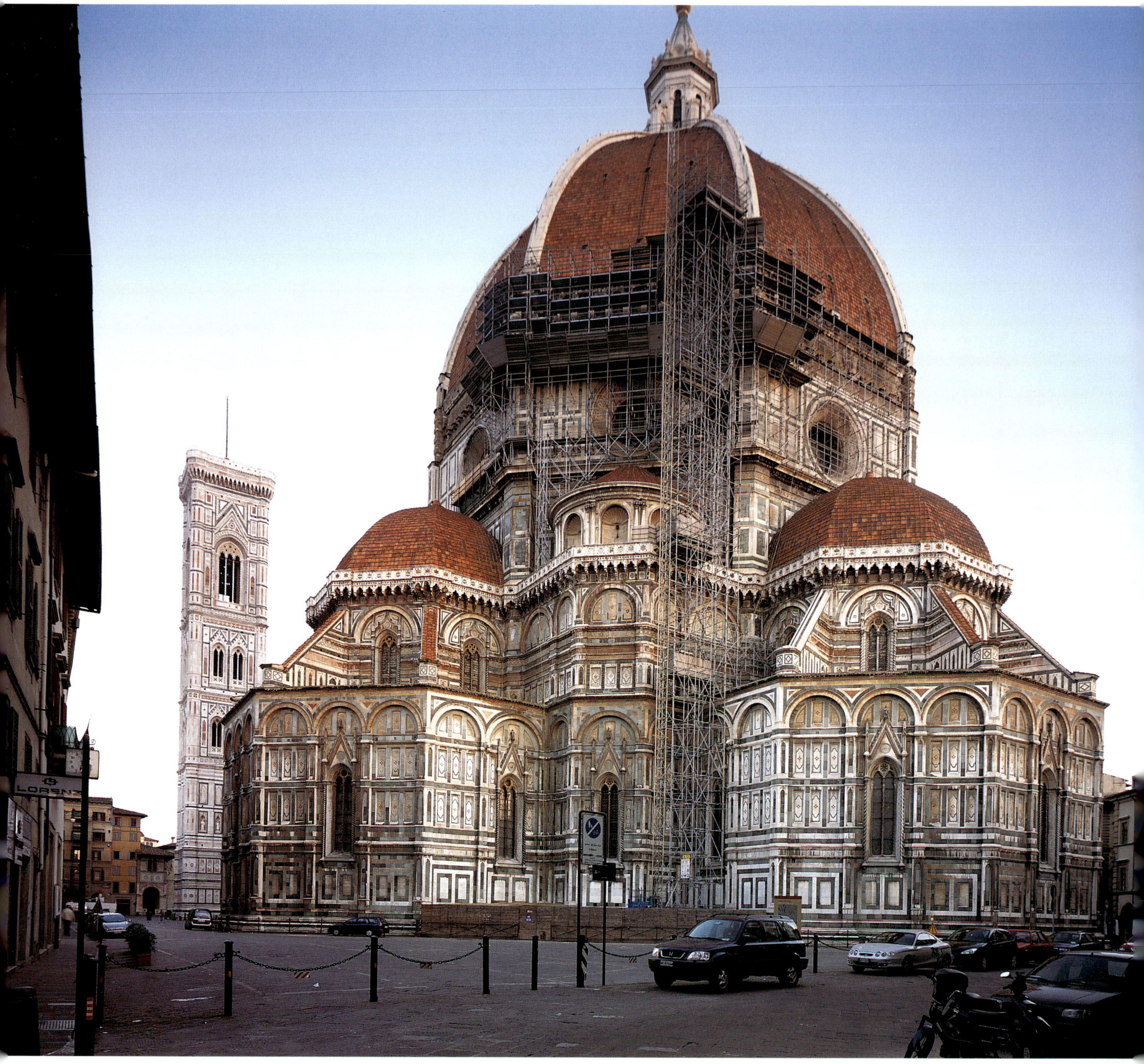

Opposite: the exterior of the eastern apses from the corner of Via del Proconsolo. This is almost the only location from which the immense volume of the eastern arm of the church can be fully appreciated. Also clearly visible is the massing of the lower apses, which help to buttress the octagon of the great cupola.

Below: detail of the south elevation, with the Porta della Canonica, the canons' entrance into the church. The medieval Canonica itself stood directly opposite, but was rebuilt in the early nineteenth century.

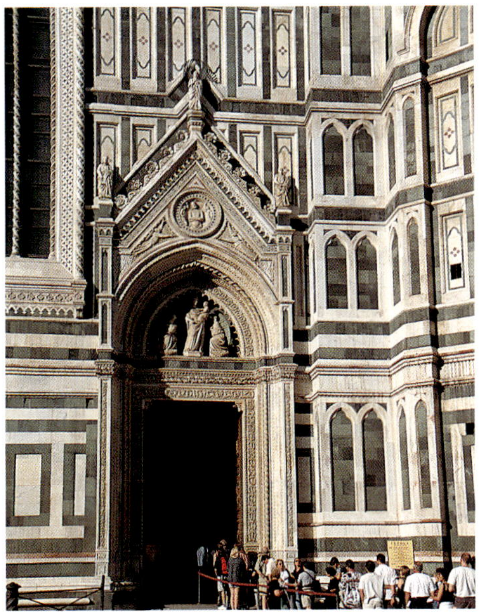

little church of Santa Reparata, which was only finally demolished in 1375, when it became impossible to continue working around it. At the same time the decision was made to proceed with the massive nave, new proposals were put forward for the continuation of the facade, and over the next couple of years, Talenti and Alberto Arnoldi developed the facade that had been frozen since the death of Arnolfo. In practice, though, little more was achieved; but had the entire facade been completed on the basis of extrapolation from Poccetti's drawing of the Arnolfian design, the result undoubtedly would have been one of the most extravagantly ornate facades in Italy.

Through the 1360s work proceeded slowly on the great nave, following Talenti's model. A written document from 1360 gives the dimensions of the entire structure, including what was to be a massive domed space above the crossing; although the precise configuration of the east end, and in particular the number and arrangement of chapels, was altered before their final construction, the overall scale of the work appears to be that of Talenti's proposal: The height of both the nave and the drum of the crossing as it was completed by Brunelleschi many decades later conform to those presented by Talenti.[25] It was left to his successors to face the formidable task of spanning a central octagonal space no less than 72 *braccia* (nearly 138 feet, or 42 meters) across; no one had succeeded in spanning such a void since the Romans, well over a thousand years earlier.

The definitive scheme was therefore something of a hybrid, a cross between a traditional, purely axial church — essentially a Latin cross — and one with an immense central space at the crossing. The size of the project was its most outstanding feature; notwithstanding the grandiose but ultimately abortive plans for Siena's cathedral, it was to be the largest cathedral ever built.[26] Until today, only three churches in the world exceed Santa Maria del Fiore in size: St. Peter's in Rome, St. Paul's in London, and the vast duomo of Milan, all completed considerably later.

Talenti's position as *capomaestro* seems to have been less than fully secure, however. In 1363 Giovanni Ghini, Talenti's rival, was recorded as chief master, and again in July 1364, by which time he seems to have replaced Talenti permanently. In this period, too, important decisions were made as to the design of the upper part of the nave, and the height and details of the vaulting. In this period Talenti's proposals were apparently being passed over in favor of Ghini's, who thereby undermined Talenti's authority. Major decisions were made in 1366 with the appointment of three separate advisory groups of painters, goldsmiths, and sculptors. All three groups concluded that work on the nave should be suspended for a time so that the great crossing and east end could be developed further. At this time, too, on the recommendation of the goldsmiths' *arte*, the extension of the nave was decided upon, so that it would have four huge bays instead of the original three, as can be seen today. In August 1366, models were called for to show how the eastern end might be resolved. Both Ghini and Talenti's son Simone put forward proposals, but both were rejected, and instead a scheme by the judging committee itself was selected. But the debate continued, and further models were made, until the discussion was widened to involve the city's population, whose views were recorded. In December 1368 the commission's model was confirmed as the definitive proposal.[27] All the other projects were destroyed, and a legal contract was drafted such that all future *capomaestri* were bound to continue work according to the approved model. As work was to continue for several decades, two or three generations of future masters were bound on oath to adhere to this design. It is clear, therefore, that the building that can be seen today — particularly the resolution of the east end — faithfully reflects this definitive scheme. Work continued slowly on the eastern end and the four-bay nave during the next three or four decades, until Brunelleschi was called upon to solve the enormous challenge of spanning the central octagon.

The manner in which the saga of the cathedral's construction developed is in many ways characteristic of the pragmatic approach that is often considered typical of the era. In this case, two important aspects of the story should be taken into consideration. One is the high level of debate

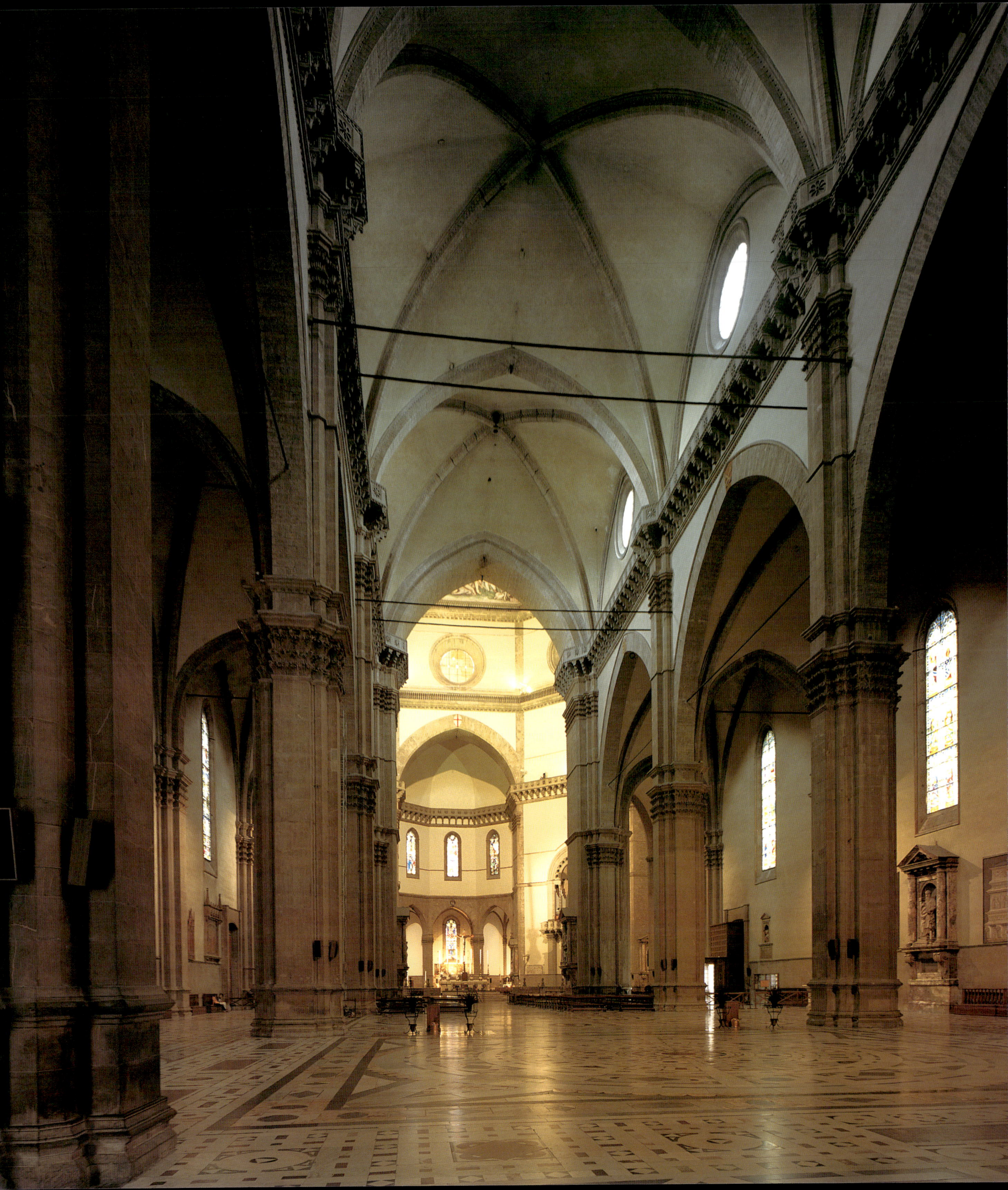

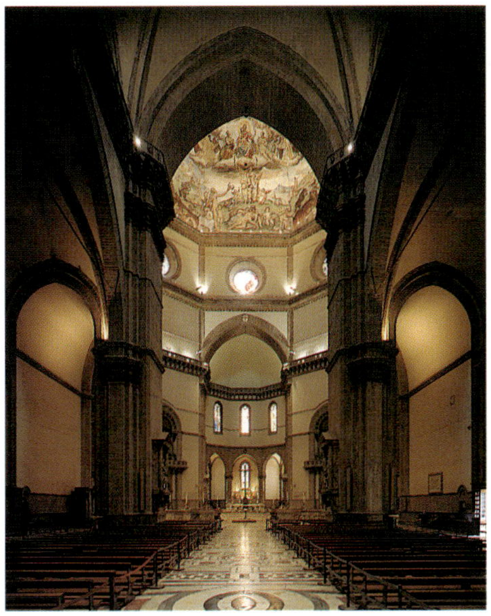

SANTA MARIA DEL FIORE

Above: the crossing and the octagon. The basic form of the crossing had already been established before Brunelleschi was faced with the challenge of vaulting this great space.

Opposite: the nave. Massive and imposing in its simplicity, the cathedral remains one of the largest churches in the world.

that took place in the city over these aesthetic matters, which were, after all, to affect the daily lives of Florentine citizens for centuries to come. What is perhaps more surprising, despite the long series of debates and apparent changes of direction, is the extraordinary visual unity, the balance and serenity of the completed structure. Even before Brunelleschi rose to the challenge of the cupola, the majestic nave and side aisles evinced an awesome quality of integrated harmony, combining great simplicity, even austerity, with carefully modulated richness — the former, for example, in the unadorned cross vaulting of nave and aisles, the latter in the complexity of the capitals, the high-level pilasters, and the cornice from which the vaulting springs. This overall appearance thus has a gravitas that is only partly the result of the immense spaces — in which a feeling of humility can hardly be repressed — but also of this powerful design discipline, in which even the richer elements are clearly and sharply defined and controlled.

The plan of the church is highly unusual. If the four huge bays of the long nave are fairly traditional, the eastern end marks a radical departure from the Latin cross plan. The massive octagonal crossing embraces the width of both the nave and the two side aisles, and from this octagon radiate the three equal arms of the chancel and transepts, the perimeter of each of which is subdivided into five appended chapels, fifteen in all. The entire spatial hierarchy is logical and rational, not simply on plan (which is easy enough to appreciate) but also in the third dimension. Structurally, the three equal eastern arms provide an almost perfect arrangement of buttresses and supports for the octagonal drum in the center of the composition, from which Brunelleschi's cupola was to rise. This hierarchy, or accumulation of volumes, is most clearly seen from the exterior of the eastern end, where the composition builds in a crescendo toward the great cupola.

The plan had many practical and liturgical advantages. The immense nave, with its wide bays, allowed a very large number of congregants (up to ten thousand, it is claimed) to have as clear a view as possible of the rites at the high altar, in much the same way that the open naves of Santa Croce and Santa Maria Novella were suited to the preaching requirements of the mendicant orders. The central crossing also provided ample space for the large numbers of officiants and dignitaries who attended special festivals here, and with the high altar located at the very center, allowed equally generous space for processions around it. The spacious transepts and eastern apse again provided for many combinations of choirs, which could be divided into groups for polyphonal choral works. Processions could go up the two side aisles toward the central crossing, or could proceed up one aisle, into the transepts, and down the other aisle without impeding the congregation in the central nave. This hybrid form of an axial church combined with a centralized plan thus had no significant disadvantages, but the inherent advantages of both. It was an unqualified triumph, arguably the most imposing work of architecture that had been built in Italy since the classical era. It was to be the responsibility of the greatest master of the next generation, though, to bring this work to its conclusion, and to bridge the void that still remained at the center of the cathedral.

Brunelleschi and the Vault of Heaven

"Who is so stubborn or so jealous that he can not praise Pippo [Filippo Brunelleschi] the architect, when he sees before him so great a structure, rising above the heavens, broad enough to cover with its shadow all of the people of Tuscany, built without the aid of any centering or other timbers, an achievement, if I have judged correctly, which in our own time has been believed to be impossible, and perhaps even among the ancients was unheard of and unknown." **Leon Battista Alberti**, *Della pittura* (1435–36) [28]

Progress on the church continued slowly but steadily, and by 1378 the nave vaults were complete; two years later, the side aisles were also complete and vaulted. The octagonal drum above the crossing was also completed in about 1400. At the same time the three eastern apses were progressing, although they were not complete until as late as 1421; the tambour or octagonal base from which the cupola was to rise was also completed at about the same time. In 1418 a competition was arranged to call for proposals for the construction of the cupola.[29] The statement gives no indication of the immensity of the task that lay ahead; an octagonal space 138 feet (42 meters) across, was to be covered with a cupola larger than any that had been constructed for well over a thousand years. The adjacent dome of San Giovanni was modest by comparison; the cathedral's octagon was not only almost twice the span of that of San Giovanni, it was to be built from a springing nearly three times higher, almost 200 feet (60 meters) above the floor of the nave. The two chief contenders in the competition were Lorenzo Ghiberti and Filippo Brunelleschi.

Filippo ("Pippo") di Ser Brunellesco was born in 1377 and, unlike his friend Leon Battista Alberti, had not received a classical, humanist education. He had been educated in a more traditional manner, largely in the workshop, although an early visit to Rome with Donatello in 1402 had been the first of many such visits to study the classical legacy. His early work as a sculptor was soon to be overshadowed by his interest in architecture, and he is first recorded working in the cathedral workshop in 1409. Here his fascination with the technical and aesthetic challenge of the cupola was awakened, but it was not before the formal 1418 competition that he was able to offer concrete proposals. The project was to occupy him for almost the rest of his life.

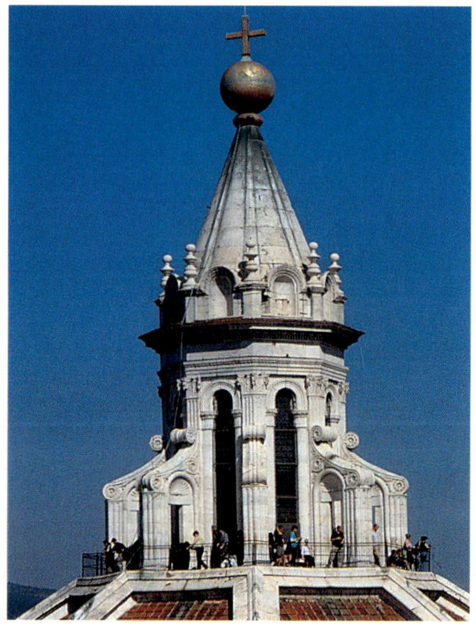

SANTA MARIA DEL FIORE

Detail of the lantern, completed as late as 1471, long after Brunelleschi's death.

Fortunately many of the documents relating to the building of the cupola have survived, although a number of tantalizing knowledge gaps remain; the most serious loss is perhaps the fact that none of Brunelleschi's own original sketches and drawings have survived, so that most of our knowledge derives from written sources alone. The first specification for the cupola was drafted on 30 July 1420, and was amended twice later, in 1422 and in 1426.[30] The problem was an extraordinary one because all of the basic decisions regarding the cupola had in fact already been made years or even decades earlier. The principal piers had all been built, and the fundamental supporting members thus established; the drum that was to support the cupola itself was complete; and two of the three "part domes" that roofed the three eastern arms of the church were also complete. (These apse domes could be described as octagonal faceted cupolas, which had three of the eight facets removed, so that the cupolas could abut the main drum of the cathedral's central cupola.) In addition, the 1367 model to which all subsequent masters had to declare their allegiance was still valid. It therefore seems very likely that this 1367 scheme had incorporated an eight-sided dome, similar to that depicted in the well-known fresco by Andrea Bonaiuti in the Spanish chapel at Santa Maria Novella. Bonaiuti's fresco was painted in about 1365, and indicates a faceted octagonal cupola, so it was presumably based on the extant authorized model, although he omits the tall drum from which the cupola was to rise; at that time, no Florentine could have had any idea as to how it could be built. The 1418 competition was, therefore, not intended to produce new designs, but rather to stimulate practical methods by which this essentially technical problem could be solved. In 1420 Brunelleschi was given the commission, but not alone, as he was joined by Ghiberti and Battista d'Ancona, who were to help supervise construction. Ghiberti's intended role is less than clear, although it seems to have been subservient to that of Brunelleschi, while d'Ancona appears to have been intended as Brunelleschi's right-hand man, a practical clerk of the works.

The basic premise of Brunelleschi's design was an octagonal cupola, broadly like Bonaiuti's illustration, and in a general sense based on the San Giovanni cupola. There were a number of inherent advantages in designing a faceted, "pointed" dome, or more accurately, cupola, rather than a pure hemisphere; one was that each of the facets is simply a curved, flat plane, and therefore comparatively easy to set out, each facet rising directly from one face of the octagonal drum. More important, perhaps, is the fact that there is considerably less outward thrust at the base of such a form than there is with a true hemispherical dome — in fact, only about half as much. This meant that the tendency of such a cupola to spread at the base was far less of a problem, although Brunelleschi still incorporated timber ring beams to mitigate this phenomenon.[31] On the other hand, a hemispherical dome had certain advantages over an octagonal cupola, the chief one being that a dome remains stable under construction as long as each ring of masonry is complete; that is, it has to be built as a series of diminishing rings of masonry, in which each course acts as a self-supporting ring beam carried by the courses below it. However, Brunelleschi did not have a circular base from which to build such a cupola, but an octagonal one, and a series of squinches or similar devices would have been necessary to effect the geometric transition from octagon to circle.[32]

A variant of the adopted solution of an octagonal "pointed" dome would have been to construct a pointed gothic vault, with eight identical structural ribs, one on each edge. But such a form generates construction problems of its own; it requires temporary centering to assemble the ribs, and to build such centering at such a height and on such a scale had never been attempted before. It was true that the part domes of the eastern apses had recently been built using this method, but they were very much smaller and considerably lower.

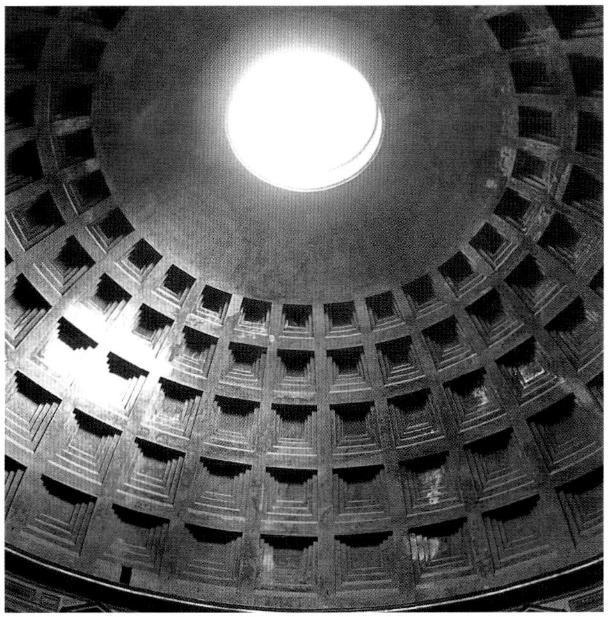

THE PANTHEON, ROME

Interior of the cupola, showing the coffered construction, some of the principles of which were adapted by Brunelleschi in Florence.

So Brunelleschi famously proposed to construct his cupola without the aid of any centering at all.[33] Alberti spoke for all of his contemporaries when he wrote with genuine wonder at the sheer audacity of this proposal, the details of which Brunelleschi apparently kept very close to his breast — understandably, perhaps, given the well-known, sometimes fierce rivalries with some of his contemporaries. He proposed two ingenious, mutually supportive methods of design that would make such a feat possible. Although the main stone ribs at the "corners" of the octagonal cupola were very strong, one fundamental difficulty was the tendency for each of the eight curved flat plates of the cupola to deflect or arch inward toward the middle, rendering them inherently unstable. Brunelleschi's solution was twofold: first, to build two stiffening ribs up the face of each of the eight facets, thus dividing them into three equal parts, and second, to construct the entire cupola out of two skins of brickwork, an inner and an outer one. The inner skin has considerably thicker walls than the outer shell, and remains the principal load-bearing structure; it is linked to the outer one by means of a network of coffered ribs, which, uncovered, would look very much like an inside-out version of the coffered dome of the Pantheon. The dome structure thus in a sense also acts like a diaphragm wall, with the two skins kept apart by the ribs, but with the whole assembly acting together. The overall thickness of this three-part structure ensures that almost all of the outward thrusts from the facets are kept within this depth of masonry and not transferred to the drum below. In order to ensure this, the structure of the brick octagon is sufficiently thick that a perfect circle can be drawn within this thickness; and because a circular dome is always inherently stable (both under construction and afterward) the whole could be built without centering. The principal role of the thinner outer dome is primarily to tie all the hidden coffers together, but it also, naturally, provides a supporting surface for the roof finish of clay tiles that cover the whole of the outer surface.

As a technical solution, Brunelleschi's scheme was brilliant. The omission of centering not only saved a great deal of money, but also obviated the huge quantities of timbers that would have been necessary, but that certainly would have proved difficult, perhaps impossible, to obtain. There was a further advantage in this form of construction: Because the structure remains self-supporting at all stages of construction, there were no difficulties with programming or resourcing of men, money, or materials — the work could proceed at any pace, depending on the availability of bricks, bricklayers, and funds. In fact, slow, steady progress, almost inevitable in a project of this size, is an advantage, as it allows time for the mortar to mature and gain strength.

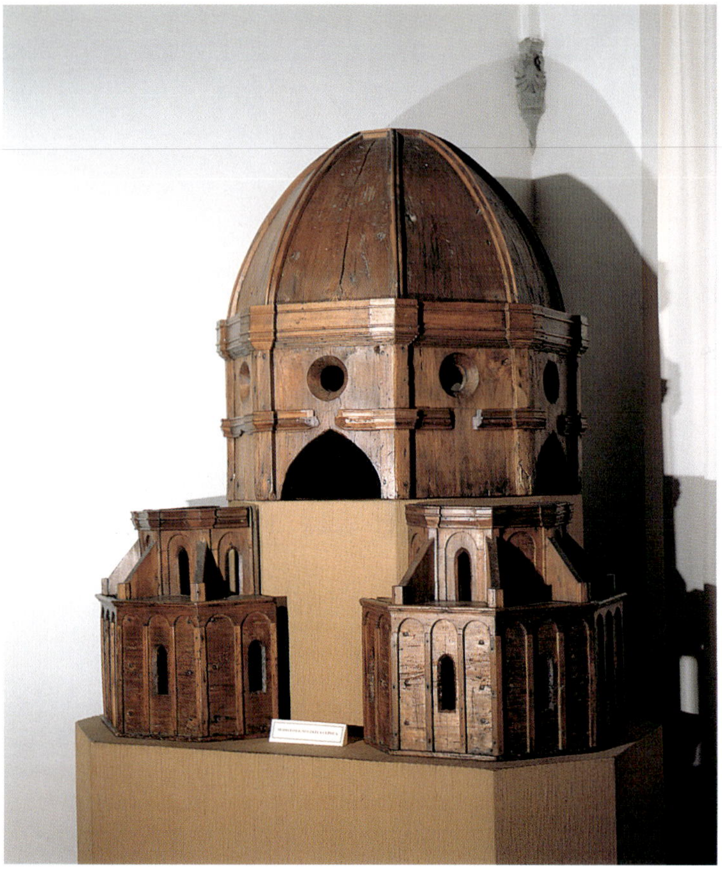

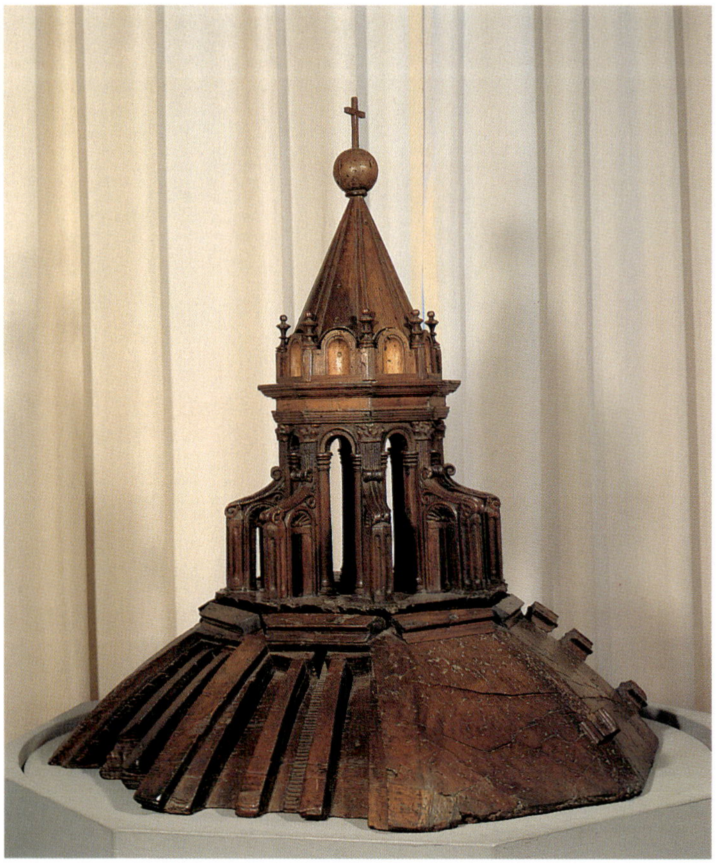

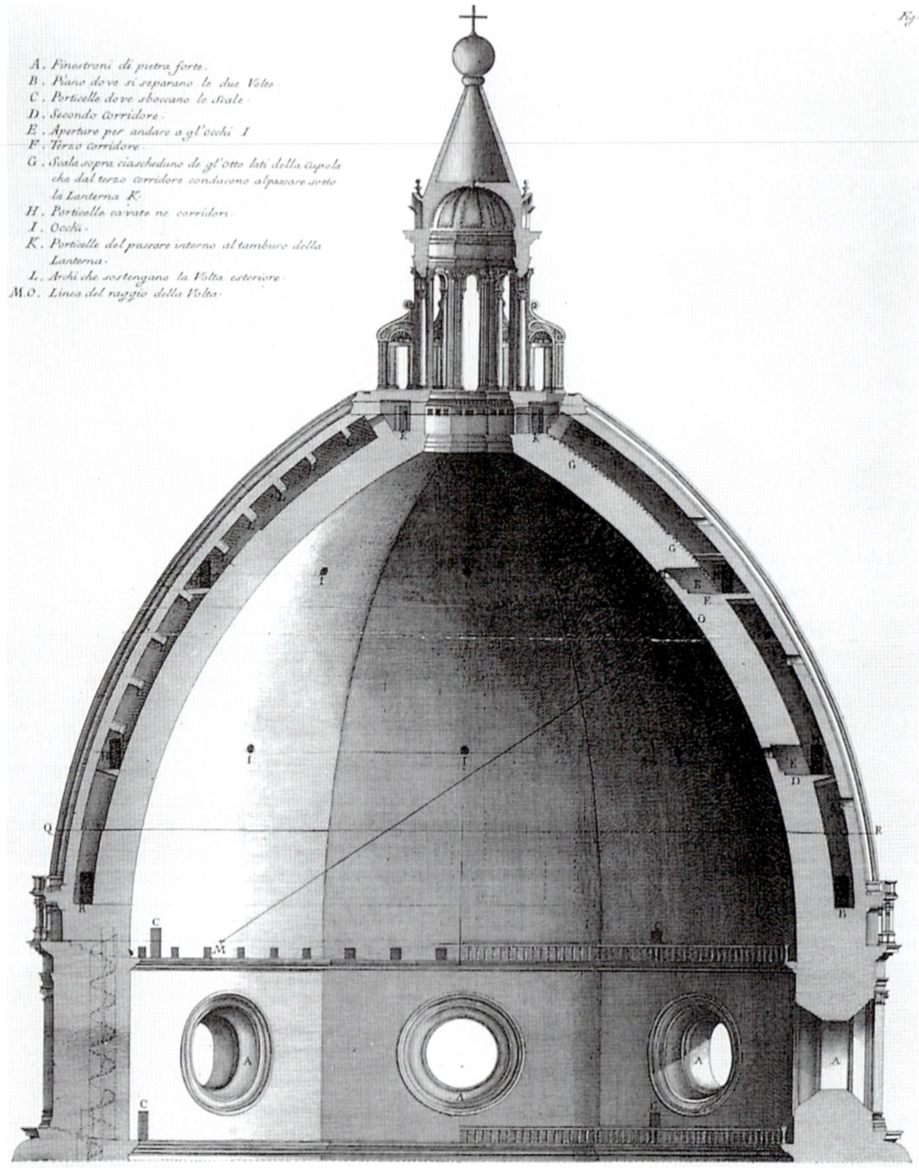

SANTA MARIA DEL FIORE

Left, top: Brunelleschi's original wooden model of the cupola, perhaps made in 1429 (Florence, Museo dell'Opera). Left: detailed model of Brunelleschi's lantern. The date is not certain, and it may have been made after the lantern itself was built. Above: detailed section of the cupola, by Giovanni Battista Nelli, 1733, showing the two layers of construction of the vaults, with a much thicker internal brick vault, and a thinner outer one.

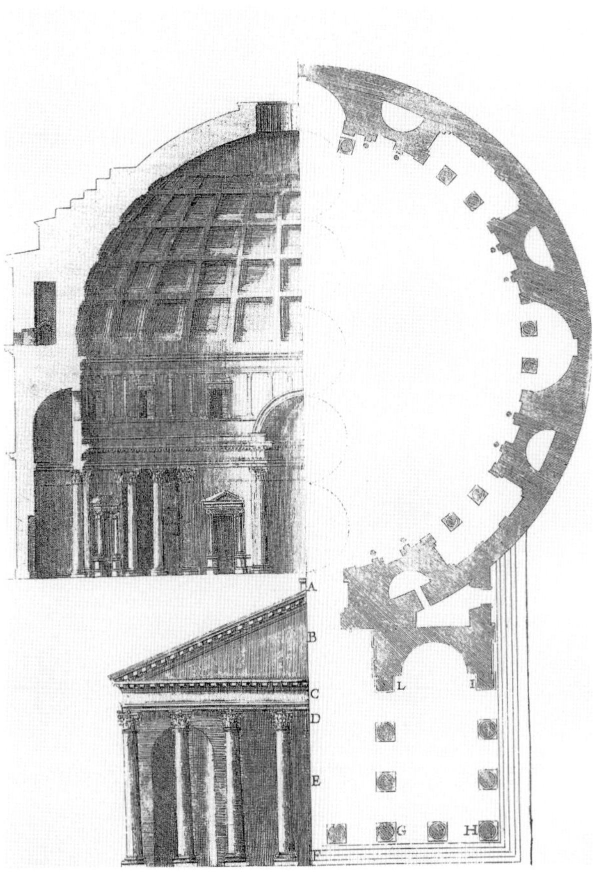

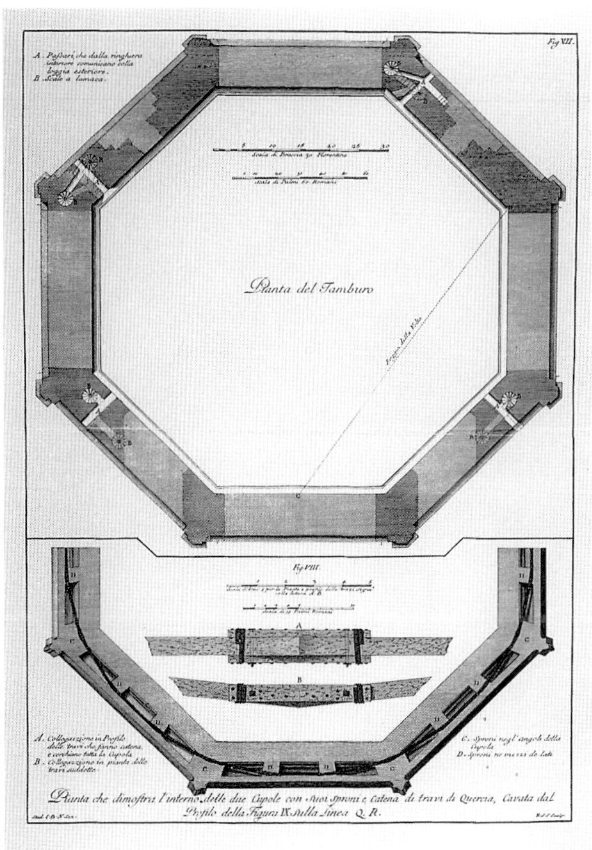

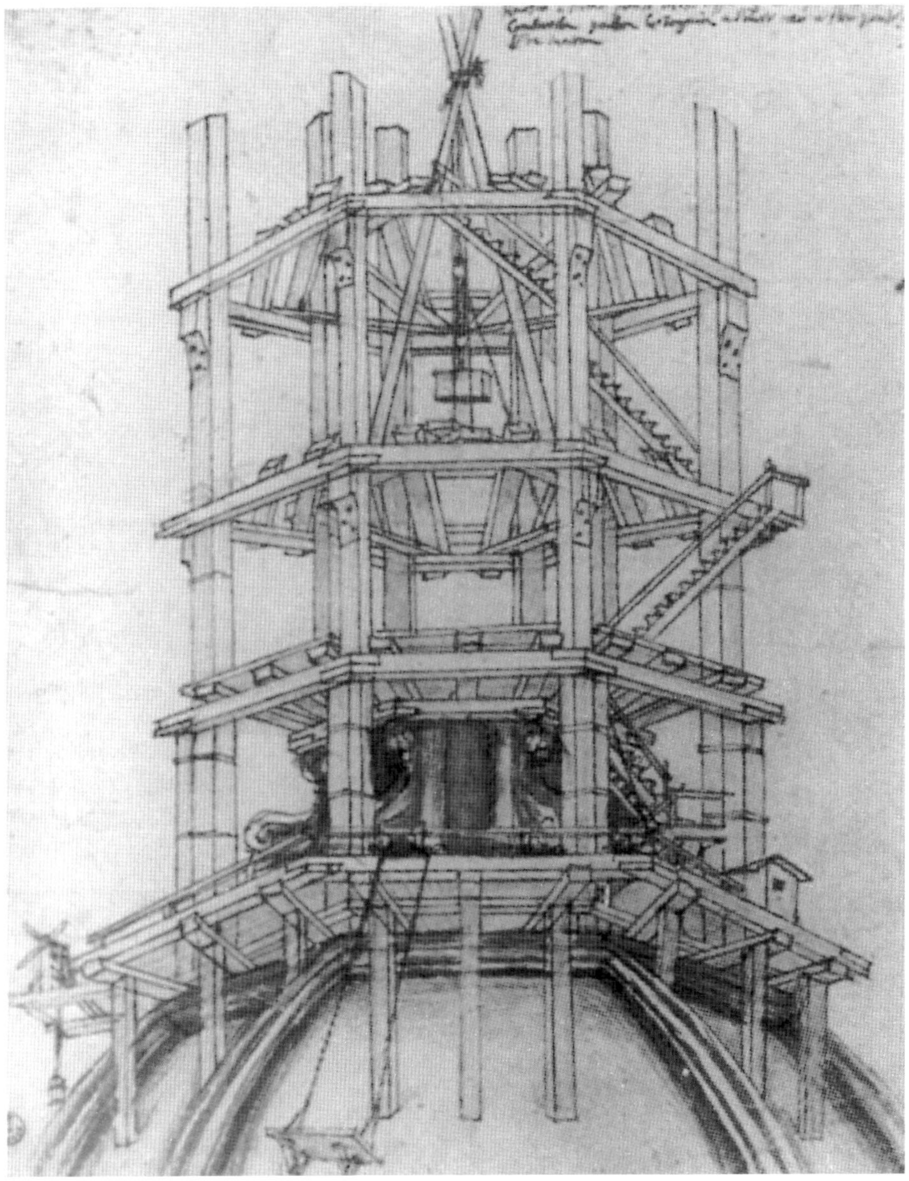

PANTHEON, ROME, AD 120–24 (Left, top)

Part plan and section.

SANTA MARIA DEL FIORE

Left: engraving by Giovanni Battista Nelli, 1733, indicating the construction of the octagonal drum on which the cupola was built. Above: drawing from Brunelleschi's workshop showing the temporary scaffolding that was to be erected for the construction of the lantern (Florence, Uffizi).

Brunelleschi's friend and colleague Alberti followed progress on the cupola closely. He was clearly aware of the basic principles behind the structural design, as he wrote later in *De re aedificatoria*: "You may likewise turn the Angular [i.e., faceted] Cupolas without a Center, if you make a perfect [circle] in the Middle of the Thickness of the Work." The cupola was finally completed in 1436; on 25 March, the cathedral was consecrated by Pope Eugenio IV.

When Brunelleschi died, in 1446, the external cladding of the drum of the cupola was still incomplete, as were the large circular windows, which were completed by Giuliano da Maiano. The cladding of the uppermost order of the drum still remained unfinished, and although proposals were put forward in 1507 by Baccio d'Agnolo, Cronaca, and Giuliano da Sangallo, only one facet of the eight was ever executed; the other seven sides remain in rough brickwork to this day. In 1430 Brunelleschi had also begun to build the so-called *tribune morte*, the semicircular colonnaded external structures that stand between the three principal apse roofs. These "half structures" are chiefly notable for their pure early Renaissance detailing, and they add a further degree of buttressing to the lower part of the central drum.

The cupola was terminated at the top by a large open ring of masonry, rather like that at the Pantheon. This open circle formed a stable ring beam, but clearly the whole composition required a suitable finish, and in 1432 a competition was launched for its design.[34] A lantern had been intended from the outset, and a surviving memorandum from 1420 mentions it, although the details of its design had not at that stage been considered. A modest precedent stood nearby at San Giovanni, but clearly something more imposing was required to crown the great new cupola.

Although Brunelleschi won the competition on 31 December 1436, work on site did not begin until 1446, the year of his death. The extreme difficulty of access was undoubtedly one of the reasons it took no less than twenty-two years to complete; the lantern itself stands the height of a small church or chapel and, when completed, added a further 40 *braccia* to the height of the cathedral. Its surrounding balcony is approximately 300 feet (91 meters) from the ground, and the task of raising and assembling the stone in such a location was no small undertaking. The design of the lantern is essentially based on that of an idealized classical temple, or Tower of the Winds, its octagonal form surmounted by a pointed octagonal pyramid roof and surrounded by an arched gallery.[35] At least as innovative as the overall form was Brunelleschi's use of stone volutes to act as buttresses to the perimeter, one of his inventions that would gain widespread popularity much later, in the Baroque and Rococo eras.[36] Comparison has often been made between the lantern as built and the little detail of a lantern made by Donatello in 1423 for the top of the staff of St. Luke in his statue for Orsanmichele. It is not clear which master inspired the other, however, since both were very close, and there must have been frequent exchange of ideas between them.

Brunelleschi's cupola transformed the image of the city, and this immense structure, quite unlike any other major work of architecture in Florence, continues to define the city today. There were simply no precedents for such a construction anywhere else in Italy. The roof of the neighboring baptistery was modest, and existing domes in Tuscany paled by comparison; that at Pisa cathedral, for example, was not a true dome but followed the rectangular plan of the crossing, and thus had a unique hybrid form. That at Siena was also somewhat odd: The dome has twelve sides, set on squinches onto a six-sided base, but its profile is quite shallow, and by no means does it dominate the exterior of the cathedral, let alone the whole city, in the manner that Brunelleschi's "vault of heaven" dominated Florence.

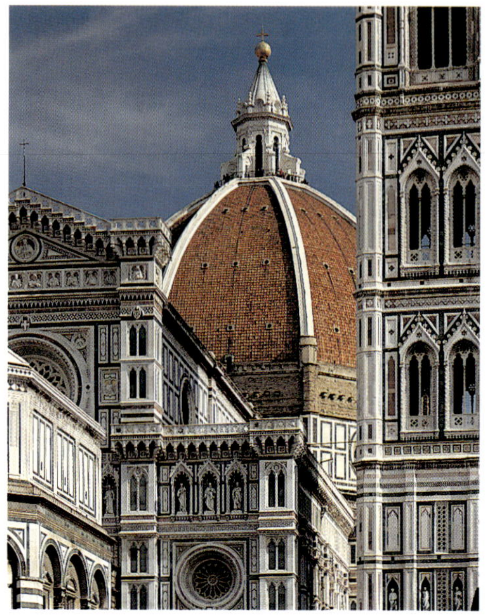

SANTA MARIA DEL FIORE

Above: detail of the nineteenth-century facade, the cupola with its lantern, and Giotto's campanile.

Opposite: detail of the cladding of the cathedral, chiefly in green and white marble.

Overleaf: view of the cupola and the campanile from the Palazzo Vecchio; this magnificent composition has represented Florence's identity in the eyes of the world for half a millennium.

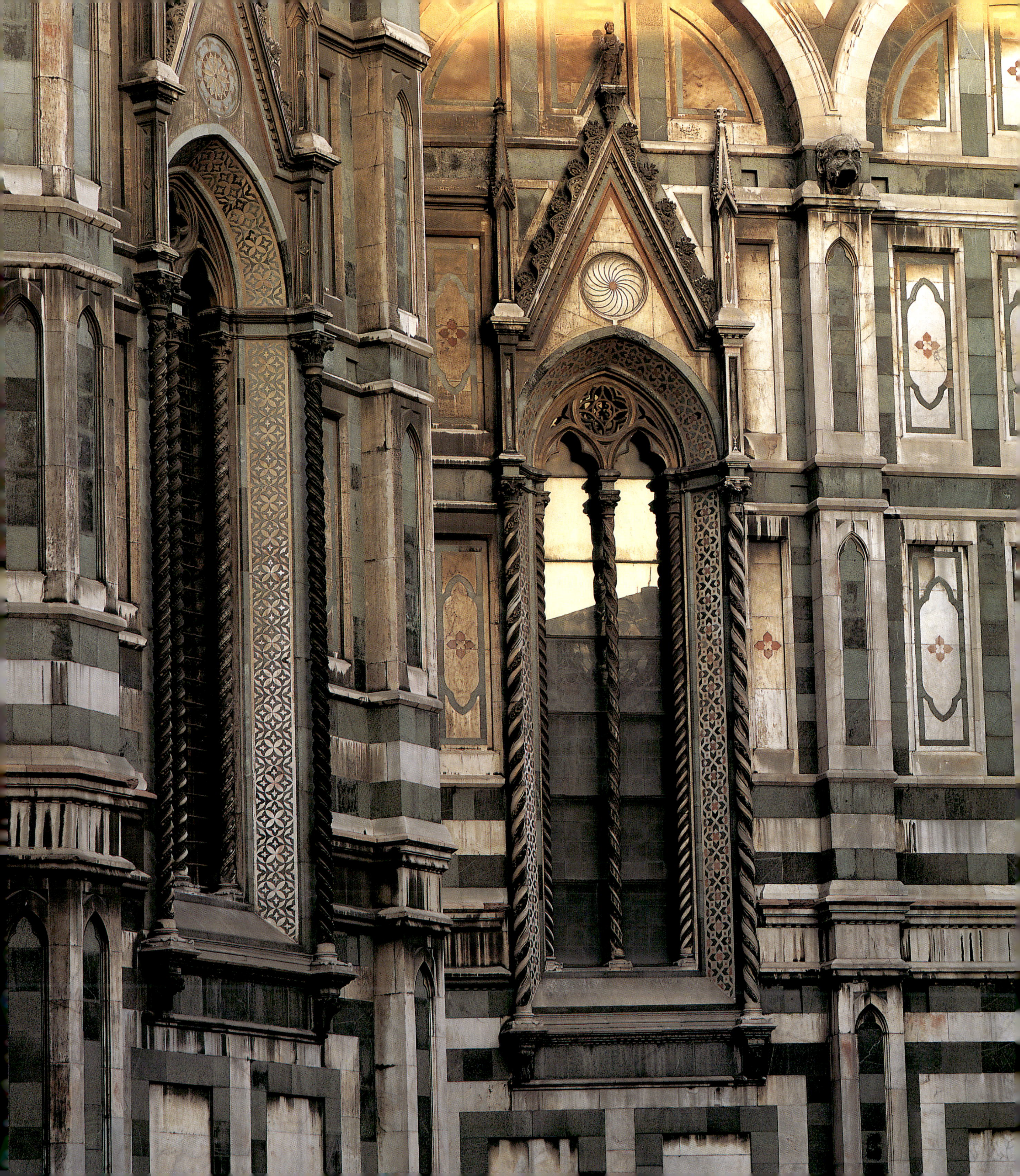

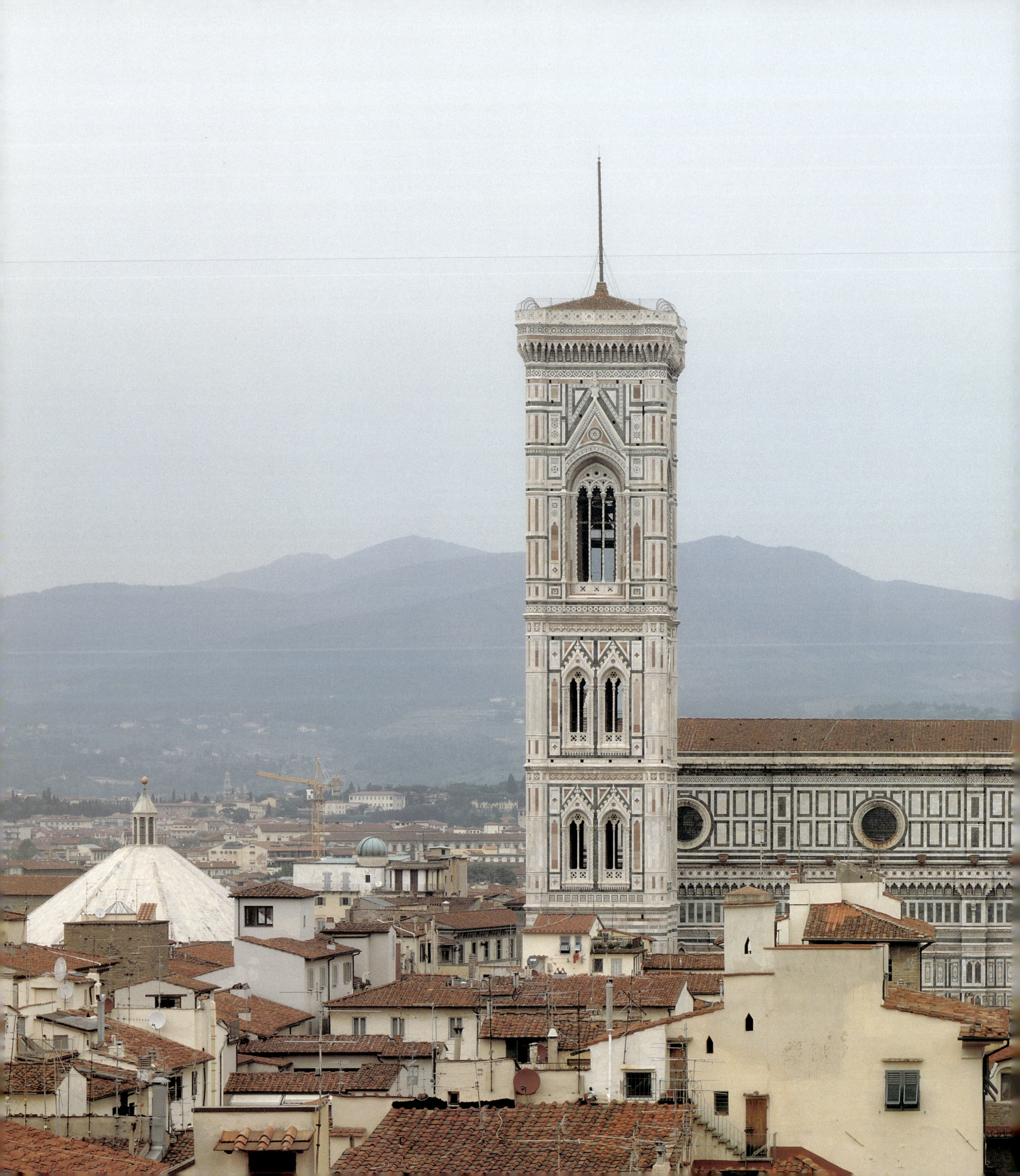

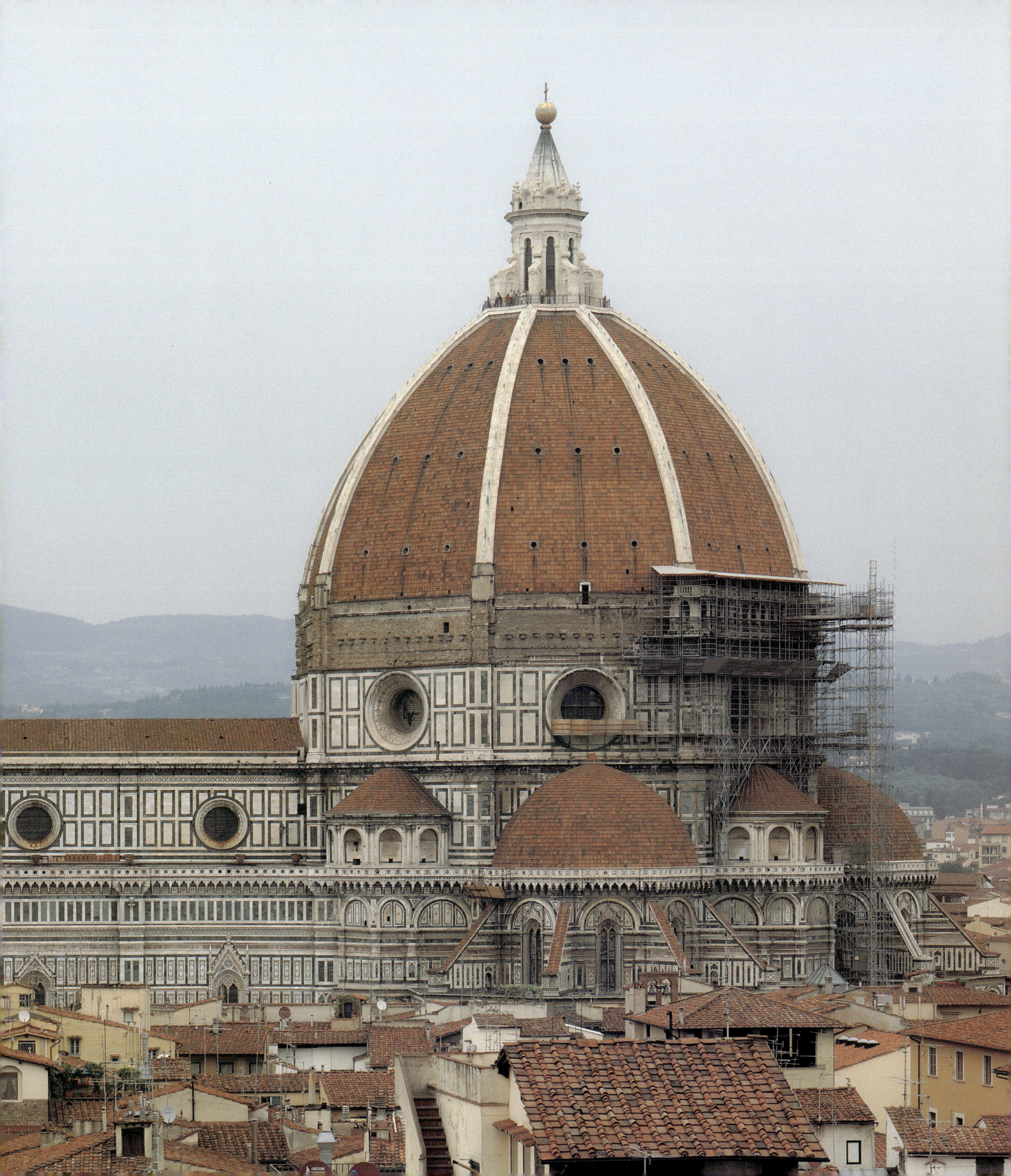

The Later History of the Cathedral

"Donato likewise executed for the same church the decorations of the organ, which stands over the door of the old sacristy, where are those figures, so boldly sketched . . . that in looking at them one almost believes them really to live and move."

Giorgio Vasari, *Lives of the Artists* (1568) [37]

Once completed, the cathedral was the site of many civic and public events as well as Church festivals. The largest single covered space in Italy reasserted the ancient role once held by Santa Reparata, where the city's government assembled to debate matters of policy long before the construction of the Palazzo del Popolo. The cathedral thus reclaimed this important civic role, as well as housed important events such as, for example, the conference held in 1439 that attempted to reconcile the Eastern and Western Christian churches. Public lectures on Dante's *Divine Comedy* were also held there.

The cathedral's structure was completed in the mid quattrocento, but decoration of the interior and fabric was to continue for some time. The windows, for example, were filled with numerous fine, stained-glass images during the period from 1434 to 1455, under the general design and supervision of Lorenzo Ghiberti. The floors of polychrome marble were begun by Baccio d'Agnolo, but completed only in about 1560 by his son Giuliano, Francesco da Sangallo, and others. Among the other important elements of the completion of the internal fittings are the works of Luca della Robbia and Donatello. Both of the *cantorie*, or singing galleries associated with the organ, one by Luca and one by Donatello, are now in the Museo dell'Opera, but Luca's sculpted group of the *Ascension* remains in situ above the sacristy doorway. Brunelleschi's intention had been to decorate the internal surfaces of the cupola with a vast cycle of mosaics, as in the baptistery, but at the instigation of Cosimo I, in 1572 Vasari began to paint the huge fresco of the Last Judgment that can still be seen today, and which was completed after his death by Federico Zuccari. The later history of the fabric was comparatively uneventful, until in 1688 the two famous *cantorie,* or choir stalls, by Donatello and Luca della Robbia were removed from their locations above the sacristy doors in conformity with the new liturgical edicts.

But the one pivotal aspect of the cathedral that remained unresolved through the centuries was the completion of the facade. The small element that had been completed by Arnolfo di Cambio was dismantled by Bernardo Buontalenti in 1587, on the instructions of Francesco I, who proposed to sponsor an entirely new facade. Buontalenti himself produced a design to clad it in a more contemporary — that is, a highly Mannerist, High Renaissance — style. Less extravagant alternative proposals were put forward by Giambologna, Giovanni de' Medici, and Giovanni Antonio Dosio. However, they all came to nothing, since Francesco died only a few months later and with him the impetus for the project. Models of these various designs survive in the Museo dell'Opera.[38]

It was only toward the end of the nineteenth century, after endless further stylistic debates, that the present facade was belatedly begun. The style adopted was, and remains, 150 years after its completion, highly controversial. In 1843 a proposal was put forward by Nicola Matas, who shortly afterward also began the facade of Santa Croce; the approach at the cathedral was similar to that at Santa Croce, a reinterpretation of the characteristic style of the campanile, with a cladding of white, red, and green marble — broadly speaking, a development of the quattrocento cladding of the rest of the body of the church. In 1861 a public competition was held, which produced continued heated debate but no clear winner. A further series of competitions and discussions finally led to the appointment of Emilio de' Fabris to execute the facade that can be seen today, completed between 1876 and 1887.[39] It has been widely criticized for its unimaginative literal historicism, the heavy crowning cornice clearly intended to marry with that of the adjacent campanile.

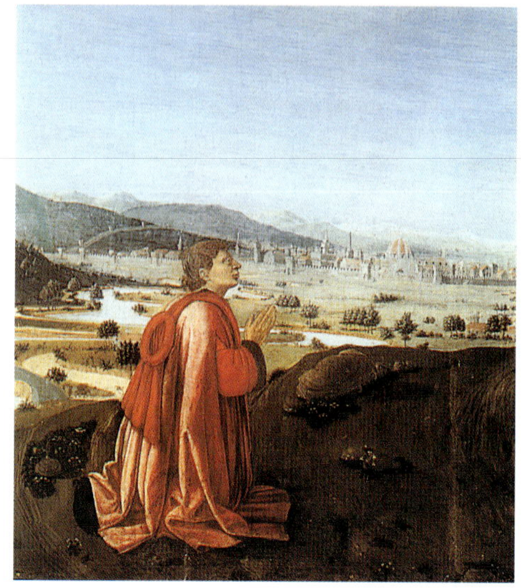

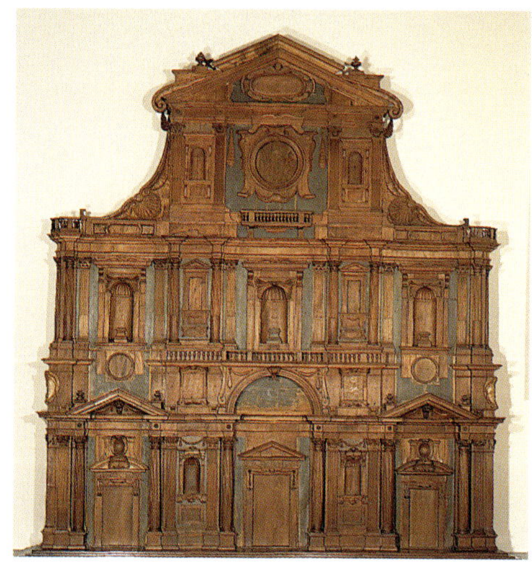

SANTA MARIA DEL FIORE

Top: detail from Francesco Botticini's *Assumption of the Virgin*, c. 1474, showing Florence, with the cupola already established as the symbol of the city. Above: wooden model of the facade for the cathedral proposed by Bernardo Buontalenti, c. 1587; this is one of a series of superb wooden models for the completion of the facade kept in the Museo dell'Opera.

Opposite: interior of the cupola. The frescoes of the Universal Judgment, designed and partly executed by Vasari from 1572 to 1574, were completed by Federico Zuccari.

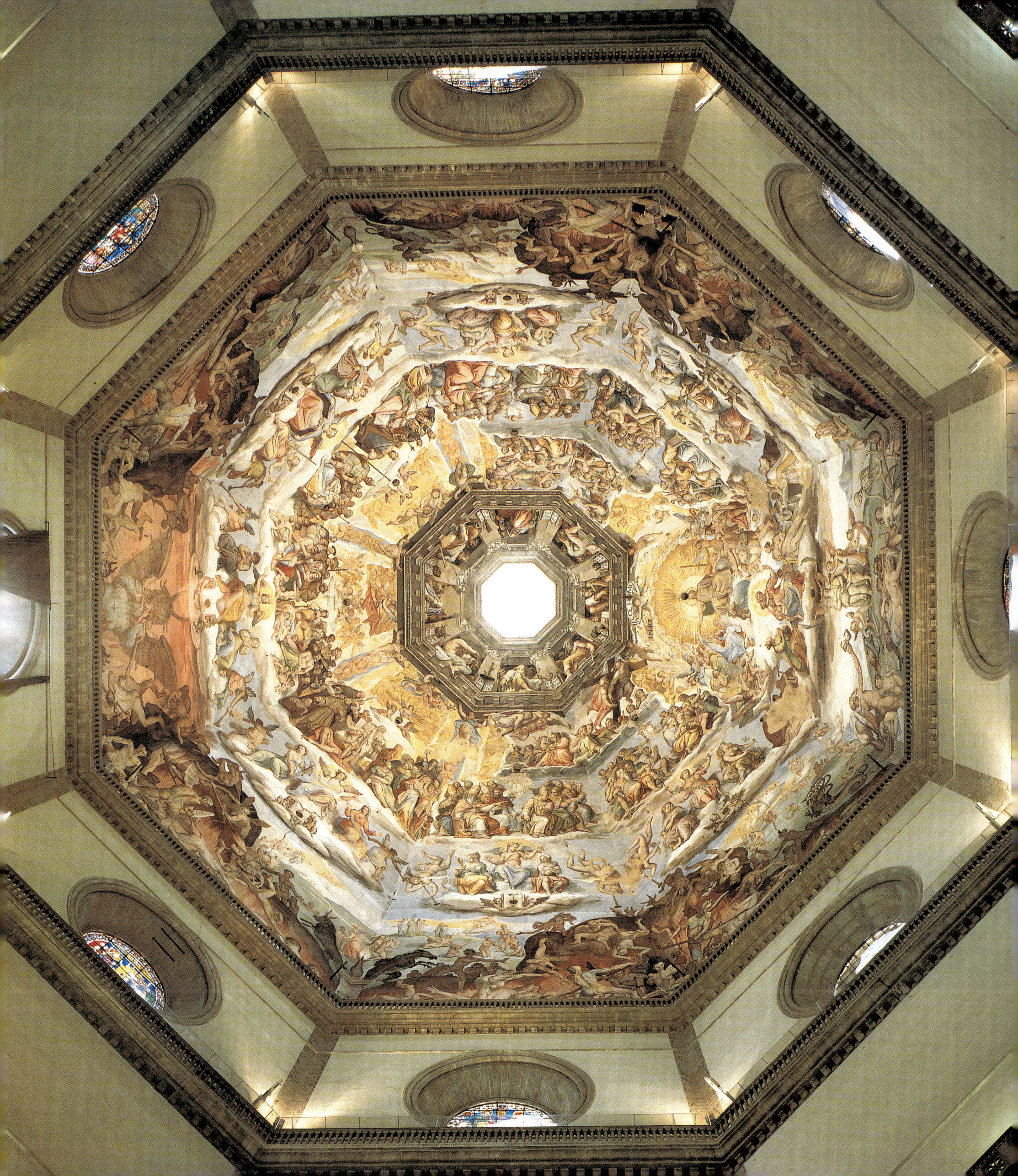

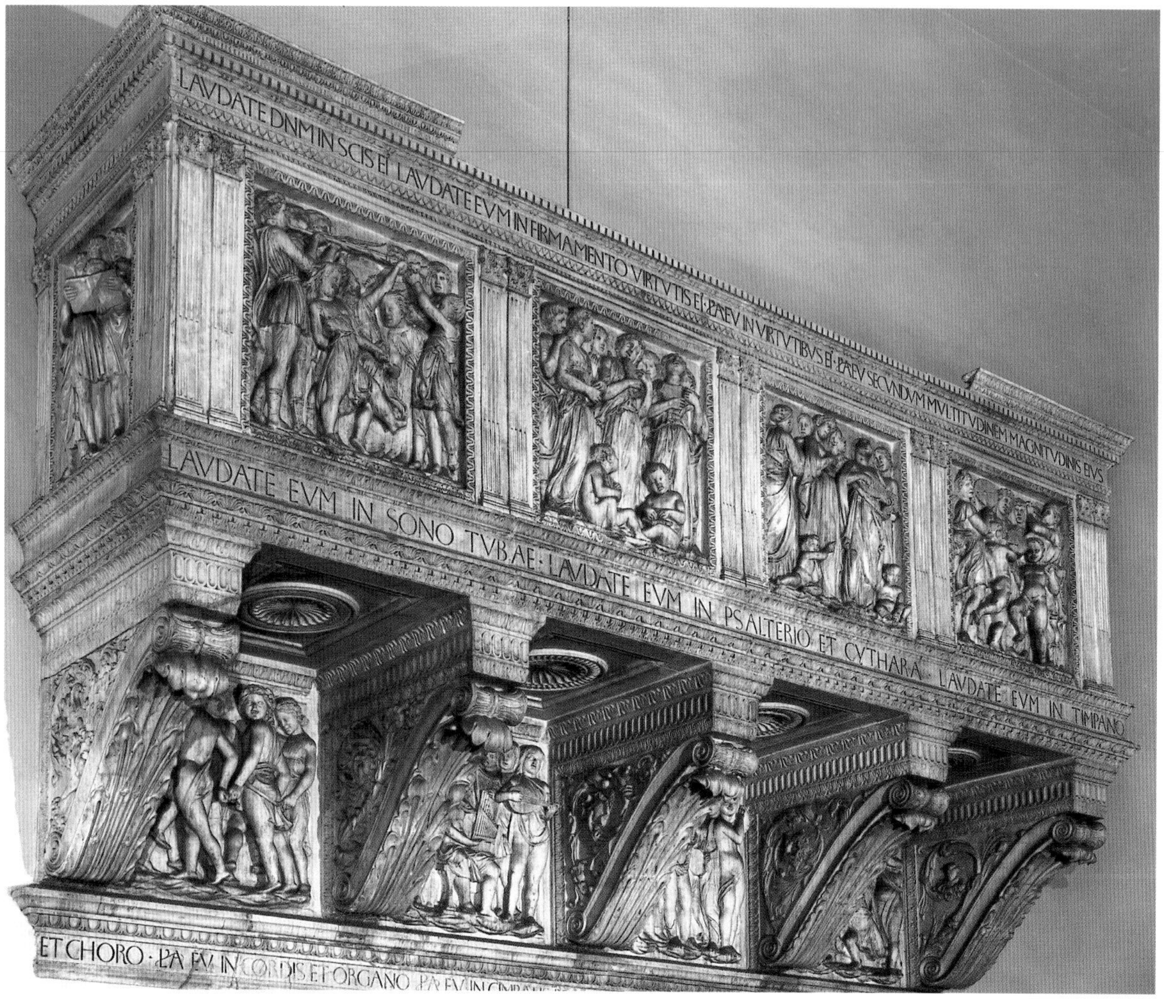

LUCA DELLA ROBBIA, *CANTORIA*, 1431–38 (Florence, Museo dell'opera)

The choir gallery of the cathedral, with details.

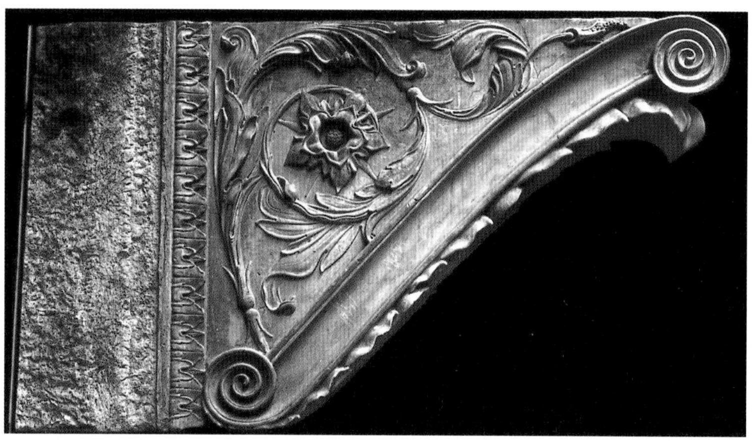

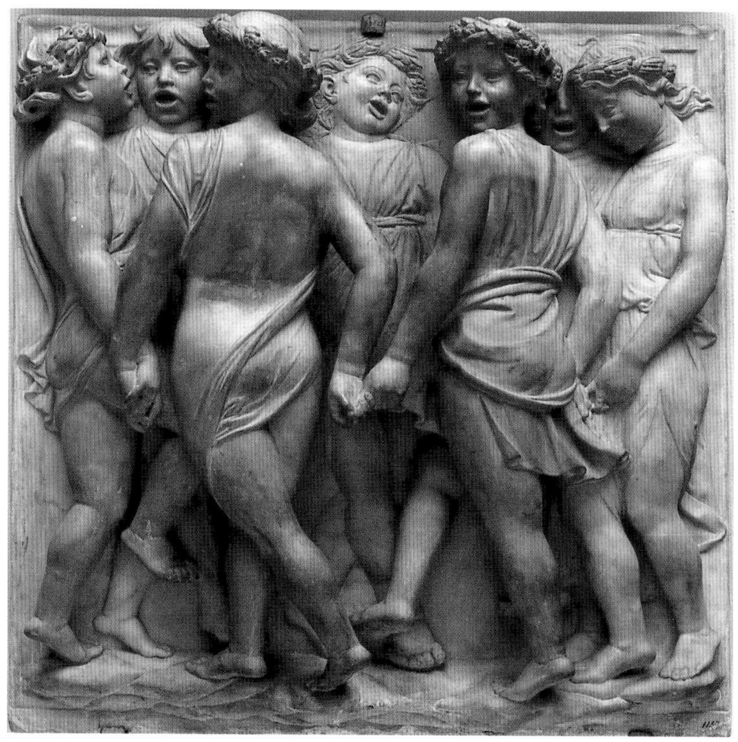

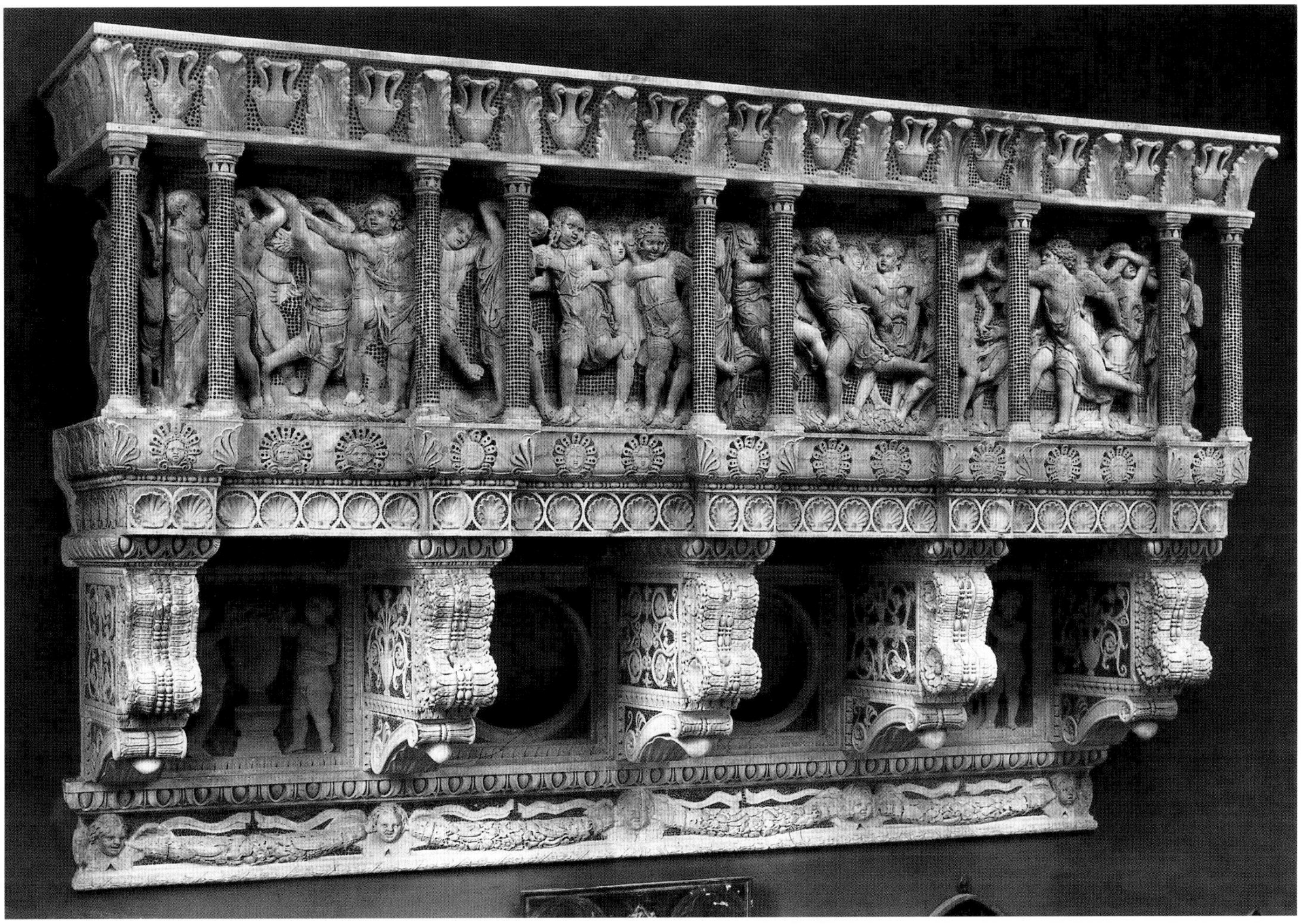

DONATELLO, *CANTORIA*, 1433–40 (Florence, Museo dell'Opera)

While della Robbia's *cantoria* depicts figures singing and playing instruments, Donatello's theme is the classical dance.

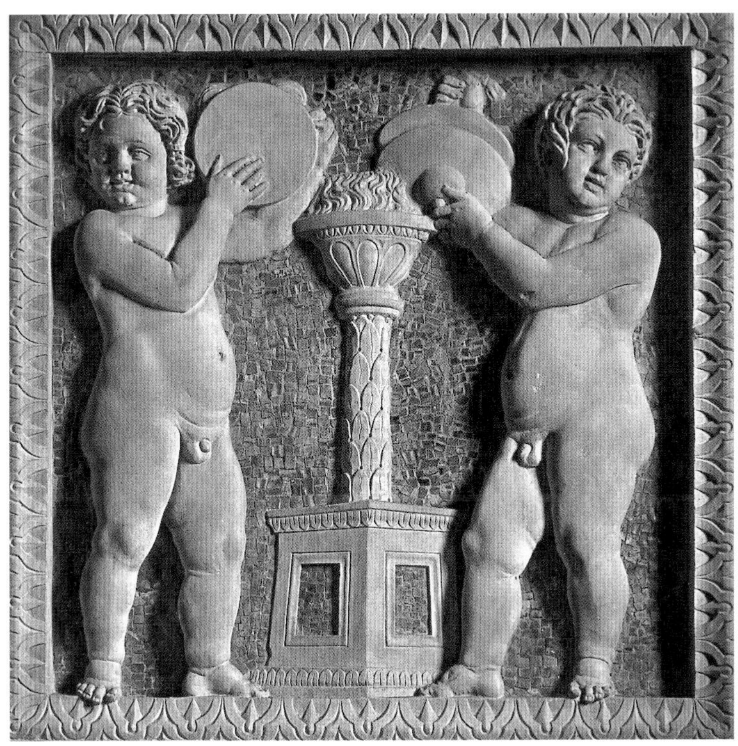

"Ahi, serva Italia, di dolorre ostello / nave sanza nocchiere in gran tempesta / non donna di proviencie, ma bordello!" (Oh, Italy enslaved, oh host of grief / a ship without a pilot in a stormy sea / no lady of fair province, but a whore!) **Dante Alighieri**, *Purgatorio* (c. 1319–20) [1]

To appreciate the practical functions that determined the construction of the complex of buildings that eventually formed the hubs of Florentine political power, some understanding of its structure is necessary. This power structure essentially crystallized at the end of the duecento and the first years of the trecento, in the time of Dante. In essence, the government of Florence then remained the same until the rise to power of Cosimo de' Medici in the 1430s.[2]

Power was vested in two distinctly different bodies, representing the judiciary and Florence's executive administration. The head of the judiciary was the *podestà*, governor or chief magistrate, who was usually a nobleman from a friendly neighboring state. The *podestà*'s duty was to render impartial justice to all citizens, and his term of office was initially one year, later reduced to only six months. In 1255 a new palazzo was begun to house the *podestà* and his legislature, the palace known today as the Bargello. The *podestà* chaired a general council of three-hundred members, with a smaller council of ninety convened on particular occasions. A few years before the Bargello was begun, in 1250 a new post was created, that of the Capitano del Popolo. One of the functions of this office was to act as a check on the powers of the *podestà*, and the *capitano* was usually also a foreign nobleman; his more specific remit was to look after the interests of the merchant classes, the *borghesia affarista*, against those of the nobility. The *capitano* himself chaired two councils, the Consiglio Generale of 150 men, and a smaller inner council of thirty-six.

The second hub of power was the executive. The example of Dante is enlightening because, not only was he the city's greatest literary figure, he was also an active, and fairly typical, participant in the government of his own city. Indeed, in his capacity as a member of the *arte dei medici e speziali* (doctors and pharmacists, spice dealers, and so on), he was elected to serve as a prior in the summer of 1300. The priors were pivotal figures in the system of government; originally, they were simply the elected heads of the guilds, or *arti*, but after the restructuring of the government in 1282 they became what has been called the driving force of the system, and membership was thenceforth limited to a precisely defined oligarchical group of families. The Consiglio dei Quattordici (Council of Fourteen), which had been a form of cabinet, was abolished the following year, and the *priorato* became the executive arm of Florentine government. At first they represented only the three most senior *arti*: Cambio, Lana, and Calimala, but later they came to represent all seven of the *arti maggiori*. The number of priors in this new cabinet also increased steadily, from an original three to six, and then to twelve and eventually to sixteen. The voting system excluded all of the old aristocracy; only members of the *arti* were eligible to vote for the priors. Voting was organized by *sestiere,* or district, and candidates who wished to stand for the *priorato* were selected by the outgoing priors and by the *capitani* (elected heads) of the relevant *arti*. Their terms of office were extremely brief — a mere two months — but during this time they were all obliged to live together under one roof, day and night, and were forbidden to leave until their term of office was over. They could not stand for reelection for at least two years. These restrictive mechanisms were intended to reduce the formation of factions or power groups that might plot against the system with the intention of taking it over. The priors were originally housed in a small private palazzo, but at the very end of the duecento a new palace was begun for them, which became known, naturally enough, as the Palazzo dei Priori, or Palazzo del Popolo, which today is generally known as the Palazzo Vecchio.

To this complex system were added a further three bodies. One was the Consiglio dei Cento (Council of One Hundred), of which Dante was also a member, whose purpose was to control the treasury and taxation. The second was the Consiglio delle Arti, the overall governing body of the trade guilds, which after 1322 had to be consulted about all major issues of government policy. The third was the magistracy headed by the Capitani di Parte Guelfa, who initially administered property and goods confiscated from the defeated Ghibellines, and who were housed in their own palazzo near the Mercato Nuovo.

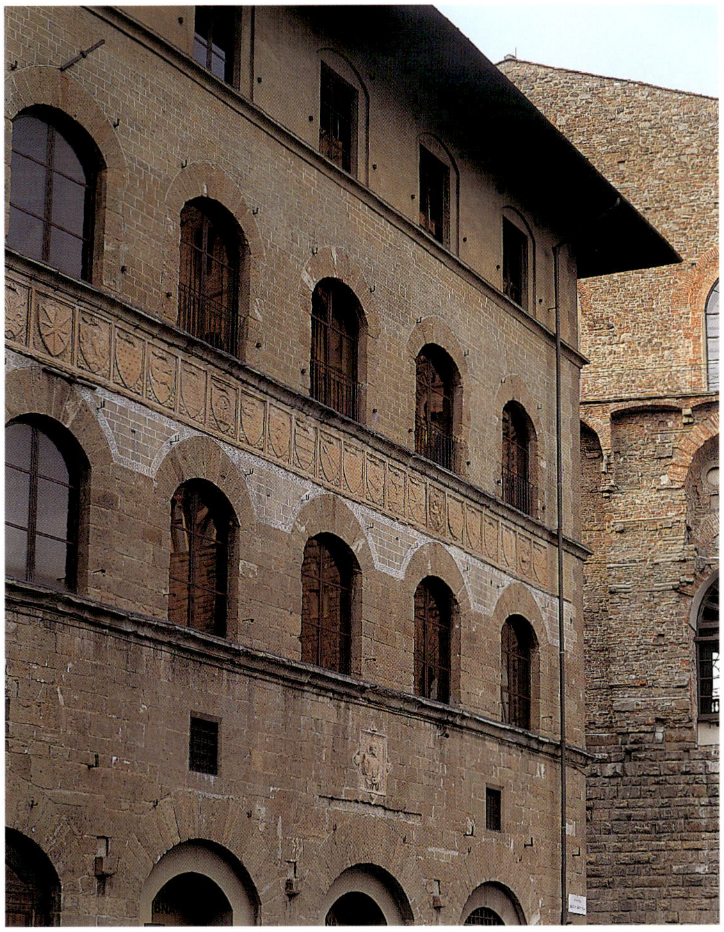

PALAZZO DEL TRIBUNALE DELLA MERCATANZIA

The facade of the palazzo shows the arms of the *arti maggiori*; among which are the eagle (Calimala), the lamb (Lana), and the star (Giudici e Notai).

The fundamental decrees of 1292 and 1295, the famous Ordinamenti, confirmed the rule of Florence by the merchant classes represented by the *arti maggiori*, while at the same time establishing its exclusively Guelf character, the Ghibellines having been defeated for the last time in 1289. This consolidation of power in the hands of the merchant class also eliminated threats from either social direction: from the common people or from the now totally disenfranchised ancient nobility. Florence's government was now "democratic" only in a highly qualified sense. While it was by no means a dynastic principality (until the rise of the Medici), neither could it be considered democratic in the modern sense. With a city population of perhaps 100,000 people, it has been estimated that, while voting rights applied to about one in five — that is, about 20,000 — almost all public posts were held in rotation by as few as 5,000 at the maximum, perhaps a good deal fewer still. However, despite all its defects, the city's government was entrusted to an elite group formed of the most dynamic, ambitious, and best educated men in Florence.

The Bargello (or Palazzo del Podestà)

"A city used to freedom can be more easily ruled through its own citizens, provided you do not wish to destroy it, than in any other way." **Niccolò Machiavelli**, *The Prince* (c. 1513–14) [3]

After the Guelfs' defeat of the Ghibellines, in 1250 a new governor was put in charge of the city to restore order. He was known as the Capitano del Popolo, and one of his responsibilities, in addition to defending the *borghesia* against the excesses of the nobility, was to administer the city's militia, which, like all of the chief posts of government, was drawn from members of the *arti*. The *capitano* needed a physical power base, and in 1255 a palazzo was begun that later became known as the Bargello. This was the first purpose-built structure in the history of Florence's government.

The present palazzo consists of three elements, but the first to be built was the section on the Via del Proconsolo. A fortified tower already stood at one corner of the site, at the junction with the Via Ghibellina, the Torre Volognana, and this tower was incorporated into the new building, which was completed in 1261. Between 1316 and 1320 it was extended by two upper stories, although a serious fire in 1332 caused considerable damage, and as a consequence the vaults of the first-floor halls had to be rebuilt. In this period, too, the uppermost level was completed, with its corbeling and crenellations. These works were carried out from 1340 to 1345 and are ascribed to Neri di Fioravanti; they also incorporated an imposing new hall for the Consiglio Generale — which today houses the

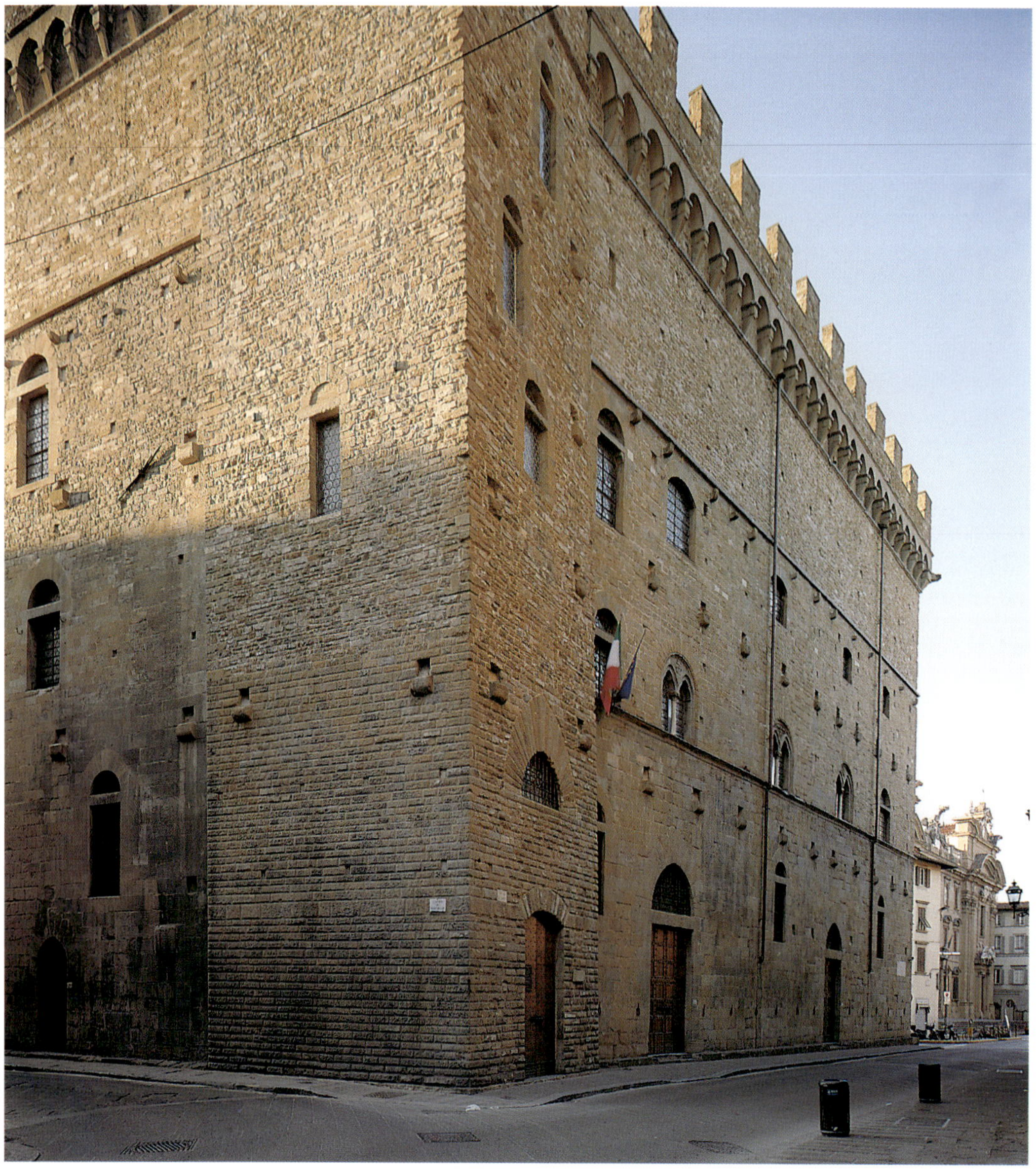

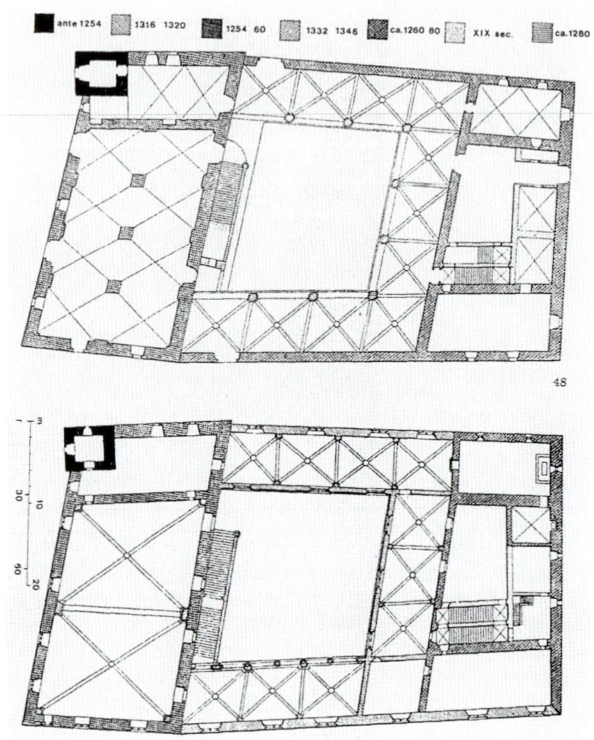

PALAZZO DEL BARGELLO

Left: the exterior has a semifortified appearance. The earlier Torre Volognana can be identified on the corner nearest to the viewer; the upper story of the palazzo was added after 1316. Above: plans of the two principal stories. The earliest section is the block on the Via del Proconsolo; the Torre Volognana is in the top left corner.

PALAZZO DEL BARGELLO

Right: view of the *cortile*, with its open staircase to the *piano nobile*. The stair was the last major element to be built, and was added after a fire in 1332. Bottom: the imposing Salone del Consiglio, built by Neri di Fioravante from 1340 to 1345 for general assemblies of the city's government. (Today it houses a superb collection of sculptures by Donatello.)

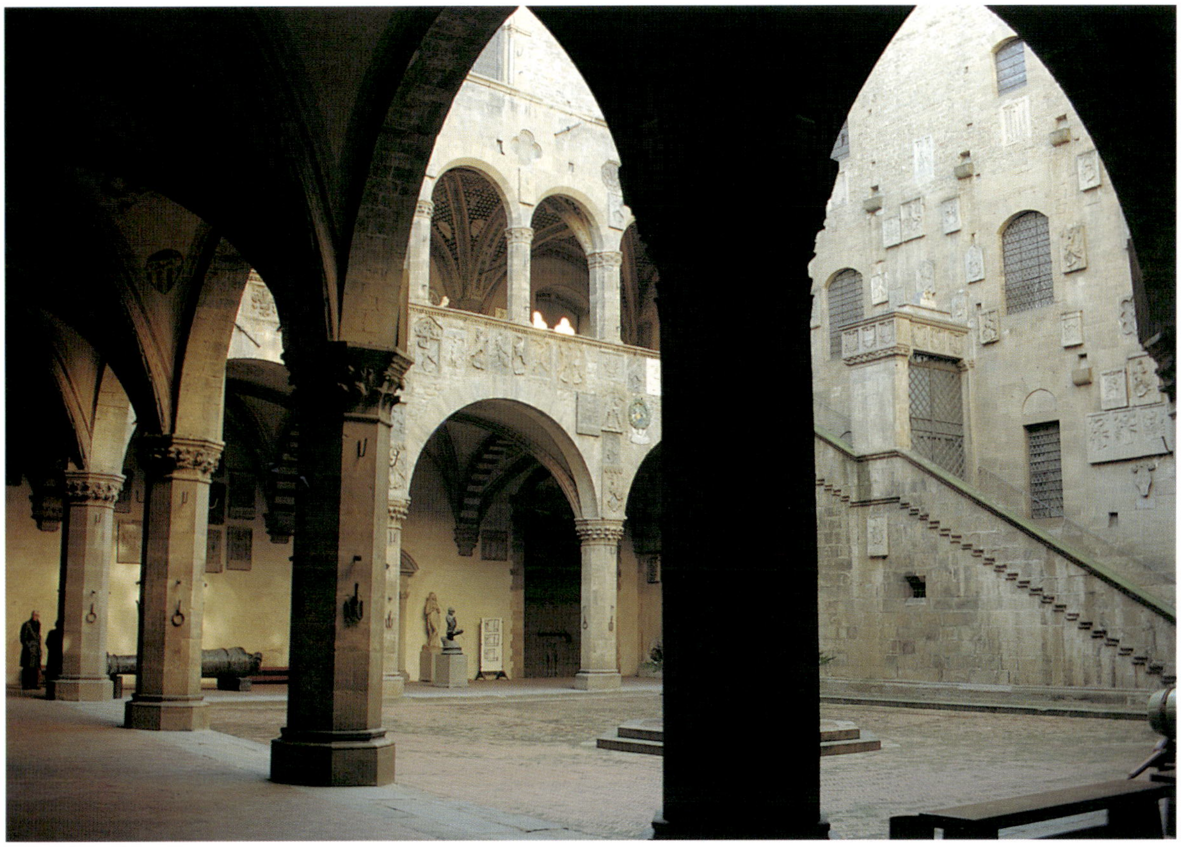

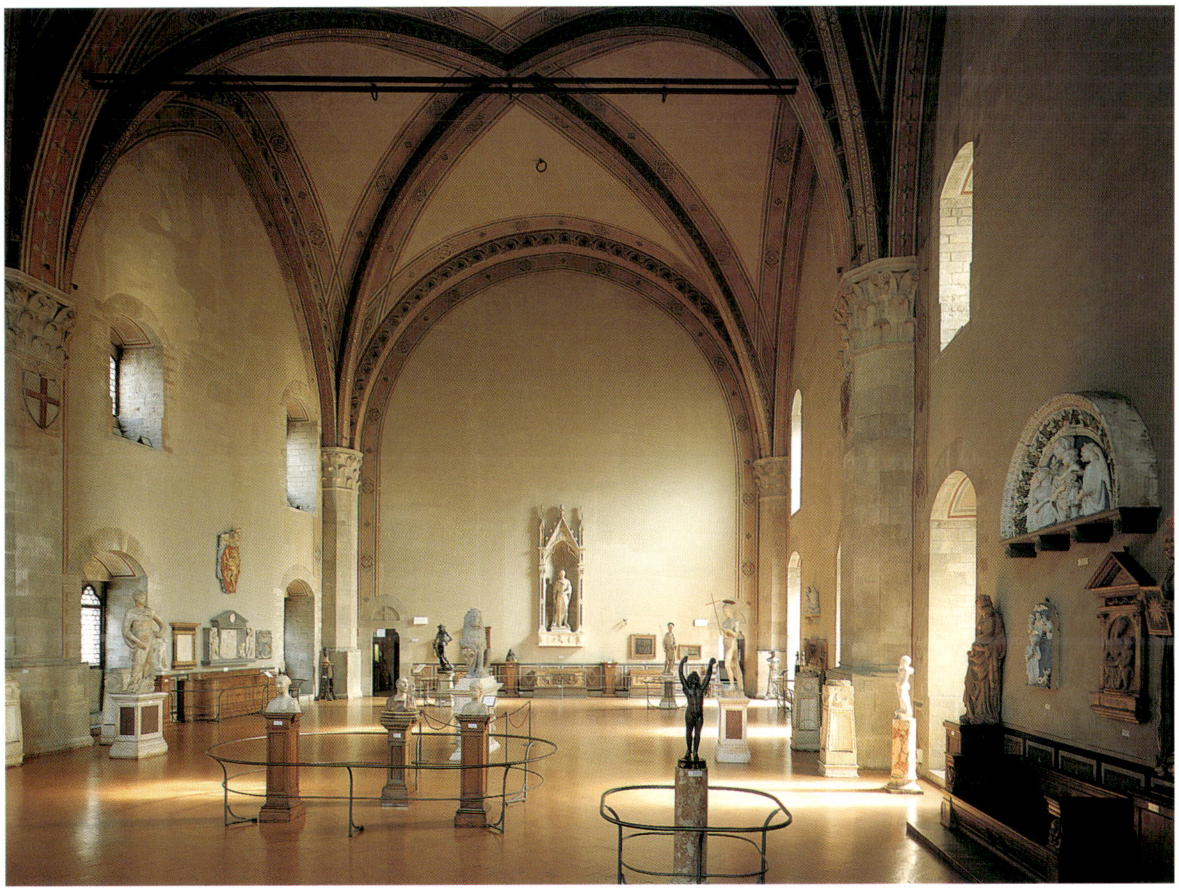

outstanding collection of works by Donatello.[4] Toward the end of the duecento, the extension of the palazzo eastward toward the rear was begun. The central *cortile* was the first new element to be completed, in about 1295, followed by the rear wing in the early 1300s. It was completed by about 1320, such that in this final form the Bargello occupies the entire city block defined by the Via del Proconsolo, Via Ghibellina, Via dell'Acqua, and Via della Vigna Vecchia. The final element to be built was the imposing new staircase in the *cortile*, which was constructed after 1345.

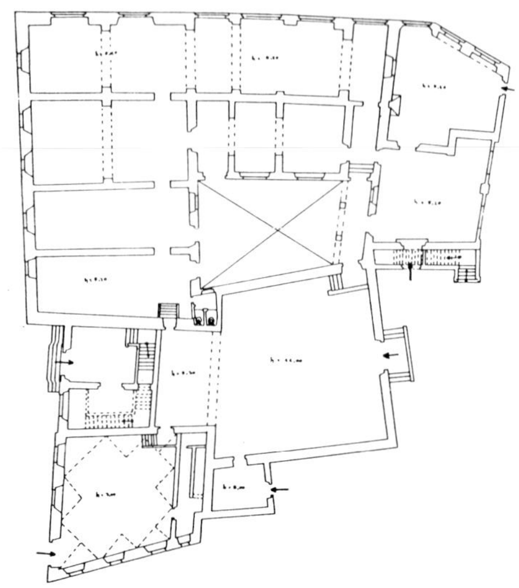

The final appearance of the Bargello marks something of a compromise. Clearly based on the contemporaneous private, semifortified palaces in the city, the palazzo naturally also had to incorporate specific requirements, such as the great hall for assemblies. Its overall appearance is noble and severe, a great monolithic block built entirely of stone, and generally symmetrical in the disposition of its principal features — that is, at least as far as the slightly irregular site and the incorporation of the Torre Volognana would allow. And although defense and security were clearly the determining factors in its external appearance, the interior of the palazzo, centered on its attractive, enclosed colonnaded *cortile*, is a clear indication that here aesthetic considerations played a major role; it is also an early example of the exterior/interior duality that was to remain a feature of all Florentine palaces, both public and private, well into the fifteenth century.[5]

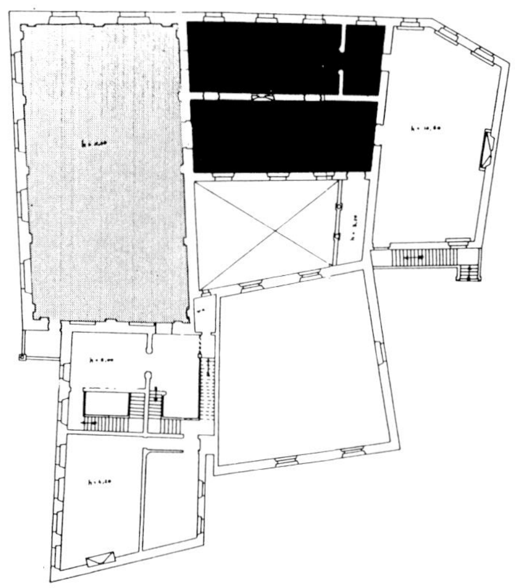

After the quattrocento the role of the *podestà* declined in importance, and with it the status of the palazzo, but it continued to house courts both civil and criminal, and the results of their deliberations were often signaled to the citizenry by the hanging of the bodies of malefactors from the facade. The name by which the palace is generally known today, the Bargello, dates from a later stage in its history thanks to the Medici who, in 1574, installed their Capitano di Giustizia, or Bargello, here. The *capitano* was the city's chief of police, and the building thenceforth contained a number of facilities associated with this post, not the least of which was the conversion of large sections of the palazzo into prisons; they included a number of the rooms on the first and second floors in the rear wings of the palazzo. Under the grand dukes the colonnades were also bricked up. The prisons survived until the nineteenth century, when, following their final removal, major restorations were undertaken; the present museum was established there in 1865.

The Palazzo di Parte Guelfa

"Lastly, in publick Buildings of this Sort, you must neglect none of those Rules which belong to the convenient and honourable Reception of a Multitude of Citizens and their easy Dismission." **Leon Battista Alberti**, *De re aedificatoria* (1452) [6]

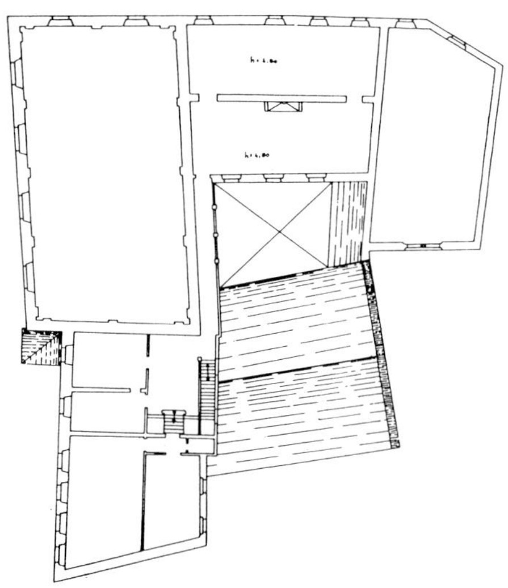

The Palazzo di Parte Guelfa, located on one side of what was then the larger extent of the Mercato Nuovo, marks another important example in the development of structures that performed specific civic and administrative functions, while at the same time in their design and general appearance clearly reflected the stresses, dangers, and social conditions in which they were built. The palazzo, begun in the duecento, has certain broad similarities to the Bargello, although it is a good deal less monumental in concept and its construction history is more fragmented. With the definitive victory of the Guelfs over the Ghibellines in 1289, the Capitani di Parte Guelfa grew to become a powerful magistracy. Although its original principal function was to administer the properties confiscated from the Ghibellines, the captaincy also became the body responsible for the building and maintenance of the city's fortifications as well as those throughout Tuscany, and for the maintenance of public buildings and highways.

The earliest nucleus of the palazzo dates from the duecento, although a complex series of modernizations and enlargements took place in the following century. From the end of the trecento dates the first order of the internal *cortile* and the base story of the great hall; in around 1420 Brunelleschi developed this wing further with the construction of an imposing new hall,

PALAZZO DI PARTE GUELFA

Right: the original body of the palazzo that dates from the thirteenth century is visible behind the external staircase, built as recently as the 1920s, on the basis of a fifteenth-century drawing.

Opposite: plans of the three stories, with the lowest floor at the top. Brunelleschi's hall is shown in gray on the second level.

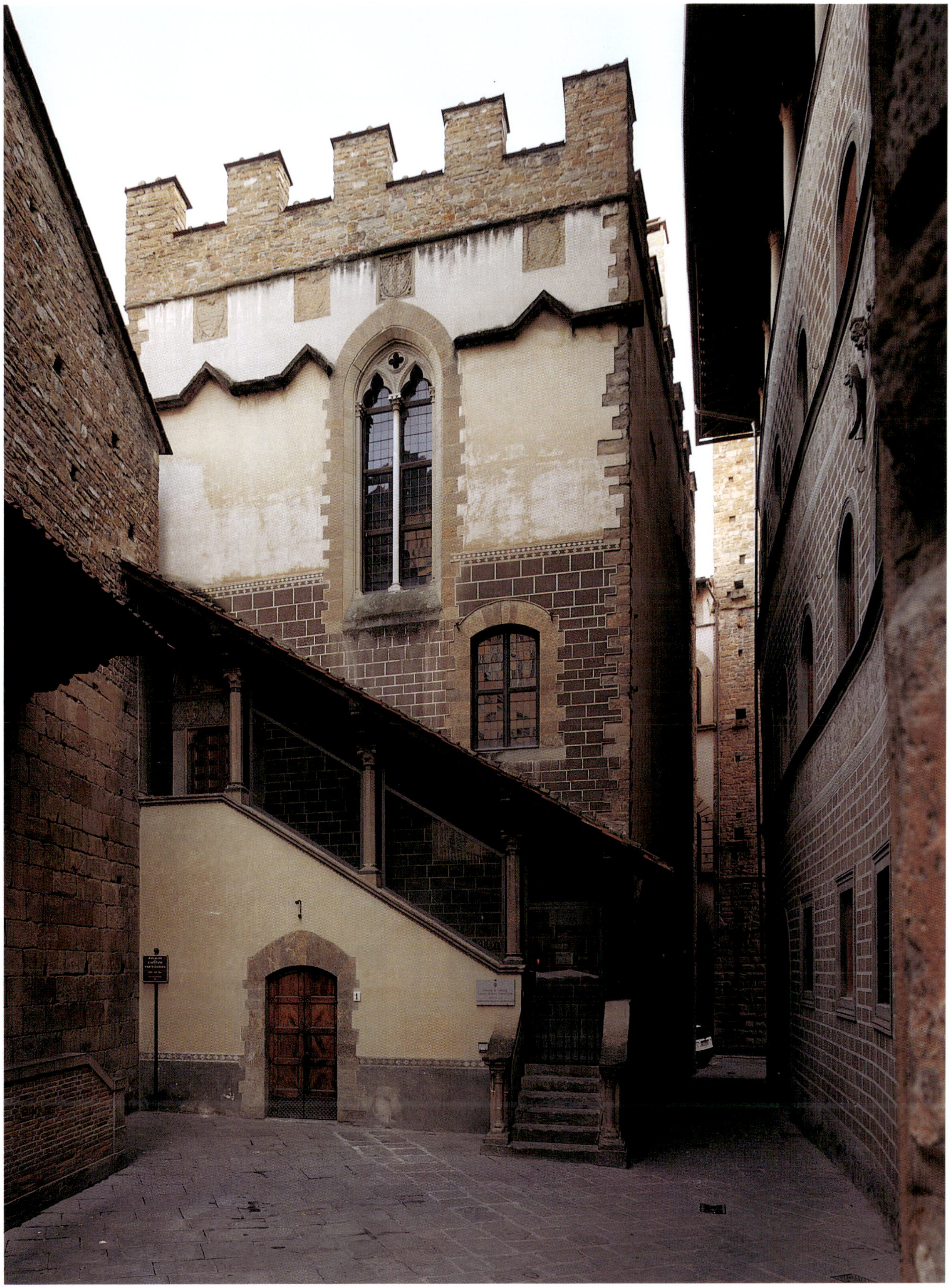

containing an audience chamber, on top of the earlier structure. This spacious hall, clean and uncompromisingly modern, with four bays of tall, arched windows, was a radical departure in stylistic terms from the older elements.[7] The interior has a similar clarity and simplicity, which was later compromised by the insertion of Vasari's coffered ceiling. Brunelleschi's new corridor linking this hall with the older parts of the building provides a stylistic link between the trecento and this new era. Nevertheless, the palazzo remains an archetypal late medieval semifortified palace, with its irregular plan, its open *cortile*, and its covered external staircase. The whole embodies the essentially evolutionary nature of many such structures, which were often adapted, modernized, and enlarged on a number of occasions to change with their evolving functions.

The locations of both the Bargello and the Palazzo di Parte Guelfa within the city's urban fabric are of some significance. Both were located at the very heart of the oldest nucleus of Florence; the Bargello is on the Via del Proconsolo, one of the streets of the grid originally set out by the Romans; the Palazzo Guelfa is even more centrally located, a few yards from the Mercato Nuovo and just west of the principal north–south axis of the Via Calimala and Via Roma. In its immediate surroundings were concentrated the city's major guildhalls, banks, and merchants' offices. The palazzo thus reinforced the importance of this zone as a hub of administration and governance; but it was the last of the triumvirate of medieval palaces, the Palazzo del Popolo, that was to complete this concentration of governmental structures, and thus, located halfway between the two earlier buildings, provided the link in the chain, the heart of Florentine government for three centuries.

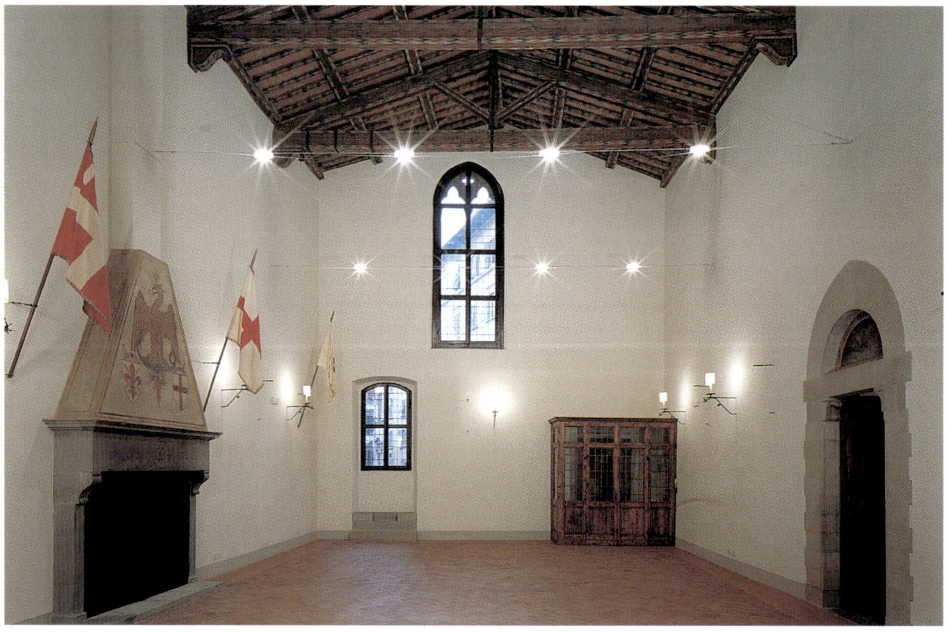

PALAZZO DI PARTE GUELFA

One of the medieval upper halls; this part of the building was not modernized by Brunelleschi.

The Piazza della Signoria

"In the midst of the city — in the Piazza of the Grand Duke, adorned with beautiful statues and the Fountain of Neptune — rises the Palazzo Vecchio, with its enormous overhanging battlements, and the Great Tower that watches over the whole town."

Charles Dickens, *Pictures from Italy* (1844) [8]

If the complex of ecclesiastical structures around the cathedral represents the hub of Florentine faith and spiritual identity, then the Piazza della Signoria, a few hundred meters to the south, represents the institution of Florentine temporal power. The square is dominated by the imposing volume of the Palazzo Vecchio, which represents the power and prosperity of the era when Florence was a free Comune.

The location of the piazza is close to the heart of the city's built-up form since the Roman foundation. Two series of archaeological investigations — in 1974 and from 1982 to 1989 — have established much of the pre-medieval urban structure, and in particular the chief buildings from the Roman and early Christian eras. In the Roman era the area of the piazza was close to the forum, which lay two blocks farther north, and even closer to the city's southern gate. A large bath complex was built in the time of Hadrian, covering the eastern part of the present piazza; on the south side, near the loggia, remains of a substantial gate have also been identified, as well as a structure built for dyeing fabrics on a large scale. From the slightly later early Christian period, the earliest basilica of Santa Cecilia, probably from the fifth century, was identified in the southwestern part of the square; and the locations of two churches from the medieval period, San Romolo on the north side and a later reconstruction of Santa Cecilia, were identified.[9] Among the lay buildings now also recently discovered, by far the most significant is the cluster of houses and towers of the Uberti clan, an important Ghibelline faction, whose seat of power this was; it was the destruction of the properties of the Uberti that provided at least some of the land for what was to evolve into the Piazza della Signoria. The chronicler Villani claimed that the former Uberti palazzi were turned into a paved public square to ensure that the land could never again be built upon by the Uberti or any other disgraced Ghibellines.

The great square that slowly developed here evolved in several piecemeal stages, with no clearly defined master plan. It took around a century to ultimately achieve the broadly L–shaped configuration that we see today, with the palazzo looming over the internal angle of the L, its great stone mass dominating the entire square. There are records, for example, of demolitions carried out in 1307 to expand the palazzo's setting, and again in 1318. In 1330 an important civic gesture was the decision to pave the piazza with brick and stone, in order (as it was recorded at the time) "to render its appearance more decorous, even and symmetrical than any other square or street in

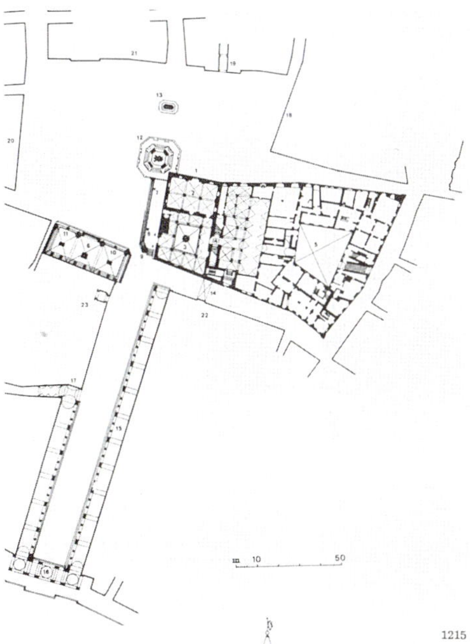

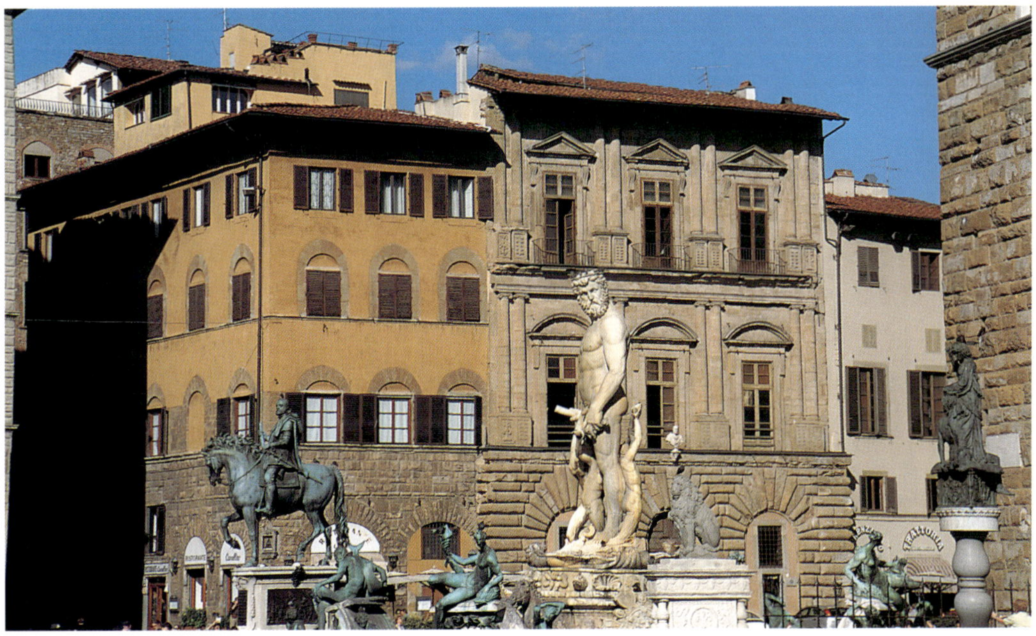

PIAZZA DELLA SIGNORIA

Above: plan with the Palazzo Vecchio to the southeast, the Loggia dei Lanzi on the south side, and the Uffizi running south toward the Arno. Above, right: view of the piazza from the west, with Palazzo Uguccioni dominating the center of the north side.

the city" — a clear indication of the desire to render the square preeminent in civic dignity. As the form of the piazza evolved, its symbolic role in relation to the Palazzo del Popolo (later Palazzo Vecchio) became steadily clearer and more important. Physically, the square wrapped around two sides of the palazzo, such that the latter became the fulcrum of the spatial composition; and functionally, the piazza became the parvis or external space annexed by the palazzo for numerous public and state events and ceremonies.

The configuration of the urban fabric in this location immediately prior to the decision to build the Palazzo del Popolo is still not easy to establish with precision. However, the site of the palazzo itself, the original nucleus, that is, had great significance in the city's overall structure. It was located just to the east of the Via de' Calzaiuoli, the axis that connected the putative new piazza with the cathedral, and that originally continued south to the city's walls. The city's hub of political power was thus to be quite distinct, and at a clear distance from the hub of religious power: Church and state defined and separated. In this period, though, the Via de' Cerchi, one block east from the Via de' Calzaiuoli, retained much more importance than it has today, and the original nucleus of the palazzo, the main entrance of which was at the northern end, was thus approached almost directly on this axis from the direction of the cathedral. It was only with the later, staged westward expansion of the piazza that its center of gravity also shifted westward, and the Via de' Calzaiuoli increased in importance (while that of the Via de' Cerchi declined) as the principal direct link between Church and state. Conversely, the palazzo itself has expanded in stages toward the east, well beyond the compact confines of this original nucleus on the piazza.[10]

The parcel of land on which the first stage of the Palazzo del Popolo was to be constructed had been the property of the Foraboschi family before its acquisition by the Comune for the new edifice. According to Villani, this fact, together with the desire not to build on Uberti land, led to the curiously rhomboidal plan of the palazzo (a decision that Villani himself considered, for aesthetic reasons, to be highly regrettable). The history of the development of the palazzo is essentially a process of eastward expansion from the original nucleus on the corner of the piazza. The direct effect onto the piazza of these later stages of expansion was therefore fairly limited, although the form of the square also continued to evolve in a sense parallel to, but distinct from, the physical expansion of the palazzo.

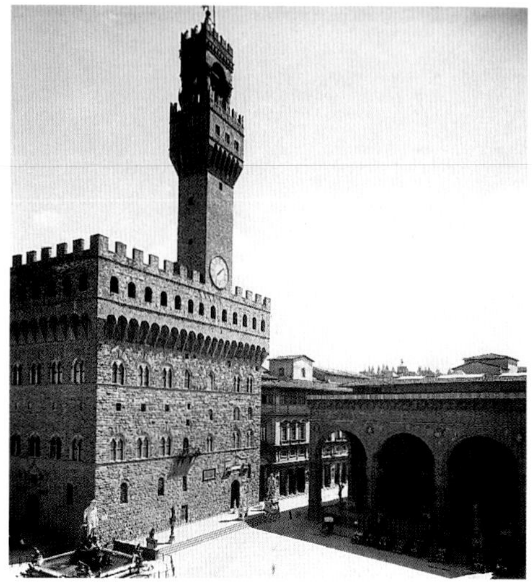

LOGGIA DELLA SIGNORIA
(LOGGIA DEI LANZI)

Above: sometimes attributed to Orcagna, it was built between 1376 and 1382 for the Comune but later was taken over by the Medici as a combined guardhouse and sculpture gallery.

Opposite: as is evident in this detail, the style is a late Gothic, and has several affinities with the detailing of the interior of the cathedral. It is decorated with the Florentine lion, or *marzocco*.

Much of the definitive expansion and regularization of the piazza took place in a series of measures during the course of the trecento. The first stage of the palazzo, the "palazzo pubblico," was built during the period from 1316 to 1319, and to coincide with this enhancement of the piazza's role, two figures of a stone lion, the Marzocco, a symbol of the city, were transferred there from the Bigallo, near the cathedral, and re-sited in the location where the loggia presently stands.[11] In 1342 the Florentines nominated Gualtieri di Brienne as their overlord *in perpetuo*, for the first and only time; Gualtieri at once set about transforming the immediate environs of the palazzo. Although his despotic rule was to be very brief, he strengthened the entrances to the palazzo by building new outer defenses, and commenced demolitions to the south and west, principally to form an open cordon sanitaire or field of fire, around the building, the more easily to defend it from armed insurrection. The measures enhanced the urban context of the palace, although despite his precautions an insurrection did, in fact, take place, and Gualtieri was forced to renounce his role.

On the west side of the piazza, Santa Cecilia was reconstructed in 1341. (Both the church and the Loggia dei Pisani were demolished in the nineteenth century, just before the present Palazzo Lavisan was built, in 1871.) A little later, from 1349 to 1356, the north side of the piazza was defined in the manner that can be seen today; this expansion involved the demolition of the church of San Romolo and its reconstruction farther north to conform to the new building line. The eastern end of the piazza also received its definitive late medieval form when, in 1359, the Palazzo del Tribunale della Mercatanzia was built there. Founded in 1318, the *tribunale* was the magistracy at which all issues relating to the *arti* and their membership were debated; it was concerned chiefly with legal and financial matters, and was usually headed by a foreigner, following the same principle of neutrality as that which governed the appointment of the *podestà* and the *capitano*; he chaired an advisory board formed by members of the *arti*. Further demolitions took place in 1362, when "the houses that were adjacent to the Piazza of the Palace of the Signori . . . toward the north, were 'pushed' further back."[12] This contemporary description probably refers to the completion of the long northern side of the piazza in its final new alignment.

The middle decades of the trecento saw more debates as to how the physical form, and hence the civic dignity, of the piazza could be further enhanced. The first recorded debates regarding the construction of the Loggia della Signoria date from 1356, although the structure was not actually begun for another twenty years. When it was finally completed, in 1382, this ambitious project marked another key stage in the development of the monumental architectural quality of the

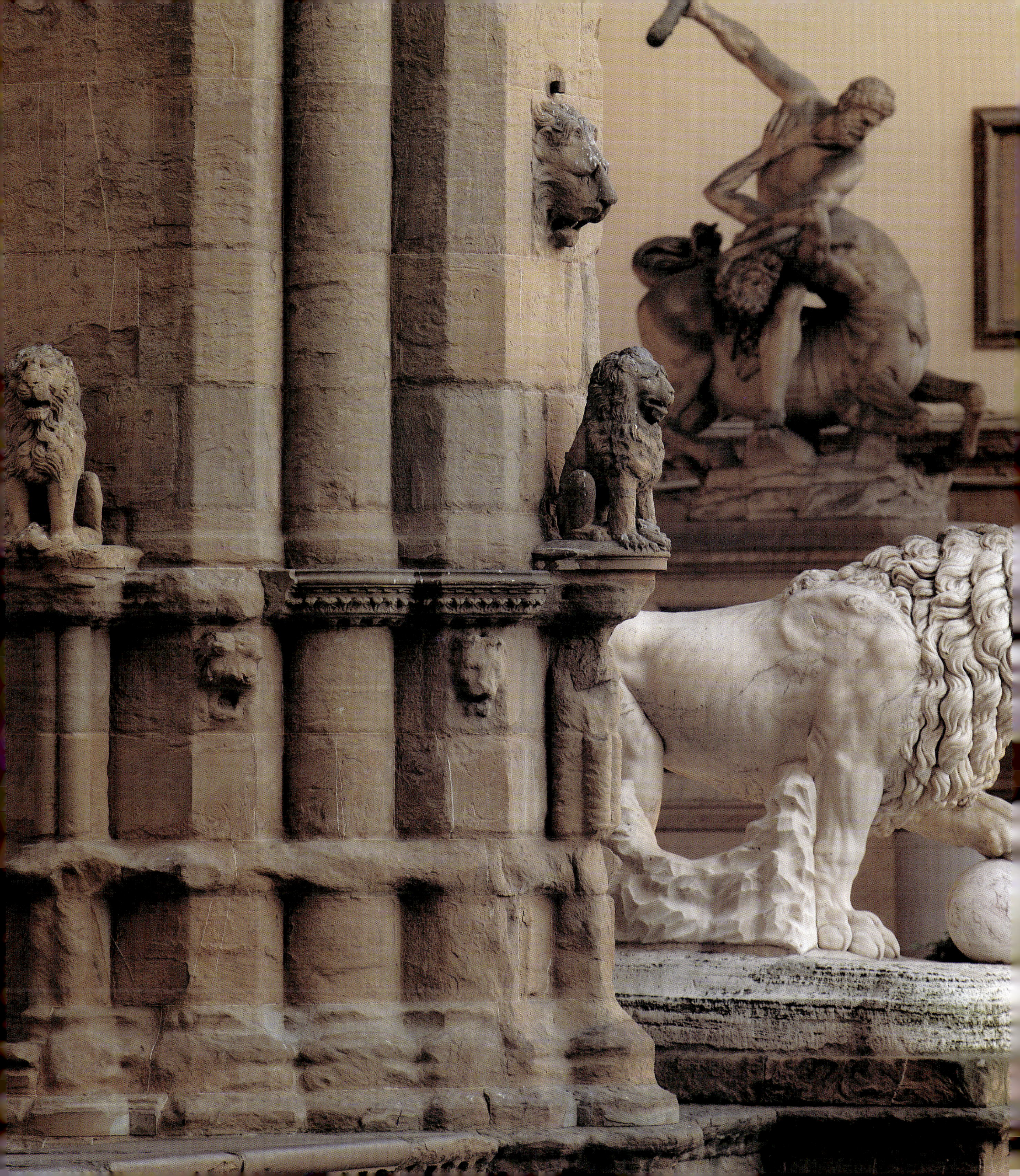

square. Yet despite the many efforts to define and dignify the piazza, many of the remaining buildings surrounding it were still by no means particularly distinguished.

The Loggia della Signoria (later known as the Loggia dei Lanzi) transformed the southern part of the square. Although inscribed in the long tradition of the development of public or semipublic logge, a tradition particularly strong in Florence, it remains a highly unusual and distinctive work. Its immediate forerunner could be said to be the Loggia del Bigallo, built two or three decades earlier on the key corner near the cathedral, but in terms of scale and grandeur the Loggia della Signoria really remains in a class of its own. It was built between 1376 and 1381 under the supervision of Benci di Cione and Simone Talenti in a style that represents a hybrid between the simple, spacious, and rigorously disciplined detailing of the Florentine Gothic in the tradition of Arnolfo (particularly evident in the great piers, which are closely related to those of the cathedral) and the apparently "pre-Renaissance" forms of its three massive semicircular arches. The three large cross vaults also represent a further stylistic refinement of those of the cathedral. The loggia, the original design of which is traditionally attributed to Andrea di Cione (also known as Orcagna), is still sometimes referred to as the Loggia di Orcagna, although he died eight years before the work was begun.[13]

LOGGIA DELLA SIGNORIA (LOGGIA DEI LANZI) (below, left)

Detail of *Perseus* (1554) by Benvenuto Cellini, one of many works commissioned or acquired by the Medici.

PIAZZA DELLA SIGNORIA (below)

The Neptune fountain (c. 1563–75) by Bartolommeo Ammannati, assisted by Giambologna, was installed under the patronage of Cosimo I, one of his many works of urban development, as was the adjacent equestrian statue, again by Giambologna.

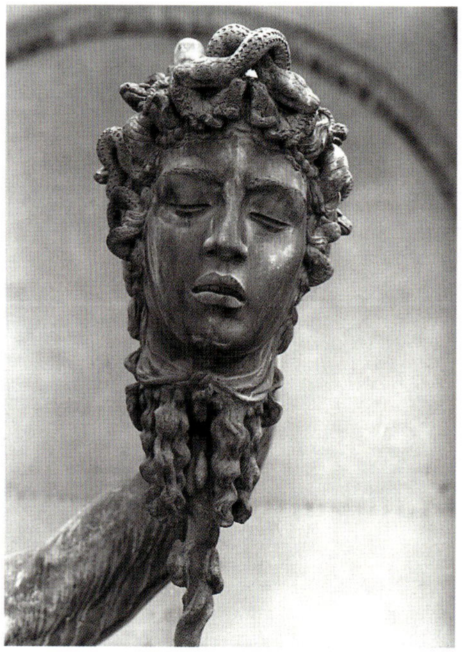

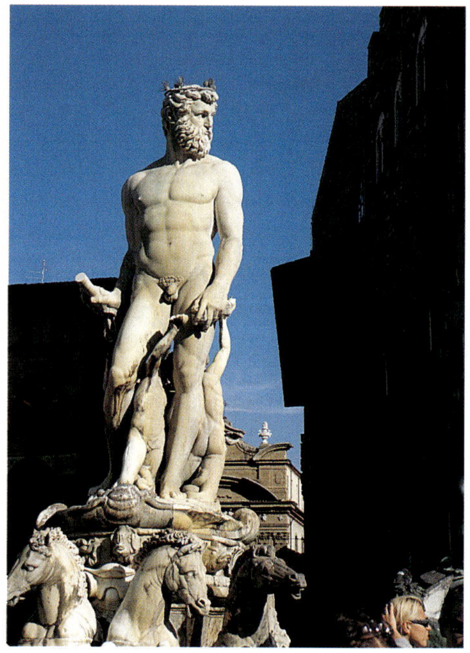

Both Benci and Talenti were closely associated with the construction of the cathedral in this period, hence the clear analogy of the detailing of the piers. The structure as a whole has a simple majesty whose light, spacious form contrasts sharply with the solid, massive severity of the adjacent palazzo, a contrast that can be read as that between the more enlightened aspects of Florentine *civitas* and *campanilismo* in this period and the expression of pure political power (and potential physical force) represented by the palazzo.

The loggia addresses the piazza directly and forms a kind of covered extension of it, so broad and tall are its arches, almost cathedral-like in scale themselves, and very much grander and more imposing than those of any other public loggia built elsewhere in this period. The four figures of the Virtues in the spandrels, contemporaneous with the building itself, were designed by Agnolo Gaddi and further emphasize the civic nature of the building; the elegant crowning parapet, itself something of a hybrid between civic and militaristic models, masks an extensive rooftop terrace, to which access was later gained from the Uffizi galleries.

Historically, like the city itself, the loggia has had two rather different "lives," the first under the Comune and the second under the Medici. In its first life the loggia played a vital civic role as the place from which the priors were elected and proclaimed, as well as performing a number of other public functions. Its floor level was raised somewhat above that of the piazza so that it formed a kind of stage for the assembled populace below. However, after the establishment of Medici dynastic rule, and particularly after the duchy was recognized, the loggia's civic role declined considerably. Its alternative name, the Loggia dei Lanzi, represents this second life, when the guard of Alessandro I and Cosimo I, formed of Austrian *Landsknechts*, was based here; their name was Italianized to Lanzichenecchi, and hence abbreviated to Lanzi. The present general appearance of the interior of the loggia also dates from the reign of Cosimo I, who began to turn the space into a form of semipublic art gallery for his collection of classical sculptures. This new use is a further example of

GIOVANNI STRADANO, *I FUOCHI DI SAN GIOVANNI*, 1558 (Florence, Palazzo Vecchio)

The painting depicts the fireworks display in the piazza on the patronal festival of San Giovanni; the Loggia della Signoria dominates in the background.

the annexation of what was formerly a Comune facility to become another element among the properties of the principate, a transfer symbolized by the installation of Benvenuto Cellini's *Perseus* in 1554, as recorded in Cellini's autobiography. Ultimately, the Medici collection assembled here included both antique Roman works and more recent sculptures commissioned by members of the family; among the latter pieces was Giambologna's *Rape of the Sabines* of 1583.

In the later trecento, though, at about the same time that the Loggia della Signoria was being constructed, another loggia was debated and built fairly rapidly, the now-destroyed Loggia dei Pisani, which stood on the west side of the square, next to Santa Cecilia. It was so called because it was built by Pisan prisoners of war, following their decisive defeat by the Florentines in the battles of 1362 to 1364, and made a further important contribution to the civic dignity of this end of the square.

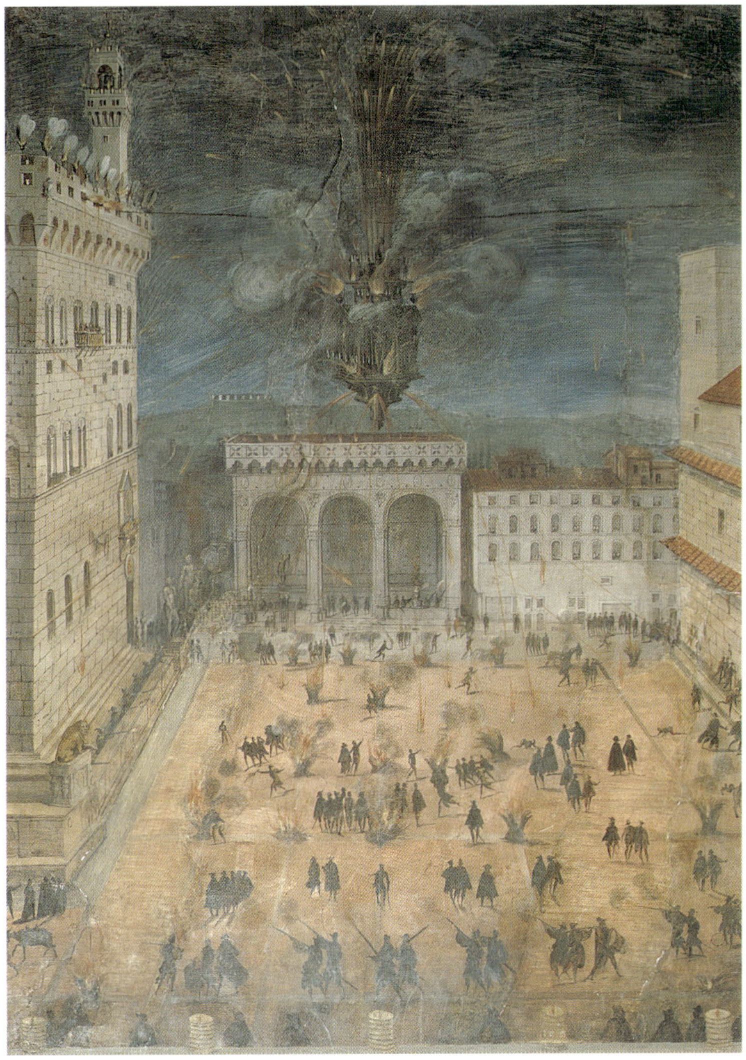

The 1380s saw the final series of legislative measures to regularize and impose order and discipline onto the piazza. In 1386–87 Santa Cecilia was rebuilt slightly farther west, yet again enlarging the extent of the square, while at the same time ordinances were issued to unify the appearance of the west and north sides with continuous colonnades. To accompany this architectural enhancement, in 1385 measures were taken that forbade certain unsuitable trades in the piazza, including prostitution; henceforth, only trades that would not be detrimental to the square's dignity would be permitted. But no major building intervention was carried out in the piazza until the later Renaissance era, when two important transformations finally gave it its present appearance, with the exception of the nineteenth-century reconstructions on the west side.

The first of these two interventions was the Fontana del Nettuno, one of many celebratory works initiated by Cosimo I. The fountain was largely the work of Bartolommeo Ammannati, assisted by Giambologna and others, and although it has great importance in scenographic and urbanistic terms, the quality of the principal sculpture has been the butt of severe criticism, most famously in a pithy comment Michelangelo is alleged to have uttered: that, in effect, Ammannati had ruined a perfectly good piece of marble. Nevertheless, the fountain was arguably the first attempt to lighten the severe, though undoubtedly imposing, appearance of the piazza, dominated by the austere mass of the Palazzo Vecchio. The gleaming white marble fountain brought not only a new material, but also the element of water, into the square for the first time. It was soon joined by the new equestrian statue of Cosimo I, a late work in bronze by Giambologna, completed in 1598. Ammannati's fountain had been located in what appears to be a rather awkward position, just beyond the projecting northwest corner of the palazzo, with its surrounding steps and railings physically linking it to the palazzo. This location is in fact on the direct axis into the piazza from the Via de' Cerchi, the route that was formerly the important link between the cathedral precinct and the seat of government. The new statue of Cosimo reinforced this axial progression even further, since it was positioned at the very center of the space left between the fountain and the north face of the piazza, again exactly on the Via de' Cerchi axis. Including Vasari's two long blocks of the Uffizi, all of these elements now linked together to form a straight axis right through the entire complex, the elements in this important axial progression now consisting of — from north to south — the Via de' Cerchi, leading from the dome of the cathedral; the statue of Cosimo; the Neptune fountain; the west facade of the Palazzo Vecchio; and finally, the long route down the center of the Uffizi, terminating in the loggia in front of the banks of the Arno.

THE DEATH OF SAVONAROLA, LATE FIFTEENTH CENTURY

Anonymous painting probably dating from shortly after the event of 1498 (Florence, Museo di San Marco).

Since 1302 when the first element of the Palazzo Vecchio was built, the Piazza della Signoria has formed the hub of Florentine political life, despite the fact that in many periods, particularly the

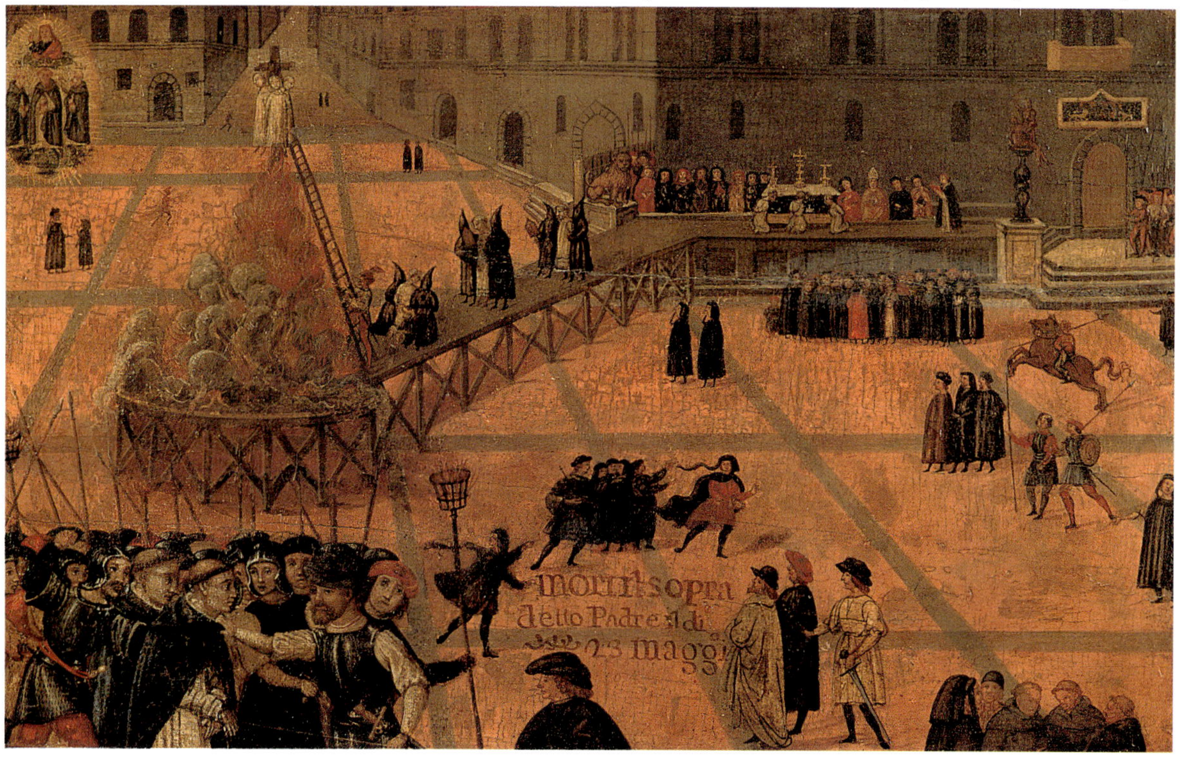

trecento, much of it must have appeared to be a permanent construction site. The bell in the tower of the palazzo summoned the citizenry to assemble to debates and to vote, while the nearby loggia was the focus of many civic events, three significant examples of which were the presentation of priors before their election, public proclamations of the law, and the reception of foreign ambassadors to the city. Almost all of the most important episodes of Florence's political history have been played out in the piazza, from the Ciompi (wool-workers') riots of 1378 to the epochal speeches given here by Mussolini 550 years later. A sample handful of the more outstanding events, although by no means comprehensive, will nevertheless give an indication of the vital role that the piazza has always played in Florentine life.

The Ciompi revolt represents perhaps the most dramatic example of the piazza's crucial role in Florence's turbulent social history. Between June and August 1378, a series of disturbances by the widely unemployed wool workers culminated in a large popular revolt on 12 July in the piazza. The demonstrators burned down the nearby palazzo of the Arte della Lana (the wool guild), and in the piazza itself they stormed the Palazzo del Popolo, drove the priors out, and installed their own representative as *gonfaloniere*, or standard-bearer. The Ciompi revolt was doomed to fail, but the group's attack on the very seat of power symbolized clearly the function of both palazzo and piazza as the hub of entrenched political power.

The brief and equally tumultuous episode of the Savonarola Republic offers another example of the function of the piazza as the scene of violent political change and upheaval. On at least two occasions during the phenomenal rise and equally dramatic fall from power of this incendiary priest, the piazza formed the very heart of the turbulent events. Having risen with extraordinary rapidity and widespread support for his fiery, apocalyptical messages, Savonarola called for the physical destruction of all goods and possessions deemed to be idolatrous or lascivious. There followed a dramatic bonfire of the "vanities" in the piazza in 1497 during Carnevale, a time of year when Florentines normally engaged in the opposite extremes of behavior. A great pile of goods and property was assembled in the square around a large wooden scaffold, and accumulated into a giant pyramid of luxuries: books, clothes, paintings, jewelry, and any artifact that was considered blasphemous or idolatrous, including gaming cards, carnival masks, and so on; all were consumed in the flames. Savonarola's mesmeric power was to be short-lived, however, and just over a year later, on 23 May 1498, a second bonfire was assembled. Savonarola had in a short time alienated many of the powerful Medici faction, as well as the new pope, Alessandro VI — Roderigo Borgia — and was summoned to Rome. After refusing to rescind his fiery theological philosophies, he was excommunicated. Returning to Florence, he found that there, too, his opponents were gathering force, and a mob set fire to the entrance of the monastery of San Marco, where he had fled for safety. He was arrested and brought to the Palazzo Vecchio, where he was twice tortured before confessing and was found guilty of heresy. The priest was condemned, together with two of his followers. As the contemporary diarist Luca Landucci described the final episode of the story: "When all three had been hanged, a fire was made on the platform upon which gunpowder was put and set alight, so that the said fire burst out with a noise of rockets and cracking. In a few hours they were burnt, their legs and arms gradually dropping off. . . . Then they fetched carts and carried the last bits of dust to the Arno, by the Ponte Vecchio, in order that no remains should be found."[14]

Three centuries later, when Florence conceded its government to the seemingly invincible Napoleon in March 1799, the piazza was crowded with different images: The French tricolor flew from the palazzo and the loggia, and a temporary amphitheater was built in the piazza to welcome the arrival of the occupying General Gauthier. Napoleon's symbolic tree of liberty, supposedly representing the death of tyrannical regimes, was erected in the piazza, although the honeymoon between natives and occupying forces did not last long; within weeks there were disturbances and demonstrations, and the tree was destroyed. These were the foretastes of widespread revolt throughout Tuscany, and after barely three months the French withdrew from the city.[15]

It was to be a tricolor of slightly different hues that was displayed in the piazza in 1859: the symbolic green, white, and red of the forces of Italian unification. The ministers of the last grand duke's crumbling government resigned on 25 April of that year, and two days later another vast, popular crowd assembled in the Piazza Maria Antonia (the present Piazza della Indipendenza) before marching to the Palazzo Vecchio. Grand Duke Leopold left the city quietly that evening, and after a few months of provisional government Florence joined the kingdom of Italy. For five years thereafter the city was the capital of the newly unified nation.

In more recent times, during the Mussolini government, the square witnessed violent conflicts between the Fascists and their opponents on several occasions. In June 1924 one of the city's leading Fascists, Renato Ricci, headed a huge parade through Florence, culminating in a rally in the piazza. On another occasion, in 1930, Mussolini gave a speech to as many as 100,000 Florentines gathered in and around the piazza.

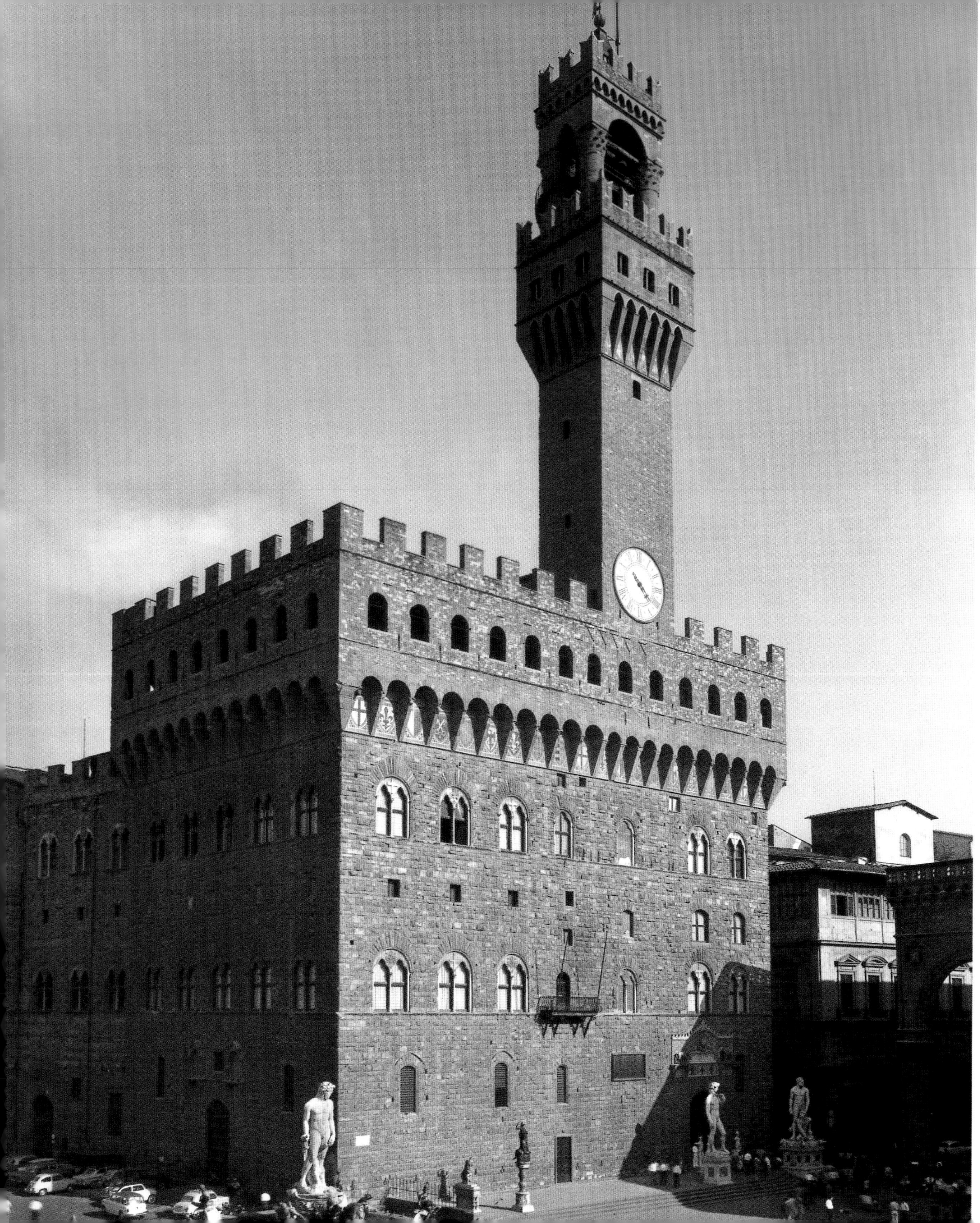

PALAZZO DEL POPOLO (PALAZZO VECCHIO)

Opposite: view of the facade onto the Piazza della Signoria. Its appearance represents a balance between the needs of defense (chiefly against local insurrection) and the dignity appropriate to the seat of government.

Below: the main *cortile* of the palazzo, remodeled by Michelozzo in 1453 and decorated by Vasari in 1565.

But this brief sketch of some of the defining roles this great square has played in Florence's political history should be balanced by a note on how it functioned in more peaceful times. The piazza was the focus of countless festivals, weddings, state visits, and other pageants over the centuries. The great patronal festival of San Giovanni was one such occasion. The long procession that wound around the city center met in the piazza, with a series of models of castles mounted onto wagons, each representing one of Florence's subject cities. The festival skillfully combined the devout with popular spectacle, and the procession of sacred relics that culminated in the Piazza del Duomo was one further element in a day of festivities that also included a horse race, much like the famous Palio still held today at Siena. Equally typical of the more festive events that still enliven the piazza today is the *calcio storico*, the soccer match played on midsummer's day. It originated in 1530, with the celebration of Florence's heroic — although ultimately unsuccessful — resistance to the imperial armies during the infamous siege. Similar spectacles enliven the other great squares in the city, notably that of Santa Croce, but the football match in the Piazza della Signoria has a clear symbolic link with the hub of Florentine government, and with civic and patriotic identity.

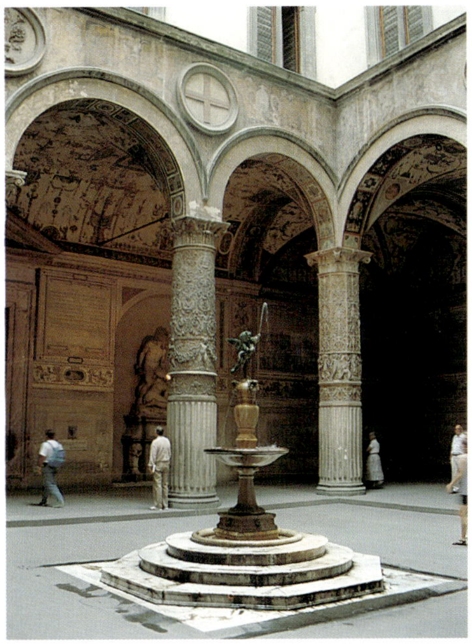

The Palazzo del Popolo (Palazzo Vecchio)

"In the said year of 1298 . . . where the said palace was built, there stood formerly the ancient houses of the Uberti, rebels of Florence, and Ghibellines, and on this place there was set out a piazza, so that they may never be rebuilt here."

Giovanni Villani, *Cronica fiorentina* (c. 1330) [16]

The noble, daunting mass of the Palazzo del Popolo was the defining image of Florentine power in the Middle Ages. From its original nucleus, hurriedly erected in a mere three years in 1299, this great, sophisticated edifice grew in stages to become the nerve center of one of the wealthiest states in Europe. Just as its complex construction history reflects the many stages of Florence's evolving systems of government, so has the name of the palazzo itself changed to reflect these phases. When it was built, it was generally known as the Palazzo del Popolo, or Palazzo dei Priori, since its original raison d'être was to house these highest officers of the government. Later, in the fifteenth century, it was more generally known as the Palazzo della Signoria; then, after the Medici had made the palazzo their own definitive power base in 1540, it became identified as the Palazzo Ducale, reflecting Cosimo I's new status. Still later, after Palazzo Pitti had, in turn, become the center of the Medici court, the building began to be referred to as the Palazzo Vecchio (old palace), not simply because of its intrinsic age, but because Palazzo Pitti was the "Palazzo Nuovo" (new palace) of what was now the grand duchy. Today it is still typically identified as the Palazzo Vecchio.[17]

The immediate political context of the construction of the earliest part of the palazzo is of considerable significance. Before building began, the priors had met in the private palace of the Cerchi banking family; however, in 1299 the violent factionalism that had divided the city between Guelfs and Ghibellines for decades saw new rivalries between "white" and "black" Guelfs. The Cerchi were leaders of the "white" Guelf faction, and so it was urgently necessary to find a more impartial place of assembly. Bloody and ferocious incidents on Florence's streets continued intermittently for three or four years, during which time the palazzo was hurriedly being built. Its general design and appearance can thus be seen as a compromised response to a highly volatile political situation, but one that, at the same time, had to provide the city with an appropriate emblem for civic pride and patriotic identity.

The original design is traditionally attributed to Arnolfo di Cambio, although according to many, he died in around 1302 — that is, just when the main body of the building was approaching completion. However, others have dated his death as late as 1310, in which case he would have seen the entire work, including the imposing tower, through to its conclusion. This first palazzo was freestanding on three sides, and its long eastern flank faced a narrow lane, which was built over when the later extensions were added. The church of San Pier Scheraggio bounded the site immediately to the south. The extent of the original palace is represented today by the purely symmetrical, five-bay north facade onto the piazza, with its great central portal, together with the longer west facade, dominated by its massive tower. If we consider this first element in isolation from the later accretions to the east, we can clearly appreciate how the palazzo's design derives from that of the slightly earlier Bargello, although it is considerably more grandiose and self-confident in execution. The great rectangular mass of stonework is broken by only two major elements, the boldly overhanging uppermost story, with its supporting arcade, and the dramatic form of the campanile, which rises sheer from the face of this cantilevered upper story. The tower was, and remains, the highest in the city, rising 320 feet (97 meters) above the pavement of the piazza.

The first and second stories were lit by a series of elegant two-light windows, all identical, while on the uppermost story a series of simpler arched openings defined the covered walkway that circumscribed the perimeter of the building. Among the comparatively few purely decorative elements were the four stone patronal lions, originally gilded, that stood on each of the outermost corners of the top story. More prominent is the long series of coats of arms that fill the arches supporting the topmost story. These arms represent the Capitano del Popolo, Florence and Fiesole, the Papacy, the Signoria, the Guelf party, the Ghibellines, and the House of Anjou. Further touches of color were also provided by the arms of the city's chief clans, again painted and gilded, above the centers of the windows of the first and second floors. The palazzo was crowned with a Guelf crenellation, while the campanile, by contrast, is terminated with the characteristic swallowtail battlements of the Ghibelline faction — a symbolic gesture of unification. More decoration was added in the trecento to the two principal doorways, and in the same period a platform known as the *aringhiera* was added, with an enclosing marble parapet wall that was built against the northwest corner of the palazzo. The purpose of this dais was to serve as a grandstand for the Republic's most senior officials and important guests to watch ceremonies and spectacles in the square. The parapet was demolished in 1812, although the stepped platform itself survives. The daring, dramatic form of the soaring campanile was constructed from the base of the Torre della Vacca, one of the fortified towers of the Foraboschi family, whose houses were demolished to build the palazzo itself. Its pivotal role in the townscape is perhaps most dramatically appreciated from the approach by the Via de' Cerchi, from which its cantilevered form is most impressively apparent.

The interior of Arnolfo's original structure has been considerably altered. On the ground floor, entered through the north door — the original principal entrance — nearly half of the space is occupied by the Camera dell'Arme, built in 1312; it is the only part of this earliest building that retains its original appearance, with its six bays of simple cross vaulting supported on stout but elegant octagonal stone columns. These columns reflect the characteristic Arnolfian vocabulary: strong, planar, linear forms reminiscent of Santa Croce, although here they are even more pared down and severe, with truly minimal capitals. The simplicity and severity of this internal vocabulary thus matches the strength and discipline of the exterior. The remainder of the ground floor is today occupied largely by the colonnaded *cortile*, which was remodeled by Michelozzo in 1453 for Cosimo Il Vecchio. Although the overall scale and dimensions of Arnolfo's original *cortile*

PALAZZO DEL POPOLO (PALAZZO VECCHIO)

Right: plan of the ground floor. The original nucleus of the palazzo is the westernmost block, centered on the *cortile* later modernized by Michelozzo. Bottom: plan of the second floor, with the rooms of the Quartiere degli Elementi directly above those of Leo X. In the center is the great Sala dei Cinquecento.

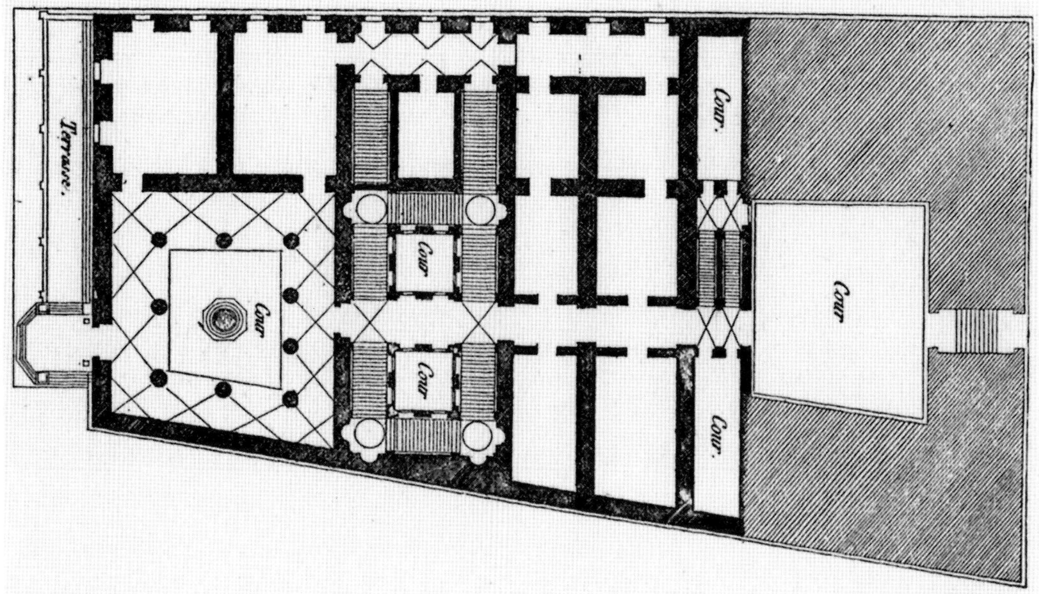

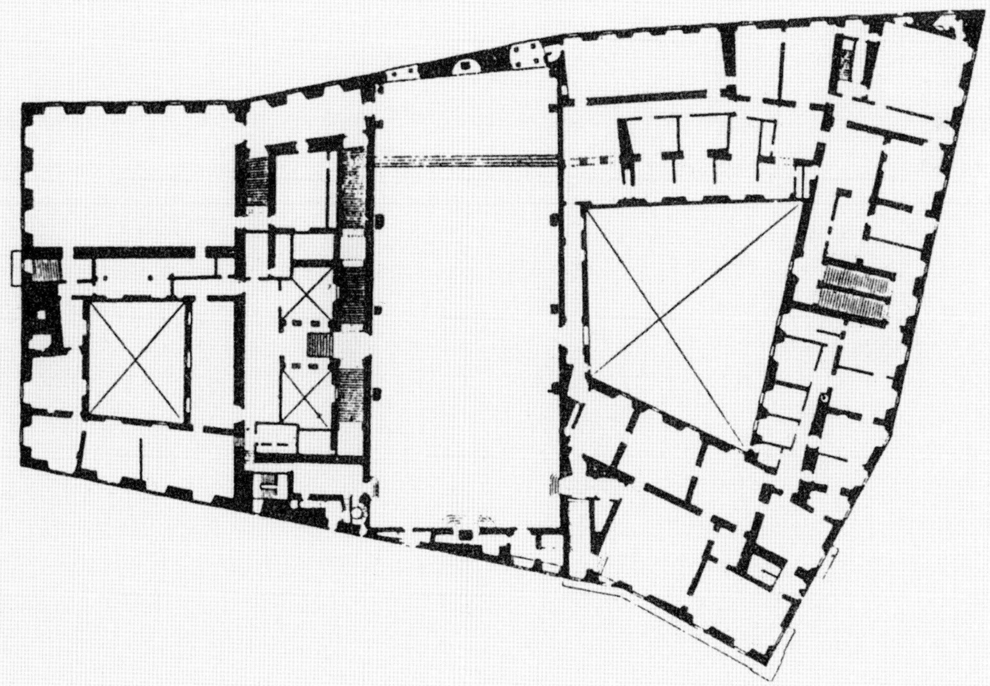

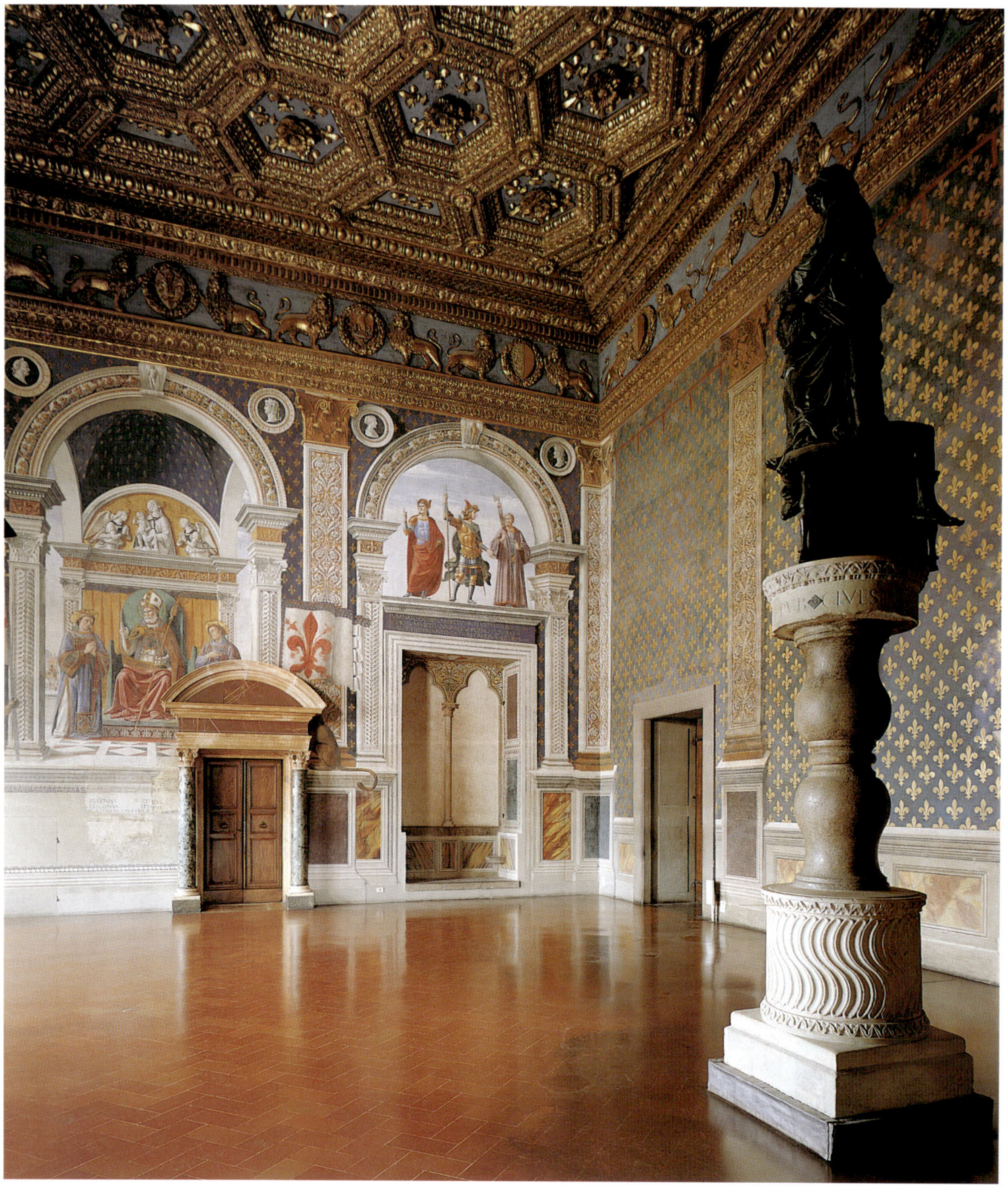

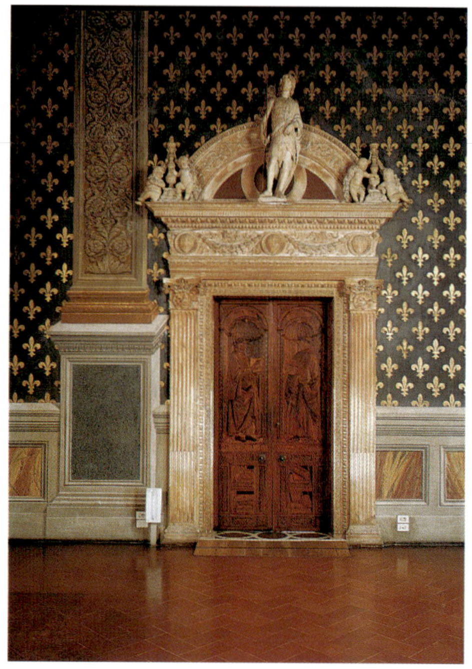

PALAZZO DEL POPOLO (PALAZZO VECCHIO)

Left: Sala dei Gigli. This beautiful hall was decorated by Giuliano da Maiano in the 1470s, after the large hall in this corner of the palazzo was divided into two. The other part forms the Sala dell'Udienza. The lily (*giglio*) is the symbol of the Virgin and of San Zenobio, both patrons of the city. Above: doorway into the Sala dei Gigli by Giuliano and Benedetto da Maiano, with the figure of Justice in the lunette.

Opposite: Sala dei Cinquecento. This immense hall was built in great haste after the reorganization of Florence's government in 1494, but was remodeled by Vasari for Cosimo I after 1540.

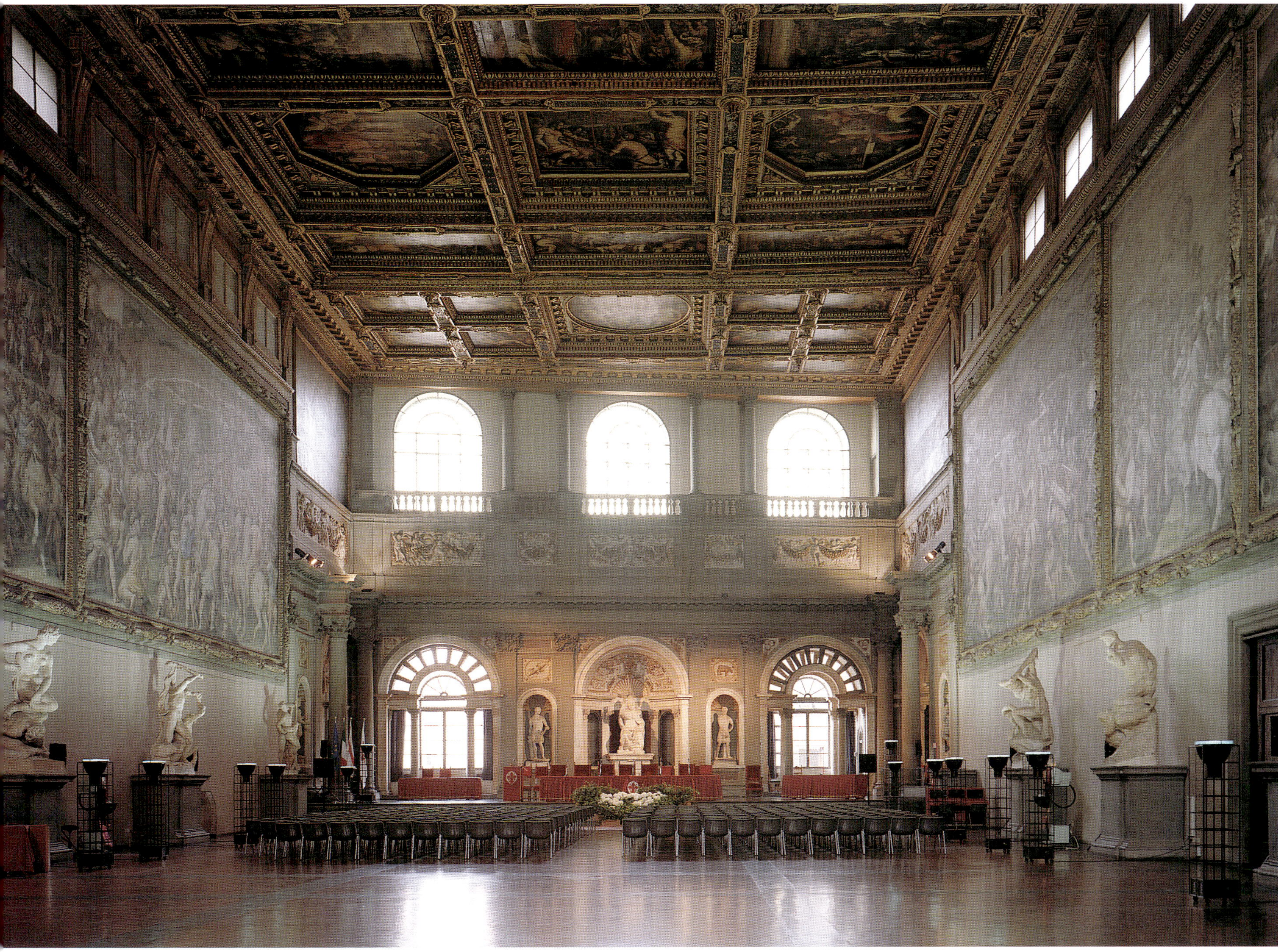

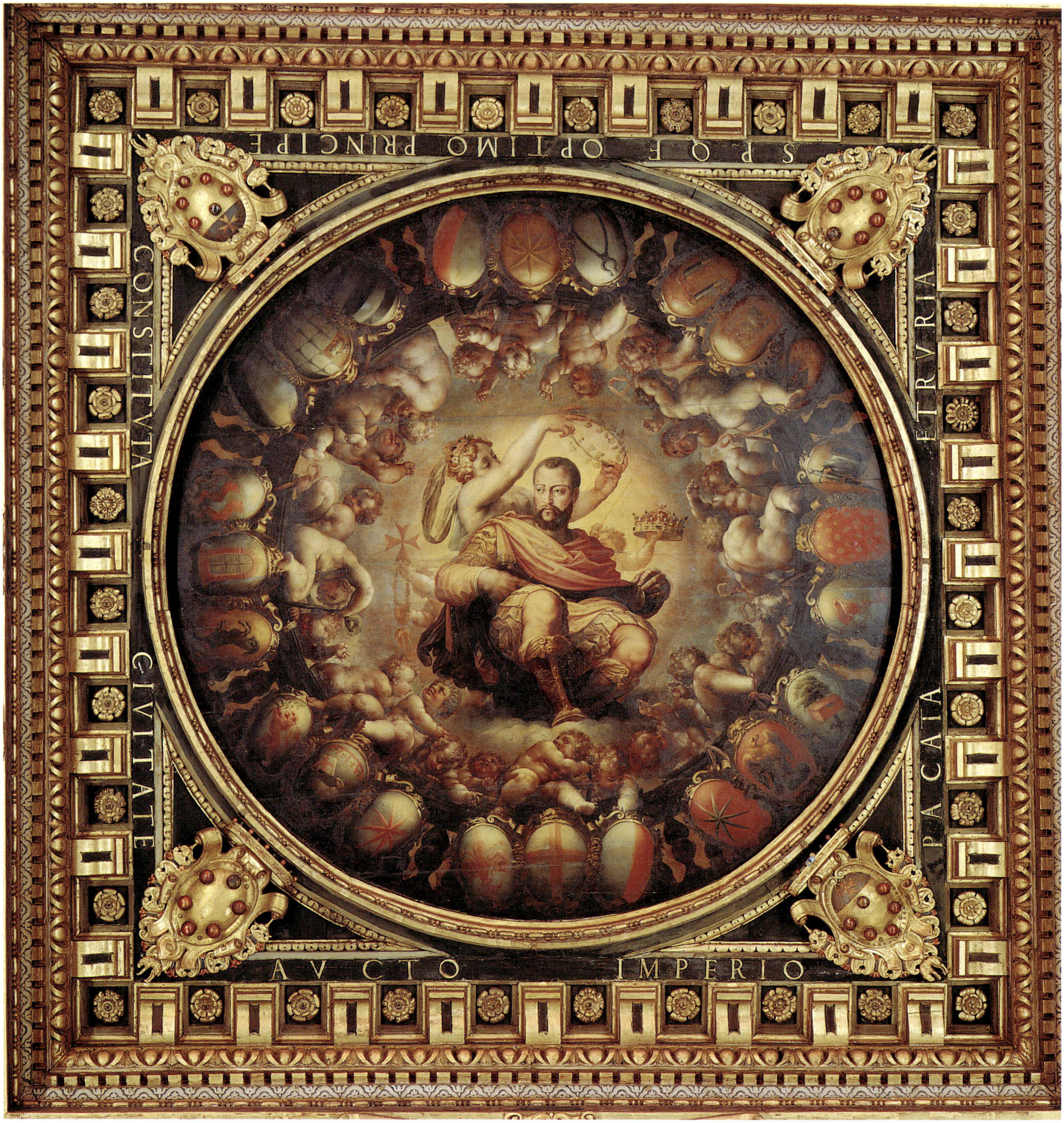
S P Q F OPTIMO PRINCIPE
CONSTITVTA
CIVITATE
AVCTO
IMPERIO
PACATA
ETRVRIA

Opposite: *Apotheosis of Cosimo I* by Giorgio Vasari (c. 1565), in the Sala dei Cinquecento. No other work depicts so well the quasi-monarchical, almost mythical self-image that Cosimo promulgated.

Below: Sala di Giove, one of the halls in the Quartiere degli Elementi, decorated by Vasari in the late 1550s. Below, right: the *studiolo* of Francesco I, richly decorated to represent his broad and eclectic range of cultural and other interests; it is a collaboration between Vasari and Vincenzo Borghini, as well as many other craftsmen.

survived this modernization, Michelozzo transformed what was almost certainly a restrained, highly disciplined work into something far richer and more elaborate, with complex bas reliefs on the columns and *tondi* in the spandrels of the arches. His modernization of the upper levels around the *cortile* was far less ornate, though, with a series of simple but elegant two-light windows in both upper stories. The final, even more elaborate part of the ground-floor *cortile* (as we see it today) is largely the work of Vasari, who in 1565 decorated all the wall surfaces with a series of frescoes celebrating the marriage of Francesco de' Medici to Giovanna of Austria.

The interior of the upper floors of the Arnolfian edifice have also been much altered over the centuries. In essence, the northern part of the earliest palazzo contained two large halls, one directly above the other, and both built directly over the Camera dell'Arme. The hall generally known as the Sala dei Duecento is on the first floor, and currently serves as the city council's debating chamber. Its original spartan appearance was modernized by Benedetto and Giuliano da Maiano in 1472, when the coffered ceiling was also installed. The two fine marble doorways date from a second modernization in the cinquecento by Baccio d'Agnolo. Directly above the Sala dei Duecento is the upper great hall; this, too, was altered by Giuliano da Maiano and divided into two smaller halls, known as the Sala dell'Udienza and the Sala dei Gigli. The ceiling of the latter hall was decorated by Giuliano with the Florentine lily (*giglio*), which also symbolized the House of Anjou, protectors of the Guelf faction in the city. The hall has a beautifully refined doorway by Benedetto and Giuliano da Maiano.

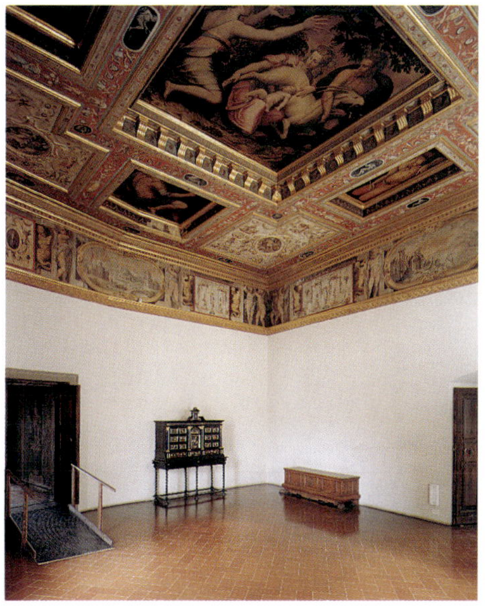

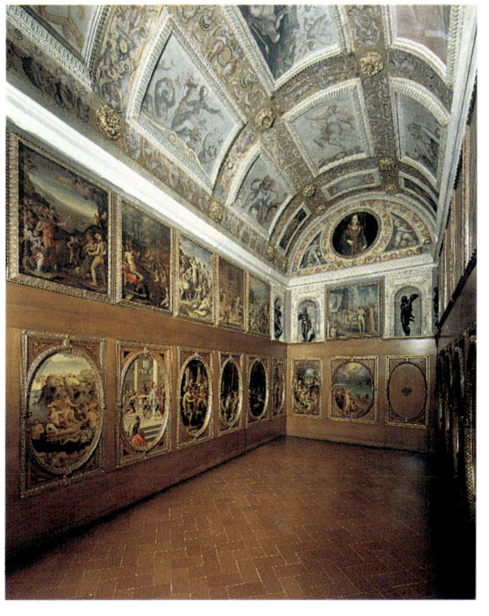

The palazzo's history after 1302 — date of the completion of the original structure — was marked on one hand by a series of eastward extensions, and on the other by a series of modernizations of earlier parts of the fabric. The first expansion stage took the form of a large new structure immediately to the east of Arnolfo's original compact block.[18] This work was begun in 1343, and roughly doubled the plan area of the original palazzo; toward the end of the following century the vast new hall, the Salone dei Cinquecento, was constructed on the upper floor. Much of this element of the palazzo was later modernized by Vasari between 1558 and 1571. The second expansion stage consisted of a further, smaller section in the southeast corner, along the Via della Ninna. Although this wing was built in the years after 1507, it, too, received its present appearance after Vasari's later sixteenth-century modernizations. The third and final stage of growth consisted of the building up of the whole city block to the east and northeast of the site, as far as the junction of the Via de' Gondi and Via dei Leoni. This stage, known as the Fabbrica Nuova, was the work of Buontalenti from 1588 to 1596. With its completion, the palazzo reached its final overall size and shape; it now occupied the entire city block between the piazza to the west and the Via dei Leoni to the east, and between the Via de' Gondi to the north and the Via della Ninna to the south.

The first stage of expansion, begun in 1345, centered on a new courtyard, the Cortile della Dogana, but this work was comprehensively remodeled after 1494, following the expulsion of the Medici from the city. This was the era of the brief republic of the charismatic Savonarola, at whose instigation the ruling clan was now replaced by a Consiglio Generale, a great assembly modeled on the Maggior Consiglio of Venice. It was thus necessary to construct a great hall large enough for such an assembly, and it was built in considerable haste. The basic structure of the present Sala dei Cinquecento was

THE UFFIZI

The central *cortile*, by Giorgio Vasari, begun in 1560. The long axial space between the two wings is a hybrid between a *cortile* and a purely linear street. The southern loggia terminates the vista toward the Arno.

begun on the first floor of this second-phase wing, and a number of additional columns had to be built in the Cortile della Dogana to support the new floor. A grand, spacious staircase was also constructed to reach the new hall from the east side of Michelozzo's courtyard. All of these works were undertaken by Simone del Pollaiuolo (also known as Cronaca), with the assistance of Antonio da Sangallo and others. As with the original building of the Arnolfian block, abrupt political change led to urgent constructional necessity, and the new hall was built in a little over a year. On its completion, the new *gonfaloniere* for life, Piero Soderini, commissioned Michelangelo and Leonardo da Vinci to decorate the vast hall, with frescoes depicting two Florentine victories, the Battle of Cascina and that of Anghiari. Only that of da Vinci was begun, but was quickly abandoned, due — reportedly — to technical difficulties with his fresco technique; today only a number of preparatory sketches survive.

The next major stage in the modernization and expansion of the palazzo took place in the decade after 1555, chiefly under the coordinating master — and Medici house architect — Giorgio Vasari.[19] In 1540 Cosimo I had transferred his family seat there from the palace in the Via Larga, and this symbolic relocation began the long process of transformation of the palazzo from the seat of the elected government of the Comune into the palace of the dukes (and later grand dukes) of Tuscany. Two aspects of the palazzo were affected by these transformations: the requirements of its physical accommodation and its iconographic imagery. The great hall in the center remained the heart of the palazzo, but it was remodeled; no longer the general assembly of Florentine government, it became the Sala di Rappresentanza, effectively the audience chamber of an absolute ruler. To improve access to the chamber, Vasari constructed the present imposing two-branch staircase, which terminates at the *salone*, with entrances at either end. The next stage was the transformation of the great hall itself; the walls were raised in height by 12 *braccia* (about 23 feet, or 7 meters) to enhance its imposing appearance, and between 1563 and 1565 Vasari also added the richly coffered gilded ceiling. Forty-two new paintings were incorporated on walls and ceiling, the program of which was under Vasari's coordination, and some of which he painted himself; the theme of these works was the glorification of both the state of Tuscany, with depictions of victories over Siena and Pisa, and of Cosimo himself, with the *Apotheosis of Cosimo* the hub around which the other images revolved. To further accommodate Cosimo's perception of the new function of the hall, a raised dais was constructed at the northern end, the "Udienza"; it was assembled in 1542 especially for the new ducal throne, in the form of a Roman triumphal arch, an allusion that would elude few notable visitors. The southern end of the hall, though, still retained the rather awkward rhomboidal plan of the building, and the attempted regularization of this end by Ammannati was never completed. A new screen wall was built across the end of it, at right angles to the parallel east and west walls, thus "squaring off" the shape of the hall; the overall theme is again that of a triumphal arch, the whole forming something of a trompe l'oeil effect in front of the real south wall beyond it. The *salone* was further enhanced by the addition of Michelangelo's sculpture *Genio della Vittoria*, which had been intended to adorn the tomb of Pope Julius II della Rovere but was never installed; instead, it was brought here in 1565.

Roughly contemporaneous with these modifications was the completion and modernization of the comparatively small, compact wing that occupies the southeast corner of the palazzo, and that is reached via the great *salone*. This wing consists essentially of two suites of apartments, one directly above the other, and the lower of which (on the *piano nobile*) is generally known as the Quartiere di Leone X; the upper is referred to as the Quartiere degli Elementi, after the themes of its decorations. Both suites were essentially private apartments, and here, again, much of the decorative iconography is a result of Vasari's overall program, with contributions by Marco da Faenza and others. The lower suite of rooms is reached directly from the *salone* and the unifying theme is the genealogy of the house of Medici. The hall of Leo X gives its name to the whole suite, which contains a series of small halls, each dedicated to one of the outstanding members of the clan: Cosimo Il Vecchio, Lorenzo Il Magnifico, Cosimo I, and the great *condottiere* Giovanni dalle Bande Nere, father of Cosimo I. Almost

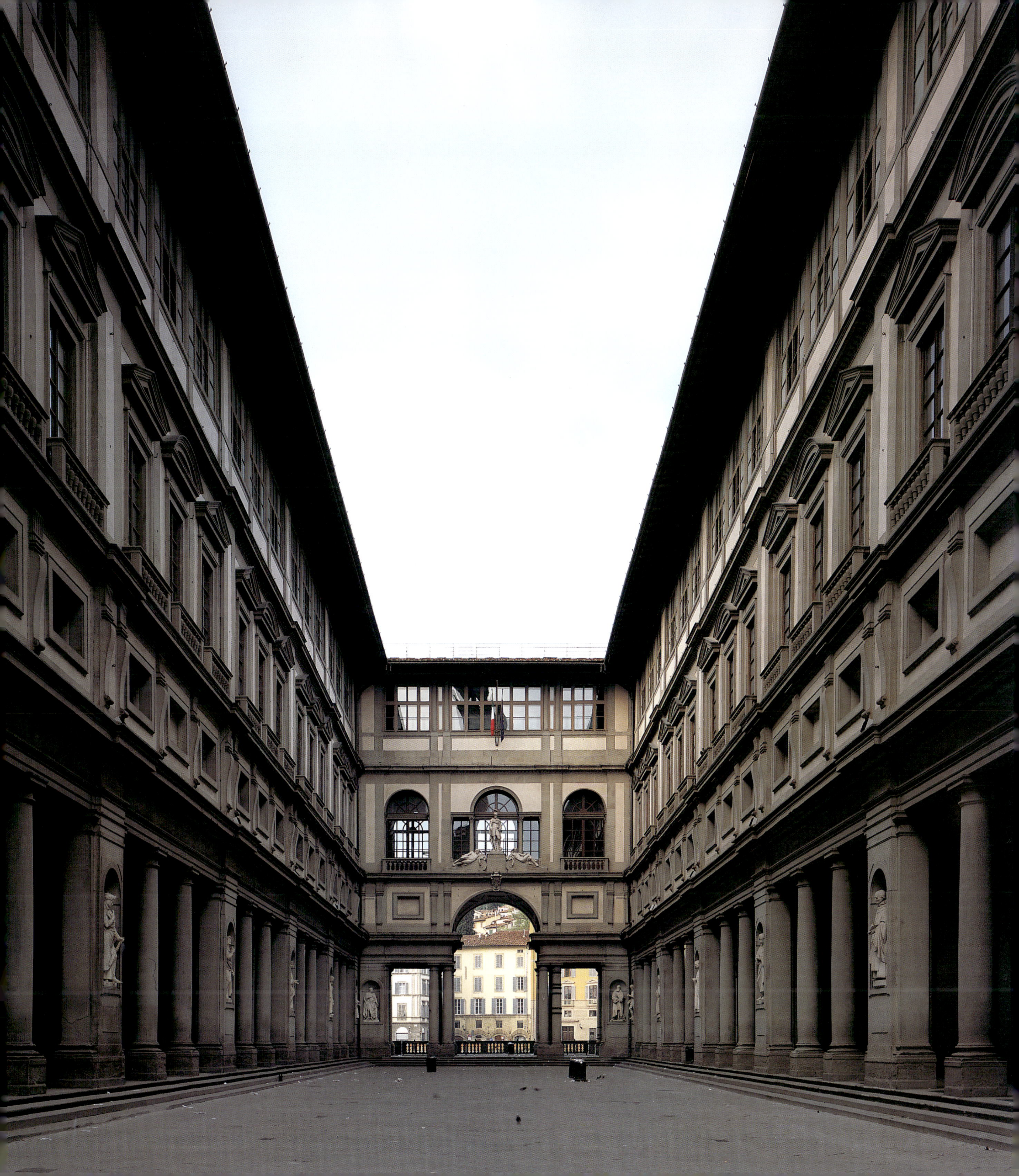

precisely echoing the arrangement of these rooms, directly above is the Quartiere degli Elementi, that is, of fire, water, earth, and air. Once more the principal master behind the concept is Vasari, but here the theme is more abstract, a series of allegories of the origins of the stars, the planets, the elements, and the classical gods. There are rooms dedicated to Jupiter, Hercules, Saturn, and Minerva, complete with cycles of paintings on these themes. The location of these rooms directly above the Medici's own quarters was a conscious arrangement intended to create the association between the great dynasty and the elements. There are direct correlations between the themes of the upper and lower rooms. Thus, for example, the hall of Cosimo I stands directly below that of Jupiter (Giove), a direct association of supreme power; the chamber of Cosimo Il Vecchio, on the other hand, stands below that of Ceres, goddess of earth and fertility, signifying the origins of the Medici succession.[20]

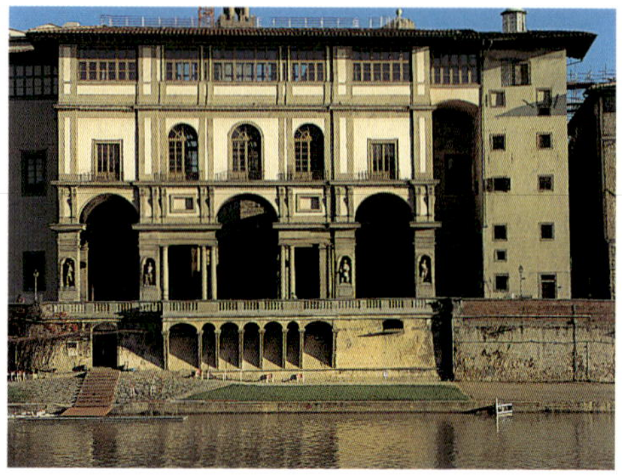

THE UFFIZI

The southern loggia, which frames the views south across the Arno. The galleries on the two upper levels link the east and west wings of the Uffizi together.

The final section of the palazzo to receive its definitive appearance during these comprehensive modernizations ordered by Cosimo I were the apartments of Eleonora of Toledo, Cosimo's wife. These apartments were formed chiefly out of the southernmost wing of the second story of Arnolfo's original building, directly facing the site where the Uffizi were to be built. Outstanding in this group of chambers is the little chapel built between 1540 and 1545, Bronzino's masterpiece. Another small but significant element is the doorway that connects these rooms to a bridge suspended high above the Via della Ninna, and that formed the Medici's private, secure link from the palazzo to the Uffizi. The little study of Francesco I was one of the very last of the later sixteenth-century modernizations; it was located adjacent to the southwest corner of the great *salone*, and represents a masterpiece of Mannerist art, reflecting Francesco's personal interests in magic, alchemy, and science.[21]

The Uffizi and the Corridoio Vasariano

"Above [the Ponte Vecchio] the Gallery of the Grand Duke crosses the river. It . . . takes its jealous course among the streets and houses, with true despotism: going where it lists, and spurning every obstacle away, before it." **Charles Dickens**, *Pictures from Italy* (1844) [22]

In 1549 Cosimo I's wife, Eleonora, acquired Palazzo Pitti, which stood on a rise a little way beyond the southern end of the Ponte Vecchio, in the Oltrarno. The decision of the Medici to transfer their court here was followed only a few years later by Cosimo's victory over Siena, and the incorporation of these extensive new territories into the Florentine state. These two events had profound consequences for the fabric of the city, and resulted in the creation of a dramatic new dynamic in the structures of power. The necessity to physically link Palazzo Pitti with the old nucleus of the Palazzo Vecchio, together with the necessity for a radical reorganization of the state's administration, resulted in the construction of the imposing Uffizi, of the vital link formed by Vasari's new corridor, and in the long, staged expansion of the Pitti itself, ultimately to become one of the grandest palaces in Italy.

In 1555, after a long war and a siege that endured for more than a year, the city of Siena finally capitulated to the forces of the Medici and the imperial armies. Cosimo was well rewarded for his loyalty to the empire, and was given the new title of Dux Senarum, duke of the territories of Siena, which were nearly as extensive as those of Tuscany itself. Florence's bitter historical rival had finally fallen to the Marzocco, the Florentine lion, and Cosimo was now sole controller of one of the wealthiest and most extensive states in Italy. One of the longer-lasting results of this considerable territorial expansion was Cosimo's urgent need to absorb the government of these new lands into that of the Tuscan state, and to rationalize its administration. In 1560, therefore, construction began on the two imposing parallel blocks of the Uffizi, the new offices of Cosimo's government. Thirteen different departments of state were to be housed there, each with its own separate entrance from the long, broad avenue that was to run down the center between the two wings. From the beginning the Uffizi were intended to form a literal administrative appendage of the Palazzo Vecchio, where the great halls of state — principally the Sala dell'Udienza — would continue to be located. Eventually the little bridge across the Via della Ninna provided Cosimo

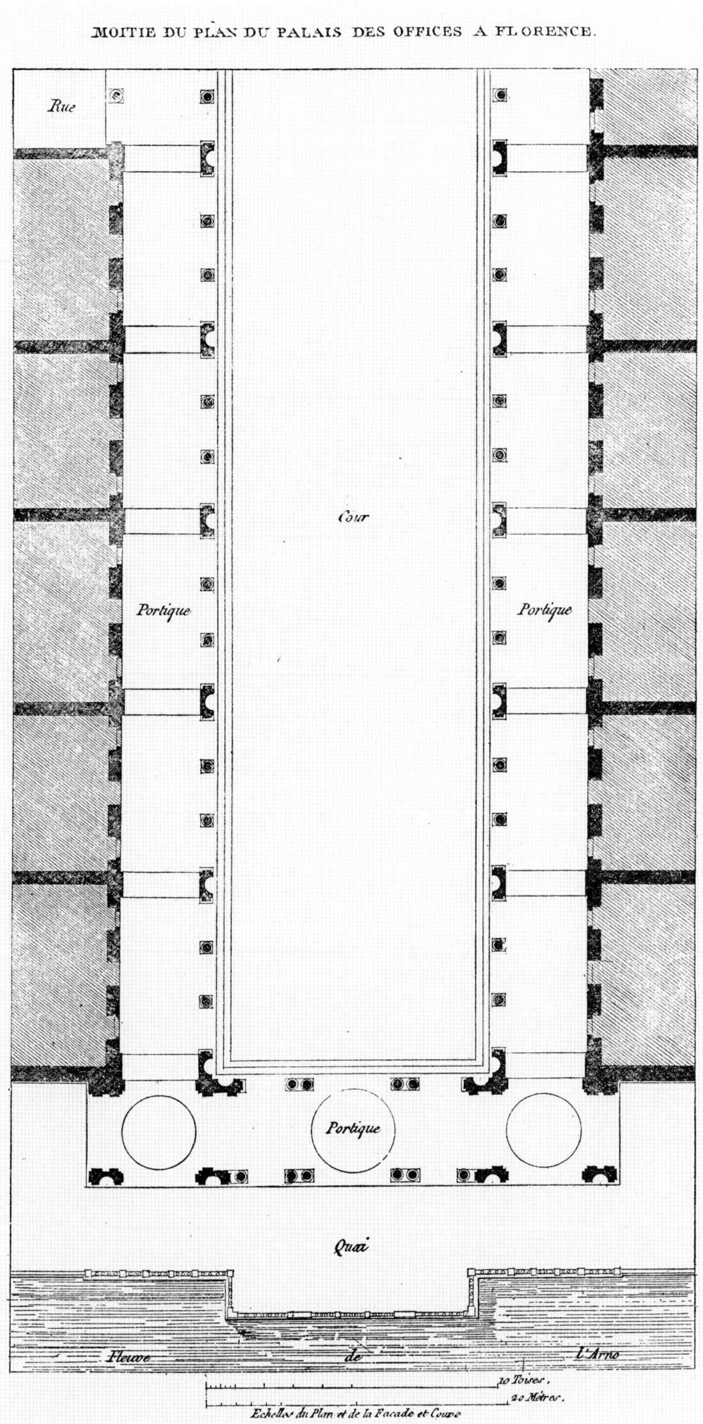

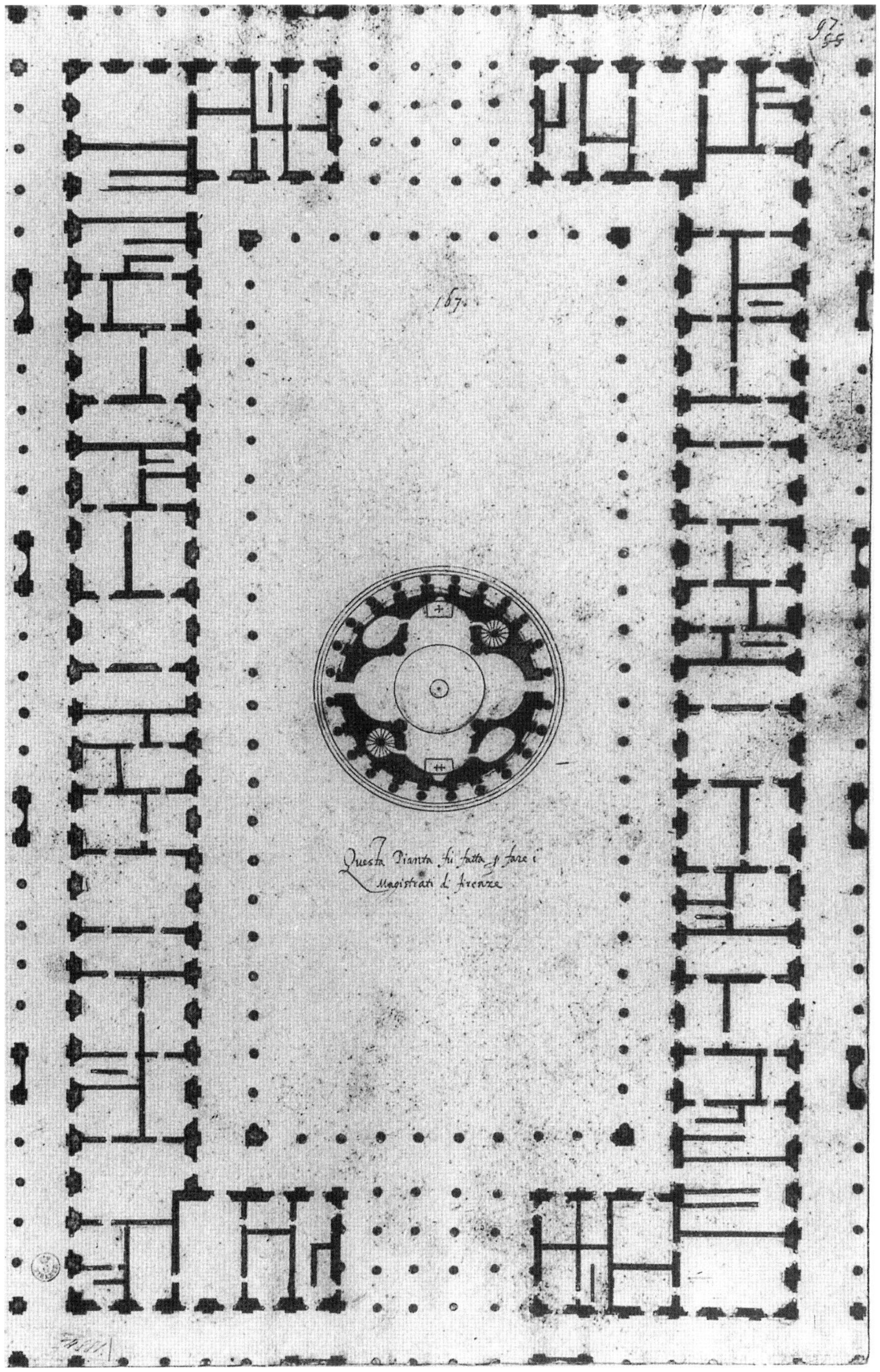

THE UFFIZI

Above: part plan of the ground-floor colonnades and loggia onto the Arno, by Grandjean de Montigny, 1806–15. Above, right: Vasari's grandiose original plan for the Uffizi, probably from 1559, was never realized.

with his own direct link between the two buildings. A narrow street that led from the south side of the Piazza della Signoria down toward the Arno already existed; however, this narrow axis had to be enlarged considerably in order to provide sufficient space, and dozens of adjacent houses were expropriated (without recompense) and demolished, particularly at the southern end. With some form of southward expansion already in mind, Cosimo had commenced acquisitions and demolitions there as early as 1546.[23] One of the victims of this dramatic urban intervention was the Romanesque church of San Pier Scheraggio, which had stood for centuries on the south side of the Via della Ninna, just across the street from the southwest corner of the Palazzo Vecchio. Vasari absorbed certain parts of the church fabric into the northern end of the east wing of the Uffizi, but its north aisle was lost in the widening of the Via della Ninna. Remains of the church can still be seen, just inside the present entrance to the Uffizi art galleries.

THE UFFIZI

The Tribune gallery. This octagonal hall was designed specifically to house the Medici's most highly regarded works of art. It is the oldest surviving part of the Uffizi, and was designed by Buontalenti in 1584. It still contains some of the gallery's finest works, including the classical Medici Venus and paintings by Bronzino, Andrea del Sarto, Giorgio Vasari, and Jacopo da Pontormo.

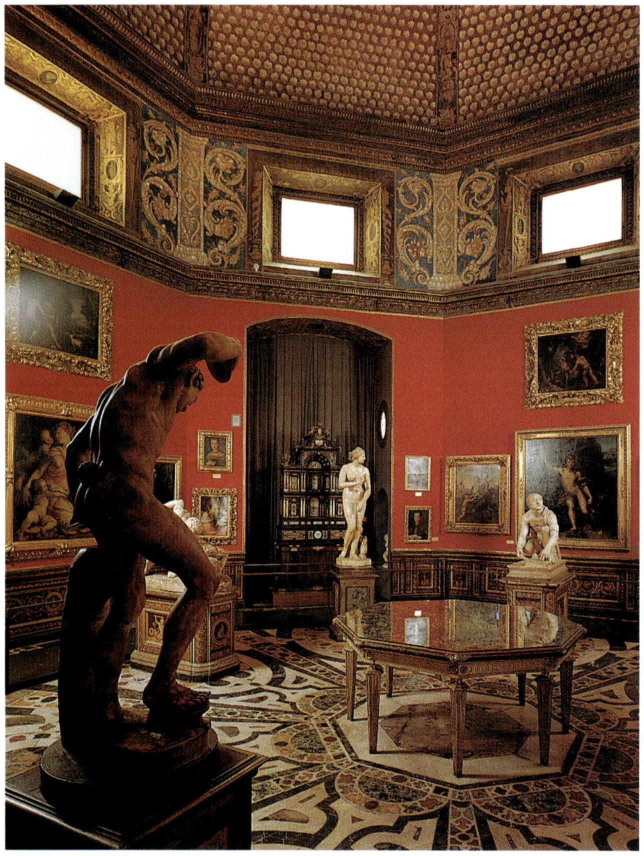

Cosimo's architect for the new offices was the ubiquitous Giorgio Vasari, whose task here was radically different from his long, phased program of works of elaboration and glorification within the Palazzo Vecchio; here he was faced with a clean slate, and was thus able to develop a design that was clearly and rationally ordered, with no historical encumbrances to constrain him. Vasari's design was rational, based on a fairly broad central avenue, which provided light and air to the various departments, as well as a logical series of points of access to them. The central space was something of a cross between a street and a *cortile*, and it served an important function in visually linking the Piazza della Signoria and the Palazzo Vecchio with the river, and thus, symbolically (and to a qualified degree, visually, too) with the Pitti and the green hill of Boboli on the far side. As a new urban intervention it was dramatic indeed, opening new vistas of the tower of the Palazzo Vecchio as one approached from the river, and introducing a strong linearity and dynamism into the basically static spaces in which the palazzo itself was set.

Construction began in 1559, and although it proceeded fairly rapidly, it was not yet complete at the time of Vasari's death in 1574. The Uffizi were continued by Buontalenti, Vasari's successor, and then by Alfonso Parigi in about 1580, according to Vasari's original scheme. Vasari's design for the two blocks was simple, elegant, and rational; in many ways it can be seen as a very early prototype for the modern office block, an essentially repetitive, modular container in which various administrative departments could be housed. Internally, therefore, it contains a large number of fairly neutral, flexible spaces, which could be used and adapted for the secretaries and administrative staffs of the various departments. According to Vasari himself, the chosen order, Doric, was the most appropriate for such a building type, because it was "more firm and solid, [a style] that is always highly favored by the Signor Duca"; characteristics such as firmness, solidity, and endurance were considered desirable administrative attributes, which reflected the dynasty itself. The facing material that dominates the exterior is *pietra serena* from the valley of the Mensola, just to the east of the city, a highly regarded stone that, according to Vasari, was used

CORRIDOIO VASARIANO

Part of the corridor is built on a colonnade along the north bank of the Arno before it turns to cross the river at a high level on the Ponte Vecchio.

"only with the authority of he who rules"; in other words, its use was effectively confined by Cosimo to only the most important buildings. The basic design of the Uffizi consisted of a ground-floor colonnade, with a mezzanine directly above it, followed by the *piano nobile*, and finally the top floor (the present gallery). This uppermost story was originally surrounded by an open colonnaded loggia, which was later filled in with large windows. At the southern end, the two long, parallel wings are linked by a dramatic Serlian arch. This arch, with its distinctly triumphalist appearance, is the most architecturally forceful element of the whole complex, particularly when seen from the northern end of the central *cortile*, where it often reads almost in silhouette, with glimpses of the green hills across the Arno beyond it.

Construction of the Uffizi continued for a considerable time. The northern section of the west wing was completed in 1580, and about halfway down this west side a new arch was inserted at the point where the Uffizi cross the existing Via Lambertesca. The adjacent doorway, designed by Buontalenti in an early but highly Mannerist style, was known as the Porta delle Suppliche, and was crowned by a quite new architectural device, a reversed broken pediment.

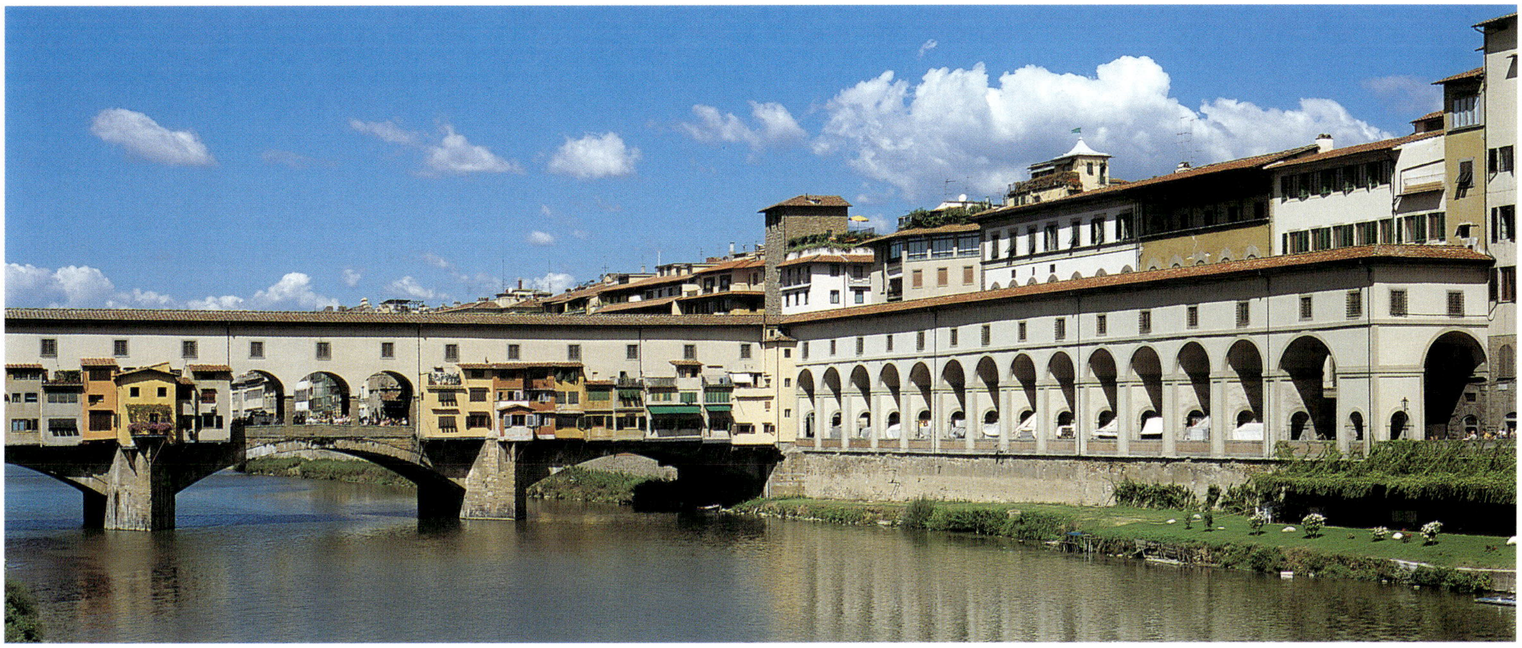

Five years after work had begun on the Uffizi, Cosimo decided to proceed with another significant element in the complex of structures that was evolving into his seat of power: the Corridoio Vasariano, the long, tortuously routed corridor that formed a direct link from the Palazzo Vecchio to the north side of Palazzo Pitti across the river, a distance of less than a mile (approximately one kilometer). The initial idea of the link is said to have been Vasari's own, and, as recounted by the architect, it was constructed in a remarkably short period of time, five or six months, between spring and fall 1565. Evidently proud of this achievement, Vasari himself records that one would think that such a work would take five years to complete, rather than five months.[24] The fundamental purpose of the corridor was to provide Cosimo — and his family, retinue, and successors — with an enclosed, weatherproof, and, above all, secure link between the Pitti, the Uffizi, and the Palazzo Vecchio. The very fact that such a link was considered necessary says a good deal about Cosimo's relationship with the citizens of Florence, and the physical danger of his position. In this respect, the design of the corridor contains a further telling detail: The string of large rectangular windows along the entire length of the corridor all open on the "outside," that is, toward the river. At the section where the corridor crosses the Arno, however, on top of the eastern rows of shops on the Ponte Vecchio, the corridor has only very small, barred windows on the vulnerable side, toward the bridge itself — where rebellious citizens might be expected to gather — and larger, rectangular windows on the side toward the river, from which little threat could materialize, and that, incidentally, give superb views up the Arno valley.

The general design of the corridor is, as one might expect, simple and utilitarian, repetitive in its detailing. However, its construction required considerable ingenuity and presented Vasari with a number of challenges, none of which were beyond his ability to resolve. The route from the Palazzo Vecchio begins in the Camera Verde, one of the chambers of Eleonora's apartments on the south side at second-floor level; it bridges the Via della Ninna and thus enters the Uffizi. It then continues down the east wing of the Uffizi via the spacious logge on the top floor, and thence across the top of the Arno loggia at the southern end. From the southwest corner it parts company with the Uffizi and turns westward, supported by an imposing colonnade, until it reaches the Ponte Vecchio. The corridor then traverses the bridge in the manner described above, although it was necessary to span the gap in the middle of the bridge by a new structure of three arches, supporting the link. When the corridor reaches the south bank, further ingenuity was necessary, since in its path stands the ancient fortified tower of

PALAZZO PITTI

Below, left: view of Bartolommeo Ammannati's cortile from the Boboli gardens along the principal axis, which commences with the amphitheater and leads up the hillside with a succession of ramps and terraces, enlivened by ponds and statuary. Below: detail of the facade.

Opposite: plan of the principal story, by Grandjean de Montigny in 1806–15, which shows the relationship between Ammannati's cortile and the amphitheater in the gardens.

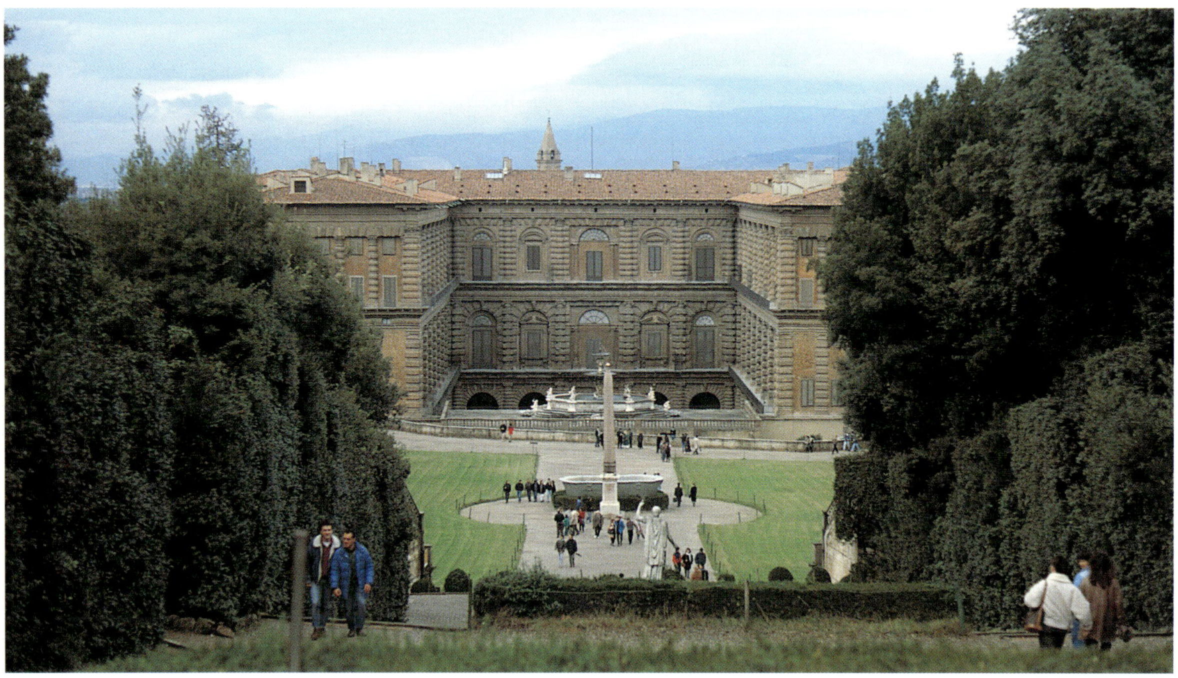

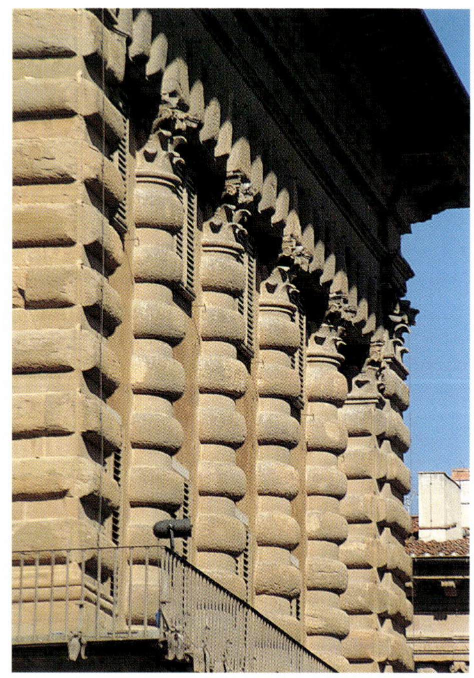

the Mannelli, so that Vasari had to wrap the corridor around the tower, followed by another new bridge to span the busy Via de' Bardi. A little farther on, more creativity was necessary to incorporate a section of the corridor into the facade of the church of Santa Felicità, which again stood in its path. Here the high-level link not only provided a new covered porch for the attendants at the church, but also allowed Cosimo a direct link into the church without having to enter the public realm at all. Finally, after several more changes of direction, the corridor arrives at the north end of Palazzo Pitti.

The building of the corridor was thus a triumph of ingenuity and planning as well as a feat of construction. The chief impetus for its extremely rapid conclusion was the wedding, in 1565, of Cosimo's heir and successor, Francesco, to Giovanna of Austria, for which event Vasari also decorated the *cortile* of the Palazzo Vecchio. With the completion of the corridor, the entire Medicean complex was linked securely together. It was also to serve another function, however, since from the outset Cosimo had envisaged it to house part of his extensive art holdings, including an outstanding collection of portraits. The otherwise rather tedious journey from palazzo to palazzo was thus not only enlivened, but enlightened, and several hundred paintings from the Medici collections still line the corridor's walls today.[25]

Pl. 2

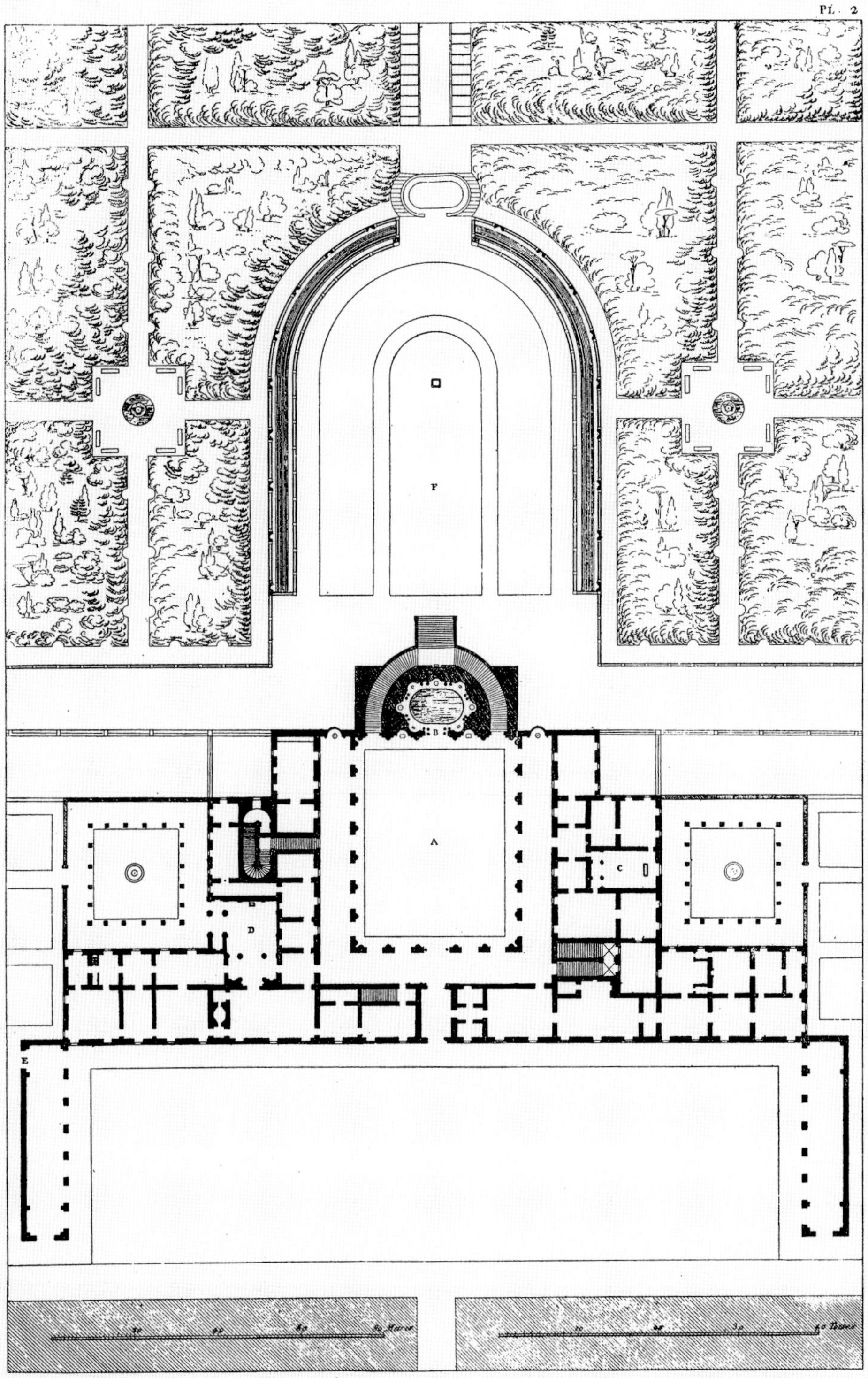

PLAN GÉNÉRAL DU PALAIS PITTI A FLORENCE

A *Grande cour*
B *Grotte*
C *Chapelle*
D *Petite Cour*
E *Entrée publique des Jardins*
F *Amphitheatre*

PALAZZO PITTI

The imposing *cortile* facade, with its bold rustication by Bartolommeo Ammannati, was built in 1558–70 for Cosimo I.

Discussion of Cosimo as a direct patron of the visual arts brings us back to the Uffizi and to what is undoubtedly today its most famous feature: the Medici art collections, which are among the finest in the world. Although perhaps projected by Cosimo, it was Francesco I who began the development of the top story of the Uffizi complex as it can be seen today. His architect, Buontalenti, began in 1581 by glazing in the open logge along the west face of the eastern wing of the building. This provided a long, spacious corridor fully protected from the elements and with a series of rooms giving off it down the east side. Francesco's collections initially comprised both paintings and sculptures, and the most highly valued of these treasures were to be housed in the tribune, the octagonal room toward the southern end, which was built specifically for this

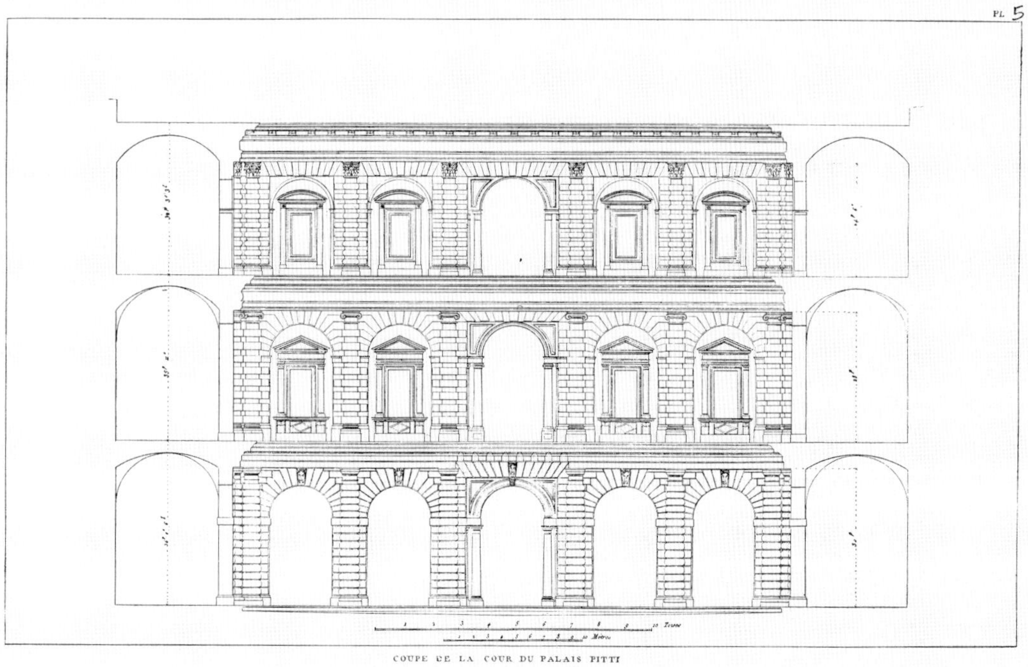

purpose by Buontalenti in 1584. Two years later, a theater was also incorporated into the east wing, adjacent to the principal staircase, now known as the Vasari stairs. The theater survived in its original form only until 1628; later it was used for various other functions (including, for a short time, the seat of the Senate when Florence was capital of the newly unified Italy), and still later was altered further.

Francesco's brother and successor, Ferdinando, increased the Medici collections considerably, particularly by his acquisition of antiquities. During a number of visits to Rome, entire collections were purchased intact. Ferdinando was also an enlightened patron of more recent artists, and contributed works by Donatello, Michelangelo, and others to the collections. He also placed an embargo on the export of works of art to ensure that the patrimony was not drained by foreign monarchs anxious to increase their holdings of Italy's artistic legacy. As well as increasing its extent, Ferdinando broadened the scope of the gallery by incorporating elements in the field of natural science, collections of arms, and other applied arts and crafts.[26] Further notable purchases include those by Leopoldo, brother of Ferdinando II, who concentrated on Venetian artists, including Titian, as well as Raphael and Piero della Francesca. During the course of the seventeenth century, the later Medici added still more to the collections, until space to display them became completely

PALAZZO PITTI

Below, top: section through the *cortile* and terraces of the Boboli garden, showing the way in which the complex follows the natural slope of the hillside.
Below, bottom: the principal facade toward Piazza Pitti. Only the seven central bays were built by Luca Pitti in c. 1458; all of the remainder was added in stages by the Medici and Lorraine grand dukes.

inadequate. The west wing of the top story of the Uffizi originally had been intended by Francesco to house a series of workshops, where works of art could be restored and repaired; shortage of space now meant that the galleries expanded into these rooms as well.

The last member of the Medici line was Anna Maria Luisa, who in 1737 ceded the entire collection to the Lorraine dynasty, with two principal conditions: that the works were to remain in the city, and that they were to be permanently retained in the public domain. The collections were, in fact, expanded yet further by the Lorraine grand dukes, and Anna Maria Luisa's conditions have been respected to this day, with only two brief exceptions, when Napoleon, and later Hitler, looted some of the treasures and took them, respectively, to Paris and Berlin. But virtually all of the works were eventually returned to Florence.

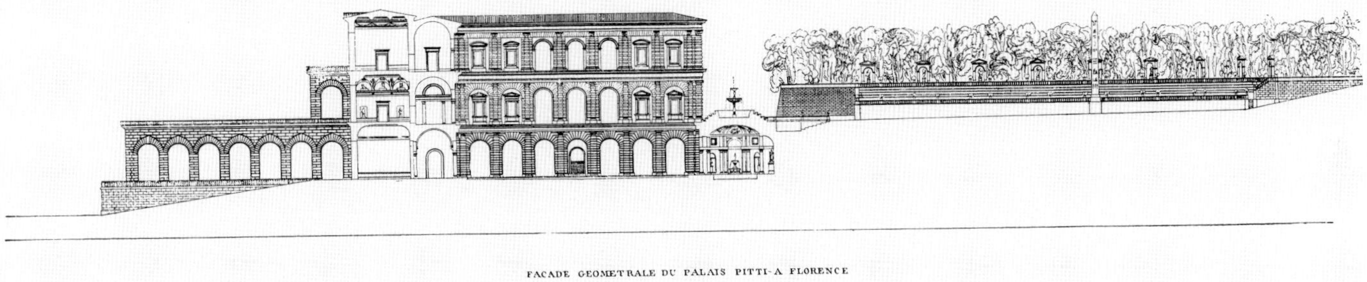

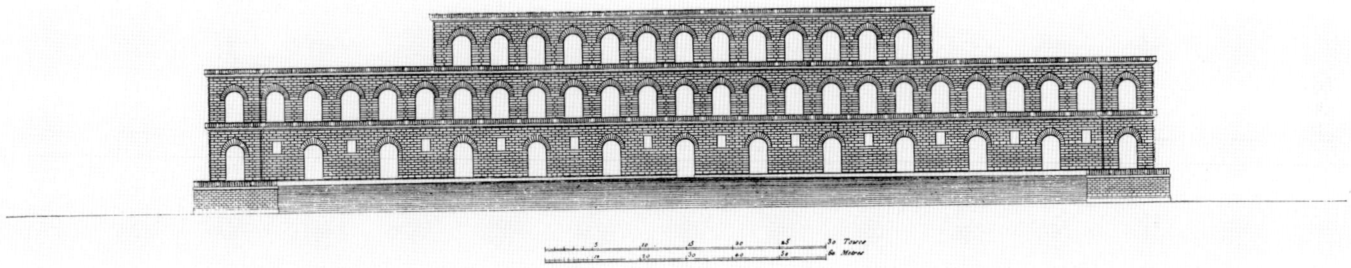

Palazzo Pitti

"Prodigious palaces, constructed for defense, with small distrustful windows heavily barred, and walls of great thickness formed of huge masses of rough stone, frown, in their sulky state, on every street." **Charles Dickens**, *Pictures from Italy* (1844) [27]

The Palazzo Vecchio represented the Medici citadel of power after 1540. However, only nine years later, Cosimo's wife, Eleonora, acquired the imposing Palazzo Pitti, across the Arno, from another famous banking dynasty and sometime principal rival of the Medici. The decision to transform Palazzo Pitti into one of the greatest quasi-royal palaces of Europe, although slow in maturation, was to have a profound effect on the political topography of the city. For the first time in Florence's history, it introduced a major element of political power onto the south bank of the Arno. Hitherto, all of the city's foci, religious, mercantile, civic, and political, had been located on the north bank, and almost all (with the sole exception of the Medici quarter around San Lorenzo) were concentrated within the small, compact area between the cathedral and the river. Now the court of the grand duchy was to be based in the Oltrarno, and this decision raised the question, How was the city, four-fifths of which lay on the north bank, to be governed — or controlled — from a private palace on the "wrong" side of the river? The question was to be answered in stages, over a period of some fifteen years.

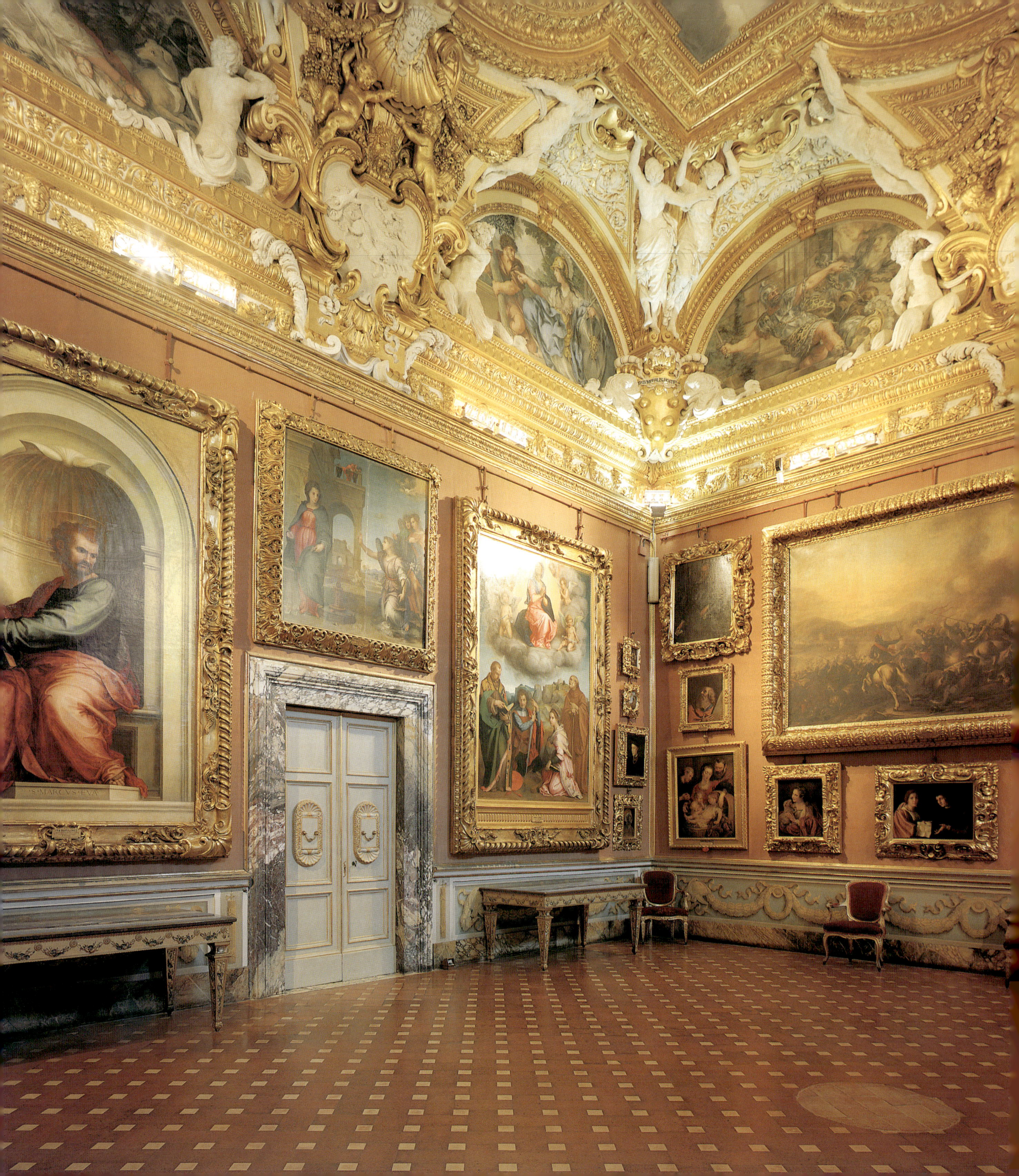

PALAZZO PITTI

Opposite: the Sala di Giove, now one of the Palatine galleries, was built as the throne room, with decorations by Pietro da Cortona.

Right: the Sala Bianca is the most imposing of the halls in the western wing of the palazzo, which became the royal apartments of the Lorraine dynasty and then the official residence of King Victor Emmanuel II.

Palazzo Pitti, final resting place of the peripatetic Medici court, was the last element in the chain of buildings that began at the Palazzo Vecchio. The history of this immense structure is one of staged expansion, from a compact, but still very substantial, mid-fifteenth-century nucleus to the impressive monument that can be seen today, by far the largest palace in Florence and one of the most remarkable in Italy, product of three centuries of enlargement and adaptation. Over the centuries the palace has retained the name of the patron of the original nucleus, Luca Pitti, the banker, contemporary and bitter rival of the Medici, who probably planned its construction in about 1440. His choice of location, on the far side of the river, was quite unprecedented at the time, when there were hardly any significant palaces in the Oltrarno — and those few were considerably earlier, semifortified structures such as Palazzo Mozzi. In terms of the size and scale

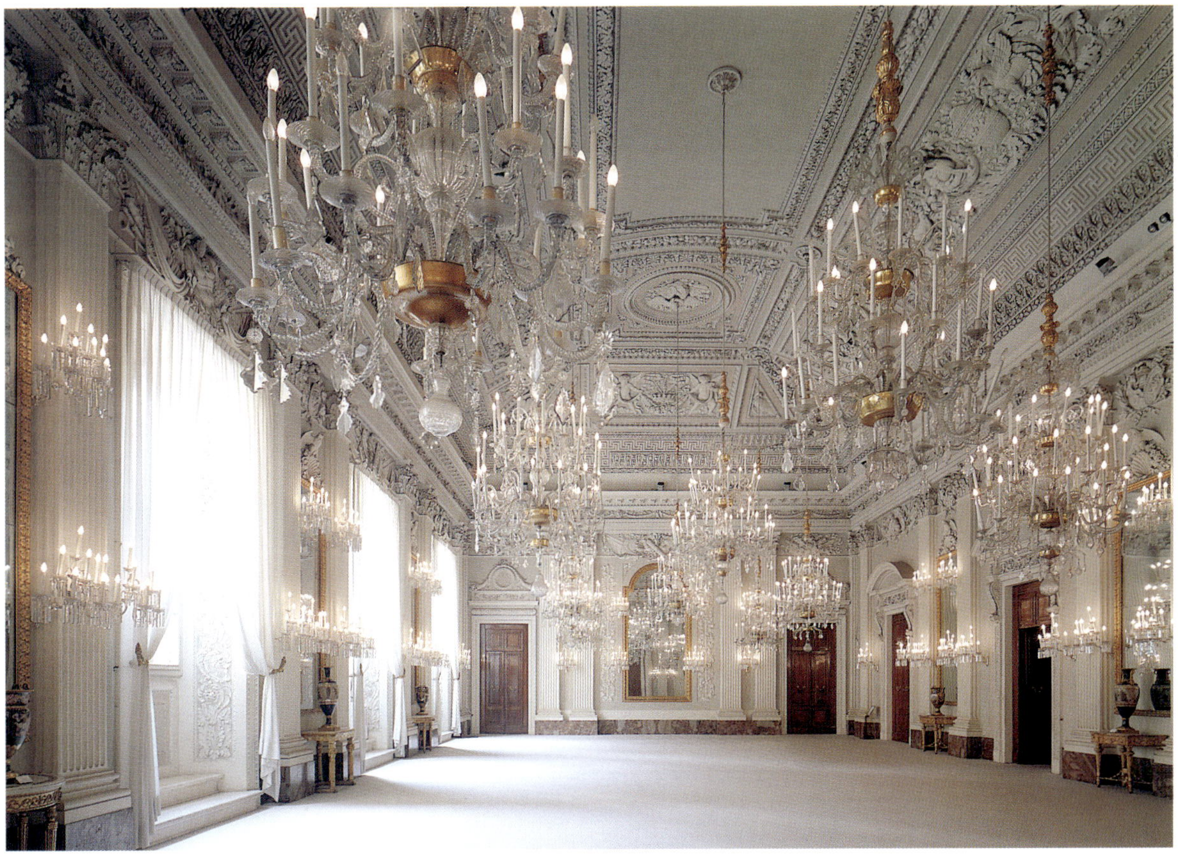

of his palace, together with a considerable degree of "daring" in crossing the river, Luca Pitti combined a gesture of defiance to the Medici and their own new palace in the Via Larga.

Luca Pitti made a bold statement in building in the Oltrarno, and closer analysis of the site reveals a shrewd intelligence. It was located only a very short distance from the Ponte Vecchio bridgehead, thus providing quick and easy access to the city's commercial heart around the Mercato Nuovo. It also stood on a rise above the existing street, the Via de' Guicciardini, which the palace was bound to dominate; the Via de' Guicciardini is one of the principal routes south out of the city, and the palace would be clearly visible to suitably impressed visitors. Behind the site of the palace rose the hill known as Bogoli, or Boboli, some parts of which — to the south and east — were quarried for stone. Pitti thus obtained a large, prominent plot facing a major artery within minutes of the city center. There has been endless debate as to the origin of the design of the seven central bays that formed the initial palace. Some degree of acknowledgment to Brunelleschi cannot be entirely ruled out, although he died in 1446, and the palace was begun only in 1458. It is often claimed that the palace was executed by Luca Fancelli after an original design by Brunelleschi; documentary evidence, however, is not conclusive.[28]

Following her acquisition of the palace in 1549, Eleonora de' Medici appointed the architect Bartolommeo Ammannati to modernize and enlarge it. The basic fabric at that time consisted of a single wing across the front of the site, containing a single row or chain of rooms, and with a *cortile* at the rear; Ammannati made several important alterations to the building, among them the transformation of the two outer portals of the main facade into windows, and the clearing of the piazza in front, one of several stages of improvement of the setting of the palazzo intended to reflect the importance of its new role. More significantly in terms of its structure, Ammannati added two projecting wings at the rear, so that the house was now built in the form of a U around three sides of a large *cortile*, with the fourth side open toward the hillside and gardens. These new wings were designed in a powerfully bold, Mannerist, rusticated style, with split pediments, but also with the correct classical use of three superimposed orders, Doric, Ionic, and Corinthian. The whole *cortile* element generally matched the strength and massive stonework of the original nucleus, and the upper levels facing the *cortile* contained open, superimposed logge, which were, however, later filled in with windows. The *cortile* facades are strongly reminiscent of the bold rustications of the work of Sanmicheli in Venice and Verona, but were unique at the time in Florence. Ammannati seems to have felt freer to experiment in such forms here than he perhaps would have in the city center; after all, the *cortile* facade not only lay outside the city's immediate urban context, but it was virtually a secret facade, visible only to the Medici and their courtiers and visitors.[29] The palazzo's public facade, by contrast, forms part of the developing palazzo tradition, and can be closely related to its original contemporaries such as the Medici palace of Via Larga and Palazzo Strozzi. Another significant aspect of Ammannati's new garden wings lies precisely in this relationship between palace and garden; the section of the Boboli garden directly behind the *cortile* forms a long series of terraces, paths, and fountains, all aligned on its axis.

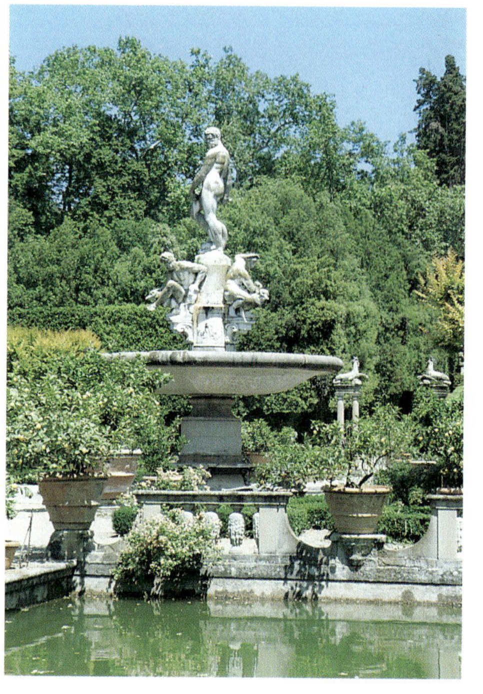

THE BOBOLI GARDENS

View of Giambologna's fountain at the center of the Isolotto.

The main facade of the palace onto Via de' Guicciardini was extended on no fewer than four occasions, to result finally in the majestic, overpowering elevation visible today, fully 670 feet (205 meters) long, and with the central block 120 feet (36 meters) high. The first of these expansions was the work of Giulio Parigi; it resulted from a competition organized by Cosimo II in 1616, and Parigi's winning proposal, begun on site in January 1620, consisted of an extension of Pitti's original nucleus by three more bays on either side — north and south — and on three equal stories. The southern extension was not begun until 1631, but the final result was the grandiose central block of thirteen bays, with a considerably more pronounced horizontal emphasis than the original palace. This phase of expansion alone made the Pitti the largest palace in the city, but Parigi's extension was expanded further by Alfonso, his son, in 1640, by the addition of two more five-bay wings at each end of the facade. However, these new wings were built on only two stories rather than three, so that the already exceptionally broad facade now spread even wider, but was lower at the two ends. In general, the design vocabulary of the earlier sections was followed very closely, with the same rustication, the same continuous balconies, the same tall, arched windows. The last extensions to this now immense facade were the two projecting colonnaded wings at each end. The first *rondo* — that to the south — was begun in 1764 by Giuseppe Ruggieri, while the final element, the north wing, was added as late as 1839 by Pasquale Poccianti. The two wings provided an important degree of enclosure to the vast, empty *cortile* in front of the palace.

The history of the incremental growth of Palazzo Pitti directly reflects its perceived importance to a dynastic court whose real power and influence, however, forms an almost precise counterpoint: The ever more massive appearance of the palace contrasts with the slow, steady decline in the power of the dynasty within. The grand ducal apartments on the *piano nobile* reflect this transformation of the palazzo from its origins as the family home of an ancient Florentine banking clan (which traditionally would have been richly but sparingly decorated) to the palace of the grand duke of Tuscany and his court. Much of the decoration, including that of five of the principal halls, is the work of Pietro da Cortona and was installed under Ferdinando II in the 1640s, following the expansion of the palazzo by Parigi. These halls, which run in enfilade across the main facade onto the piazza, exhibit a unity of thematic imagery based on the allegorical celebration of the Medici dynasty, clearly evinced by the names of the halls themselves: the Sala di Venere (Venus), di Apollo, di Marte (Mars), di Giove (Jupiter), and Saturnio. The penultimate of these halls was the Medici throne room, decorated appropriately, by Pietro da Cortona, with the fresco of Jupiter about to crown the prince. The appearance of much of the remainder of the palace's interior reflects its changing roles over the last three centuries. Indeed, almost all of Florence's most significant political developments since the Medici transferred their court to the Pitti took place within its constantly expanding walls. From this role to that of the court of the Lorraine dynasty, though, there was comparatively little functional difference. Later, for a few years after 1809, it became the residence of Napoleon's sister Elisa, grand duchess of Tuscany, who redecorated some of the staterooms. With the return of the grand dukes, first Ferdinando III and then Leopoldo II, the palace once again played its former role as home to a traditional ducal court. With the unification of Italy, the Pitti became the royal palace of Victor Emmanuel from 1865 to 1871, and it remained the property of the House of Savoy until 1912, when it was passed on to the city of Florence.

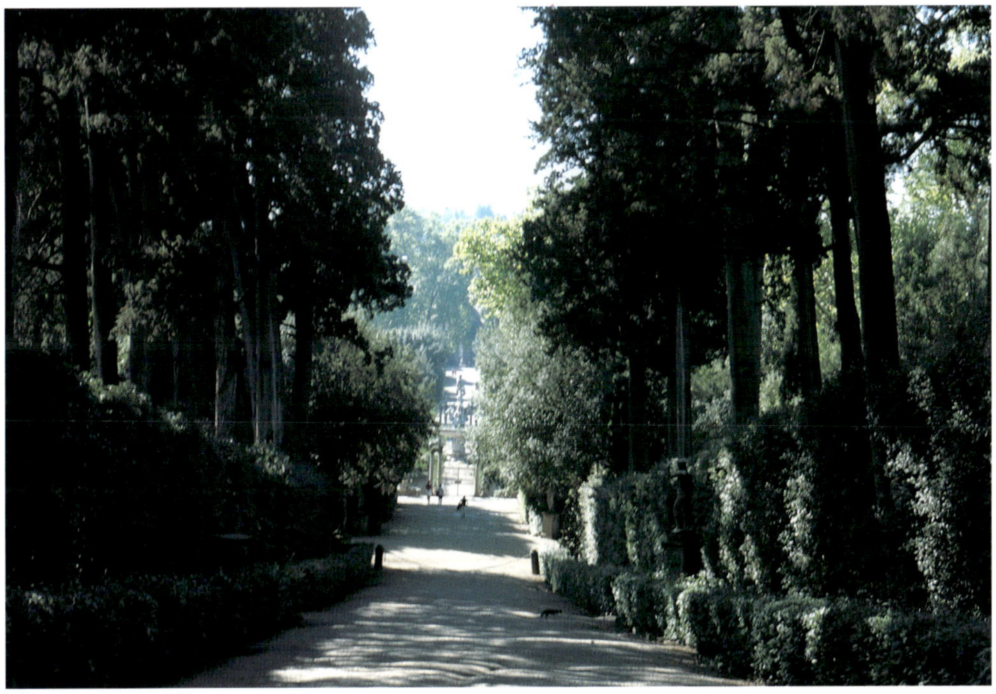

THE BOBOLI GARDENS

View of the imposing avenue of cypresses known as the Viottolone, which descends steeply down the flank of the hill toward the Isolotto and the Porta Romana.

Most of these successive changes left at least some mark on the palazzo.[30] The reforming Grand Duke Pietro Leopoldo, for example, not only opened the Uffizi to the public in 1769, but he also began to reorganize much of the interior of the Pitti, including the Sala Bianca, the white ballroom, executed with complex stucco decoration in the later 1770s by Gaspare Maria Paoletti. Pietro Leopoldo expanded the palazzo itself by the construction of the single story wing or pavilion known as the Meridiana, at the southernmost end of the south wing. This long annex, rather resembling a conservatory or orangery, was built in a simple, refined classical style, again by Paoletti; today it houses the costume museum. Pietro Leopoldo's modernizations were continued by his son and successor, Ferdinando III, by which time the contemporary style had shifted toward a more restrained neoclassical form. Napoleon's brief role as Italy's foreign emperor is also represented at the Pitti, in a modest if appropriate manner for the great modernizer, in the highly refined neoclassical bathroom, which, however, he apparently never used. The architect, Giuseppe Cacialli, was also responsible for the music room, a rather more substantial work in the north wing, which was intended to be one of Napoleon's principal reception rooms, with a colonnaded screen at each end, again in a rich but refined neoclassical idiom.

Today the Pitti contains no fewer than eight separate collections of works of art and crafts.[31] The chief of these, the Palatine collection, has at its core the paintings collected by the Medici, initially Cosimo II, and then Ferdinando II and his wife, Vittoria della Rovere. It was expanded principally by Ferdinando II and Cosimo III, but is essentially an accretion or amalgamation of formerly separate collections, to which a large number of works were added by the Lorraine dynasty. Cataloged and opened to the public in 1828, the collection contains many masterpieces, but remains highly eclectic. As with the Uffizi collections, Anna Maria Luisa bequeathed all of the works to the house of Lorraine, under the same conditions that they remain in the city and always be publicly accessible.

The Boboli Gardens and Their Buildings

"To these Delicacies we must add those of well-disposed Gardens and beautiful Trees, together with Porticoes in the Garden, where you may enjoy either Sun or Shade. To these add some little pleasant Meadow, with fine Springs of Water bursting out in different Places, where least expected." **Leon Battista Alberti**, *De re aedificatoria* (c. 1452) [32]

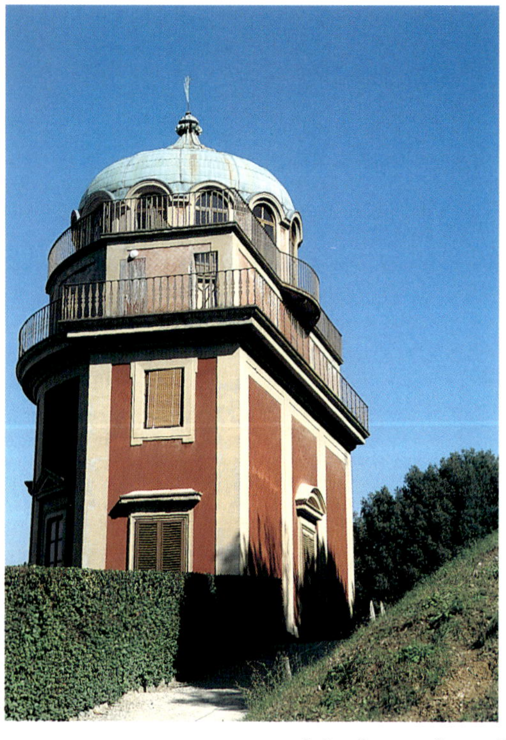

THE BOBOLI GARDENS

The Kaffeehaus, commissioned by Grand Duke Leopoldo in 1775.

In their final form the Boboli gardens covered some 2,750,000 square feet (250,000 square meters) of the hillside behind and to the south of Palazzo Pitti.[33] The gardens were a natural extension of the palace itself from the very start; indeed, the earliest attempts to design and expand the property at the rear of the palazzo began in 1550, the year after its purchase by Eleonora. The first architect employed here was Tribolo (Niccolò Pericoli), but after his death, just after the works had begun on site, he was succeeded in around 1560 by the Medici architect Ammannati; with the construction of the two new wings of the palace at the rear, Ammannati ensured that the gardens would be fully integrated with the palace.

The gardens are among the finest in Italy; from the first stage of expansion by the Medici they were always intended to integrate the natural with the formal, with liberal application of the element of water, and with a generous scattering of works of artifice by man, including grottoes, fountains, pavilions, and so on. They also contain many statues, a custom that became widespread in gardens of the seventeenth century, but that was revived here on a large scale in the sixteenth century, one of the first such applications since Roman times.

Although in their final extent the gardens are fairly complex, in essence they consist of two principal elements. The first is the section directly behind the palace and is planned directly on axis with it. It rises in a series of steps and terraces, which broadly follow the natural rise of the land. The second, larger element is a southwestward extension of this first part, at a right angle to it, and it, too, is planned around a long central axis, the Viottolone, which runs approximately northeast–southwest and terminates at the far end near the Porta Romana, the ancient southern gate of the city.

The axial progression from Ammannati's massive rear *cortile* begins with the amphitheater, which acquired its present form in about 1620, following the interventions of Giulio Parigi. From the amphitheater, whose form derives from the natural falls of the land, the sequence of ramps reaches the terrace of the Neptune fountain, set in a large shallow pond, while the vista is terminated at the summit with the colossal statue of *Abbondanza* by Giambologna. Above and to the left of this carefully orchestrated sequence of spaces and events rises the Belvedere fort, with its villa in the center. The villa, too, formed part of this scenographic program, since it was built by Ammannati in the 1570s, and despite its semi-urban location, must be regarded as yet another of the numerous

Buontalenti's grotto, built in 1583, is an extraordinary example of the Mannerist taste for exotica that flourished during this period.

Medici country villas, or *case di delizie,* that were scattered over much of Tuscany by the later sixteenth century — and form a distinctly evolving typology of their own.

The first major period of the development of the gardens, that is, from about 1560 to the end of the century, coincides with mixed stylistic developments in Florentine architecture: Restrained Roman classicism becomes tinged with increasingly self-indulgent Mannerism, and, indeed, examples of these and other styles can be found in the many structures within the gardens, which are liberally scattered with such visual incidents. One of the most extraordinary is Buontalenti's grotto, where, on the base of a highly restrained rational facade, he applied a richly sculpted mass of stone stalactites, with the kind of naturalistic fluidity that would be associated, more than three centuries later, with the work of Antoni Gaudí.[34] The grotto was intended to house the four famous unfinished *Prisoners* by Michelangelo, its naturalistic character in harmony with the raw power of these works.

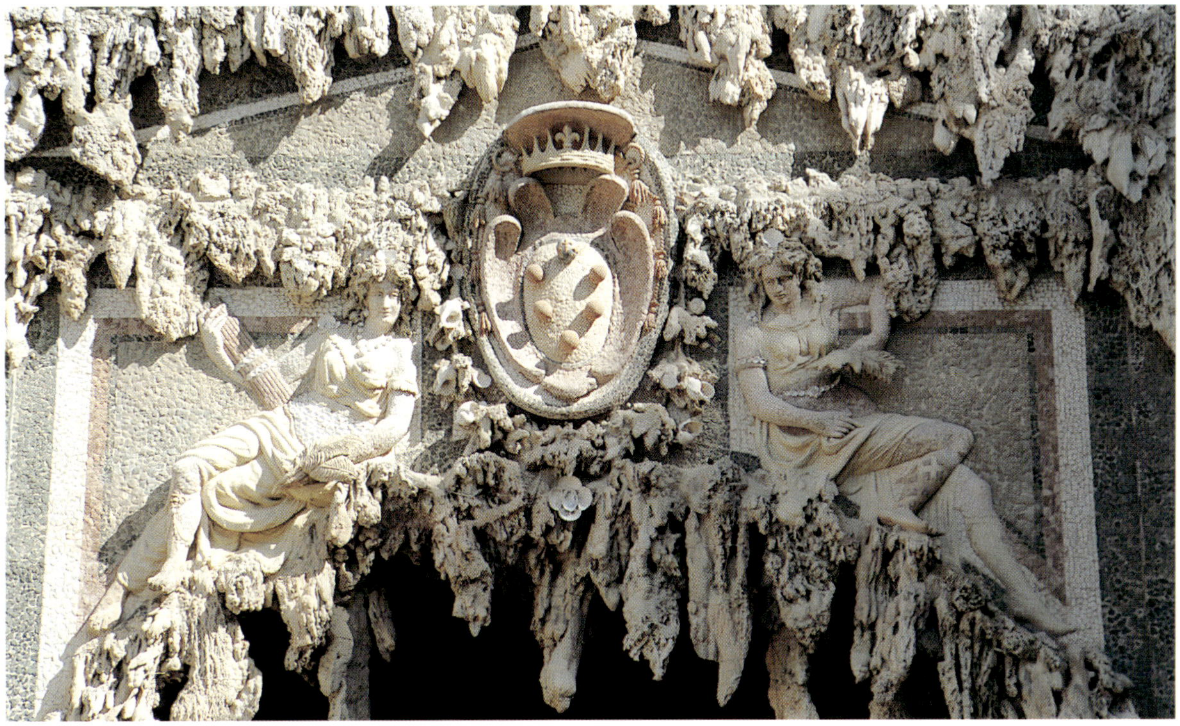

The extensive southwestern part of the gardens was planned around the long axis of the Viottolone, or avenue, which bisects the site. Much of this section was planned by Buontalenti's successors, Giulio and Alfonso Parigi, who extrapolated from the earlier section and, on a significantly larger scale, terminated this grand, sweeping avenue of cypresses with a *piazzale*, set out in 1618, much of which was occupied by the basin of a large pool. In the center of this pool was built an island, the Isolotto, reached by two stone bridges. The style is a rather late Mannerism, but the whole delightful ensemble, with the islet surrounded by stone balustrades and planted with orange and lemon trees, is highly characteristic of the period, although the fountain at the center of the islet, by Giambologna, was made as early as 1576 and was relocated here to add the final touch to the work.

The gardens continued to be further embellished by the later Medici. One of the last works to be built here was the Kaffeehaus, commissioned by Grand Duke Leopoldo in 1775 and designed by Zanobi del Rosso. The pavilion was conceived as another *casino di delizie* by Leopoldo, and thus represents something of an atypical departure from the rationalism that typified his rule. An architectural *capriccio*, the Kaffeehaus was built to take advantage of the magnificent panoramic views across the Arno to the city center, with a terrace in front; its semicircular facade is capped by a delightful little cupola.

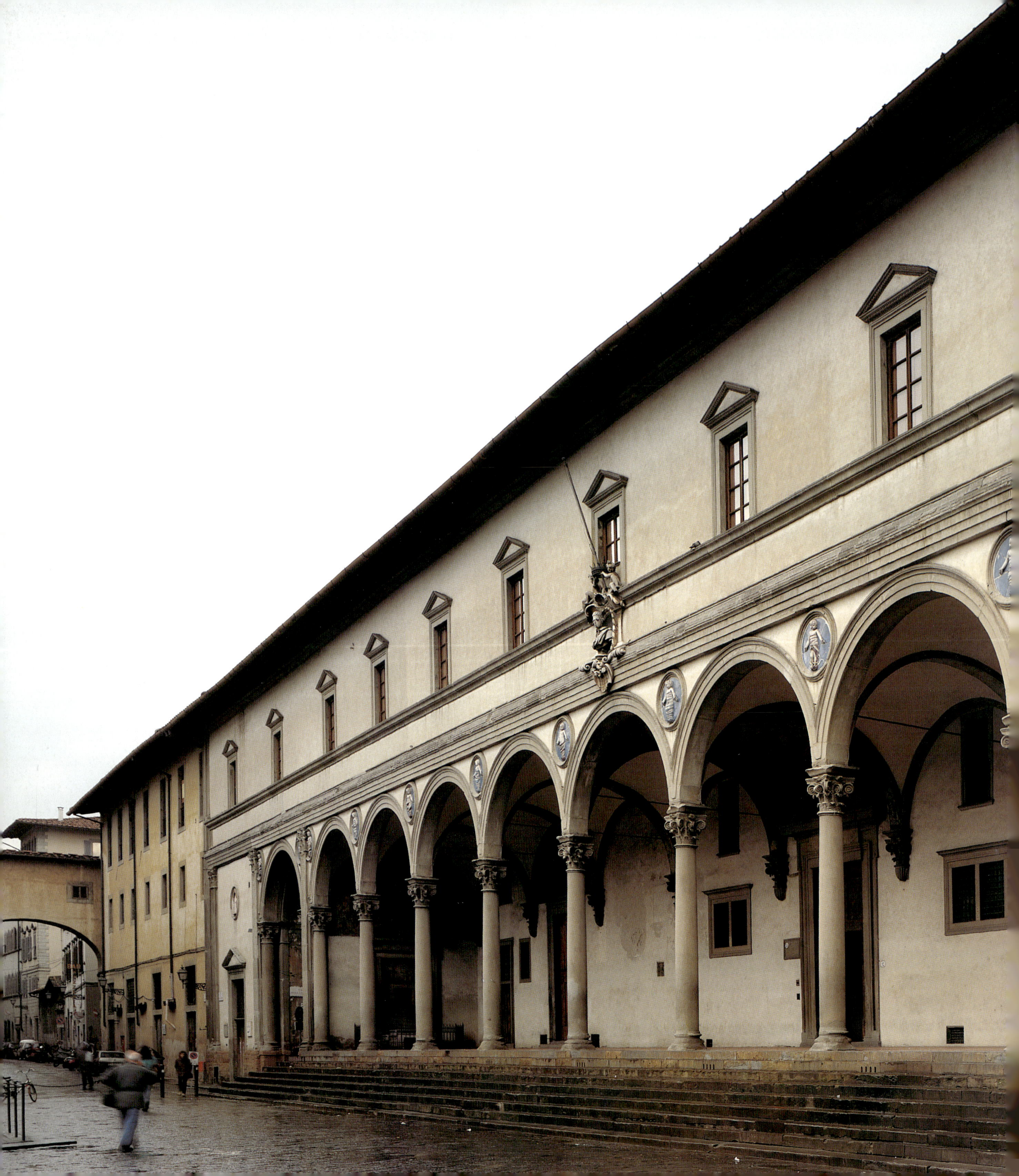

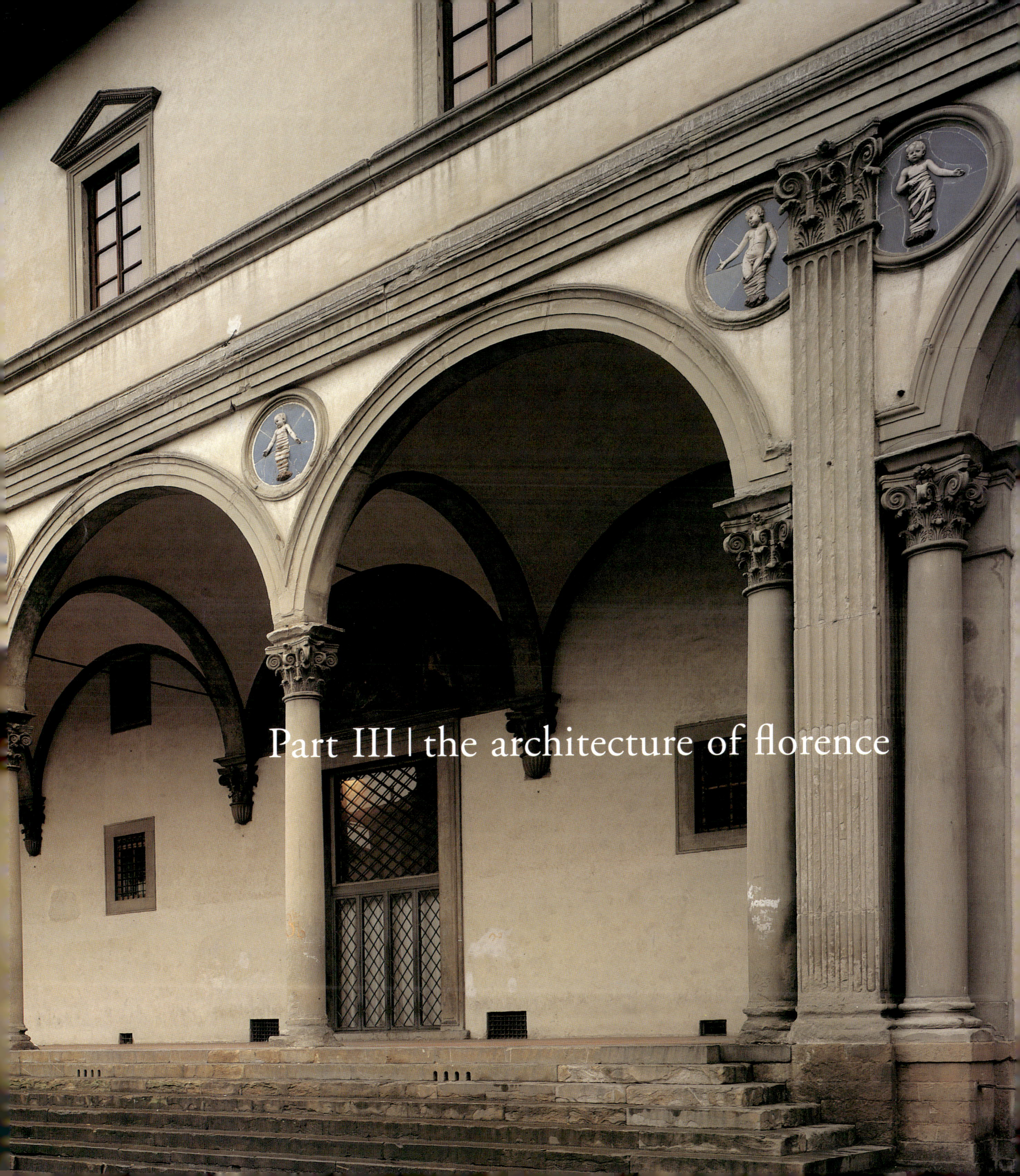

Part III | the architecture of florence

"The whole Business of the working Part of Building is this; by a regular and artful Conjunction of different Things, whether square Stone or uneven scantlings, or Timber or any other strong material, to form them as well as possible into a solid, regular and consistent Structure." **Leon Battista Alberti**, *De re aedificatoria* (c. 1452) [1]

OSPEDALE DEGLI INNOCENTI (previous pages)

View of the famous loggia by Filippo Brunelleschi begun in 1419.

Florence is built in a shallow bowl, where the Arno emerges from the lower hills of the Apennines. The Florentines were very fortunate with this location in finding sources for the basic materials of construction from which to build the city: The immediate *contado* yielded not only bricks for the the fabric of most of Florence's buildings, but there were also many stone quarries of different types and qualities, again extremely close to the center of the city itself.

Until the end of the trecento Florence was in fact a largely brick-built city. Despite the generous quantities of available brick clay, however, there never developed in the city a tradition of fine decorative brickwork that is such a characteristic feature of many other Italian cities, particularly those north of the Apennines: Bologna, Padua, Ferrara, even Venice. In Florence, brickwork was not used decoratively, nor was it generally left exposed, but was protected by a thin coat of plaster or, occasionally — but with increasing frequency in the quattrocento and cinquecento — was clad with stone. The significant shift in emphasis toward stone cladding, and indeed sometimes to entire structures of stone, can be traced not only to an increasing desire for more noble and imposing facades, but also to the influence of Renaissance writers and theorists, above all Alberti, many of whose writings were based on his knowledge of classical precedents, where stone and marble were both used generously. Later instances of finished external brickwork in the city are rare, and Palazzo Grifoni from about 1557 is perhaps the only well-known example.[2] But most of Florence's major monuments, although they give the impression of being built of solid stone, are constructed of brick. Palazzo Strozzi, for example, one of the noblest (and best documented) palaces in the city, has a substantial stone face but is built of brick; the long construction process required around 50,000 bricks per year over the many years of its building.[3]

Brickmaking in Tuscany itself has a classical origin. The Romans built in brick on a very large scale, and although the Florentines were never to match the decorative skills of the inhabitants of Emilia or Romagna, the skill of brickmaking itself continued throughout the medieval period. Brick production remained almost exclusively in the hands of the artisans themselves; the making of bricks, which involved fairly significant initial capital investment, but showed only fairly low, though steady returns, did not attract the interest of the mercantile classes. The kilnmen were highly regulated and were subject to the authority of a body called the Grascia, which, among other responsibilities, controlled the sale of foodstuffs and weights and measures. Bricks were classed in three different sizes: the *mattone* (the standard brick), the *mezzana* (half brick), and the *quadruccio* (quarter brick).

There were numerous kilns in the city's immediate surroundings in this period, but very few within its walls, as they constituted a serious fire risk; the most productive clay pits were located just beyond the city walls as well, particularly to the south beyond the Oltrarno. Some, however, remained within the walls, and there are records of kilns in the Via dell'Agnolo and Via della Mattonaia (hence the name, which means brickworks) in the eastern part of the city, and in the Oltrarno, in the Via de' Serragli. These small to medium-sized establishments were perhaps the most dominant feature of the immediate *contado*, and attached to the structure of the kilnhouse was frequently a fairly capacious colonnaded portico, which was used as a drying shed for the product. Most if not all of the kilns produced lime as well as bricks and tiles, and the Tuscan climate permitted their manufacture throughout the year, unlike other regions and cities in the north — such as Venice, for example — where firing was permitted only during the summer.

The great new construction projects of the late duecento and early trecento — the Bargello, the Palazzo del Popolo, and the cathedral — all led to a notable expansion of the stonemasons' guild and, naturally, to greater demand for both quality and quantity of the product from their yards. This demand continued into the Renaissance, with many fine new palace facades, all of stone, which dominated the city by the end of the fifteenth century. At this time there were probably more skilled masons in Florence than in any other urban center in Europe, even though it was by no means in the front rank of European cities in terms of its size or population.[4]

Fortunately there was building stone of more than one type within sight of the city walls, and even within the walls themselves. The buff-yellow *pietra forte* became the general building stone of Florence, and its extensive use unified the appearance of much of the city center. *Pietra forte* (also known as *macigno*), a calcareous sandstone, was quarried just inside and outside the walls as well as in the immediately surrounding hills. Major quarries were located at Monte Ceceri near Fiesole, Santa Margherita a Montici, San Michele a Monte Rinaldi, and at Monte Oliveto, just west of the walls in the Oltrarno; there were even quarries within the Oltrarno walls, between Santa Felicità and the Porta Romana.[5] While *pietra forte* remained the general construction stone of the city, the Renaissance also brought with it the increasing demand for *pietra serena*, a fairly soft but fine-grained gray stone, also found very close to the city. It was most probably the early use of this stone by Filippo Brunelleschi at the Ospedale degli Innocenti and San Lorenzo that greatly increased its popularity, although easy accessibility was certainly another factor: the quarries of *pietra serena* were located just beyond the eastern walls of the city, between Fiesole and Settignano, and chiefly around Monte Ceceri, Maiano, and Vincigliata, in the valley of the little Mensola stream. Florence may thus have been unique among Italian cities in the availability of such extensive stone quarries so close to the city center.

Some noble and merchant-class Florentines owned quarries, but the financial returns, like those from brickworks, were fairly low, and most were rented or leased to professional quarrymen; the large majority of the quarries were owned by the men who worked them. All stone brought in through the city gates was subject to an import duty, or *gabelle*. Some stonemasons restricted their activities to managing or owning quarries, and supplying stone for final working or dressing by others, and some ran their own shops in the city, while others not only owned their quarries but also worked the stone right through to its completed state, ready for building in on site.

Masons' workshops were generally small; nevertheless, they represented a significant investment on the part of the craftsmen in terms of the building and the yard itself, in tools and in materials held in stock — which, however, were often very modest. The total number of workshops in the city varied widely over time; in 1470 Benedetto Dei recorded as many as fifty-four, although in the census of 1562 the number registered had apparently fallen to twenty-one. This latter figure represented only those within the city walls, however, and there were probably a good number more in the immediate environs where land was cheaper, and at the quarries themselves.

Florence was equally fortunate when it came to sourcing marble, the far more expensive stone that became necessary for the cladding of the major monuments of the city. Tuscany had (and still has) great quantities of fine marble, perhaps most famously that from Carrara, but in contrast to stone, marble was used very little in the Florentine building industry. The cathedral and its campanile were really the only major projects in the city that required marble in large quantities for cladding,

NANNI DI BANCO, TABERNACLE OF THE ARTE DEI MAESTRI, c. 1408

Orsanmichele, north facade.

and the Opera del Duomo, or works department at the cathedral, acted as wholesaler or middleman to supply the very modest quantities required elsewhere in town. Most of the marble used at the cathedral was white Carrara, or green marble from Prato, which was considerably closer to the city. These marbles thus had little impact on Florence's buildings, but Carrara marble was used for fine works of sculpture.

One reason for the scarce use of large quantities of marble in the Florentine building industry was the practical difficulty of transport. The quarries of Carrara are approximately 80 miles (130 km) by land from Florence, a considerable distance in an era when road transport was slow and expensive. Carrara had been quarried extensively by the Romans on a very large, efficient scale, but the use of its marble died with the Western Empire. Most of the marble quarries brought back into use in the medieval period were located right on the coast, thus benefiting from easy transportation by sea. But transportation from Carrara to Florence by ship was still slow and fairly costly, and the quarries there really only revived significantly with the demand generated by the building of the vast new cathedral in the later duecento and trecento.[6] Commercial quarrying thus generally remained small in scale and highly localized to minimize the overhead costs of both the winning and transport of the stone.

Other building materials were required, such as sand, both for mortar and for rendering walls. Both sand and gravel were freely available from the bed of the Arno, which brought down large quantities from the surrounding hills; sand was reclaimed from the river by a group of specialists known as *renaiuoli*. Timber, although clearly essential for the industry, did not represent such an important element in the guild structure or in overall economic terms. Timber supplies were generally plentiful from the extensive upland forests of eastern Tuscany; much of it was brought down the valley of the Ombrone, and also from the Mugello, as the valley of the Sieve, a tributary of the Arno, was known. Timber was naturally used for many purposes other than construction; among these, for example, was the shipbuilding industry at Pisa. In Florence the use of timber in smaller-scale manufacture such as furniture making was contained within the guild of *legnaiuoli*, as distinct from the building carpenters and joiners, who fell under the umbrella of the building crafts, the Arte dei Maestri di Pietra e di Legname.

The Building Guilds

The organization of the Florentine *arti* reached its definitive form in the time of Dante with their division into three classes dictated by the 1293 Ordinamenti. The *arti maggiori* consisted of the following seven groups: the Giudici e Notai (judges and lawyers); the Mercanti, or Calimala (merchants); the Lana (wool workers); the Por Santa Maria, or Seta (silk workers); the Cambio (bankers and money changers); the Medici e Speziali (doctors, apothecaries, spice dealers); and the Vaiai e Pelliciai (furriers and leatherworkers). The building-crafts guild formed one of the *arti mediane*, or middle-ranking guilds, together with the guilds of smiths, butchers, shoemakers, and flax workers. The final, largest group, with nine members, was that of the *arti minori*, which included bakers, innkeepers, food vendors, and other similar trades.

Before the complete reorganization of the 1293 Ordinamenti, Florence, like most other sizeable medieval cities, had contained a large number of smaller, more specialized *arti*, in this case around seventy in number. This was still, however, a good deal fewer than the guild structure in Venice where, for example, as many as two-hundred highly specialized *arti* were registered. Indeed, much of the history of the Florentine guild system is one of consolidation rather than fragmentation. The definitive move in this direction came in 1293, when these seventy were regrouped into a total of just twenty-one altogether. The umbrella guild for the building industry, the Arte dei Maestri di Pietra e di Legname (literally, the masters working in stone and timber), became known simply as the Arte dei Maestri.[7] This consolidation into such larger groupings remained a characteristic

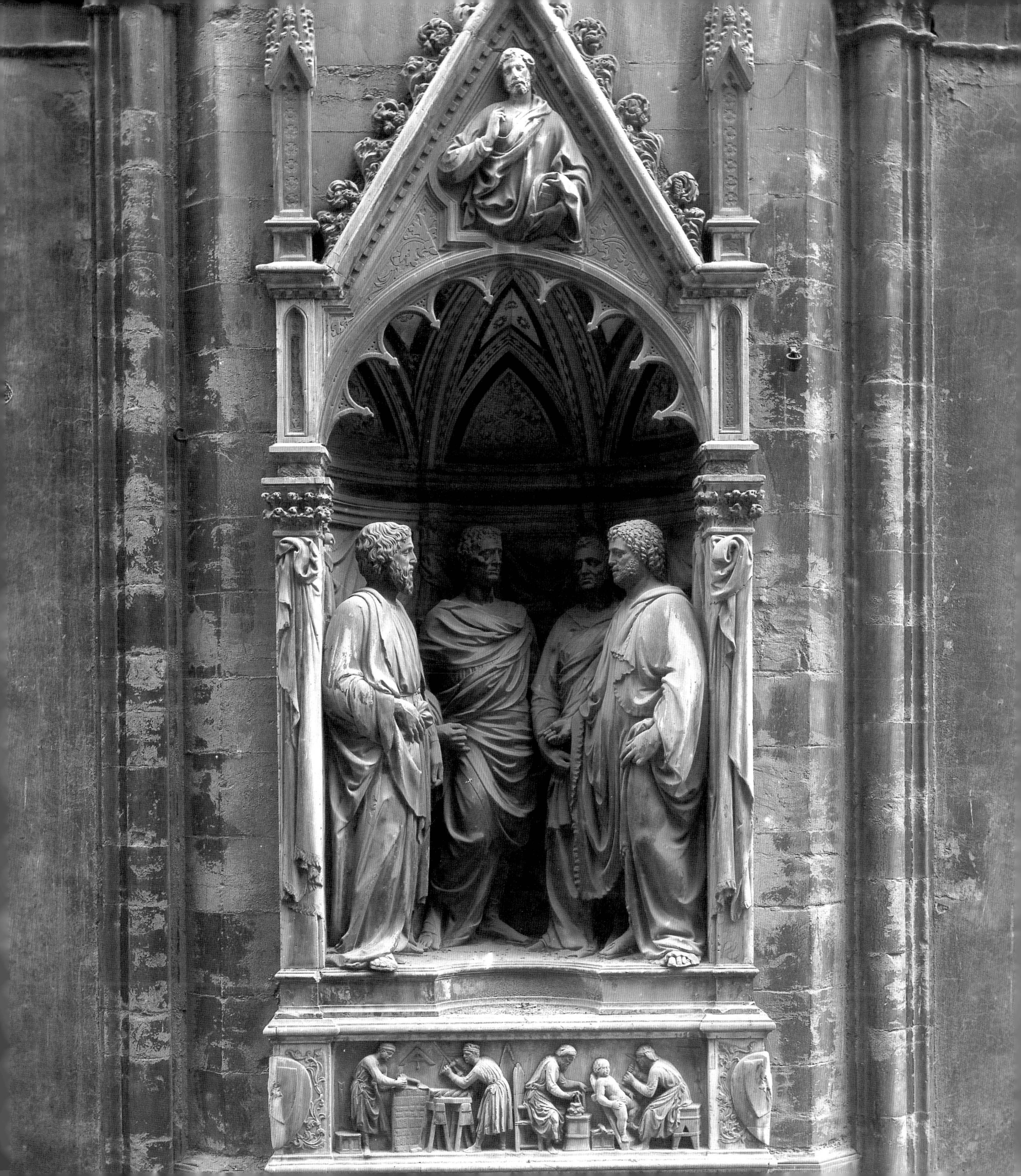

Florentine feature that was not followed elsewhere; in Venice, for example, the guild system remained highly fragmented, and in the building industry there every trade had its own guild: one for masons, one for builders, one for carpenters, and so on, each with its own regulations and statutes. Siena, on the other hand, tried the Florentine system of umbrella guilds for a time, but after a fusion in 1355, the building crafts fragmented once again a few decades later.

NANNI DI BANCO, TABERNACLE OF THE ARTE DEI MAESTRI, C. 1408

Detail of the frieze along the base of the tabernacle showing construction craftsmen at work.

Since the Florentine Arte dei Maestri had to cater to a number of different crafts, its statutes and general codes of conduct were drafted in a looser, more general manner than they were elsewhere. But since this *arte* was not one of the *arti maggiori*, and despite the fact that it had numerous members, it slowly became more and more marginalized, as were all the other *arti mediane* and *arti minori,* from the ever more dominant role played by the *arti maggiori*. A survey in 1391 recorded over nine hundred members of the Arte dei Maestri, and there must have been still more beyond the city walls. Almost all of its members were fairly modest craftsmen; it remained a very modestly run guild, with a minimum of staff and few assets; the only significant income that it received was a registration fee from its members, moneys that still barely covered the guild's costs. So, the Arte dei Maestri was quite unable to invest significantly in any field, whether in works of

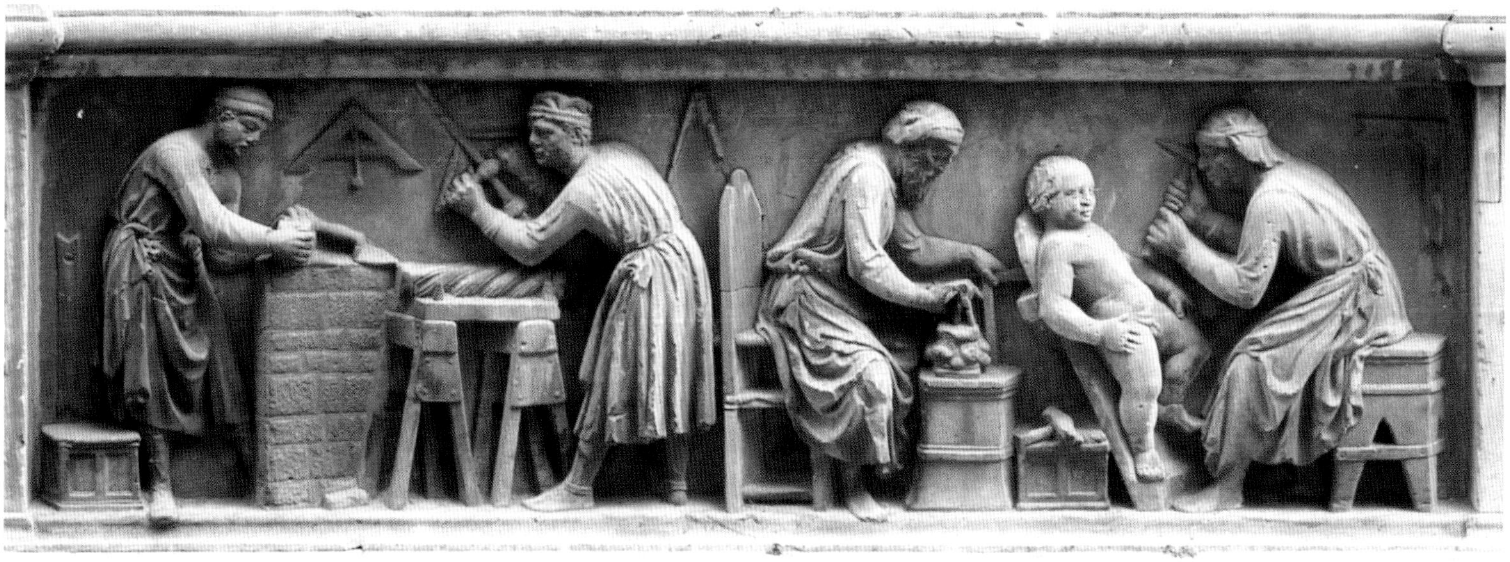

charity or in construction activity.[8] The guild's hall was thus a modest structure in the Chiasso de' Baroncelli, just behind the Loggia della Signoria. The only other grouping that infringed upon the building industry was the Confratèrnita di San Luca (the patron saint of artists), established in about 1349; not strictly a guild, this confraternity became something of an "umbrella" organization for the applied arts and incorporated in its membership, for example, goldsmiths and workers in glass.

Another important stage in the guild consolidation process took place in 1534, when the Arte dei Maestri was incorporated into the even larger grouping of the Fabbricanti. This guild now included all of the building crafts and formed an element in Alessandro de' Medici's plan to consolidate further all of the city's *arti*. The Fabbricanti (literally, "makers") now contained the previously separate guilds of smiths (*fabbri*), locksmiths and key makers, armorers, carpenters, joiners and furniture makers, as well as the Maestri themselves. This rationalization was combined with the relocation of the administration of this consolidated guild to the Uffizi, a move that also signified the loss of any remaining independence of the guilds, as they now all became fully submerged by the state's central bureaucracy.[9]

Over time the *arti maggiori* became so powerful by comparison to the other two groupings (*mediane* and *minori*) that, in practice, the system became polarized into the *arti maggiori* on one

ANDREA DELLA ROBBIA, *LA MADONNA DEI MAESTRI*, 1485 (Florence, Bargello)

The work was commissioned for the building craftsmen's guild, as can be seen by the details of their tools along the base.

hand, and all the rest on the other. At the same time the Calimala, or guild of the merchants, rose above the power and influence of the other *arti maggiori* to become a kind of paramount guild, with its own court of adjudication established in 1309; eventually, it exercised control over the manner of election of all the other *arti*, not only the *maggiori* but the rest as well. In such a system, those who were selected to be eligible for office in guild elections were effectively prenominated by the Calimala to ensure that a suitable candidate emerged; by the middle of the fifteenth century the apparently sophisticated, democratic process of electing guild officers had become so highly controlled and politicized that the guilds were all in the hands of a small, rotating inner group or coterie, who were directly answerable to the government more than they were to their own members. Administration of the guilds was now in the hands of consuls, who were "elected" (if that is still the appropriate word) to a characteristically short term of office of only four months; they were given administrative support by a small committee of eight or nine men.[10]

The Florentine Building Site

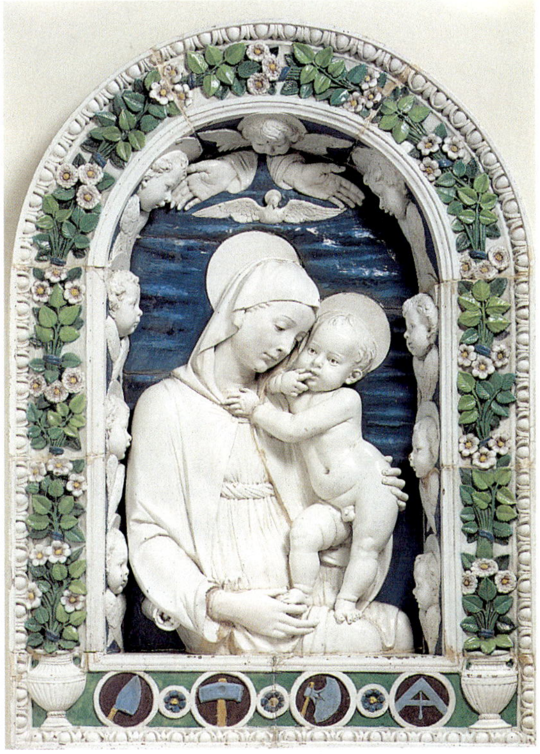

The large majority of craftsmen in Florence's construction industry worked on the basis of a daily wage. Wage rates varied fairly widely, and there was no central mechanism for controlling or establishing these levels; they were basically subject to the laws of supply and demand of the marketplace.[11] The only significant exceptions to this day-wage pattern were the permanent, senior masters retained on major building projects, who were generally paid on a monthly basis, sometimes on the base of an agreed-upon annual salary. They had the additional security of continuity of employment and pay. The day worker, on the other hand, was paid only for the days that he effectively worked, with no guarantee of work, or of any income at all if he was sick. The working week was generally six days, including Saturdays, but, as in most other important Italian cities, a large number of religious and other festivals ensured that in many weeks only five days were actually worked. Typically there were as many as fifty such holidays over the course of one year, so that the total working year was about 270 days. Although the construction industry always demands considerable amounts of physical toil, therefore, working conditions in Florence during the medieval and modern periods were not excessively arduous. The length of the working day was regulated by the Comune, as it generally was in medieval and early modern Italy, and was marked by the tolling of a bell at the Palazzo Vecchio. This working day was probably rather longer than that of today, but not excessively so, and in winter, of course, it was curtailed by the available hours of daylight.

Construction workers, as elsewhere in Italy during this period, were required to provide all of their own tools and equipment, and they generally brought their midday meal to site with them. Occasionally the employer on a major building project distributed free wine to the men on site; this was usually to mark a special event in the progress of the work. Sometimes, too, a banquet was held, again typically at the completion of an important stage of the project, such as the final tiling and weatherproofing of a roof, or the completion of a stone vault. The Ospedale degli Innocenti seems to have been particularly generous with such festivities during the quattrocento. These events represent very old, widespread customs in the construction industry, vestiges of which, such as the "topping out" ceremony, still survive today.[12]

The level of wages that a construction craftsman could expect to earn varied considerably according to his skill and experience. Stonemasons in Florence were generally referred to as *scalpellini* (literally, "stone chiselers"), but this term covered a wide range, from those who hewed the stone directly at the quarry to those engaged in refined carving in their workshops or on site. The simplest tasks were paid at a rate only slightly higher than that paid to unskilled site laborers, while the more experienced and skilled work was rewarded with rates considerably higher; typically in the quattrocento, wages could range from perhaps 10 *soldi* per day up to 20 or 22 *soldi*, only very rarely exceeding these levels. Although we are still lacking detailed corroborative documentation on prices, it has been suggested that, in the period prior to the Black Death in 1348, a skilled worker could afford to keep himself and a family of four at a modest but sufficient level of nourishment. However, the acute shortage of manpower after 1348 gave rise to sharp increases in incomes, and thereafter, a typical craftsman could have expected to see an increase of 50 percent or more in his living standard. Senior masters employed on a large, long-term construction project, such as the cathedral, had two important advantages over the day worker: security of employment, sometimes over many years, and frequently a significantly higher level of income; Giuliano da Sangallo, for example, was paid 30 *soldi* per day for his work at the important church of Santa Maria delle Carceri at nearby Prato.[13]

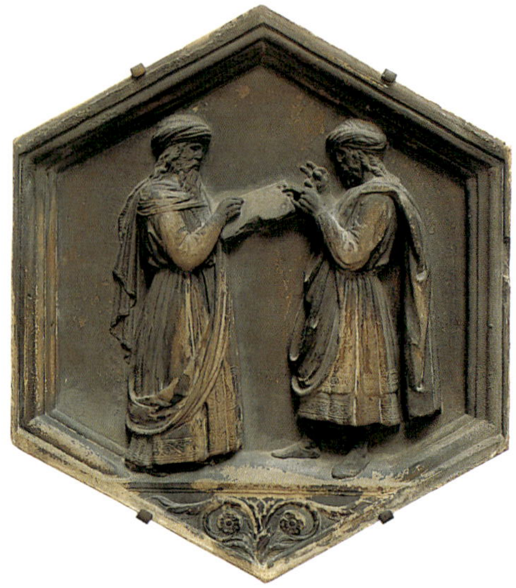

The medieval mason was essentially a craftsman, heir to an ancient tradition in which change usually came slowly, in a basically evolutionary manner. Many masons did not require much if any creative skill, since the large majority of their work was built — metaphorically, stylistically, and occasionally literally, too — on the work of their own predecessors. In this context, it is interesting to note the manner in which the city appointed the chief masters to take charge of the great project of the new cathedral and its campanile. Giotto di Bondone, Orcagna, and Andrea Pisano were none of them master masons by training; they were, respectively, primarily a painter, a sculptor-painter, and a sculptor. The reason for their appointment was thus not their construction skills, but rather, their skills in creative design, which it was hoped and intended would be transferred from their own workshops to the masons' yards of the Opera del Duomo. The technical skill required of the sculptor rather resembles that of the goldsmith, whose design talents were also very highly regarded; indeed, flexibility in working in different fields is one of the most pronounced features of the creative crafts in Florence both in the medieval era and during the Renaissance. Links between the creativity of the goldsmith and the sculptor are closer than might perhaps be thought; both worked in three dimensions, often to a small scale, and indeed many of the works created by goldsmiths bore a sometimes close physical resemblance to works of sculpture or even of architecture: Reliquaries, altarpieces, candelabra, and so on were often designed to resemble miniature buildings, complete with aedicules, windows, towers, and spires. A number of architects of the later medieval and early Renaissance periods, therefore, as the profession slowly developed and consolidated its role, had been trained in one or more of the other creative crafts, frequently as sculptors or masons, but sometimes as painters or goldsmiths.[14] And this strong tradition of multi-faceted skills continued well into the High Renaissance with Giorgio Vasari, Leonardo da Vinci, Michelangelo, and Raphael, all of whom worked as architects but also excelled in at least one other field, sometimes in several.

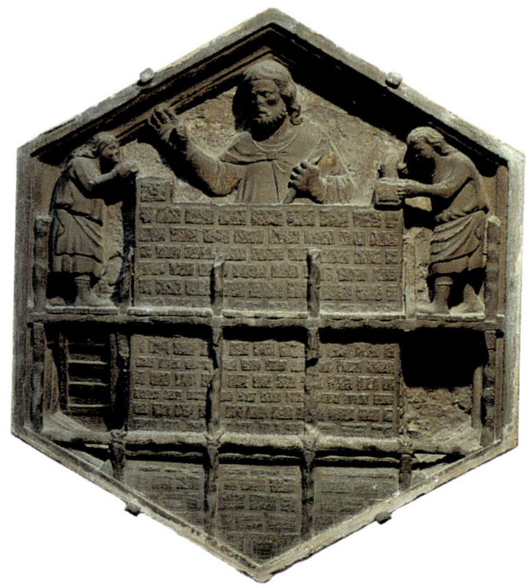

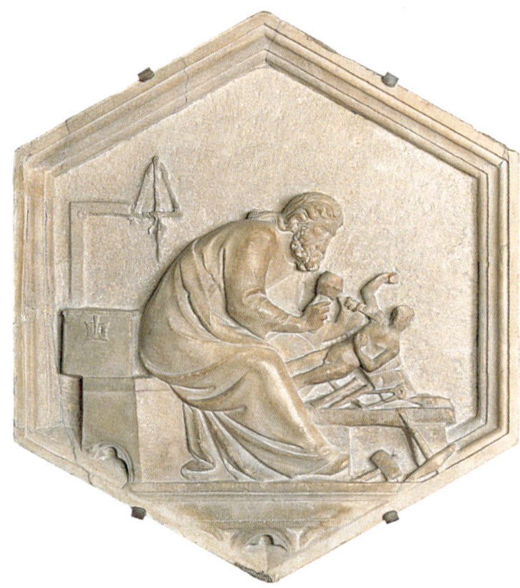

The various titles of architect, engineer, *capomaestro*, and others were still used almost indiscriminately in the late medieval period, and different titles were frequently applied to the same man working on the same project; only slowly did the roles of the architect and engineer become more or less permanently defined: the architect as the chief creative designer of a building and usually — but by no means always — the man who supervised its execution; the engineer was usually the principal master involved in public works in much the same sense as a civil engineer today.[15] During the earlier quattrocento, for an architect who wished to seriously advance his knowledge and experience, the road inevitably led to Rome. Brunelleschi, Michelozzo di

GEOMETRY (ALSO KNOWN AS *ARCHITECTURE*) (opposite top)
ARTE DI CONSTRUIRE (THE ART OF BUILDING) (opposite center)
THE SCULPTOR (opposite bottom)

Relief panels from the campanile of the cathedral, by Andrea Pisano, c. 1340 (Florence, Museo dell'Opera).

Bartolommeo, and Alberti all studied the classical legacy extensively, made careful, measured drawings of the orders, but also noted constructional details and the use of materials, from which they would later draw extensively — a knowledge that Alberti later codified in his famous treatise. Several parallel strands of development therefore led to the slow definition of the requirements for the role of the architect: the knowledge and awareness of the timeless principles of the classical heritage; a comprehensive practical knowledge of construction methods and techniques and the properties of materials; and finally, the comprehension of a sound body of theory to support one's aesthetic judgment. However, neither terminology nor practical roles were by any means settled by the quattrocento.

As the role of the architect as chief creative designer became more clearly defined in the quattrocento, so, too, did it become necessary to refine and codify his means of communication of these designs, both to his clients, usually a board or committee in the case of major public buildings, and, to some degree at least, to those who were to execute the works. Drawings, of course, remained the primary medium for the purposes both to indicate general design intent and to represent specific details; in addition, it was necessary to produce many templates — sometimes dozens or even hundreds — for the stonemasons to carve profiles for vaulting ribs, capitals, columns, and many other elements. But models, too, became used increasingly after the later trecento to convey three-dimensional ideas. Although expensive to make (they were nearly always of wood, but occasionally of papier-maché or even stone) they had great benefits: They were extremely easy for a lay committee to understand, and they were virtually permanent, an important consideration when a great work like the cathedral took several decades to complete. They therefore also served as a reminder to succeeding generations of board members and masters of the works of the approved model, from which (again, particularly strikingly in the case of the cathedral) no deviations were permitted.[16]

The two men who transformed the Florentines' perception of the design process and the role of the architect were Brunelleschi and Alberti. Although both were highly educated men, their backgrounds were significantly different, as, too, were their respective contributions to the aesthetic revolution that took place in Florence in the first few decades of the quattrocento. Filippo di Ser Brunellescho was born in 1377, the son of a fairly wealthy notary, a pillar of educated Florentine society. He received a traditional, well-rounded education, which included an appreciation of the liberal arts. It seems likely that his father's original intention had been that he should succeed him in the practice of the law, but he developed an acute and highly perceptive interest in the visual arts from an early age, and so, at fifteen, his father placed him with a goldsmith to learn the intricate skills of this craft during a six-year apprenticeship. He qualified and was enrolled in the guild in 1398. After this qualification, Brunelleschi's interests developed further to embrace mathematics, mechanics, and what today one would call structural engineering. It was this universalist, broad-based education that produced a master whose greatest achievement would demand the fusion of many skills to accomplish the immense cupola of the cathedral, symbol of the city's strength, power, and creative and technical genius.[17]

The role of Alberti formed a slightly later, but in a sense almost perfect, counterpoint to Brunelleschi's disciplined design skills and ingenious structural resourcefulness. Leon Battista Alberti was born in Genoa in 1404, the natural son of Lorenzo Alberti, from an ancient noble Florentine clan that had been exiled from the city.[18] Alberti received a fine education, at Genoa and then at Padua, one of Europe's oldest and most highly respected universities. In 1421, at the age of seventeen, he began to study canon law at Bologna, and graduated in 1428, when he took holy orders. Alberti continued his studies in Bologna, broadening his fields of research to encompass mathematics and science, as well as humanist studies. Unlike Brunelleschi, who wrote comparatively little, Alberti was a prolific writer and theorist from an early age; he probably wrote his famous treatise on painting, *Della pittura*, when in Florence from 1434 to 1436, but it was not until the 1440s that he began drafting some of the first sections of *De re aedificatoria*, his world-renowned treatise on architecture, which was not completed, in all of its ten books, until about 1452. This treatise gave the quattrocento a coherent body of theory and principle to set against the practical achievement of Brunelleschi, and thus provided a template for succeeding generations. The 1450s were also Alberti's most prolific decade in practice, since in that period he designed the facade of Santa Maria Novella and other works for the Rucellai clan. In 1459 he moved to Mantua, where he worked on Sant'Andrea and San Sebastiano. Despite the rather fragmented nature of his built oeuvre, much of which was completed by others after his death, analysis of those works that can be securely attributed to him are telling examples of the link between theory and practice that was to provide inspiration for so many.

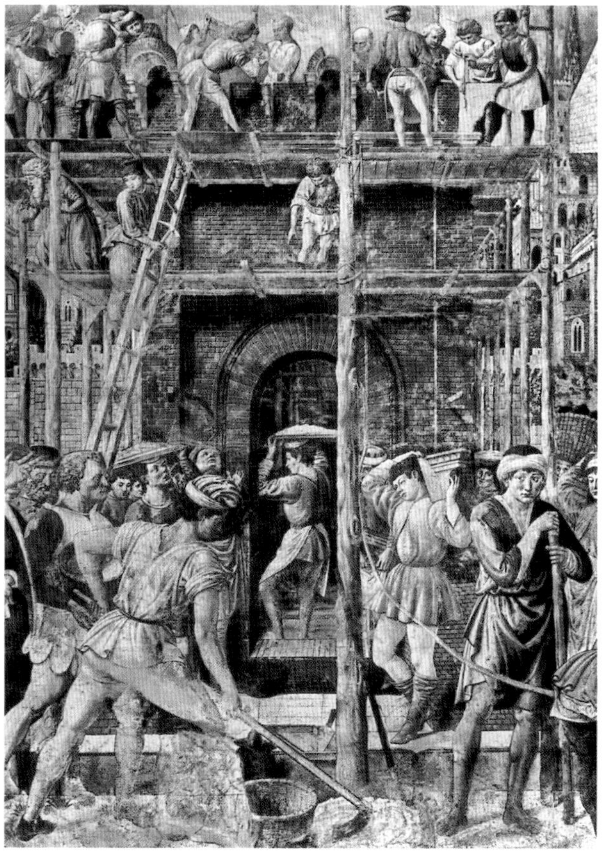

BENOZZO GOZZOLI, *BUILDING THE TOWER OF BABEL*, C. 1475

Detail of the fresco in the Camposanto at Pisa, showing contemporary building techniques.

In *De re aedificatoria* the famous guiding triumvirate, established by Vitruvius, of *firmitas, utilitas, et venustas* was modernized and reinterpreted by Alberti in the context of careful mathematical analysis and application. These Vitruvian principles had never before been clearly defined in terms of their practical application; they had remained essentially abstract concepts with little meaning for the layman. Alberti now redefined these terms as *finitio, numerus, et collocatio*, all brought together in what he termed *concinnitas*. While there has been widespread debate as to the precise meaning of these new terms, which essentially derived from some of the guiding principles established in his earlier treatise on painting, in particular *finitio* and *dimensio*, the former term is fairly easily rendered as "outline," "finish," or "form" and is thus equally applicable to architecture and sculpture as it is to painting. The second of Alberti's new architectural triumvirate, *numerus*, really forms the basis for design according to proportion and ratio, that is, an essentially mathematical approach to design striving for "perfection," an approach that Brunelleschi, for example, had already adopted with clarity and discipline in his two great churches, San Lorenzo and Santo Spirito. Alberti's third term, *collocatio*, can be translated as "composition," or the relationships between elements. Finally, these attributes are all brought together in *concinnitas*, a term that is very difficult to translate with precision, but that might be rendered as "the completed work skillfully assembled," and is really a conflation of the two Vitruvian terms *dispositio* and *symmetria*.[19] In the development of this theory Alberti was attempting to provide a universal framework, a philosophical approach to design that would give the architect, any architect, a coherent discipline to match the more practical aspects of design that are also expounded at great length in *De re aedificatoria*. For the first time in well over a thousand years, the architect had a firm foundation from which to build both the theoretical and practical elements of his architecture.

Between them, therefore, Brunelleschi and Alberti transformed the public's and their patrons' perception of the ability of the architect to design and execute a work as a coherent entity, based on a firm intellectual and theoretical foundation, which would inform an equally coherent, integrated, completed work of architecture.

LEON BATTISTA ALBERTI,
DE RE AEDIFICATORIA, C. 1452

Title page of Alberti's seminal work on the theory and practice of architecture (Eton College Library, Windsor, England).

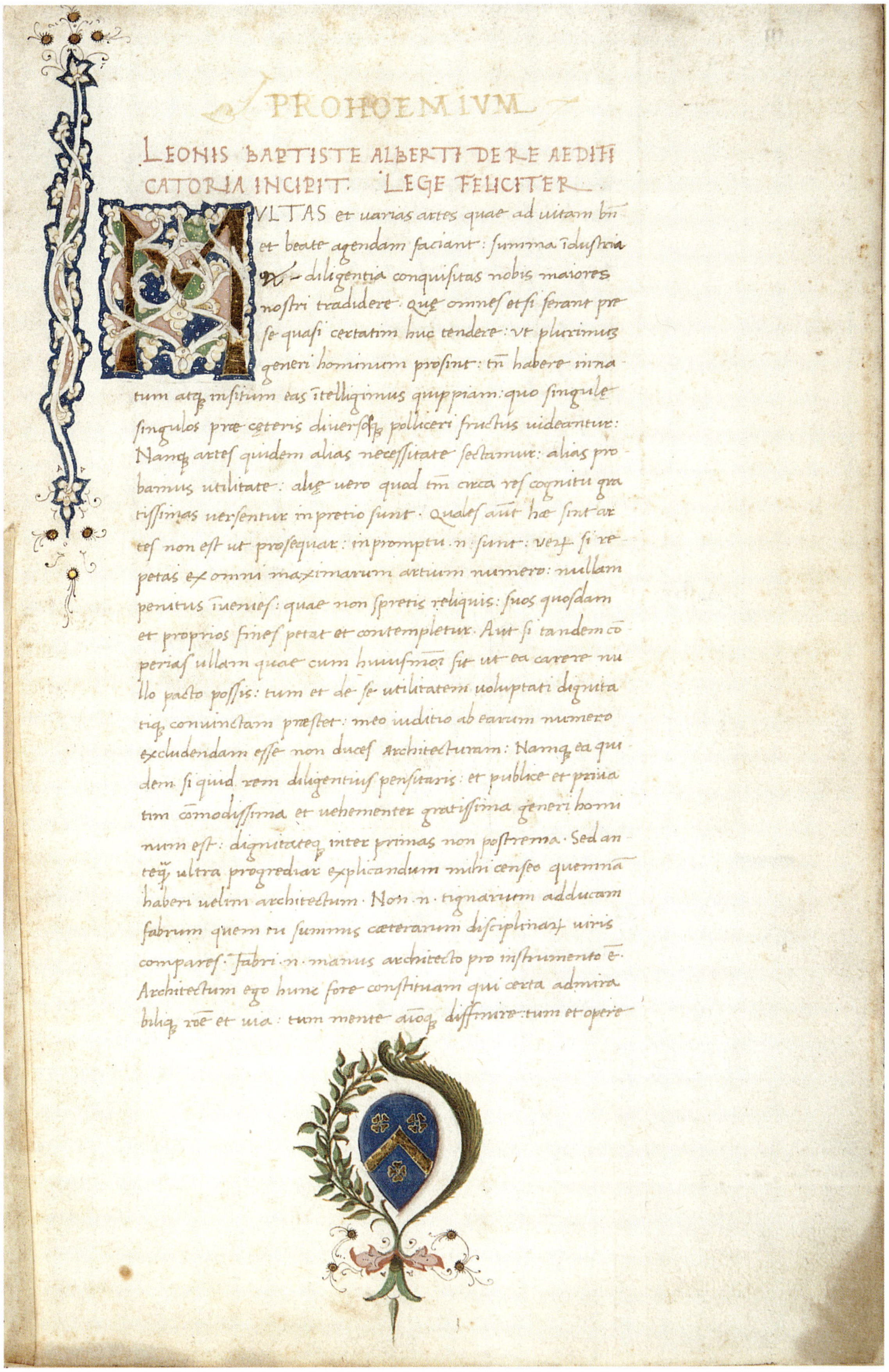
PROHOEMIVM

LEONIS BAPTISTE ALBERTI DE RE AEDIFI
CATORIA INCIPIT LEGE FELICITER

MVLTAS et uarias artes quae ad uitam bn
et beate agendam faciant: summa idustria
& diligentia conquisitas nobis maiores
nostri tradidere. que omnes etsi ferant pre
se quasi certatim huc tendere: ut plurimus
generi hominum prosint: tn habere inna
tum atq insitum eas itelligimus quippiam: quo singule
singulos pre ceteris diuersosq polliceri fructus uideantur:
Namq artes quidem alias necessitate sectamur: alias pro
bamus utilitate: alie uero quod tm circa res cognitu gra
tissimas uersentur in pretio sunt. Quales aut he sint ar
tes non est ut prosequar: in promptu .n. sunt: uerum si re
petas ex omni maximarum artium numero: nullam
penitus iuenies: quae non spretis reliquis: suos quosdam
et proprios fines petat et contempletur. Aut si tandem co
perias ullam quae cum huiusmodi sit ut ea carere nu
llo pacto possis: tum et de se utilitatem uoluptati dignita
tiq coniunctam prestet: meo iuditio ab earum numero
excludendam esse non duces Architecturam: Namq ea qui
dem si quid rem diligentius pensitaris: et publice et priua
tim comodissima et uehementer gratissima generi homi
num est: dignitateq inter primas non postrema. Sed an
teq ultra progrediar explicandum mihi censeo quemnam
haberi uelim architectum. Non .n. tignarium adducam
fabrum quem tu summis ceterarum disciplinarum uiris
compares. fabri .n. manus architecto pro instrumento e.
Architectum ego hunc fore constituam qui certa admira
biliq roe et uia: tum mente atq animo diffinire: tum et opere

8 The Defense of the City

"... and at the Distance of every fifty Cubits are Towers, adjoining to the Wall like Buttresses, projecting out in a round Figure forwards, and somewhat higher than the Wall itself; so that whoever offers to approach between these Towers is exposed to be taken in Flank and slain."

Leon Battista Alberti, *De re aedificatoria* (c. 1452) [1]

There are no remains of the earliest of the defensive walls that once surrounded Florence. The stages of the city's expansion were delineated by the succession of expanding "belts" of walls, successively Roman, Carolingian, and communal, each circle superseding its predecessors. Although for a long period several successive walls did survive, one inside the other, today the only significant traces are those of the last circle, the dramatically expanded walls built between 1284 and 1333. These last walls were by far the most extensive, multiplying the area within their secure confines by a factor of five, and extending to embrace all of the former *borghi* outside the earlier walls. So generously planned were they that Florence did not expand to fit them until the nineteenth century, and it is for this reason that a few tracts survive today, although the large majority were demolished in the nineteenth century. The total length of the wall was around 5 miles (8.5 km), and it was reinforced with towers 75 feet (23 meters) high.[2]

Because the wall took several decades to complete, a degree of evolution in the design of the gates and towers can be traced. Three of the earliest surviving gates, built as early as 1284, have a strong resemblance: the Porta San Gallo, the Porta al Prato, and the Porta alla Croce. The first two are very similar in appearance, and all three are characterized by massive arched openings, and by their simple, but immensely powerful, monumental appearance. The three other gates date from the 1320s and 1330s. The Porta San Niccolò, built in 1324, is the only one that still stands to its full original height of 110 feet (33 meters), and retains its crowning machicolation, as well as three superimposed chambers within it; the Porta San Niccolò has a matching twin across the Arno on the north bank, the Porta alla Zecca (the mint), so that together they formed a fortified gateway into the city from the east. The two other surviving gates were lowered in height considerably by Clement VII in 1526 so that gun emplacements could be installed at the top; their appearance is thus much more squat than it was originally. Among the last gates to be built were the Porta Romana in 1326 and the Porta San Frediano in 1332, both very similar in appearance: quite undecorated, with a relieving arch above their great central arches, both massively simple. The latter is the largest of all the surviving gates, and is sometimes attributed to Andrea Pisano. It is also unique in retaining its original timber gates, of equally imposing dimensions, 42 feet (13 meters) high and 26 feet (8 meters) wide. But the Porta Romana is the only gate that today retains significant tracts of the city wall on each side, and can thus be seen in something like its original context; all of the other surviving gates now stand quite isolated, as individual monuments, bereft of the urban fabric that provided their context.

The 1333 city wall, with its gates and towers, remained Florence's basic line of defense for around two centuries, effectively unaltered. However, the nature of warfare was to change significantly in the early sixteenth century, and this era saw two major new additions to the defenses of the city, which both reflected not only technological advances, particularly the development of new heavy siege artillery, but also the fundamental political changes within the government of Tuscany itself. The first stage of this new program came with the appointment of Michelangelo as governor general of fortifications in April 1529. The immediate task was to strengthen the city's defenses

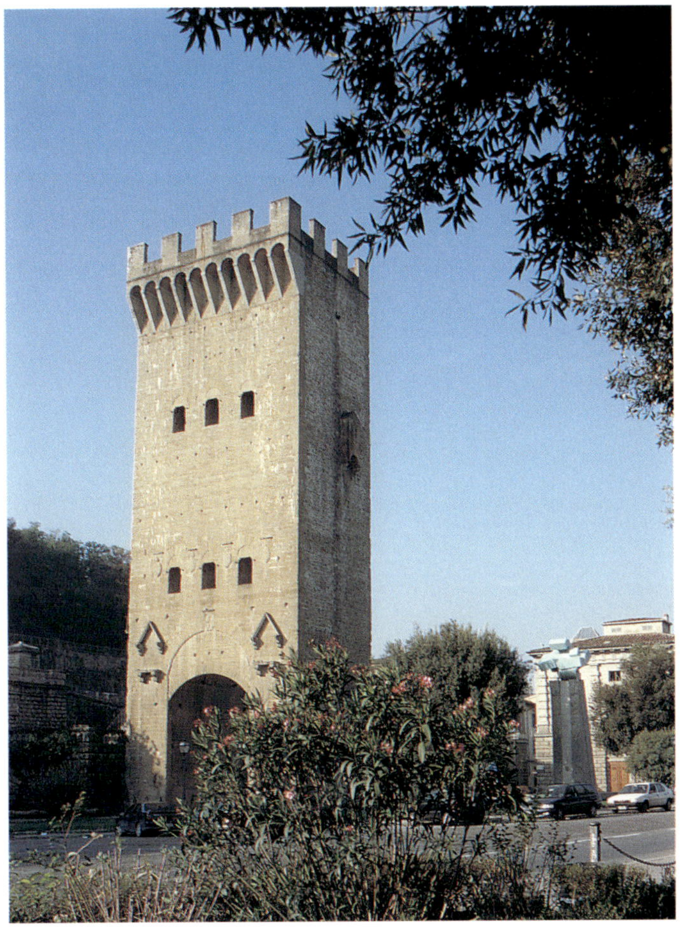

PORTA SAN NICCOLÒ (left)

Built in 1324, this is the only surviving city gate that still stands to its full original height.

FORTEZZA DA BASSO (below)

View of part of the massive surrounding walls; the fortress was built by Antonio da Sangallo in 1533–35.

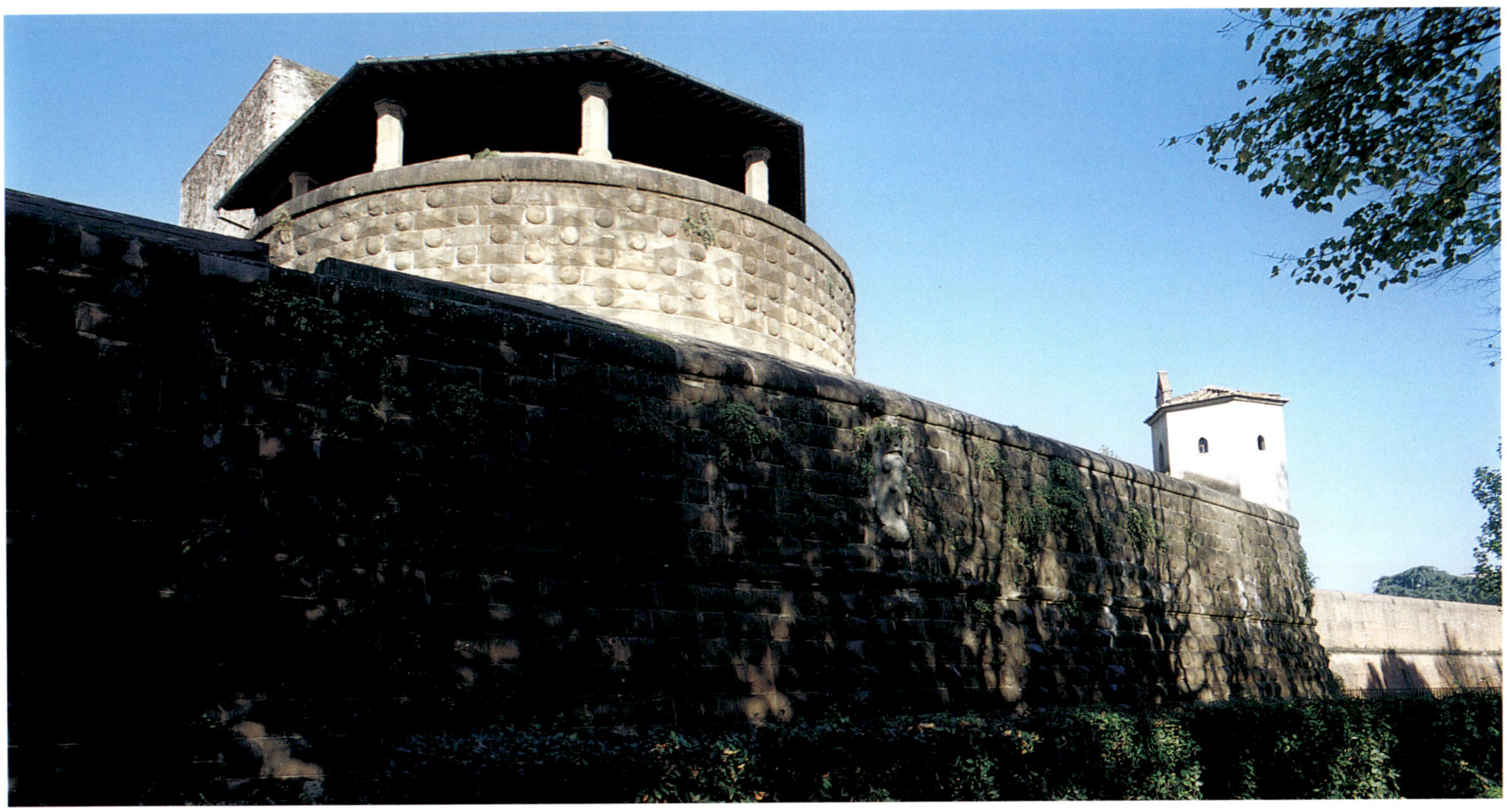

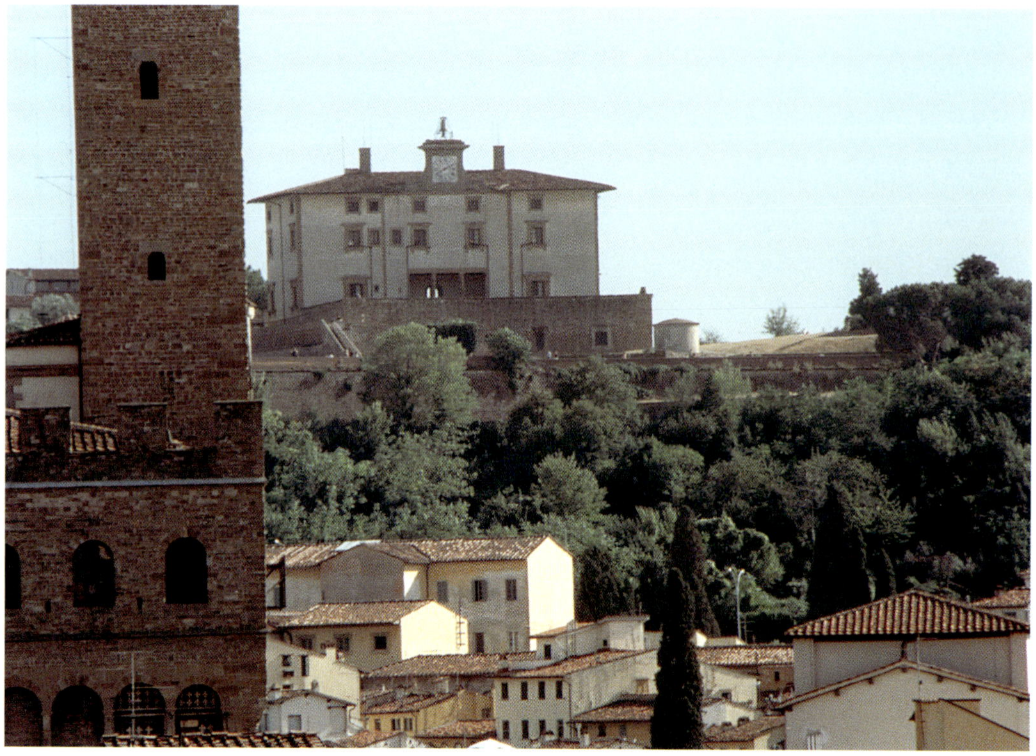

FORTEZZA BELVEDERE

Left: view of the fortress, so called for the superb views it affords over the city; the fort itself was modernized by Bernardo Buontalenti in 1590, when the villa for the captain was also built. Below: detail from Ferdinando Ruggieri's 1731 plan of the fortress.

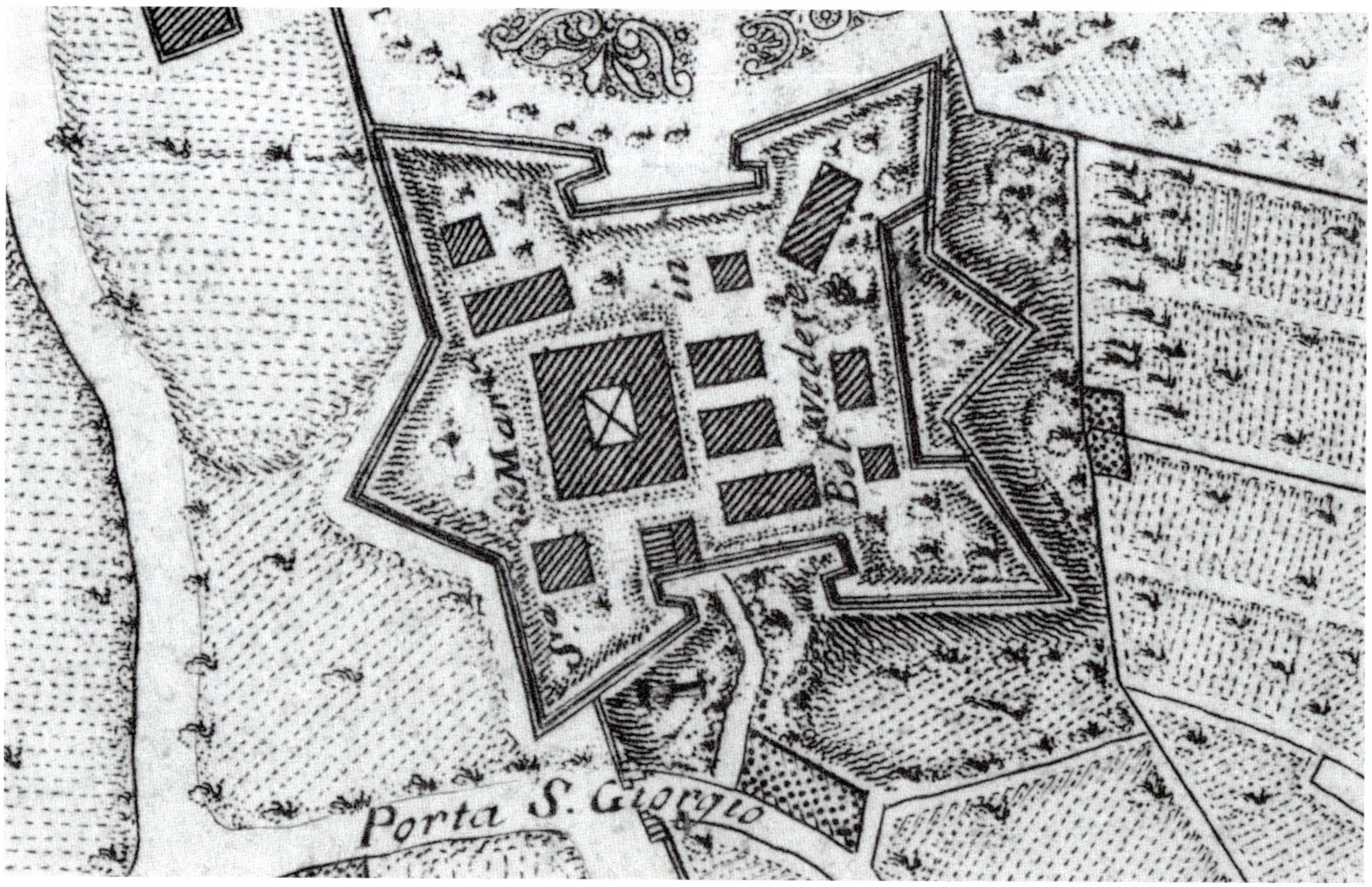

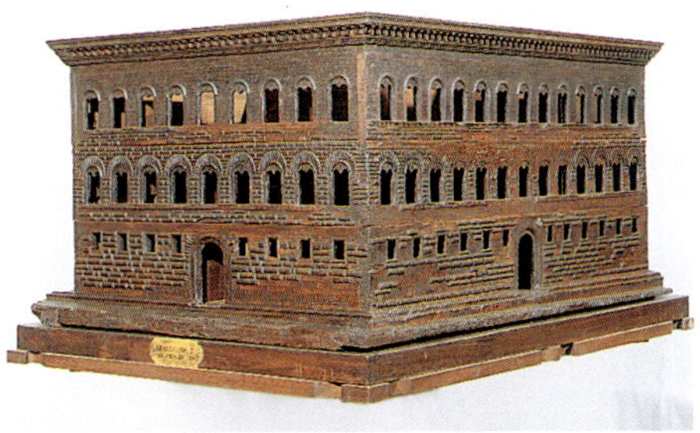

PALAZZO STROZZI

Wooden model made in about 1489 to demonstrate its final appearance to the patron, Filippo Strozzi.

against the imperial siege, and Michelangelo built bastions in front of the city gates as well as extensive reinforcements on the hill of San Miniato. His short-term expedients, which consisted of the strengthening of the whole circuit of the city walls with ramparts of earth faced with bricks, have not survived. After 1534, some of these temporary works were replaced by the Medici with more permanent reinforcements of stone. Michelangelo also produced a series of design proposals for more permanent reinforcement works; although the works themselves were never executed, the surviving drawings evince a highly original, inventive, and dynamic approach to the new exigencies. The locations for some of the designs in these drawings can be identified; they include the Porta al Prato, the Porta Romana, and the Porta alla Giustizia.[3]

A few years later Alessandro de' Medici began construction of the massive Fortezza da Basso, also known as the Fortezza di San Giovanni Battista, patron of the city. The *fortezza* was the first full-fledged permanent fort in Florence's modern history, and was intended to serve three functions: protect the northern approaches to the city from external aggression from across the vulnerable plains in the direction of Prato; protect the Medici from insurrection within the city itself; and form a kind of city within a city for the ruling dynasty, who could flee and live there on an almost permanent basis in times of social upheaval, knowing that within the *fortezza* were sufficient supplies to withstand prolonged attack from either direction. The building of the fortress proved difficult. The terrain was marshy, since the much-diverted Mugnone stream ran just outside the city walls in this location. Designed by Antonio da Sangallo, it was begun in 1533 with its principal entrance in the present Viale Filippo Strozzi; one of the existing city gates, the Porta Faenza, was to be incorporated within its massive structure. Despite the difficulties of the site, construction proceeded rapidly, principally the result of very large numbers of forced labor: Three thousand men worked on its construction, receiving food and shelter but no wages. It is said by some contemporary reports to have been built within six months. The symbolic role of the fortress was highly significant: Henceforth the Medici were to rule the city by force, either direct or clearly implied. The fort, with its pentagonal plan, remains immensely imposing today, and its design again reflected the need to take account of recent developments in the design of siege cannon: Each angle is reinforced by a massive corner bastion. The most impressive facade is that toward the city, with its brick walls clad with rusticated stonework, the alternating pattern of diamonds and balls said to refer to the Medici arms and their *palle*, as well as, more prosaically, offering an ideal surface to deflect the firepower of an attacker.

Toward the end of the sixteenth century, Ferdinando I de' Medici commissioned the second of Florence's two fortresses, the Fortezza San Giorgio, or Forte Belvedere. The site this time was diagonally across the city from the Fortezza da Basso, on a spur to the southeast, just behind the Pitti and the Boboli gardens. The land was surveyed in 1590, and the fort itself largely built in the period from 1591 to 1595. Ferdinando's architect, the ubiquitous Bernardo Buontalenti, again took full cognizance of modern developments in cannon and weaponry; his fort was built to a star-shaped plan, with powerful corner bastions. In the center stood a preexisting villa, which Buontalenti also modernized for the Medici in his characteristic manner. The Belvedere fortress, at least as much as the Fortezza da Basso, was designed principally as a means of subjugating the Florentines themselves, thus forming, in the words of John Hale, the noted military and cultural historian, "the second jaw of a vice, squeezing the principate on the people."[4] The design of the fort took the form of two bastions, one facing north toward the city, the other facing south, and piercing the line of the 1333 walls from which it projected. The fort was planned on two levels to follow the general natural contours of the land; buried deep within the subterranean vaults of the villa in the center was the Medici treasury. The panoramic vista of the city from the windows and terraces of the villa on the very highest point of the hill, which gave the fortress its popular name of Belvedere, provided the Medici not only with a powerfully reinforced citadel in times of strife, but an elegant balcony over their city in times of peace.

9 **The Social Networks**

"The Squares must be so many different markets, one for Gold and Silver, another for Herbs, another for Cattle, another for Wood, and so on; each whereof ought to have its particular Place in the City, and its distinct Ornaments."

Leon Battista Alberti, *De re aedificatoria* (c. 1452) [1]

OSPEDALE DI SAN GIOVANNI DI DIO

Entrance hall and staircase by Carlo Marcellini, c. 1735, a rich Baroque scenographic ensemble.

The Florentine medieval charitable network was very extensive. The chronicler Giovanni Villani proudly claimed that over a thousand hospital beds could be found in the city in 1339, and the quality of care offered, as well as the sheer numbers that could be cared for, was highly regarded throughout Italy.[2] Many hospitals were already long established when Villani was counting his beds; that of San Giovanni Evangelista, for example, which stood next to the baptistery, had been founded in the early eleventh century, initially for pilgrims and to aid the poor, but it was demolished in 1296 to make way for a larger, more capacious successor a little farther away. The most famous, though, was Santa Maria Nuova, which remains the oldest surviving hospital in Florence today, although much of the present fabric dates from a major reconstruction in the seventeenth century.

Among several prominent characteristics of the once numerous medieval hospitals was the fact that none were built or funded directly by the state, which considered that it had no direct role in such works. They were therefore all built and funded by groups of the citizenry, many by the *arti*, but above all by the religious orders. As was the case in most Italian cities, the institutions generically described as "hospitals" often fulfilled several roles, some of which overlapped with one another. They often, for example, fused together the roles of a true hospital for the sick; a place of shelter and sustenance for the poor and indigent, the maimed or the unemployable; a lodging place for pilgrims; and, occasionally, an isolation ward for those with contagious diseases. Although they were financially supported by the *arti* or other groupings of citizens, the administration of these numerous establishments was almost always in the hands of the religious orders. Santo Spirito, for example, was run by a specific order of Hospitallers; most of the others were administered by the principal mendicant orders. Sadly, little evidence remains in Florence today of these formerly widely scattered hospitals, except for four trecento foundations of which at least fragments survive, as well as the exceptional examples of the Innocenti and Santa Maria Nuova.[3]

The Ospedale della Scala is the oldest of these four, built on Via della Scala, and founded in 1313 by the noble Pollini family. Part of the portico of the church has survived, although as a hospital it was closed in 1531 and became a nunnery. To the north of the city center the Ospedale Bonifacio, on Via San Gallo, was established in 1377 by Bonifacio Lupi, but the medieval fabric was replaced in 1787 by Giuseppe Salvetti. The final two were founded within a few years of each other at the end of the trecento. The Ospedale di San Giovanni di Dio was established in 1382 by Simone Vespucci, close to the house in which Amerigo Vespucci was born in 1454; in 1587 the hospital passed to the friars of San Giovanni. The earlier structure was enveloped in a major phase of expansion by Carlo Andrea Marcellini in the early eighteenth century, which survives today; the church was rebuilt in 1702, but the most prominent feature is the reconstruction in about 1735 of the majestic Baroque entrance hall of the hospital itself, with its sinuous double-branch staircase and rich stucco decoration. Finally, much of the fabric of the Ospedale di San Matteo has also survived, although again much altered and extended. It was originally built between 1388 and 1410, under the patronage of Guglielmo di Vinci di Graziano da Montecatini, and the colonnaded

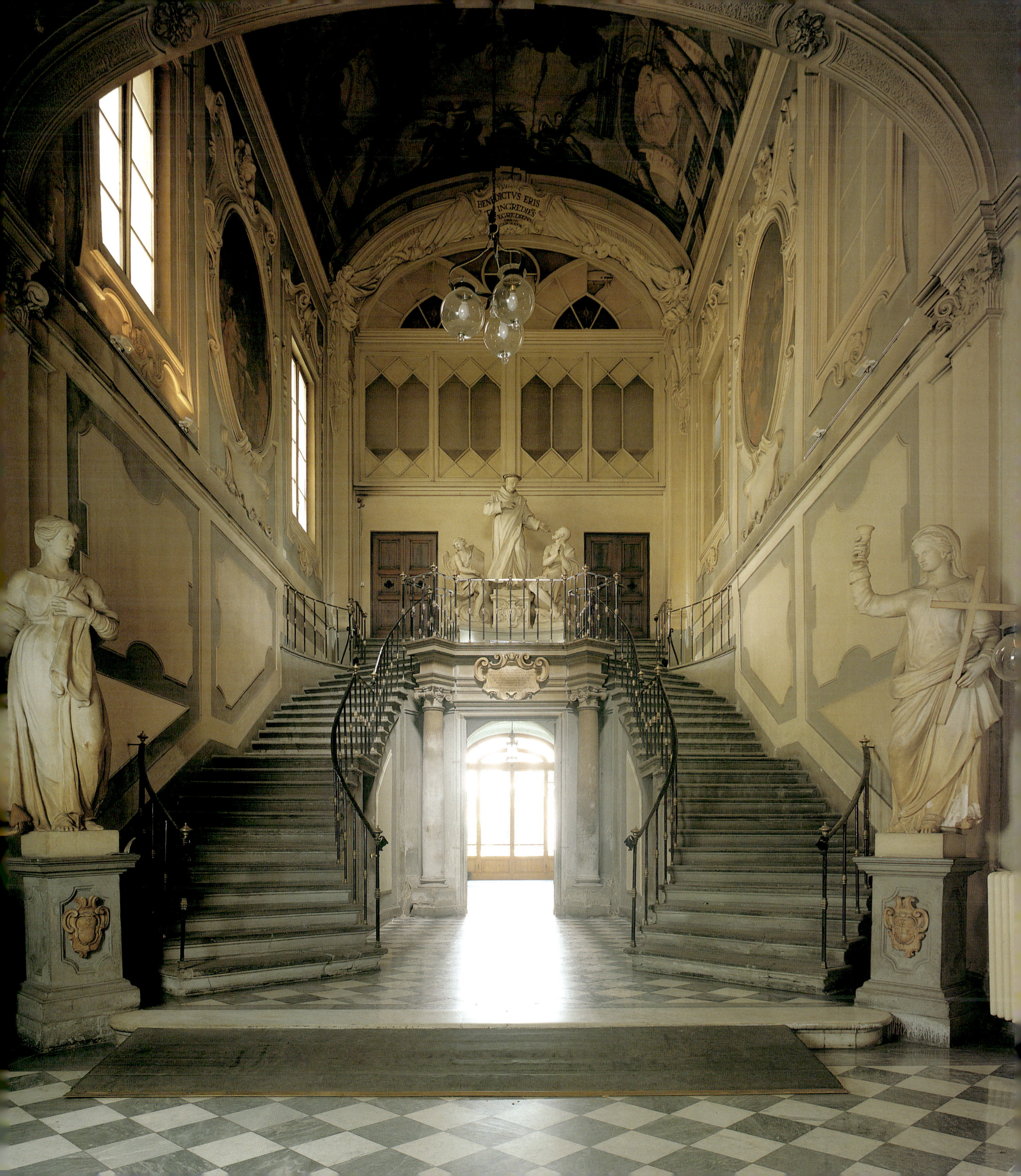
BENEDICTVS ERIS
INGREDIES
EGREDIENS

portico dates from this first construction. However, the hospital buildings were later subsumed within the complex constituted by the present Accademia delle Belle Arti, the Galleria dell'Accademia, and the conservatory of music. All four of these establishments reflect a notable expansion in charitable and hospital activities, partly as a result of the devastating plague of 1348, and partly the result of a more enlightened, humanistic awareness of the need to provide an adequate safety net to the less fortunate of Florentine society.

It was very much in the same spirit that the famous Ospedale degli Innocenti was conceived. The Innocenti marked a watershed in the city in several ways; in purely architectural terms, Filippo Brunelleschi's elegant, refined colonnade was not only one of the great seminal works of the early Renaissance, but also marked the first stage of what was to become one of the most significant urban set pieces, the first formally designed public square of the modern era, the Piazza della Santissima Annunziata. The Ospedale was also, of course, a prime example of Florentine social patronage, and is often cited as the first establishment in Europe to care for orphaned or abandoned children.[4]

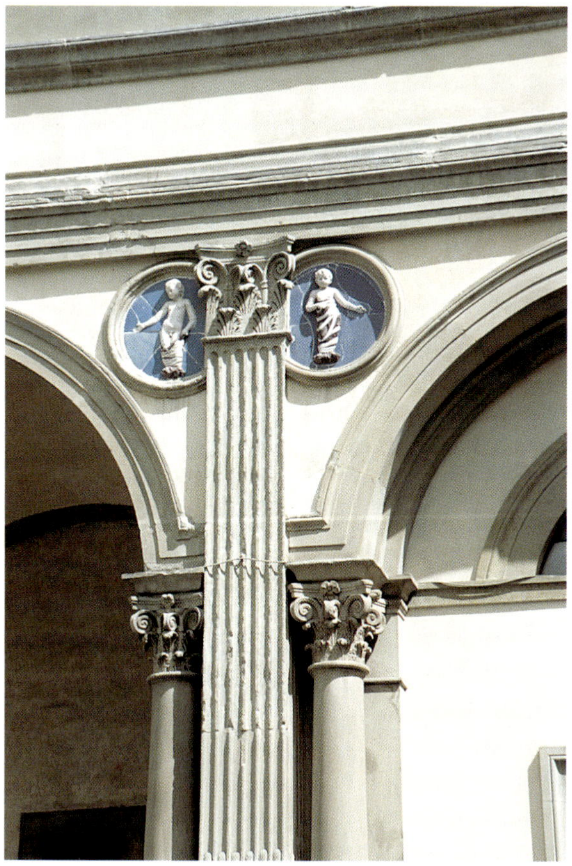

OSPEDALE DEGLI INNOCENTI

Detail of the colonnade. Brunelleschi's work of extraordinary refinement was to be highly influential (see also pages 160–61).

A product of enlightenment in several senses, therefore, the Innocenti was Brunelleschi's first major public building, and made a major contribution to the city's fabric. At the time of its commencement the square in front of the church of the Santissima Annunziata barely existed in a properly defined sense; although the Via de' Servi entered the space from the south, the only important structure there was the old church itself, the facade of which stood significantly farther north than the present portico built in 1601. The church was rebuilt in the 1440s by Michelozzo di Bartolommeo and completed by Alberti, but the significance of Brunelleschi's setting out of the loggia of the Innocenti was that it was aligned to one side of, but on exactly the same axis as, the church, thus forming what was almost certainly intended to become a spacious, formal, three-sided piazza. Brunelleschi's great loggia was not yet balanced on the west side of the square until Antonio da Sangallo built the Loggia de' Servi in 1516, but the seeds of this famous, highly influential urban composition had already been sown. The form of Brunelleschi's loggia emphasizes the theatrical setting that he intended to create. The spacious nine-bay colonnade runs across the full width of the building behind it, which in its original conception, although it actually contained several different elements, was precisely and symmetrically aligned on the central bay of the colonnade. Nowhere before had such a clear, bold urban statement been made; traditionally, in a building of this type, only the central entrance bay would have been singled out for special emphasis, but here the colonnade unites the whole facade. It can be read as an interpretation of the traditionally hidden monastic cloister, here extended and increased in scale to form a startling new urban element. It could also be read as a further variant of the traditional and ubiquitous Florentine public loggia, although here, unlike the Loggia della Signoria, it functions as an essentially transitional zone between the general public realm and the specific world within, in much the same way the considerably smaller loggia of the Pazzi chapel does.

OSPEDALE DEGLI INNOCENTI

Right: the internal *cortile* continues the architectural vocabulary of the external loggia. Bottom: plan. Behind the famous loggia the elements are planned symmetrically around the square central cloister, with the chapel to the north and the girls' cloister to the south.

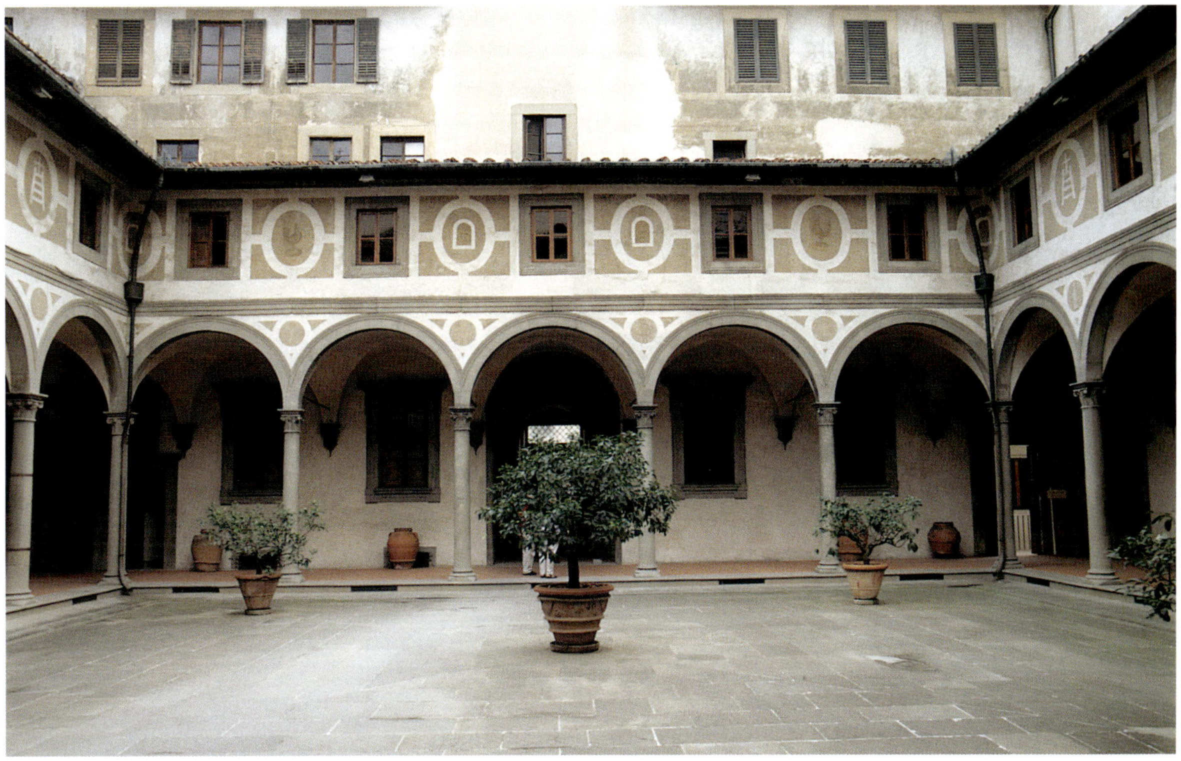

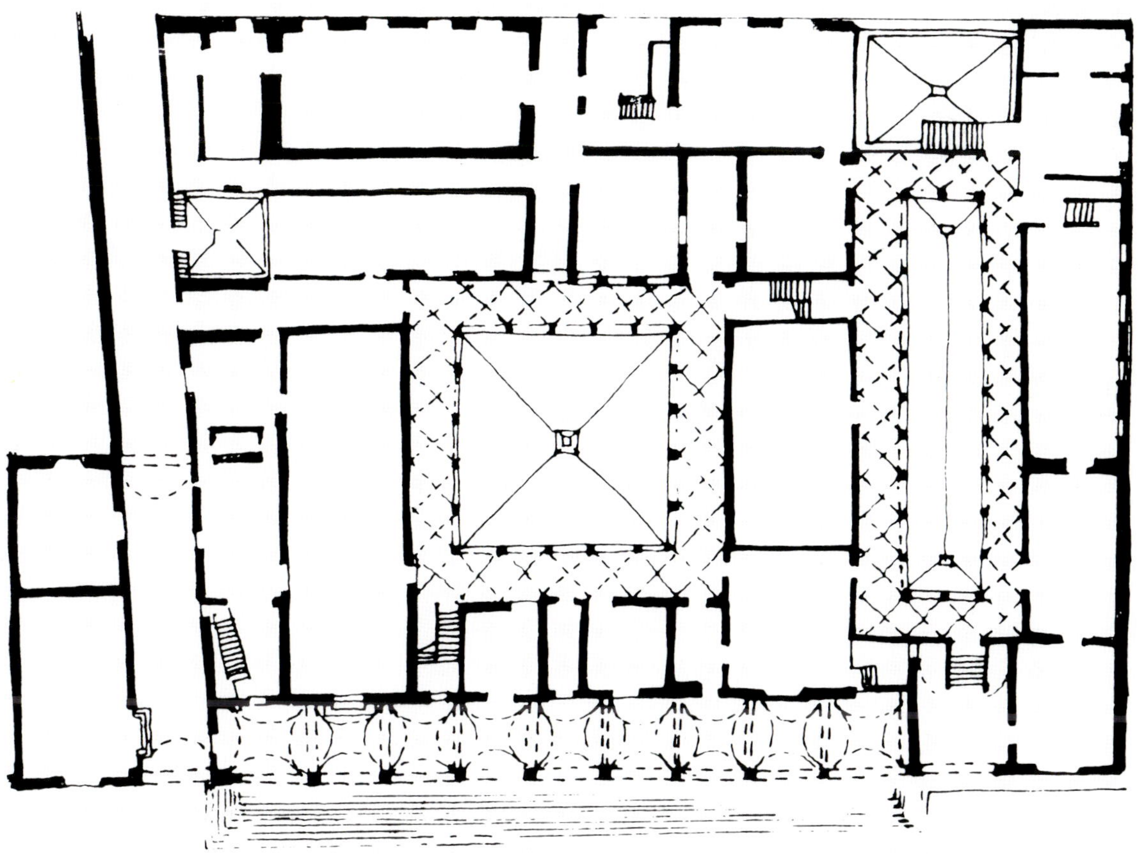

Within this grand, refined loggia, there are in fact three entrances: The central one, precisely on axis, leads into the cloister, the Chiostro degli Uomini, the hub of the whole complex; that on the left gives direct access to the church; while to the right (south) is the entrance to the main accommodation block, the Abituro dei Fanciulli.

The Ospedale was funded by the wealthy Arte della Seta, or Por Santa Maria, and was begun in 1419. The construction work was well documented, and much detail survives today regarding its progress. By 1426 Brunelleschi's portico was complete, and covered by a temporary roof; the church was also built under his supervision, as was the *abituro*. Brunelleschi also planned the main central cloister, although it was built only after he was replaced by a new master, Francesco della Luna. Work continued under della Luna in 1436 after a hiatus, and the cloister was finally completed only in 1470, when Stefano di Jacopo Rosselli built the first floor accommodation. Della Luna also built the annexed extension to the south, including the second narrow cloister, the Chiostro delle Donne, and the women's wing. In 1439 della Luna added the first story above Brunelleschi's original loggia, closely following his original intentions. Finally, on 25 January 1445, the entire complex was formally inaugurated, but the eight famous tondi by Andrea della Robbia that adorn the spandrels of Brunelleschi's arcade were not added until 1487.

The key seminal element of the whole complex remains Brunelleschi's spacious, unifying loggia. Its design contains a number of the characteristic basic elements of his later, mature work: the simple harmonic proportions, based on the circle, the square, and the cube; the spare, refined detailing in *pietra serena* set against white stucco; the simple light semicircular arches; and the richly detailed Corinthian capitals with their prominent corner volutes. Much of this vocabulary was developed further at San Lorenzo and Santo Spirito.

The only other important surviving hospital from Florence's medieval past has a very different history, although it, too, made an important contribution to the urban fabric. The Ospedale, or more correctly, because it is the oldest and most important in the city, the Arcispedale di Santa Maria Nuova was established in 1286, under the patronage of Folco Portinari, the wealthy banker whose other claim to posterity is that he was the father of Dante's beloved Beatrice. Its beginnings were modest indeed, with a mere twelve beds, but it was enlarged in 1296, and in 1312 was divided into two sizeable elements, one for men and one for women; the former stood just to the east of the church of San Egidio, while the women's wing stood across the street in the present Via Folco Portinari.[5] Thus, by the time of the disastrous plague of 1348, it contained two hundred beds. In about 1420 the Chiostro delle Medicherie was built just to the right of the church, which was itself enlarged at the same time. The church was the original seat of the Compagnia di San Luca, the confraternity dedicated to the patron saint of painters, and the new choir of the church was indeed decorated by many of the finest artists of the era, including Domenico Veneziano, Andrea del Castagno, and Piero della Francesca; however, all was destroyed in the final stage of enlargement of the church by Buontalenti at the end of the sixteenth century. Buontalenti was appointed by Francesco I to embark on a major phase of expansion, and, in addition to the works at the church, he began the first stage of the noble, classical loggia at the front of the complex. But only the central bay and the five to the right were completed after 1612 — after Buontalenti's death — by Giulio Parigi; it was not until the early 1660s that the composition was completed by the balancing five bays on the left side of the entrance. As Brunelleschi had done at the Innocenti nearly two centuries earlier, therefore, Buontalenti — and later, Parigi and his followers — united a large, rather sprawling complex of structures by facing them with a grandiose lateral loggia. It incorporated the entrance of the church of San Egidio at the center of the composition, whose location was emphasized further with the balcony added in 1699. The final and present appearance of this imposing structure was not completed until the two side wings that reach forward to enclose the

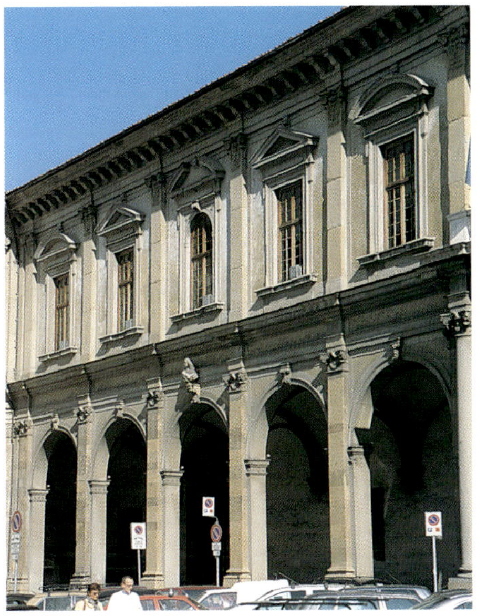

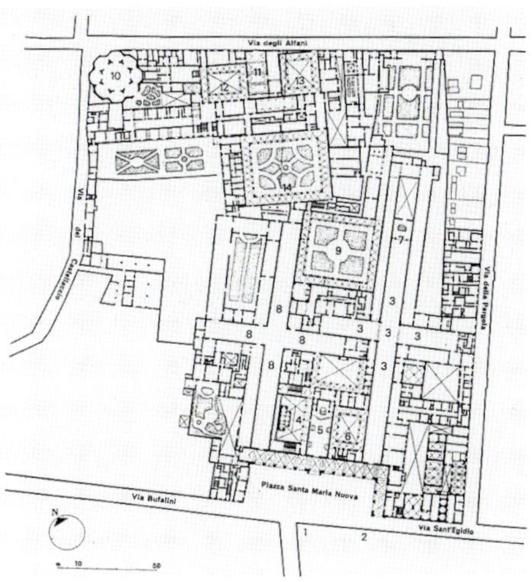

ARCISPEDALE DI SANTA MARIA NUOVA

Top: view of the colonnaded loggia begun by Buontalenti in 1606, which masks the complex building behind. Above: plan of the whole complex. The two outermost wings were built in 1707 and as late as the 1950s.

piazza were added. The right wing was built from 1707 to 1710, to the same design as the existing colonnade, but its partner to the left was added only in very recent times, in 1957.

The Arti

For a long time, many of the *arti* had no guildhall or place of assembly of their own, but instead simply met at their patronal altar in one of the city's churches; for many of the *arti* this base was at Santa Croce. Before the end of the thirteenth century, and despite the great prosperity of the city generally, only three are known to have had formal homes. The earliest was that of the Calimala, established in 1237, which met in one of the tower houses of the Cavalcanti family near the Mercato Nuovo. The next to establish a regular meeting place were the judges and lawyers, who after 1269 met in the crypt of the church of Santo Stefano alla Badia. Six years later they obtained the right to meet in a room within the Palazzo del Podestà, while in 1304 they moved again, this time to the church of San Procolo. The last of this early trio was the guild of the *tintori* (dyers), who after about 1280 met at San Onofrio.

The early trecento, though, saw a proliferation of guild headquarters. The *beccai* (butchers) found home on the north side of Orsanmichele in about 1320; the Arte di Por Santa Maria rented premises nearby in 1313, in the street that still bears its name today. In the following year the *medici, speziali e merciai* also put down roots in one of the houses of the Lamberti clan near the Via della Pelliceria, although they moved again later. In this same period the wealthiest of the *arti* also began to construct their own purpose-built halls.[6] They were usually fairly modest structures, though, the typical accommodation consisting of a ground-floor office, where the guild records were generally kept, and a first-floor room or hall (known as the *sala magna,* but which was in fact quite modest), where meetings of the members were held. The first to set this new pattern was perhaps the Arte della Lana, whose hall was built in 1308; it was significantly altered in 1331. The judges and lawyers also built their own hall on Via Pandolfini in the mid-fourteenth century, as did the Calimala (which survives today on the street of the same name), and the Arte della Seta. The *albergatori* (innkeepers) and the *rigattieri* (secondhand dealers) followed the same pattern. In fact, a new statute published in 1335 had established the requirement that all of the *arti* build or acquire a formal meeting place; by then a number had clearly already done so. Most of those concerned with trade and commerce were grouped together in a small, compact area around the Mercato Nuovo; there was also a second small cluster between the Piazza della Signoria and the Ponte Vecchio, where the *calzolai*, *fabbri*, and *mercanti di legname* (shoemakers, smiths, and timber dealers, respectively) could be found. Sadly, only a handful of these guildhalls have left any significant surviving fabric.

Architecturally, the most prominent is the hall of the Arte della Lana, which still stands today. This was originally built, in 1308, as a semifortified house by the Campiobbesi family, in the characteristic style of the period. In the trecento the Arte della Lana was one of the wealthiest and certainly the largest guild, with several thousand wool workers as members, based in two hundred commercial workshops. The guildhall that they acquired has two principal facades, one at each end of the block between the Via Calimala and Via Orsanmichele, and the finely proportioned stone facade has two upper stories above a ground floor of workshops, and a crowning crenellation. The hall also preserves some important trecento frescoes inside, while an internal staircase leads to a bridge at high level, providing a direct link into the upper level of Orsanmichele itself, where the archives were kept. The fact that the *arte*'s new home was a converted private house indicates that its spatial requirements were not particularly specialized, and clearly they could be accommodated in premises originally intended for other purposes.

The second hall, that of the *beccai* (butchers), was also an adaptation, in this case of the former palazzo of the *capitani* of Orsanmichele. The basic surviving building is of the trecento, but the present facade of stucco conceals the original stonework. In this case the facade shows an inventive mixture of rectangular windows in the lesser stories (mezzanine and attic) and more typical radiused arched windows in the principal *piano nobile*. Toward the end of the sixteenth century the hall became the seat of the new Accademia delle Arti del Disegno founded by Cosimo I, the oldest such academy in the world. The two remaining surviving guildhalls are architecturally less prominent, that of the Calimala and the Arte della Seta. The latter, a trecento structure on Via Capaccio, also preserves some valuable frescoes on its internal vaults. In general these halls remained modest structures, with few architectural pretensions; often their original function is identifiable only by the coat of arms of the guild on their facade.

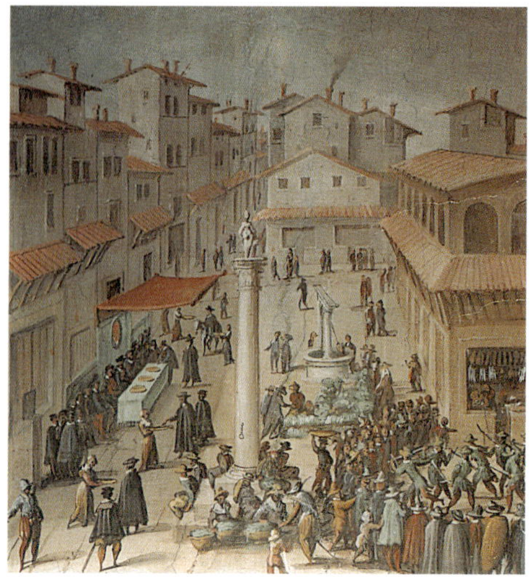

GIOVANNI STRADANO, *VEDUTA DEL MERCATO VECCHIO*, C. 1561 (Florence, Palazzo Vecchio).

The entire Mercato Vecchio district was completely destroyed in the nineteenth-century clearances of the city center.

Trade, Commerce, and Markets

Historically, the requirements of those who traded in real goods and produce, and those who traded in "invisibles," that is, banking, insurance, and moneylending, were very different. Indeed, the spatial requirements of a medieval banker or money changer were very modest: a few chairs, a desk or bench (the *banca* itself), a vault or strongbox, weights and measures perhaps, and ledgers, pens, and a stock of stationery. The real worth of a Florentine banker was itself invisible: Security, reliability, and trust were the qualities from which fortunes could be made — by, for example, the Peruzzi and the Bardi, and later, of course, the Medici — or sometimes undone — the Pitti. The places from which these men built their fortunes were, therefore, virtually devoid of architectural pretension, in sharp contrast to the vast, imposing palaces that this wealth was used to construct.

Trade, of course, was different. The city center marketplace has been one of the pivotal features of urban life in Europe throughout its history, and here again, basic requirements were fairly simple: a suitably located open space of sufficient size for the purpose, and that, more importantly, was specifically identified with and known for this purpose. Some marketplaces were known all over Europe, in much the same way the great trade fairs were known; places of lay pilgrimage, one might call them, for thousands of merchants who made long, difficult journeys to these foci for international trade. Almost infinite are the sizes, shapes, and configurations of the traditional European marketplaces, and no really meaningful generalization can be made.[7] Sometimes city markets were large and general, although more typically there were many smaller, more fragmented specialized markets clustered together. Some were located just outside the city's gates, others on the banks of a river, still others in a great central square, others again congested in a warren of adjacent courtyards, streets, and squares, like the famous Rialto markets of Venice.

Florence's patterns of market trading were comparatively simple. The Roman market had been established in the forum, near the crossing of the two main axes, and the medieval market that came to replace it was also located there. However, already by the thirteenth century, a second market, or rather, an offshoot from the first, had been established in the *slargo* of Por Santa Maria, which had been paved as early as 1270. Both of these locations were the site for weekly markets, while the larger annual fair was held outside the city walls, as there was clearly insufficient space within.

By the flourishing early fourteenth century the Piazza del Mercato was feeling the strain of its constricted size, and it was enlarged by demolitions in 1303 and again in 1356. Sadly, there remains no trace today of the Mercato Vecchio, since it was completely destroyed in the "improvements" to this part of the city in the nineteenth century. Archival photographs do exist, however, showing that the Mercato formed a compact rectangle of open space, just to the west of the Via Calimala, and occupied approximately the northern half of the present vast Piazza della Repubblica.[8] Its southern boundary was formed by the line of the Via Strozzi and Via degli Speziali. The only structure of any architectural pretension that stood there was the Loggia del Pesce, built to a design by Vasari in 1567, which formed a sturdy, stately, classical double colonnade near the

MERCATO NUOVO (below)

The building by Giovanni Battista del Tasso (1547–51) was one of Cosimo I's many works of urban improvement, although the market itself had been established here since the medieval era. Each bay was devoted to a single specialized craft, including those of goldsmiths and jewelers.

GIUSEPPE ZOCCHI, *VEDUTA DI UNA PARTE DI FIRENZE PRESA FUORI DELLA PORTA DELLA CROCE*, 1744 (overleaf)

The view has considerable historical value, as it illustrates the old Ponte alle Grazie and the fortifications around the Porta San Niccolò (left), both now lost.

western edge of the market square. It was taken down and reassembled on its present site in the Piazza dei Ciompi after the late-nineteenth-century clearances. The Loggia del Pesce had essentially commercial and practical functions, offering shelter from the elements for at least some of the market traders, while at the same time adding somewhat to the dignity of this public square.

The chief feature of the second market, the Mercato Nuovo, is also a colonnaded loggia. Here, though, the immediate urban context was significantly different from that surrounding the former Mercato Vecchio. The Mercato Nuovo has been for centuries the real commercial, mercantile nucleus of the city, and was surrounded by banks, moneychangers, the headquarters of the *arti* (including the wealthiest, the Calimala and the Lana), with all the associated connections with international trade and commerce. It is a fairly small, compact rectangle, although its extent has been encroached upon over the centuries, and it was formerly larger in the east–west direction. Its

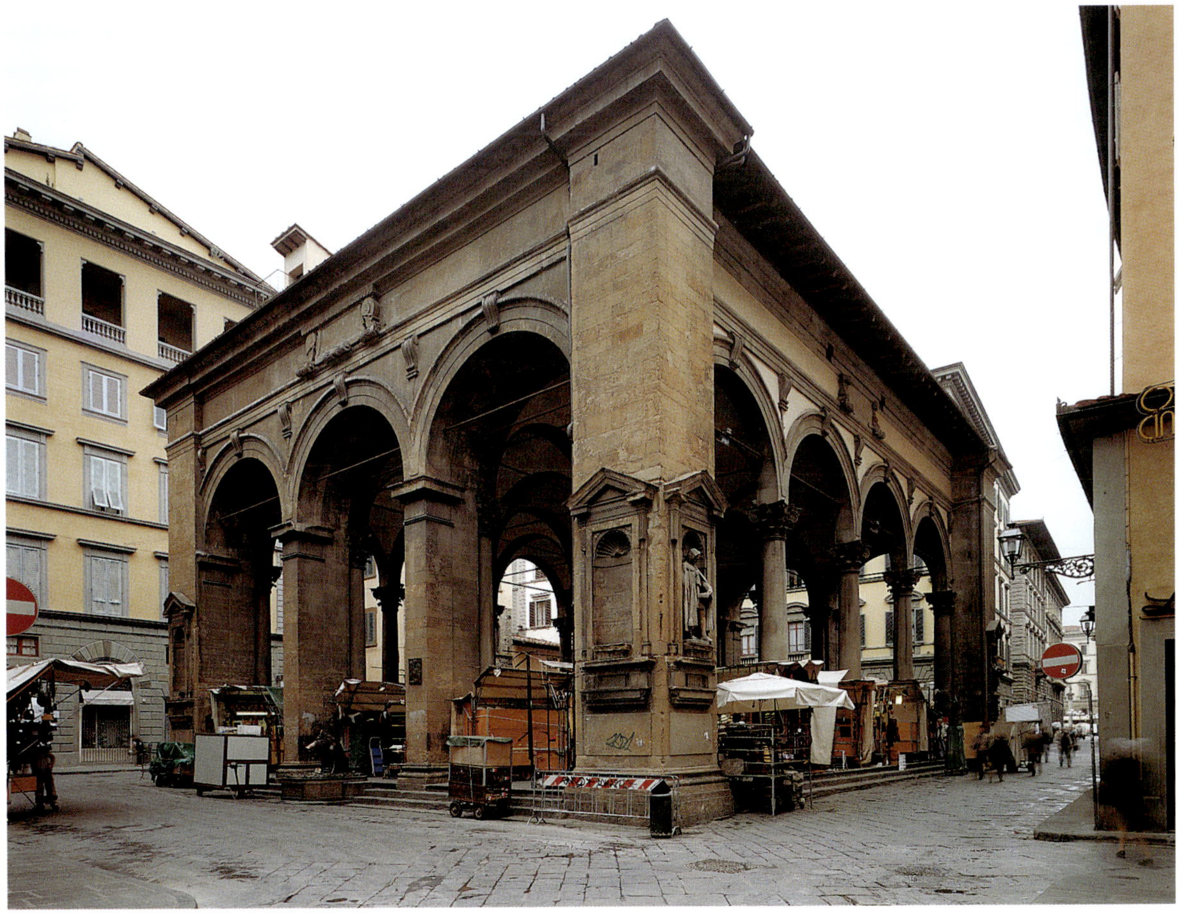

identity today is symbolized by the covered, arcaded market hall, designed by Giovanni Battista del Tasso, and built from 1547 to 1551. It was to shelter not the quotidian necessities of the Florentines but luxury goods of high value: gold and silver, silks and jewelry, each of which specialty was allocated one bay of the colonnaded structure. The loggia itself, sponsored by Cosimo I, takes the form of a rectangle four bays long and three bays across, with very simple, rather heavy, almost neoclassical detailing, particularly in the entablature and the massive corner columns. Its appearance was lightened somewhat by the addition, in the nineteenth century, of three statues within their aedicules, but it was in 1612, only a few decades after its construction, that the loggia received its best-known attribute, the famous bronze figure known as *Il Porcellino* (in fact, a wild boar), cast by Pietro Tacca, and based on a Hellenistic original in the Uffizi collection.

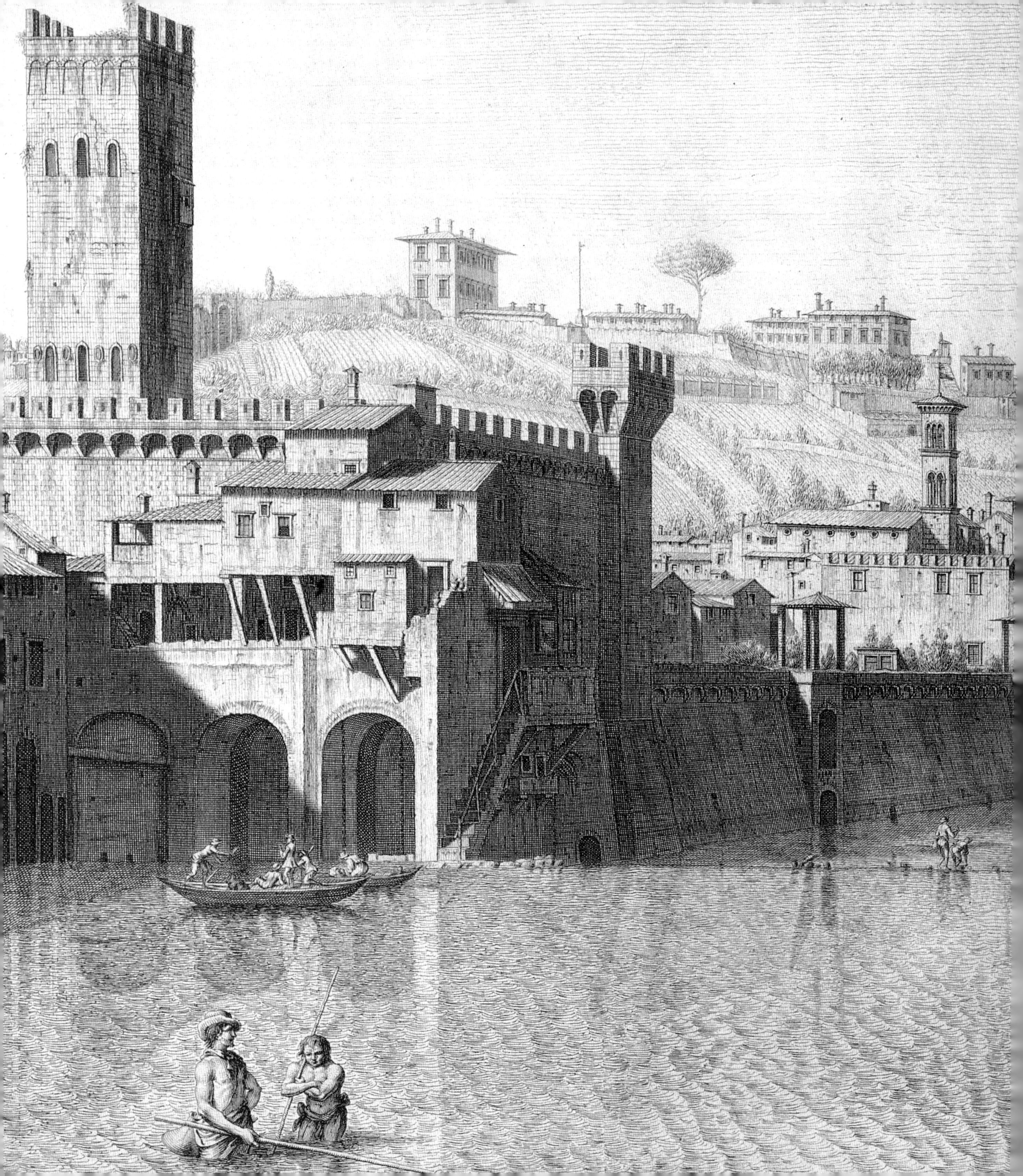

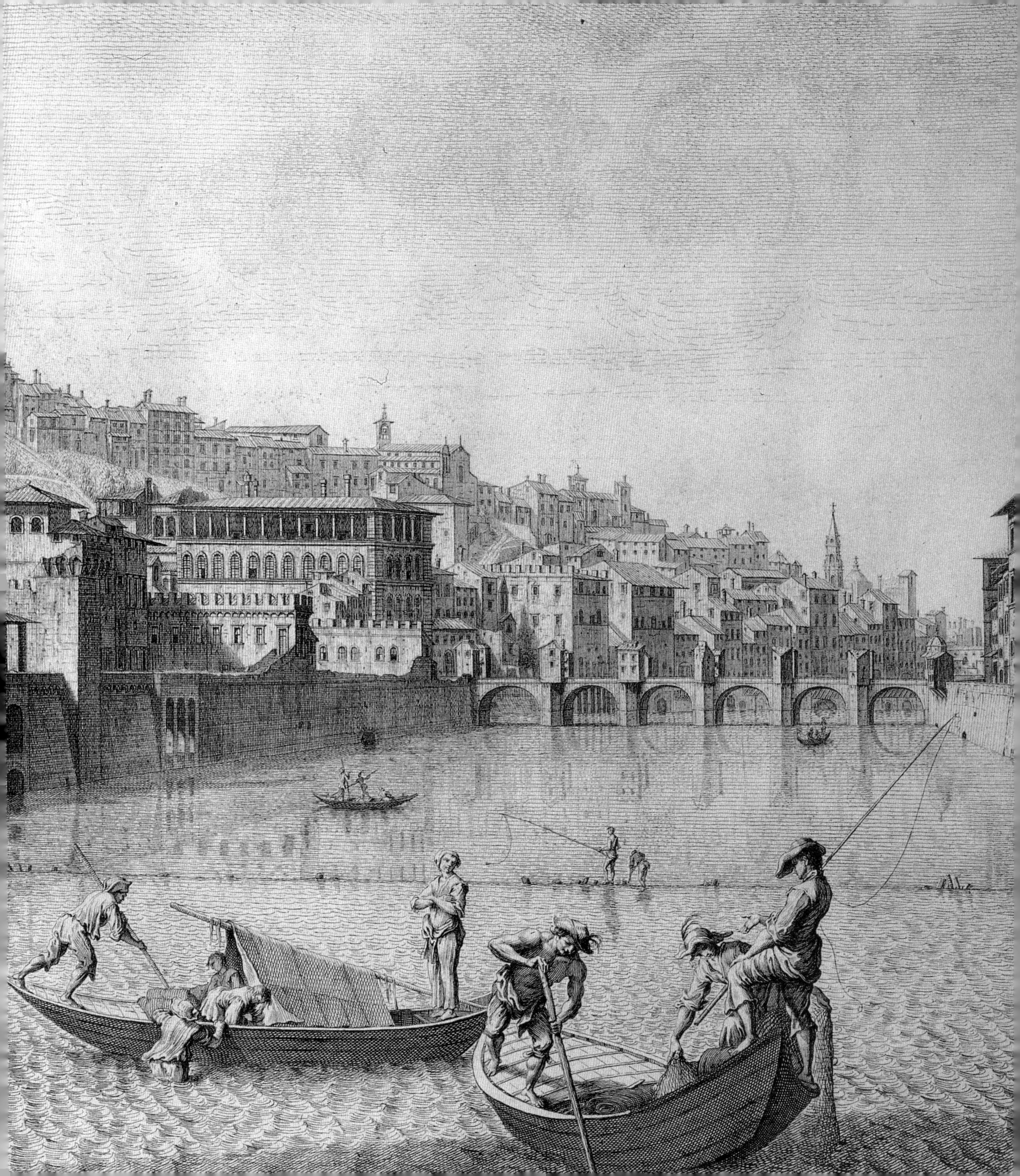

"In the whole Compass of the Art of Building, there is nothing in which we ought to employ more Thought, Care and Diligence than in the laying out and adorning [of] a temple. . . . I would have the Temple made so beautiful, that the Imagination should not be able to form an idea of any Place more so." **Leon Battista Alberti**, *De re aedificatoria* (c. 1452) [1]

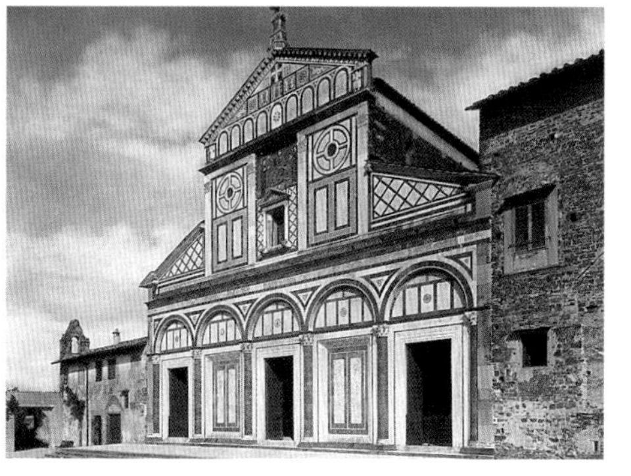

SAN MINIATO AL MONTE

View of the famous Romanesque, marble-clad facade.

The church of San Miniato al Monte is one of the most famous sights — and sites — in Florence, its refined, elegant marble facade gleaming among the somber cypresses and silvery olives of the hills above the Oltrarno. It represents the finest flowering of the earliest of several distinctive architectural traditions in the city: that of the Romanesque church facade, completely clad with fine marbles of different colors. The church, which was constructed by Bishop Hildebrand after 1018, retains much that is archetypal in its facade as well as in its planning, particularly its typical basilican form, with a long nave and two side aisles, from which it is divided by two colonnades, and with the nave culminating in a raised semicircular apse. As such, San Miniato is a member of a broad family that included the much earlier church of Santa Reparata and Santi Apostoli, both in Florence, as well as numerous other examples in the peninsula from the fifth or sixth centuries onward. As the apogee of this particular tradition, San Miniato forms part of a much broader stylistic picture, the origins of which are obscure and fragmented. A number of roughly contemporary early churches survive in the city, and although none exhibit such a fine, complete facade, in their structure and in their plans they are all members of the same basilican family. Naturally enough most of them have been very much altered and adapted over the centuries, sometimes on several occasions. These can be categorized as either monastic foundations or the smaller but more numerous parish churches, several of which survive in the city's historic center.

The most significant early surviving churches are two Cistercian nunneries, that of San Salvatore at Settimo, a few miles to the west of the city, and the Badia Fiorentina, at the very heart of the historic center.[2] San Salvatore was founded in 998, originally as a Benedictine house; its Cistercian history began in 1236. The extensive complex was begun with the church itself, which, together with the crypt below it, still evinces its original regular basilican form, with a central nave and two lean-to aisles. The Benedictine cloister and the lowermost order of the highly distinctive campanile, with its cylindrical shape, also date from this first stage. The plain, rather broad, low facade was left undecorated, however, and the present fenestration dates from considerably later. Much of the monastic complex was transformed after the Cistercian occupation, during the trecento, when the large cloister was built, together with the refectory, chapter house, and other accommodation. In this period, too, the upper part of the facade was modernized, and the hexagonal upper levels of the bell tower were added.

The Badia Fiorentina, within the city just northeast of the Piazza della Signoria, was founded by Benedictines in around 980, within a few years of San Salvatore at Settimo, on a site then on the eastern edge of the Matildine walls. It, too, was much altered later. The original body of the church was at a right angle to the axis of the present church; once again, it has a classic basilican structure, but this time with a single broad nave terminating in three apses, and with a detached campanile that was square externally but with a circular internal plan. Like the tower at Settimo, this was completed at a later period, in about 1330, and here, too, the upper order has a hexagonal plan, capped by a tall, elegant spire, which remains one of the most prominent features of the skyline of this part of the city. The entire complex was radically reorganized — probably by Arnolfo di

Cambio — in 1285, when the church was reorientated such that the original nave now formed a kind of transept, with the new nave orthogonal to it, and with a choir on the same new axis, parallel to the Via del Proconsolo.[3] This replanning was an ingenious method of enlarging the church on its highly restricted site, but it was not to be the last remodeling of the nunnery; a further series of enlargements took place in the early fifteenth century. Bernardo Rossellino added the cloister, the Chiostro degli Aranci, in 1436, in a refined Renaissance style, and toward the end of the century, in about 1494, Benedetto da Rovezzano built the atrium in front of Arnolfo's reorientated church, with its two flanking rows of colonnades. In the early sixteenth century, Benedetto also added the Pandolfini chapel giving off the eastern colonnades, which was formed by the adaptation of the existing chapel of Santo Stefano. In its final form the plan of the *badia*, which eventually covered an entire city block, remains an essentially urban but introverted complex, much of which is quite invisible — and even unidentifiable — from the street. The most distinctive urban contribution is its tall, elegant Gothic campanile, its signal to the outer world. The history of the *badia* thus forms a fairly eclectic, and sometimes ingenious, series of responses to the exigencies of changing requirements on a very difficult urban site.

The third of the *badie* of Florence and its surroundings provides the clear stylistic link back to San Miniato. The Badia Fiesolana on the foothill below the hilltop village of Fiesole was begun in 1025, and is thus almost exactly contemporary with San Miniato; although considerably altered in the fifteenth century, it retains one vital element of the original construction in the beautiful though fragmentary central section of the church facade. This fragment exhibits all the characteristic qualities of the Tuscan Romanesque church facade. Such rich, geometric polychrome marble treatment was never applied to buildings other than churches; such splendor — and such expenditure — was to be lavished solely on the house of God. The surviving fragment of the *badia*'s facade consists of only the three central bays of the lower order, with three blind arches, an entablature, and a unique, if modestly scaled, upper order consisting of geometric patterns into which are set three small, blind marble "windows." The whole is a refined exercise in the reduction and regularization of architectonic elements into planes rather than three-dimensional forms, and this process was to reach its even more refined conclusion at San Miniato.[4]

There, indeed, one finds a facade completely encrusted with geometric marble forms, serene, symmetrical, and balanced. The basilican volumes of the church behind are projected directly onto the overall profile of the elevation, with the main body of the nave represented by the tall central section, crowned by its triangular pediment reflecting the double pitched roof behind it. The lower roofs of the two side aisles are equally logically represented by the lower half-pediments that flank the central bay. The lower of the two orders, though, has a more pronounced horizontal emphasis than the upper, and is unified by the five elegant bays of the blind arcade, with their Corinthian columns and the three portals alternating with two blind, marble-clad panels.

The facade of San Miniato also has clear affinities with the cladding of the great baptistery of San Giovanni. There, the regular octagonal form of the church's perimeter enclosing wall lent itself readily to an extensive, repetitive decorative sheathing of rectangular marble panels; the principal structure, or modeling, is provided by blind arcading, in that case three arched bays on each of the eight faces of the church. The three-bay blind arcade of the facade of San Salvatore al Vescovo, also a close relative of San Miniato, is refined enough, but confined to the lower order of the facade and a decorative frieze or entablature. The rest of the facade rises plain and undecorated above, while the body of the church has been engulfed by later reconstructions of the archbishops' palace, in which it is now embedded. San Miniato, whose facade has an unequaled balanced serenity, thus remains by far the most outstanding Florentine example of this particular style, all the more so because the decorative marble cladding is applied equally consistently to the rich interior as well as to the facade.

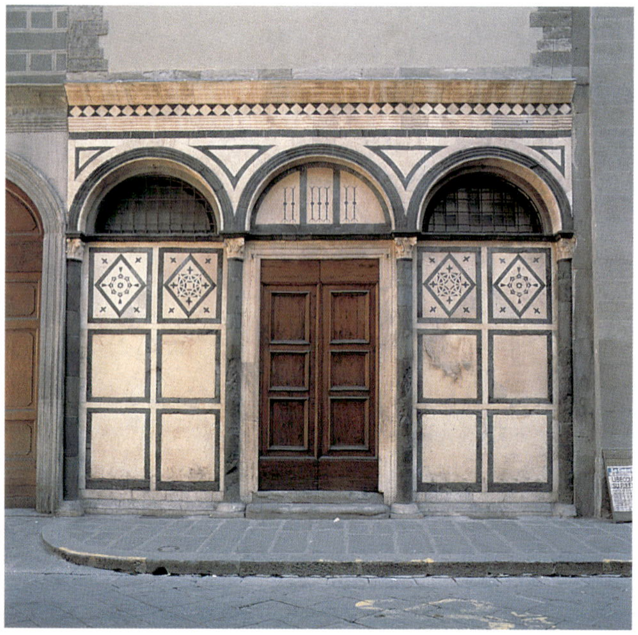

SAN SALVATORE AL VESCOVO

Detail of facade. The body of the church is now enveloped within the fabric of the archbishop's palace.

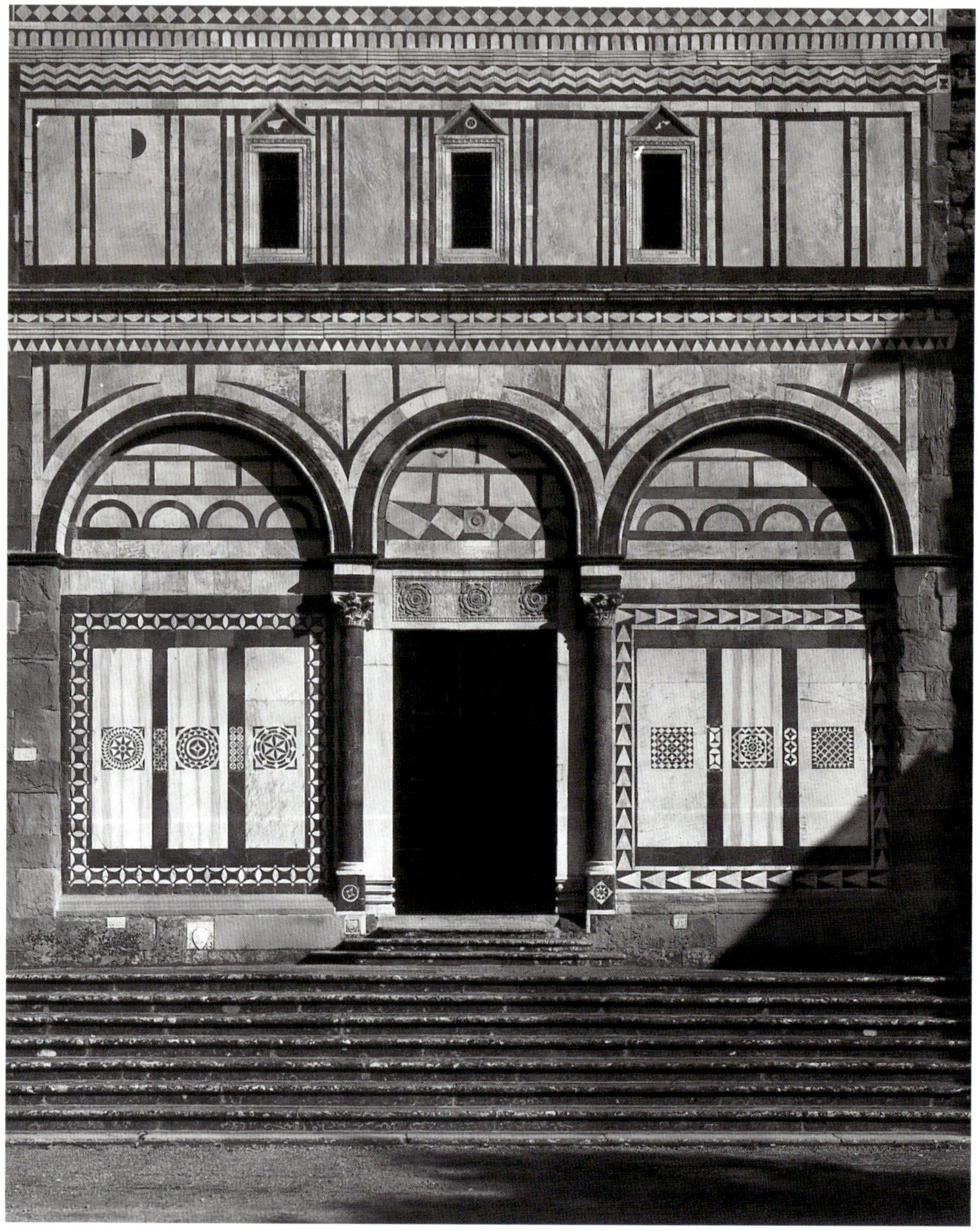

BADIA FIESOLANA

Above: detail of facade. Only the lower central section was ever completed in the characteristic Florentine Romanesque manner.

Opposite: view of the whole complex.

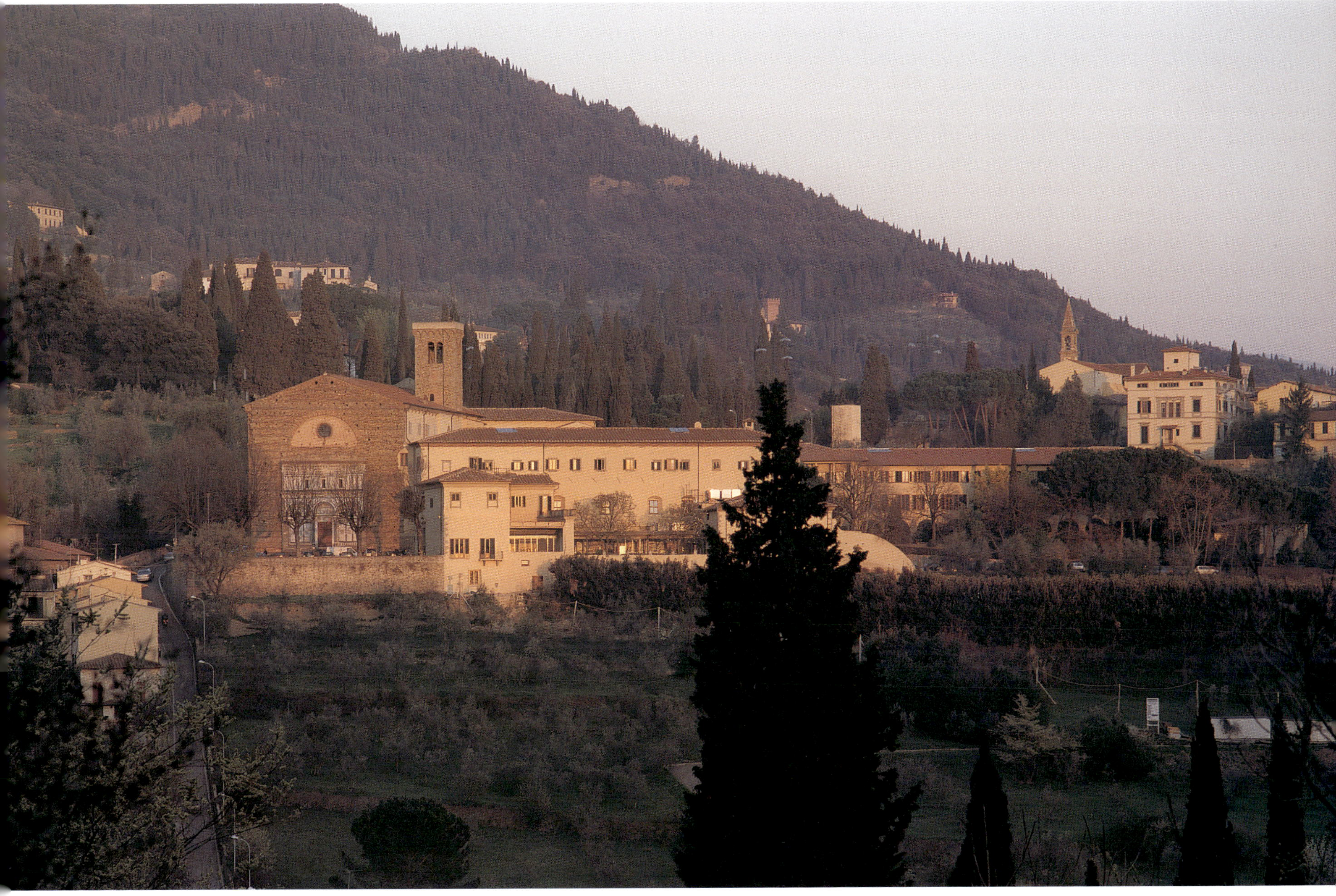

The marble facade cladding cannot be dated with precision, but similar examples exist, which extend beyond Florence to a limited number of other Tuscan cities. One is the facade of Sant'Andrea at Empoli; another is the Pistoia cathedral, the facade of which is in fact something of a hybrid, owing rather less to Tuscan Romanesque and more to the characteristically striped, colonnaded Pisan style. But Empoli's lower order, also of five bays, closely resembles San Miniato, as indeed did the whole facade originally, but the upper order was altered in 1803 and is now the same width as the lower one, the whole being crowned by a large, triangular tympanum. It seems highly likely that Empoli, built in the 1090s, was modeled on San Miniato, to which church it was also administratively subordinate.

SANTI APOSTOLI (left)

The nave is basilican, with columns of green Prato marble and an apsidal east end.

SANT'ANDREA, EMPOLI (opposite)

One of the few striking examples of the Florentine Romanesque style at some distance from the city itself. The lower order was built in 1093, modeled on San Miniato; the upper part and the crowning pediment were added in the early eighteenth century by Ferdinando Ruggieri.

The origins of this distinctive central Tuscan style and technique of "veneering" a facade in this manner continue to be the subject of considerable debate. Although rich and refined, the style is also highly formalized and disciplined, seeming almost to deny, or at least minimize, the physical mass and substance of the building behind it. There were other, roughly contemporaneous stylistic

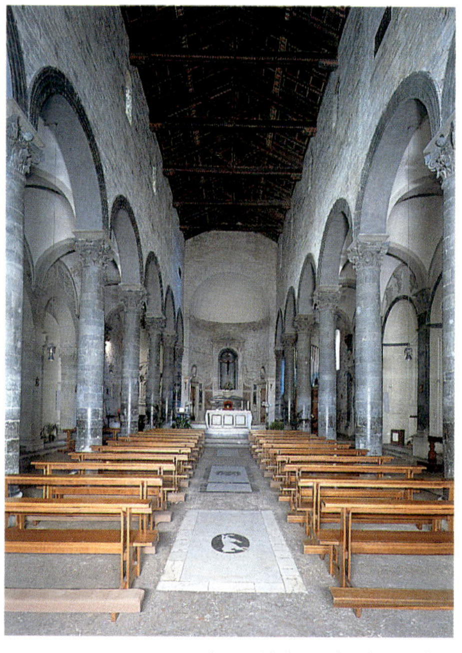

developments in this part of Italy that took a rather different route, most famously perhaps at the cathedral group in Pisa. In this alternative tradition, visual richness was achieved by banding using two different colors of marble. But the fundamental difference between the Pisan style and the Tuscan Romanesque lay in the fact that the Pisan approach was used not for "veneering" a facade but also characterized all the chief structural members of the building: columns, vaults, pilasters. (This same principle was also to be adopted later at the magnificent cathedrals of Orvieto and Siena.) The Tuscan Romanesque "veneering" tradition may have derived from earlier examples now lost; there also were many examples of classical Roman structures whose basic construction of brick was clad with panels or sheets of marble. The particularly Florentine manner in which this technique was refined did not spread very far beyond the city and its immediately dependent territories. However, the veneering of facades was by no means a local tradition confined solely to the Romanesque era; it was later revived, continued, and refined at Santa Maria Novella and at the cathedral complex. Although these facades were often described as polychrome, the materials used were in fact fairly limited, the richness being obtained by strong tonal contrast, and by geometric patterns and articulation. At San Miniato, for example, the materials are white Carrara marble and the characteristic green marble of Prato; the *badia* at Fiesole uses the same two materials, as does the Baptistery of San Giovanni. It is only at the cathedral and its campanile (together with some very minor details at Santa Maria Novella) that a third material is introduced in the form of small panels of pinkish-red marble.

Most of the other early Florentine Romanesque churches that survive today have been very much altered in later centuries.[5] They are almost all parochial foundations in origin, and were thus modest in scale; like most great medieval cities, Florence had a large number of quite small parishes, each of which had a comparatively small population, and whose liturgical requirements and resources were equally fairly limited. Santi Apostoli is one of those churches that retain a significant proportion of their original structure and appearance, with its typical basilican plan, an apsidal east end, and an interior characterized by green Prato marble columns and Corinthian capitals. These early churches frequently recycled classical Roman elements, such as columns, capitals, and so on, often combining them with newer copies if the originals were insufficient, as

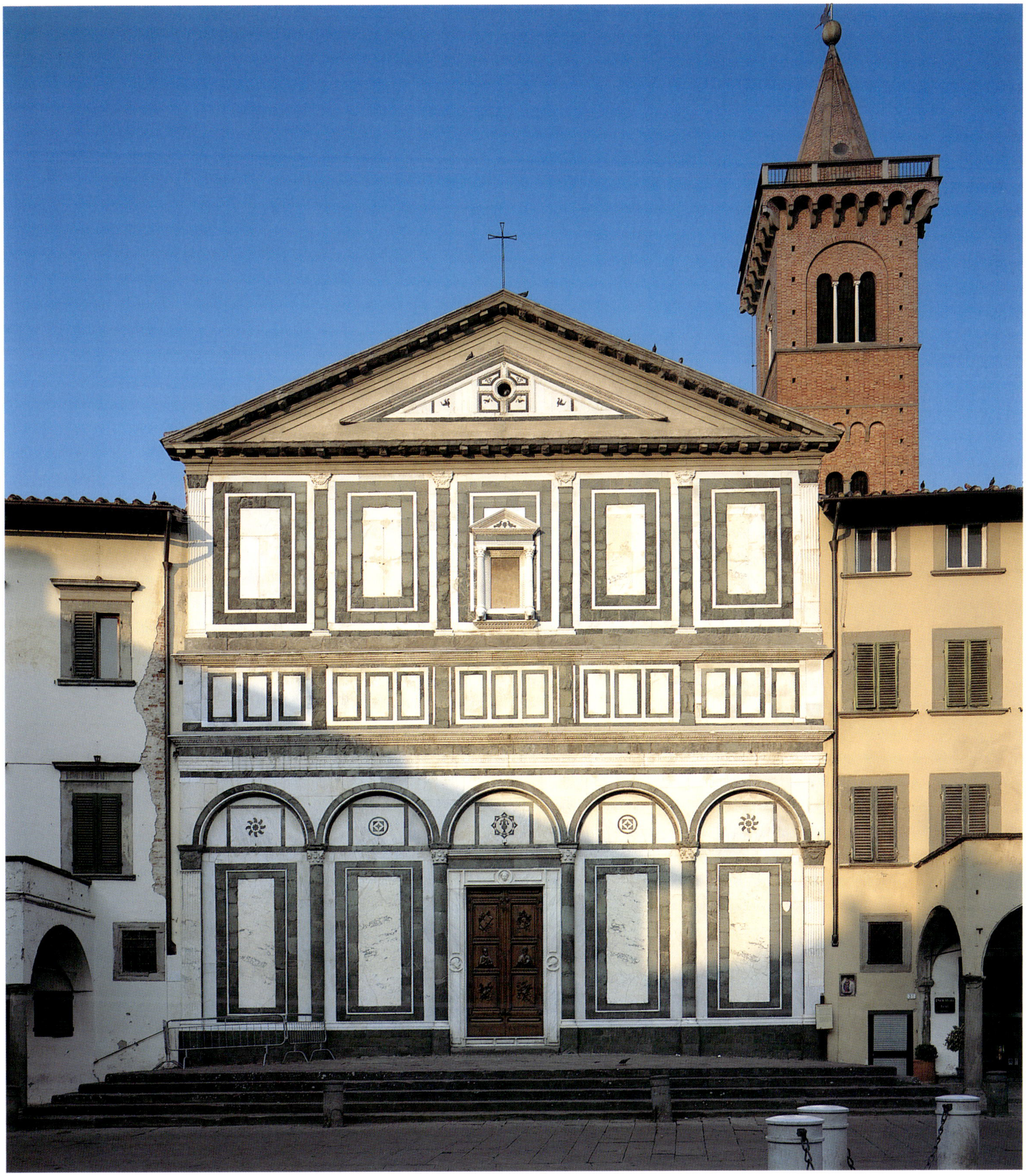

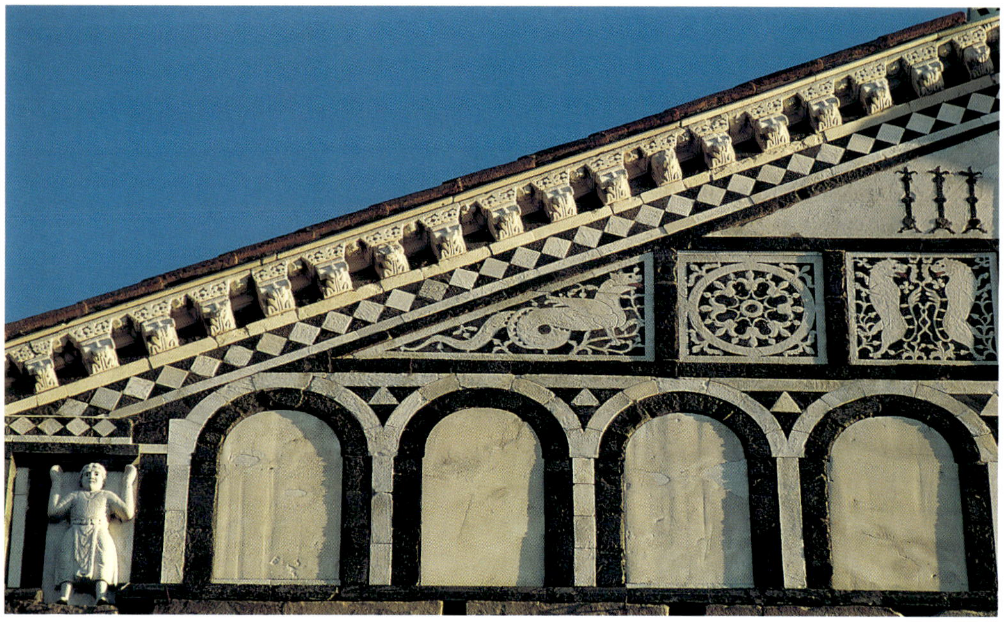

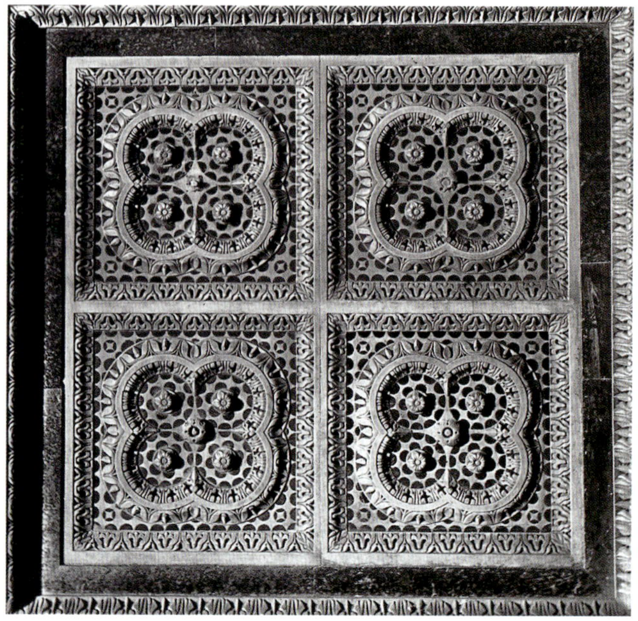

SAN MINIATO AL MONTE
(above, right, and opposite)

Above: detail of the facade, clad with white Carrara and green Prato marble. Above, right: detail of decorative paneling on the chancel. Right: plan by Grandjean de Montigny, 1806–15.

Opposite: interior of the nave, with richly decorated mosaic floor finishes; the wall cladding continues the geometric motifs of the facade.

BADIA FIORENTINA (far right)

The plan of the nunnery was altered on many occasions, notably in 1285, when Arnolfo di Cambio rebuilt the complex and enlarged and reorientated the church.

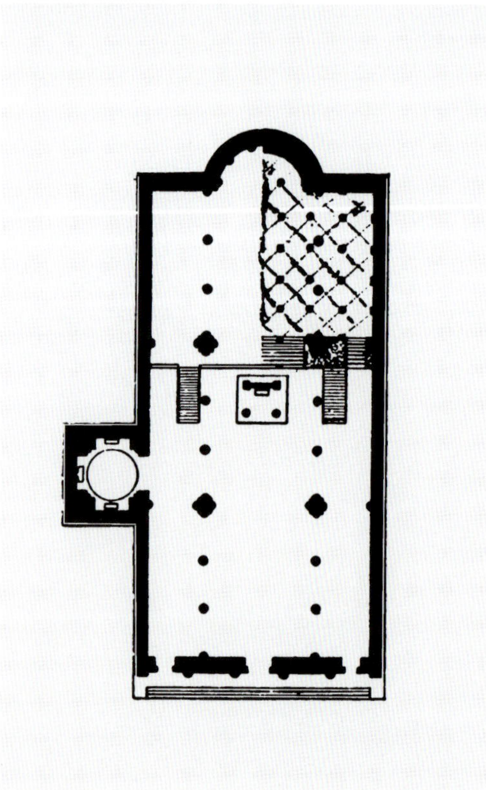

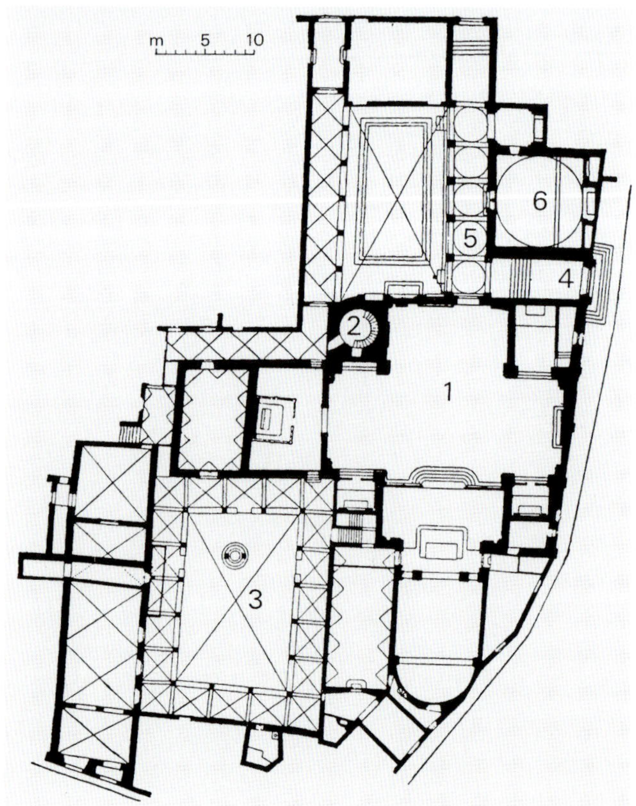

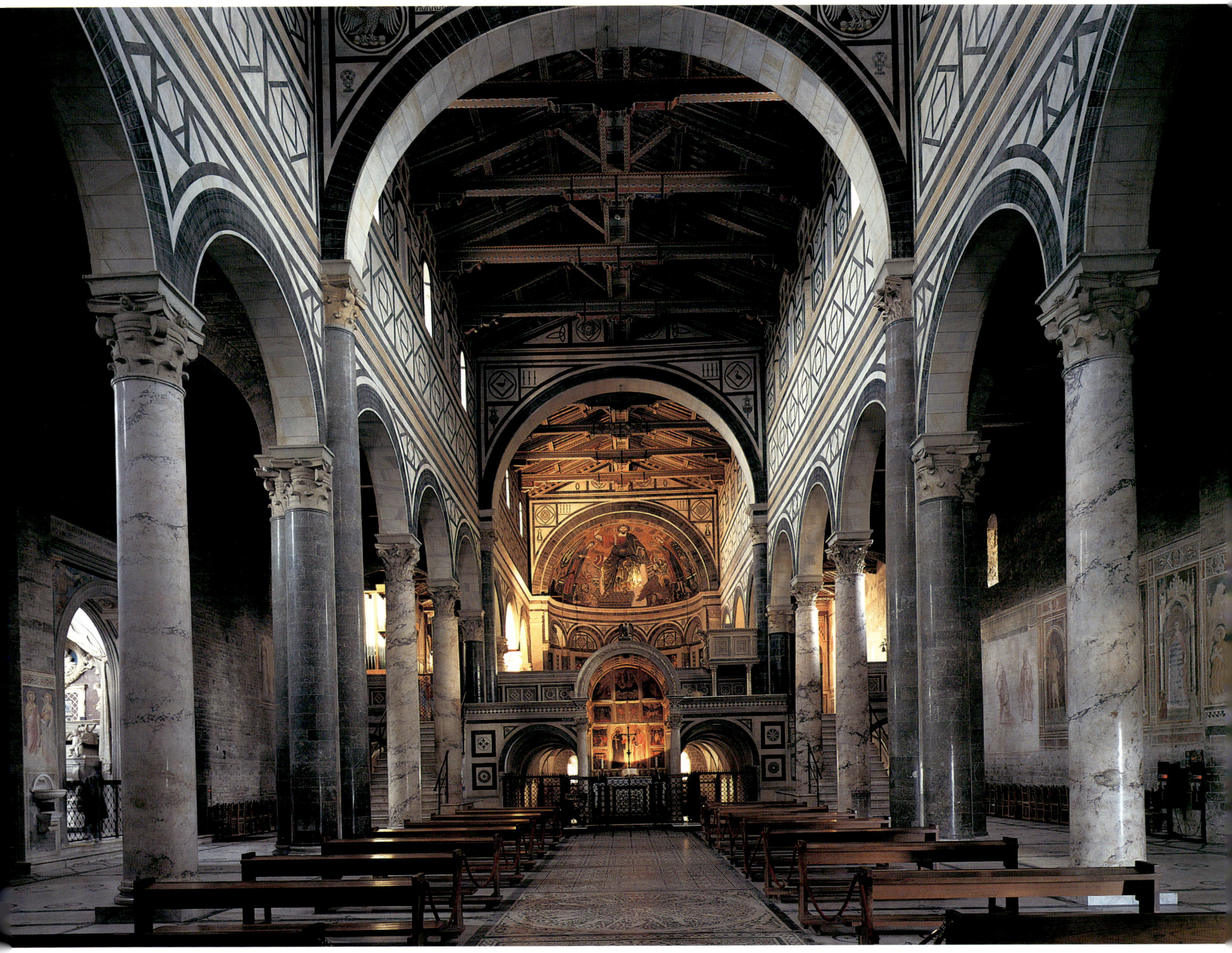

is the case at San Miniato. Sometimes, too, the careful reuse of these elements resulted in a less than perfect combination of columns and capitals, as can be observed in the cathedral of San Romolo at Fiesole, where, in some instances, there is a clear mismatch between the diameters of the columns and their capitals.

Other surviving churches roughly contemporary with Santi Apostoli include Santa Maria Maggiore and Santo Stefano al Ponte. The former is one of the oldest foundations in Florence, but was rebuilt toward the end of the thirteenth century, and is almost completely unadorned externally. Only the lower part of the Santo Stefano facade evinces its Romanesque origins, although the most prominent element there, the portal, was added in the fourteenth century in a Gothic interpretation of the Romanesque polychrome tradition, with alternating white and green marble bands to the door surround.

Two other roughly contemporary churches, both dedicated to San Jacopo, one known as that "in Campo Corbellino" and the other "sopr'Arno," each have a prominent portico across its facade. These colonnades are each of three bays, that at San Jacopo sopr' Arno rather richer and more robust than the other; both are comparatively rare surviving examples of the formerly widespread practice of constructing a porch or narthex across the full width of the main facade. The latter church was the Florentine base of the Knights of the Holy Sepulchre, later of Rhodes, and later still of St. John of Malta.

In general, these basilican churches were roofed with a simple, exposed, open timber truss, which was sometimes, as at San Miniato, richly painted and decorated. Other than the often intricately carved column capitals, most of the interiors were originally simply detailed, although some were probably frescoed. San Miniato, though, is once again the exception in this group as much for the sumptuous richness of the interior as for its refined facade. The church not only housed the holy relics of the titular saint, but also was the patronal church of the *arte* of the Calimala — represented by the eagle on the top of the facade — which endowed the building with great generosity through the centuries. Uniquely, the marble of this facade is continued inside the church, and the whole is still further elaborated with an extremely fine marble pavement. The rich choir is dominated by the powerful mosaic figure of Christ blessing, flanked by Mary and San Miniato himself; the mosaic evinces strong Venetian-Byzantine influence. The other striking feature of the internal plan is the logical spatial resolution of different liturgical requirements. The east end is split into two levels, with the choir raised high above the crypt — the earliest part of the church to have been built — in which the saint's venerated remains were housed, and that itself is significantly lower than the level of the nave floor. The choir was not completed in its final form until 1466, with the installation of the rich mosaics of Giovanni and Francesco di Domenico.

In all, therefore, San Miniato remains a very special case among the Romanesque churches of Florence, as much a result of its role as a place of pilgrimage and veneration of the saint as for the rich and influential patronage of the Calimala; no other contemporary churches in the city were as richly finished. The split-level arrangement, with the raising of the apsidal choir high above the level of the nave, and with a crypt at a half level below the nave floor, had several advantages over the more usual, slightly raised chancel with a fully subterranean crypt, and was to be influential elsewhere — for example, at San Zeno, Verona. One advantage was that the elevation of the choir greatly improved the acoustics for the liturgy, while access to and visibility of the saints' venerated remains from the nave was also rendered much more direct. A very similar arrangement can be seen at Fiesole cathedral, which is roughly contemporary with San Miniato; again the presbytery stands high above a "semisubmerged" crypt, in which the remains of the titular saint, San Romolo, are venerated.

SANTA MARIA NOVELLA

Plan of the church, with its exceptionally spacious nave and comparatively small eastern apse.

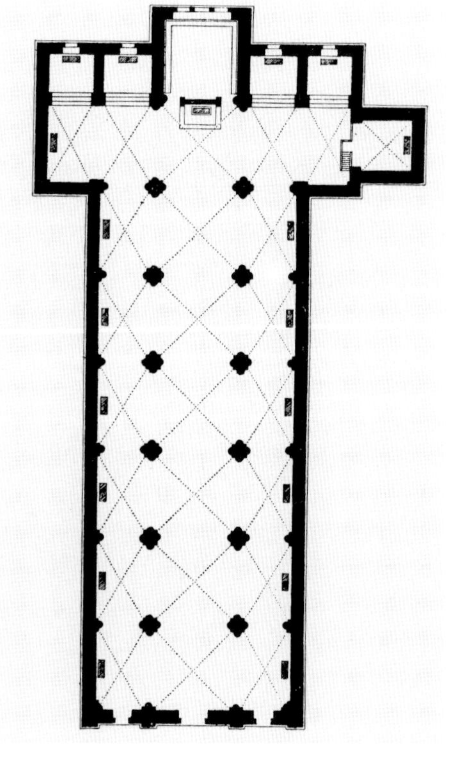

Although the external appearance of these early basilican churches varies considerably, from the rich refinement of San Miniato to the simple, unadorned brickwork of several others, the almost universal characteristic of these churches remains their basilican plan, axial and symmetrical, with a central nave flanked by long colonnades and two lower side aisles. This was the basic plan that was to evolve into the rather more complex, although still strongly axial, form of the Latin cross; the introduction of the cross axis, in the form of transepts, not only gave rise to a subtler, more complex spatial hierarchy, but also eventually led to a centralizing tendency based on the crossing at the junction of the two elements. This Latin cross form is highly characteristic of the great conventual churches of the high medieval era.

The Great Medieval Conventual Churches: Santa Maria Novella and Santa Croce

Most of the fairly small churches discussed above were built in the eleventh century, and although altered, modernized, and sometimes largely rebuilt in the following centuries, most remained small, essentially parochial structures. But with the remarkable, rapid spread of the mendicant preaching orders in the duecento, above all the Dominicans and Franciscans, together with the equally notable expansion of the city's population, wealth, and prestige, the stage was set for radical new building typologies and urban interventions that would permanently alter the topography and architectural scale of the city.

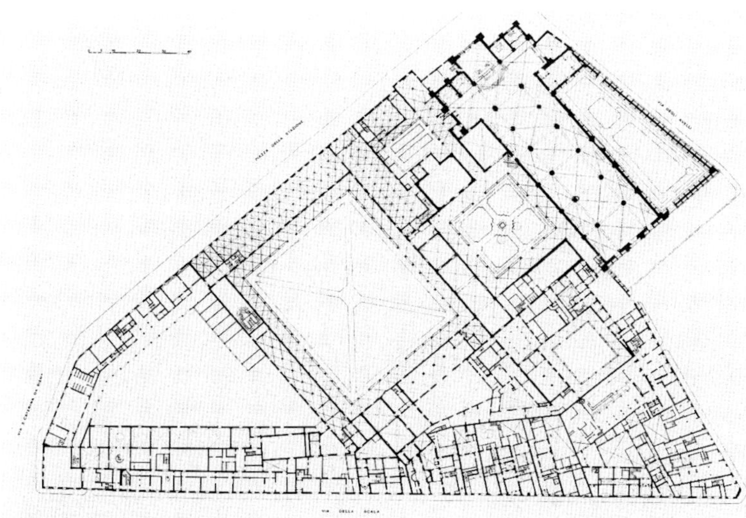

SANTA MARIA NOVELLA

The extensive monastic complex, the largest in Florence, is planned around two principal cloisters, the small Chiostro Verde, and the much larger Chiostro Grande, both built in the fourteenth century.

The arrival of these two preaching orders in Florence had a similar physical impact on several other major Italian cities, such as Bologna and Venice, to give two prominent examples. While the cathedrals of these capitals had long remained the patronal shrines and the hubs of their religious identity, the cities now became multicentered in ecclesiastical terms; the huge new churches built by these orders created major new poles within the urban form, new centers of worship, new hubs of social and communal life. The whole texture of the city became considerably more complex.[6]

In Florence the Dominican establishment of Santa Maria Novella dates from 1221, when the order acquired the church of Santa Maria della Vigna from the cathedral chapter, on a site just outside the second ring of communal walls but well within the much greater arc of the final walls that were to be begun in the 1280s.[7] The extensive monastic complex, founded in 1246, included a preliminary church structure orientated on the conventional east–west axis. It very rapidly seems to have been viewed as insufficient, and so the present, definitive building was begun on a very much larger scale in 1278–79, incorporating the earlier material within the transepts. By this time, at least some of the monastic buildings were also well under construction. The new church was begun at the liturgical east end, which was now reorientated so that it actually faced north, and construction then proceeded with the nave, which was completed by the early trecento. The initial architects for this daunting project were two dominican monks, Fra' Sisto and Fra' Ristoro, succeeded by Fra' Jacopo Talenti, who also designed the Chiostro Verde.

The liturgical eastern arm of the church (now orientated to the north), which includes the short chancel and the two transepts, is fairly compact in plan, each of the three wings consisting of a single square bay; they are all quite dwarfed in scale by the extraordinarily long and spacious nave. This arrangement reflects the importance of this great open volume for preaching to large congregations of several thousand Florentine citizens, and represents a confident adaptation and magnification of the traditional basilican aisled hall to serve this new purpose. The nave bays are broad and spacious, and the two side aisles are nearly as high as the nave itself, so that there is no real spatial break between the central volume and the two flanking ones; all three spaces flow into one another almost unimpeded, further aiding the flow and assembly (and dispersal) of these large congregations. Spatially the nave incorporates even subtler devices. The strong axial progression toward the three large but simple lancets that terminate the "east" end is enhanced by the decrease in the length of the nave bays as one approaches the high altar from the "west" end. This device engenders a false or exaggerated perspective, and serves not only to extend the appearance of the length of the nave but also to concentrate the eye on this east end; at the same time, though, the bay arrangement opens out the "western" part of the nave to improve sight lines and facilitate the assembly and movement of the crowds.

The architectural vocabulary of the interior is as coolly confident and clearly articulated as are the spatial arrangements. The basic structural columns are all of *pietra forte*, while the bays are vaulted with cross vaults, the arches and ribs emphasized with characteristic stripes, which derive from the green and white marble tradition of the Tuscan Romanesque but also have clear visual links with the striped tradition of other cities of the region, such as Pisa and Siena; in fact, new masterpieces in the elaboration of this particular design approach were being constructed contemporaneously with Santa Maria Novella at both Siena and Orvieto cathedrals. The design of the great nave of Santa Maria Novella is occasionally attributed to Arnolfo di Cambio, although there is no documentary evidence, and it is far more likely that his hand was indeed associated with the second of the two great mendicant churches, Santa Croce.

Although the upper order of the facade of Santa Maria Novella was famously completed by Alberti in around 1440, a good deal of the lower part of the facade was built contemporaneously with the body of the church itself. These earlier elements include the great circular central window, from about 1367, which Alberti had to incorporate into his design for the upper order; the six deep ground-floor niches, with their pointed arched heads; and the two flanking portals, again complete with their Gothic heads. Here again, therefore, one can see an interpretation — in green and white marble — deriving from the Romanesque tradition, adapted to the Gothic orders. The piazza in front of Santa Maria Novella, which superseded in urban importance the earlier piazza to the east (and which today is largely isolated from the church by traffic), was set out by the Comune in 1287, achieving its final dimensions only in around 1325. The great square became the social center of this sector of the city, scene of many public events and festivities, including horse races.

The church became patronized by a number of wealthy Florentine clans, notably the Rucellai, but also the Bardi, Gondi, Gaddi, and Strozzi, all of which built their own private chapels annexed to the church. That of the Rucellai is the earliest; the altars of the Bardi and Filippo Strozzi occupied the two chapels to the right of the high altar, those of the Gondi and Gaddi the pair to the left. The chancel itself was patronized by the Tornabuoni, and all of these chapels were richly decorated by some of the finest artists of the day, most outstandingly, perhaps, Filippo Lippi and Benedetto da Maiano for Filippo Strozzi, Domenico Ghirlandajo for the Tornabuoni, and Andrea Pisano and Nardo di Cione in the earlier Strozzi chapel in the left transept.

Santa Maria Novella, with its great complex of monastic buildings, cloisters, and herb gardens, ultimately occupied a sizeable part of the northwestern section of the city, and the spacious piazza in front of the facade became, like that of Santa Croce, one of the social hubs of Florence. Most of the monastic buildings spread out to the west of the church and centered on two cloisters, the smaller known as the Chiostro Verde, immediately adjacent to the church itself and, farther west, beyond the refectory block, the Chiostro Grande, the largest in the city. The majority of these monastic buildings were designed by Jacopo Talenti and built in the two decades or so after 1333; the Chiostro Verde is the most noteworthy, with sturdy octagonal piers supporting cross vaults, its

SANTA MARIA NOVELLA

Opposite, top: the lower, gothic order of the west facade dates from the church's construction in the early fourteenth century, while the upper order was added by Alberti after 1458. Opposite, bottom left: the interior of the nave was complete toward the middle of the trecento. The simple open space was designed to preach to congregations of several thousand. Opposite, bottom right: the Spanish chapel was built in the 1350s as the chapter hall of the monastery, it was frescoed by Andrea di Buonaiuto and others after 1367. In 1540 it was bequeathed to Eleonora of Toledo, Cosimo's wife, from whom it acquired its present name.

Overleaf: the walls of the Chiostro Verde, from about 1350, are decorated with a famous fresco cycle, now badly deteriorated, by Paolo Uccello and others.

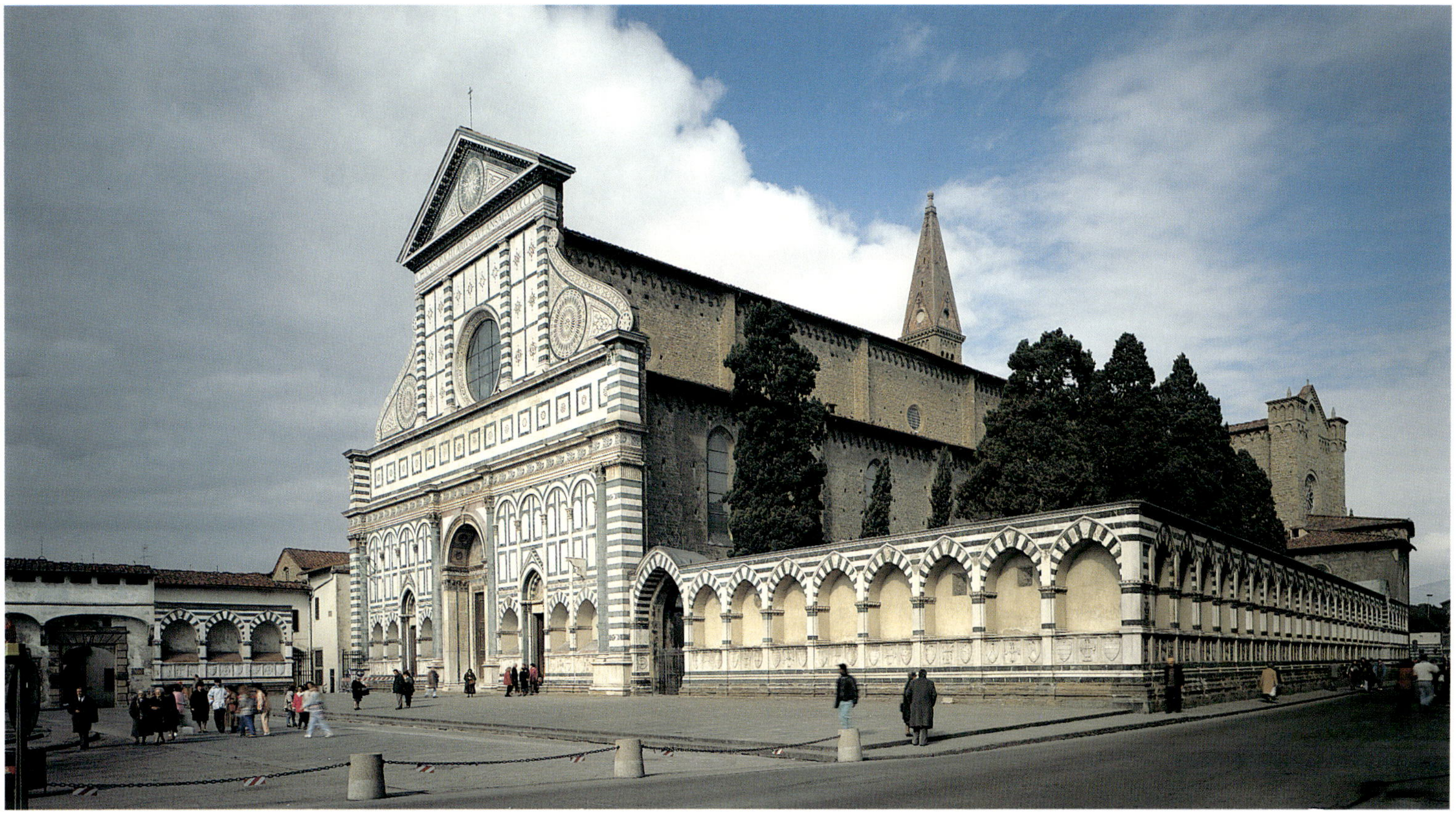

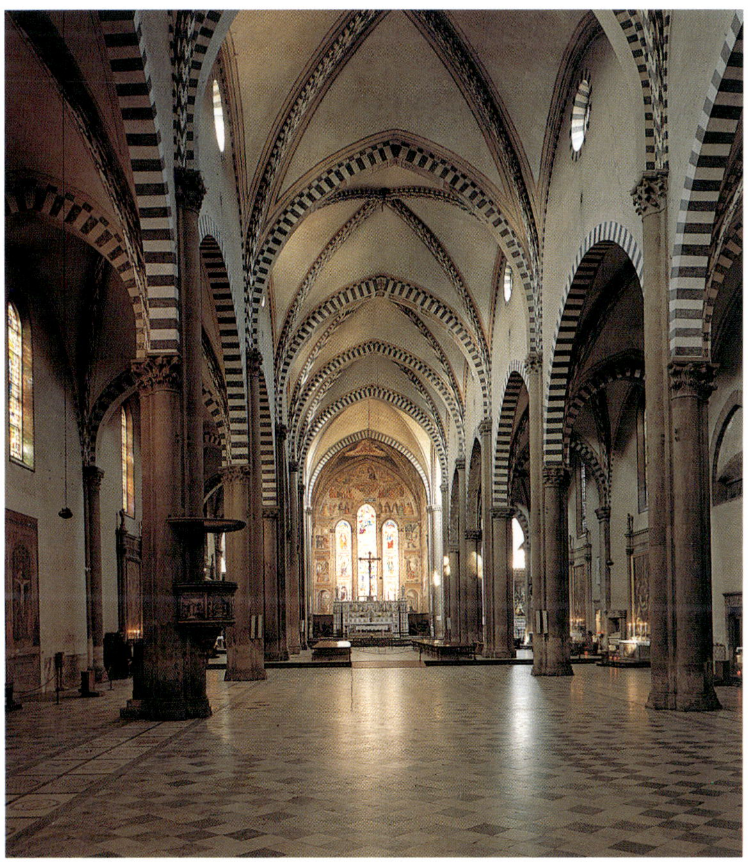

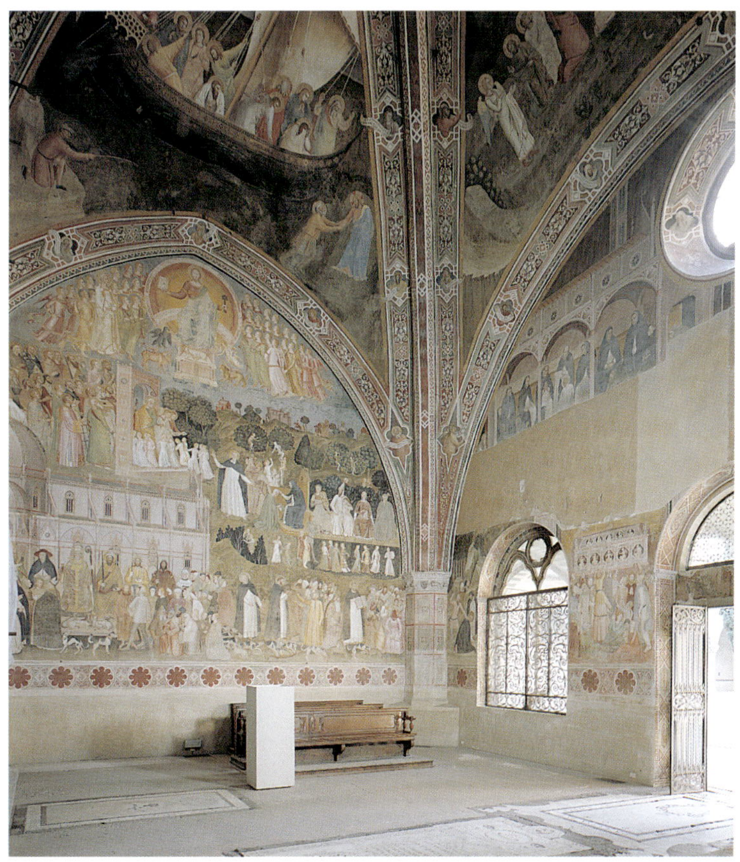

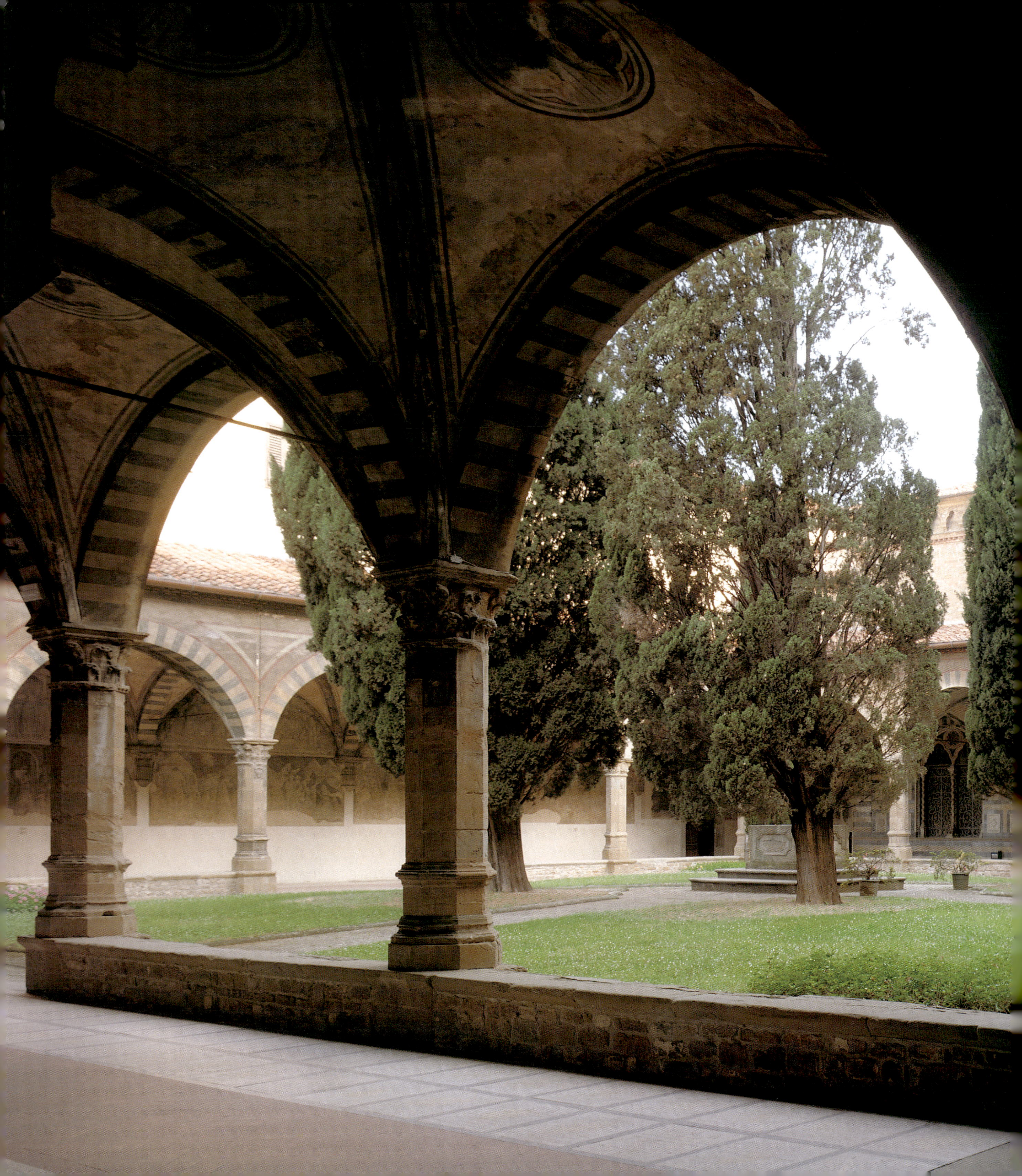

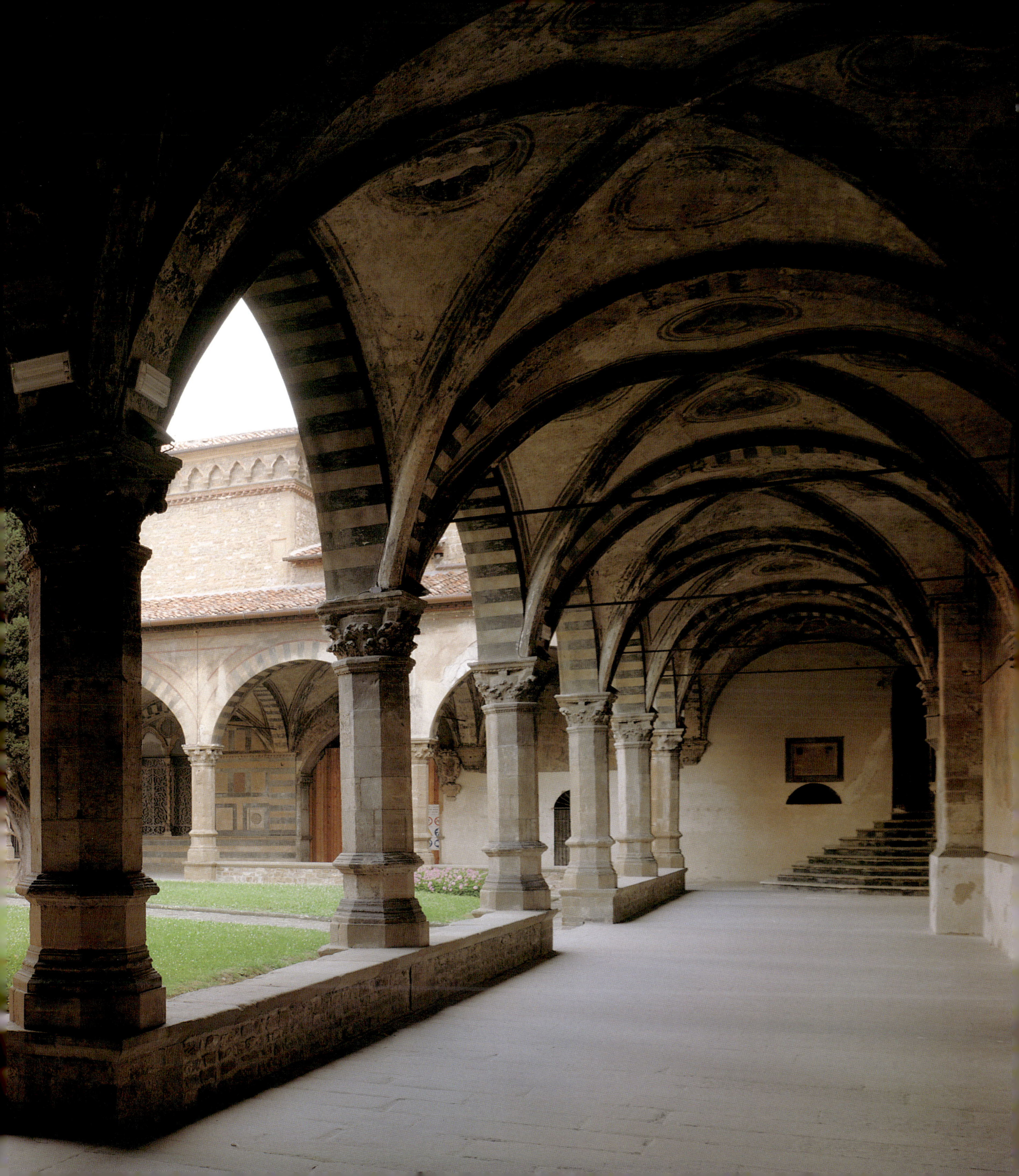

surrounding walls decorated with frescoes on a green background (from which the cloister derives its name), including some celebrated works by Paolo Uccello.

Much the same urban and cultural importance and effect was achieved by the establishment of the other mendicant order, the Franciscans, on the other side of the city center with the foundation of Santa Croce.[8] Saint Francis himself had originally founded a modest monastic house here in 1211–12, and a church is first recorded in 1225. But, as was the case with so many of these earliest foundations, the building rapidly became quite inadequate to accommodate the extraordinary expansion of the order, and was already enlarged or replaced by 1252. By 1285 a finer edifice was proposed, and the result was the magnificent structure that can be seen today, now generally acknowledged as the work of Arnolfo di Cambio.[9]

As with the construction of Santa Maria Novella and many other such churches, the rebuilding of Santa Croce commenced at the east end, so that the essential liturgical elements — high altar and monks' choir — were completed first, and the divine offices could thus be conducted while the long, slow progress of work on the body of the church continued. By 1302, the likely year of the death of Arnolfo, the choir and transepts were probably completed, together with their adjacent chapels; work then began on the huge, spacious nave, which itself was completed only in around 1385. It was not consecrated, however, until as late as 1443, by Pope Eugenio IV.

The plan of Santa Croce takes the design principles of Santa Maria Novella even further, arguably to their ultimate conclusion. The church is very large indeed, one of the largest in Italy, but the eastern end is highly compressed, with a short, projecting central apse and two narrower, rather stubby transepts, the eastern sides of which are terminated with ten small chapels, five on each side. The immense, spacious nave dominates the entire ensemble; it has seven bays, and is roofed not by a vault but by a continuous series of open timber trusses, a close echo of the earlier basilican halls. The more complex rhythm of the ribbed cross vaults of Santa Maria Novella is here replaced by a clear, open, arcaded hall, rather like a magnificent, elegantly detailed great barn. The overwhelming impression is of immense flowing space and of evenly distributed light; the vast rectangular piazza in front of the edifice seems to be continued, roofed and "tamed," to become the interior of the church itself, its essential structure rationalized and minimized. The eastward vista down the nave is terminated by the flat transverse wall of the choir, which is itself pierced by one very tall, elegant central arch and two smaller flanking arches, beyond which is the dazzling concentration of light from the three tall lancets of the faceted apse.

The nave bays are very broad and the side aisles tall, so that the entire tripartite space reads almost as one. Different again from Santa Maria Novella, though, is the crisp, sharply detailed vocabulary of the stone structure itself, with its flat planes and sharp edges, and this refined minimalism, as well as the spatial qualities of the interior, are the chief reasons for the attribution to Arnolfo. All of the detailing is clean and pared down, with very little applied decoration; only the nave capitals and high-level corbels and trusses are anything other than utilitarian — albeit a highly refined utilitarianism. In this the friars were following the basic precepts of the order's founder, but there were, in fact, major tensions and schisms within the city, and indeed within the order itself, over the construction of the church, the grandiose scale of which offended many purists. Even more ironic than this debate, perhaps — the grand scale could, after all, be justified in practical terms by the vast crowds to whom the friars preached — was that Santa Croce was to be patronized by many of Florence's wealthiest citizens, including the famous banking dynasties of the Peruzzi and the Bardi. Santa Croce thus marks a culmination of this particular stylistic development, that of the vast, open, Gothic preaching hall, derived from the long tradition of the earlier basilican typology but now achieving new heights of space and scale.

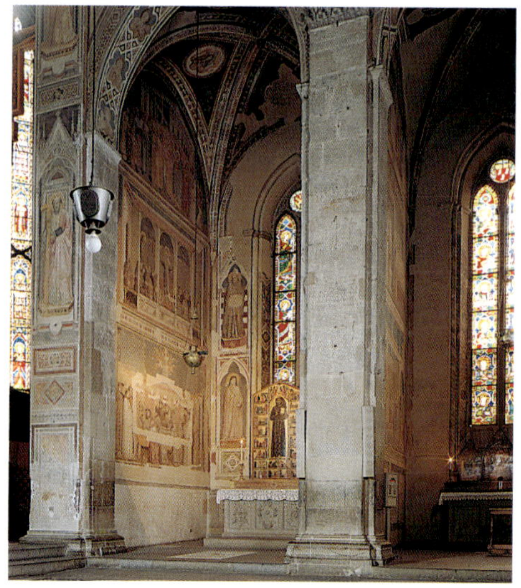

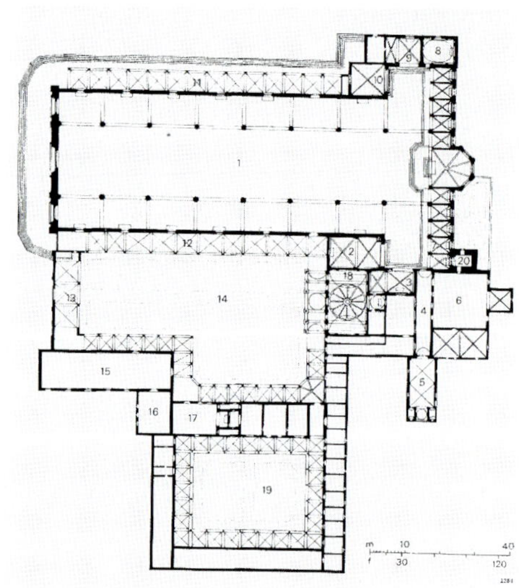

SANTA CROCE

Top: the Bardi chapel, which contains, together with the adjacent Peruzzi chapel, the last two fresco cycles by Giotto from 1320 to 1325. The church was patronized by many notable Florentine families, among whom the Bardi and Peruzzi were perhaps the wealthiest. Above: plan of the church and monastic buildings; the monastery occupies the land to the south side of the church. Most of the trecento monastic buildings survive, including the refectory.

Opposite: interior of the nave. The massive, simple, but imposing church was begun by Arnolfo di Cambio in 1294. Much like Santa Maria Novella, it was basically a great preaching hall; its architectural vocabulary is linear, planar, and extremely plain.

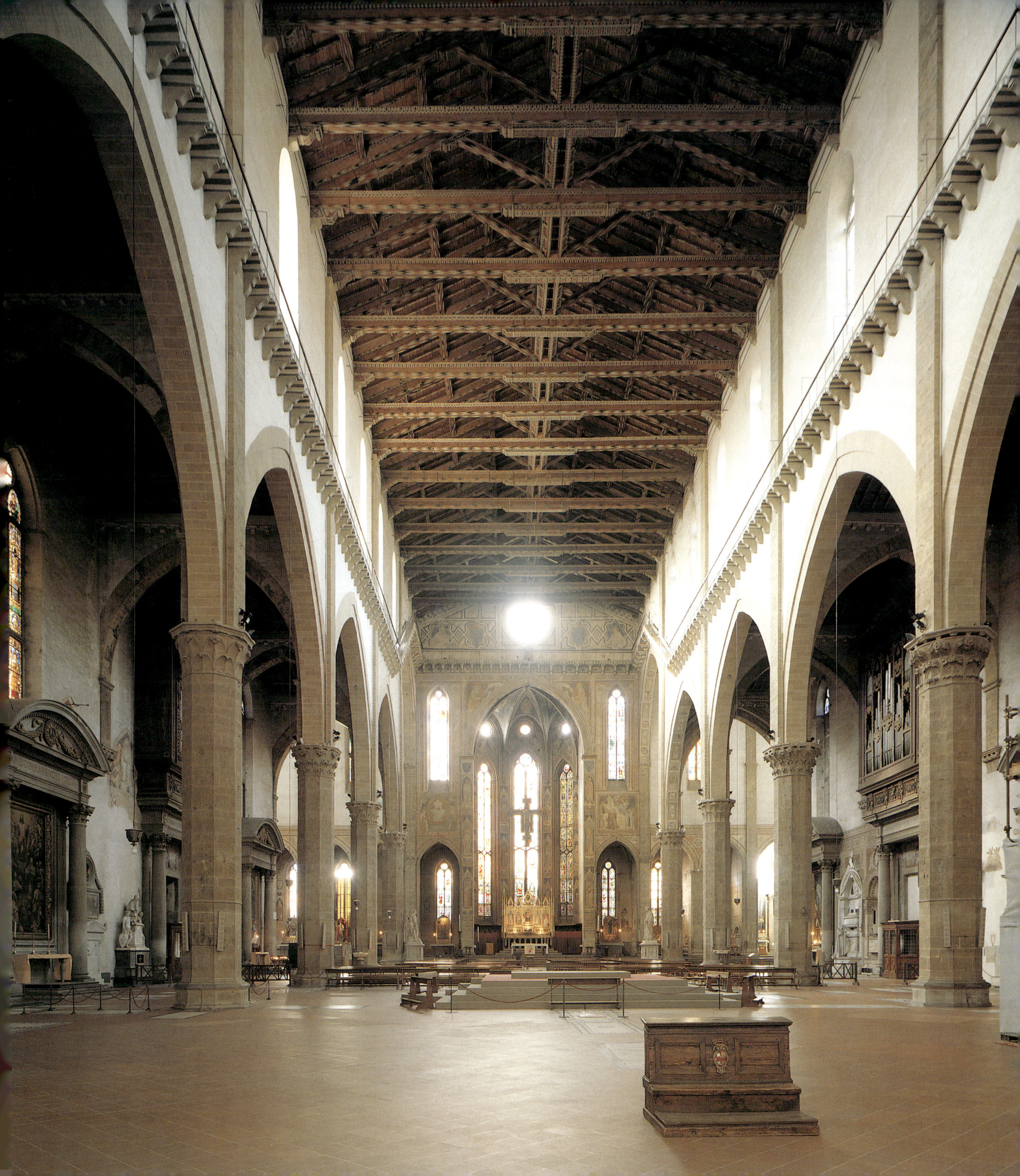

As at Santa Maria Novella, annexed to the great church was an extensive monastic complex, in this case all on the south side toward the river. The unusual L-shaped first cloister originally was divided into two, and on the south side was built the great refectory and the other monastic accommodation. Later the complex was extended further, with Benedetto da Maiano's second cloister, built in 1453 in a refined Renaissance manner. Within the church itself the patronage of a number of wealthy Florentine dynasties was expressed in the typical manner, by the adoption and decoration of chapels, particularly in the transepts: the Riccardi, Peruzzi, and Bardi in the righthand arm, the Spinelli, Capponi, Ricasoli, and Bardi (again) on the left side. Also prominent in the patronage of Santa Croce were the Baroncelli, while the imposing sacristy from 1340 was funded from the banking fortune of the Peruzzi.

SANTA TRINITÀ

The compact plan, with its five very short nave bays, reflects its constricted urban site.

How does the design of these two great churches relate to that of the third major medieval Florentine church, the cathedral itself, the construction of which continued during much of the trecento? All three buildings share certain fundamental characteristics, although they differ considerably in detail. The common features in general terms are the grandeur and simplicity of their interiors, with very large, broad nave bays and comparatively high side aisles, such that the three parallel spaces flow together with little visual impediment. From Santa Maria Novella the cathedral takes its simple ribbed cross vaulting of the nave and aisles, while the clean, refined detailing of the main structure — columns, capitals, arches, and piers — and the high-level cornices owes more to the linearity, the planar forms, of Santa Croce than to the more rounded, more typically Gothic forms of Santa Maria Novella. In plan there are major differences between the two mendicant churches and the cathedral, not so much in the design of the naves but in the treatment of their respective east ends. Santa Maria del Fiore, with its hybrid, part-centralized, part-linear plan, has no parallel in the other two churches, where the compact cruciform plans of the east ends reflect their liturgical needs. (The choirs in both churches were located in the liturgical eastern bays of the nave.) The cathedral was clearly intended to be terminated in its highly unusual manner, with three equal wings giving off the central octagon, in part, at least, to serve its specific functions, for processions and other festive public occasions, for which there was no equivalent or need in any other church in the city.

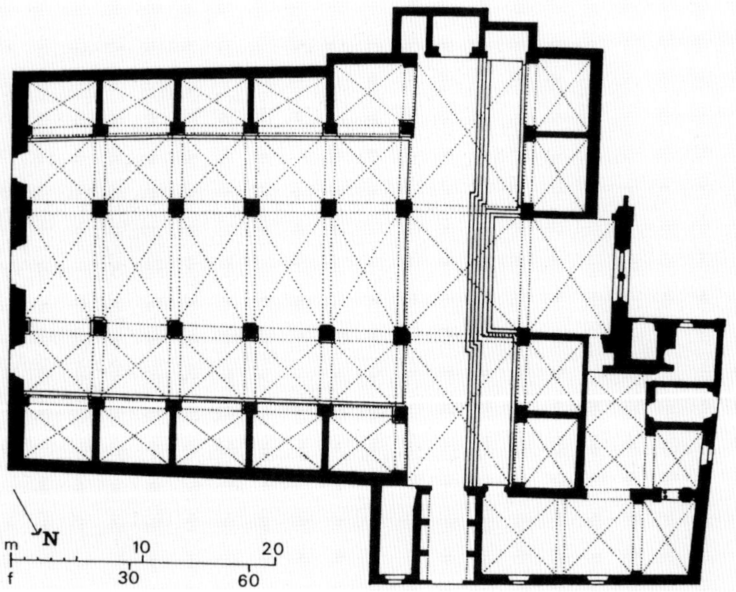

Although Santa Croce and Santa Maria Novella dominated their respective halves of the city, they were not the only significant Gothic churches built during this period, and a few others deserve specific mention. Santa Trinità, although considerably smaller in scale than the Franciscan and Dominican foundations, nevertheless represents a good example of the later refined, rather minimalist approach to Florentine Gothic church design that derived from these earlier examples, particularly Santa Maria Novella. Its foundation dates from the eleventh century, when it was the Florentine home of the Vallombrosan order; the earlier structures, however, were largely lost in the definitive rebuilding of the monastery that took place from 1300 to 1330, although the church itself

SANTA TRINITÀ

Below: view of the chapels. The church was completed in about 1400, and is one of very few surviving gothic church interiors in Florence, other than the two great monastic houses. Below, right: detail of the fresco by Lorenzo Monaco depicting scenes from the life of the Virgin, from about 1420–25.

was not reconstructed until after 1360; the bulk of the fabric is thus contemporaneous with at least part of the decades-long process of reconstructing the cathedral. The definitive rebuilding of Santa Trinità is usually attributed to Neri di Fioravanti, who is also associated with the cathedral in the same period.[10] Not surprisingly, therefore, it shares some features with Santa Maria del Fiore, albeit on a considerably reduced scale. Construction took place in two distinct stages, the first, from 1360 to 1370, comprising three of the five bays of the nave, and the second, from 1383 to 1405, consisting of the rest of the nave, the apses, and transepts. In its cross vaulting, Santa Trinità can be seen to be related to Santa Maria Novella, but in the sharply defined linear approach to the nave articulation, with square piers and simple, engaged pilasters rising to carry the ribs of the vaulting, it has more in common with Arnolfo's refined minimalism at Santa Croce. The substantial sense of enclosure provided by the strong piers and lines of the vaulting ribs (and the much smaller nave bays) serves to emphasize the verticality of the space. The plan is fairly complex, although it is

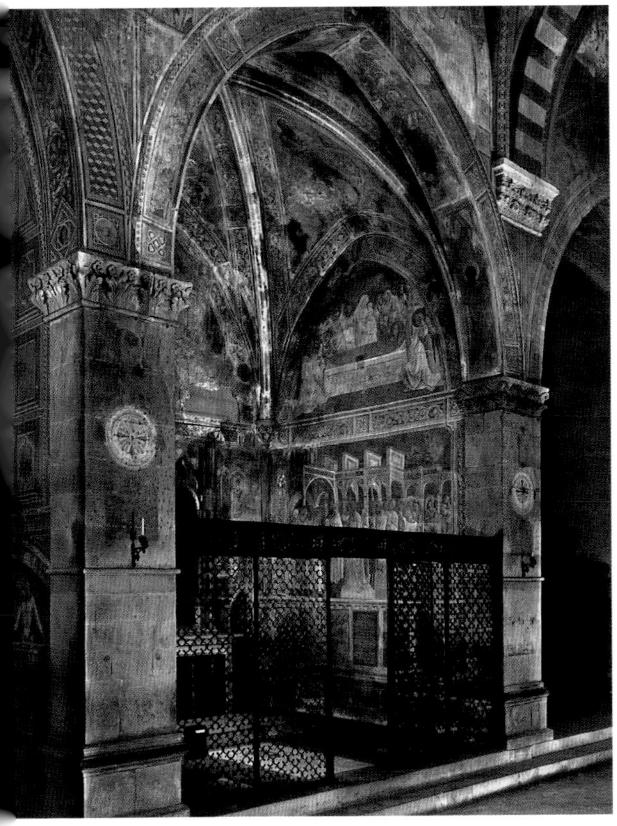

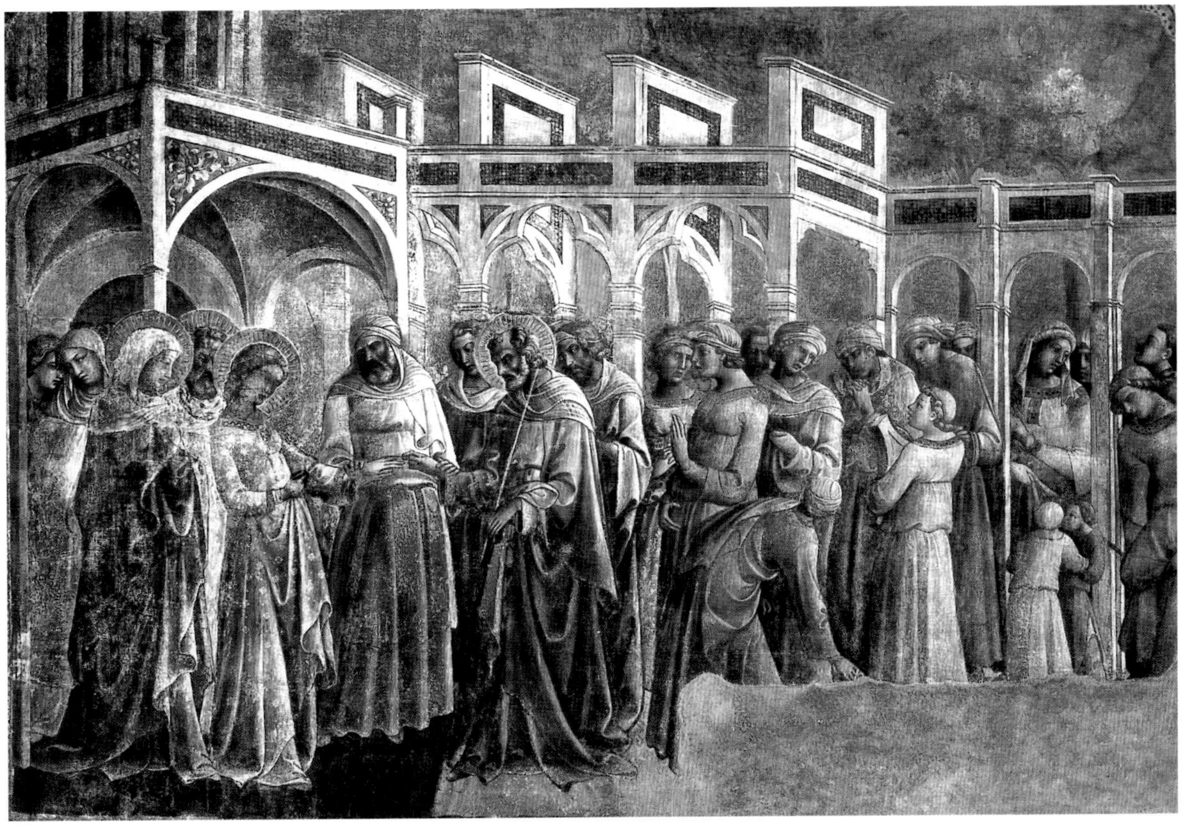

basically a Latin cross, with a five-bay nave; the side aisles are both lined with chapels, which were patronized by a number of important Florentine clans, including the Davanzati and Sassetti.

San Francesco at Fiesole is perhaps the most important of these other mainly trecento constructions. Founded as the Florentine base for the order known as the Romiti in 1330, it became a Franciscan house in 1399; the attached conventual buildings were added after about 1405. Much altered internally, the church retains a characteristically simple early quattrocento facade, with a fine central *occhio* ("eye") window and a deep, projecting stone porch.

The Certosa (Carthusian monastery) at Galluzzo is another important complex much added to and modified over the centuries.[11] It was founded by the wealthy Niccolò Acciaiuoli in 1342, and was also patronized by the Visconti. The site, southwest of the city on a spur above the confluence of two streams, had strategic importance and was formerly a fortress known as Montagudo. The new

Carthusian house was the work of Jacopo Passavanti, under the direction of Acciaiuoli himself, and the complex became very extensive indeed; the many monastic cellblocks were built around a vast central *cortile*; there were also picture galleries and libraries. The hub of the complex, though, lay in the imposing structure that today still dominates the site, the Palazzo degli Studi, built to contain three large halls for teaching, all patronized by the same Niccolò, a friend and patron of both Boccaccio and Petrarch. Construction of the extensive complex took several decades, and the present church, by Giovanni Fancelli, was not built until the 1540s. The Certosa remained an important center of learning until the Napoleonic dissolutions, and since 1958 has been occupied by Cistercians.

Orsanmichele

The extraordinary structure that for centuries has been known as Orsanmichele, which stands only yards away from the Mercato Nuovo, has played a special role in the history of Florentine civic life.[12] Describing Orsanmichele simply as a church gives no indication of the richness and complexity of the history of this unique, almost unclassifiable structure. Its story illustrates perhaps better than that of any other building the characteristic Florentine fusion of civic, social, commercial, and religious elements, which is reflected in the architectonic styles of the building itself; Orsanmichele's history reflects the interdependent, overlapping nature of these elements of Florentine culture and society as a whole.

The earliest structure on this site was a small oratory, built — it is said — as early as the eighth century, and dedicated to San Michele "in Orto" (in the orchard), from which misty origins the popular title has derived. In around 1285 this small early chapel was replaced by a public loggia, or open hall, the first in Florence, dedicated to the storage and selling of corn. The design of this loggia is often attributed to Arnolfo di Cambio, and has been identified as one further element in his reordering of the key monuments of the city; but very soon after its completion, the site began to be venerated, as the result of the miraculous powers of a painting of the Virgin that the loggia contained.[13] It was to be a short-lived structure, though, which was destroyed in the disastrous fire that afflicted this part of the city in 1304. A rather hurried reconstruction followed in 1307, but it was not until 1337 that a more permanent rebuilding of the loggia was begun, on the instructions of the Comune. This was completed in the 1350s, but the new market loggia did not take full account of the religious pressures and needs that had arisen due to the earlier visions and miracles; so, during the 1360s and 1370s, the loggia was enclosed by the present perimeter walls and thus effectively became a more conventional votive chapel. The basic structure of the loggia was retained, however, as can still be seen today, with two rows of three bays, and with strong, semicircular cross vaulting to the interior. The rebuilt loggia is usually attributed to Francesco Talenti, Neri di Fioravanti, and Benci di Cione, all three of whom were masters for the rebuilding of the cathedral in this period. The work of enclosing the hall in the years after 1367 was that of Simone Talenti, Francesco's son, and is remarkable chiefly for the extraordinary refinement of the complex tracery of the windows. The importance of the chapel for pilgrimage and votive offerings called for the creation of a grandiose, complex tabernacle, which also served as the high altar, built in one of the two eastern bays by Andrea Orcagna in 1359; it is an incredibly rich and refined work which frames the subject of the church's veneration, the painting of the Virgin and Child by Bernardo Daddi.

But the transformation of the former loggia into an enclosed votive chapel meant that the Florentines had lost their grain store and market, which had to be replaced. In this extremely densely built up part of the city, with no spare land available at all, the only direction to go was upward, and so the grain stores were built directly above the chapel, in two stories, with one spacious great hall constructed directly above the other. By 1383 the second, uppermost hall was

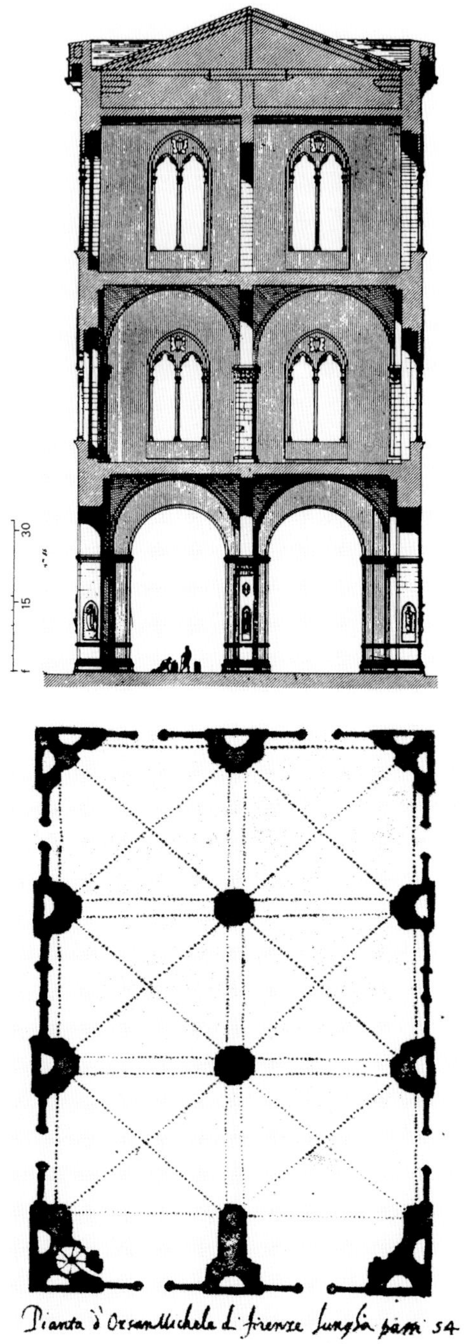

ORSANMICHELE

Top: section showing the two spacious stories of grain storage above the church. Above: the church's original function as a covered loggia for the grain market is clearly visible in its plan, in the form of a regular rectangle, three bays long and two bays wide.

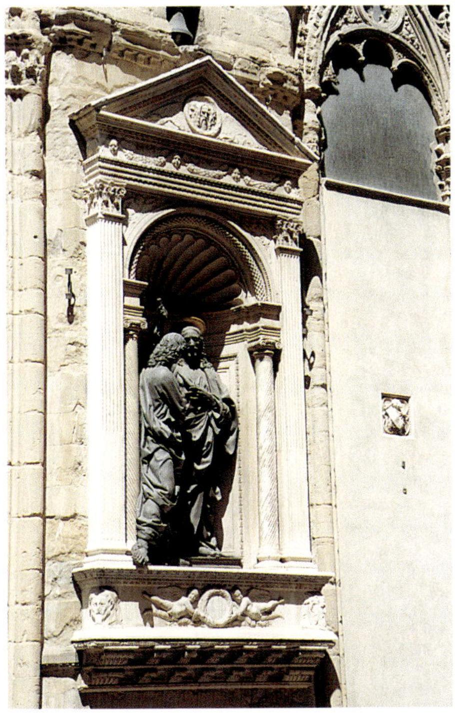

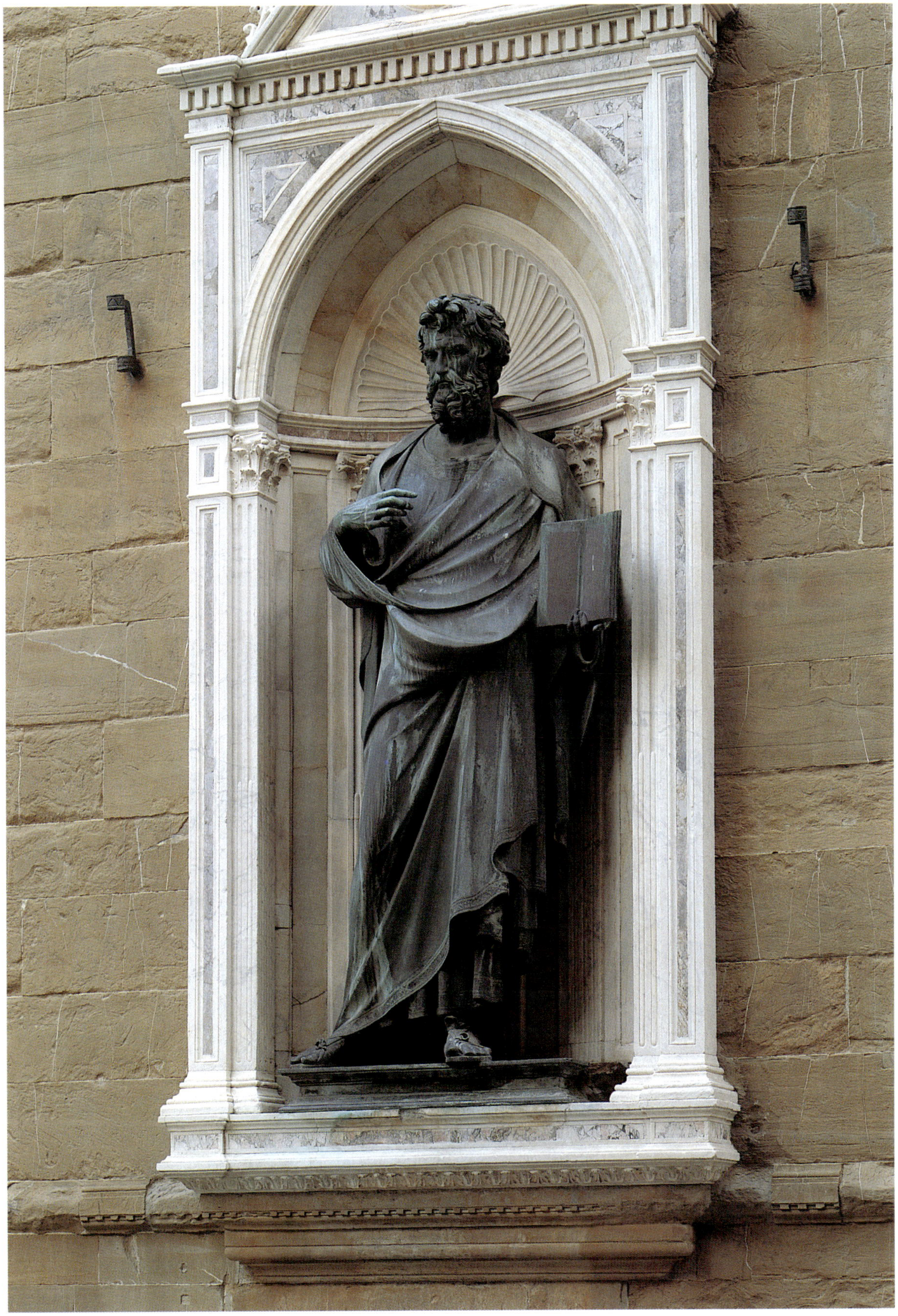

ORSANMICHELE

Above: niche that decorates the exterior. The Florentine government instructed the chief *arti* of the city to "adopt" and fund the tabernacles and the sculptures that they were to house. Right: St. Matthew by Lorenzo Ghiberti, 1419–22.

completed, and in 1404 the rich crowning crenellation was added to the skyline. Practical evidence of the use of these upper stories for grain storage can still be seen today in the "pipes" cut into the pilasters so that grain could be brought down to the lower levels.

The church also formed a vital hub for the activities of the *arti*, many of whose halls were nearby; in 1339, the niches around the exterior of the ground floor were allocated by the Comune to the principal *arti*, one to each; there are fourteen niches in all, four on each of the longer sides and three on each of the two shorter faces. Although it took some time before the niches were all occupied, eventually they housed a magnificent collection of sculptures by the city's finest masters. Directed to fund the sculptures to fill these niches were the seven *arti maggiori*, together with the Tribunale di Mercatanzia and the six *arti mediane*, among whom were the smiths, butchers, shoemakers, builders, and sculptors. Most of the works that were first installed here date from the period from 1410 to 1420, and were by Nanni di Banco, Niccolò Lamberti, Orcagna, Ghiberti, and Donatello; later some were replaced, and among the new replacements were *San Luca* by Giambologna, to replace Lamberti's original; Verrocchio's *St. Thomas*; *St. John the Evangelist* by Baccio to replace Orcagna's original; and a bronze copy of Donatello's *St. George*.[14]

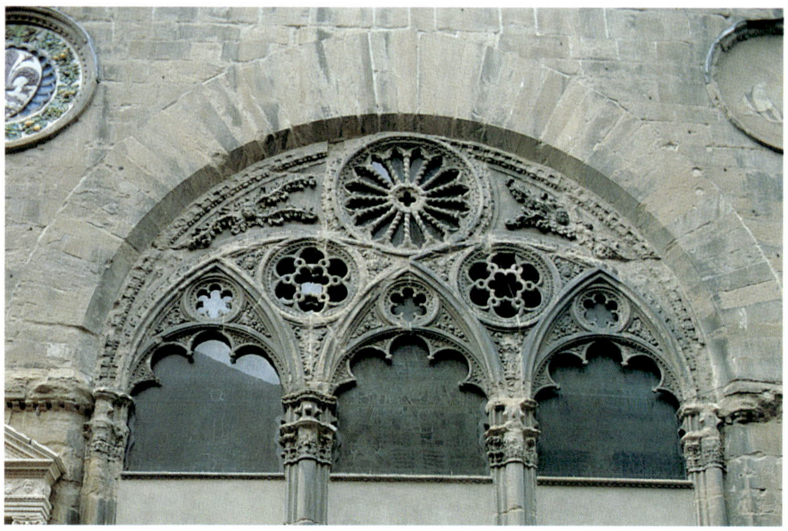

ORSANMICHELE

Left: detail of one of the elaborately traceried ground-floor windows, added after 1367 by Simone Talenti.

Opposite: detail of the high altar. The extraordinarily rich tabernacle, or *baldacchino*, from 1355–59 is Andrea Orcagna's masterpiece, and frames Bernardo Daddi's painting of the Madonna.

Orsanmichele is therefore, as finally completed and decorated in the mid-quattrocento, a complex, hybrid structure, the appearance of which reflects these various stages of construction and very different practical requirements. The richly detailed exterior of the ground floor clearly evinces the importance to the people of the city of the votive chapel inside, while the equally richly sculpted aedicules in which the statues of the *arti* are set reflect their own pivotal importance to the city's society and its economy. The exterior of the two upper stories, however, has features that can be traced back to the semifortified civic tradition of palaces like the Bargello and even the Palazzo Vecchio. All are characterized by fine ashlar masonry walls in which two-light windows are usually set at fairly wide intervals, with the whole capped by a crenellation, part practical and part symbolic. It is essentially a refined but highly functional building.

Early Renaissance Churches: Brunelleschi, Michelozzo, and Alberti

If the first great civic architecture of Florence was instigated by Arnolfo di Cambio in the late duecento, then it was Filippo Brunelleschi who, a century later, transformed the ecclesiastical architecture of the city with a series of profoundly important buildings, from those early works such as the Ospedale degli Innocenti and the Sagrestia Vecchia at San Lorenzo to the churches of Santo Spirito and San Lorenzo itself, and all culminating, of course, with the great cupola of the cathedral. Brunelleschi is the pivotal figure around whom revolves Florence's early Renaissance architecture.

In 1419 he was appointed by the Medici to transform the family's patronal church of San Lorenzo. The appointment was almost exactly contemporaneous with the commencement of the elegant loggia of the Ospedale degli Innocenti, which was to be completed in 1425. These years were exceptionally active ones in his professional career, since he was also closely involved with the

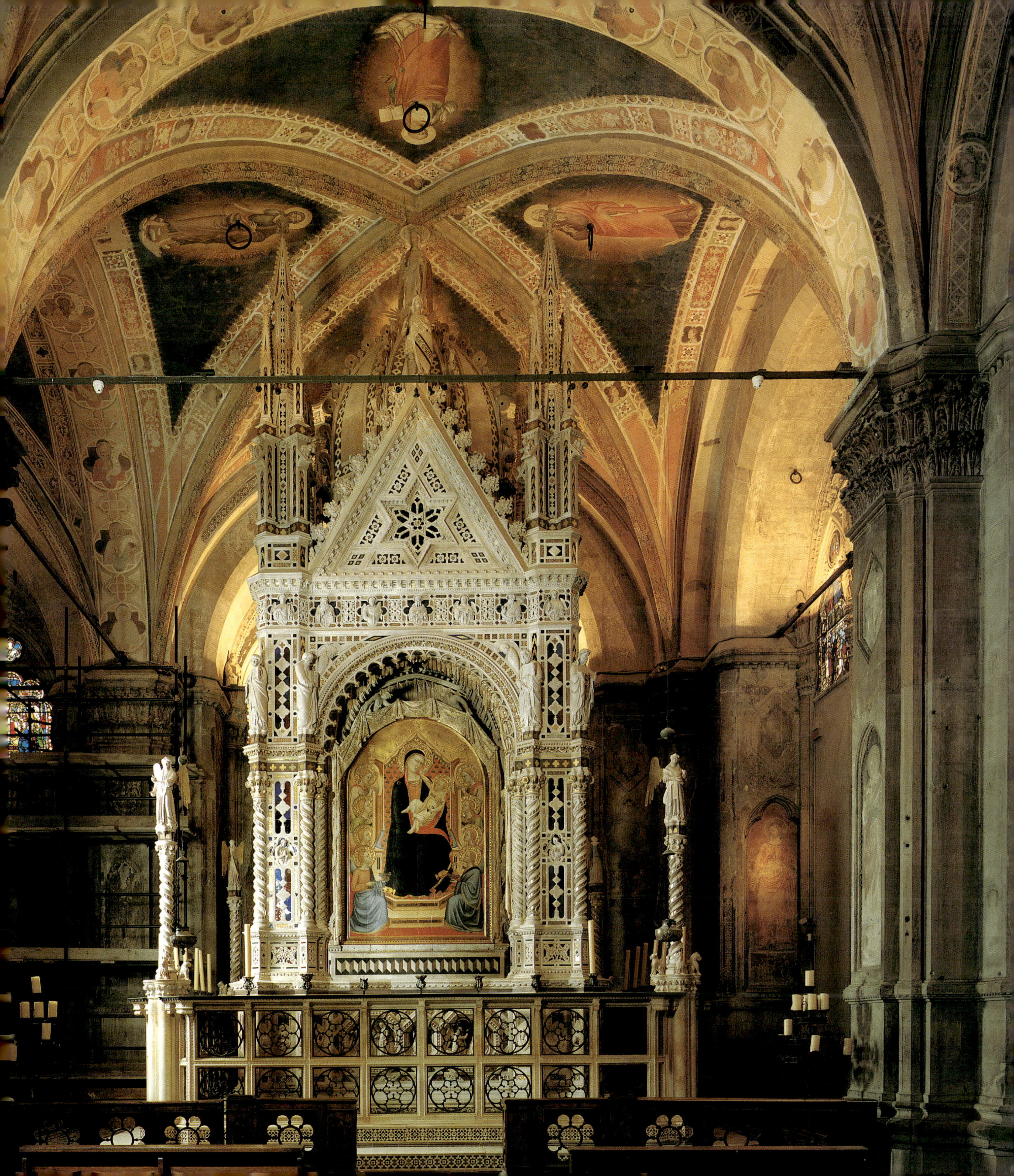

cupola at Santa Maria del Fiore through much of the 1420s.[15] On 10 August 1421, a solemn ceremony was held to mark the laying of the first foundations of the new church of San Lorenzo. This was the first stage of the Medici clan's endeavors to honor and glorify the dynasty through a series of self-laudatory buildings; the program thus begun was only finally concluded with the grandiose Cappella dei Principi, well over 150 years later.

Before San Lorenzo, a much lesser known fragment from Brunelleschi's oeuvre, roughly contemporaneous with the Innocenti, should be examined: the Barbadori chapel at Santa Felicità, which is interesting because in this modest structure there is early evidence of some of the characteristic features of Brunelleschi's later interiors, particularly the Sagrestia Vecchia, and the Pazzi chapel at Santa Croce.[16] (The Barbadori chapel was to be considerably altered in the later sixteenth century by Vasari, however, when he built the section of the Corridoio that runs across the upper part of the facade of the church on its way to Palazzo Pitti.) The chapel was originally projected by Bartolomeo Barbadori in around 1420, and was built about five years later. It is square in plan, surmounted by a cupola on pendentives. Brunelleschi refined and developed these basic forms further at the two later chapels; here, therefore, is a prototype, extremely simple, almost minimalist in its detailing, of the later, richer works. Those few key elements picked out in *pietra serena*, though, give a preliminary hint of the manner in which his interior architecture was to develop in the future.

Although the foundations for the presbytery of San Lorenzo were begun in 1425, the Sagrestia Vecchia was complete by March 1429, before the church itself, and shortly before the death of Giovanni di Bicci de' Medici, patron of the work.[17] Dedicated to San Giovanni Evangelista, the sacristy is perhaps more accurately identified as Giovanni di Bicci's memorial chapel. It was to be attached to an outer corner of the left transept of the slowly emerging new church, but is effectively a separate, autonomous structure; it remains a seminal work in Brunelleschi's development, and has often been described as a personal philosophical statement, a humanist manifesto. In proportions, the sacristy is very simple: The body of the chapel is a precise cube, surmounted by an equally precisely defined hemispherical cupola. The precision of volume and proportion that these simple statements convey was to become a constant theme in his work, refined to perfection in the two great churches; equal precision and discipline was applied to his use of materials, another constantly evolving theme in his oeuvre. The basic structure and architectural vocabulary is all in gray *pietra serena*, while all of the nonstructural planes (wall surfaces, spandrels, the "sails" of the cupola) are finished with plain white plaster. Such a rational, functional, but highly refined approach was profoundly influential in the development of Renaissance architecture, not only in Florence itself, in the later work of Michelozzo and Sangallo, for example, but also in Venice in the work of Mauro Codussi. However, despite the underlying purity and perfection of these Euclidian forms, in its final manifestation the sacristy was more complex visually. It was completed only in the early 1440s, when Donatello added the two entrance portals, as well as the bas-reliefs directly above the doorways and the high-level tondi. In the design of the upper orders of the chapel, Brunelleschi's approach was both reactionary and highly original. The chief reactionary aspect is perhaps the form of the cupola, the *volta a vela*, or sail vault, as it was known, which is not, in fact, a true dome, but is essentially constructed of "sails," or umbrella panels, which themselves are based on medieval rib-vaulted precedents. Here the ribbed vault is translated into a rational, structurally very strong form, using the new architectural language. Far more original is Brunelleschi's "rediscovery" of the form of the pendentive to span the transitional zone between the square plan of the cornice and the circular plan of the springing of the cupola itself. The pendentive had not been part of the classical Greco-Roman vocabulary, where it appears to have remained unknown, but was frequently used later in the "new Rome," Constantinople, and throughout the

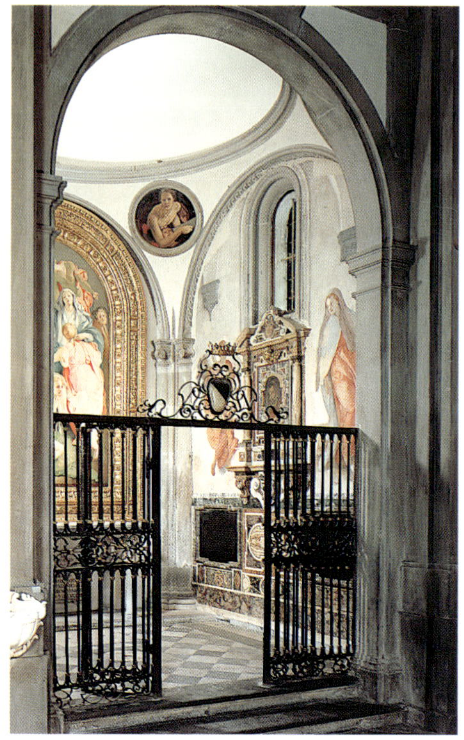

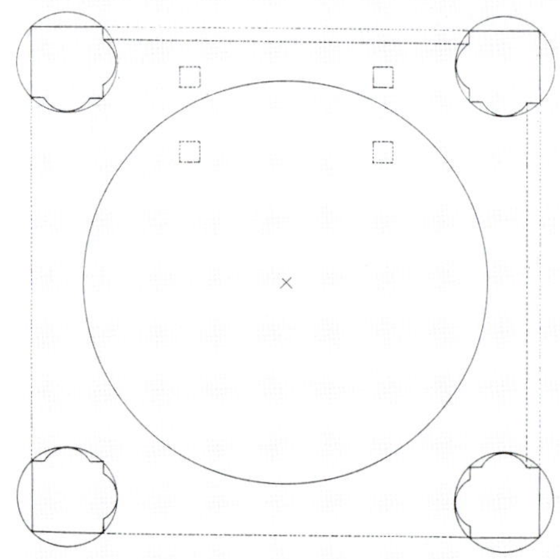

BARBADORI CHAPEL, SANTA FELICITÀ

Top: this modest work is one of Brunelleschi's earliest, but already incorporates characteristic elements, including the pendentives and his restrained use of materials: plaster and *pietra serena*. Above: plan of the chapel.

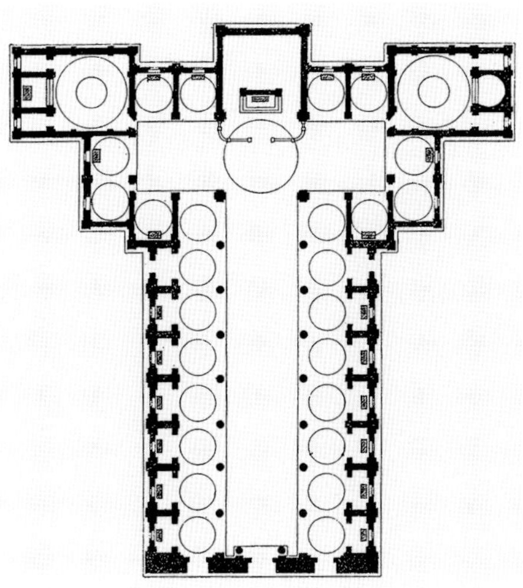

SAN LORENZO

Plan by Grandjean de Montigny, 1816–15. The Sagrestia Vecchia is in the top left corner of the plan, the Sagrestia Nuova in the top right.

Eastern Empire. For this reason, it was comparatively widespread throughout the Venetian overseas empire, the *impero da mar*, and was therefore probably introduced in Italy through Venice's close trading and cultural links with the east; San Marco is the supreme evidence of its westward spread. But the pendentive had few precedents in Tuscany, the Romanesque cupola of San Paolo a Ripa d'Arno in Pisa being a rare example, together with Brunelleschi's own previous tentative use of the form in the Barbadori chapel. In the sacristy, therefore, evidence can be seen of what were to become Brunelleschi's developing preoccupations: proportion and Euclidian geometry; structural soundness and rationality; the development of a logical, classical matrix of architectural elements; the clarity of his decorative vocabulary; all of these elements then unified by the defining structural framework of the spaces — columns and capitals, cornices, arches, ribs.

Brunelleschi's plan for the San Lorenzo church itself was designed by 1421, although it was only completed after his death by Antonio Manetti, his pupil and biographer; Manetti supervised the final stages of the work after 1461.[18] The prior, Padre Dolfin, had originally planned an enlargement of the old church, and had already begun the construction of a new choir, so Brunelleschi was faced with some constraint; the fabric of this partially completed element had to be incorporated into the liturgical east end of his own proposal (San Lorenzo is orientated almost precisely in the reverse of the traditional manner, with the "east end" lying almost due west). Although the basic plan of the church retains the traditional Latin cross form of its medieval predecessor, with a long central nave, two side aisles, and square-ended transepts, the whole was now reinterpreted by Brunelleschi with rigorous attention to proportions, harmony, and to a clear classical vocabulary. The entire plan of San Lorenzo is generated from a square, a single large square for each of the spaces at the east end — crossing, chancel, and the two transepts — and four large squares for the length of the nave. However, this module of the large square is subdivided into two for the lesser, or secondary, elements of the plan; thus, the four large nave bays are each divided into two to produce an eight-bay nave colonnade, and these same smaller, half-bay dimensions are repeated in the bays of the side aisles and in the small square chapels built around the east end. The entire plan is thus strictly modular, and all based on a simple ratio of 2:1 both in the two-dimensional proportions of the structural bays and in their heights. The order of San Lorenzo is refined Corinthian; the plain, monolithic cylindrical nave columns are surmounted by classical capitals, but above them again are tall blocks of trabeation in the form of "dosserets," or short sections of entablature, which support the springing of the semicircular nave arches. The whole ensemble marks a dignified, restrained interpretation of classical forms, using the same two materials: *pietra serena* for all the elements of structure and white plaster for the essentially "neutral" surfaces between the elements of this principal architectural vocabulary. The modular restraint of the nave is completed by the use of a flat, coffered ceiling, the rhythm of which complements that of the main colonnade.

The church of San Lorenzo became the center of a long series of additions and further works over many decades after Brunelleschi's church was completed; to this nucleus were added Michelozzo's cloisters, Michelangelo's Sagrestia Nuova and the Biblioteca Medicea Laurenziana, and finally, Matteo Nigetti's overpowering Medici chapel in the early seventeenth century. But it was to be at Santo Spirito that Brunelleschi was to develop still further his principles and philosophies of church design.[19]

Brunelleschi's original proposal for Santo Spirito represented a radical innovation in the urban sense, while further refining the architectural vocabulary developed at San Lorenzo. The urban proposal was to completely reconstruct the church but with reversed orientation, such that its facade was to face the Arno toward the north, Brunelleschi's intention being that it should be approached by an imposing new public square, extending as far as the riverbank. This was a new

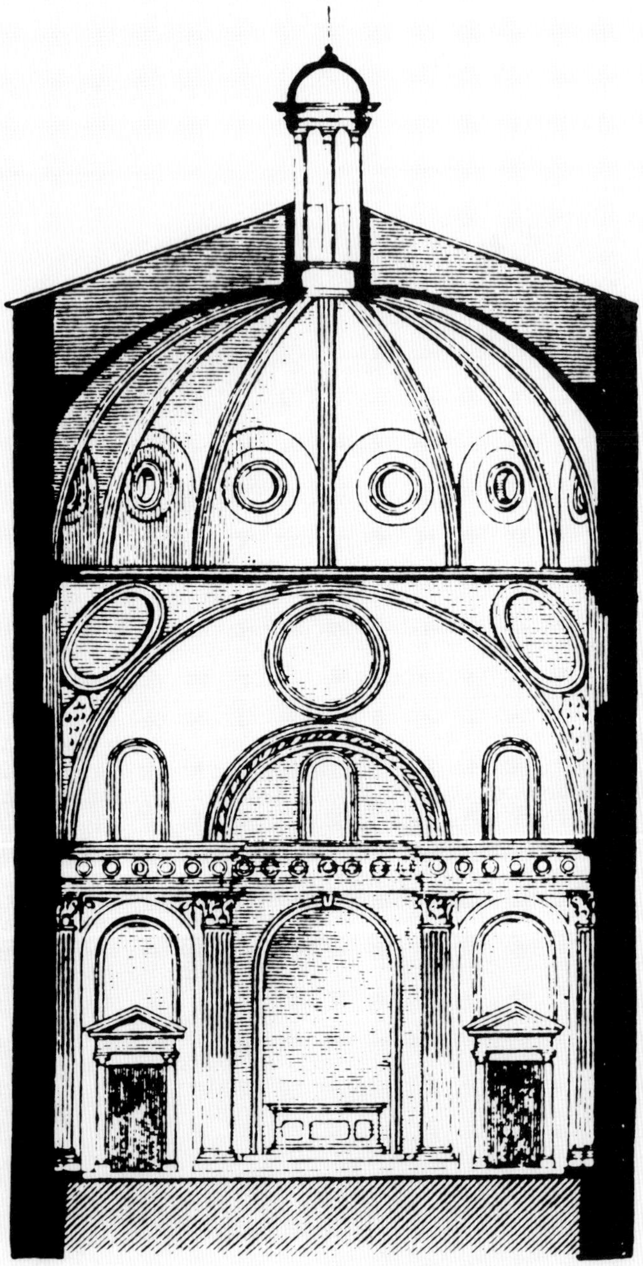

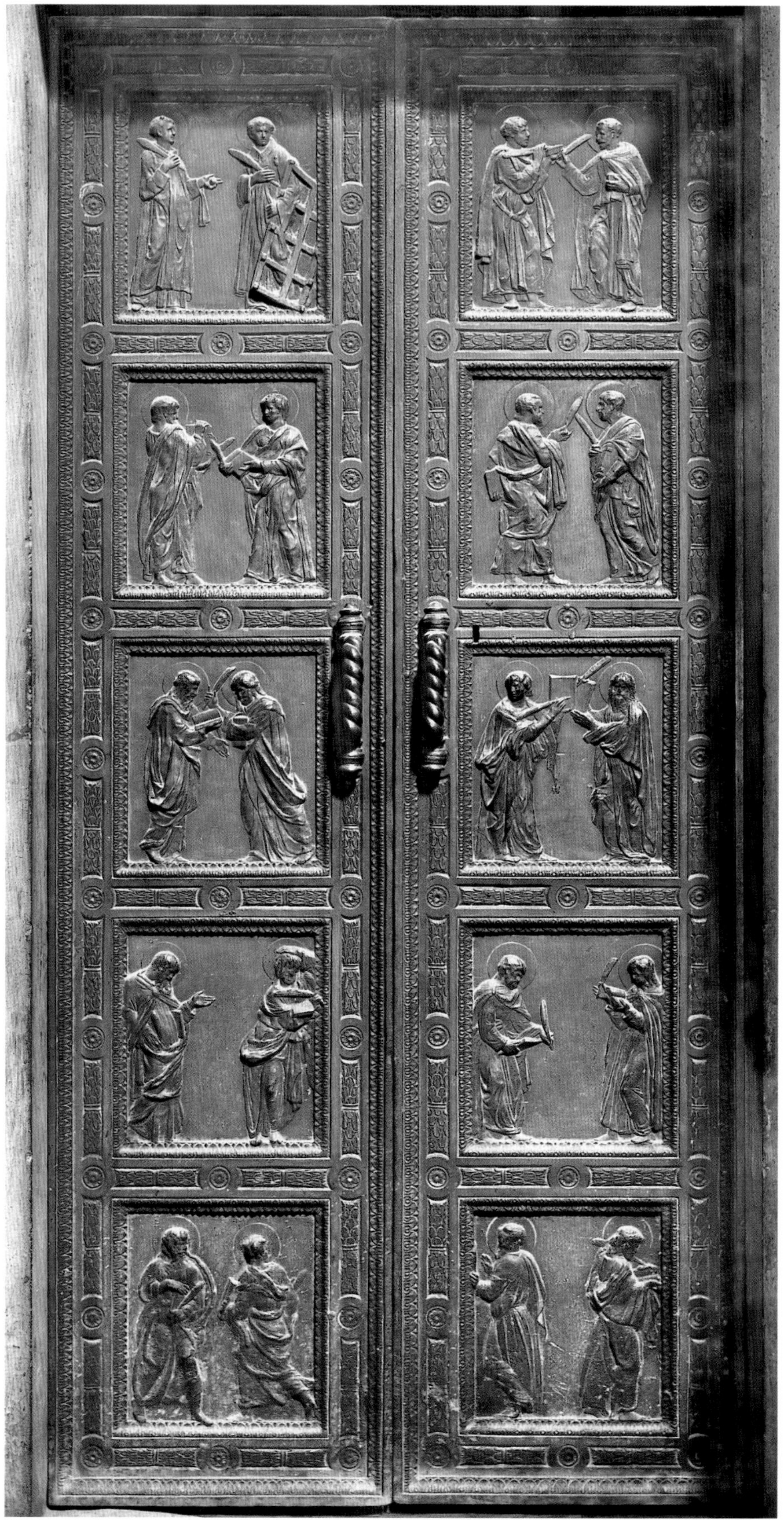

SAGRESTIA VECCHIA, SAN LORENZO
(above, right, and opposite)

Above: section of Brunelleschi's sacristy.
Right: entrance doors.

Opposite: the internal space is designed to precise mathematical volumes: a cube for the lower part, surmounted by a hemispherical cupola. The tondi were added in about 1440 by Donatello.

SAN LORENZO (overleaf)

Interior of the nave. The church's harmonious appearance results from the application of rigorous mathematical proportions to all of the elements, and the equally rigorous vocabulary of materials.

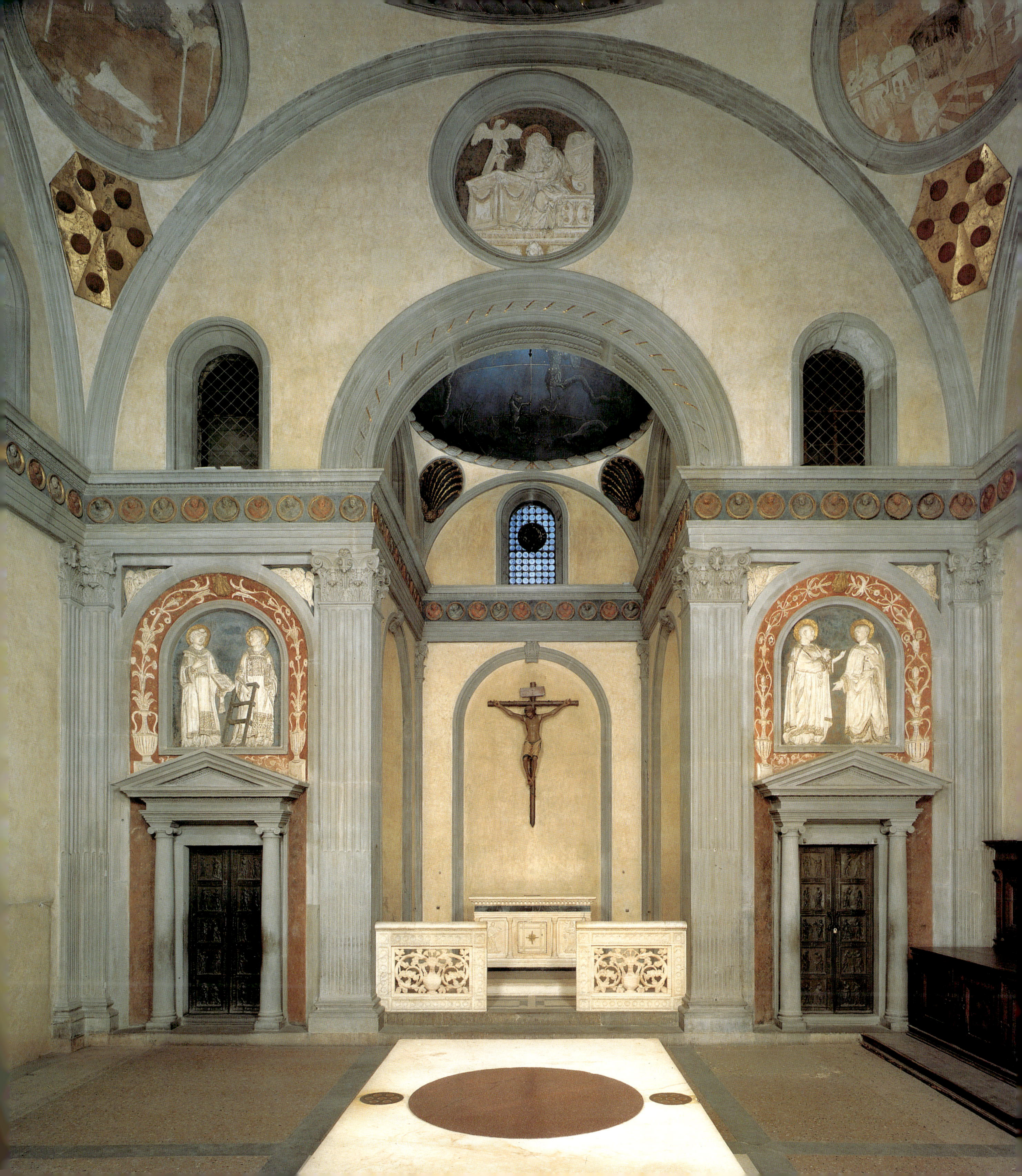

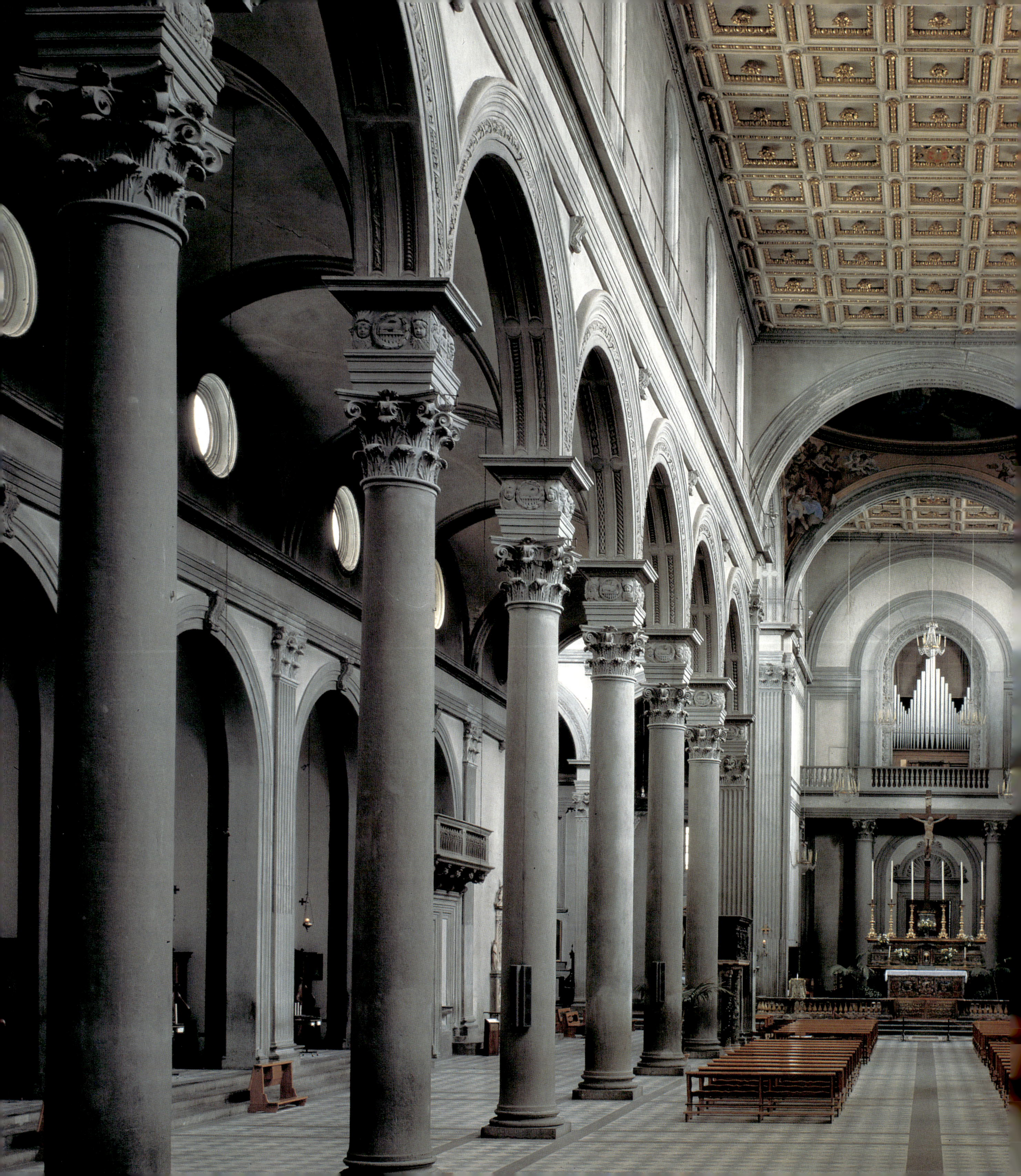

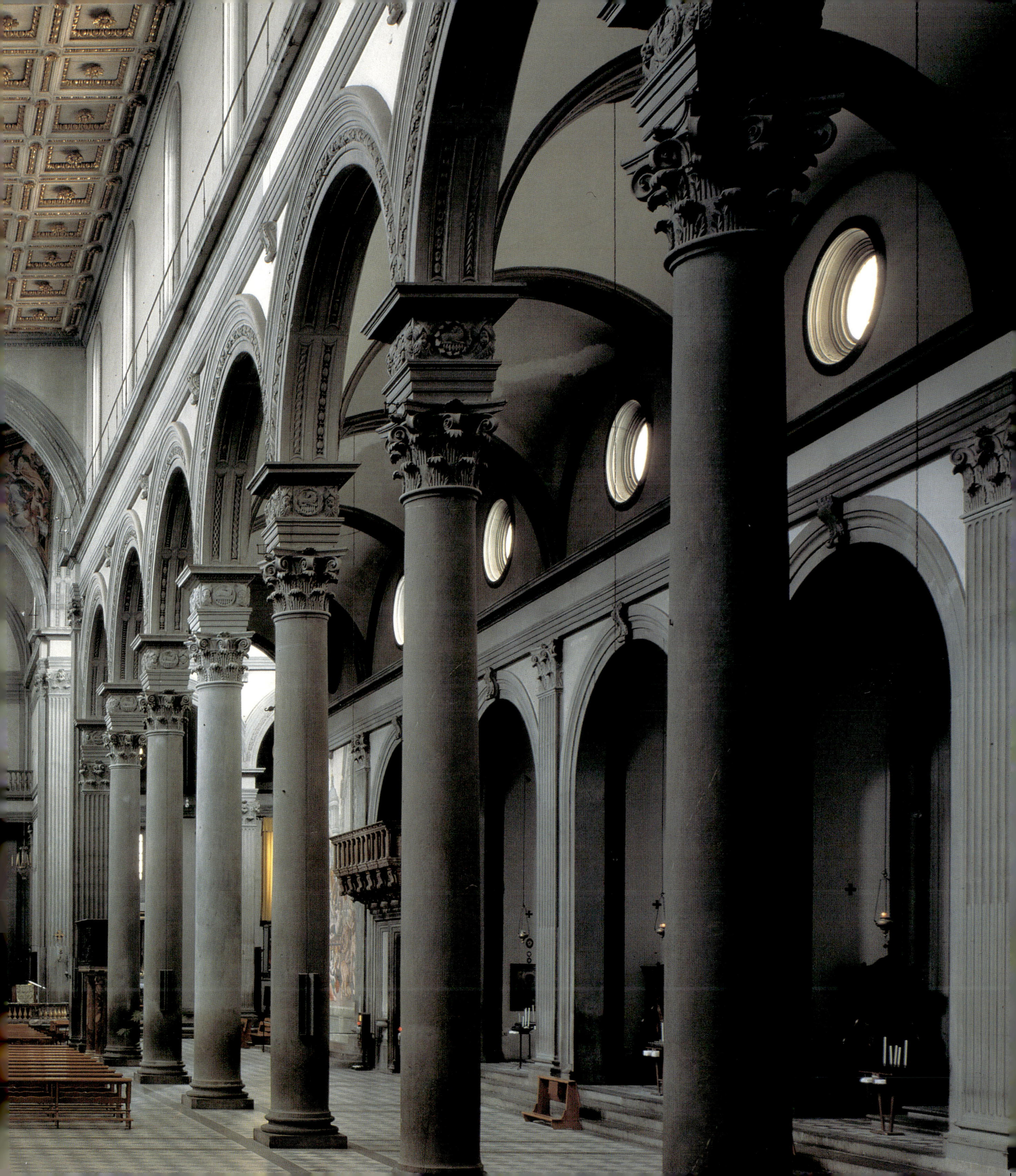

concept indeed, one that would have introduced a major new element into the city's urban structure: a monument with its piazza on the south bank worthy of comparison with some of those on the north bank — Santa Croce, the Palazzo del Popolo — which would significantly increase the importance of the Oltrarno within the city.

This first proposal was drawn up in 1434, although the present church was not begun until twelve years later, in the year of Brunelleschi's death. Despite the fact that more reactionary counsels prevailed over the church's orientation, it remains the only one of Brunelleschi's major works that was not constrained by previous structures or by their physical context: The site was virtually a tabula rasa, and for this reason the result offers the purest example of Brunelleschi's unfettered application of module and proportion. The module employed by Brunelleschi throughout Santo Spirito was eleven *braccia*. The plan of Santo Spirito is a rigorously disciplined Latin cross, with the same major bay configurations as those at San Lorenzo, that is, one large square bay for each of the two transepts, for the crossing, and for the chancel, and four identical bays for the nave. Here, however, the entire Latin cross plan is surrounded by an ambulatory of secondary spaces or continuous aisles, which wrap around the perimeter with a further series of small square bays, again, as at San Lorenzo, with dimensions half of those of the main bays. These are not aisles in the conventional sense, since they do not simply flank the two sides of the nave, but are constructed around the entire perimeter of the plan, including the transepts, the east end of the chancel, and the facade. Nor was this the end of Brunelleschi's spatial innovations, since his plan developed further the concept of a hierarchy of subordinate perimeter spaces by adding to this ambulatory an equally continuous series of semicircular chapels, which also follow the outermost enclosing walls of the building. These little chapels were intended to be expressed externally, but after Brunelleschi's death, Manetti, who was chiefly responsible for the execution of the works, clad them with a plain wall so that their semicircular form cannot be discerned from the exterior.

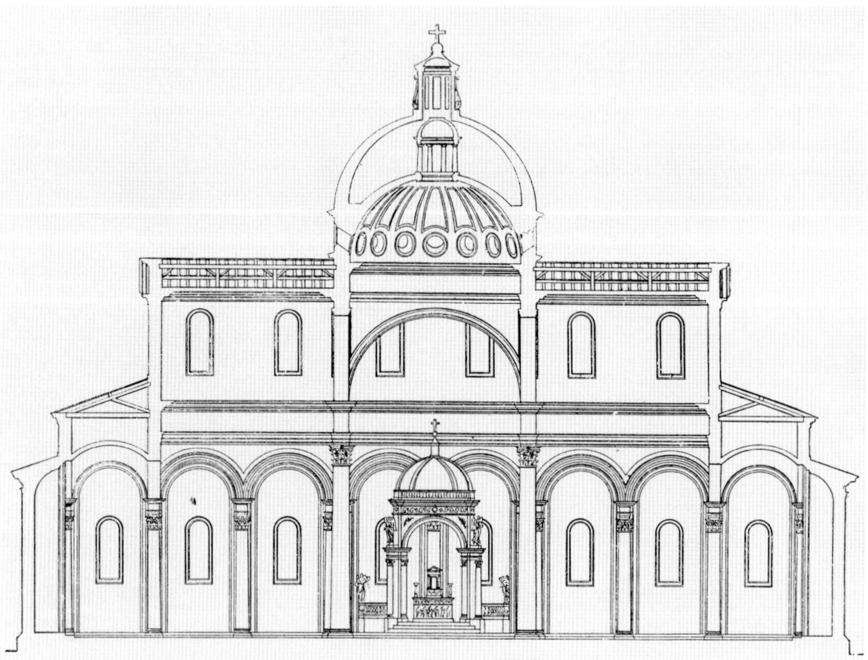

SANTO SPIRITO

Left: section of the church by Grandjean de Montigny, 1806–15. Like San Lorenzo, the structure is designed to precise geometric proportions.

Opposite: plan of the church and monastery by Grandjean de Montigny, 1806–15. The plan is more complex than that of San Lorenzo, with a series of small niches or chapels surrounding the perimeter of the entire structure.

The general internal appearance follows Brunelleschi's scheme very closely, and the whole evinces a stately, regular discipline close in spirit to that of San Lorenzo. The same Corinthian order is employed, with the same basic vocabulary of elements, but the effect of the continuous perimeter ambulatory and chapels around the whole of the east end gives more centrality to this hierarchy of spaces; the careful gradation of volumes, together with the spacious, well-lit crossing, has the effect that the crossing itself can be read almost as easily as the hub of a centralized, Greek cross plan (which has one arm extended to form the nave) as it can be read as a traditional Latin cross. It is interesting to compare this spatial duality with the plan of the great cathedral; although the

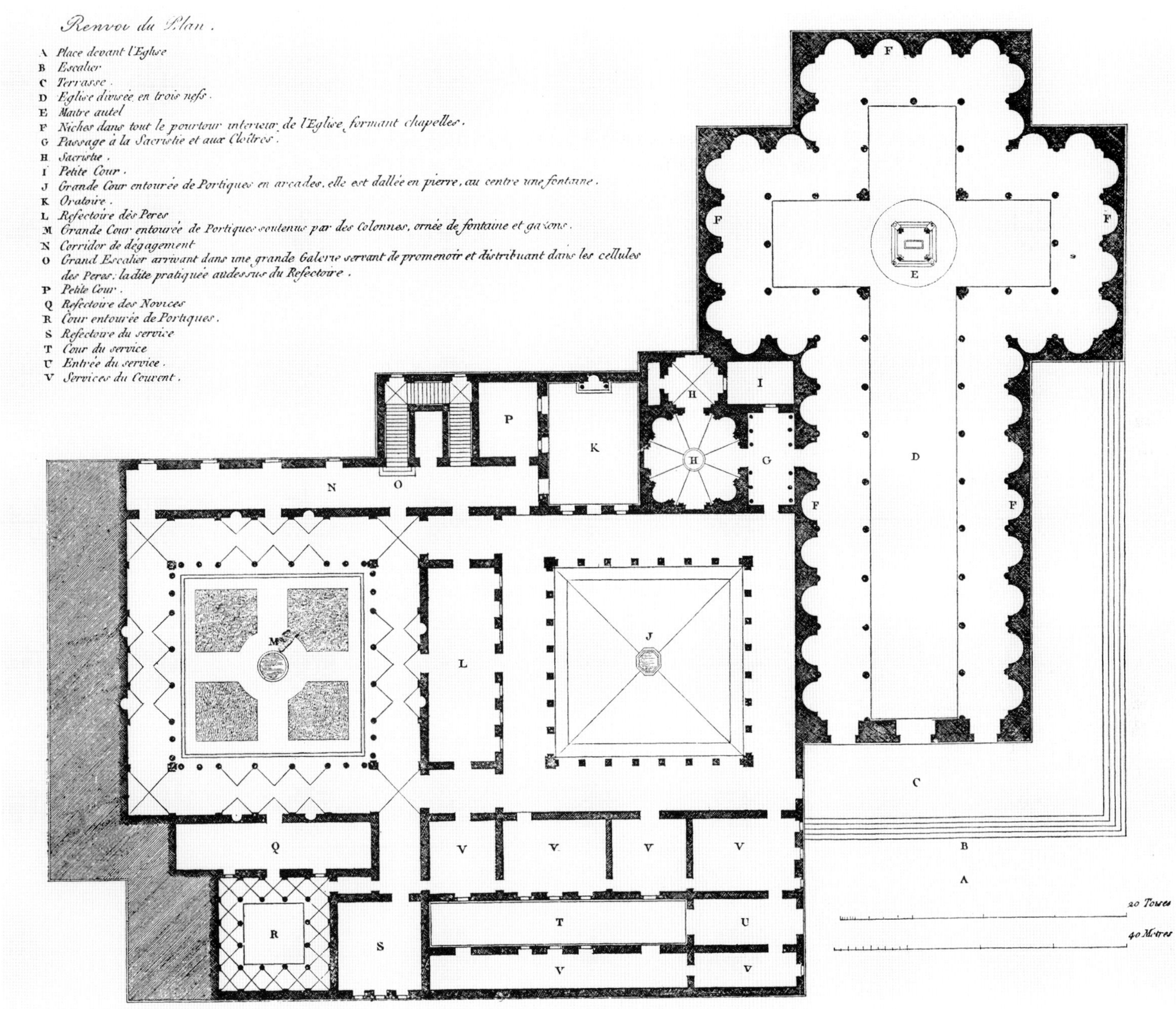
Renvoi du Plan.
A Place devant l'Eglise
B Escalier
C Terrasse.
D Eglise divisée en trois nefs.
E Maitre autel
F Niches dans tout le pourtour interieur de l'Eglise formant chapelles.
G Passage à la Sacristie et aux Cloîtres.
H Sacristie.
I Petite Cour.
J Grande Cour entourée de Portiques en arcades, elle est dallée en pierre, au centre une fontaine.
K Oratoire.
L Refectoire dés Peres
M Grande Cour entourée de Portiques soutenus par des Colonnes, ornée de fontaine et gazons.
N Corridor de dégagement
O Grand Escalier arrivant dans une grande Galerie servant de promenoir et distribuant dans les cellules des Peres: ladite pratiquée audessus du Refectoire.
P Petite Cour.
Q Refectoire des Novices
R Cour entourée de Portiques.
S Refectoire du service
T Cour du service
U Entrée du service.
V Services du Couvent.
20 Toises
40 Mètres

architectural vocabulary is completely different, the two have a common link in the emphasis given to the three equal eastern arms, and in this ambivalence of plan, whereby an axial form contains within it much of the essential quality of a centralized plan. In both cases, the importance of the crossing as the focal point is emphasized by surmounting it with a cupola, concentrating light at the hub of the plan where the four arms meet.

SANTO SPIRITO

Interior of the nave, begun in 1446. Both Santo Spirito and San Lorenzo epitomize Brunelleschi's rational, disciplined, and strictly mathematical approach to their design, and his clarity in the use of materials: *pietra serena* for the structure and white plaster for all of the nonstructural surfaces.

The analogy to a centralized Greek cross plan raises a fundamental issue in the development of the Florentine Renaissance church, that of centrality as opposed to axiality, and of the intellectual development and application of different but perfect Euclidian geometric forms. Following the classical precepts, many believed, as did Brunelleschi and Alberti, that pure geometric forms such as the square, cube, and sphere were inherently perfect, and because of this perfection were the most appropriate forms to employ in architecture, particularly in the house of God. The nucleus of the centralized plan form, in effect a cube surmounted by a cupola, represented the concentration of perfect space, the cupola itself representing the vault of heaven. The Dome of the Rock in Jerusalem, also a centralized plan surmounted by a cupola, was a frequently cited example of this spatial symbolism and perfection, and was itself, of course, located in the city that represented the hub of the world.[20] In *De re aedificatoria*, Alberti makes the following observation on the church plan:

". . . some Temples are round, some square, and others, lastly, have many sides. It is manifest that Nature delights principally in round figures, since we find that most Things which are generated, made or directed by Nature, are round."[21]

Brunelleschi's early use of these "divinely ordered" forms at the Sagrestia Vecchia was the first of a long series of explorations of this alternative, centralized convention, one that he developed further at the Pazzi chapel at Santa Croce. The theoretical aspects were discussed by Alberti in his treatise *De re aedificatoria*, and later architects such as Sangallo, at Santa Maria delle Carceri in Prato, and Cola da Caprarola, at Santa Maria della Consolazione in Todi, gave further physical expression to these theories.[22] Centralized planning, of course, has profound liturgical implications as well as a purely intellectual, theological, or even spatial justification, and it is revealing that these earliest examples of new, centralized forms were initially applied to secondary or subsidiary spaces rather than to the body of a church itself. Both of Brunelleschi's examples were private chapels, where, it could be argued, a small centralized form was at least as appropriate to their function as a strongly axial one would be; it needs to be pointed out, though, that the debate was both a practical and an intellectual one, as were the bitter disputes over Michelozzo's proposals for the completion of the Santissima Annunziata. The famous saga over the great project of St. Peter's in Rome probably represents the apogee of this debate over the relative merits of such forms.

Brunelleschi's Pazzi chapel at Santa Croce, his second centralized chapel, has a complex history, much of which still remains obscure and the subject of debate, despite centuries of research and analysis.[23] Although the commission was given to him by Andrea de' Pazzi as early as 1429, we know little of progress on the building until considerably later; the cupolas of the chapel and of the portico are respectively dated (on the fabric itself) to 1459 and 1461. Both dates are more than a decade after Brunelleschi's death, and there must be at least a small degree of debate as to precisely how closely his own designs were followed in these last elements of the chapel to be completed. Although part of an earlier cloister was demolished as early as 1433 so that work could begin, it seems that a definitive start was really only made in 1442. By the following year, though, much had apparently been achieved, and the walls were complete up to the level of the trabeation. Andrea de' Pazzi left a sizeable sum of money in his will in 1445 specifically to ensure the chapel's completion, but the death of Brunelleschi himself the following year seems to have resulted in a

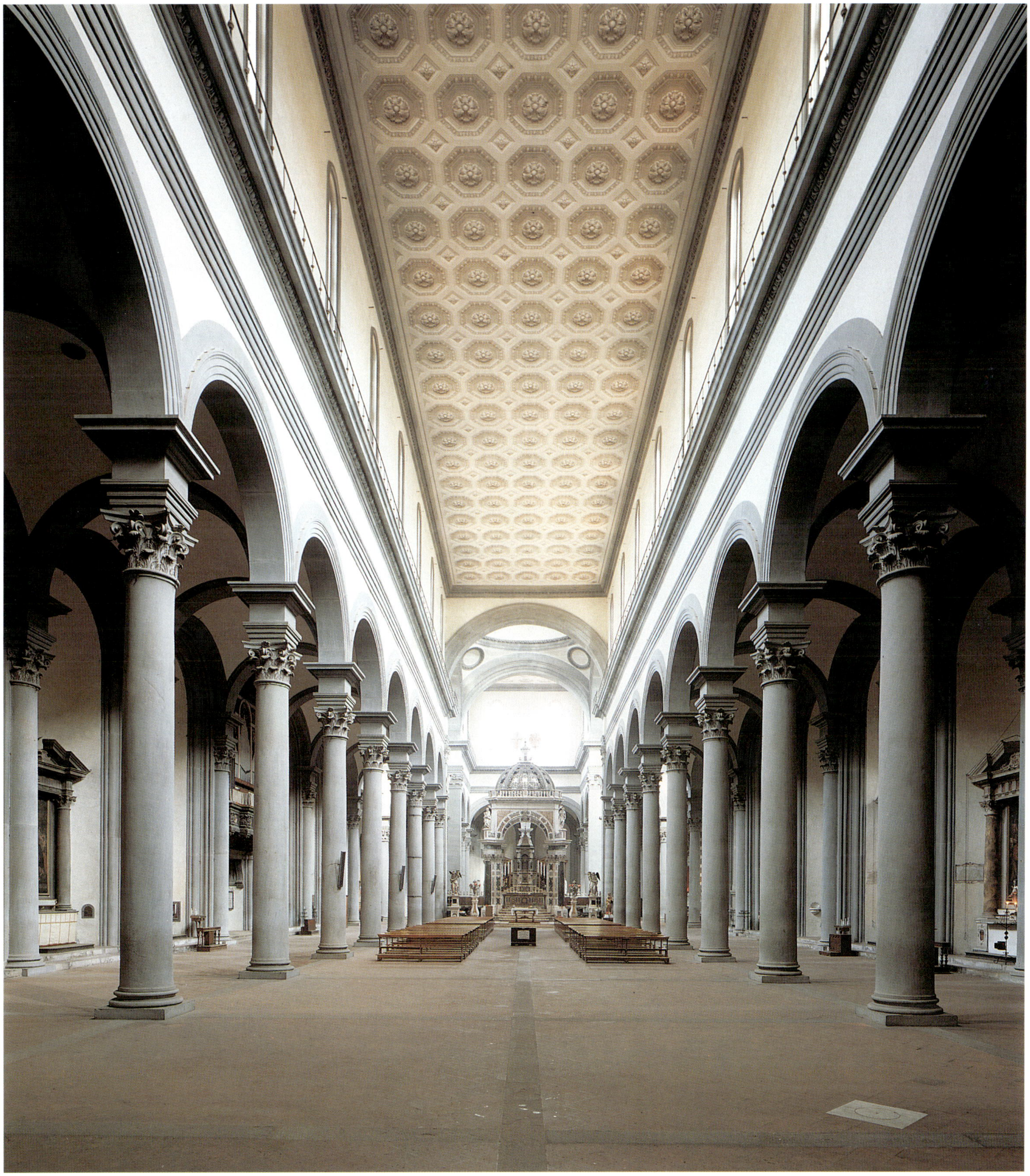

prolonged interval before the roofs were covered and the portico completed. Supervision of these latter stages was probably carried out by Bernardo Rossellino.

The building has two principal component elements, the chapel itself and the portico that precedes it. While there is little doubt that the design of the chapel was indeed that of Brunelleschi, there are dissenting views as to whether Brunelleschi had also envisaged a portico, which, it has been suggested, did not form part of his original design.[24] This does not mean, of course, that he did not intend the chapel to be approached by a portico or narthex, which, after all, has a very ancient tradition in early Christian and Romanesque churches, at least two of which Brunelleschi could see in his own native city; even closer at hand were the traditional cloisters of the adjacent Franciscan monastery. The portico can thus easily be read as a Brunelleschian reinterpretation of one or the other of these earlier forms, to provide a narthex for the chapel. It is clear, however, that it was completed after his death, probably by Rossellino, although attributions to Manetti, Michelozzo, and Giuliano da Maiano have also been suggested.

The chapel itself is a rectangular hall, with its slightly longer axis at right angles to the direction of approach. Its square central bay, which is by far the most dominant element, is surmounted by a hemispherical cupola, again of the "sail vault" type, supported on pendentives; the projecting chancel, containing the altar, is again itself surmounted by a miniature cupola. All of these elements derive directly from the Sagrestia Vecchia. The dimensions of the principal spaces are the same as those of the sacristy, but here the main space is extended to left and right by the addition of two fairly narrow, barrel-vaulted bays. The chapel is not a purely centralized space, therefore, and this was partly perhaps a reflection of its dual purpose; in addition to serving as the Pazzi family chapel it was also the chapter house for the friars, a function that is evinced by the integration of continuous stone benches around the inside of the perimeter walls. The principal orders of the chapel, once more all in *pietra serena*, derive from the earlier work, with the main articulation in the form of fluted Corinthian pilasters and a rich cornice. Equally carefully integrated into the whole are the twelve tondi depicting the apostles, some of the finest works of Luca della Robbia, and the four polychrome roundels of the evangelists set into the pendentives, often attributed to Brunelleschi himself. The overall effect of the interior is thus extraordinarily well balanced and carefully composed, with every element fully integrated into the harmonious, disciplined whole.

The portico serves an important spatial function precisely by forming a transitional space between the open cloister garth and the interior of the chapel itself. Its form, too, is most unusual because the flat trabeation of the colonnade, with two bays on each side of the central entrance, is broken in the center by a large semicircular entrance arch. The soffit of the portico, formed by a tunnel vault, broken in the same central bay by a small, shallow cupola, is equally original. In the sense that these elements form a prelude to the larger-scale elements within, the portico is indeed fully integrated with the chapel itself, even though aesthetically it appears to be a slightly foreign element when approached from across the cloister. This axial approach is of great importance, since it establishes the chapel's presence as a clearly expressed entity, not buried within the fabric of the church like the Sagrestia Vecchia; the

PAZZI CHAPEL, SANTA CROCE

Below: plan and front elevation by Grandjean de Montigny, 1806–15.

Opposite: principal facade from the cloisters. The chapel was planned in about 1430, but built in the years after 1440. Its facade and loggia were the last elements to be completed.

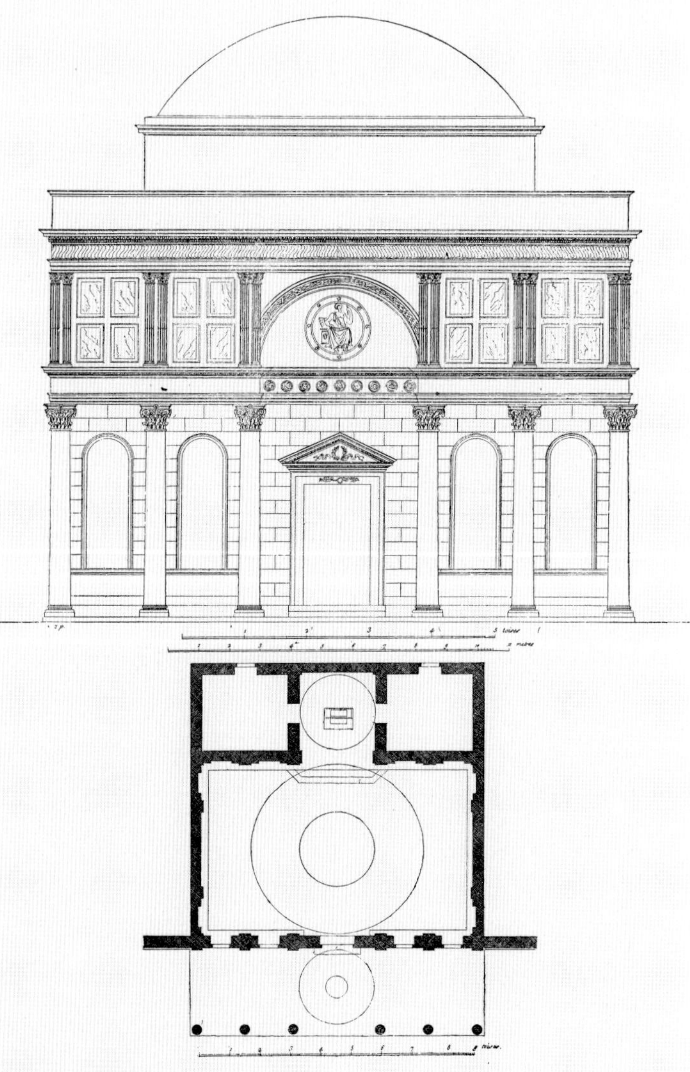

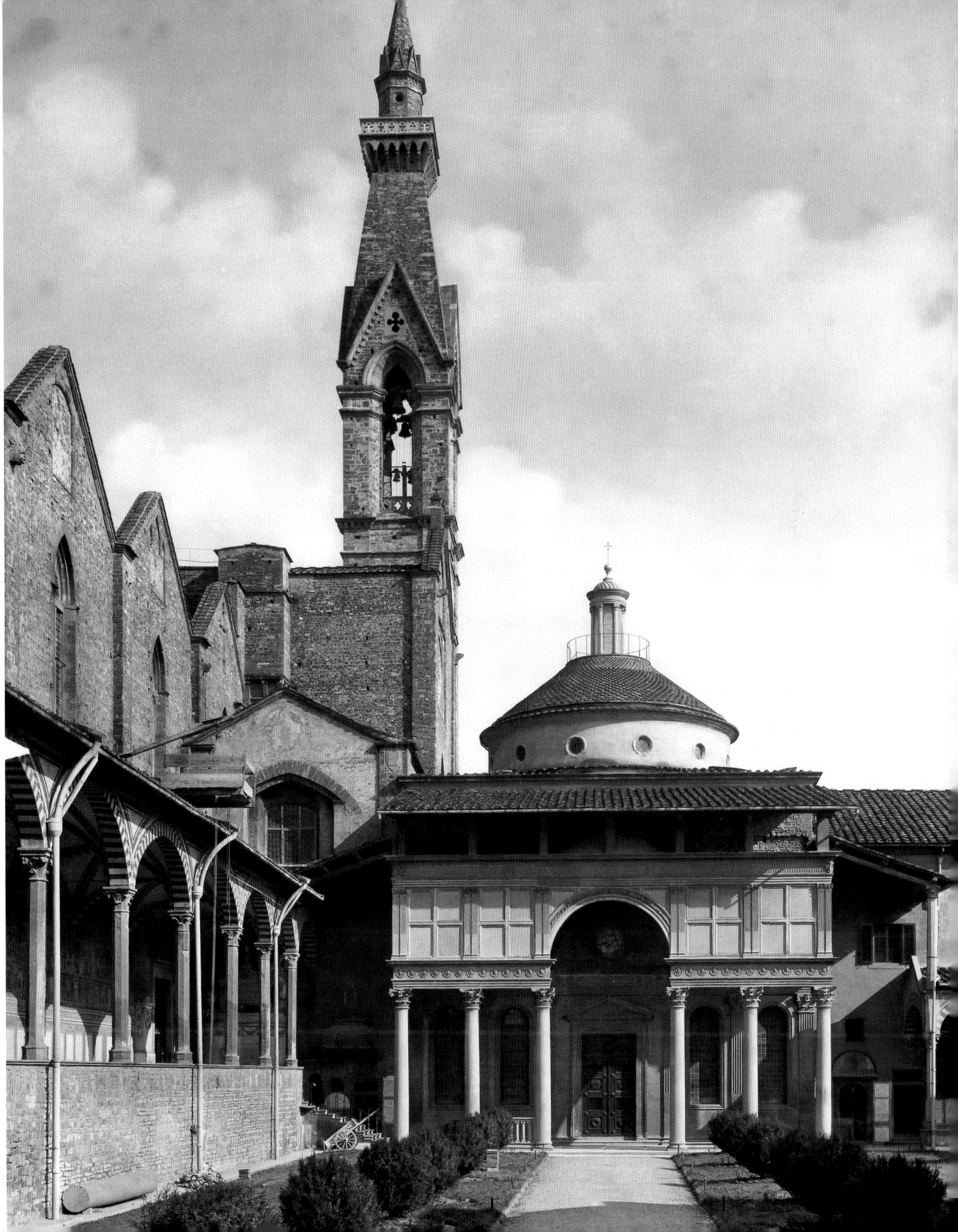

scenographic importance of this approach is also expressed by the raising of the outer conical roof of the cupola considerably higher than the inner one, so that the real importance of the cupola as the hub of the internal spatial relationships is signaled to the outside world. Despite the fact that the chapel was completed so long after Brunelleschi's death, it remains a superb example of refinement, integration, and structural discipline and ranks among his finest works.

PAZZI CHAPEL, SANTA CROCE

Like Brunelleschi's great churches, the chapel is built to precise mathematical proportions; it was completed after his death, perhaps by Manetti, Michelozzo, or Giuliano da Maiano.

The last of Brunelleschi's ecclesiastical works, the oratory church of Santa Maria degli Angeli, which stands very close to the Ospedale degli Innocenti, is also probably his least known.[25] He was commissioned to design the work, which was to take a highly radical form, in 1435. In the center of the plan was a tall, inner drum, octagonal in plan, with eight piers, and it was to be surrounded on all sides by a series of lower, secondary spaces or chapels. The outermost enclosing wall was to have sixteen facets, eight flat surfaces alternating with eight panels containing niches. Of the eight chapels of the interior, one contained the entrance vestibule, while that directly opposite was the choir; the remaining six — three on each side — were each dedicated to two of the apostles. The building has considerable importance in the history of the development of the centralized church plan, although Brunelleschi completed only the lowermost order, the upper parts being completed as recently as 1936. (The surviving elements, badly altered and virtually buried by later accretions, have only recently been restored, and their significance reappraised.) The origins of the building's form, though, remain somewhat enigmatic; among others, perhaps the most obvious local precedent is the centralized octagonal form of the baptistery, although other, more distant examples are closer in volumetric terms: the early Christian churches in Rome, in particular, and especially Santa Costanza and Santo Stefano Rotondo, both of which Brunelleschi may have studied when in the city. The Dome of the Rock may again have played a part here, perhaps indirectly, since volumetrically, it is very similar to the Roman churches. However, there is little doubt about the influence of this church on Michelozzo's highly controversial choir for the Santissima Annunziata, which is very close by.

Brunelleschi's legacy in the field of ecclesiastical architecture is of immense importance. In addition to the extraordinary technical achievement of the cupola of Santa Maria del Fiore, the churches and chapels that he designed represented the physical embodiment of profoundly important principles and theories. These principles were based, above all, on a fully integrated approach, whereby every single element forms a vital part of the whole, and in which each relationship is based on clear, precise geometric ratios and proportions. The even broader importance of such an approach was that it was universally applicable, to any building type, in any location. Not only did Brunelleschi evince these universal principles in his built oeuvre, on a more specific level he rediscovered and developed an entire vocabulary of architectural forms and elements, most of which had not been seen since antiquity, while some were quite new, such as the use of the double-shelled cupola at the cathedral; the reintroduction of the pendentive to support the cupola; the "invention" of the volute as an element both structural and decorative; the use of coupled orders; the deployment of a rigorous internal architectural framework based on pilasters, cornices, architraves, and plinths; the application of an equally rigorous approach toward the definition of structural and nonstructural elements. When he died, in 1446, Brunelleschi was one of the most famous men in Italy; in Vasari's well-known words, he had been "sent from heaven to invest architecture with new forms after it had wandered astray for many centuries."[26]

Michelozzo di Bartolommeo was born in 1396. His professional career offers an instructive comparison with that of Brunelleschi; although he did not rise to the heights of creativity and influence of his mentor, who was a generation older, his work represents a more instinctive, although still refined, interpretation of earlier forms and languages. Without Brunelleschi's strong intellectual background, Michelozzo's oeuvre is characterized by a development essentially derived

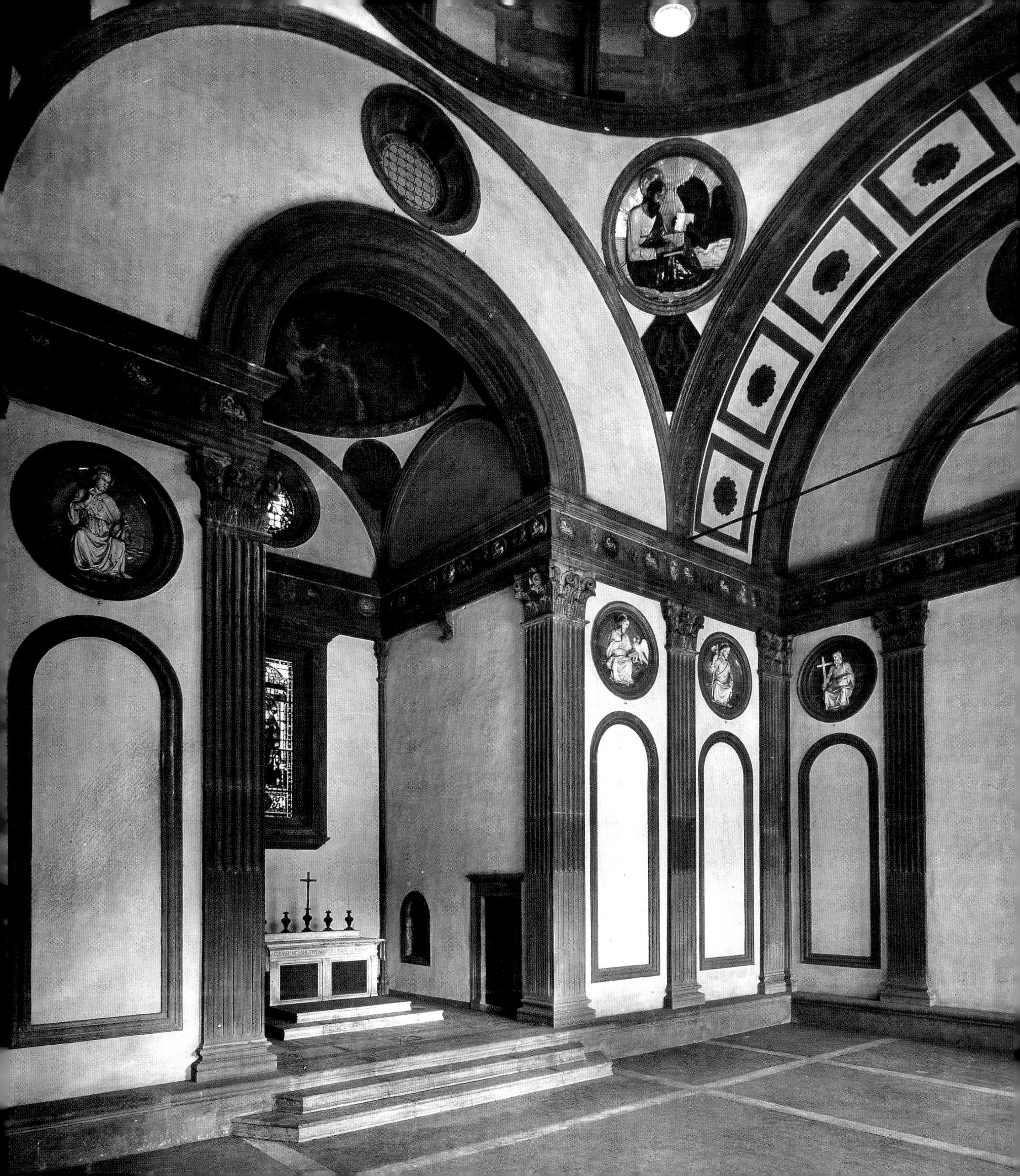

from Gothic forms, rather than from a radical, intellectually based new classicism. Nevertheless, his technical skills and, in some projects, his sheer inventiveness, are without question. He was closely associated with both Donatello and Ghiberti for many years (his early training as an engraver at the mint rendered him a suitable assistant to the latter on the baptistery doors).

Michelozzo's known body of work is surprisingly varied both in style and substance, from the noble palazzo for the Medici in the Via Larga (the present Via Cavour) to the rather eclectic villa for the same dynasty at Cafaggiolo.[27] But his most refined and archetypal work is the convent of San Marco, from about 1436 to 1443, which was the object of generous Medici patronage.[28] Michelozzo embarked on a radical, comprehensive modernization of this complex group of buildings, the spatial hubs of which are the two elegant cloisters. The first cloister, that of Sant'Antonino, was modernized before 1440; it incorporated the refectory and lodgings for guests, and houses a famous series of paintings by Fra Angelico, notably the *Deposition* commissioned by the Strozzi family and completed in 1432. The larger, rear cloister, that of San Domenico, was entirely new, and is all the work of Michelozzo. But Cosimo Il Vecchio's intention at San Marco was to create not only a religious center, but also a flourishing hub of intellectual and cultural life; in this sense the real heart of the complex is Michelozzo's new library, which stands on the first floor next to the rear cloisters. This imposing space is articulated by twin rows of Ionic columns dividing the large hall into three zones, the central one for circulation and the outer pair for study. It is said to have been the first such library in the Western world intended from its inception to be open and available to the general public. As a seminal new building type, the library set an important model or precedent for many libraries elsewhere: a long, airy, light space, rationally articulated and clearly planned. Although it spans the space in a single, clear volume, Michelangelo's later library at San Lorenzo clearly benefited from Michelozzo's influence.

Michelozzo's second major ecclesiastical work, the remodeling and extension of the Santissima Annunziata, was in many ways a radically different type of project. It was also much more controversial.[29] Of the two chief components of the existing church, the Gothic nave was transformed, while an extraordinary new element was built at the east end in the form of a circular rotunda to house the choir and high altar. The nave remodeling was a characteristically elegant, restrained affair: the two side aisles were transformed into a series of chapels by introducing cross walls at each bay position; unfortunately, however, much of this remodeling was obscured by the later rich seventeenth- and eighteenth-century decorations. Michelozzo's choir, however, was a far more radical addition. The work was begun in the late 1440s, that is, a decade or so after Brunelleschi's Santa Maria degli Angeli, so there was some precedent very close at hand. But what was apparently uncontroversial for a semiprivate oratory was far less acceptable here, and a highly charged debate surrounded the proposal. Building was still well short of completion in 1455, when Michelozzo ceased working on it; in 1460 the project recommenced under Manetti, but it was only finally completed by Alberti in the early 1470s, after a generous donation by Lodovico Gonzaga, marquis of Mantua. Alberti produced a new model, still following Michelozzo's basically circular form, but there followed two years of bitter argument in the city over the design. The principal opposition was led by Giovanni Aldobrandini, and essentially centered on the perceived unsuitability of such a form for the house of God, since it was claimed to be essentially pagan in origin (derived from the plans of circular Roman temples and mausolea), and thus only suitable for pagan, or at least lay — and not divine — buildings. It was also claimed to be inappropriate liturgically, and this consideration may have partly influenced Brunelleschi's own objection to the original proposal of attaching a basically circular form to a basilican church. Despite the disfavor, however, Gonzaga persevered with the project until its conclusion in 1476, four years after Alberti's death.[30]

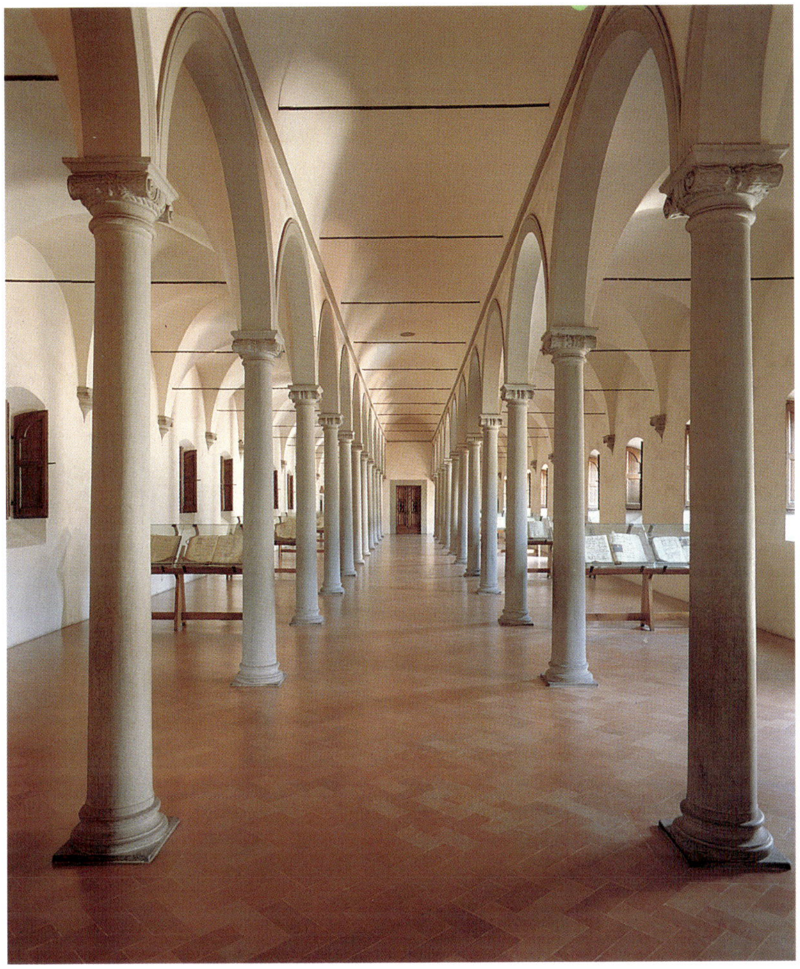

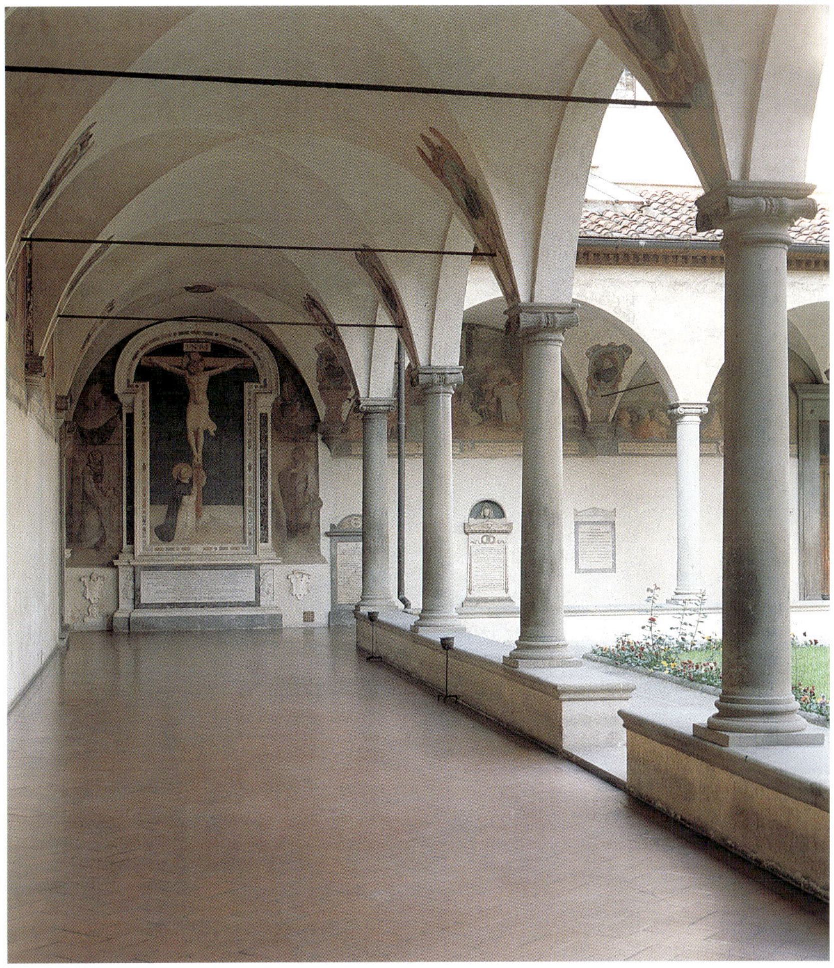

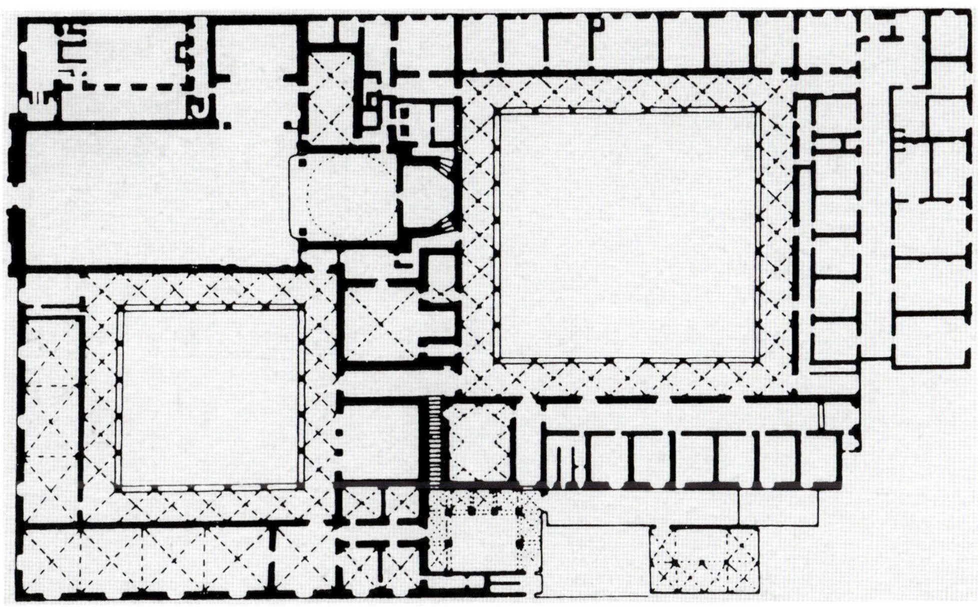

SAN MARCO

Above, left: the library. This refined, elegant interior, with its twin colonnades, initiated an important new building typology, and became a prototype for many later libraries elsewhere, including that of Michelangelo at San Lorenzo. Above: the cloisters, a characteristic example of Michelozzo's restrained, harmonious style. Left: plan. Michelozzo was responsible for the comprehensive reordering of the monastic complex, including the cloisters and library, after 1437.

Michelozzo's original concept remains remarkable, as it was indeed modeled directly on the classical temple of Minerva Medica in Rome. The plan has ten sides, which internally are resolved into a purely circular form, with nine radiating chapels, the tenth side forming the arch that connects the choir to the existing nave. The chapels are expressed externally as shallow radiused projections from the body of the building, rather like Brunelleschi's original intention at Santo Spirito. As classical as the origin of the design was the means of roofing the central space: a shallow masonry dome in the Roman manner, similar to that of the Pantheon. The original radical plan was undoubtedly Michelozzo's, but it was retained and developed by Alberti, and later clearly found an echo in Alberti's own developing theses on the ideal centralized church plan. The interior of the whole church was radically modernized in the seventeenth century, however, when the complex stucco decorations were added, obscuring the much simpler lines of the original structure.

Michelozzo's involvement at the Santissima Annunziata was not confined to the church itself; he was also responsible for a general reorganization and modernization of the conventual buildings, rather as he had done at San Marco. The two principal elements here were the new church atrium, or Chiostrino dei Voti, and the large main cloister, the Chiostro dei Morti, at the side of the church. The vocabulary is also familiar from San Marco: light, simple, and highly refined, with the colonnaded porticoes of the main entrance similar to those employed in a rather different context in the *cortile* of the Medici palace. The rectangular colonnaded atrium was the forerunner of that built later by Giuliano da Sangallo at Santa Maria Maddalena de' Pazzi, in a much more restrained, even severe manner; although the detailed architectural treatment is quite different, spatially the two works are closely related.

SANTISSIMA ANNUNZIATA

Below, left: view of the Chiostro dei Morti. Below: plan of the church by Grandjean de Montigny, 1806–15. Michelozzo modernized the monastic buildings here after 1444, much as he had done at San Marco, and with a similarly refined, minimal vocabulary. The eastern end of the church is occupied by the unusual circular choir.

Opposite: the interior of the choir was originally built to a striking (and highly contentious) circular plan by Michelozzo, later continued by Alberti; the church was comprehensively modernized by Giovanni Battista Caccini after 1605, and completed by Giovanni Battista Foggini in the 1690s.

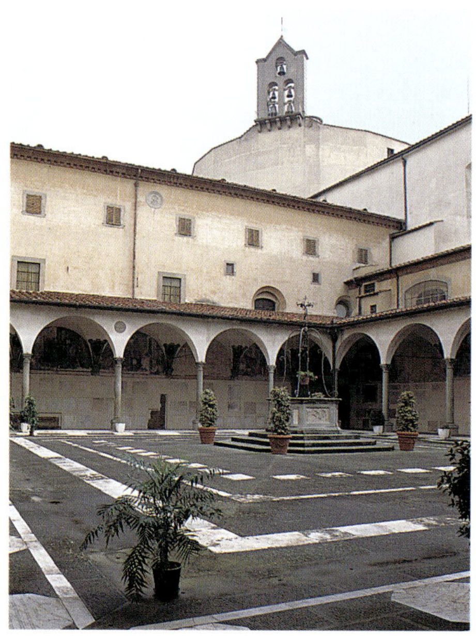

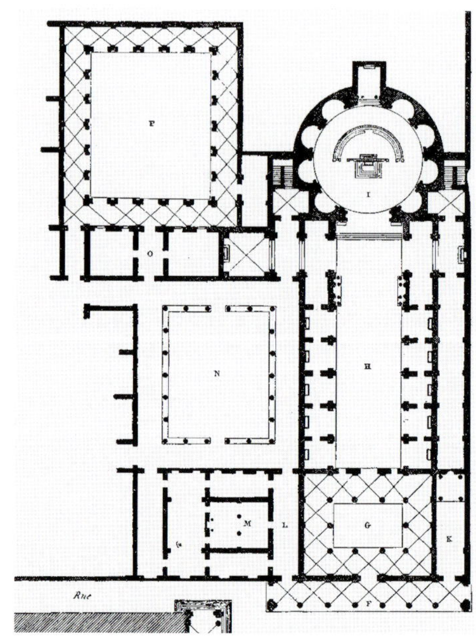

Most of the remainder of Michelozzo's major works were lay projects for the Medici, one small but notable exception being the *baldacchino* for the high altar at San Miniato al Monte. The *baldacchino*, which also forms the Cappella del Crocefisso, was carved in 1448, and is a fine example of Michelozzo's inherent sculptural creativity, almost amounting to playfulness, with four different capitals supporting the barrel-vaulted canopy above the altar.

The third of our triumvirate of central figures in the development of early Renaissance churches in Florence is Leon Battista Alberti, who was a few years younger than Michelozzo. As we have seen, his professional career was very different; he was neither a highly disciplined design and engineering genius like Brunelleschi, nor was he a practical master who matured his craft through experience like Michelozzo. Instead Alberti was perhaps the finest example of that rather clichéd figure, the universal man of the Renaissance: Highly educated, he possessed many skills and had a broad, humanistic interest in all of the creative arts, which to him were of equal importance. Unlike the other two, he also, arguably, became more influential as a theorist than for his built work.

During his career as papal secretary, Alberti traveled widely, and although he visited Florence in 1434, it was only in the early 1440s that one can say with reasonable accuracy that he began seriously to practice architecture; by this date, the drafts of his seminal treatise, *De re aedificatoria*, were almost certainly complete. In about 1450 he began work on the major renovation of San

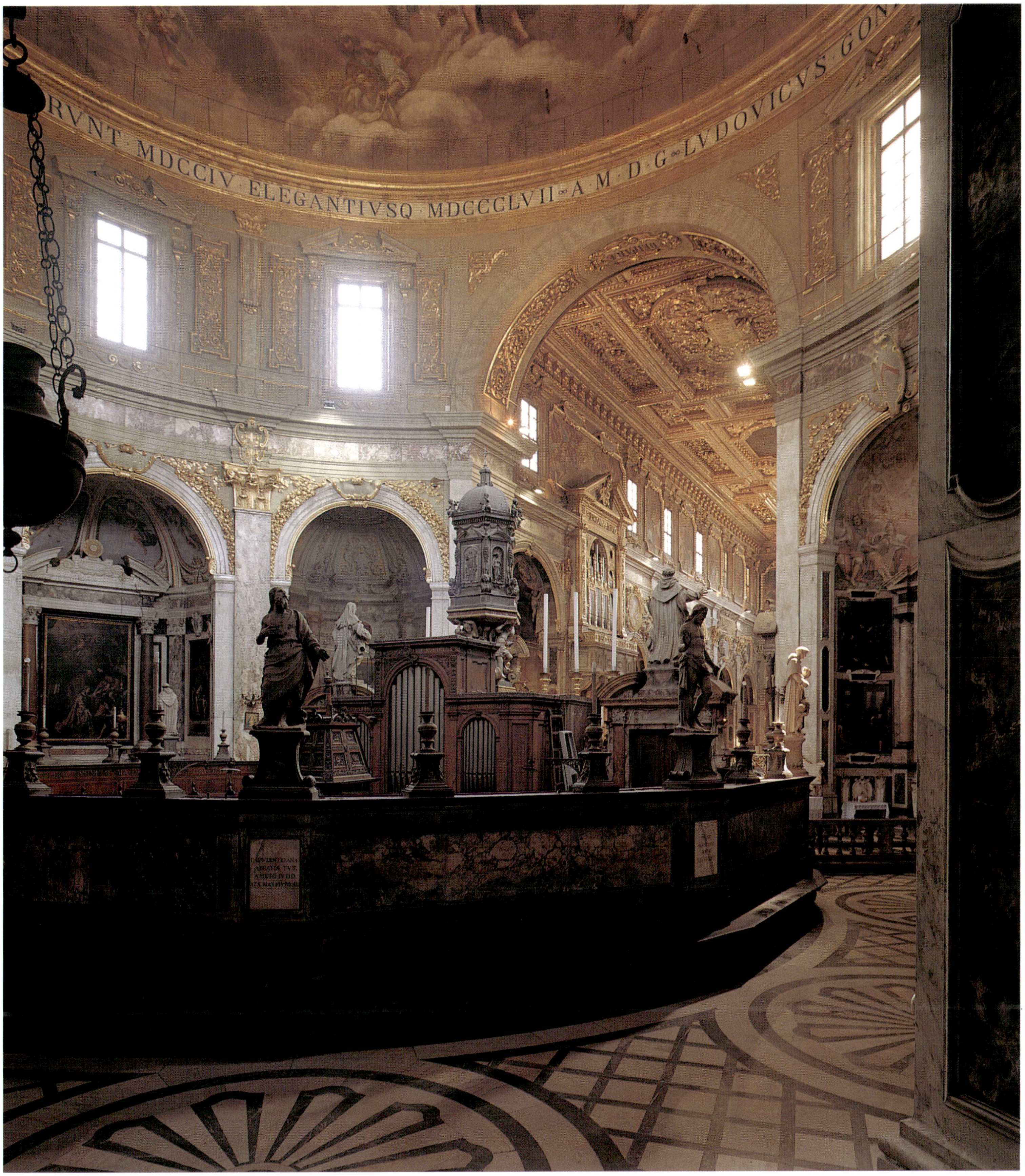
RVNT MDCCIV ELEGANTIVSQ MDCCCLVII A M D G LVDOVICVS GON

Francesco at Rimini, and shortly thereafter developed an important relationship with his most powerful and influential friend and patron in Florence, the banker Giovanni Rucellai. Rucellai's role was fundamental; almost all of Alberti's built work in the city was a direct result of his patronage: For Rucellai, Alberti designed the family palazzo, the chapel of the Holy Sepulchre at San Pancrazio, and, most important of all, perhaps, completed the facade of Santa Maria Novella.

This long-term association with one particular patron reflects a close personal rapport and empathy, but it also marks a similarity to the relationship enjoyed, for example, by Michelozzo, the Medici family's architect, and also, to a degree, to the continuing works Brunelleschi had undertaken slightly earlier, again for the Medici. These relationships themselves reflected an appreciation of the knowledge and talent that such extraordinarily gifted masters could bring to their patrons: within such deep relationships design skills could be encouraged and developed as the aesthetic appreciation of the patrons themselves also matured. The example of Alberti and Rucellai represents perhaps the closest of these long-term relationships, and reflects the attempt of one powerful patron to directly influence the appearance of his own immediate quarter of the city.[31]

The completion of the facade of Santa Maria Novella was a challenging task. The initial instigator of the program was Pope Eugenio IV, who had been in Florence in 1439 to reconvene the Council that had attempted to reconcile the eastern and western Christian churches. At about the same time, Rucellai was also developing the idea of completing the facade of the great church as his own family's contribution to their quarter of the city, a very high-profile act of public patronage. Rucellai's initial plans were, in fact, twofold: not only to complete the church facade but also within the church to construct a chapel or *tempietto*, a copy of the Holy Sepulchre in Jerusalem. The chapel was indeed built by Alberti, but not within the monastic church; it was relocated to San Pancrazio, the family's own local church, only yards from the Rucellai palazzo.

Work on the lower part of the facade of Santa Maria Novella had come to a halt in 1365. The precise extent of work that had been completed by then still remains a matter of some conjecture; certainly it had included the bold Gothic forms of the three arched niches on either side of the central doorway, and the two taller Gothic doorways set into the lower order, thereby establishing the vocabulary of the alternating colors of green and white marble. However, it is still not certain who was responsible for the elegant row of tall blind arches that rise from these rather chunky Gothic forms, up as far as the level of the great broad fascia that Alberti introduced, and that clearly divides the lower from the upper order of the facade as a whole. These tall blind arches can be read as an archaized trecento work that harks back to the earlier Romanesque traditions of the baptistery and San Miniato; but they have also been interpreted as Alberti's own ingenious compromise in completing the lower order in this classical Tuscan tradition, that is, with round arches in rather shallow relief (but still retaining the two colors of marble) before he embarked on the truly original, indeed brilliant resolution of the upper order.[32] The two zones were to be kept apart by the very broad, neutral zone of the frieze, with its bold row of green marble squares. The upper order itself, although as yet quite unadorned, was not exactly a tabula rasa, although the constraints within which Alberti had to work were in a sense simpler to apprehend; they consisted chiefly of the necessity to clothe the gable ends of the nave and the two lower side aisles, while at the same time taking into account the great circular central window.

Alberti's solution was ingenious. The central bay, representing the gable end of the nave, was terminated with an aedicule, surmounted by a bold triangular tympanum, incorporating the large circular window in the center, and with the surface articulated by means of four pilasters of striped marble. The further resolution of the relationship between this "temple front" and the lower side bays was achieved in an equally revolutionary manner, by two great curved volutes, physically and aesthetically linking the two orders of the facade. The entire tour de force was finished with refined cladding of white Carrara and green Prato marble, the regular rectangular pattern of the central bay giving way at the flanks to the rich, ornate cladding of the volutes, almost reminiscent of *pietra dura* in its complexity. The richness of the volutes is matched by a similar refinement in the detailing of the crowning tympanum, where the greater use of green marble provided an appropriately stronger visual termination. In all of this facade, Alberti reinterpreted the strong local tradition of marble cladding, but now applied to a radically different architectural vocabulary. He also incorporated a number of symbolic images carefully set within the apparently strongly disciplined and abstract paneling. The chief among them is the bold, radiant sun at the center of the tympanum, the symbolic representation of Christ (as well as Truth); the sun is also repeated, in more stylized form, in the circles that terminate the outer members of the volutes, while it appears yet again, in smaller, still more stylized form, in the squares of the central frieze. Rucellai's patronage is acknowledged in two ways: most prominently in the bold inscription on the frieze below the uppermost tympanum, but again, more subtly, in the row of motifs of a ship under sail — the family arms — in the narrow frieze above the lower order. Underlying the composition is a strict application of precise geometric units and proportions. The central aedicule, for example, is contained within a precise square, and the two flanking volutes are each formed within a square of half the dimensions of this central one.[33] Alberti's final task here was the difficult one of inserting a new central doorway, which was flanked by the striped Gothic niches. The portal is more truly classical than the screen of the upper order, bold and simple in form, its depth and modeling echoing that of the flanking Gothic elements, although it is appropriately much larger in scale, rising almost to the full height of the lower order. The completion of the facade of Santa Maria Novella took about twelve years, much of the work being physically executed by Giovanni di Bettino in the decade after 1458.

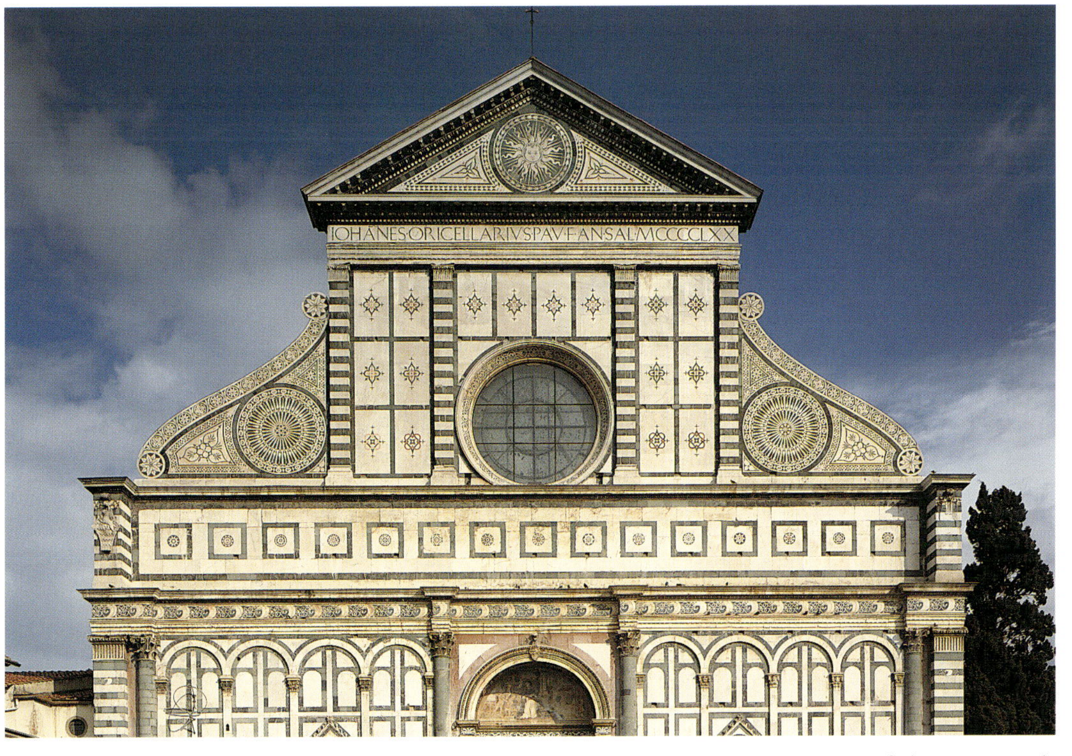

SANTA MARIA NOVELLA

The upper part of the facade was built by Alberti in 1439–42 under the patronage of Giovanni Rucellai. The refined marble cladding is equally characteristic of Alberti's Rucellai sepulchre at San Pancrazio.

By way of a summary, although certain aspects of the facade are clearly drawn from and respect the Tuscan-Romanesque tradition, the more startlingly new forms were destined to have great influence. The volutes, for example, almost certainly inspired by Brunelleschi's early use of such forms on the lantern of the cupola of the cathedral, were developed in the sixteenth century to become one of the most characteristic features of the mature Renaissance and Baroque, in Italy as in all of Europe. But it was the temple front, with its bold, beautifully proportioned crowning tympanum, that was to be even more seminal; it was developed in the succeeding decades, indeed centuries, by other outstanding architects, perhaps most famously by Andrea Palladio in his Venetian churches. Later the basic form was again interpreted and disseminated over much of Europe.

Alberti's only other ecclesiastical work in Florence could hardly be more different in scale or character than this monumental public work: the small-scale, almost secretive (or at least semiprivate) chapel of the Holy Sepulchre, again commissioned by Giovanni Rucellai.[34] The church of San Pancrazio almost adjoined the family palazzo, and together with the loggia that faces the palace, formed a small cluster of buildings entirely under Rucellai patronage. Giovanni decided to relocate the sepulchre here once work had begun at Santa Maria Novella, and it was constructed almost certainly between 1464 and 1467, the date on the inscription. The chapel was originally in direct communication with the church via a large opening in the side wall, although the physical arrangements have been altered considerably since it was formed. Alberti made significant alterations to this chapel, including the raising of the roof, and its completion by means of an impressive barrel vault. He also created the link with the church itself by forming a large, new opening, and then inserting two freestanding Corinthian columns to reduce the span, which supported a rich architrave. The walls of the enclosing chapel, too, were articulated by a framework of pilasters of *pietra serena*, and a complex architrave and cornice was then wrapped around the whole volume.

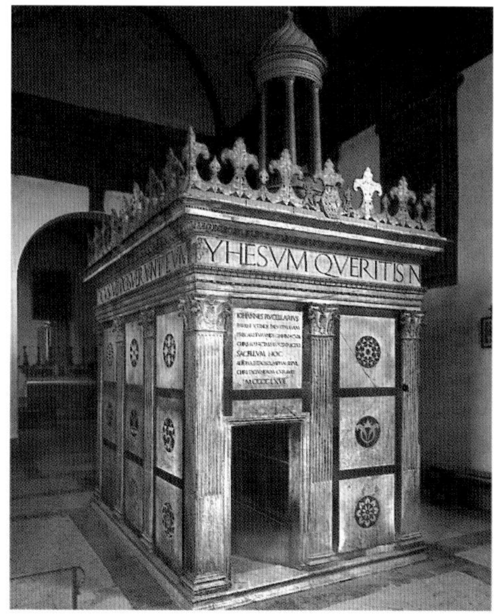

RUCELLAI SEPULCHRE, SAN PANCRAZIO

Above: commissioned by Giovanni Rucellai, the sepulchre modeled on the Holy Sepulchre in Jerusalem was begun in 1467.

Opposite: view of Alberti's refined marble detailing.

But it is the freestanding, jewel-like, casket-shaped sepulchre at the center of the chapel that captures the attention immediately, an extraordinarily refined, exquisitely detailed shrine clad entirely with fine marble. The shrine was to serve two functions: as the tomb of Giovanni Rucellai, and as an homage to the tomb of Christ in Jerusalem, on which it is said to have been modeled. In fact, the Holy Sepulchre itself has undergone so many alterations and restorations over the centuries that it is impossible to gauge its precise condition in the early fifteenth century; Alberti's intention was probably to re-create the classical Constantinian structure rather than the gothicized version that probably would have greeted a visitor in this period. The casketlike form of the tomb evinces Alberti's unique mastery of the revival or reinterpretation of classical forms. One of the most striking examples is the beautiful Latin inscription from St. Mark's gospel, executed in exquisitely proportioned Roman capitals, that runs around the frieze. Equally striking is the paneling of the wall surfaces, once again drawing on the Tuscan tradition, with refined inlays of contrasting marbles, all in precise geometric forms set into circles. Still another remarkable feature is the order of pilasters that frames the structure, with their fluting and highly inventive composite capitals. Most of Alberti's more important contributions to Renaissance architecture can be seen here, refined and miniaturized, but all unified by a rigorous geometric discipline and harmony of proportions.

If the work of Michelozzo can be seen as a direct development from the founding influence of Brunelleschi — albeit with his own particular and refined spatial sensibilities — then that of Alberti can be seen as a powerful, if physically rather fragmentary, factor that enriched and rendered more complex and sophisticated some of the tenets established by Brunelleschi. Alberti's other lasting legacy was, of course, the extraordinary influence of his treatises, not solely that on architecture, but also those on painting and sculpture. The following generations, principally Antonio Manetti (Brunelleschi's pupil and biographer) and Giuliano da Sangallo, but also a number of other lesser figures, could thus draw on a powerful range of recent influences, exemplars, and inspirations, both practical and theoretical.

One of the products of this younger generation is the complex of buildings at the Badia Fiesolana, which was largely rebuilt under the patronage of Cosimo Il Vecchio after 1456. The architect is not known with certainty; Vasari attributed the church to Brunelleschi, who had already been dead for ten years when the work began, but it is more likely to have been designed by a follower of Michelozzo, with clear influence also from Alberti. The austere barrel-vaulted church interior is sparsely decorated, but the space has great dignity and the minimal extent of richer detailing is

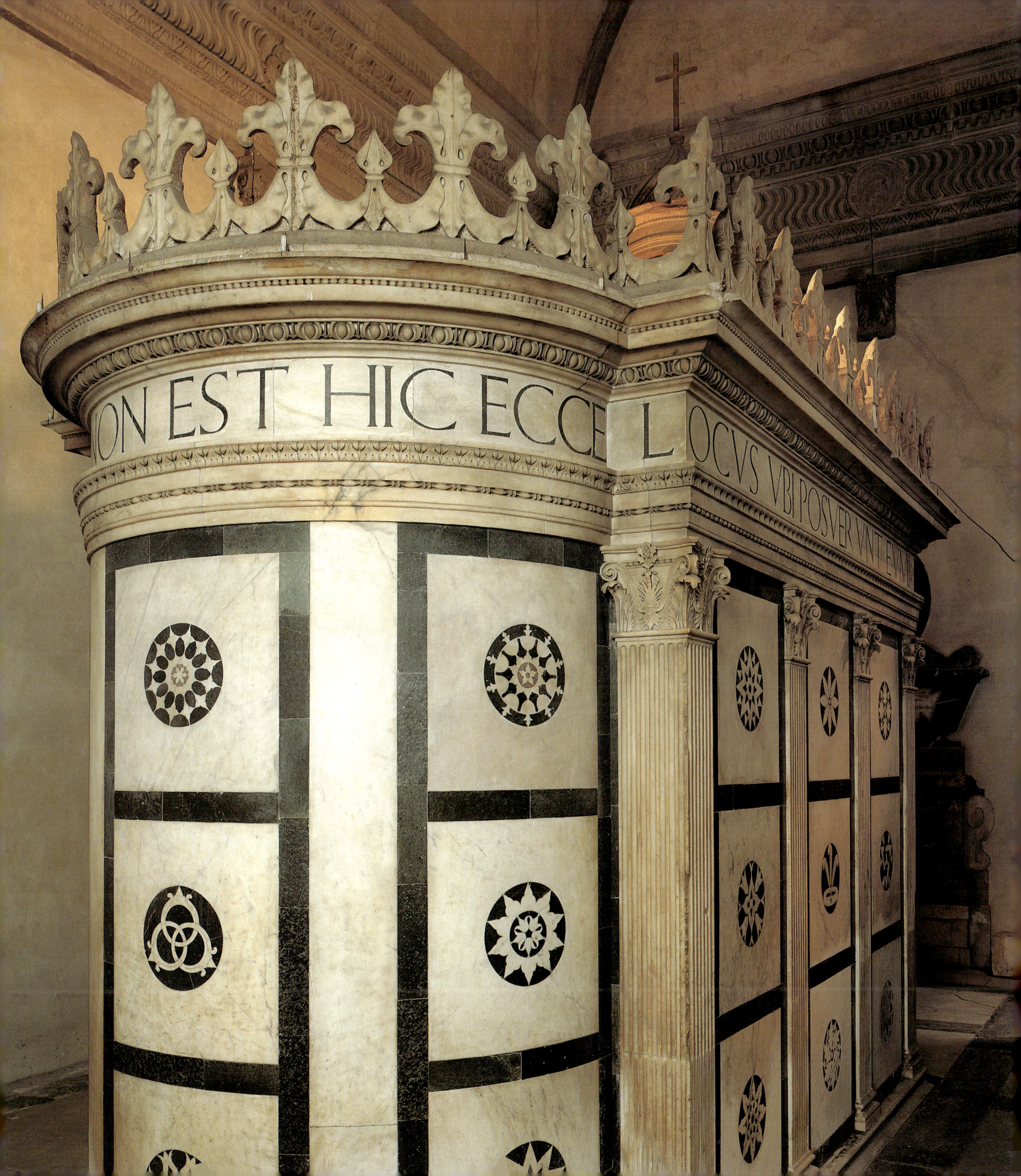
ON EST HIC ECCE
LOCVS VBI POSVERVNT

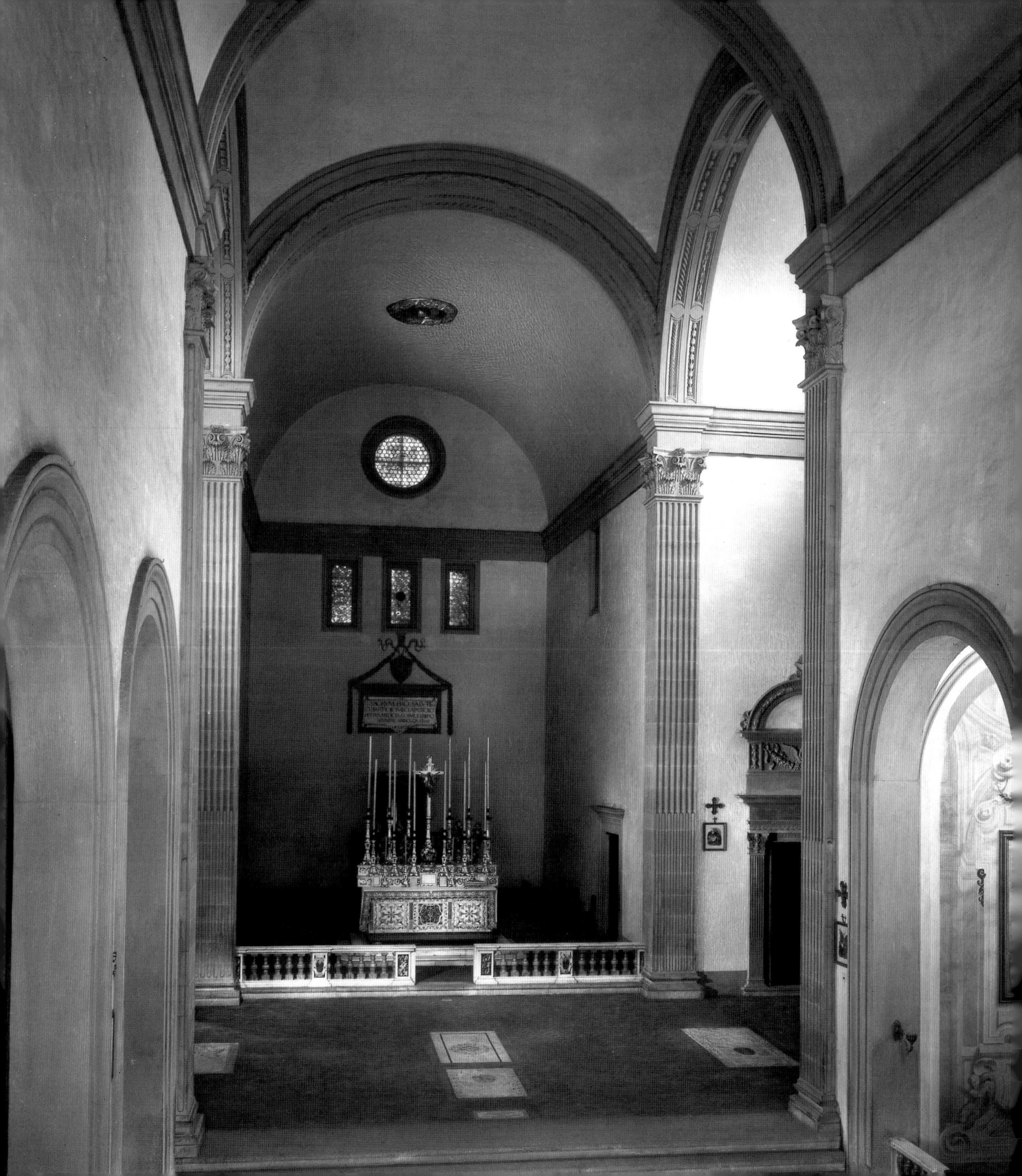

BADIA FIESOLANA (opposite)

The simple interior, perhaps by Michelozzo, is defined by the aisleless barrel-vaulted nave and its side chapels.

SANTA MARIA MADDALENA DE' PAZZI (right)

The narthex or cloister in front of the church, with its extremely simple but refined vocabulary, was built by Giuliano da Sangallo in about 1490.

highly refined in the Albertian manner.[35] The external spatial relationships, though, suggest a degree of Michelozzian influence; the church itself stands on the highest part of the site, almost detached from, and with its axis at an angle to, that of the monastic complex in order to maximize the visual impact of its facade.

The principal figure in the last decades of the century, though, was Giuliano da Sangallo, whose active career bridges the two centuries, and who spent several formative years in Rome around 1465–72. He returned to Florence with a great deal of knowledge of the classical monuments, and his most significant ecclesiastical work in Tuscany is the famous, centrally planned church of Santa Maria delle Carceri at Prato, begun in 1484 under the patronage of Lorenzo de' Medici. The church was very influential in reviving the centralized Greek cross plan for the first time in a full-size church, as distinct from smaller chapels or sacristies; Sangallo developed the vocabulary employed by Brunelleschi on a smaller scale at the Pazzi chapel into a full-scale version, more powerful and bold, but still highly refined and clearly articulated.[36]

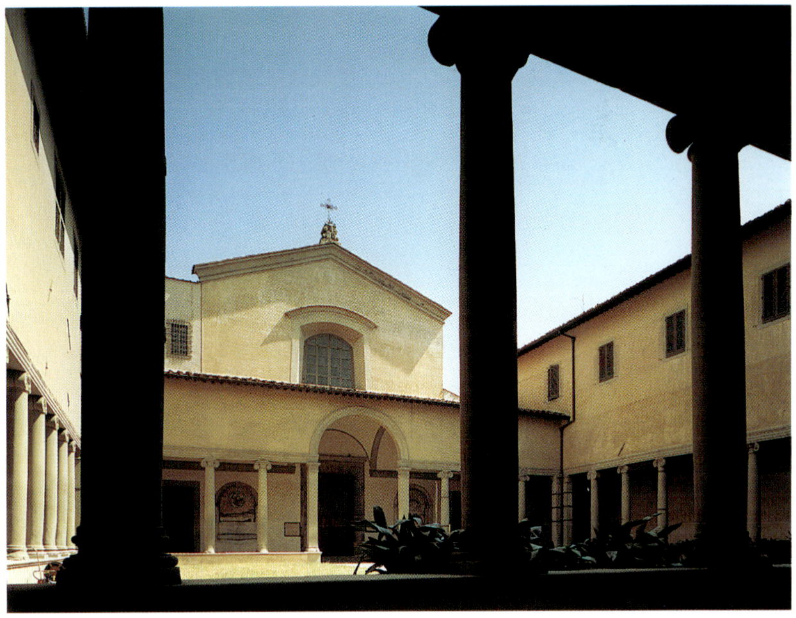

One of two significant ecclesiastical works completed by Sangallo in Florence itself is the atrium of Santa Maria Maddalena de' Pazzi in Cestello, built in the early 1490s.[37] The cloister or atrium, which stands between the church and the street, is minimal to the point of severity. Sangallo's use of a continuous, flat trabeation around the cloister, supported by Ionic columns, is broken only by the large central arches that signal first the entrance into the cloister and then that into the church itself. One can identify another reworking of the Pazzi chapel portico here, extended to a considerably larger scale, although with minimal detailing, so that it becomes a complete spatial entity.

Sangallo's second Florentine church project also has a centralized plan: the octagonal sacristy at Santo Spirito, begun in 1488, and later completed by Cronaca (also known as Simone del Pollaiuolo). The work consists of two rather disparate elements: a rectangular vestibule, with twin rows of heavy columns and surmounted by a rich, ornately coffered barrel-vault ceiling; and then the sacristy itself. In a sense the vestibule is more startling than the sacristy, since this was the first time that such a quintessentially High Renaissance form as the coffered ceiling had been seen in Florence; the sacristy, on the other hand, refined and highly restrained, derives directly from the *pietra serena* vocabulary first used by Brunelleschi and developed by Sangallo at Santa Maria delle Carceri; here, though, the frieze is simpler, and the whole has a balanced serenity in sharp contrast to the ornate vestibule.[38]

Sangallo's principal collaborator and successor at the sacristy of Santo Spirito was Cronaca, whose other important work in Florence is San Salvatore al Monte, built in the 1490s. It is the last quattrocento church in Florence in more than one sense, since its imposing single-nave interior marks a kind of culmination of one line of stylistic development. Cronaca here adopted two superimposed orders for the first time in the city, but in contrast to the traditional use of the classical orders, both were in the same, simple Doric; and his use of alternating triangular and segmental window heads was to become a motif widely adopted in the work of Michelangelo and Bramante, as well as Sangallo's younger brother, Antonio. These were the signs of a newer, more experimental generation, who would develop a more creative, flexible approach to the grammar of architecture, and who would be identified with what is popularly known as the "High Renaissance," that is, the Renaissance of Michelangelo.

Later Renaissance and Mannerism: Michelangelo at San Lorenzo

By 1516 Michelangelo Buonarroti had already established the fame of his extraordinary skills in Rome, with the completion of the Sistine Chapel four years earlier, and with his work on the tomb of Pope Julius II. Still primarily known as a painter and sculptor, his move to Florence coincided with a significant shift of emphasis in the nature of his commissions, and he was to be recognized there primarily as a sculptor-architect.[39] He was to work on three successive projects at the Medici church of San Lorenzo, where the developing Mannerist qualities of his architectural style can be clearly traced. His patrons in Florence were two Medici popes in succession, first Leo X (who reigned from 1513 to 1521) and then Clement VII (who reigned from 1523 to 1534). Leo X was Giovanni de' Medici, second son of Lorenzo Il Magnifico, while Clement was Giulio de' Medici, the illegitimate son of Lorenzo's brother Giuliano. Both of them had the intention to further develop and elaborate San Lorenzo as the fulcrum of Medici patronage in the city, but this was achieved in rather different ways in Michelangelo's three projects.

The basic fabric of the church had been completed by Manetti by about 1470, following Brunelleschi's master plan, although differing somewhat in detail, and, as was generally the case, the facade had been left to the very last; it was still *in cotto* (raw brickwork) when Michelangelo arrived in the city. Brunelleschi's intention seems to have been to complete the facade by sheathing it with marble, thus, at least in general terms, following the ancient Florentine tradition that had had its roots at the baptistery and San Miniato, and had been further developed — or rather, revived and reinterpreted — in the 1460s by Alberti at Santa Maria Novella.

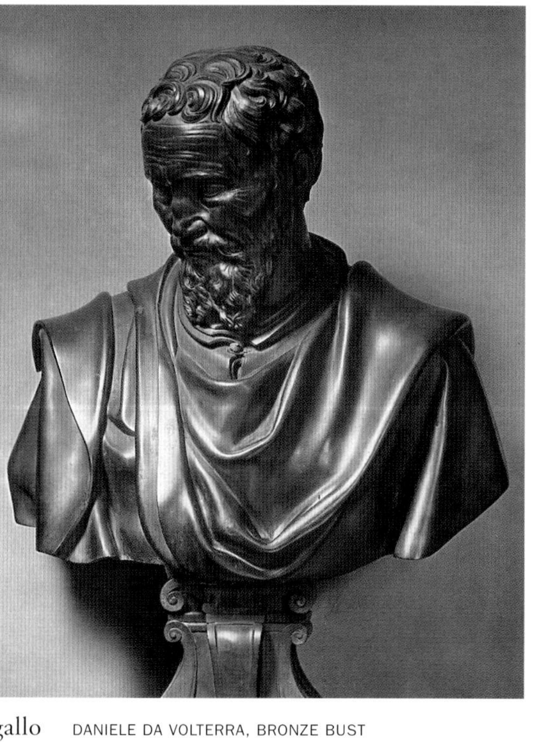

DANIELE DA VOLTERRA, BRONZE BUST OF MICHELANGELO, 1564–66 (Florence, Bargello)

In 1512 the Medici had returned to Florence in triumph, and three years later Pope Leo X promoted a competition for the completion of the facade of San Lorenzo. He demanded proposals from Raphael, Jacopo and Andrea Sansovino, and Baccio d'Agnolo, but other proposals, too, were produced, notably by both Antonio da Sangallo and his elder brother Giuliano, the latter by now very old but apparently still active. The fact that Giuliano da Sangallo developed several schemes might suggest that his proposals were the most highly favored, but he died in October 1516. The approach adopted by Raphael apparently was not approved, because the pope wished for a solution that would allow for the incorporation of a large number of statues, rather than a more purely architectural solution; although the design is lost, one can conclude that Raphael's proposal was more severely Roman, simpler and more architectonic in conception. Michelangelo, though, was perceived as a sculptor-architect, one with the skill to integrate these two elements, and on this basis was selected to develop his proposal. The model of 1517, which has survived, seems to represent the culmination of his developed ideas: It takes the form of a great monumental screen, with horizontal rather than vertical emphasis, incorporating numerous niches and plinths for statuary. The architecture itself essentially provides a grammar or framework of friezes, cornices, and pilasters, an articulated setting for the sculptures that were to dominate the ensemble. A contract was signed the following year, but two years later the entire project was postponed, never to be recommenced, as the pope now reorganized his patronal priorities, deciding to concentrate on works more directly related to the Medici.[40]

The result of this reappraisal was in fact to be Michelangelo's second project at San Lorenzo, the Sagrestia Nuova, which this time was executed.[41] The decision behind commissioning the new sacristy was essentially a practical one: to provide a new setting for the funerary monuments of later generations of the Medici dynasty, the earlier ones having been housed in Brunelleschi's Sagrestia Vecchia. The new sacristy precisely mirrors the old one in at least some respects: It is located adjacent to one corner of the right transept, mirroring the earlier structure next to the left transept, and its plan is identical but reversed. It is, however, in its height that one can see most clearly the stylistic developments that had taken place in the intervening decades. Michelangelo's new sacristy is considerably taller than that of Brunelleschi; above the lowermost order is inserted a fairly generous attic, above which four lunettes support a hemispherical cupola. This cupola, unlike Brunelleschi's "umbrella," is a pure half-sphere and is roofed with coffers along the lines of the Pantheon in Rome, albeit on a much reduced scale. The entire vocabulary of the interior is very different from Brunelleschi's dignified restraint. All four walls are articulated with a robust, monumental classical framework that contrasts strongly with the earlier sacristy, in which only the altar wall is singled out for richer treatment. The detailing is already idiosyncratic; the windows to the lunettes just below the dome are not rectangular but in the form of trapezoids, in order to enhance or stretch the sense of vertical perspective. The doorways, too, are extended upward with blind tabernacles directly above them, complete with swags and broken pediments. At the same time more solidly, powerfully classical, the sacristy is already a highly personalized interpretation of the orders and their treatment.

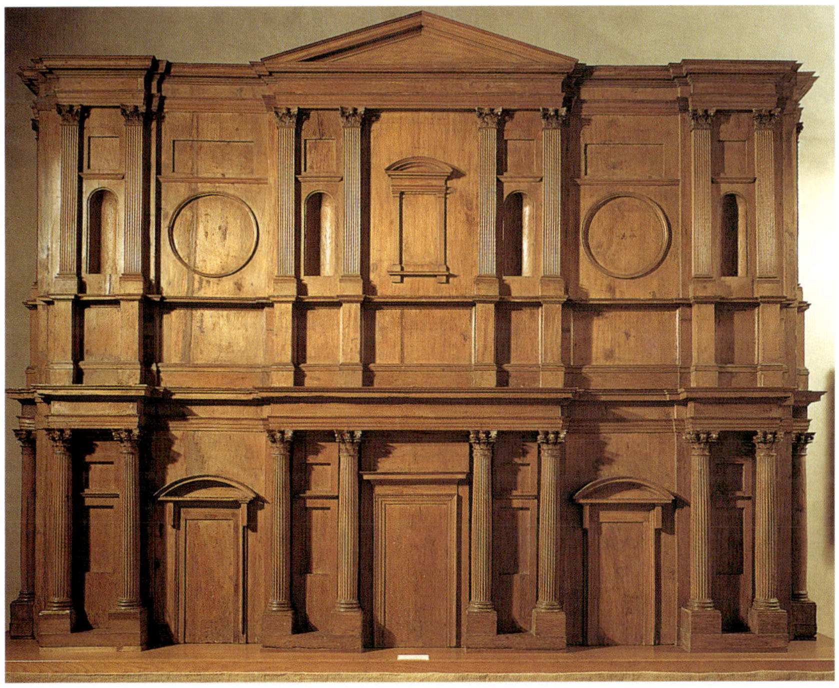

SAN LORENZO

Wooden model of the facade proposed by Michelangelo (Florence, Casa Buonarroti).

Construction began in 1520 and continued until 1524, followed by a hiatus, during part of which time — from 1529 to 1530 — Michelangelo was engaged on the city fortifications at San Miniato. After the sack of Rome by imperial forces in 1527, the Medici were forced to flee Florence, and as a result the latter stages of the building of the sacristy were protracted. But with the return of Alessandro de' Medici in 1531 the project was belatedly resumed, although when Clement VII died in 1534, and with the statues for the tombs not yet complete, Michelangelo moved back to Rome. The tomb figures were put in place in 1545, the final stages being completed by Vasari and Ammannati in 1554–55 to Michelangelo's plan.

When finally concluded, the tombs in the sacristy were those of Giuliano, Duke of Nemours (son of Lorenzo Il Magnifico), and Lorenzo, duke of Urbino. The titular figures that are set in the niches surmounting these monumental sarcophagi are among Michelangelo's most outstanding works, while the sarcophagi themselves are surmounted by the famous pairs of figures representing, respectively, Dawn and Dusk (Lorenzo) and Day and Night (Giuliano). The final figure in the sacristy was Michelangelo's *Madonna and Child* of 1521; considered as a whole, therefore, the sacristy remains a rare example of a complex work designed, supervised, and, at least to a large extent, completed by Michelangelo as an integrated whole, with the sculpture and architectural framework fully complementing each other.[42]

The third of Michelangelo's three projects for San Lorenzo, the Biblioteca Laurenziana, was very different in both form and function. Chronologically, there was a good deal of overlapping between these last two commissions, since work began on the library in 1525, although again it

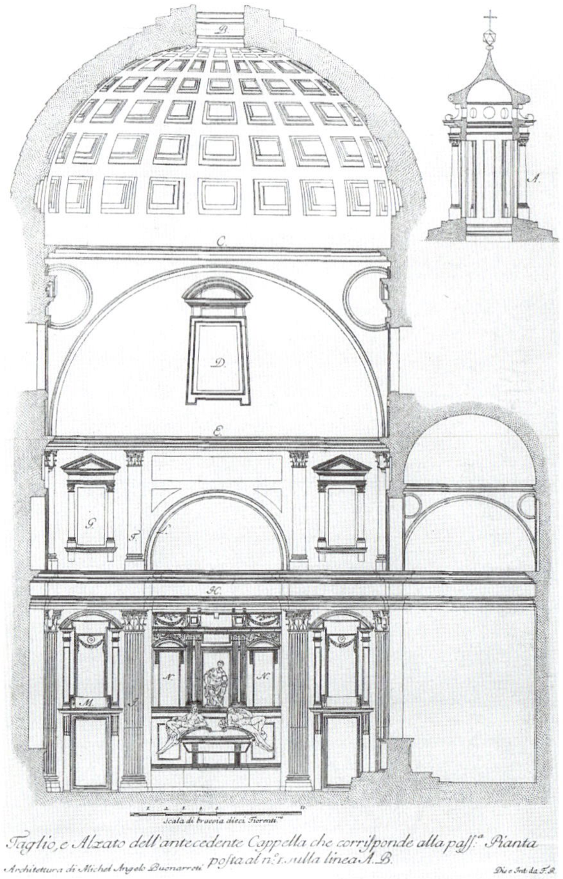

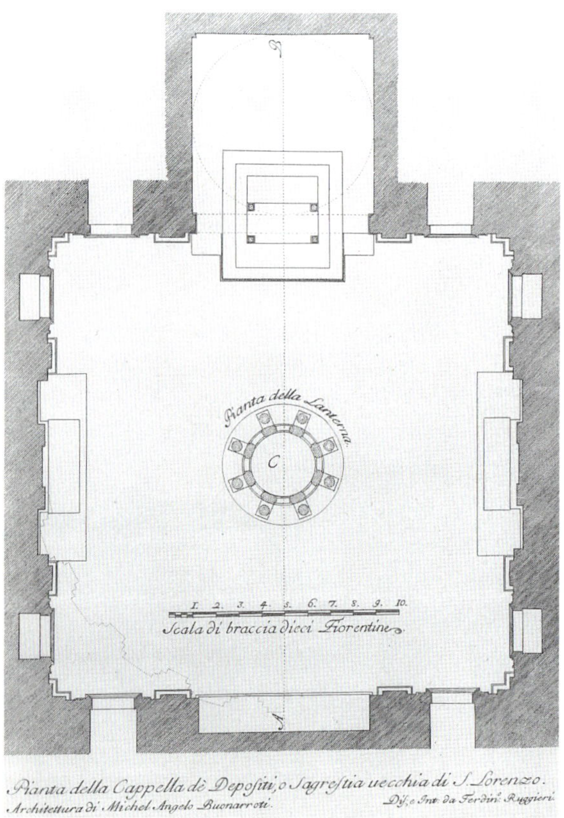

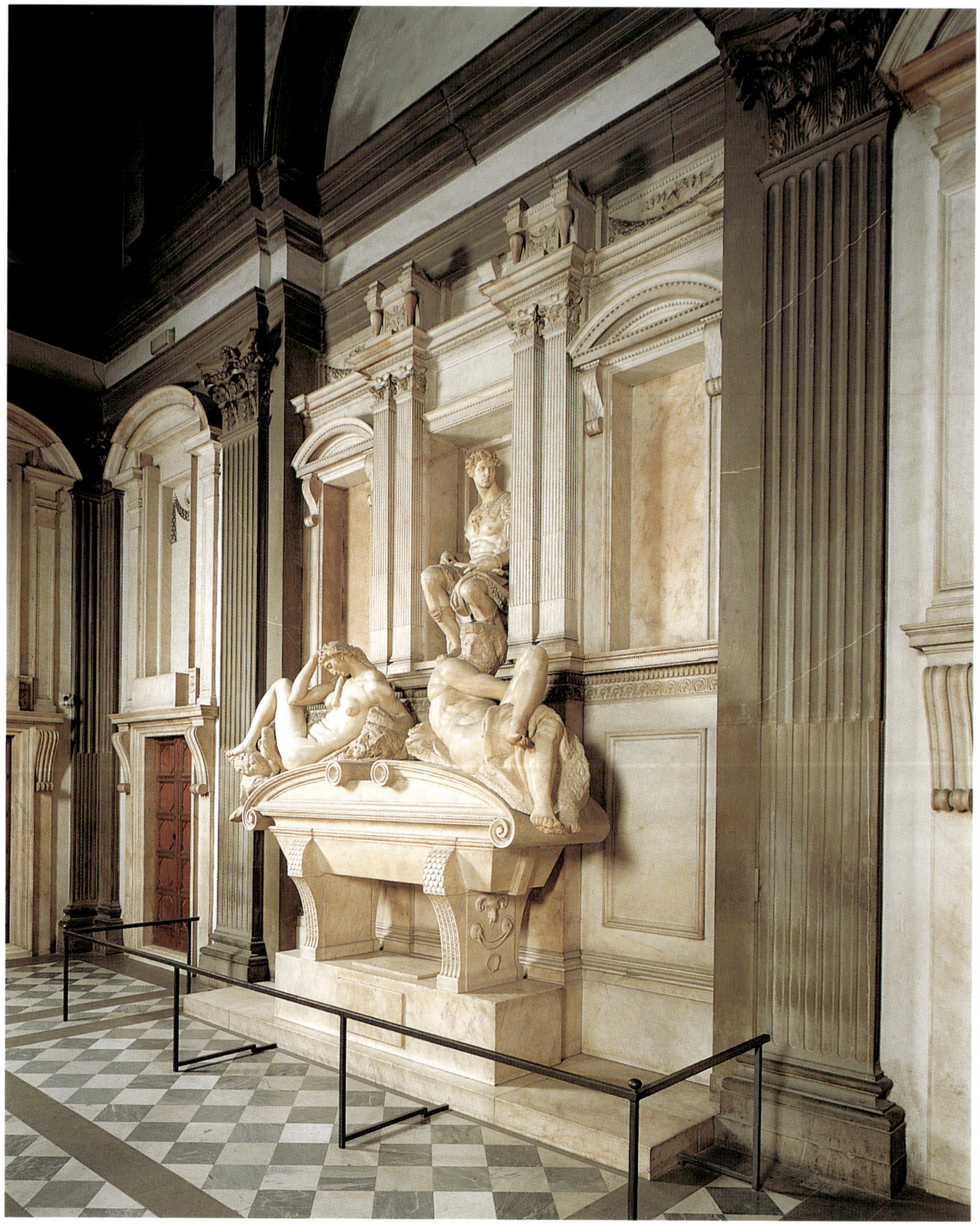

SAGRESTIA NUOVA, SAN LORENZO

Left, top and bottom: plan and section by Ferdinando Ruggieri, 1755. Above: the interior of the sacristy is arguably Michelangelo's most fully integrated work of sculpture and architecture. In the center is the tomb of Giuliano de' Medici with the figures of Night and Day.

Opposite: the tomb monument to Lorenzo de' Medici, duke of Urbino, with the figures of Dawn and Dusk.

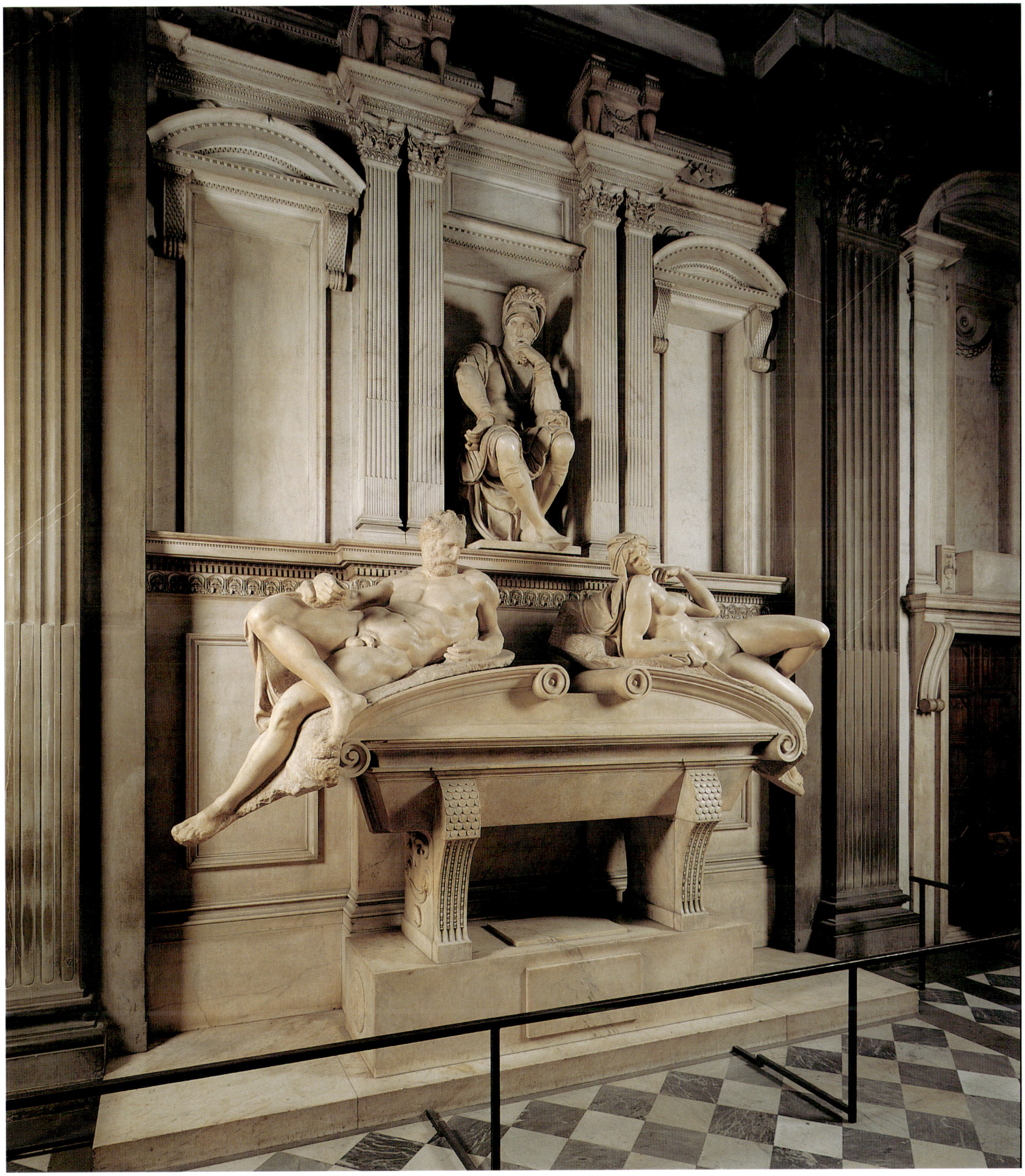

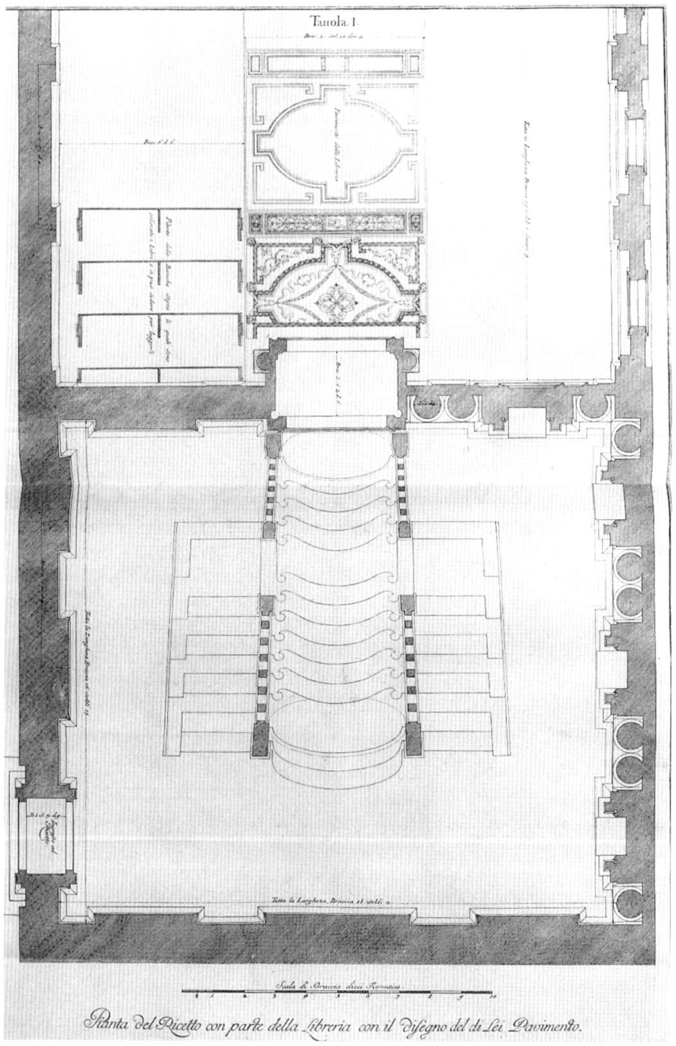

BIBLIOTECA LAURENZIANA, SAN LORENZO

Above: plan of the *ricetto*, or vestibule. Right: section through the *ricetto* and staircase. Both are by Ferdinando Ruggieri, 1755. The section illustrates well the spatial difficulties that Michelangelo had to resolve.

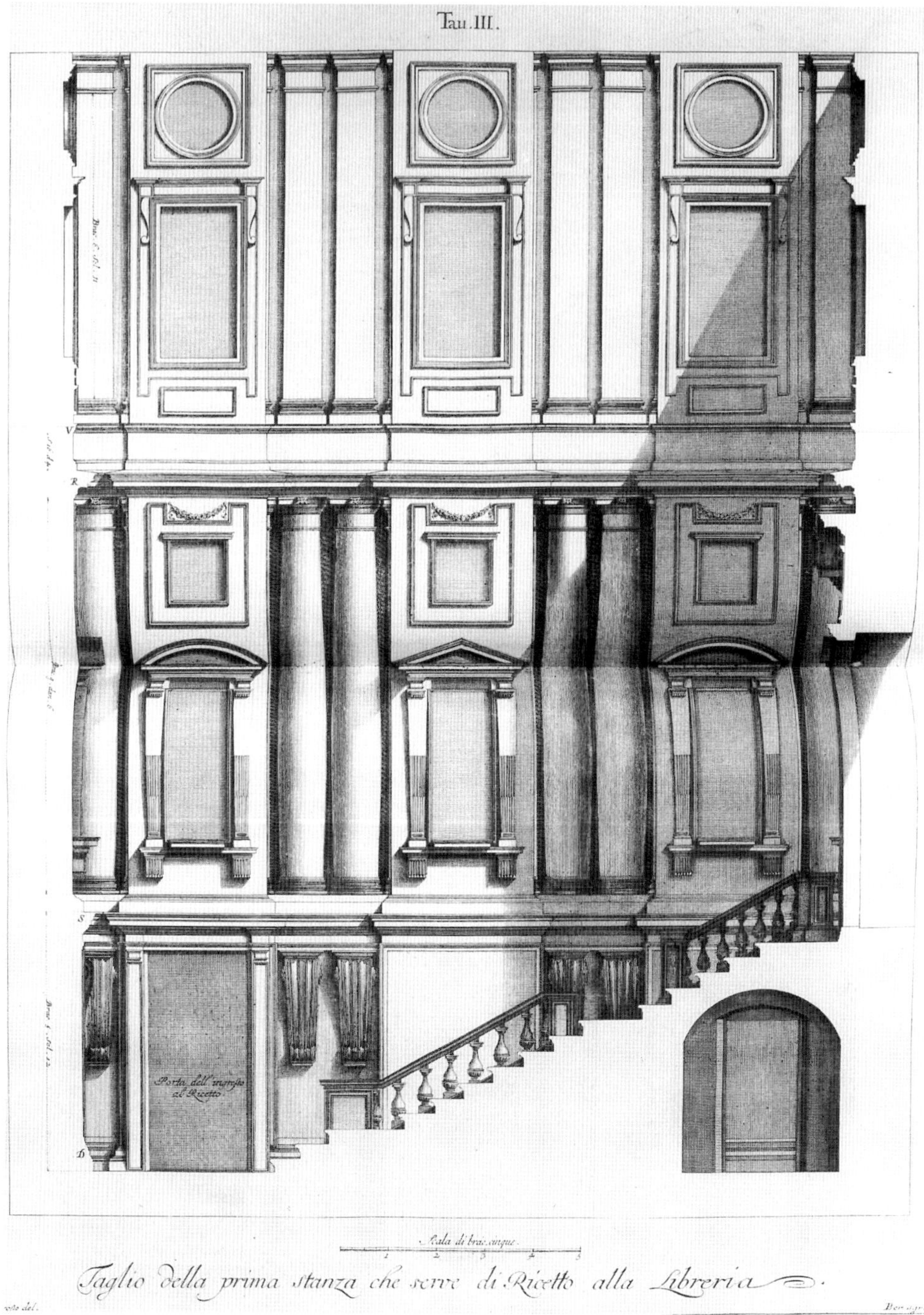

remained incomplete when Michelangelo left for Rome in 1534. The library was one of the very first works of architectural patronage inaugurated by Pope Clement in 1523, with the explicit intention of housing the magnificent, indeed unique, collection of books, manuscripts, and incunabula that had been begun by Cosimo Il Vecchio and was greatly expanded by Lorenzo, after whom the library was to be named. In a further gesture of enlightened patronage, it was to be made accessible to the public. Although the library was to be constructed on a difficult site just to the south of the church, Clement had stipulated that the large cloister that already stood next to this flank of the church — a refined, elegant work designed by Michelozzo, built on two levels — was to remain undisturbed. The result of these restrictions was that the new library had to be built at second floor level, on top of the older parts of the monastic buildings that stood immediately west of the cloisters.[43]

The location and the overall dimensions of this new structure were, therefore, determined by the preexisting structures that were to support it. This arrangement, particularly the upper-level location, did give Michelangelo certain advantages, notably in the provision of generous natural light, but it also rendered access up to this second story very difficult: A vestibule at first-floor level, sandwiched between the end wall of the church transept and the main space of what was to be the library, and known as the *ricetto*, was the only point of access. The final result, therefore, as we see it today, consists of two quite distinct and clearly articulated volumes, the tall, boxlike form of the newly reordered entrance vestibule, the *ricetto*, with its famous staircase, and the long, regularly modulated volume of the library, or more accurately, the reading room.

Construction of the work began with the library itself, which was to serve not solely as a repository for the extraordinary Medici collections, but also as a public reading room, thus, in principle at least, drawing on the precedent that Michelozzo had established at San Marco. However, although they are both long, regularly planned spaces, the interiors of the two libraries are quite different. Michelozzo's stately, refined double colonnade (clearly drawing on the monastic tradition) divides the width of the hall into three zones, the central one for circulation and the two side zones for study; Michelangelo, on the other hand, designed a single space, unbroken by colonnades but articulated more subtly, partly by means of the reading desks and cabinets themselves, all of which are still in place. The two banks of these fittings are separated by a central aisle, again producing a tripartite division of function, and this division is further articulated, again quite discreetly, by the treatment of the two end bays and by the subdivisions of the rich, coffered ceiling. The long, noble space is articulated longitudinally by the bays of the fenestration, which provides natural light down both sides and whose giant order of pilasters is subdivided into two secondary orders, the large windows themselves, and a high-level series of smaller, rectangular blind "windows" above them. The basic principles of this form of articulation, with the main structure in *pietra serena* and all the wall surfaces in neutral white plaster, had its origins with Brunelleschi in the quattrocento, but here it performs a new function in establishing a clearly hierarchical arrangement of elements: primary (the principal giant order), secondary (the subdivisions), and tertiary (the wall surfaces). By 1534 when Michelangelo left for Rome, the reading room was complete up to, but not including, the ceiling; however, he appears to have left very detailed drawings and instructions, such that we may safely regard the whole ensemble as his own work. It was opened to the public for the first time in 1571.

Both the design and construction of the vestibule were less straightforward. The floor of this *ricetto* is some 13 feet (4 meters) below that of the library itself, and it was thus necessary to devise a suitably imposing staircase to effect this transition within a very confined space, which in plan was almost exactly square. Michelangelo's first proposal dates from 1524, but in the following year he began to develop the definitive arrangement by placing the staircase at the very center of the space, with three parallel flights all meeting at an intermediate landing before reaching the level of the library in a further single flight. Some steps were made according to this design, but it was never completed, and when the staircase was finally built by Ammannati in 1558, it was on the basis of an amended design from about 1555 together with a new clay model that Michelangelo sent to Ammannati from Rome. The final work, therefore, must be seen at least to some extent as Ammannati's interpretation of the information he received. The stair itself, with its fluidly shaped treads, seems already to hint at the Baroque; although the two outer flights are rational enough, the central one has a sinuous willfulness that seems to delight in its flowing form.

The articulation of the volume of the *ricetto* itself is equally boldly and confidently articulated. This space, in its final form, is 33 feet (10 meters) square in plan but nearly 49 feet (15 meters) tall, with a basement order that is quite plain apart from the huge volutes that appear to support the principal order above it. This principal order is characterized, above all, by the bold paired columns set into recesses within the thickness of the walls, and between which deep niches remove further large parts of what logically should form the basic structure of the entire building. In a sense, the structure is less willfully illogical than we might suppose, since research has shown that these columns, rather than the walls, were, in fact, designed to support most of the load of the roof, so that there is a kind of double bluff in the way the structure is conceived. The third order, with its large windows, brings light down into this very deep volume, and is less dramatically modeled; this element was not completed until as late as 1904, together with the remaining structural articulation of the lower orders.

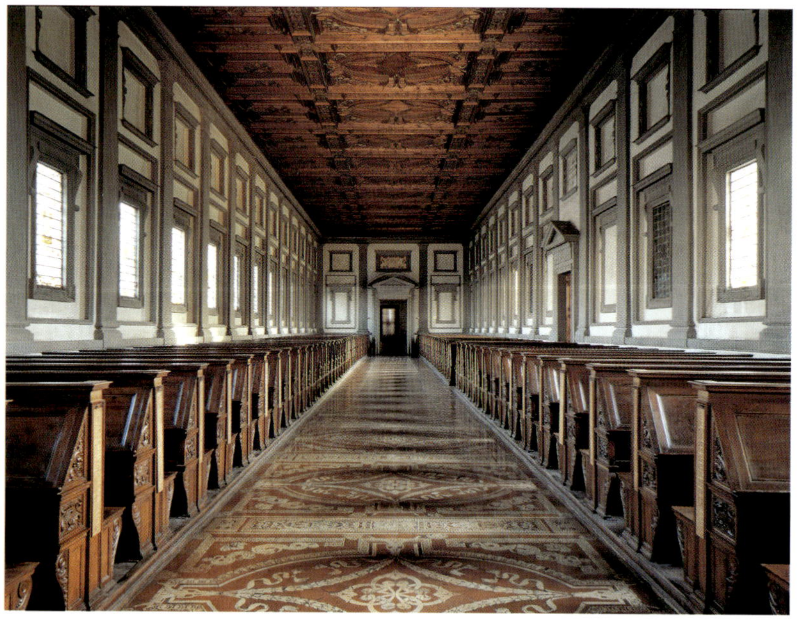

BIBLIOTECA LAURENZIANA, SAN LORENZO

Left: the interior of the library is broadly based on Michelozzo's earlier library at San Marco. Michelangelo's is a more richly developed volume, however, with no internal colonnades; every element, including the book cabinets and reading desks, forms part of a carefully integrated whole.

Opposite: interior of the *ricetto* with the monumental sculpted staircase, all in *pietra serena*.

The entire dramatic work, even in the partly completed condition in which Michelangelo and Ammannati left it, was clearly revolutionary both in the manipulation of classical forms and in the bold arrangement of the two spaces. The tall *ricetto* is constricted, dramatic, and strongly defined, lit from above, its own powerful vocabulary contrasting with the inviting fluidity of the staircase. These stairs rise quite steeply because of the restricted space, and reveal a dramatically different space at the top: the second element, the library itself, long, formal, rhythmic, and ordered, and lit from the sides. Michelangelo had shown the way to a new, more daring, more plastic, more manipulative approach to the design of space and light.

The Later Baroque: Buontalenti and Nigetti

With the unique and highly personal exception of Michelangelo's early-sixteenth-century works, later examples of Mannerism in Florence are generally more carefully modulated affairs. There is comparatively little evidence of the spatial fluidity, the modeling of structures such as Giacomo da Vignola's work in Rome, for example, nor was there any activity remotely resembling the extraordinary works of urban improvement undertaken in Rome under the dynamic patronage of Sixtus V toward the end of the century. In Florence the principal building projects were governmental; that is, they were exclusively Medicean: The modernizations at the Palazzo Vecchio,

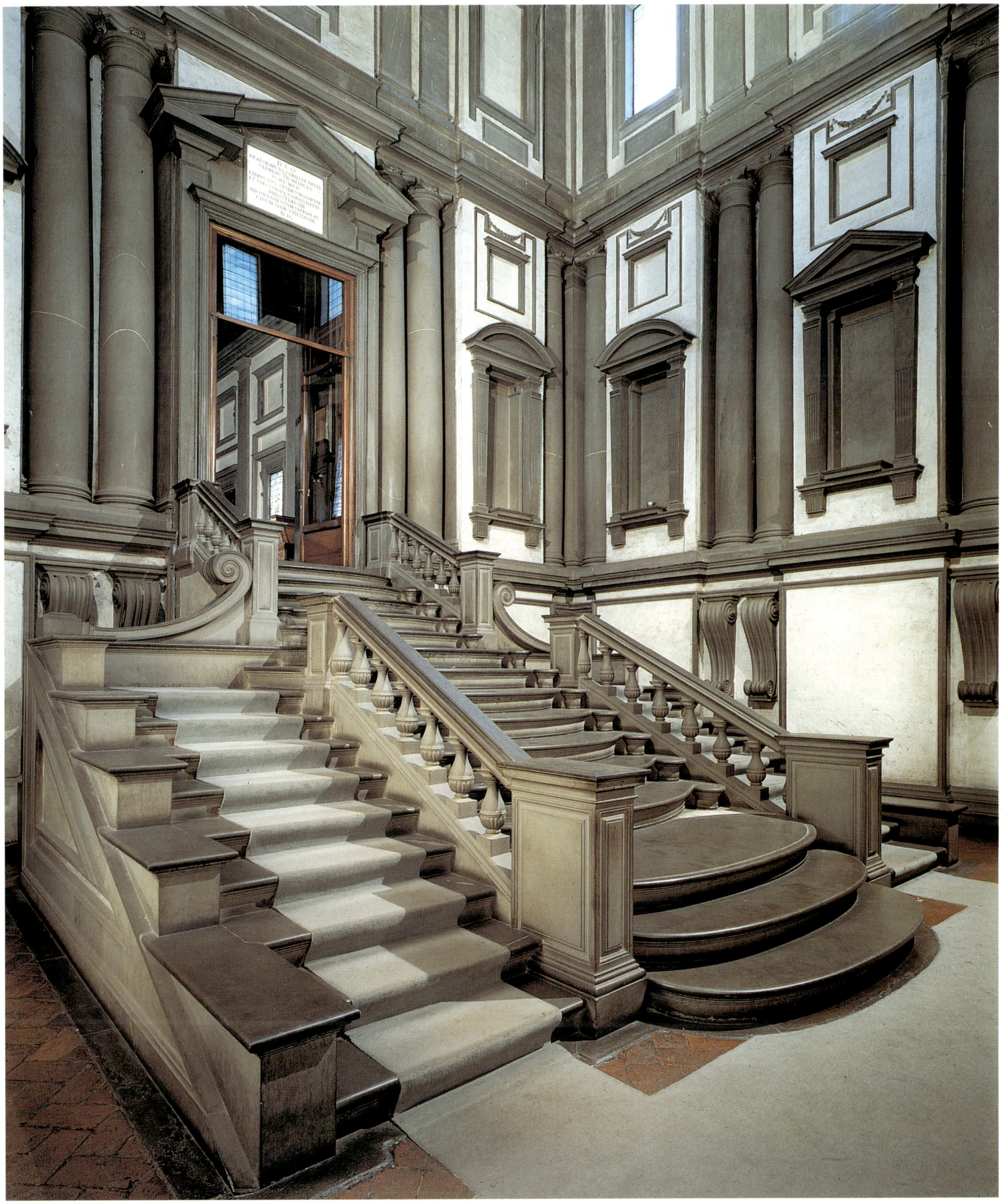

the expansion of Palazzo Pitti, the Uffizi, and the Corridoio Vasariano were all works based on the consolidation of dynastic power. Later cinquecento churches are thus probably best represented by the facade of Santa Trinità, begun by Bernardo Buontalenti in 1593, in the wake of his unsuccessful proposals for the facade of the cathedral. It is a cool, measured work despite its Baroque detailing, chiefly evinced by the pediments, some broken, some segmental, and some triangular; as a whole it is a good representation of the characteristically reserved Florentine response to the more self-indulgent fluidities of Rome.[44]

Just into the following century, however, the important works of Matteo Nigetti, a full generation younger than Buontalenti, indicate a loosening of some of these restraints. Nigetti was a follower of Buontalenti, but the maturation of his skills coincided with the rather more eclectic rule of Ferdinando I. The work that characterizes Nigetti's career better than any other is the extraordinary and highly controversial Cappella dei Principi at San Lorenzo, the last and by far the most overtly richly monumental of all the major Medicean interventions at their own church.[45] The first suggestion of a new chapel worthy of housing the mortal remains of what were now the grand dukes of Tuscany had come from Cosimo I, and Vasari had apparently produced a scheme, which is now lost. The foundation stone for the imposing structure was laid in 1604, and although its design was traditionally ascribed to Buontalenti, much of the detailing and virtually all of the supervision was carried out by Nigetti until his death in 1644. By 1625 the chapel was complete up to the level of the springing of the cupola, but thereafter work proceeded more slowly, with the cupola's basic structure complete by about 1650. The external cladding of *pietra dura* and the white marble windows were the work of Ferdinando Ruggieri, and were added as late as the 1730s.

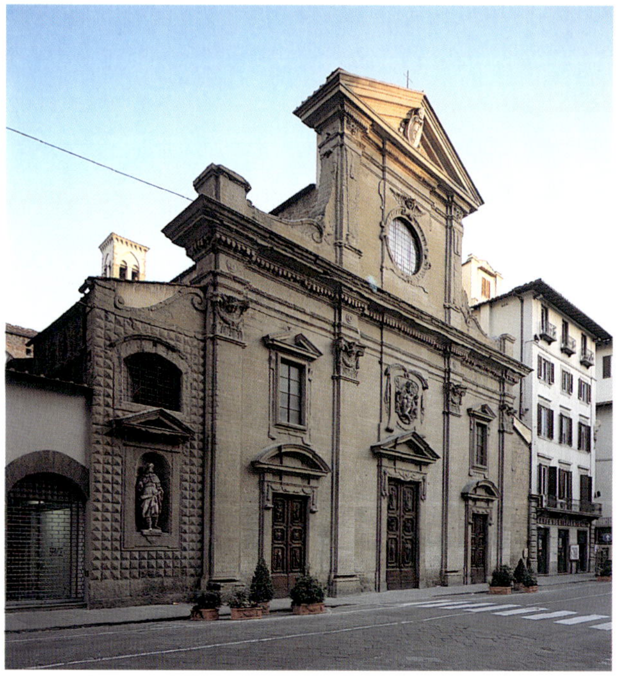

SANTA TRINITÀ (left)

The facade by Bernardo Buontalenti in 1593 shows elements of the Baroque in the profiled pediments and cartouches.

CAPPELLA DEI PRINCIPI (opposite)

Left: Matteo Nigetti's vast, monumental interior is lavishly decorated with *pietra dura* on almost all surfaces. The monuments to the Grand Dukes from Cosimo I to Cosimo III surround the interior, two of them (those of Ferdinando I and Cosimo II) surmounted by statues. Right: plan. The impressive octagonal volume is attached to the rear of San Lorenzo, and rises above a low undercroft or crypt. See also exterior of the chapel, page 76.

The chapel is the most opulent and grandiose of all the Medici works at the church, and arguably the dynasty's most elaborate anywhere; indeed, it is also one of the most ornate and ambitious family mausolea in all of Italy. In plan it has the form of an octagon, almost 100 feet (29 meters) across, and surmounted by a large segmental cupola, the second in size and prominence in Florence after that of Brunelleschi at the cathedral. The location of the chapel is unusual in that it is attached directly to the liturgical east end (in fact, the west end) of the church of San Lorenzo, behind the high altar, but with no direct connection to Brunelleschi's masterpiece. Volumetrically, therefore, although it may appear to have similarities with the centrally planned choir that Michelozzo attached to the Santissima Annunziata, the Cappella dei Principi is a separate structure, abutting the church for purely associational reasons.

The chapel's interior is extraordinarily lavish, overpowering in its deployment of *pietra dura* on virtually all of the surfaces below the cupola. Ferdinando had established the famous Opificio (workshop) delle Pietre Dure in 1588 to train specialist craftsmen to work on the chapel, and this renowned establishment has survived until today. Ferdinando scoured most of the then known world in search of the semiprecious stones with which to decorate the chapel on a scale never seen before.[46] The six monumental sarcophagi of the later grand dukes are all carefully integrated into

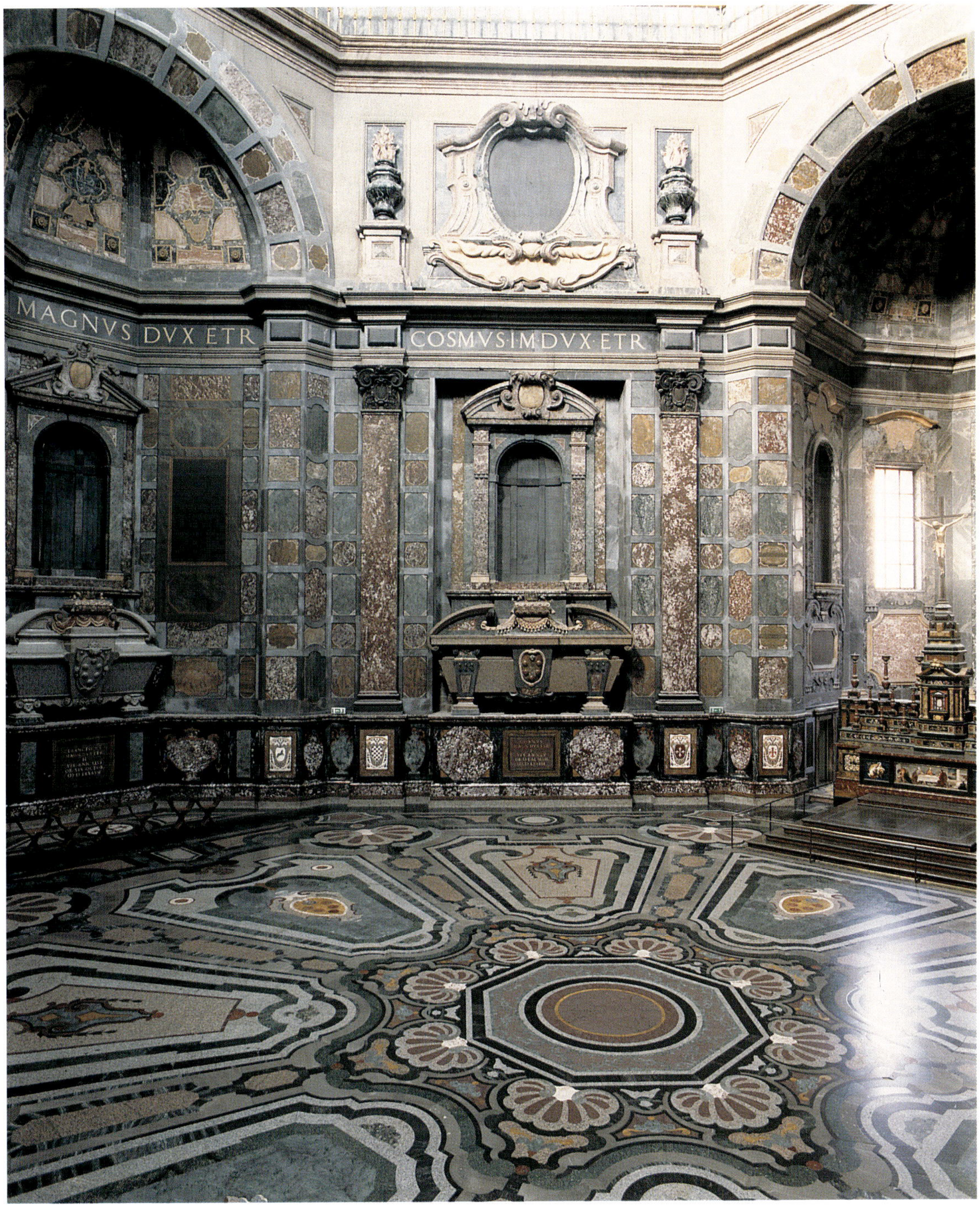
MAGNVS DVX ETR
COSMVS·I·M·DVX·ETR

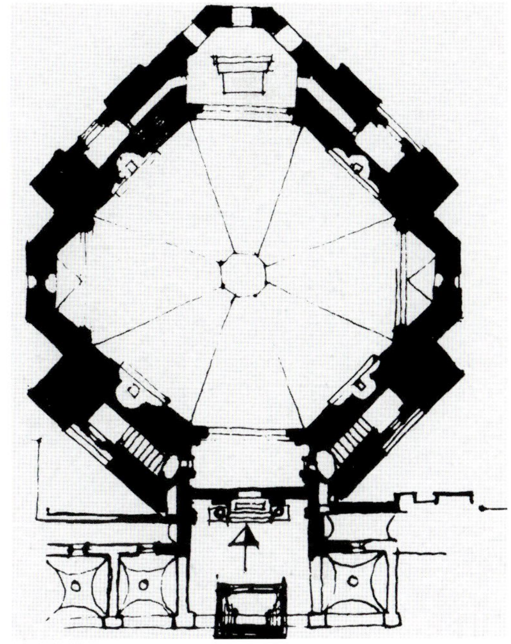

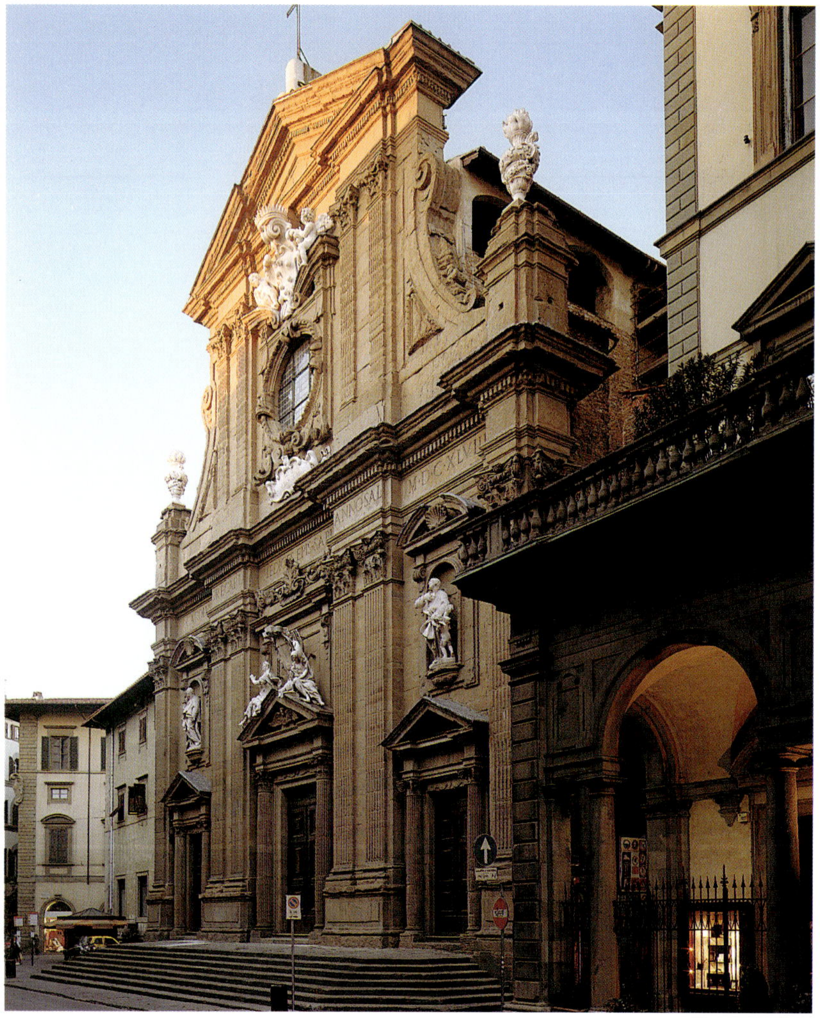

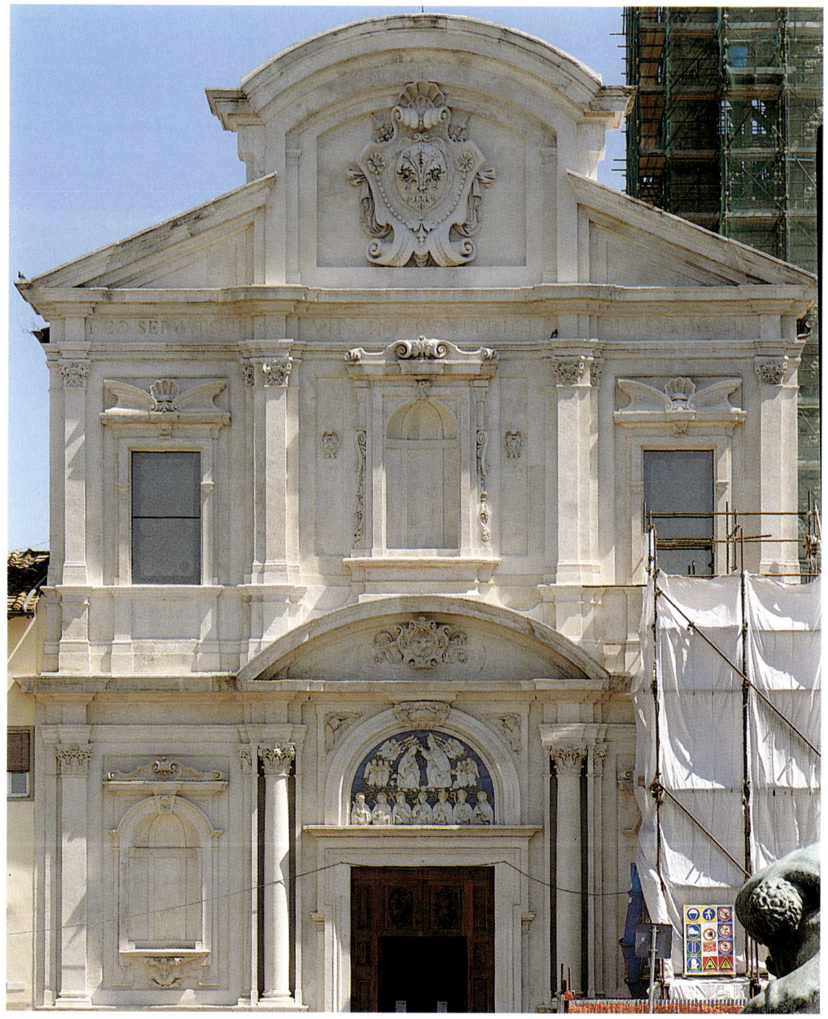

SANTI MICHELE E GAETANO (above, left)

The church, built between 1604 and 1649, is largely the work of Nigetti until 1630, while the facade is by Gherardo Silvani, and is one of the most robust and richly Baroque in the city.

OGNISSANTI (above)

Nigetti's well-balanced composition, with its Mannerist reversed broken pediments, can be appreciated from the quays on the other side of the Arno.

the overall scheme, while two of the sarcophagi are surmounted by huge arches set with statues of Grand Dukes Ferdinando I and Cosimo II by Pietro and Ferdinando Tacca. This extraordinary monument was to be the last Medici intervention at San Lorenzo, and the final completion of the cupola in the mid-eighteenth century coincided, fittingly enough, with the rule of the very last of the Medici, Gian Gastone.

The prolific Nigetti built several other Baroque projects in the city. The most notable is perhaps the Theatine church of Santi Michele e Gaetano, begun in 1604 and later continued by Gherardo Silvani. The choir and transepts at the eastern part of the church are the work of Nigetti, while the nave and facade were completed by Silvani in the 1640s. The facade in particular can be read as a reworking, in a much more exuberant Baroque manner, of Buontalenti's facade for Santa Trinità, which stands nearby.[47]

Many of these Baroque churches took several decades to construct, and were often completed by the generation that succeeded the original architect. The modernization of Ognissanti is a rare exception, since its remodeling took a mere ten years, from 1627 to 1637, but here, too, the facade was added by Nigetti to the church by Bartolomeo Pettirossi. This facade is a robust, original example of Nigetti's skills, richly modeled with niches and bold pilasters, while the oversized portal (containing a relief panel salvaged from the earlier church) is flanked by embedded columns. The whole ensemble, seen from across the Arno, forms a lively and dramatic composition.

Such well-balanced richness remains comparatively rare in the city, however, and a more characteristic example of interventions in this period is the rather earlier completion of the facade of the Santissima Annunziata. Here the immediate urban context really took precedence over any desire to make a bold, original contribution, and the tall loggia built across the width of the whole facade by Giovanni Caccini in 1604 consciously continues the motifs of the famous earlier colonnades of Brunelleschi at the Ospedale degli Innocenti on the east side of the spacious square, and the loggia of the Servites by Baccio and Antonio da Sangallo on the west side. Caccini's loggia formed an extrapolation from the earlier central entrance arch on the facade of the church, which had been built considerably earlier by Sangallo, and although in general terms the loggia does indeed finally unify the three sides of the piazza, Caccini's contribution is notably taller and, with its powerful crowning cornice, is more heavily monumental than the two earlier logge. After 1605 Caccini also began the modernization of the famous circular choir in the church itself, although this did not reach its final form until the complex stucco decorations of Giambattista Foggini were added in the early eighteenth century.[48]

The Later Seventeenth and Eighteenth Centuries: Parigi, Silvani, Ruggieri

Two or three more works from the latter half of the seventeenth century illustrate together fairly well the comparatively modest scope and extent of many of these later Baroque projects. The first is the Jesuit church of San Giovannino Evangelista, or "degli Scolopi," the rather surprisingly reserved facade of which was added by Alfonso Parigi in the early 1660s. Parigi was a member of a prolific family of architects in the city; his father, Giulio, was Ammannati's chief pupil, responsible inter alia for the enlargements at Palazzo Pitti. San Giovannino has a richly decorated interior, which is not reflected in the almost neoclassically disciplined facade, with its inset paired columns based on Michelangelo's precedent at the Biblioteca Laurenziana.

The other two works involved another prolific master of the period, Pier Francesco Silvani. San Frediano in Cestello has an unusually complex history: This Cistercian church was begun in 1670 to Silvani's design, but after four years on site the project was halted because its continuation would have necessitated demolition of some of the monastic buildings. After a second scheme was called for and begun, in 1679 the entire work completed to date was demolished, and a third structure,

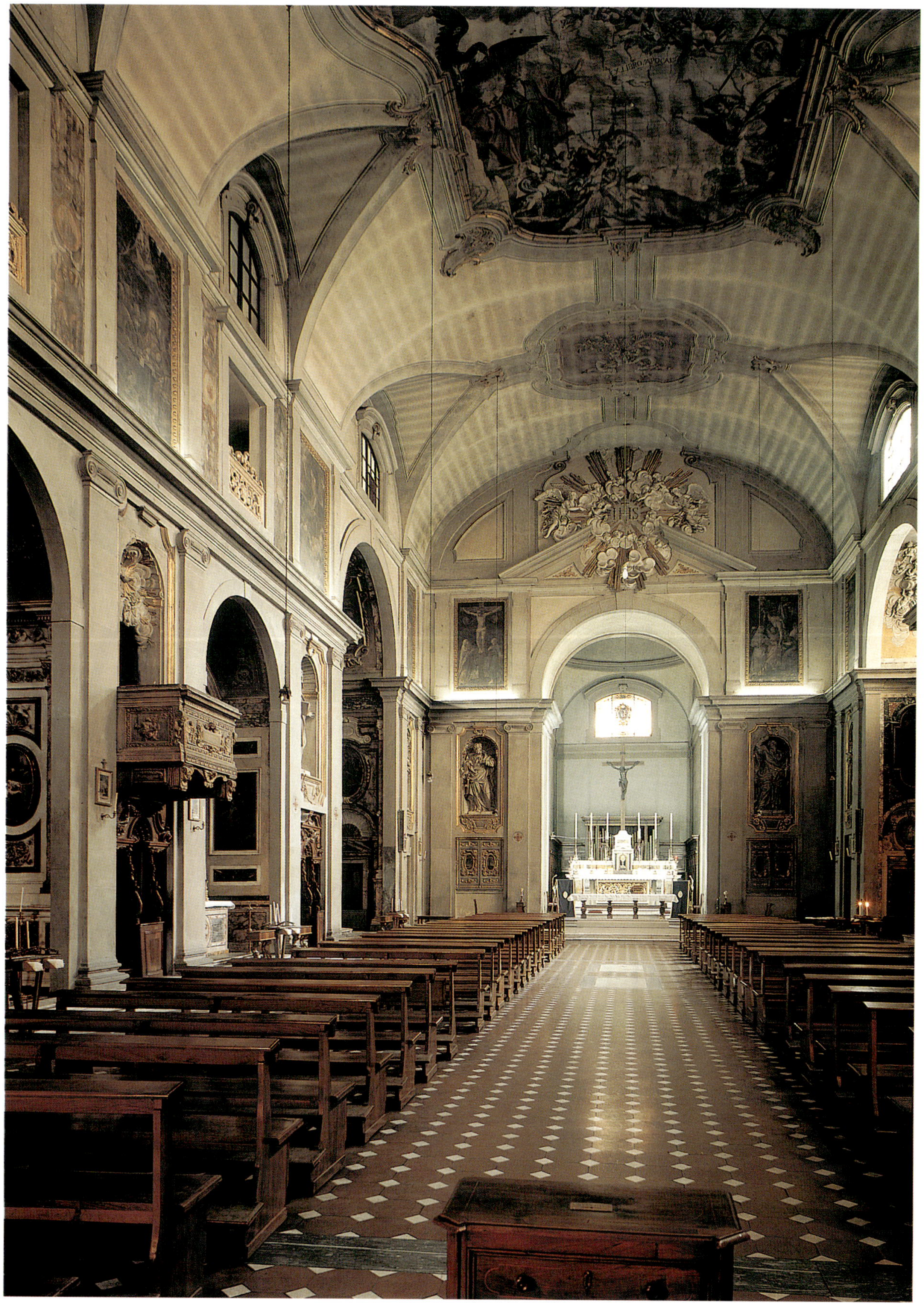

SAN GIOVANNINO DEGLI SCOLOPI

Alfonso Parigi's interior, from about 1665, is richly decorated in the typical Jesuit manner.

this time by Antonio Ferri, was begun; it was completed, including the characteristic cupola, by 1698.[49] The plan is based on a Latin cross, with chapels flanking the tall, three-bay nave, but it is above all the prominent cupola, raised on its high drum, that makes such an important contribution to the townscape of the western part of the Oltrarno. This prominent urban role is unusual in churches of this period, many of which were modernizations either of facades or interiors, but that rarely made a broader contribution to the city scene.

A similar observation can be made regarding Silvani's Corsini chapel at the Carmini, undoubtedly one of the key works of the seicento in Florence. (Silvani was also responsible for the sumptuous palazzo for the same family on the north bank of the Arno.) The chapel at the Carmini was

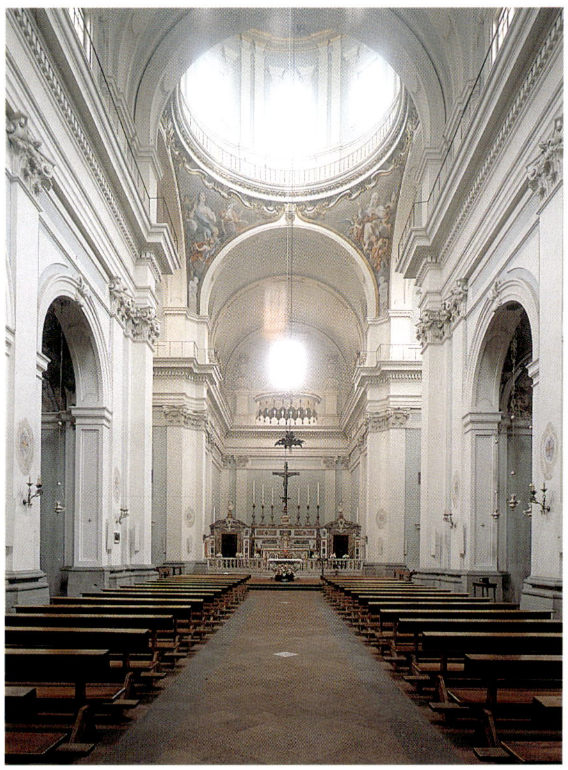

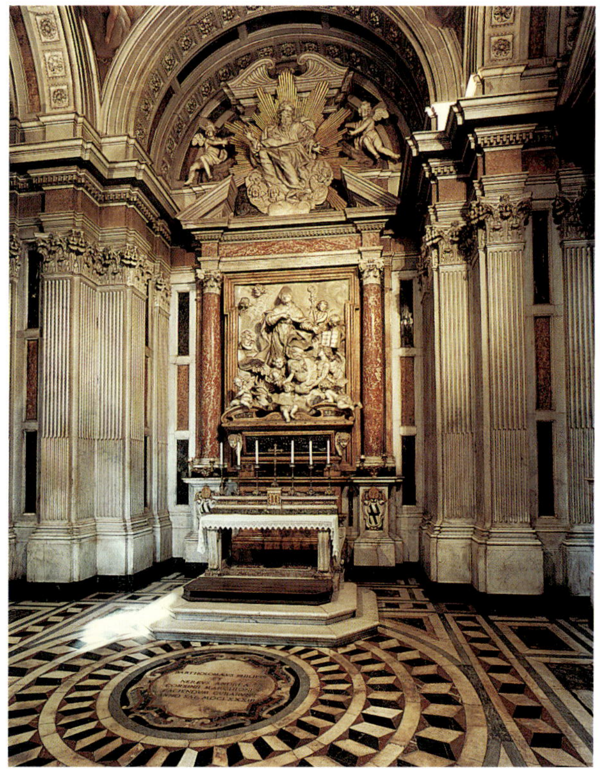

SAN FREDIANO IN CESTELLO (right)

The spacious, stately interior was completed in 1698. The church's construction has a complex history, with three architects in succession; it was completed by Antonio Maria Ferri.

CORSINI CHAPEL, CARMINI (far right)

Silvani's chapel is one of the finest and richest examples of seventeenth-century Florentine Baroque. The decoration is by Luca Giordano, Carlo Marcellini, and others.

financed in 1675 by Bartolomeo and Neri Corsini, in honor of the wishes of their antecedent, another Bartolomeo, to build a chapel in honor of another forebear, Sant'Andrea Corsini. Andrea had died in 1373, and had been canonized in 1629; it was thus to celebrate this belated canonization that the elaborate and very costly chapel was built. It occupies the end of the left transept of the church; square in plan, it is surmounted by a cupola on pendentives, all richly frescoed by Luca Giordano. The chapel was completed in 1683, and its sumptuous decoration, with marble relief panels by Giambattista Foggini, represents one of the finest, most fully integrated "Roman" Baroque interiors in the city.[50]

New church construction in the following century was not extensive, and again, much was confined to the remodeling of interiors. Perhaps the most imposing project of the period, which took many decades to complete, was the rationalization of the complex now known as San Firenze in the square of the same name. The grandiose facade that today occupies most of the eastern side of the piazza is in fact a great screen that visually unifies the several rather disparate elements that stand behind it.[51] At the north end is the church of the Filippini order, whose monastic house this complex also contains; the church was designed by Silvani in 1668 but was not completed until 1715, by Gioacchino Fortini. The second element, the comparatively neutral, rather severe central

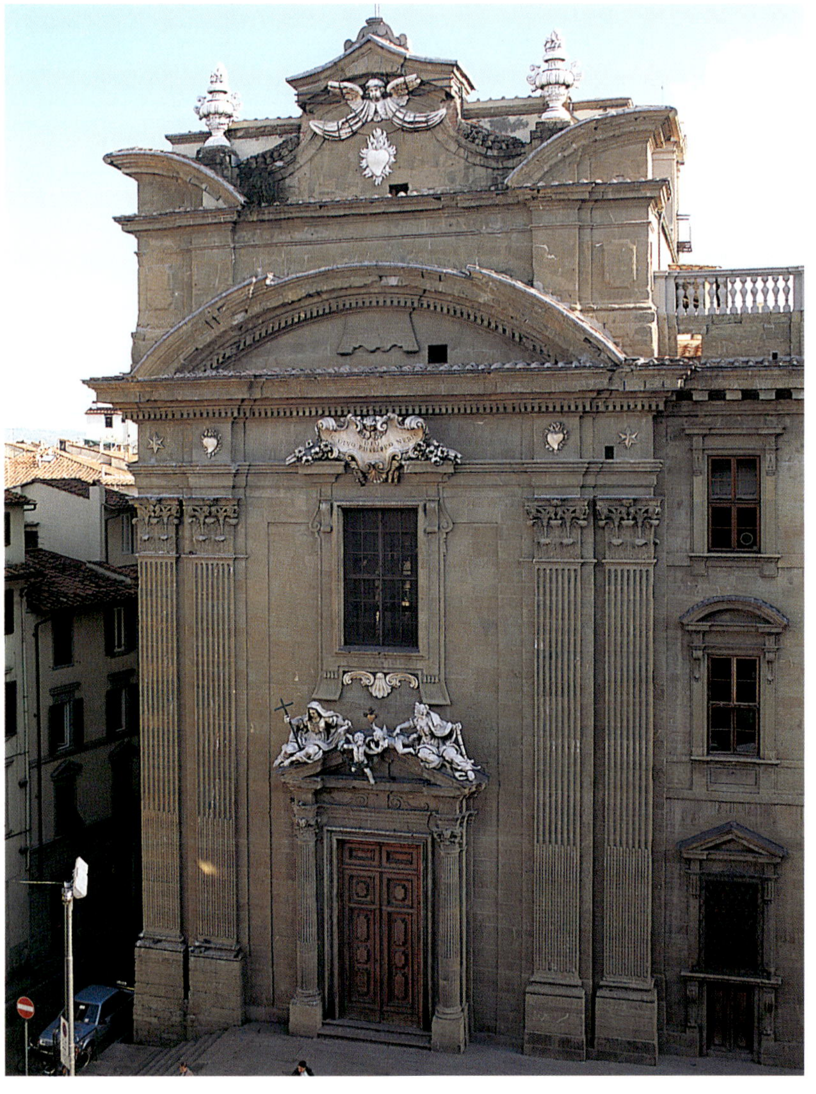

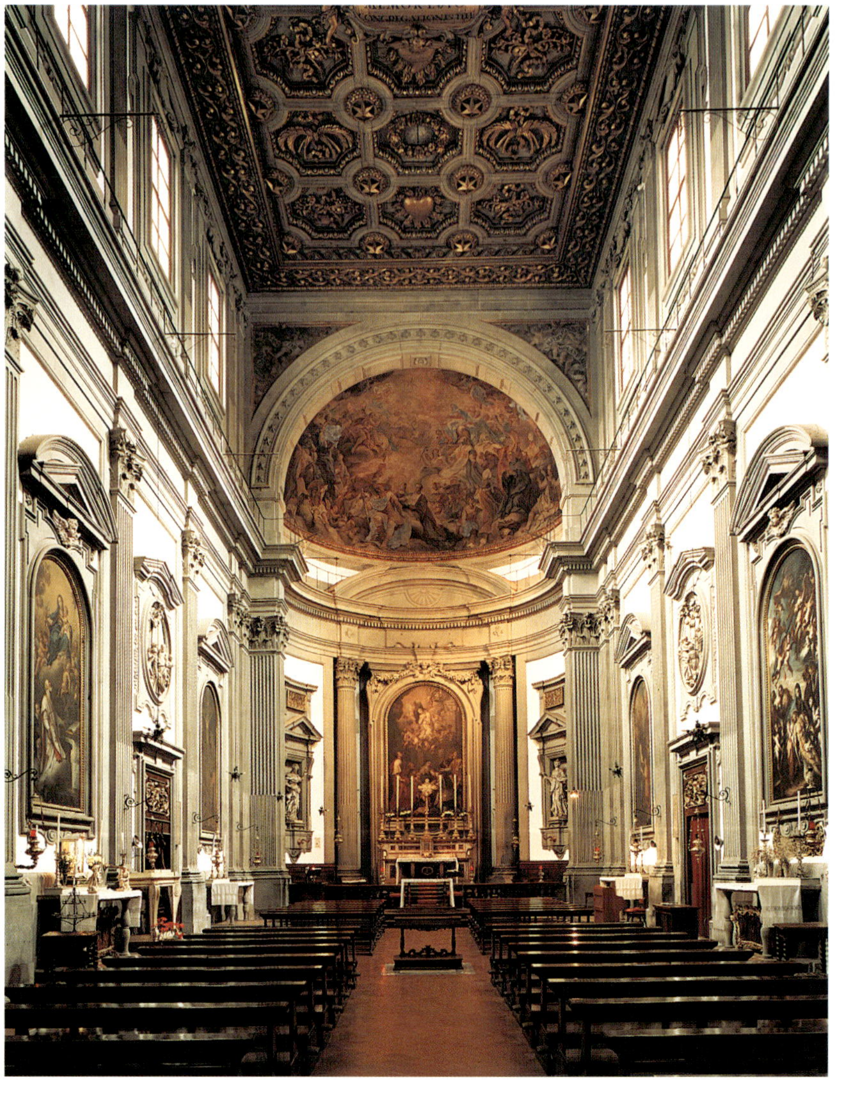

SAN FIRENZE

Above: the monumental screen onto the piazza incorporates the two church facades, the first begun by Ruggieri in 1715 and the second, modeled on the first, by Zanobi del Rosso in 1775. Above, right: interior of the church of San Filippo Neri, largely the work of Gioacchino Fortini, completed in 1715. Right: plan of the San Firenze complex showing the chief elements, the church of San Filippo Neri and the oratory; between them the central wing contains the entrance hall and stairs, with the cloisters behind.

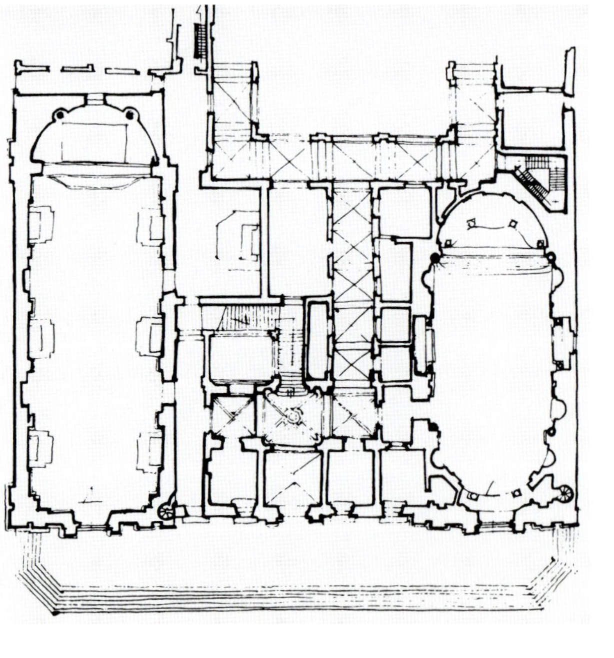

section of the long facade, masks the conventual buildings erected around an internal *cortile*, completed by Giovan Filippo Ciocchi in 1749. The third element, which occupies the southwest corner of the complex, was to become an oratory, built on the site of a much earlier church dedicated to San Fiorenzo, which gave its name to the whole complex. The oratory (today the Assize Court) has a robust, strongly modeled interior with a semicircular apse. The final architect to work on this extensive collection of structures was Zanobi del Rosso, who designed the imaginative, grandiose internal staircase, but whose imagination arguably did not extend to the rather ponderous external screen that unites the whole complex. The church facade, to the north, had in fact already been designed by Ferdinando Ruggieri in 1715, and so Zanobi simply repeated it to clad the facade of the oratory at the south end, with the two comparatively well modeled facades separated by a rather dour central block, which is enlivened somewhat by the sculpted group on the skyline.

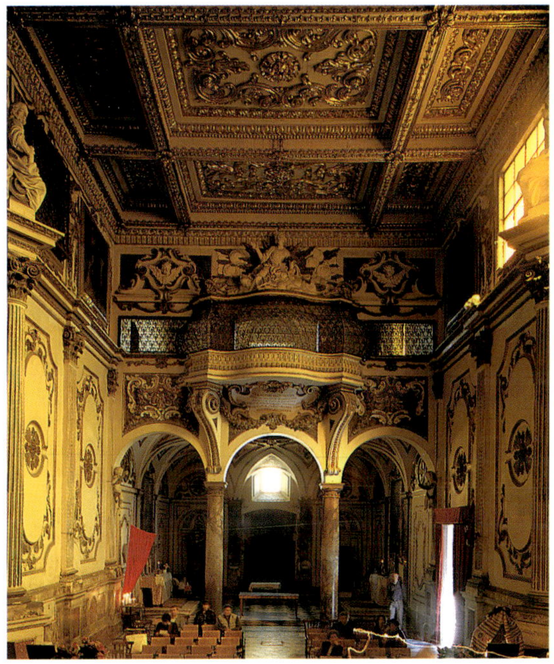

SAN GIORGIO ALLA COSTA

The interior by Giovanni Battista Foggini, from about 1705, is the most delightfully ornate and frivolous Rococo church interior in Florence.

Among a number of ecclesiastical interiors that were remodeled in this period, two stand out for particular mention, stylistically representing two distinct branches of the tastes of the era. The first is the little church of San Giorgio alla Costa, whose interior was comprehensively remodeled by Giovanni Battista Foggini in 1705 in a delightful Rococo manner — a rare example in Florence — with complex stucco and gilding. The rectangular nave is broken by a choir gallery, or *barco,* across the center, and the atmosphere of the whole is more reminiscent of a private salon for aristocratic musical entertainment or theater than a place for worship.

The second example is the restructuring of Santa Felicità by Ruggieri in the late 1730s. The church had a rather special status, as it lay on the route of the Corridoio Vasariano, and had become annexed by the Medici as a grand ducal chapel to serve the vast Palazzo Pitti nearby. The remodeling had to reflect this unique role, and Ruggieri's rebuilding is stately and imposing, the nave strongly vertical in emphasis, and framed by powerful, fluted Corinthian pilasters. There is no applied decoration; the strongly articulated structure is left to speak for itself, while generous natural light is provided by large clerestory windows. A similar, almost neoclassical restraint also characterizes the facade of San Marco. The church itself had been completely rebuilt in the sixteenth and seventeenth centuries, the facade being the very last element to be constructed, in 1776. Its self-controlled appearance dominates the north side of the tree-filled square, with a pronounced vertical emphasis crowned by a strongly modeled tympanum.

These examples show a rather characteristically measured Florentine response to the development of the full-blooded Roman Baroque, with just a handful of exceptions to this restraint, both in the field of remodeled interiors and in modernized facades. Examples of Rococo frivolity in the city are considerably rarer still. There were no further significant ecclesiastical works built in Florence until the nineteenth century, which era of stylistic revival brought the very belated completion of the facades of some of the greatest churches of earlier centuries: Santa Croce and the cathedral itself.

"I have already observed elsewhere, that a House is a little City. We are therefore in the building of it, to have an Eye almost to every Thing that relates to the Building of a City; that it be healthy, furnished with all Manner of Necessaries, not deficient in any of the Conveniences that conduce to the Repose, Tranquillity or Delicacy of Life." **Leon Battista Alberti**, *De re aedificatoria* (c. 1452) [1]

Before we begin to discuss the history of the most important and dominant building typology in the city, the noble or merchant's palazzo, it is important to be aware of the stylistic development of the more modest, and thus more typical, Florentine house, from which, at least in some senses, all of these imposing palaces derive. The Florentine palazzo can be said to have its most distant origins in the fortified tower houses of the bloody period of the Guelf–Ghibelline struggle. The major stages of this development, which reached its culmination in the vast Palazzo Pitti, include important surviving examples of the true early medieval palazzo, such as Palazzo Spini Feroni; the definitive monuments of the early Renaissance, such as the palazzi of the Medici, Rucellai, and Strozzi; and the numerous examples from the later Renaissance and Mannerist periods.

TORRE DELLA CASTAGNA

The thirteenth-century tower offered protection and security to the adjacent *badia* convent.

Much remains unknown about the early stages in the development of the Florentine palazzo, and it therefore seems appropriate to try to sketch the domiciliary background of the era of the famous tower houses of the Guelf–Ghibelline struggle, which is also one during which most of the citizens of Florence lived in humble cottages. Despite the law of 1250 that limited the height of these early tower houses to a maximum of 50 *braccia* (about 100 feet, or 30 meters), and despite later ordinances as well as many centuries of adaptation and losses, a surprising number of the remains, or stumps, of such edifices remain in the old city, some indeed still looming rather menacingly over the tiny courtyards and narrow alleys of the city center.[2] The Torre della Pagliazza is generally accepted as being the very oldest, whose plan is uniquely circular, testifying (it is also generally agreed) to its sixth-century Byzantine origins. Recently restored and cleared of many later accretions, the form of this building, with its single large doorway at ground level and an irregular arrangement of windows on the upper levels, can be seen more clearly now than had been possible for centuries. Excavations in 1983 indicated that the tower was built on the base of an earlier Roman structure, part of a baths complex, which was almost certainly the reason for its unusual plan; the sixth-century tower itself also seems to have stood on or very close to the line of the Byzantine city walls. This particular tower remains a special case both in its form and in its antiquity; far more typical is a fairly large group of later survivors, the most important of which are the tower houses of the Corbizi (or Donati), Marsili, Alberti, and Amidei, and the towers known as the Torre della Castagna and the Torre delle Vedove. There are several other, less prominent but well-known examples, including the Torre Baldovinetti, the Torre dei Greci, and the Torre Mannelli. Nearly all probably date from the thirteenth century, and although they differ considerably in detail, in their surviving height, and in their arrangement of doors and fenestration, they all equally clearly represent responses to the same urban climate of insecurity and uncertainty.[3]

As an urban typology, of course, the tower house was by no means confined to Florence; it was widespread in many cities subjected to the internecine struggles of the Guelf and Ghibelline factions. Elsewhere in Tuscany, for example, are the famous examples of San Gimignano and Volterra, handfuls of survivors of the many dozens that originally stood there. Less well known, and rather more difficult to identify today, too, are those that survive in nearby Pisa. Most of them, in these and other locations, have several common features: They are usually square or nearly square in plan, for clear reasons of stability; they are constructed of stone, often only roughly dressed and coursed; their window openings

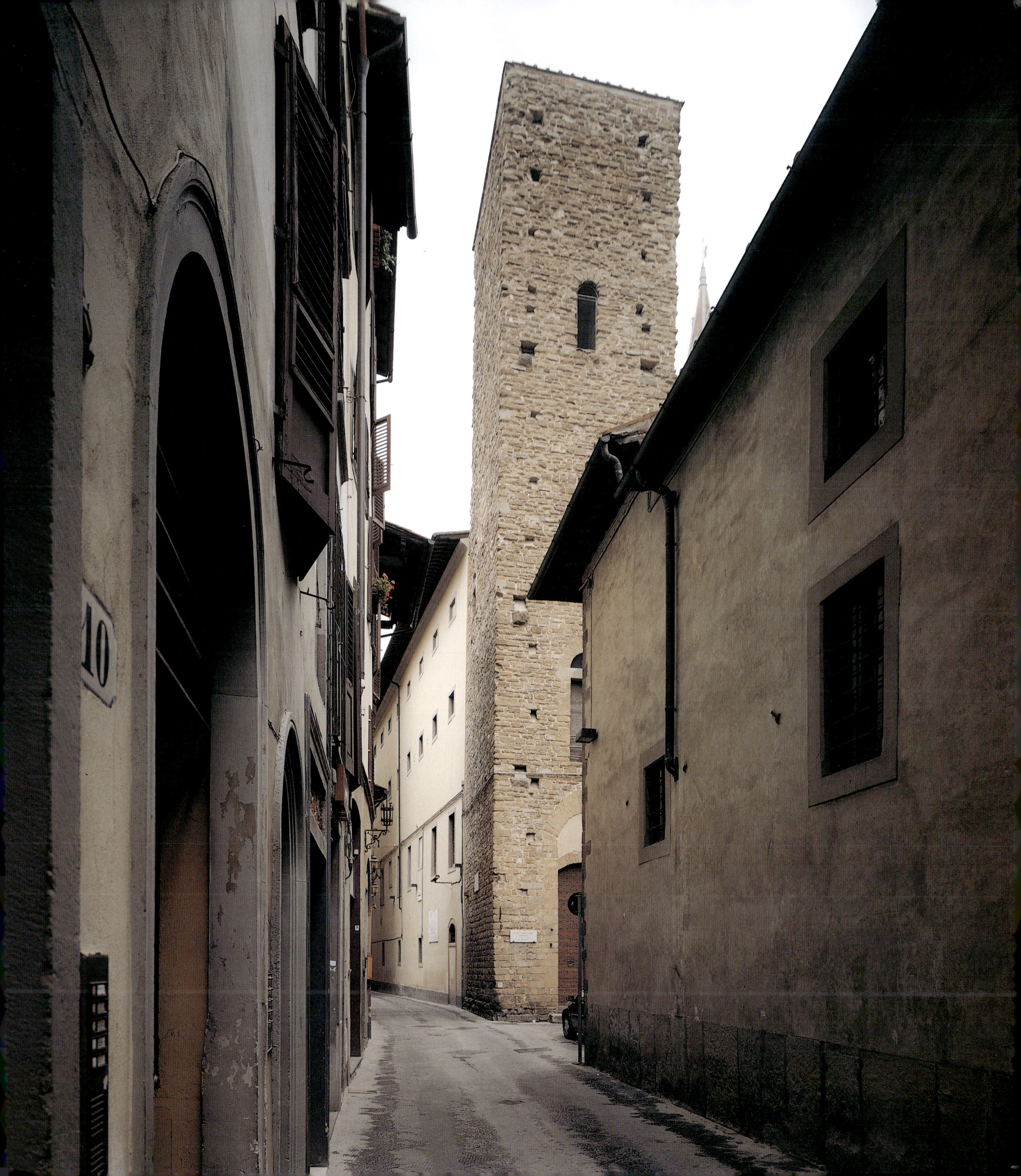
10

are small; and they are built on several stories. Those that survive in Florence vary in height from three stories to six, those of the Corbizi and Marsili being the best preserved of the group.

It is important to appreciate that these towers were not built as isolated, individual "one-family" dwellings, but as elements in complex groups of structures best defined as clusters — that is, a number of such towers were erected fairly close together, all on the same city block, or *insula*, and connected to one another in various ways, generally by means of lower, more conventional blocks of housing or by *palazzetti*. These clusters belonged to the same clans or to closely related clans that had the same allegiance (that is, Guelf or Ghibelline, or later, *bianchi* or *neri*), and were grouped into *consorterie,* or associations. Access was usually possible at the upper levels between many or all of these different elements, both palazzi and towers, without the necessity of venturing down to the dangerous streets below. In between the towers, the more conventional accommodation at lower levels represented the normal living quarters of the various families in times of peace, so that the towers themselves, usually reached by a single small doorway from an upper floor, remained essentially places of retreat in times of urban unrest. They were also often used as storehouses for bulk domestic supplies. Another characteristic feature of the upper floors of these houses were the contiguous wooden balconies, or *ballatoi*, from which projectiles could be thrown to repel aggressors. These balconies represented a timber variant of the overhanging stone upper galleries that still can be seen today, for example at the Palazzo Vecchio, but that, because of the impermanent nature of their materials (and later ordinances to remove them) have long since disappeared from the city.

The Torre dei Corbizi (or Donati) originally defended a key point of access into the center of the city, via the important Borgo degli Albizi. On the other side of the same *insula* today still stands a second tower, which, together with the *palazzetti* between them, formed a compact complex of accommodation all once owned by the prominent Guelf family, the Donati. Within this defensible "island," several alleys and *cortili* gave access to the various elements of the complex. The Torre della Castagna was also built in a prominent corner location and offered similar protection to the Badia Fiorentina; it was donated to the nunnery by the emperor Corrado in 1038, and is thus one of the oldest such survivors. Later the tower was given to the city by the *badia* in 1282 for the use of the priors while the nearby Palazzo Vecchio was being constructed. The tower has only four stories, which are all particularly tall; the lower two were built in coursed ashlar, but the upper parts are constructed in uncoursed rubble. A similar approach was followed at the Torre dei Marsili, just across the river in the Borgo di San Jacopo, which again formed one of a cluster of six such towers, in this case built to defend the *insula* of the Ghibelline Ramiglianti family. It passed to the Marsili, Guelfs by allegiance, after the decisive defeat of the Ghibellines in 1265; in the following century the Marsili connected it to their adjacent palace on the Via Toscanella. The unusual trapezoidal plan of the Torre degli Alberti, near Santa Croce, on the other hand, marks a specific response to the unusual shape of its site, an acute angle at the junction of Via de' Benci and Borgo Santa Croce; its three facades still dominate this important street junction. Many such towers contained a shop or loggia at the base. The Torre degli Alberti still retains one, which was added in the fifteenth century, when the civil climate of the city had become rather more secure, and by which time, too, the outermost city walls had long been completed to offer an outer ring of defense against external aggression.

All wealthy Florentine clans formed themselves into *consorterie* and built such complexes for themselves, but the lower classes of society clearly had no such resources. Their living accommodation was often very humble, the poorest of all often built from the rubble and remains of houses destroyed in the civil wars, notably the struggle between the *bianchi* and *neri* in 1300–01.[4] The humblest Florentines lived in a single room that served as a bedroom and kitchen together. It was built, if not from reclaimed rubble, then from brick or timber, and was roofed with thatch; the floor was of beaten earth, and there was a hearth in the center, smoke escaping through a gap in the thatch: an archetypal primitive medieval "hovel," therefore, into which the only light was provided from the doorway or from a single window opening, which, of course, had no glass.

The larger majority of citizens, though, lived rather better than this. After all, Florence was a very wealthy city, and a skilled craftsman in any trade could probably make a passable living. His accommodation probably consisted of two rooms, a bedroom and a kitchen, the former being used to receive visitors, a pattern that, incidentally, also persisted through much higher levels of society. The kitchen, however, was still fairly rudimentary, and the windows were closed by means of wooden shutters. Wealthier Florentines made use of waxed cloth to allow light in and keep out the weather; glass was only found later in the houses of the wealthy, and was criticized by the Church as being too luxurious. The main living room, the *stanza principale*, combined the functions of bedroom and living or reception room even in rather large houses. Although daily meals would be taken in the kitchen, the *stanza principale* was used for festive occasions or special events. Here the floor was finished with brick or timber boards. Higher-quality floor finishes such as stone or marble were naturally a further reflection of status and wealth. A similar gradation applied to the treatment of wall surfaces. In the humblest cottages, they were of bare brick or rough stone; the next stage was to finish the surfaces with plain plaster, while wealthier houses would have the plaster painted and frescoed. Later still, wall hangings became widespread. The treatment of upper floors and ceilings reflected this hierarchy of finishes, too. Upper floors were constructed with substantial timber beams, usually set fairly close together and usually left exposed to form the ceiling of the room below. In the wealthier houses, these beams were often quite elaborately painted and decorated.

The houses of wealthier Florentines naturally developed a more complex hierarchy of spaces and their uses.[5] A hall designed specifically for the reception of visitors was an important stage in this process of refinement; known as the *sala prima* or the *sala madornale,* it was used solely to receive important guests and for banquets and other special or celebratory occasions. For a long time, though, even in the houses of the wealthy, it remained the custom to receive personal guests or relatives in the bedroom, a common custom in much of Europe. Bedrooms would thus be furnished as "day rooms" as much as purely for sleeping. The substantial step toward greater comfort represented by the construction of fireplaces and chimneys spread among the *borghesia affarista* (the merchant bourgeoisie) as well as the nobility in the period immediately after Dante's time — that is, from the mid-trecento onward — and within a few decades had become very widespread.

An important adjunct to the houses of Florence's moneyed families was the external loggia; this architectural feature was widespread in the duecento and trecento, and although many such structures have been lost in the centuries that followed, a handful of later examples survive today, including the very well known loggia of the Rucellai, directly in front of the family palazzo; that of the Frescobaldi is the only one to survive from the era of Dante. Some were built by congregations, or quasi-religious confraternities, many others by private families. The form of the logge varied considerably; some were formed out of part of the ground floor of the family palazzo itself, while others, like that of the Rucellai, were built as separate structures nearby.[6] They served a number of functions, chiefly for family festivals (baptisms, weddings, and so on), or were sometimes simply used as a gathering place for the clan and its friends and associates. Later, these activities tended to become relocated to the top floor of the palazzo itself, where a covered colonnaded balcony was often constructed. Palazzo Dei (later Guadagni), offers a good example of this new trend, dating from the very early cinquecento; the much older Palazzo Davanzati was also augmented around the end of the same century by the loggia that is visible today, standing atop the original palace, already three hundred years old when this addition was made. Placing the gallery at a high level naturally offered greater privacy and security than did the loggia at street level, and there were further advantages of such a rooftop location during the stiflingly hot Florentine summers: some breeze, and sometimes beautiful views to the surrounding countryside.

"Of the adorning of private Houses . . . in town you must not raise your Platform or Basement too high above your Neighbors, nor let your Portico project too far forward from the Line of the adjacent Buildings." **Leon Battista Alberti**, *De re aedificatoria* (c. 1452) [1]

There is a fairly substantial number of surviving palaces from the later duecento and the trecento in the city that represent what was arguably Florence's greatest period of wealth and prosperity. Most of them can be seen, in their general appearance, to be members of the same extended family. Not surprisingly, though, none has survived the centuries completely unaltered, although some have fared better than others in retaining their original appearance.[2] One of the earliest is the important Palazzo Mozzi, in the *borgo* of San Niccolò, in the Oltrarno. The Mozzi were a Guelf banking family, who had become wealthy in the eleventh and twelfth centuries and had branches in a number of European cities. In 1260, though, their houses were destroyed by the Ghibelline faction, chiefly because they were strategically located at the southern bridgehead of the Ponte Rubaconte (the present Ponte alle Grazie). The principal palazzo was reconstructed quickly — it had already been rebuilt by 1273 — on the axis of the bridge, where it still stands today. In that year Pope Gregory X was lodged in the palazzo, which was considered "the most noble building in the city."[3]

Palazzo Mozzi, with its solid stone facade and its regular arched windows, remains a good example of the transition from semifortified tower house to the more open palazzo; it is stoutly built and defensible, incorporating a towerlike section (with Guelf battlements) within the body of the house, but the windows of the upper stories are comparatively large, allowing ample light inside. The facade is refined but regular and severe, faced with *bugnato rustico* stonework — that is, stonework that is semi-coursed and dressed on the face; the ground floor is articulated by a series of large, arched openings giving access to warehouse accommodation or shops, often leased to other Florentines. A single portal, again easily defensible, gives access to the central *cortile*, around which the palazzo is built. Adjacent to the *cortile* were stables and stores for bulk provisions such as oil, wine, timber, and grain, while behind the palazzo itself orchards originally extended up the steep hillside as far as the city walls. Above a low, barred mezzanine, the first floor contained the principal apartments, reached by a stairway from the *cortile*. A large hall, the *sala di rappresentanza*, occupied the whole width of the front facade, while bedrooms were also on this level, in the side wings ranged around the *cortile* and at the rear. The second story generally contained servants' quarters, kitchens, and other ancillary accommodation. Originally the roof of the palazzo was completely surrounded by a stone parapet, which later was replaced by the present large, overhanging cornice.

There is a further handful of roughly contemporary surviving palazzi in the city, the most prominent of which are Palazzo Davanzati and Palazzo Spini, later Feroni. The latter, even in its now truncated form, remains the most soberly impressive of these early semifortified palazzi. It was begun in 1289, on a prominent site on the north bank of the Arno, immediately next to the Santa Trinità bridgehead. In a sense, therefore, its strategic importance mirrored that of Palazzo Mozzi on the eastern edge of the city. It is also an exact contemporary of the Palazzo Vecchio, and offers a valuable comparison between the design of a lay palace and that of the seat of Republican power in this important era. Palazzo Spini Feroni forms a massive rectangular block, occupying an entire island site that was formerly even larger,

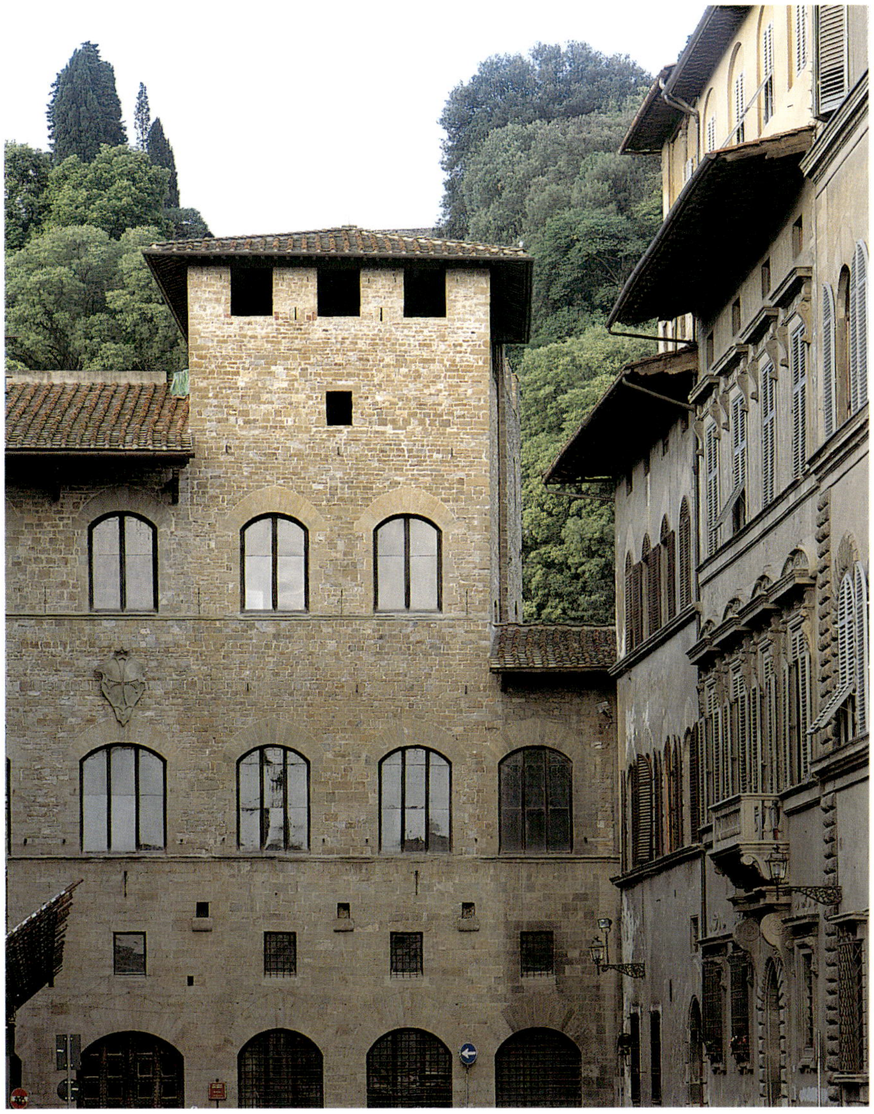

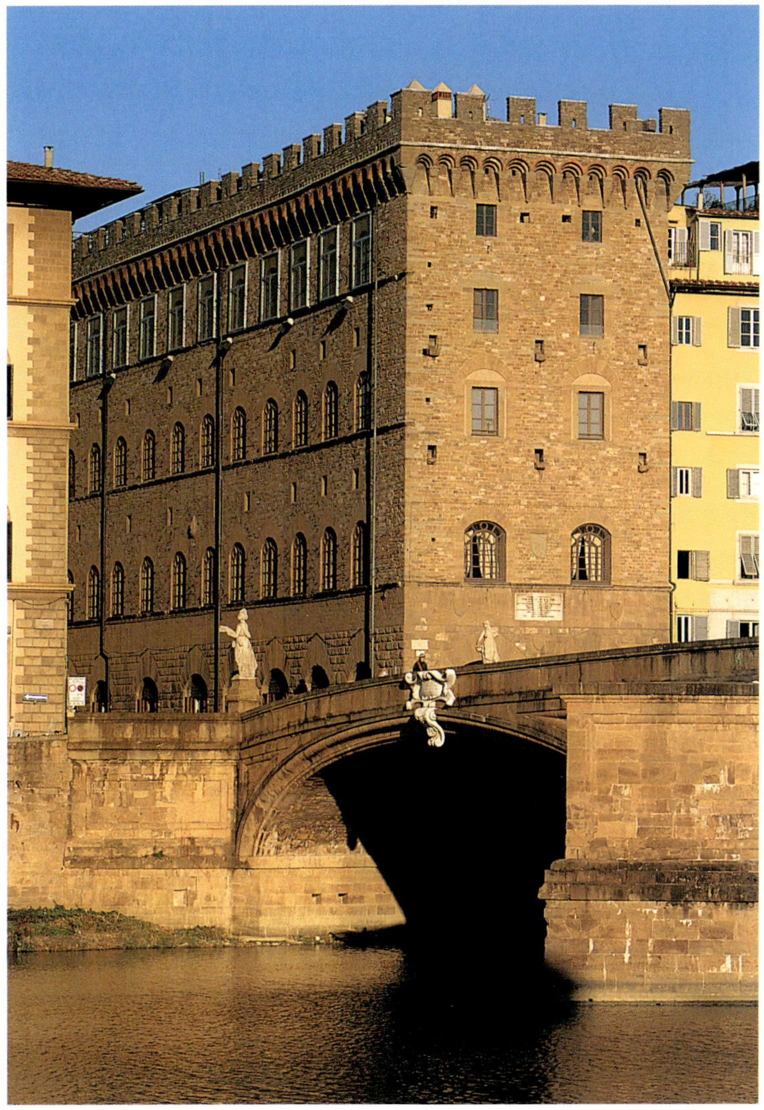

PALAZZO MOZZI (above)

Facade onto the piazza. This is a fine example of the severe, minimally detailed palaces of the later thirteenth century.

PALAZZO SPINI FERONI (above, right)

One of the most prominent of the surviving early palaces (begun in 1289), this edifice dominates the northern bridgehead of Santa Trinità.

as it extended for another three or four bays across the present *lungarno* to the river's edge; we therefore see today about three-quarters of its original imposing mass. Palazzo Spini Feroni established the basic vocabulary of the Florentine palazzo for the early trecento. It has no towers, although its defensive capabilities are signaled clearly enough by its crowning Guelf crenellation, built above prominent machicolation. The ground story, as usual, was used for commercial activities, represented by a series of arched openings, and above this three further stories were built, all with simple, regular, segmental-arched windows. The palazzo retained important defensive functions in the city as a whole, too; it was matched on the south bank of the Arno by the similarly imposing Palazzo Frescobaldi, the two palaces together thus forming a fortified gateway defending the heart of the city from the west. Palazzo Gianfigliazzi stands on the west side of the square on which stands Palazzo Spini Feroni; they are almost exactly contemporaneous, and, although the former is less monumental, they are similarly detailed, and the two together thus form an archetypal ensemble from this period.[4]

The slightly later palazzo today known as the Palazzo dell'Arte della Lana, although generally identified as the headquarters of this important *arte*, was in fact built in 1308 as a private house.

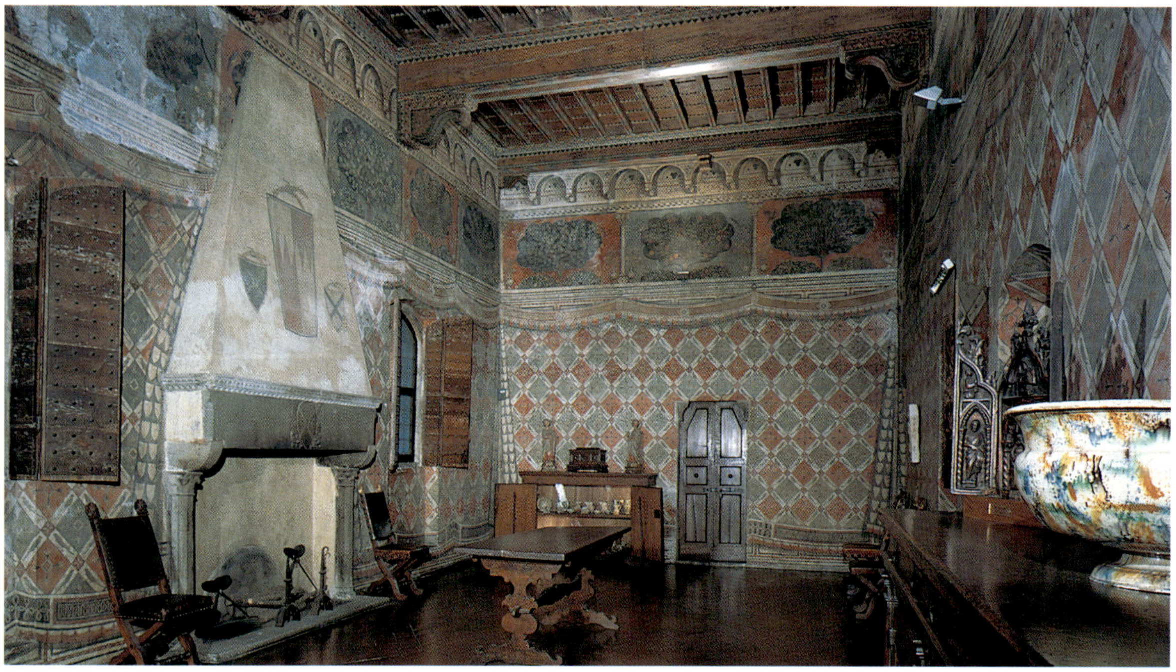

PALAZZO DAVANZATI

The Sala dei Pappagalli is a largely intact late-fourteenth-century interior. Well-preserved internally, in 1905 the palazzo was established as a museum of medieval Florentine life, with contemporary furniture and fittings.

Built on a restricted city center site with one facade onto the Via Calimala and the other onto Via Orsanmichele, the palazzo has two upper stories, crowned by the characteristic Guelf crenellation. It became the seat of the *arte* in the fourteenth century, but the original clarity of its form was considerably obscured by "romantic" remodeling in the early years of the twentieth century, when, among other alterations, the tabernacle of Santa Maria della Tromba was reassembled on the corner, following the wholesale demolitions in the Mercato Vecchio.

Palazzo Davanzati (originally Davizzi) represents a further degree of refinement and rationalization from the earlier Spini Feroni and Mozzi palazzi, particularly in the detailing of its regular facade. It was built in around 1350 on a constricted city-center site near the Mercato Nuovo, its four-story facade originally surmounted by a crenellation was later replaced by the present loggia.[5] Although austere, the facade is highly refined in its minimal detailing, with the ashlar carefully graded from the large dressed stones of the ground floor up to the rougher, smaller stones of the top story. There is a small internal courtyard with a prominent open staircase up to the principal apartments, supported on a series of arches and corbels; this staircase, however, like much of the interior, was "restored" in the early twentieth century, and much of it is a rather imaginative reconstruction. The

PALAZZO DAVANZATI

Below: the original, simpler medieval appearance of the *cortile* was elaborated by the rebuilding of the complex external staircase in the early twentieth century. Below, right: space was already extremely limited in the heart of the medieval city, so the house was built on four stories, to a very compact plan.

palazzo, though, also exhibits features that were innovative in the mid-quattrocento, reflecting a further stage of refinement in patterns of living. For instance, toilets are built into the thickness of the wall on every story, which are the earliest surviving examples, and a well shaft rises to the full height of the building, allowing water to be drawn up to each story. The *piano nobile* has a large hall occupying the full width of the palace behind the facade like that at Palazzo Mozzi, and also retains its original, richly decorated timber ceiling. The palazzo was acquired by Elia Volpi in 1906, from which date the interior was elaborated with a collection of artifacts from the fourteenth and fifteenth centuries; these were to form the basis of its present function as a museum of Florentine domestic life during those periods.

Roughly contemporary with the refined Palazzo Davanzati are Palazzo Acciaiuoli and the Palazzo dei Giudici; the latter is of particular interest, since there one can see the rationalization in the grading of rustication that was to be reinterpreted by Michelozzo for the Medici a century later: A robustly rusticated ground story is surmounted by two stories of flat-faced ashlar; the uppermost loggia here again is a later addition.

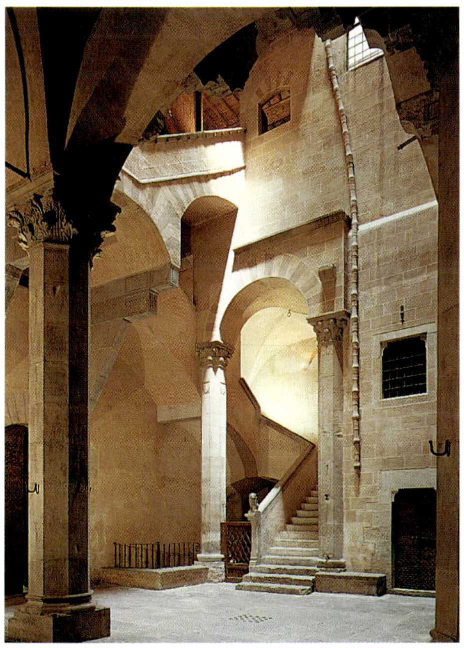

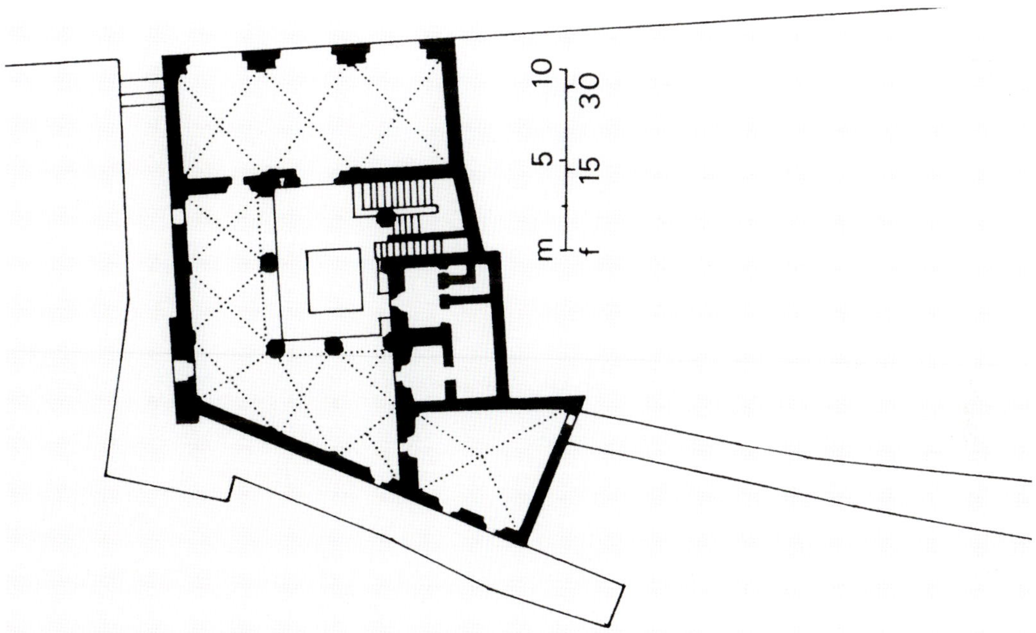

Palazzo Typology in the Quattrocento

"I think I have given myself more honour, and my soul more satisfaction, by having spent money than by having earned it, above all, with regard to the building I have done." **Giovanni Rucellai** [6]

The mature palace of the mercantile bourgeoisie, the wealthy, thriving merchant class, is the predominant building typology of quattrocento Florence. The scale and sheer size of some of these palaces represented a completely new order of magnitude when compared with even the most imposing of the older generation of palazzi; they reflected, in the clearest possible manner, the power, prestige, and political preeminence of this class. The majority were constructed on the last remaining sizeable plots within the penultimate ring of city walls, in the districts immediately surrounding the grid of streets of the original city center. These locations are highly significant; the Medici, Rucellai, and the rest built their impressive new palazzi just beyond the dense, congested heart of the city, some distance away, that is, from their own banks and businesses. The banks still remained clustered in the immediate environs of the noisy, crowded Mercato Nuovo, but the Strozzi and others were now to receive their clients and other notable visitors not at the banks

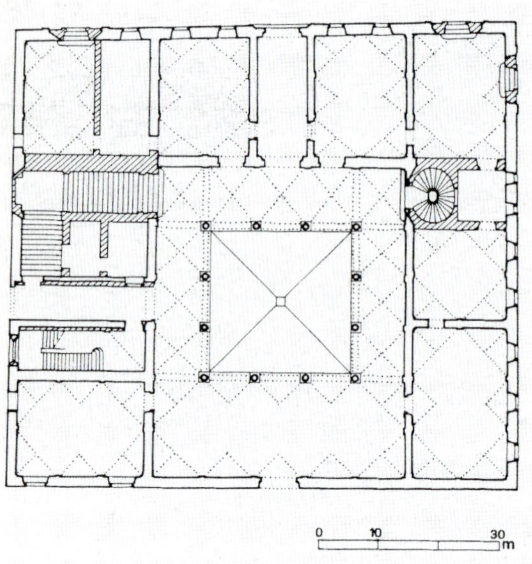

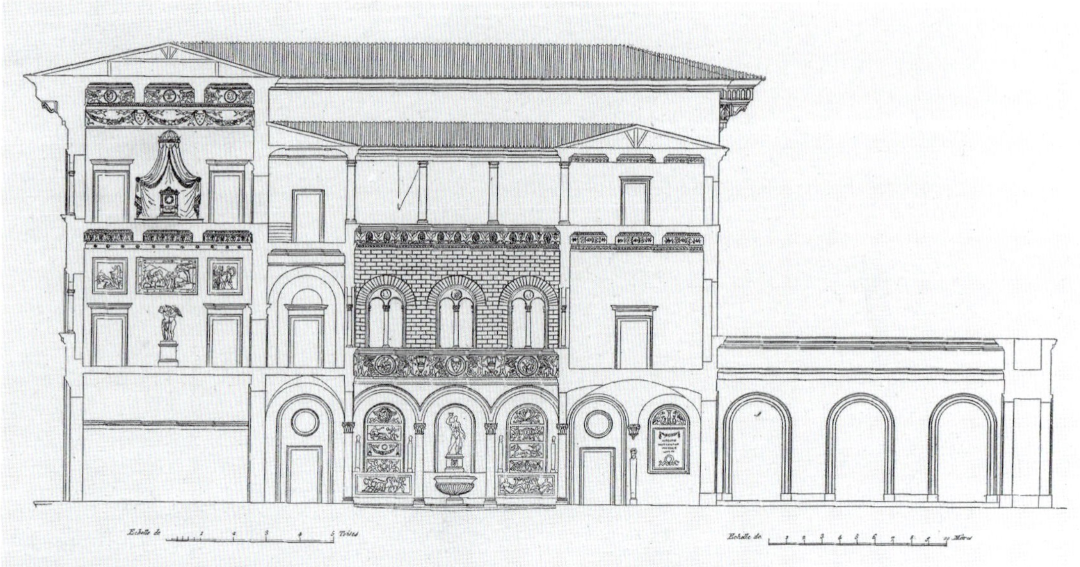

PALAZZO MEDICI RICCARDI

Above: plan by Grandjean de Montigny, 1806–15. Michelozzo's original house lacked the northern wing, which was added in 1685 by Foggini for the Riccardi. Above, right: section through the *cortile*, also by Montigny. Right: exterior by Michelozzo, 1444–69. The building established a new scale and architectural vocabulary for the mature Renaissance palace that was to be followed by other patrons such as Luca Pitti and Filippo Strozzi. The open loggia on the corner was later filled in by Michelangelo, who added the two "Roman" windows.

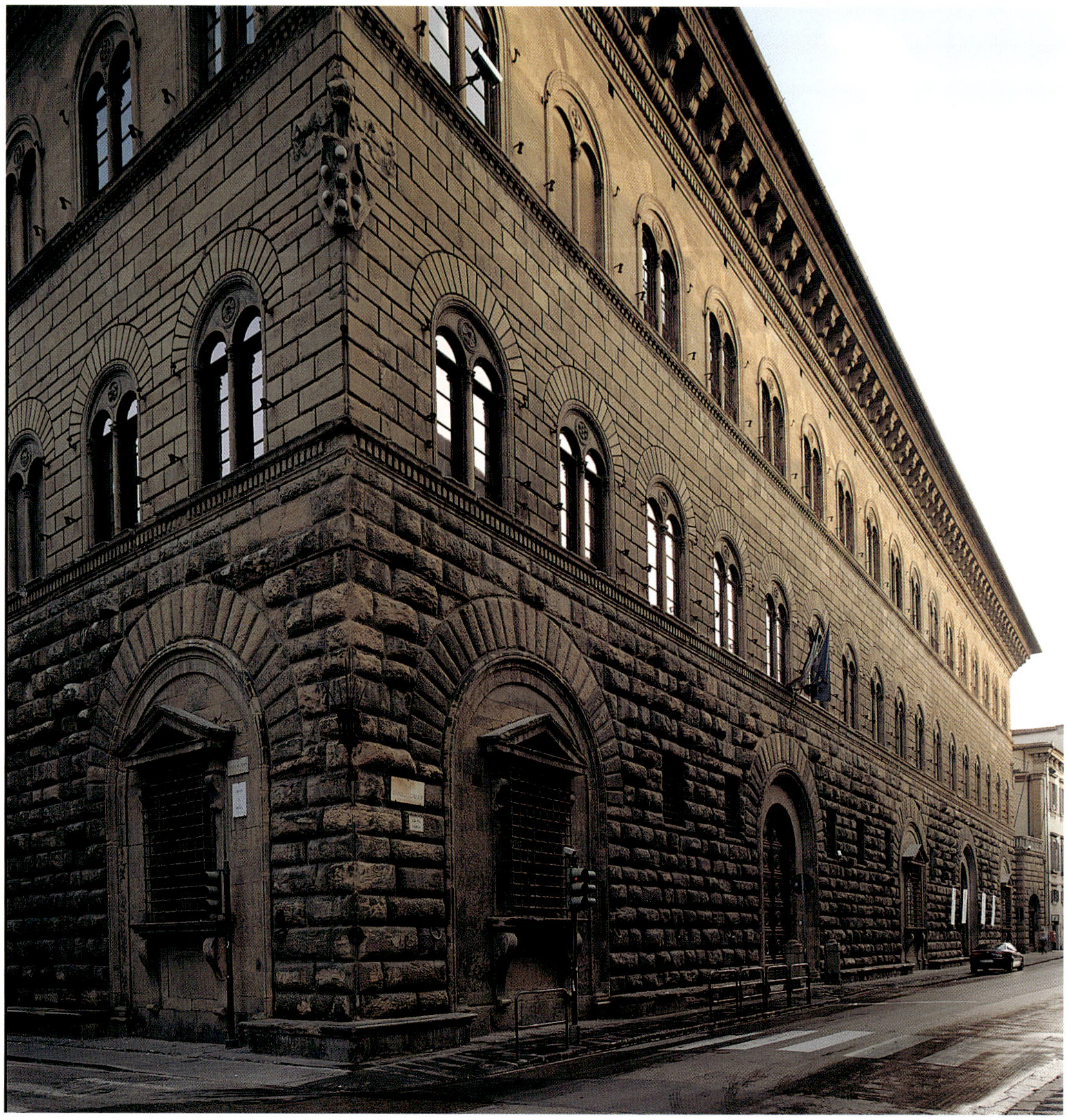

themselves, but in the elegant, secluded *cortili* of their impressive new palaces. This new "bipolarity" has been identified by some as the very first separation of functions that characterized the development of almost all Western cities in the centuries that followed, as the business core of the city slowly became more and more exclusively devoted to trade, banking, and commerce, while the magnates themselves resided farther away from the city center. While it would be an exaggeration to describe the short walk, or carriage ride, from Palazzo Rucellai to the Mercato Nuovo as "commuting," nevertheless, the separation of functions is significant.

Many of the palaces themselves, too, radically altered the scale and fabric of the city. Instead of being embedded within this fabric, as many of the earlier semifortified palaces — such as Palazzo Davanzati — had been, they now often formed large, monolithic structures, sometimes occupying an entire city block; four-square, self-contained, essentially introverted, while at the same time their powerfully imposing, daunting facades presented the external image that they wished to convey to the rest of the world. The building of these edifices was made possible only by the accumulation of enormous wealth, and by the often painstaking acquisition of many small parcels of land to achieve a plot of sufficient size on which to erect these monuments to wealth and power.

As is almost always the case in the development and refinement of a completely new building typology in the city, a phase of transition preceded the mature stage of these great palaces, a time during which not only were late Gothic forms supplanted by the new language of the Renaissance, but the typology itself was still being developed. Such an early transitional example is Palazzo Bardi, built around 1410 and traditionally ascribed to the young Brunelleschi. Already apparent here is the focal importance of the internal *cortile*, itself stylistically something of a compromise between the Gothic and the new language, but with an elegant colonnade supported by proto-Corinthian columns.[7] A slightly later example is Palazzo Capponi da Uzzano, which was built in 1427 for Niccolò da Uzzano, a patron and personal friend of Donatello. The palazzo is ascribed to Lorenzo di Bicci, and although the facade is something of a hybrid, with two roughly rusticated lower orders surmounted by flat, squared ashlar, the internal *cortile* clearly represents the tendency toward refinement and elegance that became such a prominent feature of the next generation of palaces. It is often suggested that Donatello himself also contributed to the design of the palazzo, particularly since the heraldic lion on the main stair bears a resemblance to Donatello's lions on the tomb of Pope Giovanni XXIII.

The most outstanding of the next-generation palaces are undoubtedly those of the Medici, Pitti, Rucellai, and Strozzi, to which one must add a second group that includes the Strozzino, Pazzi, Antinori, Gondi, and a number of others. Given that even this second group contains such outstanding and noble edifices, one can perhaps begin to appreciate the real scale and monumental grandeur of the palaces of the first group.

In 1444 Michelozzo was commissioned by Cosimo de' Medici to design the new family headquarters in the Via Larga (the present Via Cavour). In many senses the project was to have a profound effect on the future development of the city. While the site of the new palace reinforced the family's close links with San Lorenzo, which is only about 325 feet (100 meters) away, it also established the precedent of the new noble palace built quite separately and distinctly apart from the family's place of business. Via Larga was then on the very edge of the built-up part of the city center, one clear advantage of which was the availability of a large, prominent piece of land. The site itself not only stood at the junction of the Via Larga and the important cross-axis toward San Lorenzo composed of the Via de' Pucci and Via dei Gori, it was also on the route toward San Marco farther north, that other vital hub of Medici patronage. In addition, this location addressed the city center directly, since its southeastern corner is connected by a direct line of sight to the baptistery of San Giovanni, the city's old spiritual heart. It is no coincidence that the Medici family arms are so prominently displayed on this corner of the palazzo, in this key symbolic location.[8]

Laden with symbolism, therefore, the location demanded a powerful architectural statement, one that Michelozzo most certainly provided. The palace derives from the medieval tradition in that the entire block is built around a central internal *cortile*, and is surrounded by four ranges of accommodation. But the external image of the palace was quite unlike any ever seen in the city before: simple, powerful, and repetitive. The external facades consist of graduated orders, the first of which is defined by huge, rough, rusticated blocks of stone of a quite unprecedented size and scale; these massive elements testified to the power and wealth of the Medici dynasty. This was building on a Roman scale, with a confidence that was intended to echo through the centuries, and that made even its most substantial predecessors appear almost transitory by comparison.

The principal facade on the Via Larga was originally only ten bays long, with three giant orders, and with the rustication carefully gradated toward the huge, ponderous cornice — whose monumental scale was again unprecedented in Florence — that crowns the whole composition. (The additional seven bays on Via Larga were added by the Riccardi in 1659.) The fenestration of the two upper stories is regular, rhythmic, and restrained, all composed of the repetition of a single element, a two-light window with a semicircular head. The detailing of the ground story, though, is far more massive, with much larger arches alternating with small square, heavily barred, cell-like windows. The larger arches define the central entrance bay and two of the flanking bays, although it is important to note that the two arches on the prominent southeast corner toward the baptistery were originally open, forming a covered loggia in the characteristic Florentine manner. This original arrangement thus provided a degree of spatial relief at this all-important junction, a direct continuation of a strong Florentine tradition, that provided the only acknowledgment of the palazzo's relationship with the broader urban texture. The corner loggia was later filled in by Michelangelo in 1517, when two classical windows were set into the now-blind arches.

Internally, the entire palace was focused on the square central *cortile*, with its strong but elegant ground-floor colonnade. Here, too, was originally a three-part graduation of these courtyard facades: an open colonnade at ground-floor level, a solid wall to the first *piano nobile*, in which were set the same two-light windows as those on the facades, and a colonnaded loggia on the second floor, which was also later filled in. The design of the *cortile*, surrounded by a characteristically refined Michelozzian Corinthian colonnade, itself became something of a prototype for the quattrocento Florentine palace interior, an oasis of refined tranquility set apart from the noisy, often dangerous city beyond, a layman's interpretation of the monastic cloister. The whole ensemble was crowned by an open colonnaded loggia in which to take the air on warm summer evenings, while the sgraffito decoration to the upper level seems to reinforce the sense of detachment and artificiality. All of the principal upper apartments as well as the chapel (later to be memorably decorated by Benozzo Gozzoli) were reached from the *cortile*, thus rendering the palazzo virtually a self-contained, self-sufficient world apart.

A very similar approach was followed at the almost exactly contemporary Palazzo dello Strozzino, which is also attributed to Michelozzo, largely on the basis of the facade design. The graduated treatment of the rustication is very similar indeed, as are the two-light windows in the upper stories. Although the palace was probably designed by Michelozzo, the upper story was completed by Giuliano da Sangallo in the later 1460s.

With Cosimo's new palazzo Michelozzo had established a new standard, a new image, above all, a new sense of scale, to which the wealthy Florentine could now aspire — a precedent that was indeed to be challenged, albeit by only a handful, in the following decades. Because it was, at the simplest level, a statement of wealth and power, there were certainly a few in the city with sufficient

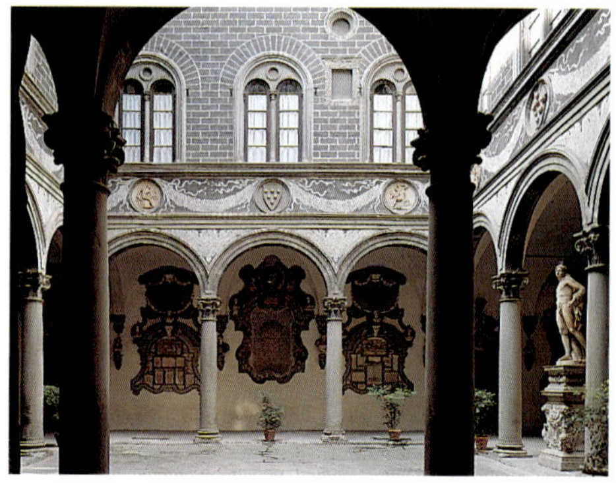

PALAZZO MEDICI RICCARDI (above)

In sharp contrast to the powerfully rusticated exterior, the *cortile* epitomizes the calm and serenity of the intellectual Renaissance, an oasis of tranquility from the pressures (and dangers) of life in the city beyond.

CHAPEL, PALAZZO MEDICI RICCARDI (opposite)

Detail of the famous cycle of frescoes by Benozzo Gozzoli, depicting the Medici.

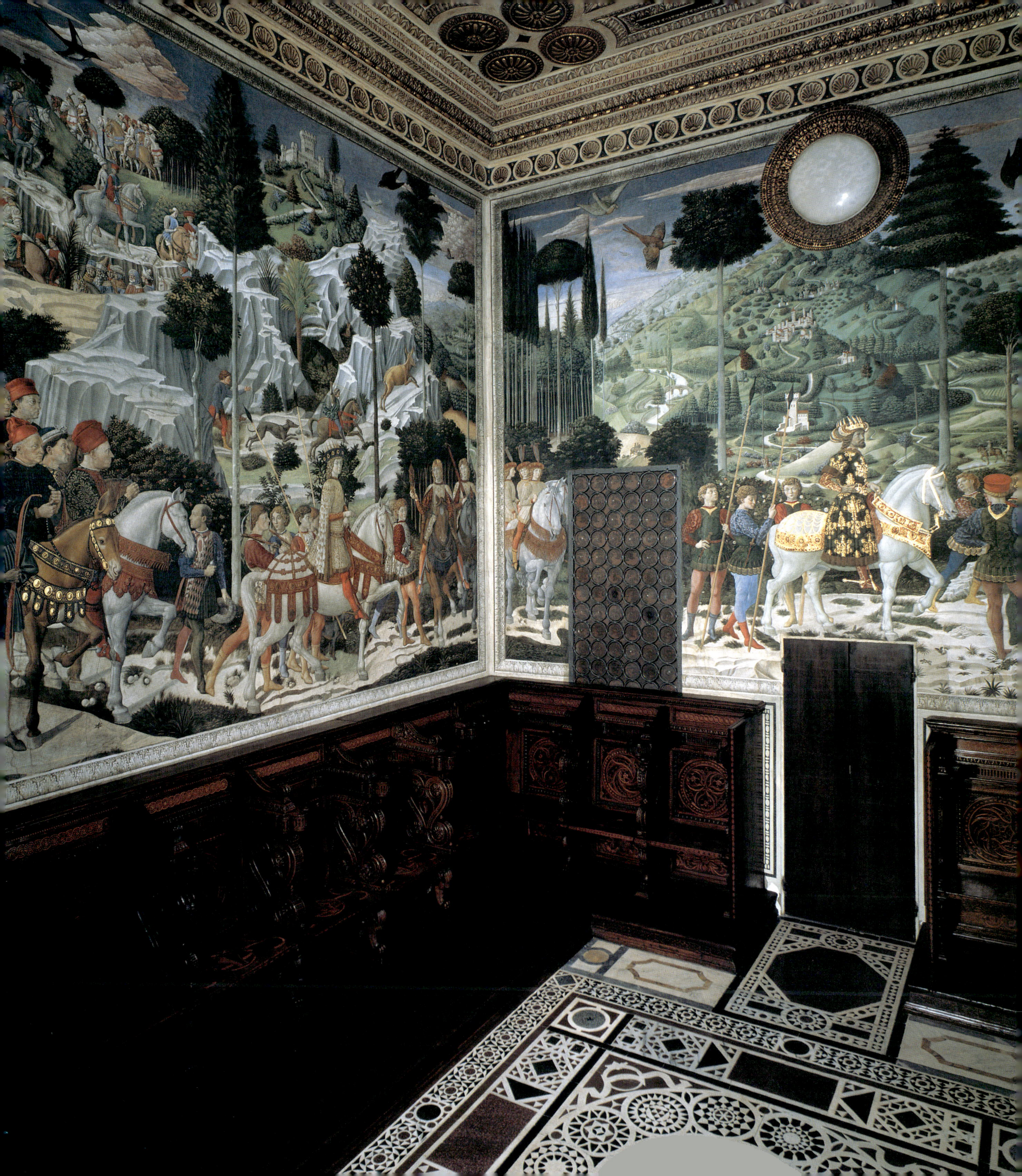

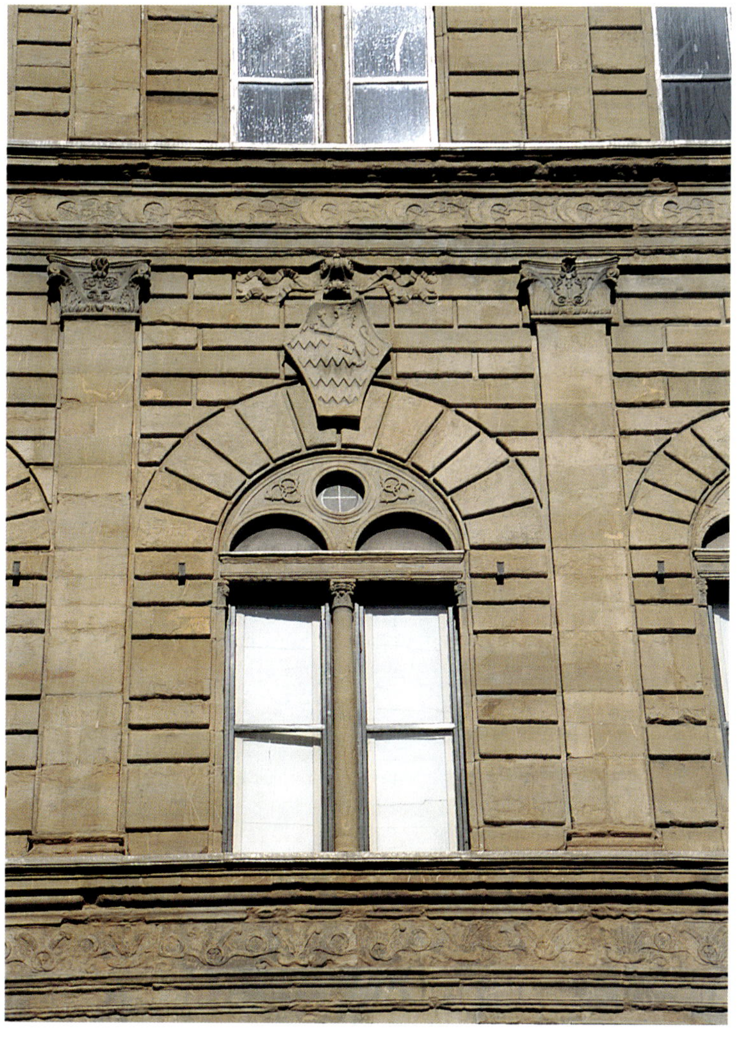

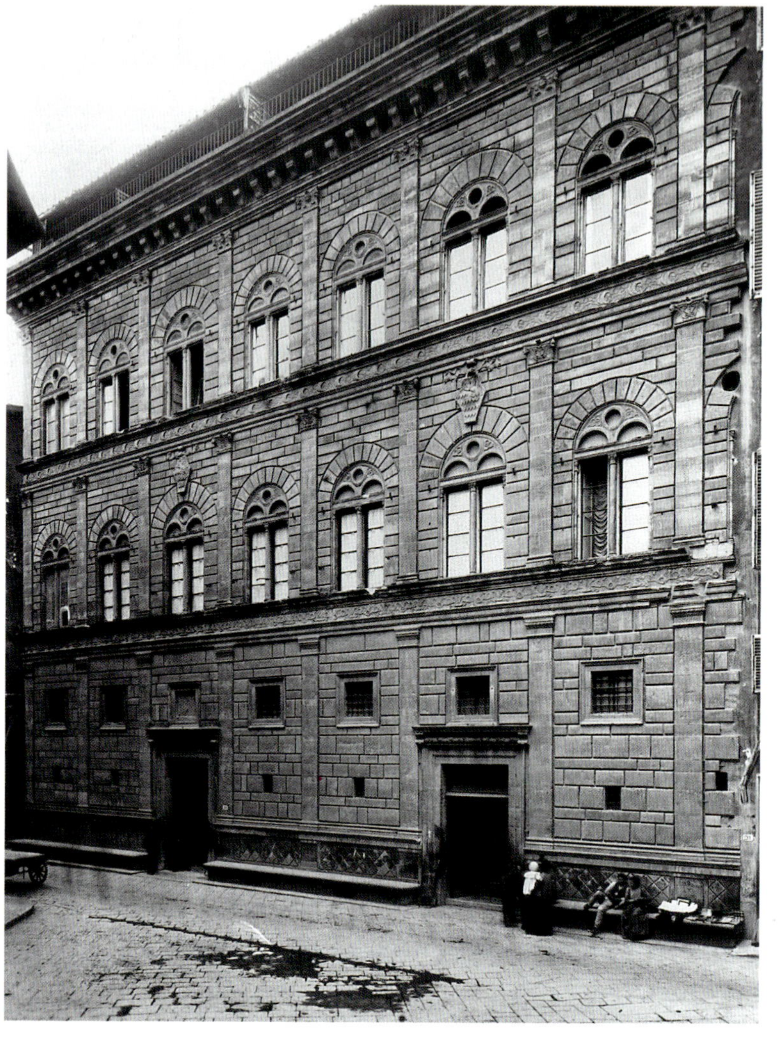

PALAZZO RUCELLAI

Above: facade detail. The motif of the sailing ship (which can also be seen on the frieze of the facade at Santa Maria Novella) is the family symbol of the Rucellai. Above, right: Alberti's facade is an exercise in the application of mathematical proportions, and its refined, shallow, more elaborate detailing contrasts strongly with the images of power epitomized by the facades of the Medici and Strozzi palaces. Right: Alberti's plan, 1446–51. The palace's construction required the acquisition of several smaller properties, hence the awkward-shaped plan, unified by the refined facade.

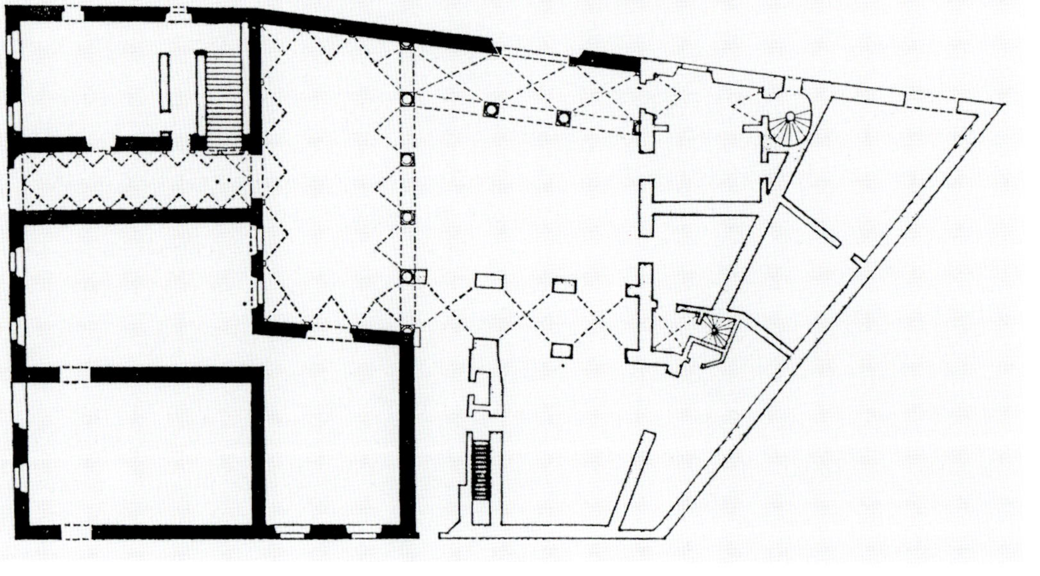

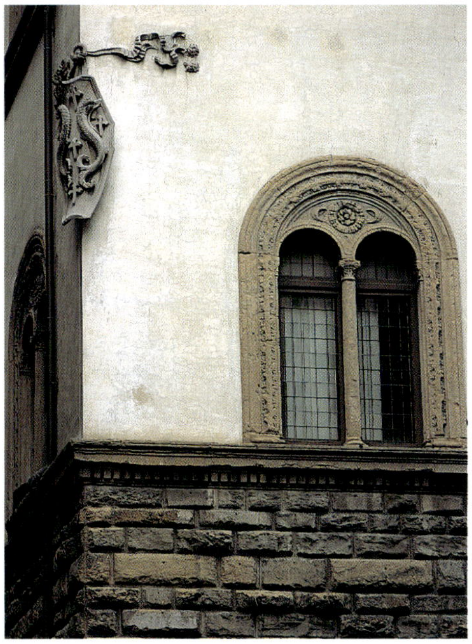

PALAZZO PAZZI

Detail of exterior usually attributed to Giuliano da Maiano, 1458–69. The detailing is more restrained than that on the Medici palace, and the site, on the narrow Via del Proconsolo, is less prominent. The family arms depict dolphins and the sacred flame brought back to Florence from the Holy Land.

motivation to challenge this palatial preeminence, as much to reflect their own perceived position and ambitions in the political sphere as to represent their patronage of the mother of all the arts. Among these few were the Rucellai, Pazzi, Strozzi, and Pitti.

While Michelozzo remained the Medici's principal architect, Alberti had established a similar relationship with the Rucellai, whose zone of patronage in the city lay a little farther west, around Santa Maria Novella and the family's parish church of San Pancrazio. When Alberti was asked to remodel their palazzo, his approach was radically different from that of Michelozzo; here there was no hint of development from the powerfully fortified, traditional Florentine palace.[9] Alberti's new facade for Giovanni Rucellai is an open, intellectual exercise in the application of Vitruvian principles; there are no overwhelming rustications, but instead the facade is essentially treated as a screen, with flat, subtly modulated stone coursing, and with three correctly superimposed classical orders: Doric, Ionic, and Corinthian pilasters are here set together with friezes and cornices to form a regular framework of articulation. This was the first time in Florence that the three orders had been applied in this truly classical manner.

The building was probably designed by Alberti in around 1450, but construction took place in two distinct phases, probably under the supervision of Bernardo Rossellino: The first stage, from 1455 to 1458 (or perhaps a little earlier), was followed by a second, from 1465 to 1470. Giovanni Rucellai's original ambition was for a facade of eight or even nine bays, and the seven executed bays remain unfinished on the right side of the facade to this day. An initial proposal from Alberti seems to have been based on only five bays, with a single portal in the center, and Rucellai had had to acquire a number of adjacent properties in order to increase the plot available to him. The later eastward expansion of the seven bays that we see today included the incorporation of a second doorway, which increased the horizontal proportions, in comparison to the original five-bay facade, which was almost square. The facade unified the rather disparate structures behind it, some of which were preexisting and were in part retained, and, like all of Alberti's facades, was based on the precise application of rules of ratio and proportion. The immediate influence of the work is clearly visible in the slightly later oeuvre of Bernardo Rossellino, notably at the Palazzo Piccolomini of 1461 at Pienza, where he employed an almost identical vocabulary of flat rustication, a grid of pilasters, broad, square portals, and two-light windows.[10]

Directly opposite the facade of the palazzo, the tall, three-bay loggia was built for the same Giovanni Rucellai; the loggia, which dominates the diminutive triangular piazzetta, was built from 1463 to 1466, in a rather more robustly classical form than the refined, carefully planned palazzo. The loggia is a sober, restrained work about which almost nothing is known. In principle, its existence reflects some of Alberti's own precepts regarding the development of urban sites and the importance of public meeting places, and it was used partly as a kind of covered market to display some of the family's own products; however, it is difficult to establish the degree of Alberti's involvement in either its design or execution.[11]

The Later Quattrocento Palazzo

The 1450s and 1460s saw considerable building activity in the city on the part of the wealthy merchants and bankers. No projects, though, were laden with more political significance than those of the Medici and Pazzi, whose bitter political rivalry reached its bloody climax in the 1478 Pazzi conspiracy in which Giuliano de' Medici, Lorenzo's brother, was assassinated in the cathedral.

The imposing new palace built by the Pazzi was begun later than that of the Medici, after 1458 (perhaps in 1462), and was completed around 1470; it was thus begun a full generation before the rivalry between the two clans erupted in the famous rebellion. Although the architect for the Pazzi palace has not been conclusively identified (Brunelleschi's name has sometimes been suggested), the general consensus today attributes the palazzo to Giuliano da Maiano.[12] The site in the Via del

Proconsolo is closer to the city center, but it is considerably less prominent than that of the Medici, since the street is narrow, and the all-important facade can be seen only from a fairly acute angle; for this reason, the ground story is boldly rusticated, while the two upper stories are both simply detailed with the now familiar two-light windows, here set into narrow stone frames, and with the general wall surfaces completely plain. The refined internal *cortile* is colonnaded on three sides, with heraldic dolphins, symbol of the Pazzi, ingeniously incorporated into the capitals. Also incorporated was a vase, another old symbol of the Pazzi, representative of the sacred flame that Pazzino de' Pazzi had reportedly brought back from the First Crusade to the Holy Land. After the 1478 conspiracy the palazzo was confiscated by Lorenzo de' Medici and kept during the continuing vendetta between the two clans in the years that followed.

As can be inferred from the examples of the Pazzi and Medici, there was considerable variety in the manner in which the design of the palace facade was approached in this period. Palazzo Pazzi is an example of the approach that incorporated the use of substantial areas of plain plastered wall surface, which was sometimes decorated with fresco or sgraffito. The application of sgraffito decoration was becoming more widespread. The first Renaissance example can be seen in the *cortile* of the Medici palace, and the technique, first used in the trecento, experienced a considerable revival in the later quattrocento. Unfortunately, of course, sgraffito and fresco are both inherently a good deal less permanent than heavily rusticated stonework, and many examples are now lost. Of those that have survived, many are confined to the inner facades of *cortili* rather than the street facades. The other principal line of development was that of the all-stone facade, but with a variety of treatments for the various orders. Probably the finest example of the highly disciplined ashlar facade is that of Palazzo Antinori; it was first built for the Boni family, although the Antinori, who were originally bankers and silk weavers from Lucca, acquired the palace in 1506 and still own the house today. With its precisely defined stone coursing, its refined, severely minimal detailing, the palace seems to combine a slightly anachronistic antiquarianism with a cool humanistic rationality. It is datable to around 1465, and is usually attributed to Giuliano da Maiano.[13]

But the culmination of the rusticated, all-stone facade can be said to have been reached with the vast monumental palace built by Luca Pitti in 1458. The general history of the palace has been recounted in an earlier chapter, but it is useful here to place it stylistically in the context of the quattrocento Florentine palazzo. Pitti's motivation in beginning this imposing monument was at least as clear as that of Francesco Pazzi, who in fact began his architectural riposte to the Medici at the same period that Pitti began building works, in 1458. It is traditionally said that Pitti's intention was to build a palace so monumental that the newly completed palace of Cosimo de' Medici could be fitted within its courtyard. However, Pitti's attempted overt display of wealth proved to be a classic example of pride preceding disaster; he completed only the central seven-bay section of the new palace before his abrupt fall both from favor with the Medici and also in his financial standing. Pitti died in 1472, his personal monument well short of completion.[14] However, and although it was greatly enlarged later, even the section of the palace that was completed by Pitti exceeded in size, and in its overwhelmingly powerful rustication, any other palace yet seen in the city. The three stories, each of an equal height of 40 feet (13 meters), loomed over the piazza, which was itself raised high above the level of the ancient Via de' Guicciardini, further emphasizing its dominance. The original design of the facade has traditionally been attributed to Brunelleschi, who had famously produced a design for the Medici palazzo in the Via Larga, which had been rejected as being too grandiose and monumental; it has often been suggested that this same design (in essence, at least) was recycled and proposed to Pitti instead. But the execution of the project is rather more securely linked to Luca Fancelli, to whom Vasari had already attributed the palace as early as the 1550s.

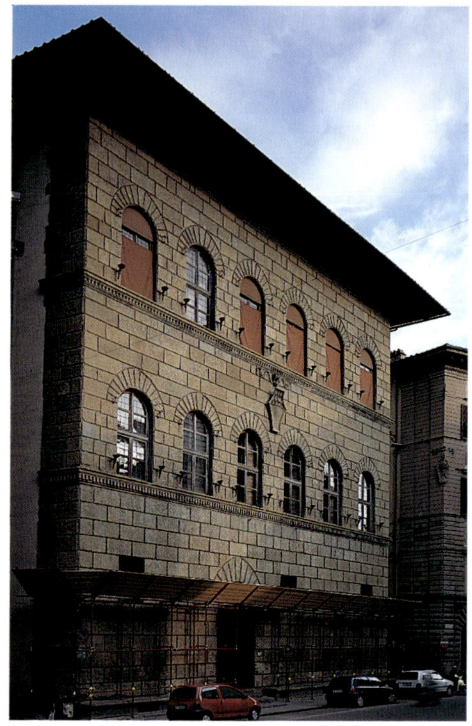

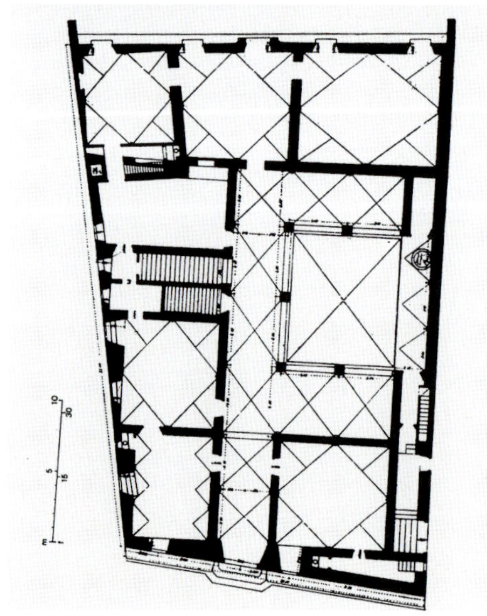

PALAZZO ANTINORI (top and above)

Top: the facade from 1461–66, attributed to Giuliano da Maiano, is a highly disciplined exercise in the arrangement of simple elements, of solids and voids. Above: the palace has a conventional Florentine plan, built around a small central *cortile*.

PALAZZO PITTI (opposite)

Detail of the facade that eventually became the largest in the city. The scale is massively imposing, and was made considerably more so by the palazzo's location on a hillside, looming over the Piazza Pitti and the road to Rome.

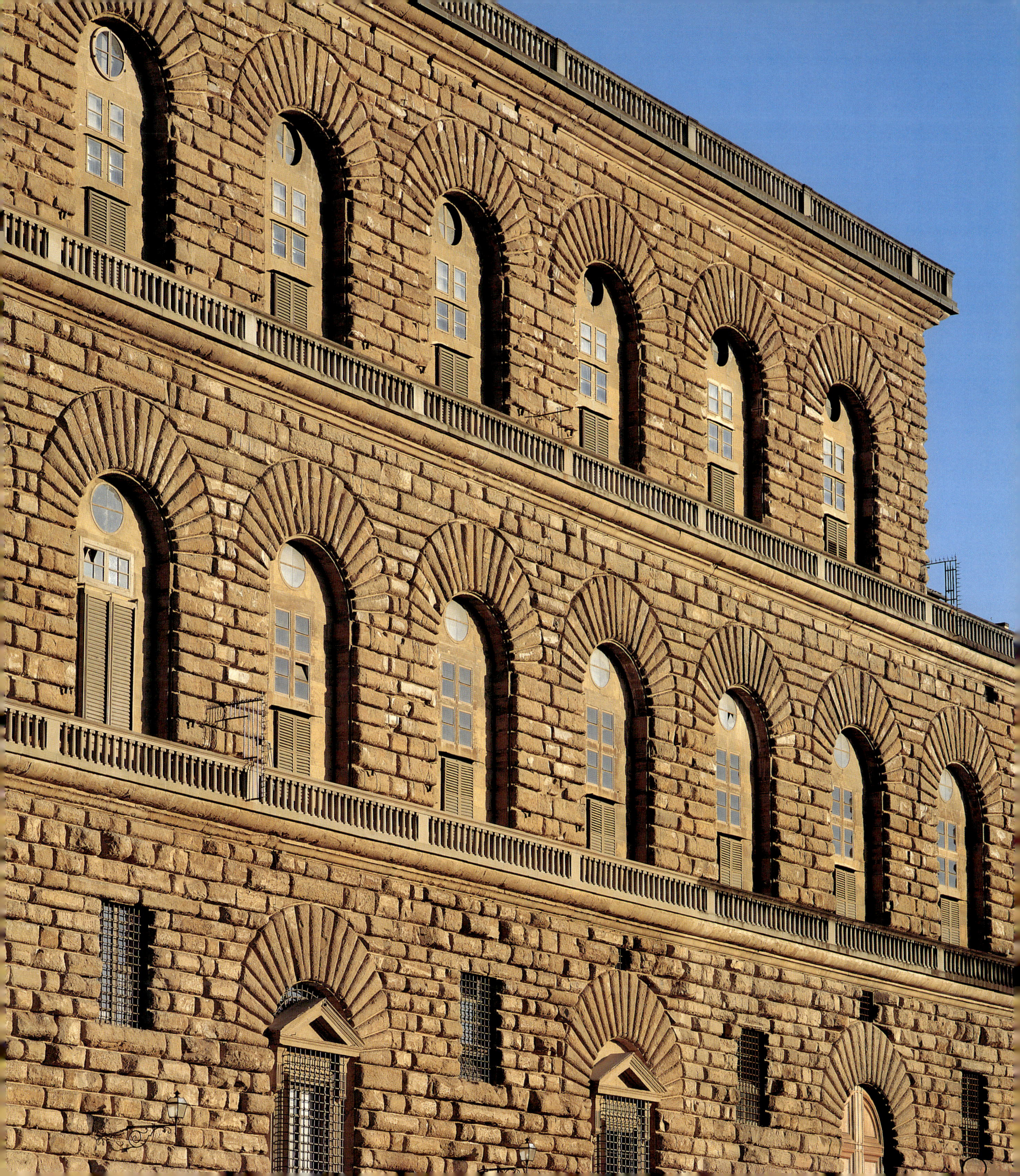

The element completed by Pitti consisted of a single chain of rooms behind the seven central bays of the monumental facade. The facade itself had a central doorway, as well as two flanking doorways later converted into windows when the palazzo was extended; the first and second floors consisted of two rows of seven identical windows. The immense rustication of the ground story is repeated, on a rather reduced scale, on the two upper stories, and is continued around the arched heads of all the door and window openings. In a sense, Palazzo Pitti marked the culmination of a certain course of development, its grandeur and Roman character seemingly unsurpassable.

Several other slightly later palazzi generally followed the guiding precepts by then long established by Michelozzo, although with a number of variable elements. In this context the work of Giuliano da Sangallo has particular significance. Sangallo had spent considerable time studying classical architecture in Rome, and when he returned to Florence in the 1470s, his first project there was probably the palazzo of Bartolomeo Scala, begun in 1472; Scala was *cancelliere* of the Republic and a notable humanist scholar. Although it was considerably altered in the eighteenth century, the palazzo evinces significant Roman influence in its layout. It was planned not around a central *cortile* but was preceded by a peristyle with a facade facing the private garden; the colonnade of this peristyle was decorated by twelve relief panels that are also the work of Sangallo. His later Palazzo Gondi shows a further stage of refinement of a facade that arguably forms a more representative example of the rusticated ashlar tradition. Palazzo Gondi, from about 1490, has an all-stone facade divided into three equal orders, each of which is faced with stone of a different gradation. The ground floor, for example, is clad with bold, cushion-shaped rustication, while the *piano nobile* is faced with squared ashlar with prominent coursing, and the top story is finished with smooth ashlar and minimal jointing; the whole exercise is capped by a monumental cornice. Palazzo Gondi, like many others, was built in stages, and the original section probably had twin entrance portals, rather than the present three, somewhat like Alberti's Palazzo Rucellai.[15]

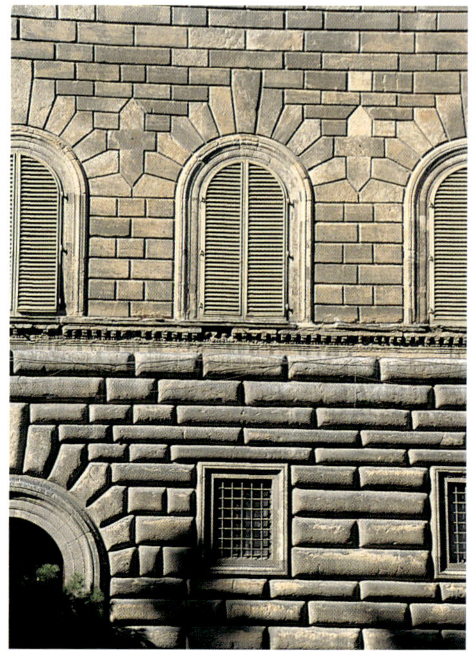

PALAZZO GONDI

Detail of the facade by Giuliano da Sangallo. The graduated rustication echoes that of Palazzo Strozzi, with which it is almost exactly contemporaneous.

The alternative approach to that based on massive rustication and ashlar was the facade on which only certain key elements were singled out for robust stone treatment, while the upper orders were generally finished with smooth plaster. This less ostentatious path is represented in the same period by Palazzo Corsi, later Horne, attributed to Cronaca, in which the rusticated stonework is confined to the surrounds of the main portal, the windows, and the quoins, the general wall surfaces being left unadorned. In this alternative approach the robust, more restrained tradition of the medieval legacy is discernable, a tradition that in a sense also mirrors more closely the archetypal Florentine aesthetic characteristics of close, precise detailing, of clarity and restraint. A very similar aesthetic approach can also be seen in another palazzo often attributed to Cronaca, Palazzo Dei, later Guadagni, in the Piazza Santo Spirito, built in the very first years of the new century, and whose severely reticent facade is relieved only by the spacious top-floor loggia that runs across the full width of the facade.

Finally, in this brief survey of the later quattrocento palaces, we come to the building that exemplifies the perfection of one of these particular traditions or lines of development: Palazzo Strozzi. The Strozzi clan had been allowed to return to Florence in 1460 after their exile, and their vast new palace was begun by Filippo Strozzi in 1489. The original design is attributed to Sangallo, who also made the wooden model that still exists today; the execution of the work, though, was largely supervised by Benedetto da Maiano (up to the level of the first-floor capitals) and then by Cronaca, until the completion of the structure in about 1498.[16]

Palazzo Strozzi marks the perfection of the great Florentine city palace as a vast, three-dimensional artifact. It is the only one of all of the great palaces that was designed from the outset to be effectively freestanding, since it occupies an entire city block, with three street

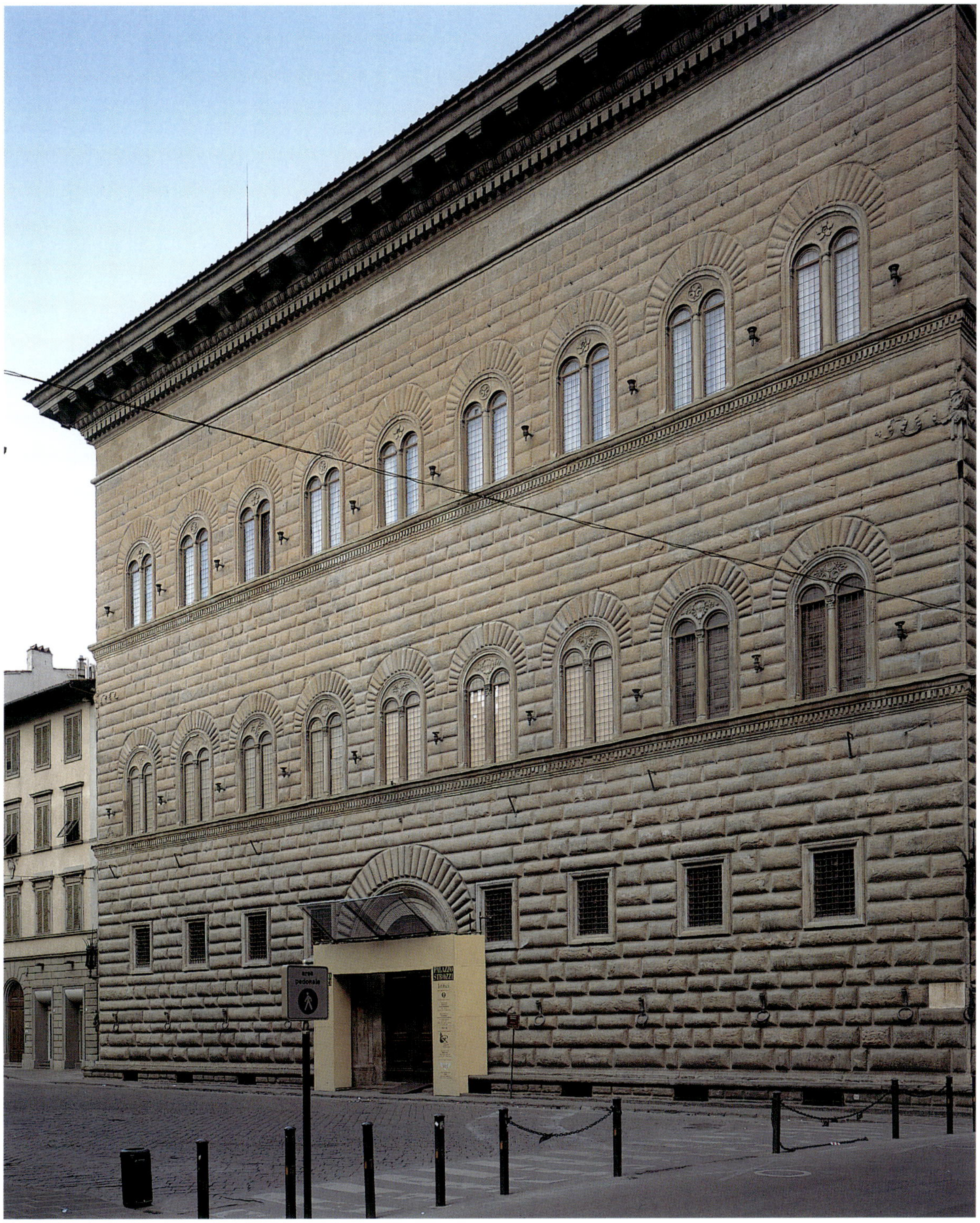

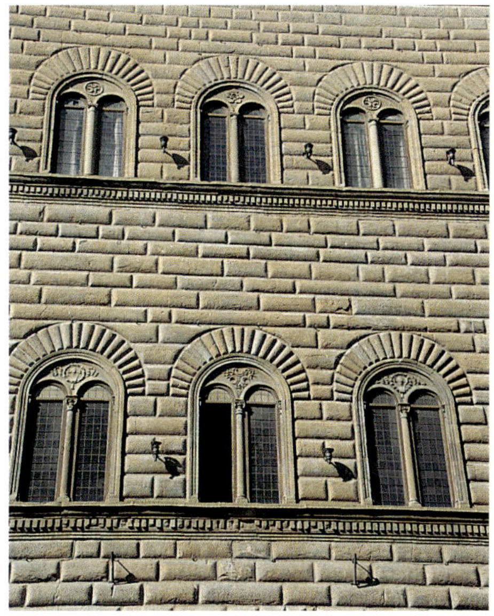

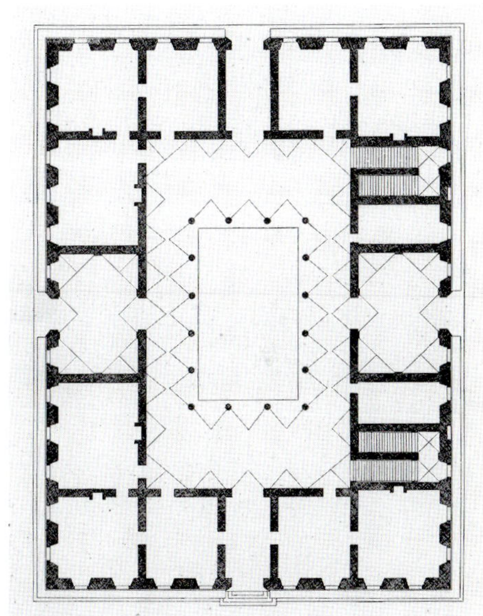

PALAZZO STROZZI

Left: east facade, begun in 1489 by Benedetto da Maiano. The palace has the most rigorously disciplined layout and appearance of any in the city. It was completed by Cronaca in about 1502. Top: detail of facade. Above: the disciplined order of the palace's exterior is reflected in the logical internal plan, which contained two superimposed apartments on the upper stories.

facades of nearly equal importance. (The fourth facade, never completed, faces a very narrow lane.) Each of these principal facades is designed as a symmetrical composition, with a massive central entrance portal; on the shorter east and west facades the portal is flanked by four bays on each side, while on the longest, the north facade, which looks onto Via degli Strozzi, there are six bays on each side of the entrance portal. The cladding of these noble facades, with their three extremely high stories, is based on graduated rustication like that at Palazzo Gondi, with the ground floor faced with huge cushion blocks of stone; the first and second floors are similarly formed but progressively shallower in their modeling. The enormous surmounting cornice, a considerable technical achievement in itself, is modeled directly on classical Roman examples. All of the detailing is consistent, logical, and refined; for example, all the windows of both the first and second floors are identical, as are the solidly square openings of the ground floor. Internally, the planning is as symmetrical and rational as the facades, with a central rectangular *cortile* by Cronaca from 1503; refined and elegant, it is closely modeled on the earlier courtyard by Michelozzo for the Medici. In both palaces the two contrasting images of the Florentine Renaissance palazzo are codified in definitive form: The external image is powerful, daunting, still — if necessary — defensible, albeit extremely carefully detailed; the interior, by contrast, is light, airy, and refined, the epitome of wealthy, sophisticated city life. Construction of the palace was sufficiently advanced for it to be occupied by the Strozzi in 1504. Work then ceased until 1523, after which date there was a further brief effort, but progress halted entirely in 1538; although most of the fabric was by then concluded, the great cornice was, and remains, incomplete. Nevertheless, no other palace in Florence was to match that of the Strozzi in its restrained yet monumental grandeur.

The mature Renaissance palace, as exemplified by Palazzo Strozzi, is distinguished in several other ways from its predecessors. One of the most pronounced differences is that the entire building was used solely by the family that patronized it; gone were the shops, warehouses, and other uses that had formerly occupied almost all of the ground stories of the earlier palazzi.[17] This break with a long tradition can be seen in all of the great palazzi discussed above, in marked distinction from the earlier palaces such as the Spini Feroni and Davanzati. It represents a further polarization in patterns of use in the city; not only was the great palazzo now purely residential and detached from the owner's place of business, it was now also "monofunctional," with no residual associations with trade or commerce of any kind. In the center was the *cortile* with its well, and somewhere on an upper story there was also usually a small chapel; these palazzi were thus self-contained "islands," insulated from the city by their imposing facades.

The total number of occupants was generally surprisingly small: simply the nuclear titular family itself, together with its immediate servants. Indeed, it must be borne in mind that, with the exception of the very largest of these palaces — the Medici and the Strozzi, in particular — the number of individual rooms was not very high. The ground story was given over to various ancillary and support functions, while the principal *piano nobile* generally consisted of a single chain of perhaps half a dozen or so rooms surrounding the central *cortile*; together with the lesser second story, there were perhaps ten to fifteen principal rooms in all. A few of these houses were built with the specific intention of accommodating two closely related branches of the same family, again the Gondi, Rucellai, and Strozzi, for example, and this arrangement is reflected in the fact that there are usually two separate street portals and two *piani nobili*, one directly above the other, for the use of each branch of the clan.[18] These august dynasties did not maintain large numbers of servants; we know, for example, that Giovanni Rucellai's elegant new palace was staffed by just four men and four or five women, although the number of servants did increase in the following century. Servants were generally quartered in a couple of rooms on the top story.

Despite the comparatively small number of rooms, all of these new palaces were very much bigger than the families' previous accommodation, the result of which was that, as Goldthwaite has put it, when they were finally completed they were "rattling around in quarters with some of the largest and grandest rooms still completely empty."[19] The practical use of many of these rooms was virtually interchangeable, although their function resulted to some degree from their orientation, such that they were sometimes arranged as summer and winter apartments, orientated to avoid the stifling summer heat and to catch the elusive winter light, as appropriate. The principal *piano nobile* of Palazzo Strozzi is, in fact, designed to contain two identical but "handed" apartments linked together by logge, one on the east side and one on the west, each with an access staircase from the *cortile*. The furniture that occupied these imposing halls was generally itself fairly massive and imposing, almost architectural in scale; examples of this monumental and expressive design approach are the great *cassoni*, or chests, which formed the most usual means of storage for many goods, particularly fabrics, clothes, and bed linens.[20] Beds, tables, and chairs were similarly substantial and robust.

Many of the palaces of the subsequent generations became highly formulaic in the external face they presented to the world. Perhaps partly for this reason, increasing use was made of the attachment of a prominent family coat of arms to the facade, usually carved in stone. The arms were also often affixed to other buildings with which the clan was associated: logge, churches, hospitals. The ubiquitous *palle* of the Medici are certainly the most widespread of these arms, but many others can also be identified; we have mentioned the dolphins of the Pazzi, and there were the crossed chains of the Alberti, the "sails of fortune" of the Rucellai (visible on the facade of the family palace and on Alberti's facade at Santa Maria Novella), the crescents of the Strozzi, the rose of the Ricasoli, the pears of the Peruzzi (punning on their name), the three horns of the Guicciardini, all badges of propriety and ancient dynastic pride.

A Rural Interlude: The *Villeggiatura*

"The spot in question was some distance away from any road, on a small hill that was agreeable to behold for its abundance of shrubs and trees, all bedecked in green leaves. Perched on its summit was a palace, built round a fine, spacious courtyard, and containing loggias, halls and sleeping apartments . . . richly embellished with paintings depicting scenes of gaiety. Delectable gardens and meadows lay all around, and there were wells of cool refreshing water." **Giovanni Boccaccio**, *Decameron* (c. 1350) [21]

The great families of Florence had always had an exceptionally close relationship with the surrounding *contado*. In the medieval period, Florence's countryside had been scattered with the castles, towers, and semifortified farms of the city's leading families. Many of the most famous and wealthiest clans themselves had originated from well beyond the city's walls; the Corsini, for example, came from the Val d' Elsa, southwest of the city. And there were the Medici, who had originated in the Mugello, the valley of the river Sieve, a dozen miles or so northeast of the city, where they had long owned castles and lands, above all at Trebbio and Cafaggiolo. The Mugello lay some distance beyond Florence's *contado*, but the more immediate environs, particularly the hills of Fiesole to the north and Galluzzo and similar locations to the south, had long been favored by the citizenry for rural escape, the *villeggiatura*, particularly during the stifling heat of the Florentine summer. Boccaccio's famous storytellers, fleeing the plague in 1348, were following the well-worn paths of many earlier generations as they retreated to rural safety.

But it was in the quattrocento that a large number of Florentines began to invest on a steadily increasing scale in rural land, developing these estates for produce while at the same time making more extensive use of the villas and their surrounding lands for the *villeggiatura*, or vacation. In many cases these newer developments evolved around a preexisting nucleus, often in the form of a

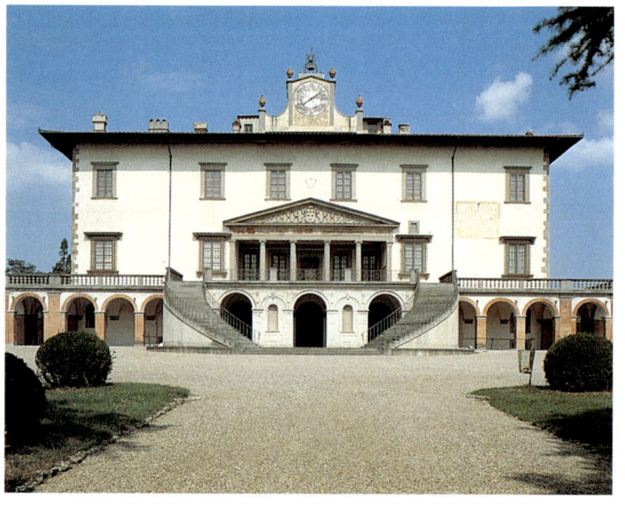

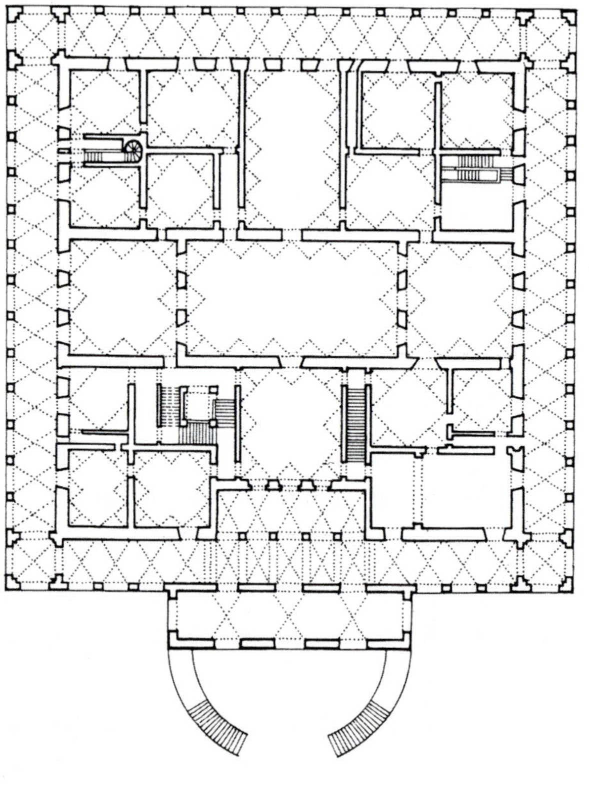

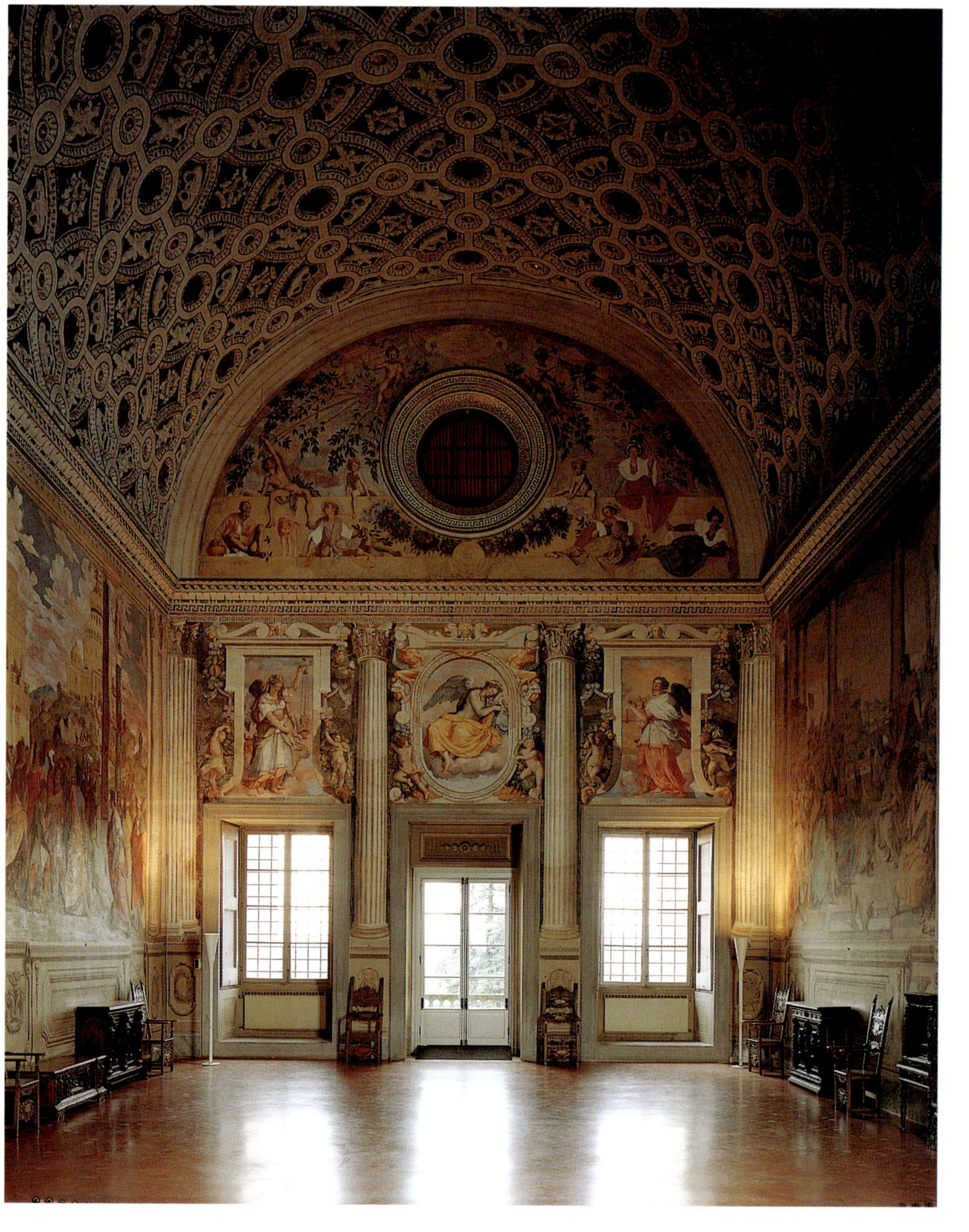

VILLA MEDICI AT POGGIO A CAIANO

Opposite, left top: the principal facade dates from after 1480, it has a classical portico and is carefully integrated with the surrounding gardens. Opposite, left bottom: plan. The concept of the villa, its symmetrical planning, and its relationship with the surrounding landscape all marked a revolutionary approach to the design of country villas for the nobility. Opposite right: interior of the central *salone*, the hub of the house, decorated with wall frescoes by Andrea del Sarto and Jacopo da Pontormo.

semifortified farmhouse or villa. Although there were naturally many others, the country properties of the Medici (which at their maximum totaled some fourteen in all) epitomized the genre and provide a valuable series of "case studies" of the manner in which these rural or semirural holdings were developed over time. Alberti stated the key principles for designing a country villa in his famous treatise: "We should build in the Middle of an open Champian [*sic*], under the shelter of some Hill, where there is plenty of Water and pleasant Prospects, and in the healthiest part of a healthy Country."[22]

Cosimo de' Medici's architect, Michelozzo, played an important role in this modernization of the rural farmhouse-villa. It was Michelozzo who was first appointed to modernize the family property at Careggi, only a couple of miles north of the city walls, and then to effect similar works at Cafaggiolo and il Trebbio, both long-established fortified farmhouses in the Mugello. The true *case di delizie* (literally, "houses of delights," places for rest, conversation, fine wines, hunting, and other pleasant rural activities) developed a little later, but these first efforts at modernization were essentially transitional in character, function, and appearance, since they were constrained by the existing fabric, much of which bore (and still bears) clear evidence of its quasi-defensive origins.

The works Michelozzo undertook at the two Mugello estates were essentially compromises, Cafaggiolo in particular still looking much more like a castle than a villa even after its modernization, with two crenellated towers and extensive machicolation. Nevertheless, according to Giusto Utens's famous illustration, the immediate surroundings of the villa of Cafaggiolo were certainly "tamed," with terraces, parterres, and a degree of man-made alterations to the surrounding lands, at least as far as the natural wooded hillsides.[23] At the more modest Trebbio, the overall impression is still that of a fortified farmhouse, albeit one that was now rather better appointed inside.

The estate at Careggi is particularly significant, though, since it had been acquired by Cosimo Il Vecchio in 1417, and thus did not form part of the old traditional Medici estates. Forty years later, in 1457, it was modernized by Michelozzo; while retaining the prominent battlements, the architect transformed the defensive walkway along the top into a covered promenade, a clear indication of less insecure times. More significantly, the plan was extended to form a U, with two new wings built toward the garden, thus creating a direct spatial dialogue between the house itself and the natural, or seminatural, world beyond. Despite its perhaps inevitably still rather compromised appearance, Careggi became the most favored of all the Medici *case di delizie*; Lorenzo founded his Platonic Academy there, and further developed the gardens.[24] The villa was sacked and badly damaged after the rout of the dynasty in 1527 and in the siege of 1529, however, but was later restored by Alessandro de' Medici. But Careggi is essentially still a transitional work, before the construction, *ex novo*, of the true *casa di delizie*.

The villa sponsored by Lorenzo Il Magnifico at Poggio a Caiano fulfilled this pivotal role. Lorenzo had bought a property belonging to the Rucellai in 1473, and later announced a competition for the design of a new villa, which was won in 1480 by Sangallo; Sangallo's design was to be extremely influential, setting a standard for the many such villas that were to follow. The site lay in the plain to the west of the city; the plan is compact and symmetrical, in the form of an H, with the two side wings connected by a large, spacious central hall crowned by a noble, barrel-vaulted ceiling. The principal story is raised above ground level, and stands on a colonnaded basement, which itself contains most of the necessary ancillary accommodation; this *piano nobile* is also surrounded by a spacious terrace on all sides, reached by an imposing external double staircase. This ingenious arrangement provided the necessary height to achieve a prospect from the *piano nobile* over the rather flat surroundings, while the terrace formed a link, a transitional zone between the villa itself and the landscaped gardens beyond. Another highly original element was the main entrance, signaled by the large, classical, pedimented portico, behind which an Ionic loggia leads into a vestibule and thence into the central *salone*. All these features reveal the work of a highly creative, original master.[25] Among the many famous later architects who drew on the design principles of the Medici villa at Poggio a Caiano, Andrea Palladio is undoubtedly the most outstanding; in the late cinquecento, Palladio developed the Renaissance country villa still further, with a series of remarkable examples built in the Veneto for the Venetian and Vicentine nobility. Construction of the villa paused with the death of Lorenzo but was recommenced in the early 1500s, when the gardens, stables, and outbuildings were developed. These last reflect the status of Poggio as a working farm, but they were set a discreet distance away from the house itself. In the same period, the internal decorations of the central *salone* were further elaborated, chiefly by Andrea del Sarto and Jacopo da Pontormo.

Poggio is thus a key work in several respects: It is purely a villa, with no residual defensive features in its design; the plan and the facades are carefully designed as an integrated whole, with the emphasis on symmetry, clarity, and logic in both planning and appearance; and the villa was fully integrated with its context, its physical surroundings, the prospects outward from the four terraces being as carefully considered as the internal plan of the house itself. The villa at Poggio was to prove an extremely influential new typology.[26]

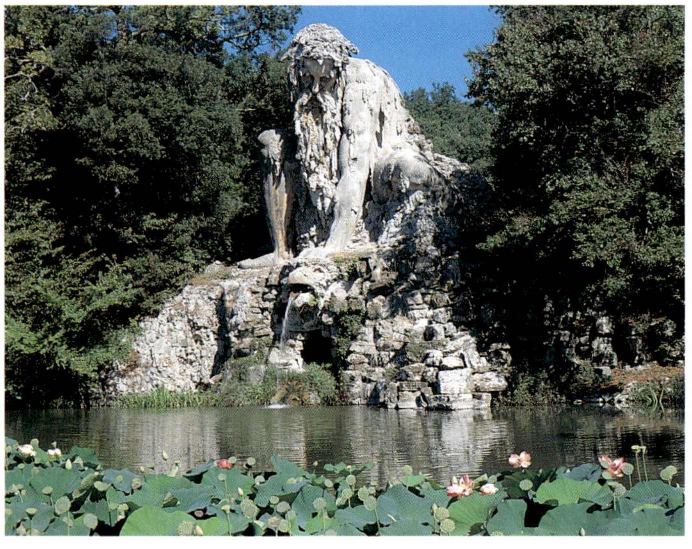

GIAMBOLOGNA, *FONTANA DELL'APPENNINO* (left)

Giambologna's extraordinary massive figure survives in the Parco Demidoff, formerly the Medici villa at Pratolino.

GIUSTO UTENS, *VILLA MEDICI, LA PETRAIA*, C. 1599 (opposite, top)

The villa was reconstructed by Buontalenti after 1594. It was surrounded by regularly planned herb gardens and terraced orchards.

GIUSTO UTENS, *VILLA MEDICI AT PRATOLINO*, C. 1599 (opposite, bottom)

An invaluable record of Buontalenti's lost villa, which was demolished in 1824, although much of the extensive surrounding parkland has survived as the Parco Demidoff.

The large villa at Castello, on a low hill northwest of the city and not far from Careggi, was the next Medici rural property to be modernized. It had been bought in 1477, but it was not until 1540, under Cosimo I, that a series of works to both the house and its estate were begun. Tribolo (Niccolò Pericoli), Cosimo's architect, was faced here with an existing structure that essentially was retained but refaced, resulting in a very long, symmetrical facade of eleven bays, with a powerful rusticated central doorway added by Buontalenti in about 1592. The villa was large and luxuriously decorated, and its very extensive landscaped grounds were arguably of equal importance: the villa was surrounded on three sides by terraces, orchards, herb gardens, fish tanks, and in front of the house were two large, rectangular ponds with fountains. These landscaping works were altogether more ambitious than any others yet attempted, with grottoes, statuary, and other delights matched only by the Boboli gardens attached to Palazzo Pitti.[27]

By now, although provided with all the requisite accommodation for a prolonged *villeggiatura*, the villas were almost overshadowed in importance by their often quite large gardens and estates. This relationship is rendered particularly clearly in the famous series of paintings of the Medici estates executed by Giusto Utens. In some of Utens's portraits of these estates — notably Pratolino — the villa appears to be almost an accessory to the surrounding expanses of greenery, some tamed (often at huge expense), and some clearly and intentionally left *al naturale*.

The overall form of the Medici villa La Petraia is more compact than Castello, its near neighbor. La Petraia was also developed around an earlier nucleus, of which the original fortified tower can still be seen rising above the house itself. Formerly the property of the Strozzi, it was bought by the Medici in 1530. Its compact, square plan represents a variant of the plan at Poggio; here, though, there is a spacious terrace on only one side, from which the gardens descend on three levels,

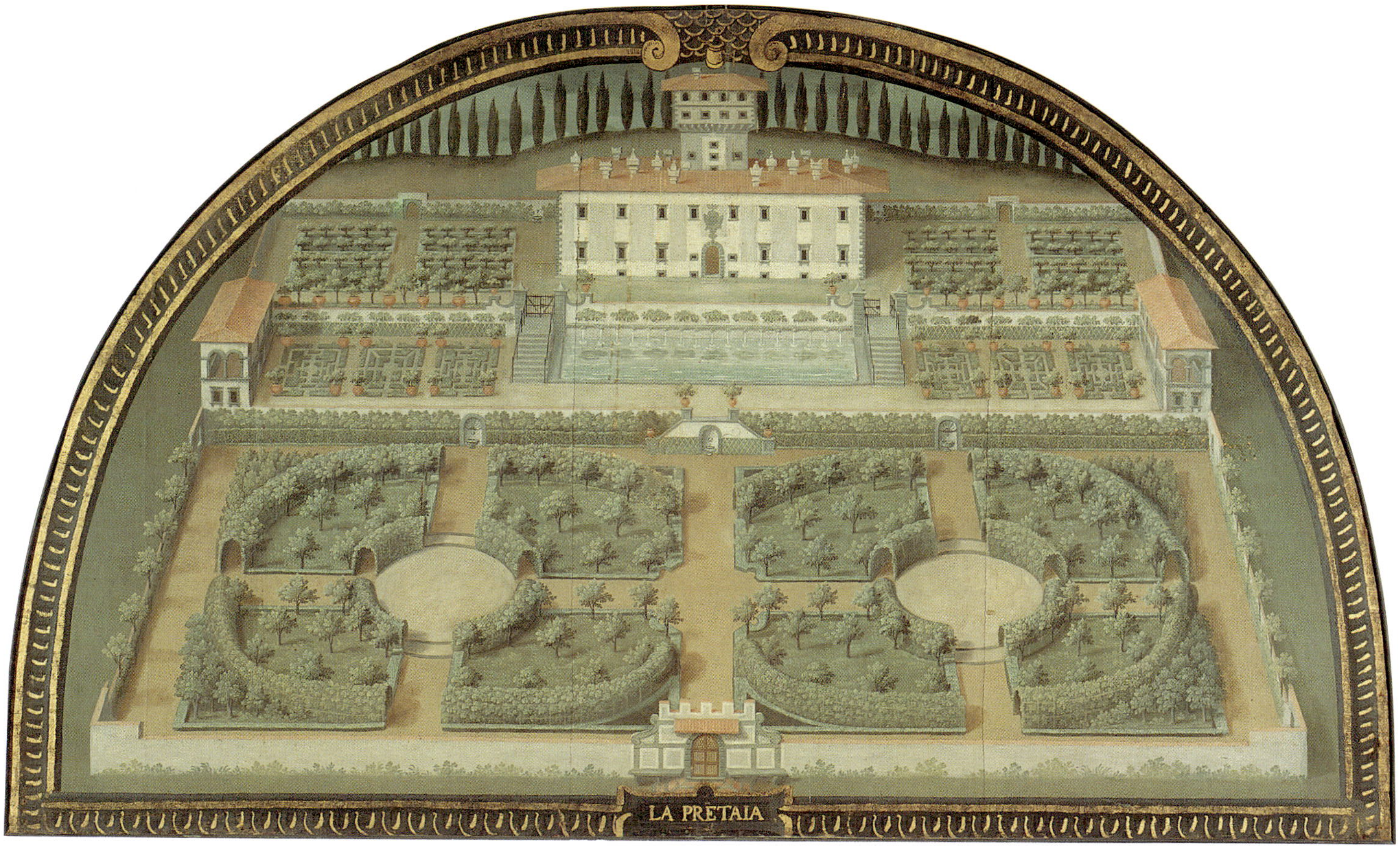
LA PRETAIA

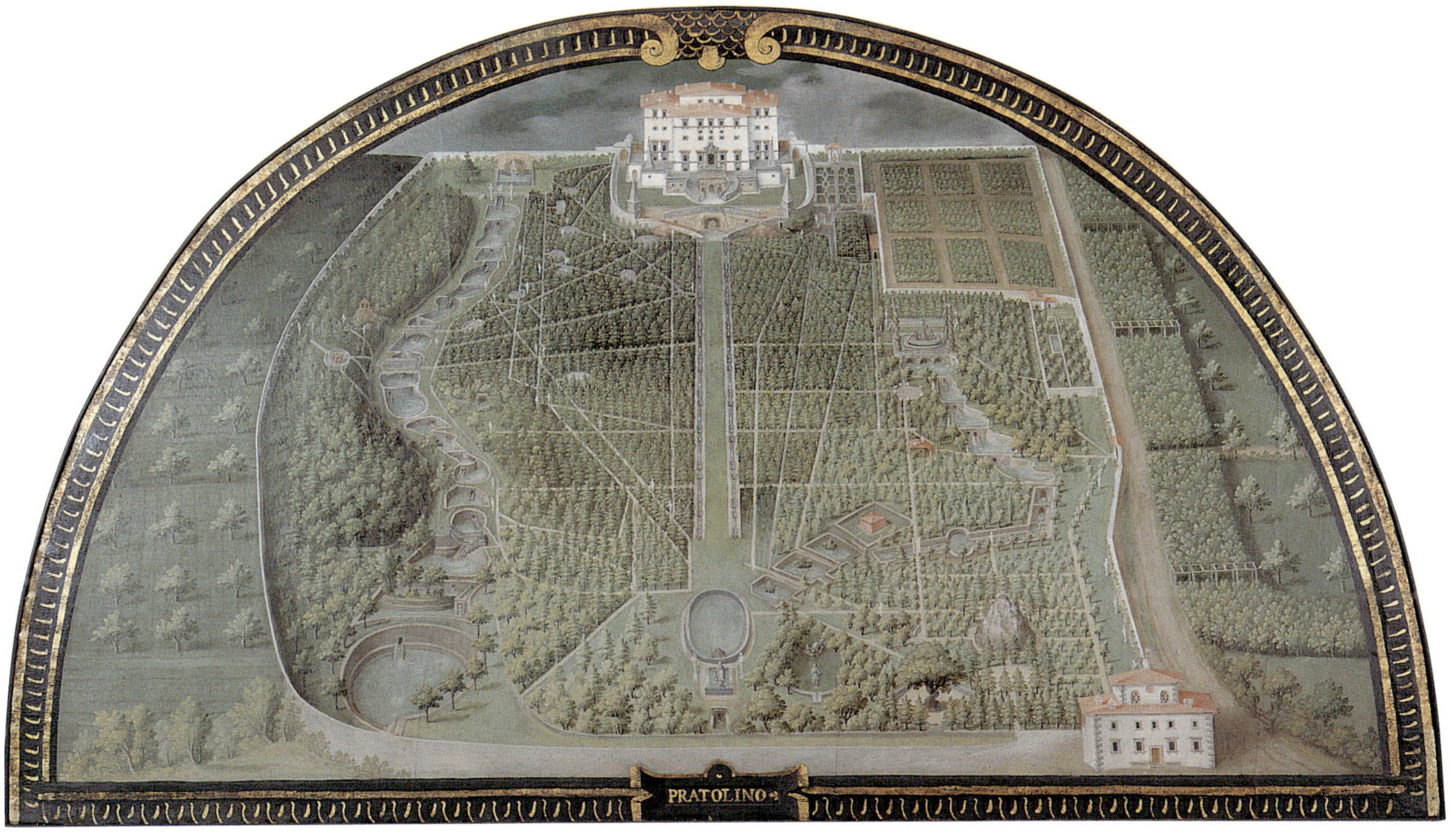
PRATOLINO

following the slope of the hill. At Castello, the basic fabric of the farmhouse was retained, and compromised, at least to some degree, the form, function, and planning of the villa itself; a similar observation can be made regarding La Petraia, which was comprehensively remodeled, this time by Buontalenti, in the years after 1576.

The rural masterpiece of the prolific Buontalenti, though, was probably the lost villa of Pratolino, which stood a few miles farther north of La Petraia, on the road toward the Mugello. Francesco de' Medici acquired a huge estate here in 1568 and commissioned Buontalenti to design a new villa and extensive grounds. The villa and its gardens became famous throughout Europe and, with their lakes, fountains, grottoes, and statuary, were the most remarkable sight to any visitor approaching Florence from Bologna and the north. But the appearance of the house is recorded in detail today only in Utens's painting, as the building was destroyed in 1822 after years of abandonment.[28] The gardens, however, survive as the Parco Demidoff, and among its more remarkable features is the gigantic carved stone figure of the Fontana dell'Appennino by Giambologna. The villa itself was also remarkable; modeled in a general sense on Poggio a Caiano, it had a compact, centralized plan,

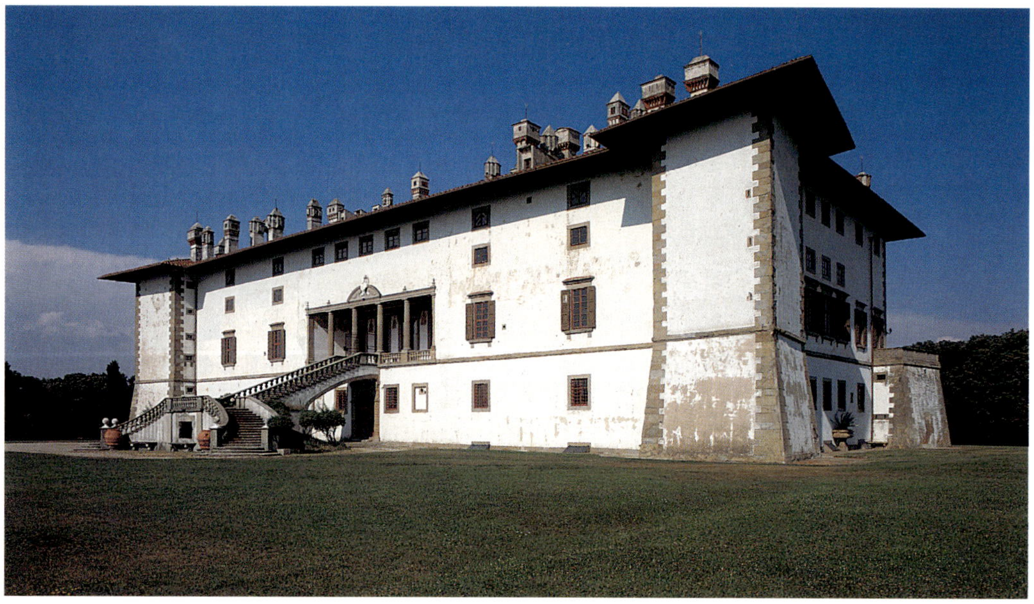

VILLA MEDICI AT ARTIMINO ("LA FERDINANDA")

Sometimes known as La Ferdinanda, the villa was built by Buontalenti for Ferdinando I in 1594. It owes much to Sangallo's villa at Poggio a Caiano in its rational planning and carefully designed relationship to the surrounding landscape.

with the principal story raised on a lower basement (the basement story elaborated with a series of grottoes and artificial caves) and surrounded by a terrace. The villa was strictly symmetrical, with prospects on all four sides, the main facade looking toward the south. This was a format Palladio was also to adopt, for example at the Villa Foscari and Villa Capra, both compact, centrally planned estates.

The development of the gardens at Pratolino is a fine example of the later-sixteenth-century love of both the natural and the grotesque; in particular, one can identify the merging of real natural forms with artificial "natural" forms — that is, forms designed to appear naturalistic, although they are clearly works of human artifice.[29] Giambologna's huge Appennino figure at Pratolino is perhaps the best example of this blurring of boundaries, although there is another, particularly bizarre example at the grotto at the Pitti. In this latter case one can see fairly clearly the distinction between the rational and ordered architecture itself and the soft, organic forms of the grotto that is set within it. Frequently, though, in this period the architecture also became full of illogicalities; broken pediments and reversed pediments, for example, are fundamentally wrong and defy reason, as do dropped keystones, twisted or "barley sugar" columns, and other similar features that had developed in the decades since Giulio Romano's Mannerist works at Mantua. By the later sixteenth century, similarly willful Mannerist features could be found all over Italy, particularly in the buildings and details associated with villas and their gardens, where the architectural proprieties and rules could be flouted with more ease, perhaps, than they could in the more aesthetically circumscribed and tradition-bound city.

Yet another of Buontalenti's many rural interventions for the Medici in this same period was the villa known as La Ferdinanda, adjacent to the hamlet of Artimino near Carmignano, west of Poggio. Begun in 1594 for Ferdinando I, Artimino was a comparatively rare example of a completely new construction, and Buontalenti's solution draws yet again principally on the seminal example of nearby Poggio; he also reintroduces references to the older, fortified tradition, most notably in the projecting corner "bastions," while a further homage to Sangallo can be seen in the inset colonnaded entrance portico. Its harmonious but rather severe appearance is lightened by the frivolous collection of chimneypots that enliven the skyline, which gave the villa its nickname, the "house of a hundred chimneys." The villa was used principally by the Medici for hunting on Montalbano, but was richly decorated and furnished; all of Utens's famous lunettes were painted for display in this villa.[30]

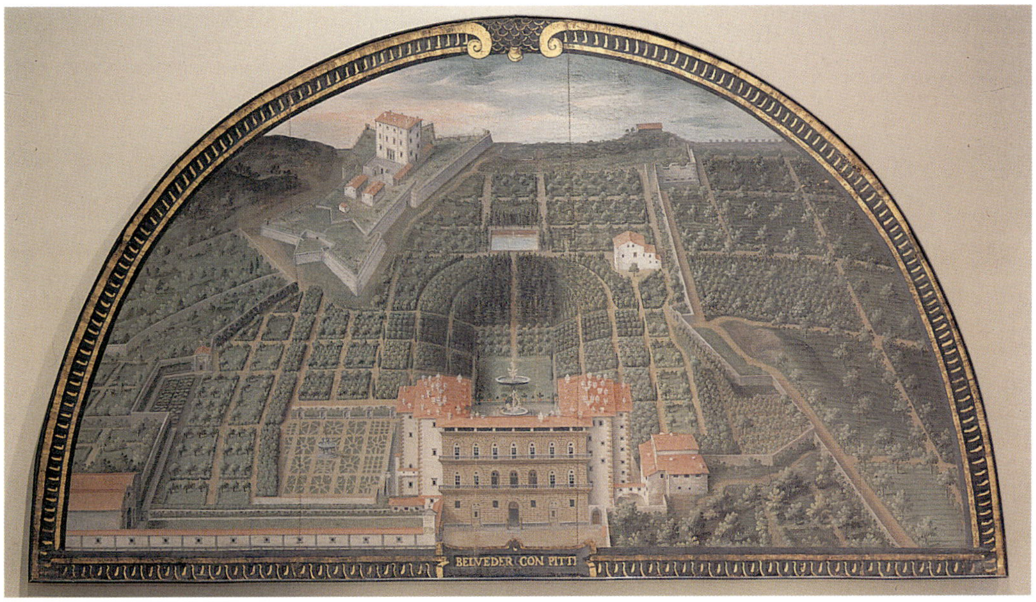

GIUSTO UTENS, *PALAZZO PITTI AND THE BELVEDERE*, C. 1599

An important reminder of the appearance of the palace (and its gardens) after the works of Ammannati but before the later expansion of the palazzo by Parigi and others. In the top left corner is the Belvedere fort and villa.

In a sense, after a villa such as Artimino the genre could not easily be developed any further, other than in purely stylistic terms. Its practical functions now well established, the rural villa had expanded and its role had evolved in stages:The original fortified farmhouse had been transformed first into a *casa di delizie*, with the farming functions set at a discreet distance; further development had rationalized the planning of the villa itself, and had embraced the progressive annexation of increasingly larger tracts of the surrounding estates. The grounds immediately adjacent to the villa were the most highly formalized, often set out geometrically with terraces and plant beds, herb gardens, and so on; farther from the house, though, the approach was more naturalistic, with subtly contrived "natural" landscapes; finally, in the distance, the seminatural gave way to nature itself, often in the form of the lowering, forested Apennines.

The very last of the Medici villas, Poggio Imperiale, lies just south of Florence, a mere mile beyond the Porta Romana and the Boboli gardens. In a sense its history echoes that of the Pitti, since it is marked essentially by staged expansion.[31] The estate was confiscated from the Salviati family by the Medici in 1565, but it was only after 1622 that Giulio Parigi began its expansion and transformation for Archduchess Maria Maddalena. Further expansion took place in the 1680s, and still more works were undertaken under the Lorraine dynasty after 1767; these last gave the imposing villa its present neoclassical character. Finally, the main facade was refaced in 1807, in the form that can be seen today. Poggio Imperiale has the impressive but rather daunting character of a palace rather than a villa, set at the end of a mile-long avenue of cypresses. Any close interrelationship between villa and its surrounding parks and gardens, though, has long since disappeared, and without this traditional, carefully balanced communion, the palace appears isolated, marooned.

The Later Renaissance and Baroque Palaces

"A noble house in the city brings considerable honor, being more visible than all of one's possessions." **Michelangelo Buonarrotti** [32]

After this brief excursion into the Tuscan countryside, we should now resume our discussion of the later development of the urban palazzo. Despite the turbulent events of the brief era of Savonarola, many new palaces were built in the city during the early years of the sixteenth century. But attempts to emulate the noble precedents established by the Strozzi and Medici were very few; instead, two

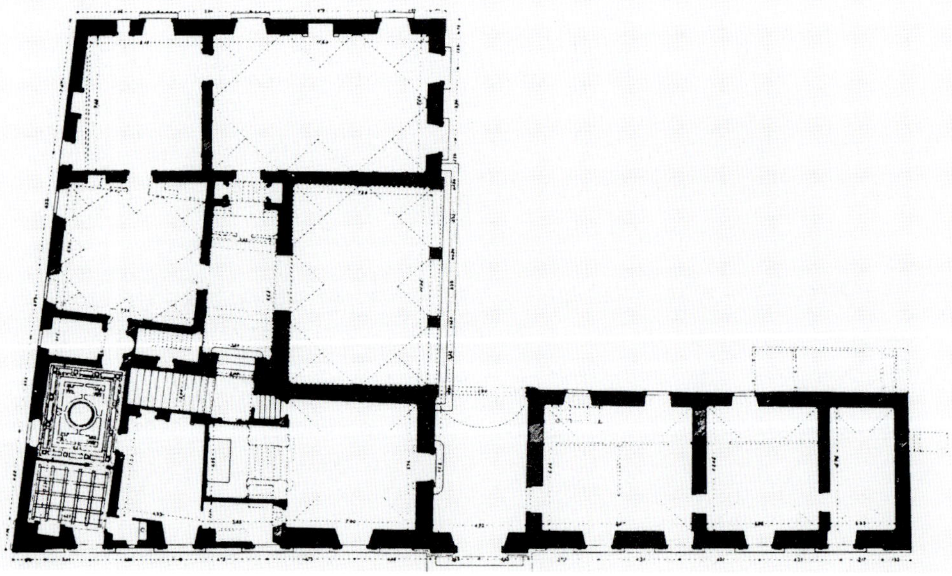

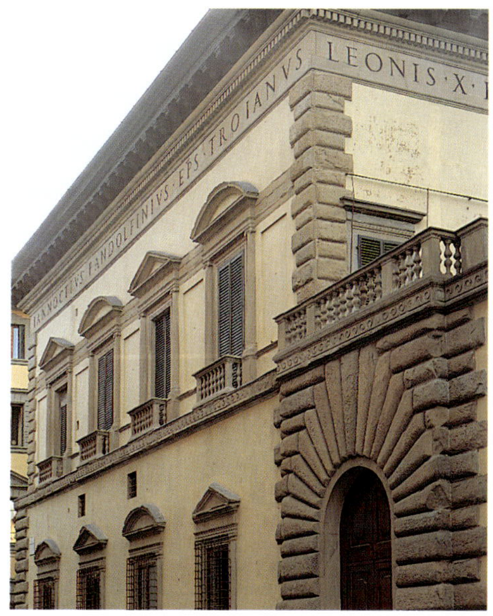

PALAZZO PANDOLFINI

Above, left: plan; the southern wing of the palace was never completed as intended. Above: the facade from about 1515–20 by Raphael was the first truly Roman Renaissance palace facade in the city.

quite different design philosophies can be traced, one essentially a continuation of an established Florentine typology, the other representing the influence of another source, that of Rome.

The most active practitioners in the first two or three decades of the new century were Baccio d'Agnolo and Cronaca. In general, their work tends to follow the first of these two paths, that is, it takes its lead from the comparatively restrained models established at the end of the quattrocento by Cronaca himself at Palazzo Corsi, later Horne, for example. This disciplined, almost minimalist approach is epitomized by Palazzo Dei, later Guadagni, again by Cronaca, in the very first years of the cinquecento. One can perhaps identify in its reticence and strict discipline something of the influence of the philosophical precepts of that tempestuous priest Savonarola, and of the Republican interlude before the Medici returned in triumph in 1512. But in fact, precedents for such regularity and restraint can be traced back to Palazzo Pazzi in the 1460s, which, with the exception of its bold ground-floor rustication, evinces an equally severe minimalism on the two upper stories. In any case, at Palazzo Guadagni symmetry and restraint were perhaps at their most rigid of any palace of this era in the city. The only note of lightness or relief is offered by the spacious loggia that occupies the whole width of the top story, with its views across the Piazza Santo Spirito. Disciplined rustication is confined to the main portal, the window surrounds, and the quoins; all other surfaces are plain plaster.[33]

Palazzo Guadagni was not the only example of Republican restraint, however, and a similarly disciplined approach can be observed in several other palaces of the 1510s and 1520s; Baccio d'Agnolo is associated with many of them, including Palazzo Taddei, Palazzo Ginori, Palazzo Albizi, and Palazzo Rosselli del Turco. In these and other examples, the degree of ornamentation is highly codified and rigidly defined; for example, flat rustication is applied in almost every case solely to the window surrounds on the upper stories and to the main portal on the ground floor. Occasionally it also extends to the quoins, while modest stone stringcourses define the levels of the upper floors. Ground-floor windows are almost always simple squares or rectangles with narrow frames of stone; roofs usually have the characteristically generous Florentine overhang. All of these houses can therefore be said to represent to some extent the return to this pre-Medicean era of restraint. But the evolution of architectural styles is rarely as tidy and straightforward as this, and indeed, in the early years of the new century Florence was also subject to another, more expressive influence, this time from Rome.

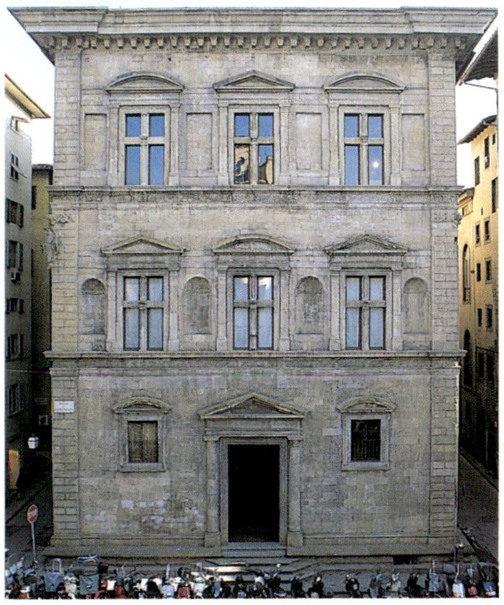

PALAZZO BARTOLINI SALIMBENI

The strong neoclassical facade from 1517–20 by Baccio d'Agnolo already incorporates some early Baroque elements, such as the niches and alternating pediments framing the windows.

By 1504 both Michelangelo and Raphael had arrived in Florence from Rome, and both were to broaden the Florentines' approach, particularly to the design of palace facades, in a significant manner. One of the most curious, and probably earliest, examples of this Romanizing tendency is Palazzo Cocchi Serristori, on the Piazza Santa Croce, where a preexisting medieval palace was given a prominent, idiosyncratic new facade, perhaps by Baccio d'Agnolo, in the early years of the new century. The new facade of the palazzo consists of an articulated arrangement of pilasters and cornices, loosely — albeit fairly clearly — derived from Albertian principles, with three generous arches on the *piano nobile*, and three large rectangular windows (really a modified architectonic loggia) on the top story. The first-floor articulation is particularly notable, as the major order of pilasters and trabeation contains within its bays a secondary order of arches, into which the large windows and smaller mezzanine openings are set; equally remarkable is the way the whole facade rises from the retained rustication of the original fourteenth-century building. Although clearly tentative and experimental, the palace hints at the more full-blooded Roman style of the slightly later works of Baccio and Raphael, among others.[34]

The pivotal work in this new phase of facades *alla romana* is Palazzo Pandolfini, built from 1515 to 1520 as a residence for the bishop, Giannozzo Pandolfini, following the publication of a papal bull by Leo X. Although Raphael, who was in Florence in 1515 and 1519, designed the palazzo, its execution was carried out under the supervision of GianFrancesco and Aristotele da Sangallo, who modified the initial proposal significantly.[35] Raphael's original scheme had a monumental palace of nine bays, although only four were actually built. Begun in 1519, work on the palace continued until the later 1520s, but progress was very slow after the disruptions and depredations of the sack of Rome in 1527. GianFrancesco died in 1530, and what was completed thereafter is the work of his brother Aristotele.

Palazzo Pandolfini is the first truly Roman Renaissance palace in Florence — Roman, that is, in several respects: in its being built on only two (very spacious) stories, compared to the almost universal three stories of the typical Florentine palace, and in the monumental treatment of the windows, each of which is framed by an aedicule and surmounted by a pediment, the profiles of which are alternated, half being triangular and the remainder segmental. The first-floor windows also have balconies, while the huge, heavily rusticated entrance portal is the only element on the facade to be treated in this manner, other than the bold quoins. (The remaining parts of the imposing facade, above and to the right of the portal, were never completed.) It is almost certain that the central window directly above the monumental doorway was strongly modeled to provide a centralizing emphasis, which, again, was a new element in the design of the Florentine palace facade.

Palazzo Pandolfini, though, was not alone in bringing the language of Donato Bramante and Raphael to Florence, since in the same period Baccio was building Palazzo Bartolini Salimbeni, a native Florentine, "Roman" palazzo that is perhaps his masterpiece. In its attempt to reclassicize the city, Palazzo Bartolini Salimbeni has great importance, its noble proportions dominating the small Piazza Santa Trinità.[36] For this palace Baccio incorporated prominent aediculed windows similar to those at Palazzo Pandolfini, but also announced some further innovations. Here, the window openings are subdivided by stone mullions and transoms into four smaller lights, to which the architect added some almost Mannerist touches, with niches scooped out from the facade's surface alternating with the windows. These niches have a different shape on each of the two upper stories, providing a lively counterpoint to the rhythm of the windows themselves, while the whole facade is capped by a huge, oversailing cornice.

PALAZZO UGUCCIONI

Facade onto the Piazza della Signoria. Its prominent and powerfully modeled Roman appearance was intended to mark the first stage of the comprehensive *renovatio* of the piazza in the classical manner.

Much criticized by his contemporaries, Baccio's palace was to have a considerable influence on succeeding generations; for example, the powerful modeling of its facade was echoed thirty years later by that of Palazzo Uguccioni, the first attempt to classicize the north side of the Piazza della Signoria. The original design for Palazzo Uguccioni, built in about 1549–50, has in the past been attributed to Michelangelo, as well as to Antonio da Sangallo the Younger, and its rich facade is the most purely Roman yet seen in the city. The strong rustication of the ground floor is surmounted by two upper stories whose bays are defined by paired half-columns standing on tall rectangular plinths, with the windows surrounded by deeply modeled aedicules.[37]

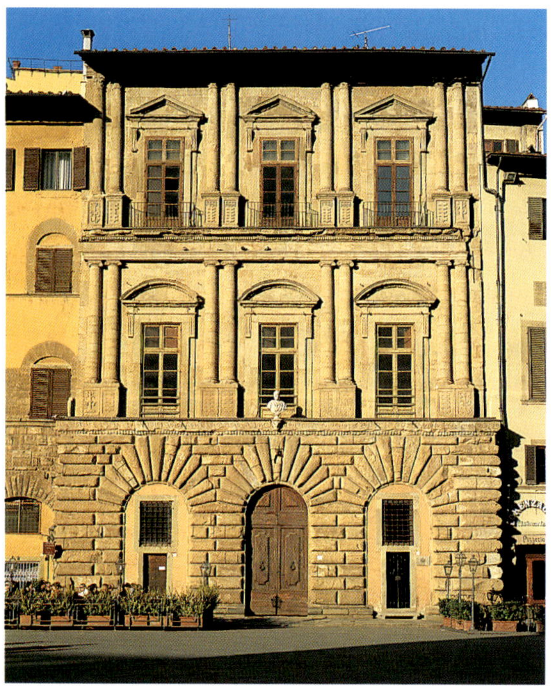

Although only a mere three bays wide, Palazzo Uguccioni had considerable urban importance, since it was the first attempt to modernize the prominent north side of the Piazza della Signoria: Contemporaneous with Cosimo I's plans for extensive clearances to the south to connect the piazza with the Arno, where the Uffizi were to be built, a similar proposal for the north side of the piazza involved the broadening of the tortuous Via de' Cerchi, which would have extended its width as far as the corner of Palazzo Uguccioni. This would have re-created a major new north–south axis linking the piazza directly to the cathedral, and Palazzo Uguccioni would have provided the first of a series of imposing classical structures along the north side of the square.

Later palaces of the sixteenth century tended to fall broadly into one of the two design typologies identified at the beginning of this chapter; that is, they were either highly restrained, disciplined, even austere works, or they were based on this more expressive Roman vocabulary, often embellished further with more overtly Mannerist interventions or "accessories." Baccio's generation was followed by that of the prolific Ammannati and Buontalenti, both of whom developed a much broader vocabulary of elements with which to articulate these later palaces.

Palazzo Grifoni, for example, was planned and begun by Baccio but completed by Ammannati in 1563. In a general sense the palazzo, which dominates the southwest corner of the Piazza della Santissima Annunziata, is of the Roman type, but is unusual in that the facade surfaces are of undecorated brick (a Roman characteristic), while all of the architectural detail is picked out in stone, including the strongly emphasized quoins, the heavy crowning cornice, and the window frames, now (revealingly) with Mannerist broken pediments.[38] A window in the center of the *piano*

PALAZZO NONFINITO (below)

Detail of the facade, begun in 1593 by Buontalenti for Alessandro Strozzi. The palace was planned on a massive scale, but the uppermost story was never completed.

CASA DI BIANCA CAPPELLO, VIA MAGGIO (below, right)

Detail of the rich, complex sgraffito decoration that covers the facade; it remains one of the best-preserved examples of this technique in the city.

nobile is another new feature in the vocabulary of the palace facade; it reflects the influence of Sebastiano Serlio and his highly influential treatise, the fourth book of which had been published in Venice in 1537. This book contains a number of proposals for the composition of palace facades; large composite windows such as that at Palazzo Grifoni form the central feature of several of them.[39]

Both of the outstanding architects of the era, Buontalenti and Ammannati, were equally capable of producing sober, traditional Florentine palace facades as well as those that were more expressive and even Mannerist. Ammannati, for example, was responsible for Palazzo Salviati and Buontalenti for Palazzo Capponi in the Oltrarno, both impeccable examples of the restrained tradition. But more characteristic of the last decades of the century, both stylistically and in the nature of their patronage, are Buontalenti's Casino Mediceo and the well-known house of Bianca Cappello.

The Casino was built from 1568 to 1574 by Buontalenti for Francesco, son of Cosimo I, as a place of retreat. It stands on Via Cavour (the former Via Larga), the traditional Medicean axis of power

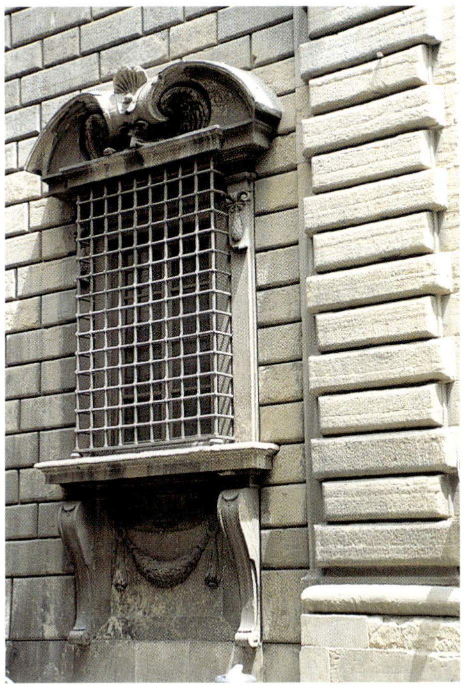

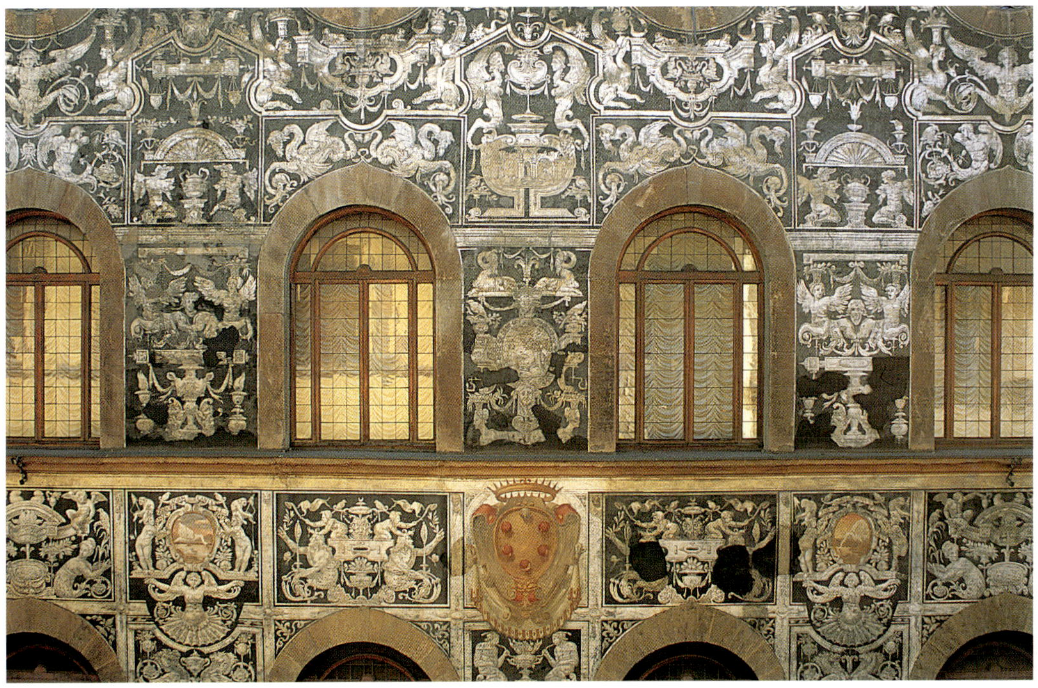

in this part of the city, but a little farther north from the Medici palazzo; in fact, the site is closer to San Marco, that other hub of Medicean patronage, and therefore far from the corridors of power of the Uffizi or the Pitti. Here Francesco was free to indulge in his other interests, principally alchemy (an interest shared by his architect) and the development of highly specialized craftsmanship techniques. The Casino was thus to be something of a mixture of laboratory, workshop, and study. The main entrance of the long facade onto the Via Larga already demonstrates a little of the Mannerism that seems particularly appropriate for a building that was to house such eclectic research activity; Buontalenti's imagination was allowed further indulgence in the sculpted motifs of various life forms — animal, vegetable, mythical — he applied to the face of the structure.[40]

If the Casino represents the somewhat eccentric patronage of the ruling dynast, then the house of Bianca Cappello represents quite a different aspect of the power and influence of the Medici prince. The Venetian noblewoman Bianca Cappello was the lover and later the second wife of Francesco I, and her house on the Via Maggio was transformed by Buontalenti in 1567. The existing typical quattrocento Florentine palazzo was modernized by the insertion of two massive new ground-floor windows and a heavily rusticated central portal, but more remarkable is the rich, complex sgraffito decoration that covers almost all of the facade's surface. The decoration by Bernardino Poccetti in 1579 is today a rare surviving example of what was once a comparatively widespread treatment of facades in the later sixteenth century. But the decoration of the Casa Cappello, all in black and white, with the exception of the full-color Medici arms, is particularly refined, with a fine array of masks, fauns, monsters, and mythical creatures of many kinds — a perfect demonstration, once again, of the eclectic interests of both patron and architect.[41]

A couple of final examples illustrate the typical character of the Florentine palace toward the end of the cinquecento. The first is Palazzo Larderel, the work of Giovanni Dosio, which represents the continuing interest in the palazzo *alla romana*; built in about 1580, the palace is harmonious if rather cold and restrained, its three-bay, three-story facade notable — at this late date — for the lack of any Mannerist embellishments. The same observations cannot be made, however, about the so-called Palazzo Nonfinito, begun in 1593 by Buontalenti for Alessandro Strozzi. It stands on the Via del Proconsolo, on the block immediately north of Palazzo Pazzi, and is an enormous structure that,

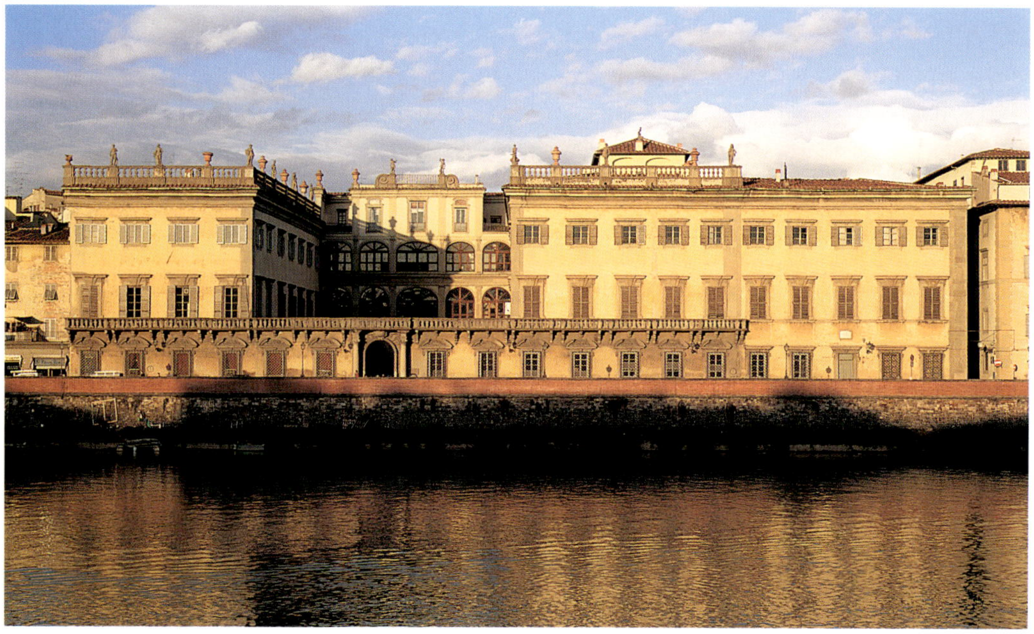

had it ever been finalized, would have been one of the largest palaces ever built in Florence. Directly representative of the Strozzi family's ambitions, its massive ground floor, with rusticated stonework and heavy windows with broken pediments, was largely completed by Buontalenti (whose hand can be seen in his characteristic zoomorphic details), but there followed a rift with his employer, and the portal was added later by Giovanni Caccini. The internal *cortile* is the work, around 1602, of Lodovico Cigoli, Buontalenti's pupil, while Vincenzo Scamozzi was chiefly responsible for the *piano nobile* and the upper parts of the facade, built in around 1600. However, the palace was never completed on the vast scale originally intended by Strozzi, and a proposed second *piano nobile* was never begun; Buontalenti's imposing lower screen thus appears rather out of scale with the single floor that was built above it.[42]

The Seventeenth-Century Baroque

The reigns of the last of the Medici generally encompassed a period of stagnation and decline in the Tuscan economy, one clear result of which was that the high Baroque is far less well represented in Florence than it is, for example, in Rome or Turin. Another, much less tangible factor to consider is what is often said to be the innate moderation of so many aspects of the Florentine character; the more truly frivolous excesses of the Rococo, for instance, are virtually nonexistent in the city, and even the more universal mature Baroque is tempered there with a degree of balance

PALAZZO CORSINI AL PARIONE (below)

Facade onto the *lungarno*. The largest Baroque palace in Florence, it was begun by Pier Francesco Silvani in 1648 but was not completed until several decades later.

VILLA CORSINI AT CASTELLO (opposite)

Detail of the central bay of the exuberant Baroque facade by Antonio Maria Ferri, 1699.

PALAZZINA REALE ALLE CASCINE (overleaf)

The 1787 Palazzina Reale by Giuseppe Manetti, in a refined neoclassical idiom, formed the administrative headquarters of the farm-estate of the grand duchy, which later became the Cascine public park.

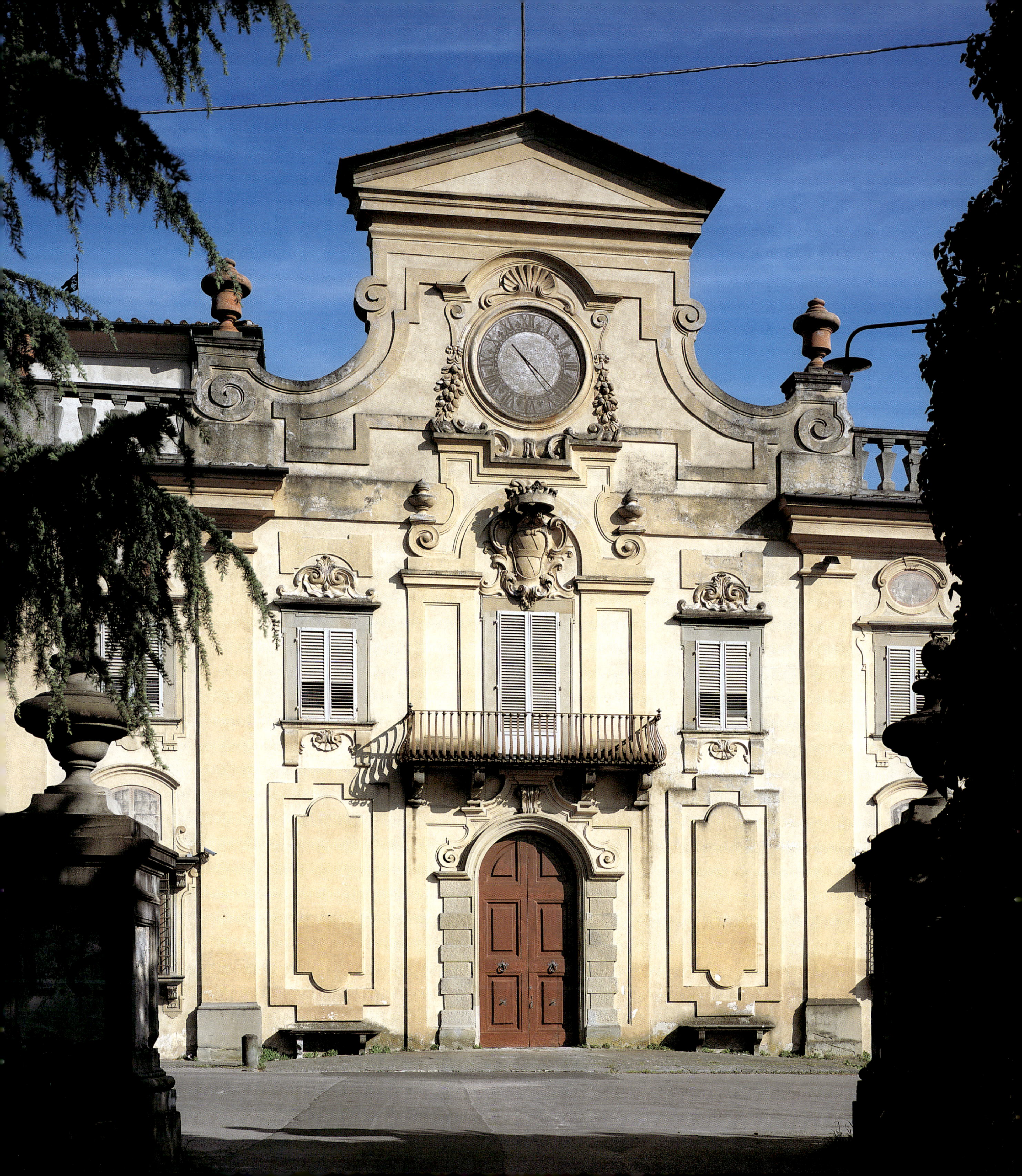

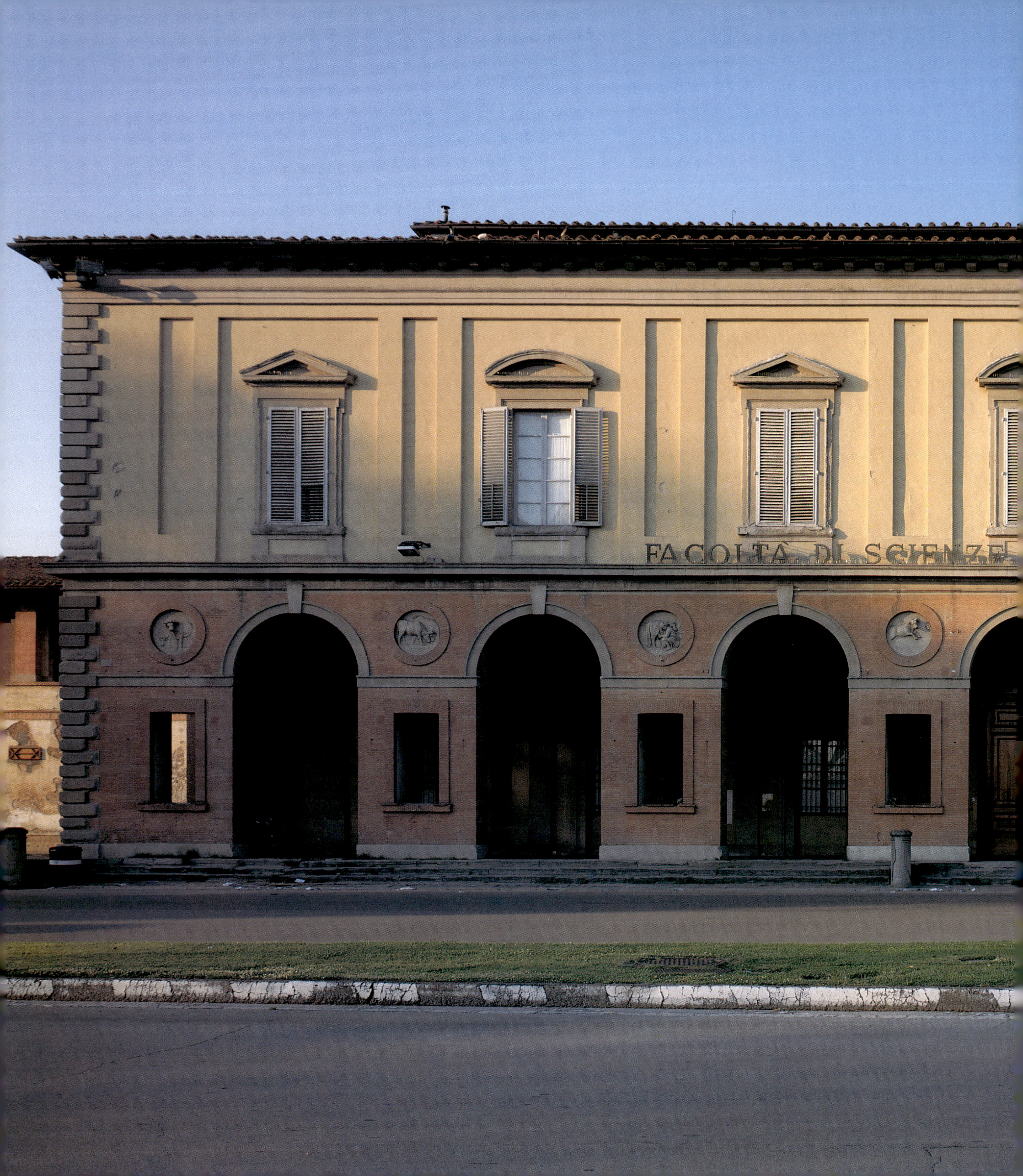
FACOLTA DI SCIENZE

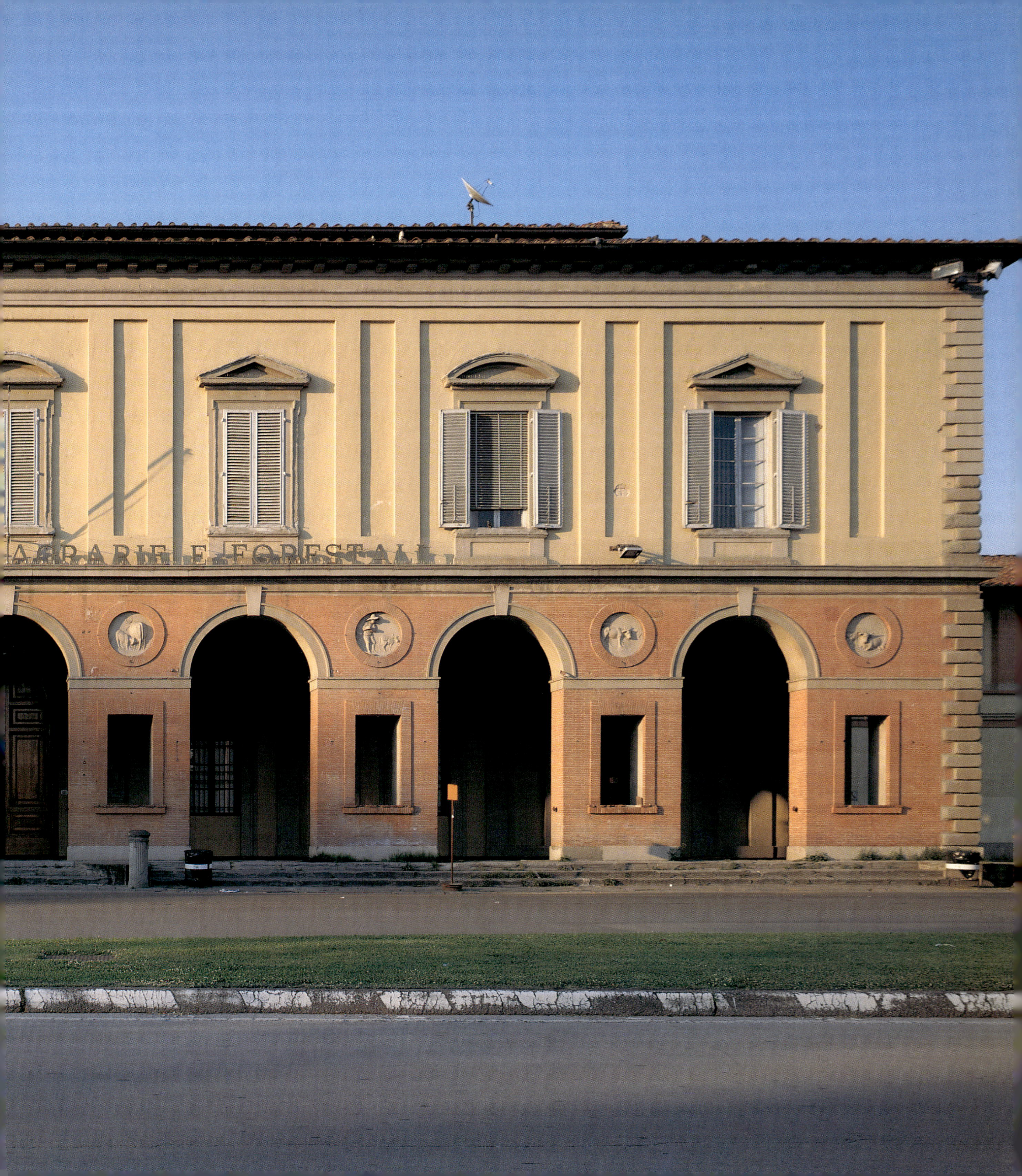
AGRARIE E FORESTALI

and restraint. Florence produced no Francesco Borromini as Rome had done, or a Filippo Juvarra, as did Turin, or yet a Baldassare Longhena, as did Venice. The palaces of the later Florentine Baroque are therefore comparatively few in number, and comparatively restrained at least in their external appearance. But if the city itself had declined to the second rank, there still remained architects of considerable ability, notably Matteo Nigetti and Gherardo Silvani in the first part of the seventeenth century, and later, Giovanni Battista Foggini.

Silvani built several substantial palaces, among them Palazzo Covoni and Palazzo Castelli, both distinguished by robust facades in which all of the architectural elements are "pulled out" from an entirely neutral wall surface; slightly more imaginative is his Palazzo Strozzi "del Poeta," with its aediculed windows and prominent central balcony, built from 1626 to 1629 for the poet Giovanni Battista Strozzi.

PALAZZO CAPPONI

Below: facade toward the gardens. The palace begun in 1699 by Carlo Fontana and others is one of the most imposing of a number of late Baroque palaces in the city.

Opposite: the grand formal staircase; in many such palaces, a comparatively restrained facade concealed lavish Baroque or Rococo interiors, notably in the staircases and ballrooms.

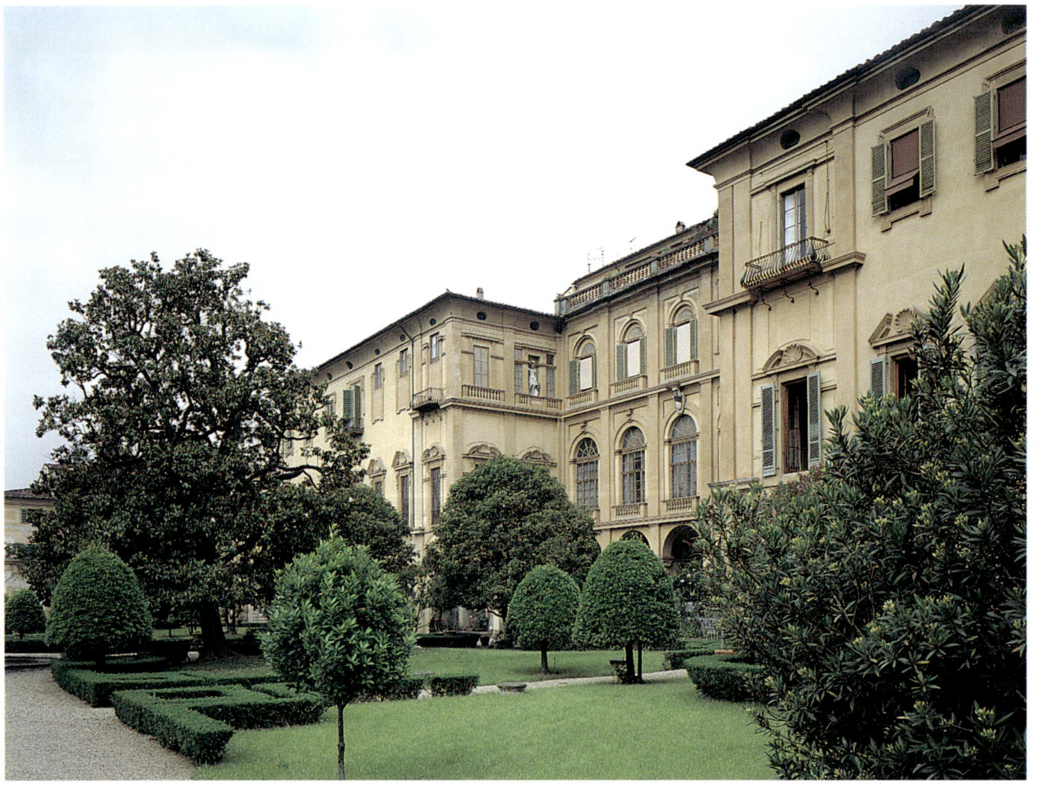

The Palazzo delle Missioni from about 1650 is the only known Florentine work of Bernardino Radi, and links the still fairly conventional Silvani with the later, more adventurous work of Antonio Maria Ferri. The facade of the palazzo is highly original, incorporating circular niches containing the busts of the four Medici grand dukes and exhibiting a lively plasticity of ornament more characteristic of Rome in this period.

The work of Antonio Maria Ferri is considerably varied in style, from the regular, heavy conformity of Palazzo Orlandini to the far more romantic facade of the impressive Palazzo Corsini al Parione. This extensive palace, the largest and most imposing built in the city in the seventeenth century, was constructed over several decades and represents the work of many architects in succession.[43] Work began on a prominent location on the north bank of the Arno in 1656, based on the restoration of an earlier casino on the site, and was undertaken by Alfonso Parigi the Younger; he was succeeded by Ferdinando Tacca, who worked on the palace until 1671. In 1679, after a hiatus of several years, Silvani was appointed in turn, and it was he who was responsible for the general configuration of the plan, with its distinctive U shape, and with the open side facing the river. Finally, the palazzo was completed by Ferri, who constructed the grand staircase with its cupola.

The long, elegant facade toward the Arno is notable for Silvani's unusual plan based on Roman examples, and for the long screen wall surmounted by a balcony that unites the two wings. The whole theatrical ensemble plays an important role in defining this section of the riverbank, and with its parapets enlivened with statues, represents the principal urban intervention along the Arno in this period. The interiors, too, are the work of the most outstanding Baroque craftsmen of the period, with stucco decoration by Giovanni Passardi and paintings by Piero Dandini, Alessandro Gherardini, and others. The fact that Ferri was capable of an even more fluid Baroque style is visible in his work at the Villa Corsini at Castello. The principal facade of this modernized quattrocento villa was radically transformed in 1698–99 in a highly theatrical Baroque manner, with a character that is difficult to imagine applied to a palazzo in the more sober confines of the city itself. In particular, the central bay of the facade was transformed with a crowning tympanum flanked by volutes, so that it resembles nothing so much as a Roman Baroque chapel.

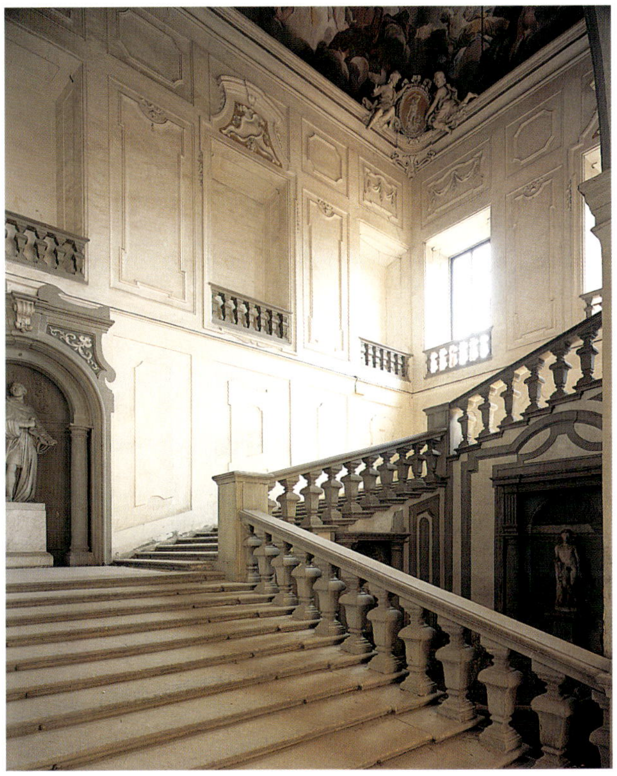

Among the comparatively few important palace projects during the very last decades of the reign of the Medici grand dukes, the imposing Palazzo Capponi is the most notable. Built on the northern edge of the city, with extensive grounds formerly owned by the Salviati family, the palace was designed by the Roman architect Carlo Fontana in 1702. However, while Fontana himself remained in Rome, the execution was supervised by Ferdinando Ruggieri and Alessandro Cecchini, and was completed in 1716. The exceptionally monumental facade onto the Via Gino Capponi presents a traditional urban face, while the plan is again in the form of a U, with two wings reaching out into the extensive gardens. The rear facade is consequently lighter, livelier, and well articulated, with an open colonnade at ground-floor level that joins the main entrance, on axis, with the gardens beyond. As with many such palaces, the comparative restraint and order of the exterior belies the opulence within, particularly the grandiose staircase, with its fountains and statues, and the sumptuous halls of the *piano nobile*; the palace represents something of a hybrid, a cross between a city palazzo and a rural (or at least suburban) villa.[44]

Only one or two of the palazzi from the Lorraine era are worthy of mention here. In general the period was far more noteworthy for public works than for expressions of individual taste; in fact, one of these few buildings, the Casa Livia, was itself originally built to house one of Grand Duke Pietro Leopoldo's offices. In appearance, however, it certainly resembles a private *casino*, which it indeed became, since it was given by Pietro Leopoldo to the dancer Livia Malfatti Raimondi in 1786 as a private residence. It had been built eleven years earlier by Bernardo Fallani in such a convincing interpretation of the late-sixteenth-century style of Buontalenti that it has been attributed to Buontalenti by more than one writer. In fact, the style is a robust revival of a rather Mannerist *alla romana* palazzetto, with rusticated quoins, prominent window aedicules, and alternating pediments. The era of revivalism was thus now well in hand in Florence, and the house is contemporary with the much more extensive, literally neoclassical works at Poggio Imperiale.

The Palazzina Reale, built on the edge of the Cascine park by Giuseppe Manetti a few years later, in 1787, exhibits similar restraint. The *palazzina* is not strictly a private palace either, since it was built to house the administration of the grand ducal estates of the Cascine, but it represents perfectly the dignified simplicity and rationalism of the best of the buildings from the Lorraine era. The *palazzina* was to be the first of a series of works undertaken by Manetti at the Cascine, the ancient Medici estate that was opened to the public for the first time by the Lorraine grand dukes.[45]

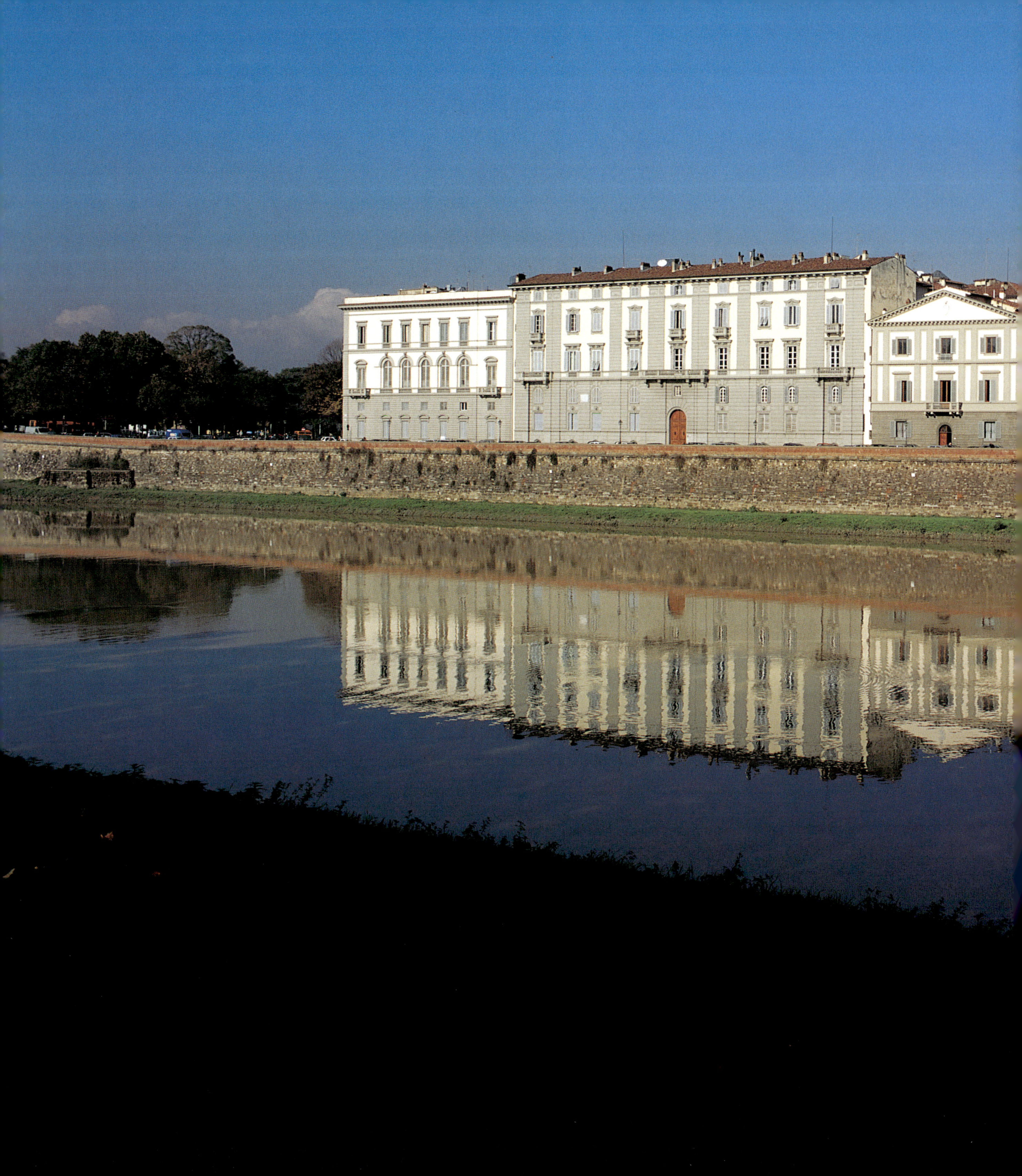

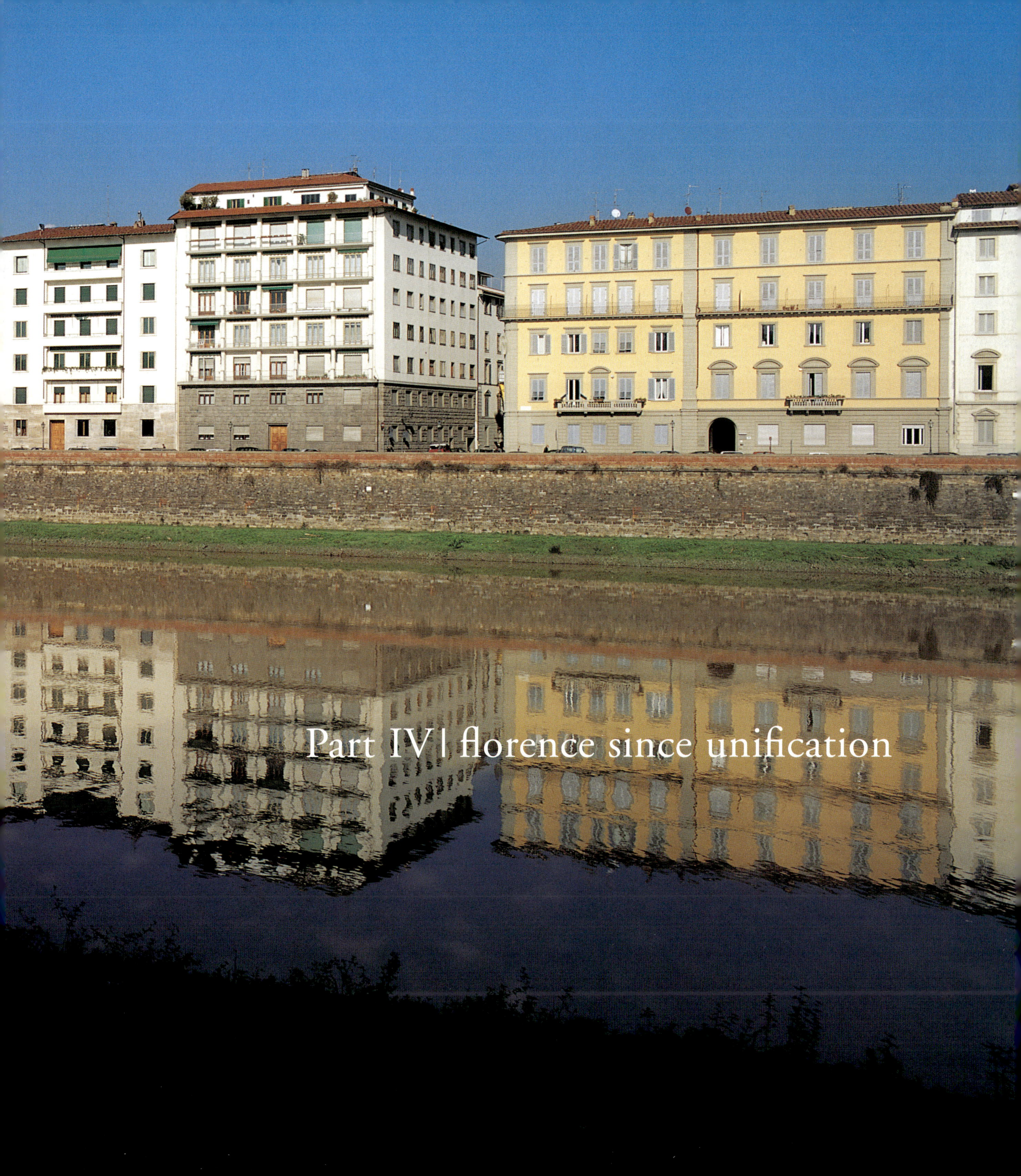

Part IV | florence since unification

"I saw our great new square [Piazza della Indipendenza] thronged this morning with near twelve thousand people, all a-bloom with red, green and white banners . . . ringing with shouts of 'Viva la *nostra* Italia!'"

Theodosia Garrow, eyewitness account, 27 April 1859 [1]

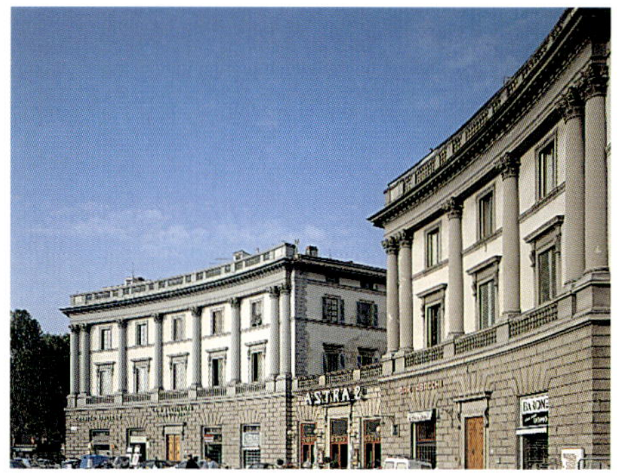

PIAZZA BECCARIA

Begun in 1865, this piazza was one of a series of key urban set pieces conceived by Giuseppe Poggi to transform Florence into a great European city in the manner of Paris or Turin.

LUNGARNO AMERIGO VESPUCCI (previous pages)

For five years, from 1865 to 1870, Florence, once capital of the grand duchy of Tuscany, found herself the somewhat unlikely capital of the newly unified Italian nation. During the few years prior to this momentous change, the city had made a few attempts to modernize the urban structure of what was effectively no more than a reasonably large provincial capital of around 150,000 inhabitants.[2] Most of these works of "improvement" inflicted considerable damage on the historic fabric, since their principal purpose was to ease communications between the city center and the new railway station behind Santa Maria Novella. Via Nazionale, for example, was cut through to link the recently set out Piazza della Indipendenza with the new station, and the Via de' Cerretani and Via Panzani were also both widened, this time to form a more spacious link between the cathedral and the railway terminus. These street widenings resulted in a series of large, monolithic new blocks, rather similar in character to those built down one side of the Via de' Calzaiuoli.[3] Still further street widening took place in the Via degli Strozzi and Via de' Tornabuoni; fortunately, perhaps, a number of others were planned but not executed.

In 1865 Italy's new capital was transferred from the elegant, orderly seventeenth- and eighteenth-century Piedmontese capital of Turin to a Florence whose basic form had hardly changed in three centuries.[4] One immediate and urgent necessity was to find suitable working accommodation for up to 20,000 civil servants and government officials, as well as housing for the daunting numbers who were expected to flood into the city within a matter of months. A sudden social and economic crisis thus arose in Florence; rents rose dramatically, throwing many of the poorer Florentines onto the streets, and the city council attempted to find temporary housing for them in hastily assembled, prefabricated timber dwellings. To secure accommodation for the many government departments, a large number of religious properties were sequestered, as were many other monumental structures, some formerly used by the governments of grand ducal Tuscany. Among the monastic buildings thus taken over were Santa Croce, San Firenze, Santa Maria Novella, and the Badia Fiorentina; the monastic houses were allowed to retain only the accommodation considered essential for the functioning of the religious orders: church, campanile, minimal living quarters; all the rest was commandeered. Among the famous nonreligious monuments hurriedly brought into use for the new national government were the Palazzo Vecchio and the Uffizi, Palazzo Strozzi, and the former ducal villa at Poggio Imperiale.

In order to cope with an estimated population increase of a further 50,000 in the years following the transfer of government, it was clear that major new urban development was essential. The man charged with planning this dramatic expansion was Giuseppe Poggi, and the results of his strategic program had a more remarkable effect on the form of the city than any other single episode in Florence's history. In the space of barely a dozen years, Florence was more comprehensively transformed than she had been even in the great palace-building era of the later quattrocento. One must go back as far as the construction of the last circle of city walls in the time of Dante to reach an era so far-reaching in its consequences for the form of the city.[5]

Completely new residential quarters had to be planned to house these large new numbers, and so the districts of Mattonaia and Maglio were set out, the former planned on a regular grid, with a spacious new square, Piazza d'Azeglio, in its center. The latter district, Maglio, completed the development of a smaller area just south of the Porta San Gallo. Both new districts, as well as a third, the Cascine "triangle," lay just inside the line of the city walls, but it was becoming clear that, with these three new quarters, there was no further possibility of expansion *intra muros,* and so Poggi made the fundamental decision to demolish all of the city walls on the north bank of the Arno — that is, around 80 percent of the total length.

The city walls were demolished with surprising ease and rapidity between 1865 and 1869, and with their disappearance the most important historic definition of Florence's urban form was gone.[6] Henceforth, the city could expand unfettered into the immediately surrounding belt of orchards, olive groves, villas, and market gardens, with the inevitable dilution of the urban fabric and the loss of the sense of identity of the ancient nucleus that had defined the city for the previous five hundred years.

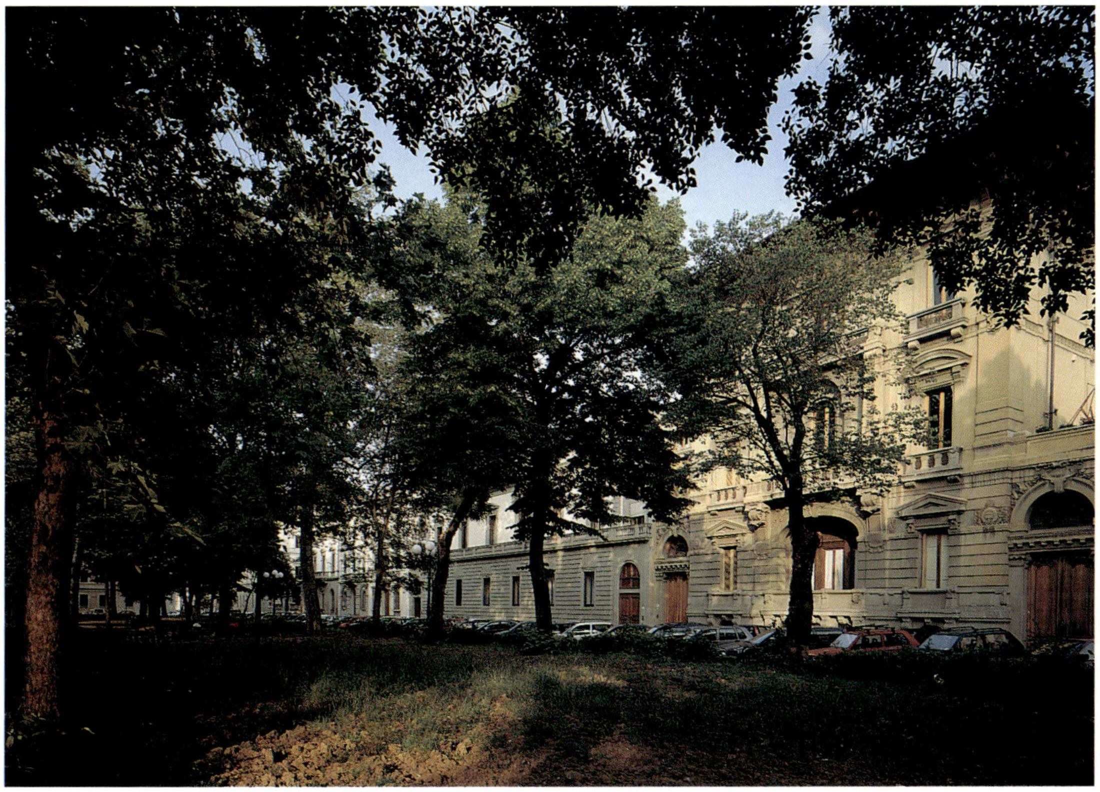

PIAZZA D'AZEGLIO

In contrast to Piazza Beccaria, this square, built by Giuseppe Poggi between 1862 and 1866, was surrounded by substantial apartment blocks, with a large private garden at the center.

A series of broad boulevards was laid out following the path of the lost walls, using the demolition material to form roadbeds and footpaths, while the surviving city gates now became stranded in the middle of a series of new squares and *rond-points*, set out in the Parisian manner. The Porta San Gallo, the Porta al Prato, and the Porta alla Croce all survived, but now as the centerpieces of large new piazze; the chief of these were the Piazza della Libertà at the Porta San Gallo, and the Piazza Beccaria at the Porta alla Croce; both squares were to be surrounded by imposing new blocks of apartments in neoclassical style. Ironically, the development of the automobile in the twentieth century once again rendered these broad boulevards barriers of a rather different kind between the inner city and the extensive modern suburbs beyond them.

Poggi also embarked on a series of further street widenings and "improvements" within the historic center. These included the northward extension of the Via Larga, various works of clearance around the Piazza della Signoria to enhance its setting, the widening of the Via de' Martelli and of the Ponte alla Carraia, and the new *lungarno* along the eastern part of the north bank as far as the Ponte San Niccolò. The final, untouched tract of land within the old circle of walls, on Via della Scala, was also now developed. Beyond the walls, in the Oltrarno, the Viale dei Colli was built, an impressive work of engineering that unfortunately inflicted considerable environmental damage upon this prominent district of the city, visible from the north bank; the approaches to San Salvatore and San Miniato were radically and permanently disfigured, with many of the cypresses and olive groves on the hillsides destroyed. The culmination of these works was the setting out of Piazzale Michelangelo, which, while offering magnificent new panoramic vistas of the city never seen before, nevertheless urbanized what for centuries had been a quiet, verdant fringe in the southeast corner of the city.[7]

The Loss of the Mercato Vecchio

In 1869 a debate began that resulted in many profound effects on the very heart of the old city, not least of which was the fate of the Mercato Vecchio. There was little doubt that the immediate environs of the old market were in need of major works of improvement; the district contained some of the most overcrowded, unsanitary, physically deteriorated parts of the city, including the towering tenements of the ancient ghetto.[8] Nevertheless, rather than a careful program of restoration, drastic measures were proposed: to demolish the entire district and replace the *mercato* with a vast new piazza, surrounded by new offices, a theater, and large shops and department stores. The market functions would be displaced entirely, and were to be reconstructed on a new site to the north of San Lorenzo, where, indeed, the present market halls were begun in 1870. This new Mercato Centrale, covering a large rectangular zone bounded by the Via dell'Ariento, Via San Antonio, Via Santa Chiara, and Via Panicale, was the work of Giuseppe Mengoni, the architect-engineer of the famous Galleria Vittorio Emanuele II in Milan, and is a fine example of the modern iron and glass approach that was to be followed in a number of other European cities for such structures; the huge nineteenth-century markets of Les Halles in Paris offered a further example of the typology.

But the future of the ancient Mercato Vecchio site was not to be resolved quite so straightforwardly, since in that same year, 1870, the capital was transferred again, this time permanently, to Rome. Almost overnight, therefore, Florence was transformed once again into a regional capital; the thousands of government employees moved south, and there was no longer any impetus or need to continue further new expansion projects. The city's population fell by 28,000 in barely three years as a result of this inevitable exodus. Certain intractable problems remained, however, one of these being the continuing congestion and difficulty of access into the historic center. But it was only in 1881 that an objective survey of the Mercato Vecchio district was undertaken, and after a series of alternative proposals were drawn up, the project which stands today was begun on site in 1885.[9] It amounted to complete demolition and reconstruction, a tabula rasa approach that would be unthinkable today, since all of the historic centers of Italian cities are now protected by law. At the time, though, the plan was regarded as a unique opportunity to provide the city with a spacious modern heart, with broader streets, substantial new palazzi, and, at the very center, a great new square, the Piazza Vittorio Emanuele, fittingly named after the new king of the recently unified nation.

In June 1885 the whole district was evacuated, and destruction began. The boundaries of this new city center were defined by the Via de' Pecori to the north, Via de' Calzaiuoli to the east, Via Porta Rossa to the south, and Piazza Strozzi and Via de' Pescioni to the west. Within this entire area only a handful of earlier structures were to survive, among them the famous Orsanmichele and Palazzo Vecchietti. Numerous medieval tower houses were lost, as well as the churches of Sant'Andrea, San Tommaso, and Santa Maria in Campidoglio. The new piazza was the first section to be set out, its location defined by the former Mercato Vecchio, although it was doubled in size toward the south. The basic plan of the new quarter was a simple rectangular street grid, much of which follows, in general terms, the lineaments of the much narrower medieval street pattern it replaced, which was itself based on the original Roman grid set out two millennia earlier. Thus, for example, the Pelliceria was widened and straightened, as were the Calimala and its continuation, the Via Roma, and, on the west side, the Via degli Strozzi. Countless narrow lanes, alleys, and courtyards, though, were obliterated in favor of large, simple rectangular blocks of new construction, which were intended not only to present imposing facades, especially those onto the new piazza, but also to maximize profits for the developers. In a particularly poignant gesture, the old Loggia del Pesce, which had stood along the west side of the old market square, was dismantled and reassembled in the Piazza dei Ciompi, half a mile

MERCATO VECCHIO

Right: model of the city's ancient market district, before its total destruction during the mid-nineteenth-century modernizations. In the background is the Loggia del Pesce. Below: nineteenth-century photograph of the market before its destruction.

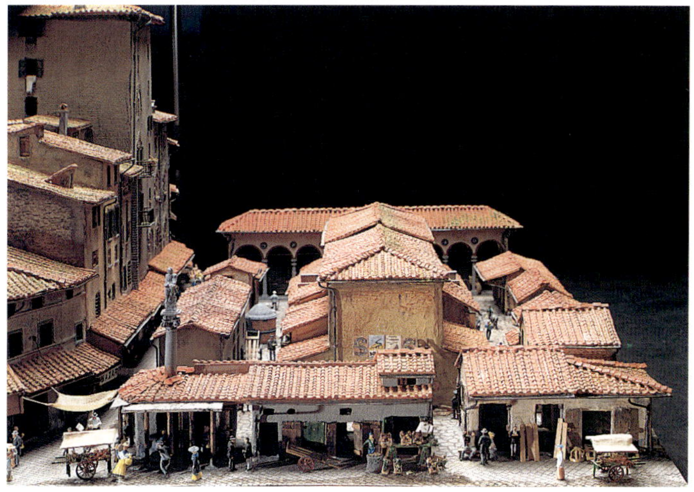

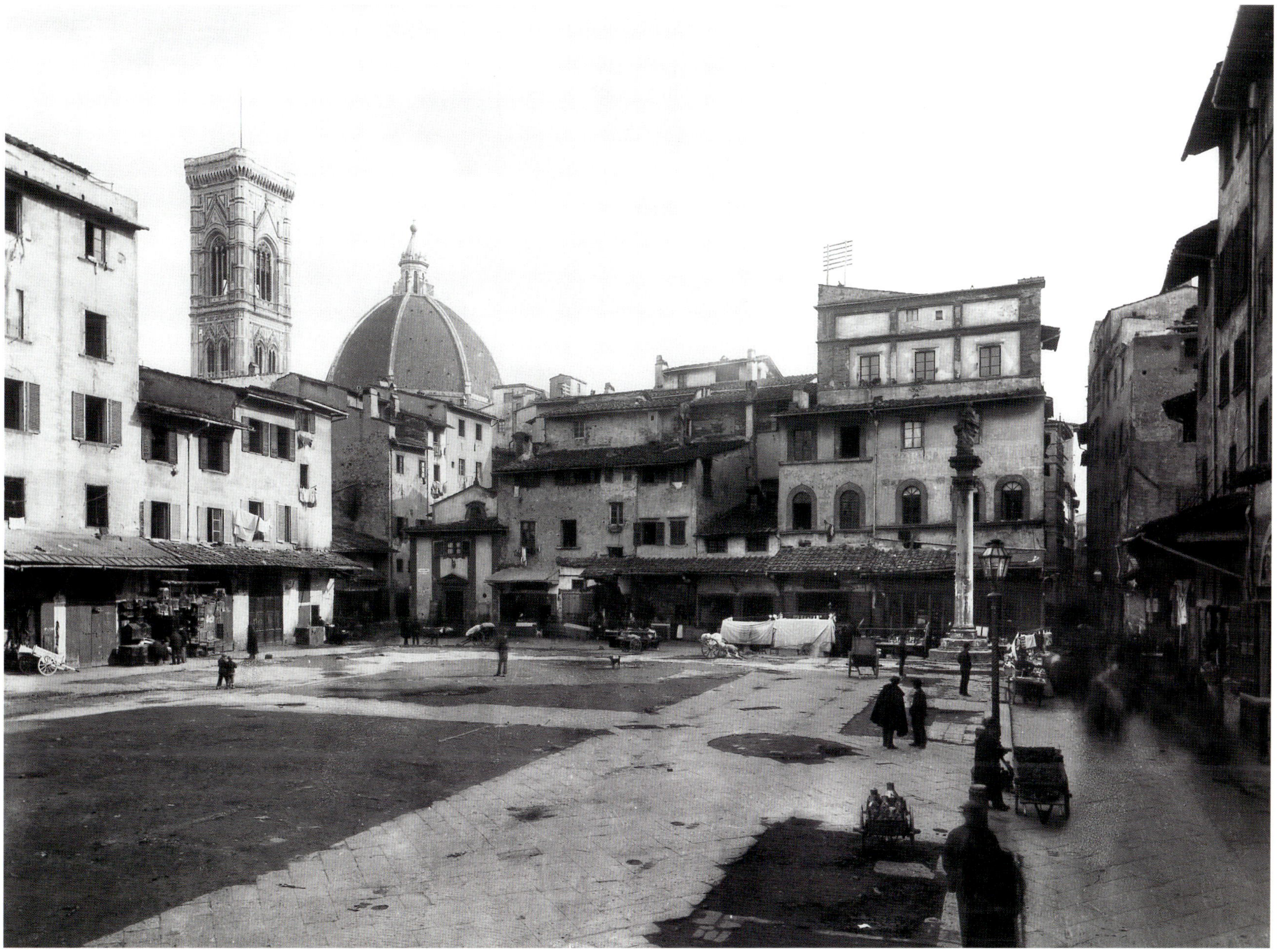

away to the east; it still stands there today, isolated and quite devoid of meaning, far from its original function as a shelter for the city's fishmongers.

At the end of the century, therefore, Florence had clearly lost the significance and impetus of its brief role as capital city, although it was left with the dramatic built legacy of those few years.

Twentieth-Century Development Plans

The city's history over the last century has been marked by a series of attempts to reach compromises with various new forms of technology and industrialization while still retaining the vital characteristics of its own identity — a familiar enough dilemma for all historic city centers. The key event in this story remains the long-lasting effect of the loss of the city walls, since without this clear definition of what was "within" and what was "without," the way was now left open for further and further dilution of the city's fabric, and ever more extensive expansion into the plain to the west and northwest, and toward the hills to the north and east.

Technological change, above all in transport, facilitated this spread, first with the railway, then with trams, and finally with the internal combustion engine. There were other pressures for expansion, too, in the years between 1890 and the First World War, when the population increased by as much as one-third. New housing was built in many parts of the periphery, much of it in the form of terraces of workers' cottages, particularly in the northeast as far as the first foothills toward Fiesole, and to the northwest around the industrial suburb of Rifredi. New bodies were established to plan and direct these works, an Ente Autonomo for popular housing, and a Comitato degli Indigenti for the truly destitute.[10] Some of these developments were concentrated, logically enough, on remaining gaps just outside the old line of the city walls. A new general development plan for Florence was tentatively proposed in 1907 but it was not begun until 1915. In essence this Piano Regolatore, a plan based on highway systems and access into the city center, also proposed a network of parks and open spaces but did little other than sanction the city's more or less uncontrolled spread toward the surrounding hills. In particular, as a result of its railway link, Rifredi was identified as a zone for major industrial expansion. Further proposals were made to modernize parts of the historic center; fortunately, though, only one of these, in the district of Santa Croce, was carried out only partially in the 1930s during the Fascist era, and was confined to a three-block sector between the Via dell'Agnolo and Via Pietrapiana. Similarly destructive proposals for the Oltrarno were not executed.

In Florence as elsewhere, a number of important modern individual buildings were erected during the Fascist period, some of considerable architectural importance. They included the new sports stadium built by Pier Luigi Nervi in 1931 to the east of the city, and the reconstruction of the Santa Maria Novella railway station in 1934–35. This latter work involved the demolition of part of one of the monastic cloisters, as well as many other local losses.

The Second World War inflicted grave damage on the city's fabric; most of the destruction was not the direct result of bombardment, but resulted from the German decision to thwart the Allied advance northward from Rome. The most catastrophic result was that all of the bridges across the Arno were blown up by the retreating Germans, with the sole exception of the Ponte Vecchio; the Allied advance was made as difficult as possible by the demolition of many buildings around the northern and southern bridgeheads of the Ponte Vecchio, and along the Via Guicciardini and most of Por Santa Maria; several palazzi and a number of ancient towers were reduced to rubble.

After 1945, almost all of the bridges over the Arno were rebuilt in simpler, more modern forms, although the Ponte Santa Trinità, the last to be reconstructed, was reopened in 1958 as a faithful replica of that which Ammannati had built four centuries earlier. The issue of reconstruction around the Ponte Vecchio bridgeheads, though, was considerably more difficult to resolve because, although not all of the lost buildings necessarily had great architectural merit, collectively they nevertheless had formed an extremely densely built-up prominent part of the city's fabric. In urban terms there were two losses, one being the vital north–south axis formed by Por Santa Maria, the bridge itself, and Via Guicciardini; and the other the east–west axis along the two banks of the river. In 1946 a competition was launched for the design of replacement buildings, and although some of the proposals were highly inventive, the end result was essentially a compromise between commercial pressures to maximize heights and densities, and the desire to re-create something of the character of what had been lost.[11]

In 1951 a new plan for the city was proposed that, although never fully adopted officially, provided sound, basic lines for Florence's development into the 1960s. One of this plan's positive features was the recognition that the city could not continue to develop solely in concentric rings, but that there was an important axis toward Sesto and Prato in the northwest that should be recognized and developed further in a controlled manner. Some of the other precepts were equally farsighted: the revitalization of inner quarters of the city such as Santa Croce and the Oltrarno was considered a high priority, as was the protection and safeguarding of the surrounding hills, particularly Fiesole and those to the southeast. Other principles included the decentralization of polluting industries, and the control of traffic in the city center; only in the last fifteen years has this last question been given any serious consideration.

Without a new, adopted general development plan, expansion during the 1960s was dramatic indeed, much of it completely unregulated and without any form of planning approvals. Finally, in 1962, a new Piano Regolatore was published; however, attempts to coordinate this plan and integrate it with the cooperation of the surrounding *comuni* were doomed to failure. Later attempts at such integration have met with only partial success.

On 4 November 1966, Florence was devastated by the flooding of the Arno. The river had inundated the city many times in its history, on rare but violent and ill-predicted occasions, usually when the tributaries in the hills and mountains to the east had been swollen with torrential rains. But in more recent times the riverbanks had been raised and strengthened, such that many Florentines believed the Arno was now tamed and civilized. In 1966, however, they were proved disastrously wrong. The floods reached the city in the early hours of the morning while the townspeople slept and the authorities were terribly ill-prepared. By midmorning the worst flood in well over a hundred years had reached the cathedral; the *lungarni* were under 6 to 10 feet (2 to 3 meters) of water, while the Ponte Vecchio threatened to collapse. The torrential waters carried off vehicles by the score, wrenched panels from Ghiberti's baptistery doors, and filled the entire city center with filthy, oil-polluted waters. By nightfall the city was still inundated. The waters began to recede on the following day, but the damage was incalculable. Barely a single monument was left without serious, and in many cases permanent, damage; paintings and archives were lost, frescoes ruined. There followed a quite extraordinary global response, with offers of assistance of every kind from every field of human expertise, and within three or four years much was restored, repaired, consolidated. An immense accumulation of specialized knowledge and expertise in restoration of every kind of material was one of the most important results of this catastrophe, and over the last few decades this knowledge has been applied to rescue works following many other disasters, and also, less dramatically but invaluably, to safeguard works, such as frescoes, subject to environmental degradation and pollution.

14 **The Architecture of Florence since Unification**

"The architect should be equipped with knowledge of many branches of study and varied kinds of learning . . . He ought to be both naturally gifted and amenable to instruction . . . Let him be educated, skilful with the pencil, instructed in geometry, know much history, have followed the philosophers with attention, understand music . . ." **Vitruvius**, *Ten Books of Architecture* (first century BC) [1]

The dramatic events associated with Florence's brief period as capital of Italy also had a strong impact on the city's architecture. The new architecture of this brief era tends to be large in scale, grandiose, formal, neoclassical (of one shade or another), its general appearance clearly intended to reinforce the image popularly conceived as that appropriate for such an august — if short-lived — role as national capital. This urban scale, evinced by the grand boulevards set out along the lines of

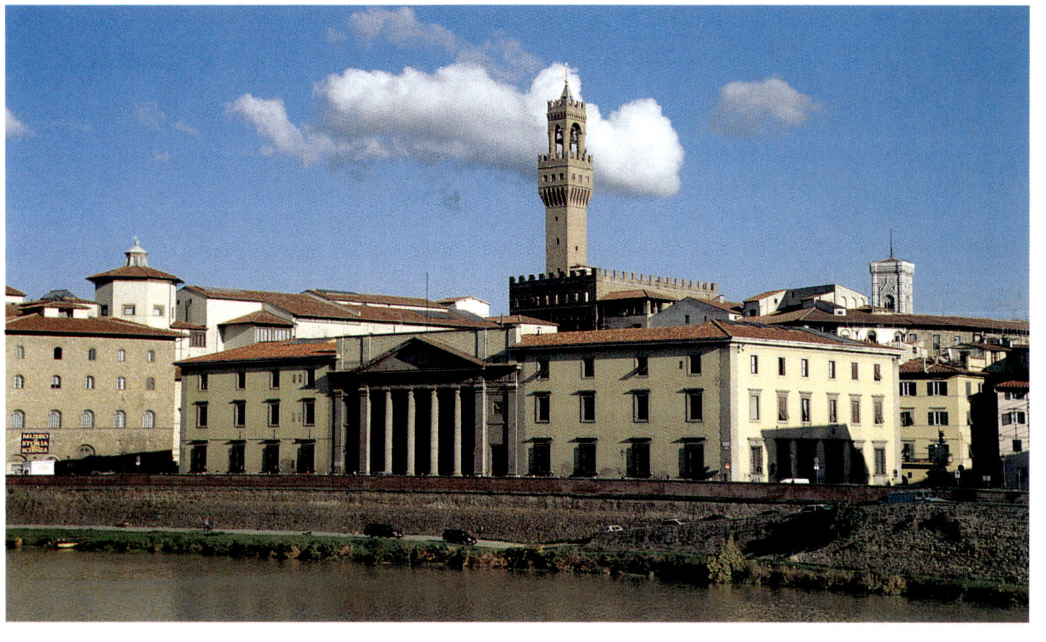

PALAZZO DELLA BORSA

The stock exchange building from 1858–60 by Emilio de Fabris and Michelangelo Majorfi was one of a number of major works along the *lungarno* in this period.

the old city walls, can perhaps be seen most clearly in the architecture surrounding these new piazze: Piazza d'Azeglio, Piazza Beccaria, Piazza della Libertà, and Piazza della Repubblica.[2] Neoclassicism in this period, though, took several forms. One of the earliest examples of midcentury metropolitan architecture was the Palazzo della Borsa, the city's new chamber of commerce, a dignified Greek structure with a prominent Doric portico on the north bank of the Arno designed by Michelangelo Majorfi and Emilio de Fabris in 1858.

But it was with the grander urban set pieces that Giuseppe Poggi was able to realize the appropriate "capital city" scale, comparable with the *rond-points* and other piazze of Paris, Rome, Milan, and Turin — all of them, of course, considerably larger, more truly metropolitan European cities. The first square, for example, Piazza Beccaria, was begun in 1865, and although the capital had moved again before its completion, the whole ensemble has a strong stylistic unity despite the rather daunting scale of the central space. It is a true *rond-point* (seven streets converge here, although not precisely symmetrically), with its focal point at least notionally formed by the surviving Porta alla Croce, which is today stranded in the center of a busy traffic junction, and with the historic remnants of the market from which the piazza takes its name long since disappeared. The surrounding palazzi, though, are elegant and well ordered, with Poggi's favored rustication to the ground floor, surmounted by a two-story giant order of Corinthian pilasters supporting a powerfully expressed cornice.

At Piazza della Libertà, Poggi resorted to a rather different vocabulary. Here again the center of the piazza is today defined — and isolated — by incessant traffic as much as by the medieval Porta San Gallo and the more prominent Arco di Trionfo. The surrounding palazzi are united by spacious ground-floor colonnades, above which are two stories of fairly simple, rhythmic classical fenestration, characteristic more of some nineteenth-century parts of Bologna than of Florence.

The third of these great public squares, Piazza d' Azeglio, was begun just before Florence became the capital, but was not completed until 1866. On the eastern edge of the city center, it is located just inside the line of Poggi's boulevards, and has thus been spared the transformation into a major traffic hub, as the others have become. The square is large and rectangular, a counterpart in the eastern districts to the Piazza della Indipendenza in the west, and was surrounded by substantial three- and four-story apartment blocks. In the center a large, well-planted public garden provides some much needed green space to this poor, crowded sector of the city; it was, in fact, modeled on the principles of the London squares, and the garden was intended solely for the use of the occupants of the surrounding palazzi.

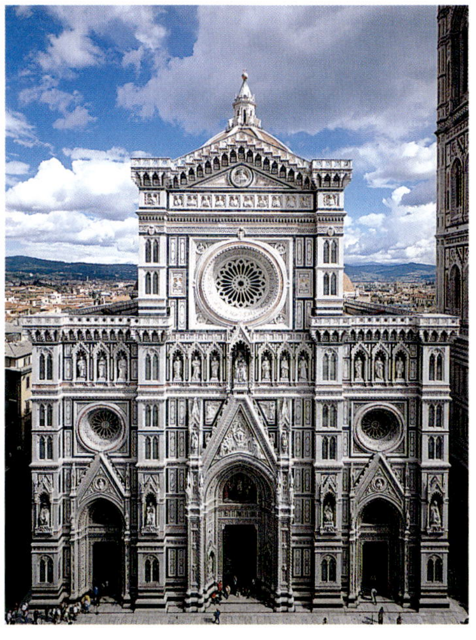

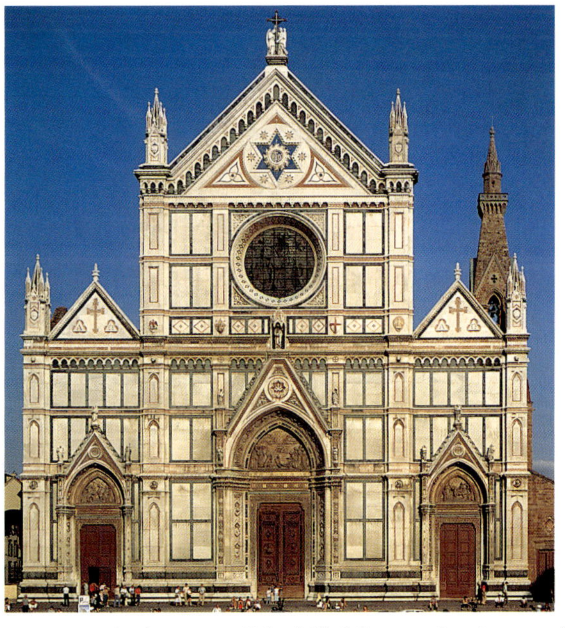

SANTA MARIA DEL FIORE (above)

The facade of the cathedral from 1876–87 by Emilio de Fabris and Luigi del Moro remains the subject of considerable debate today, well over a century after its completion.

SANTA CROCE (above, right)

Facade by Nicola Matas, 1857. The completion of the facades of both Santa Croce and the cathedral in this period, in styles that attempted to reinterpret the Florentine Gothic past, was highly controversial.

Two final works resulting from the Poggi plan should be mentioned, since not only were they important in urban terms but they also involved significant new buildings: the Piazza Poggi and Piazzale Michelangelo, which together radically altered the approaches to the hill of San Miniato. Piazza Poggi was conceived as a rationalization of the spaces around the medieval Porta San Niccolò, with a series of ramps and steps, and with four *palazzine* (only three were actually built) to define the square at the bottom of the hill. These *palazzine* are characteristic of Poggi's substantial but refined Neoclassicism, and the project was continued with the construction, farther up the hill, of the vast balcony of Piazzale Michelangelo, with its spectacular views over the eastern part of the city center. The loggia on the piazzale was originally conceived by Poggi as a museum dedicated to Michelangelo, but it became a mundane café, the nobler intentions for the piazzale remaining confined to the copy of *David* that stands at the center of the square.

While the architectural works of Poggi and his successors developed the neoclassical tradition, the other spirit of the age was technological, and found its expression chiefly in the railway station (rebuilt since), the central markets, and the tepidarium of the botanical gardens. The new Mercato Centrale, designed by Giuseppe Mengoni and inaugurated in 1874, is a fine example of the iron-and-glass rationalism of the era. The *mercato* combined the logic of the functional industrial tradition with classical cast iron detailing, in the characteristic manner of the period. The price to be paid for this admirable edifice, though, was the clearing of a sizeable area of the old city and the demolition of a number of historic structures. The tepidarium is perhaps an even more notable "palace of glass," modeled on the Crystal Palace and Palm House at Kew in London; it is remarkable for the refinement of its minimal detailing.

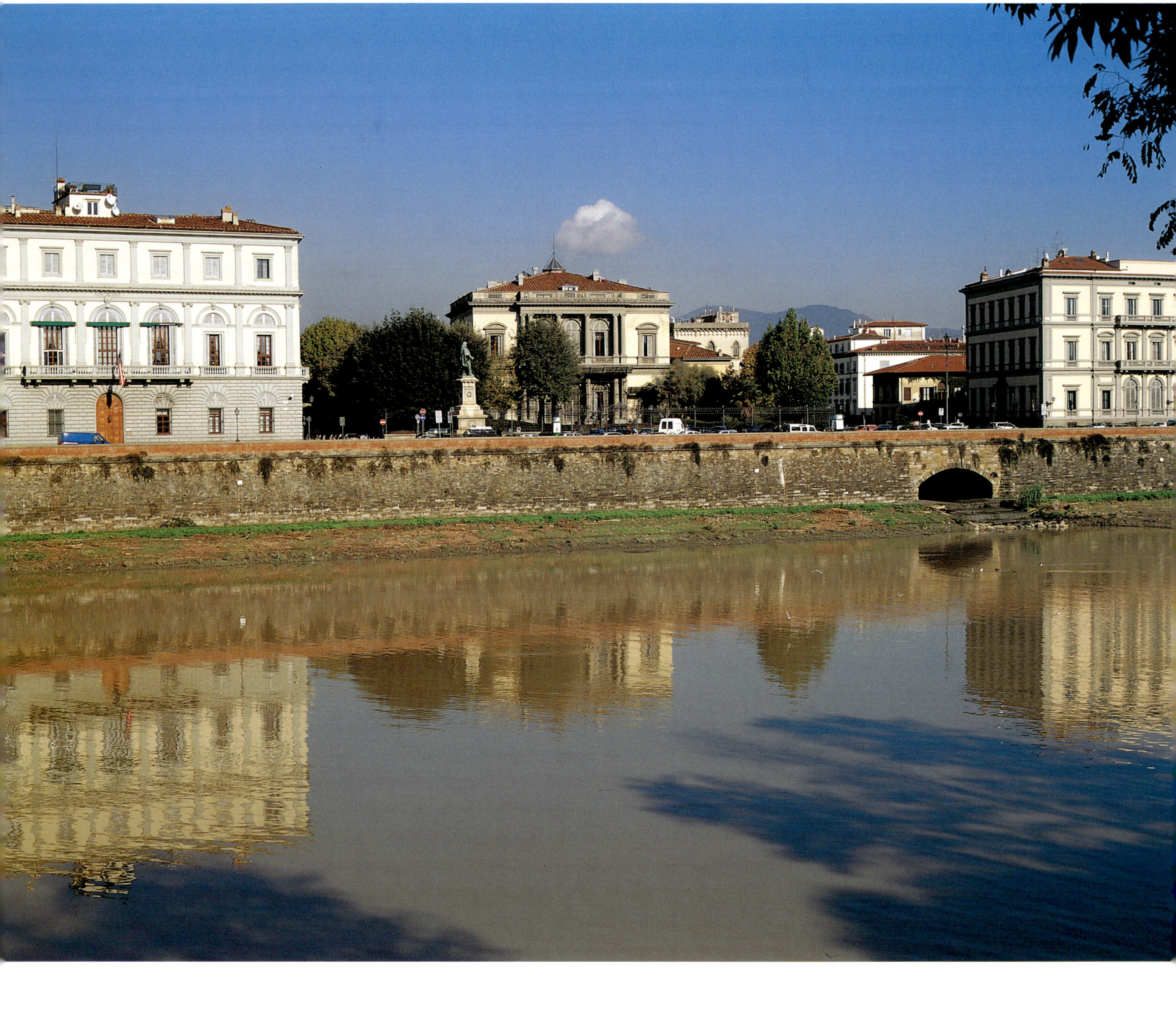

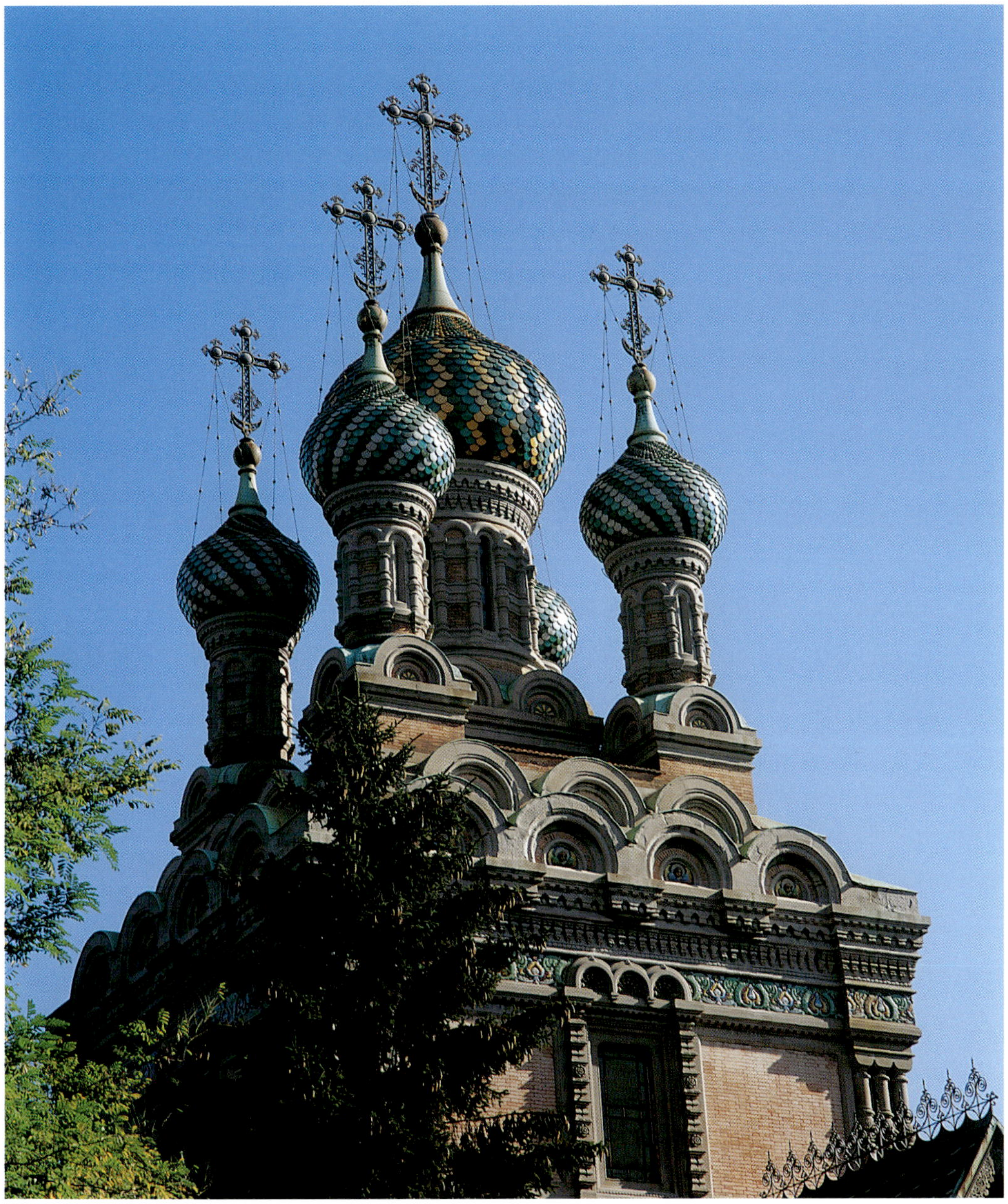

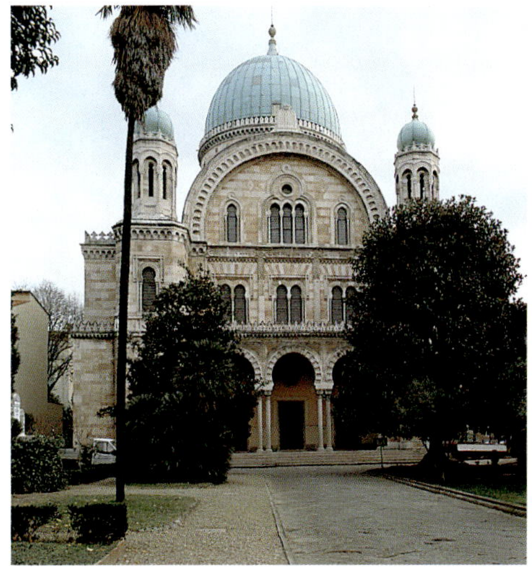

THE SYNAGOGUE (above)

The outstanding synagogue, with its mixture of orientalist elements, was built by Vincenzo Micheli from 1874 to 1882.

RUSSIAN ORTHODOX CHURCH (left)

Florence is rich in examples of eclectic later nineteenth-century architecture. The Russian Orthodox church was built by Michail Preobragenski and others in 1899–1903.

VILLA FAVARD (opposite)

The villa, from 1857, is a strongly modeled but highly refined example of Giuseppe Poggi's Neoclassicism.

Far more controversial, though, in this period of the evolving "battle of the styles" was the decision to construct a facade for Santa Croce, which, like those of most of Florence's major churches, had languished in bare brick for several centuries. The desire to complete such works was highly characteristic of the time, as one can see with the proposals for the facade of the cathedral a few years later. Although today these neo-Gothic facades may seem inevitable to many, the stylistic choice was by no means unchallenged at the time. The proposal by Nicola Matas for Santa Croce in 1857–63 was the subject of extensive polemic and debate, the result of which many regard today as an excessively literal, rather pedantic reiteration of the medieval *alla fiorentina* motifs of panels of white Carrara marble accented with green marble from Prato; in broad terms, the facade is designed after the manner of the baptistery, but with some acknowledgments to the cathedrals of Orvieto and Siena. The strong contrast, though, between this external richness and the grand austerity of Arnolfo di Cambio's great church behind it represents a tension that is not resolved, and one is left wondering how Arnolfo himself would have completed the church's facade: certainly not in this rich, opulent, "un-Franciscan" manner.[3]

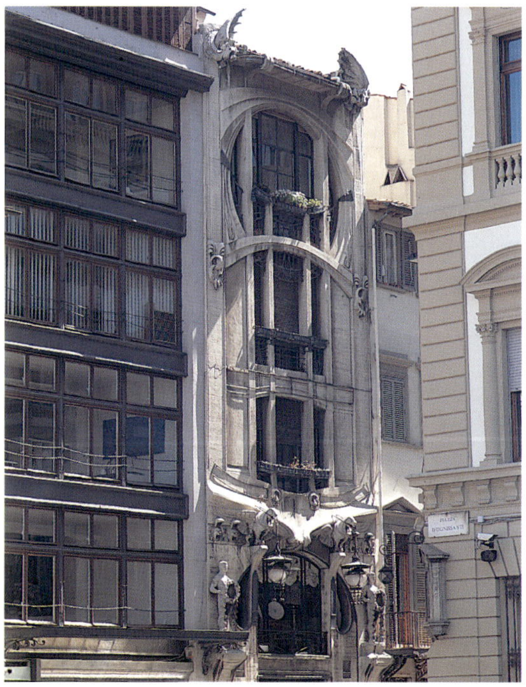

CASA GALLERIA VICHI (left)

Built by Giovanni Michelazzi in 1911, this is probably the richest and most self-indulgent of several notable Art Nouveau, or "Liberty," buildings in Florence.

MERCATO SAN LORENZO (opposite, top)

Although its construction in 1869–74 resulted in the loss of the traditional local urban fabric, the market by Giuseppe Mengoni is a fine example of the iron-and-glass rational aesthetic of the nineteenth century.

PIAZZA DELLA REPUBBLICA (opposite, bottom)

The piazza by Vincenzo Micheli and others occupies the site of the cleared Mercato Vecchio, and is surrounded by grandiose commercial developments of the late nineteenth century.

Similar observations can be made about the facade of the cathedral. Again Matas submitted a proposal, although sixteen years later, in 1859, a new public competition was announced. It was then postponed for two years as a result of the turbulent political situation, but was relaunched in 1861, when a number of Gothic variants were put forward for consideration. (Many of these alternative proposals can be seen displayed in the Museo dell'Opera.) None found favor, and so a second competition procedure was begun in 1863. The declared winner was Emilio de Fabris, who proposed to finish the facade with three gables like that of Santa Croce. Yet again, however, no clear mandate was forthcoming, and so a third and final competition was launched in 1867; once more de Fabris was declared the winner, subject to his making some further modifications to the design. The facade that we see today was therefore finally begun in 1876, to be completed eleven years later. The final conclusion regarding the manner of treating the roofline was Luigi del Moro's solution, a basilican arrangement with a central gable and two flat-topped side wings, all surmounted by a heavy oversailing machicolation, intended to echo that of the adjacent campanile.[4] Larger, richer, more deeply molded and sculpted than that of Santa Croce, the facade succeeds only in the most general sense that it superficially unites the other historic elements in this famous group, the campanile and the baptistery. But it remains essentially a stylistic exercise, rather than a genuine reinterpretation, and again there is a violent disjuncture — similar to that at Santa Croce — between the rich facade and the noble minimalism of the immense interior of the church behind this facade.

The many new nonecclesiastical works that resulted directly or indirectly from the Poggi plan generally took stylistic routes different from those at the two great churches, however, and many achieved their aims with considerable success. One of the first was Palazzo Calcagnini, designed by Poggi himself in 1857, for a prominent site on the new Lungarno Vespucci. The style is a sober, dignified Neoclassicism, which Poggi found singularly appropriate in the years following 1860, with its implications of a grand future for the city that would be comparable to the earlier eighteenth-century elegance of the former capital, Turin. The Villa Favard, on an almost adjacent but rather different site, shows an appropriately distinctive response from Poggi: This is effectively

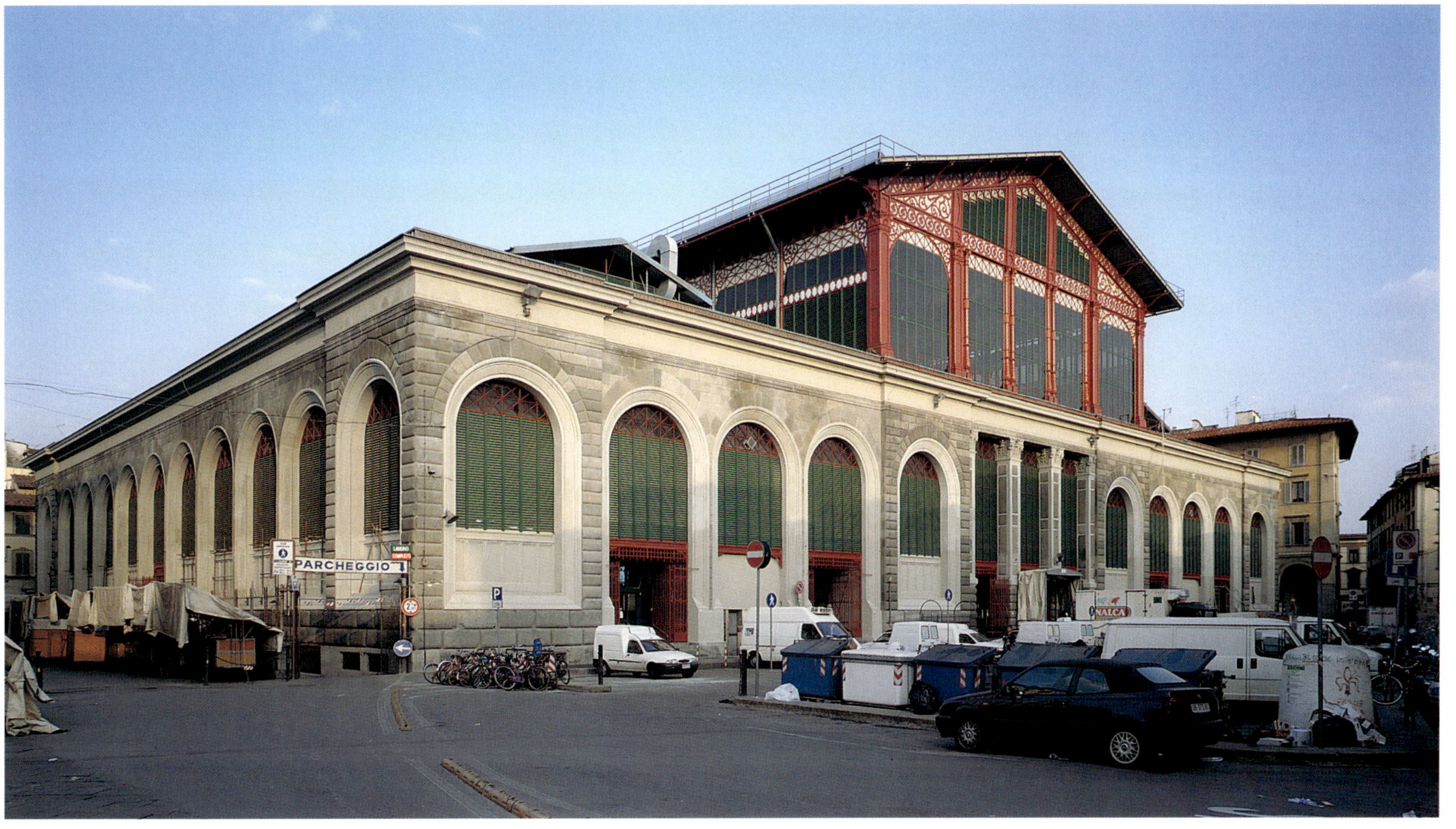
PARCHEGGIO

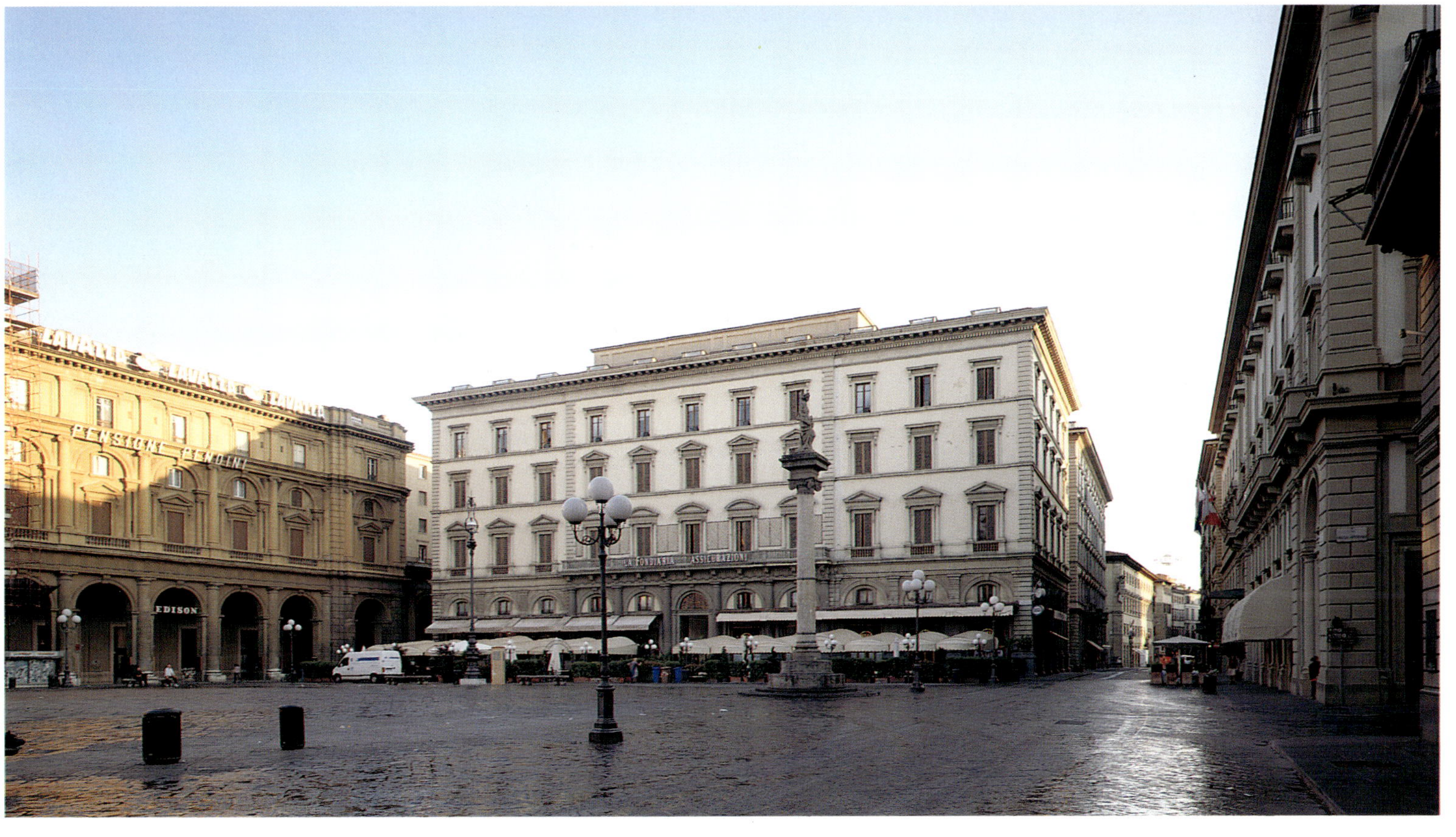
PENSIONE PENDINI
EDISON

a slightly out-of-place suburban villa, freestanding and built on two stories, but again classical and with a powerful Doric–Ionic loggia toward the Arno.

But the most monumental result of the era of Poggi, and of Florence as capital, was undoubtedly the demolition and reconstruction of the Mercato Vecchio district, which reemerged as the grand Piazza Vittorio Emanuele II, now the Piazza della Repubblica. Following the demolitions of 1885, the new palazzi surrounding the square were complete by around 1893. The centerpiece of this grand example of speculative urban renaissance is the Arcone, the arch bridging the junction where the Via degli Strozzi enters the square on the west side. The arch forms the central feature of the great block that forms the entire west side of the piazza, with its grandiose ground-floor colonnades and its unusual upper levels consisting of two further superimposed orders looming over the square. The palazzi occupying the remaining sides of the piazza are all equally imposing, characteristically ebullient examples of the speculative developments of the period. They were designed by several of Florence's leading neoclassical architects of the time, among them Vincenzo Micheli (who also designed the Arcone), Giuseppe Rossi, and Giuseppe Boccini, and lend a powerful unity and consistency to the ensemble.[5]

SANTA MARIA NOVELLA RAILWAY TERMINUS

Below, left: view of the exterior. Built by Giovanni Michelucci, Italo Gamberini, and others in 1934–36, this is a world-famous example of the Modern Movement; although constructed during the Fascist era, it was outstandingly innovative. Below: view of the interior main hall.

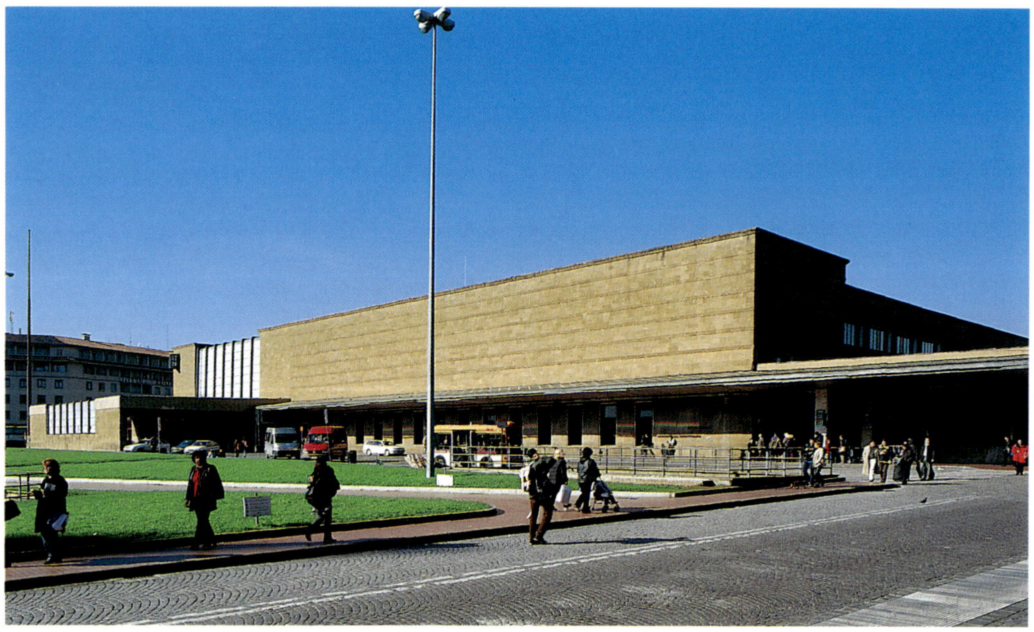

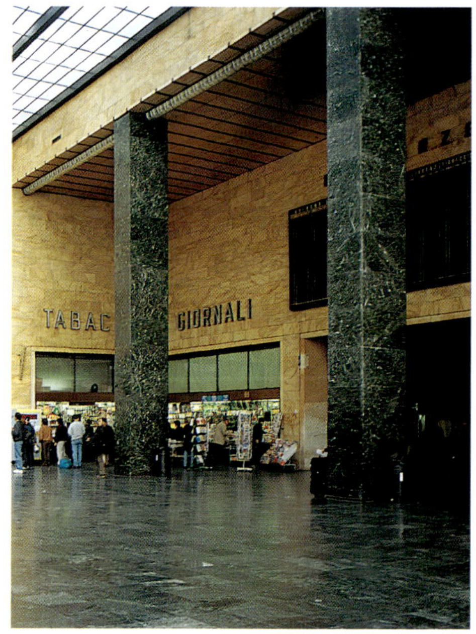

The later nineteenth century, though, was an age of eclecticism in Florence as elsewhere in Western Europe, and while much new development is characteristically Neoclassical and "Poggian" in style, the Jewish synagogue and the Russian Orthodox church, completed in 1882 and 1903, respectively, represent the more extreme, and the most literal, aspects of this eclectic approach. Both buildings are testimony to the lively internationalism of the city in this period, although the Jewish community in Florence is, of course, of very ancient origin. The ghetto had been demolished in the Mercato Vecchio clearances, and so the native Jewish population was forced to resettle, many of its members in this part of Santa Croce. The synagogue by Vincenzo Micheli and others is in a style best described as Moorish-Byzantine, with two flanking turrets and a great central arch, beyond which rises an imposing copper dome. The cladding in two colors of marble, though, clearly attempts to place the facades within the ancient Florentine tradition. If the synagogue, appropriately enough, borrows from a wide variety of Middle Eastern stylistic sources, the church, on the other hand, is far more single-mindedly Russian, with its multicolored onion domes set on tall drums and surmounted by large crosses. It was founded by the daughter of Czar Nicholas I, and its interior is as richly decorated as the spirited exterior would suggest, in accordance with the Eastern Orthodox rite.

STADIO COMUNALE

Built between 1929 and 1932 by Pier Luigi Nervi for the World Cup in 1934, the stadium is dominated by the 230-foot (70 meters) high "Maratona" tower; its refined structure was unfortunately compromised by alterations when the competition returned to Florence in 1990.

Overleaf: detail of the staircase.

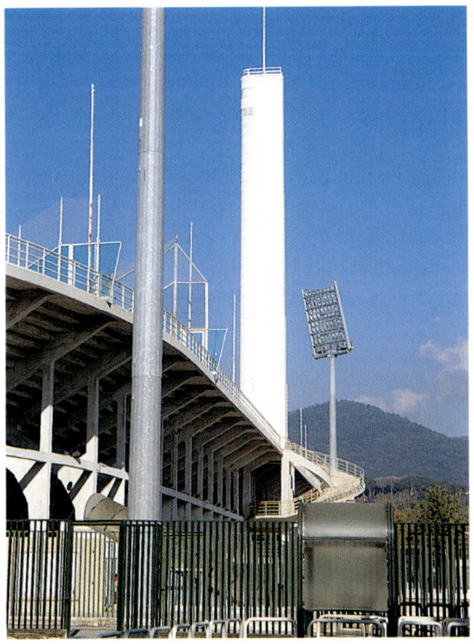

By the end of the century, the dominant style in Florence remained a rather heavy Neoclassicism, but it began to be tempered in the early years of the new century by the increasing influence of the "Liberty" or Art Nouveau style. The first rather tentative manifestations can be identified in the form of the Maggazzini Pola e Todescan, but the most exotic urban example is the wonderful facade of the Casa Galleria Vichi in Borgo Ognissanti, designed by Giovanni Michelazzi in 1911. Few works outside Brussels and Paris can be said to express the essence of the style more sinuously, more bizarrely, than this tall, elegant but highly eclectic facade.[6] Michelazzi was the foremost exponent of Art Nouveau architecture in Florence, and designed a number of suburban villas for wealthy Florentines to indulge their personal aesthetic tastes, of which the Villino Lampredi from 1908–10 and Villino Broggi from 1911 are the finest examples. At the former, a fairly conventional plan is enlivened by a highly creative facade, at the center of which stone dragons support a first-floor balcony with their wings, and where the ironwork of the ground-floor windows and first-floor balconies has a sinuous fluidity reminiscent of Antoni Gaudí. The Villino Broggi is more fluid in its structural form, however, and is unique in Florence in that the highly sculptural, three-dimensional exterior reflects the spatial flow in the internal volumes, in particular that of the helical staircase. Balconies and turrets appear to be almost extruded, and there is again a characteristically flexible, imaginative manipulation of ironwork.

Architecture Between the Wars and the Modern Era

The interwar period, dominated by the rise of Fascism, produced some important and remarkable works of architecture in the city. Although powerful conservative aesthetic interests continued to thrive in Florence as a result of the weight of its past, the city could not remain isolated against the influence of a dynamic younger generation; in particular the futuristic visions of Antonio Sant'Elia — although none were realized on the scale originally envisaged — influenced the younger architects of the so-called Tuscan Group, principally Italo Gamberini and Giovanni Michelucci, as well as the latter's contemporary, the remarkable architect-engineer Pier Luigi Nervi.

Nervi's Stadio Comunale, begun in 1929 on the site of the old Campo di Marte military base, brought for the first time a raw concrete modernism to the city. The stadium, constructed entirely of reinforced concrete cast in situ, is simple, logical, and repetitive, with just a few carefully identified features designed to raise its quality to refined architecture rather than pure engineering. One of these features is the helical staircase, the other the extraordinarily slender Torre di Maratona, which is 230 feet (70 meters) high. The stadium, although universally recognized as a pivotal work of the Modern Movement, was unfortunately altered for the 1990 World Cup, when additional staircases compromised the original clarity of its form.[7]

The Tuscan Group represented a strong regional reaction against the anonymity of the more purist Modernists, and the work of its members retains a powerfully organic element in their bold use of modern materials. The peak of their achievement is represented by the new railway station at Santa Maria Novella, which was built following a competition held in 1932. The results were highly contentious, though, and heated debate led to polarization of views in both camps: On one hand stood the Florentine modernist intellectual elite, who strongly favored the winners, while on the other was a combination of conservative, reactionary figures allied with some elements of the Fascist governing regime. The main structure was completed by 1935 and remains a remarkable (and still controversial) addition to the city's monuments, one of the earliest and still most important Modern Movement works in Italy. Its massing is insistently horizontal, with the austere principal facade toward the city center (and the back of Santa Maria Novella) clad in *pietra forte* but enlivened with a taller, fully glazed "cascade of glass," a cavernous porte cochere forming the entrance itself. The second outstanding element is the concourse, with its dominant folded roof structure, broken by a long, raking band of glazing that brings natural light into all parts of the space. With the passage of time, this huge, spacious concourse has effectively become another of

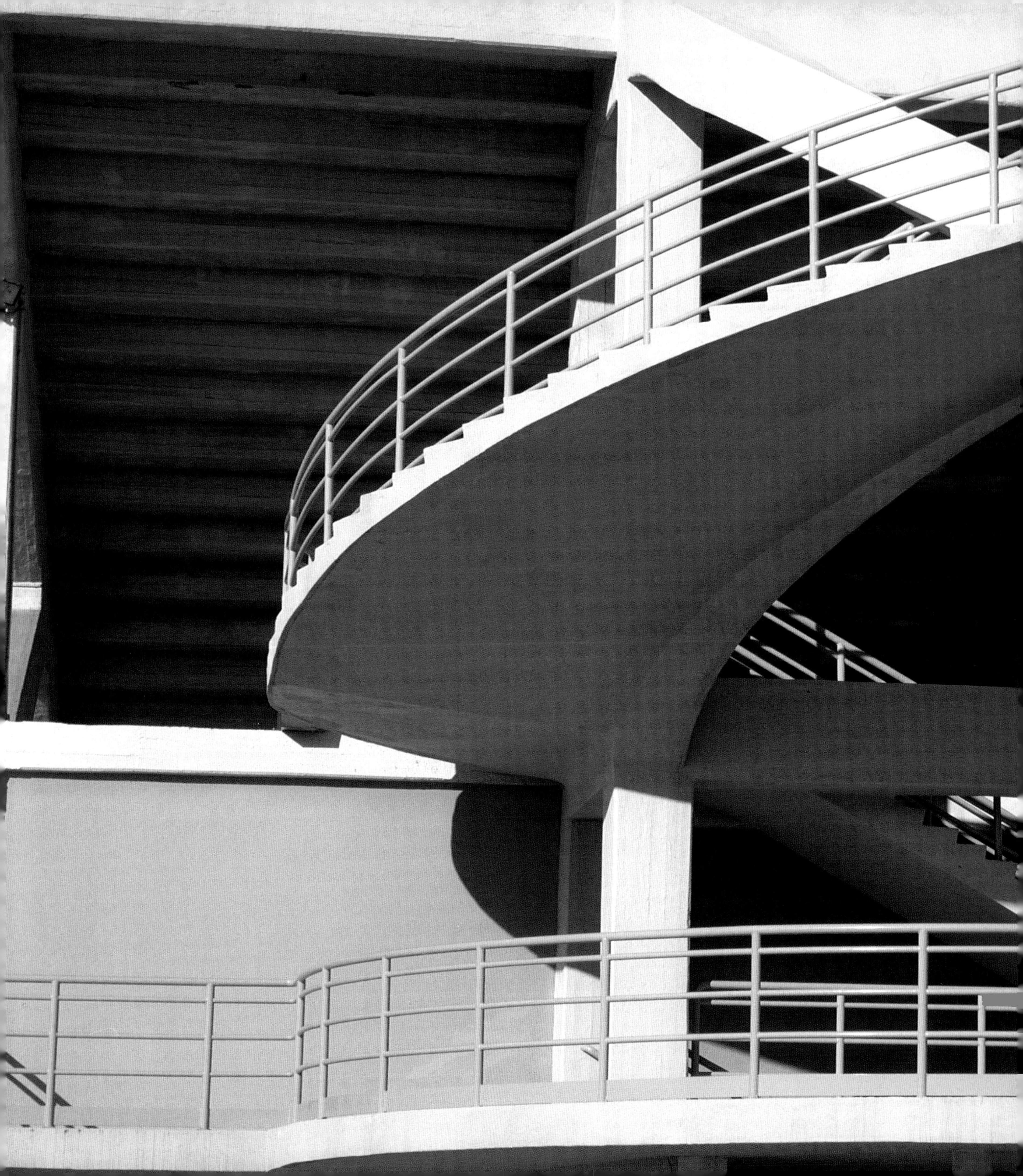

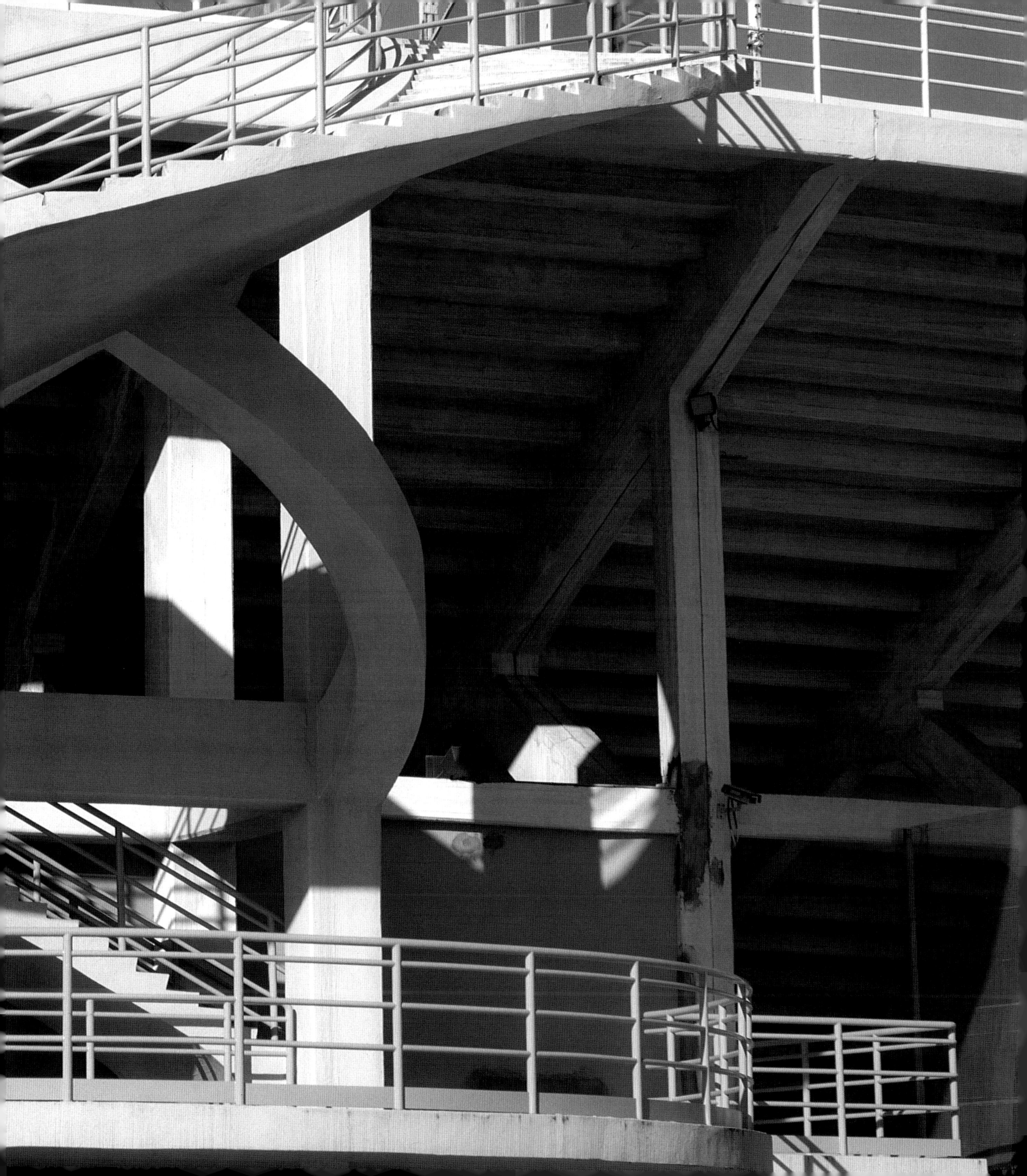

the city's great public piazze, a meeting place for thousands every day, albeit a rather less traditional one than those of Santa Croce or the Piazza della Signoria.[8]

Pure "white modern" works in the manner of the highly influential Giuseppe Terragni are lacking in Florence, however, where the inherently more eclectic and even mannerist tendencies of the Tuscan Group remained the dominant influence. Works such as the railway buildings near the station by Angiolo Mazzoni reflect a more sculptural, pragmatic response to their individual sites than do many "purer" Modern Movement works, while the reactionary monumentality of the new Biblioteca Nazionale Centrale, completed in the same year as the railway station, represents the other end of the stylistic spectrum: a grandiose and excessively pompous pile in an eclectic neoclassical idiom. Nothing illustrates better the range of responses to the city's fabric in the first half of the twentieth century than these two works, which are physically only half a mile apart, but several centuries distant in their design philosophy.

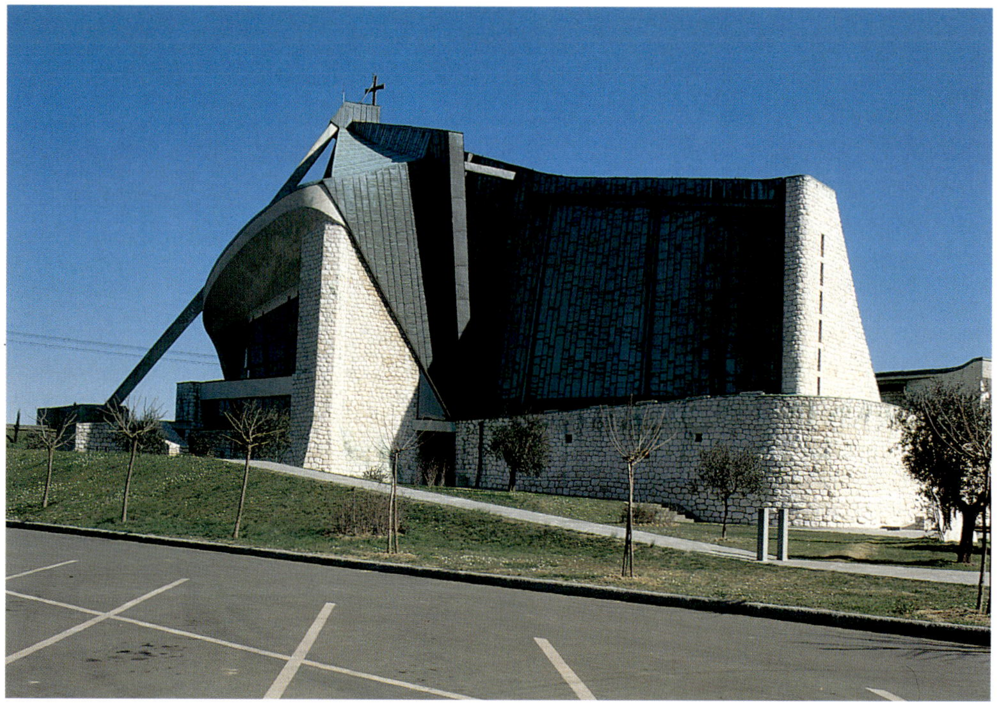

SAN GIOVANNI BATTISTA ("CHIESA DELL'AUTOSTRADA")

Michelucci's masterpiece of 1960–64 is a triumphant resolution of volumetric complexity, externally expressed by its tentlike form.

In the immediate postwar period, the most urgent priority in Florence was clearly the repair of war damage. However, three major threads can be identified in the development of architecture in the city since the 1950s: the continuation of a strong functional, engineering-led tradition, influenced above all by Nervi, and often highly refined and inventive; the development of free, more organic forms, as epitomized by some of the later works of Michelucci; and the more "mainstream" modernist tradition.

It is with the construction of several new bridges across the Arno that the development of the first of these three threads can be most easily identified. The destruction of every bridge except the Ponte Vecchio by the Germans in 1944 led to two demands: the urgent reconstruction of those lost, together with new crossings to link the city more easily with the surrounding state highway network, and in particular with the proposed Autostrada del Sole. The Ponte alle Grazie was the first to be rebuilt in a clearly modern style, on the site of the city's ancient eastern crossing. The result of a competition, the bridge attempts to fuse the honesty of exposed concrete beams with massive stone piers, echoing its earlier historic form. Ponte Vespucci, on the other hand, built in 1954–57, downstream from the Ponte alla Carraia, was a totally new construction by Riccardo Morandi, with a simple, elegant, minimalist approach. There followed a gap of a decade before the two more recent spans across the Arno were built: the Ponte da Verrazzano in 1967–69 by Leonardo Savioli and the Ponte all'Indiano in 1969–76 by Fabrizio di Miranda and others. Of the two, the former is upstream of the historic center, while the latter stands downstream, at the western end of Le Cascine. The design approach is quite different: The Verrazzano bridge has a single span of 380 feet (115 meters), supported on each side by substantial concrete abutments, while the Ponte all'Indiano, with a considerably greater span of around 700 feet (210 meters), is the only suspension bridge in Florence, an altogether more spectacular structure with two raking pylons supporting the suspension cables.[9]

While these infrastructure works were being developed in the 1950s and 1960s, other movements and tendencies were also being established in the more conventional fields of architecture — that is, less based on engineering. The extraordinarily long career of Giovanni Michelucci, who lived from 1891 to 1990 might be thought to provide a narrative thread through these decades, but in fact, his own oeuvre demonstrated a series of distinct phases, beginning with the public works projects of the 1950s, chiefly the Cassa di Risparmio in the Via Bufalina and the Poste e Telegrafi in the Via Pietrapiana. Here one can already see his characteristic modeling and manipulation of masses — albeit partially constrained by the buildings' fairly prosaic functions — which was to reach its apogee in the famous Autostrada church of 1960–64. From the same period of postwar reconstruction, the well mannered apartment blocks of the Via Guicciardini, in their highly sensitive historic context, however, give little indication of the sculptural freedom, the poetic subtleties of the Autostrada church, where Michelucci was able to model as freely as was Le Corbusier at Ronchamp.[10] The church, formerly known as San Giovanni Battista, is dedicated to those who lost their lives constructing the extraordinary engineering feat of the *autostrada*, or motorway, and is thus a place of pilgrimage; loosely based on the essentially transitory form of the tent, it is here frozen in concrete, with the treelike forms of the branched columns supporting the great copper sails of the roof. San Giovanni Battista is Michelucci's most freely expressionistic work.

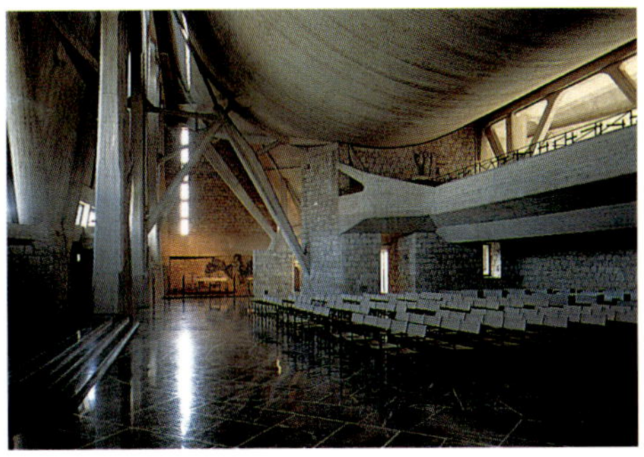

SAN GIOVANNI BATTISTA ("CHIESA DELL'AUTOSTRADA")

The interior continues the tentlike analogy, with its raking columns and subtle, carefully controlled lighting.

Roughly contemporaneous with its construction in the 1960s, slightly different, although also strongly modeled, organic and highly articulated forms were also being developed by both Leonardo Ricci and Leonardo Savioli. The group of villas designed by Ricci, for his own family among others, is perhaps the most Wrightian work to be built in Florence and its surroundings, and stands on a spectacular site carved into a hillside at Monterinaldi, just west of Fiesole. Ricci's own villa is the most expressive; it is built on a number of levels, terraced out of the hillside, with a massive stone wall forming the base, rather like a medieval defensive rampart.

Two extensive new housing projects in the peripheral zones of the city represent very different approaches to the issue of public housing. That known as the Isolotto, on the south bank opposite Le Cascine, completed in 1958, is fairly conventional, if excessively fragmented, while the other, southeast of the city at Sorgane, contains the more expressive, highly articulated apartment blocks by both Ricci and Savioli. The latter's concern with plasticity of form is seen again in a more urban context in his apartment block on Via Piagentina, while his boldly articulated forms are even more pronounced in the 1966 Villa Bayon at San Gaggio, beyond the Porta Romana, where the massive oversailing form of the roof, like a giant porte cochere, acts as a shelter for the articulation of the lesser elements of the habitation beneath it.

The work of Italo Gamberini in broadly the same period followed a slightly different path, one less boldly and three-dimensionally articulated; nevertheless, Gamberini made several attempts to deal with the issue of inserting new works into a highly developed urban context, among them the sophisticated facade of the BICA building in Via Nazionale in 1957 and the quite different, complex form of the Archivio di Stato at Santa Croce. The Archivio occupies a large pentagonal site between the Arno and Piazza Beccaria, and was developed in phases over many years, from 1972 to 1988, to form the central element in this academic district, which also includes part of the university and the nearby Biblioteca Nazionale. The Archivio focuses on an internal street, with the archive deposits themselves in a rather forbidding six-story wing along Viale Amendola, and the administration and research facilities in a more transparent, roughly parallel block on Viale Giovine Italia.[11]

More recent works on the fringes of the historic center have included further developments at Santa Maria Novella, including Cristiano Toraldo's contentious new bus station in Via Valfonda, and the additions and modifications by Gae Aulenti and others to improve access to the railway station; both of these last projects were stimulated by the necessity to control and organize large numbers of visitors to the city for the World Cup in 1990.

Florence's pivotal contribution to the cultural history of the West remains incalculable. The city emerged in the Middle Ages to become the chief commercial center of Tuscany, and the extraordinary wealth that its banking and textile industries created ensured the construction of a series of monuments, from the Bargello to the majestic cathedral, together with its enlightened program of urban improvements, which set an example of *civitas* for many other cities in Europe to emulate.

However, the city's problems at the start of the new millennium are many and acute. They are familiar to those who attempt to reconcile the numerous conflicting interests that both affect and afflict most of our historic centers, not just in Italy but in much of the developed world: the constant need for restoration and repair to the historic patrimony; the difficulties of access and congestion that make all such efforts more expensive; the management of traffic, of parking, and deliveries of goods; the high costs of living for the native residents, and ensuing drain of numbers from many such historic centers to the cheaper, more spacious suburbs; the further conversion of city center properties into nonresidential (often tourism-based) functions and the resultant loss of shops and amenities for those citizens who do remain; the huge daily influxes of tourists and the management of such numbers; the damage caused to the historic fabric by various forms of pollution. It is a familiar litany indeed, equally applicable to Venice and Rome, to Seville, Amsterdam, Prague, or Edinburgh.

Florence's most recent general development plan, that of 1985, attempted to draw on the status quo, without aiming for unrealistic and unachievable targets. Instead, it concentrated on improving infrastructures, on safeguarding green open spaces, on setting up legislation to conserve and at the same time reanimate the historic center. Although it remains to be seen how effective such a strategy will be in the longer term, it has already had tangible effects: Much of the historic center is now largely pedestrianized, the commune now uses electric- and gas-powered buses to reduce air pollution, and an extraordinary era of building conservation has recently taken place, much of it sponsored by the Church for the Jubilee Year. Major restoration has been undertaken, for example, at Santa Croce, Santa Maria Novella, and at the cathedral group, where the Museo dell'Opera was also comprehensively restored. There are further plans to rationalize and greatly enlarge the museum sector, too, partly by making far more of the Palazzo Vecchio available to the public realm; the fascinating but highly undervalued Museo di Firenze com'era is also to be relocated there.

Florence today has to fulfill many functions, some of which are apparently quite incompatible. As one of the main cultural and artistic centers of Italy, the greatest challenge is the management of the vast influx of tourists, chiefly by better dispersal and distribution both in time and in space. These problems are most acute during certain seasons, principally at Easter and in the summer. For much of the year, for example, there are long queues simply to enter the cathedral, although once inside the great space can comfortably absorb very large numbers. The Uffizi, though, remains a very special case, and this museum's difficulties are unique in the city. The present system of advance booking is only partially successful and has some serious disadvantages: It precludes any possibility of spontaneous or unplanned visits either by tourists or by Florentines themselves, and even with advance booking there is sometimes a wait of more than an hour simply to enter the building.

One of the more intelligent strategies being developed is that of planned or strategic dispersal, that is, for the promotion of a more integrated approach to the city's many other museums, churches and sites. For example, a system based on group tickets giving entry to a number of sites (at a large discount over individual entries) is partially in force in Florence, and has already proven extremely successful at the civic museums around the Piazza San Marco in Venice. One of the obstacles to further development of such integrated schemes is the different ownerships of the various major monuments of Florence: Some are the property of the Comune, others of the governmental Department of Cultural Heritage, still others of the Church, and others again remain in the hands of private bodies. Nevertheless, there is great scope for future development and coordination if such bureaucratic difficulties can be overcome. Hand in hand with such integrated schemes, visitors must be made aware of the riches of other galleries and museums — the Casa di Dante, for example, the Museo Horne, even parts of the Pitti — which are usually freely accessible, and often virtually deserted.

A much more controversial issue than the dispersal and integrated management of tourist destinations is the question of a local tourist tax, which would probably have to be levied on the basis of hotel room occupancy. Such a measure (or a version of it) has been proposed more than once in Venice, but was never implemented there as it was far too controversial. It has recently been suggested in Florence, and is currently being instigated in several other tourist destinations, including Spain and Greece. The principle of the proposal is a small daily tariff (around 1,000 lire per person per day has been suggested), generating funds that would go directly to the Comune specifically for the restoration of the city's historic fabric. Perhaps not surprisingly, there has been strong opposition from many commercial entities, which fear the loss of income for their activities, although it is difficult to envisage levies at such a modest level being a serious deterrent for most visitors. The proposal has not yet been formally developed, and there are undoubtedly many administrative issues to be resolved (for example, how does one distinguish between business visitors and tourists?); nevertheless, it represents a serious attempt to raise money for works that would otherwise have to be subsidized by the central government or by the Florentine Comune itself, by diverting resources from citizens elsewhere.

Florence has a number of other faces, though, of which the millions of tourists are naturally largely unaware. One of these derives from the medieval legacy from which the city's wealth originated: the textile industry, banking, and insurance. There are still countless workshops that provide employment for thousands, producing many of the goods for which the city has been famous for centuries: silks, fabrics, leather, and fashion. There is another, less picturesque Florence, too, that of industrial production, most of it located safely beyond the historic center, mainly in the plain to the northwest, and centered on Sesto and Prato, itself one of the most important textile centers in Italy since the medieval era. Another aspect of the city also has great importance for its economy: Florence as administrative capital of the region of Tuscany, with its four million inhabitants, and with all of the attendant bureaucracy, administration, and support services that require large numbers of civil servants and regional employees. As an indirect result of this role of regional capital, many other bodies, both public and private, have their headquarters in the city.

Many of these overlapping faces of the city are in direct conflict with each other. Tourist pressures on the *centro storico* have resulted in dramatic rent rises in recent years, driving out many of the city center's older and poorer residents. Fast-food outlets have made some inroads in displacing the traditional *osterie* and *trattorie* (although the Florentines offer strong resistance), while tourist-based retail shops replace the traditional street-corner *salumerie*. This process is by no means as far advanced as it is, for example, in Venice, where entire neighborhoods are now without a butcher or an electrician, but the tendency is clear enough. There is no doubt that mass tourism is the city's largest single employer and wealth generator, but it also remains Florence's greatest challenge in both economic and environmental terms. There is now probably more technical experience and expertise in the restoration of the city's physical fabric here than in any other city in the world (much of it learned since the 1966 floods), but the most critical aspect of the survival of the city's historic center remains its inhabitants, the Florentines themselves. Only considerable effort and perseverance (and direct financial subsidy in the form of social housing) by the Comune can prevent the city's heart from becoming an empty husk, devoid of all permanent habitation. While the vision of the Calimala thronged until well after midnight is a tribute to the successful physical regeneration of the pedestrianized city center, an even greater success will lie in the future knowledge that these crowds taking the late evening *passeggiata* are not only tourists or day visitors from the provinces but the Florentines themselves, reclaiming their own city.

Notes on the text

INTRODUCTION

1 Charles Dickens, *Pictures from Italy* (1844; new ed. London, 1973), pp. 238–39.

CHAPTER 1

1 Leon Battista Alberti, *De re aedificatoria* (c. 1452) IV, II.

2 On the early history of Florence, see also G. Maetzke, *Florentia* (Rome, 1941); and M. Lopez Pegna, *Firenze dalle origini al medioevo* (Florence, 1962). I am greatly indebted to the excellent general urban history of the city by G. Fanelli, *Firenze* (Rome and Bari, 1980), for my research for the following chapters.

3 Fanelli, *Firenze*, p. 4 (including plan).

4 A very informative model of Roman Florence is on display in the Museo di Firenze com'era, which at present is in the Via dell'Oriuolo but is to be relocated in the Palazzo Vecchio.

5 See Fanelli, *Firenze*, plan p. 4.

6 See also sketch plan of Roman Florence in *Firenze e provincia* (TCI guides, Milan, 1993), p. 42.

7 Lopez Pegna, *Firenze*, pp. 64, 66.

8 M. Lopez Pegna, *Le più antiche chiese fiorentine* (Florence, 1971).

9 On the foundation of the baptistery, which remains a highly debated issue, see pp. 94–95.

10 See also sketch plan of the Carolingian city in Fanelli, *Firenze*, p. 8.

11 These were the walls famously referred to by Dante as the "cerchia antica."

CHAPTER 2

1 Giovanni Villani, *Cronica fiorentina* (written c. 1330; new ed. Florence 1844–55), IV, VIII.

2 Especially the territorial struggles between Florence and Siena in 1174–75.

3 On the crafts see R. Davidsohn, *Storia di Firenze*, vol. 1 (Florence 1956–68), p. 1168.

4 G. Fanelli, *Firenze* (Rome and Bari, 1980), p. 14. There is also a description in Villani, *Cronica*, IV, VIII.

5 In c. 1024 bishop Ildebrando also instituted a third annual market or fair outside the city walls.

6 On San Miniato see pp. 186–87.

7 See below, p. 26; see also Fanelli, *Firenze*, p. 50, fig. 18 (the map shows the location of the towers).

8 Davidsohn, *Storia*, Vol. 1, p. 1137.

9 See Fanelli, *Firenze*, p. 20; see also P. Santini, *Le societa delle torri in Firenze*, Vol. XX (Archivio Storico Italiano, 1887), pp. 4, 5.

10 Villani, *Cronica*, VI, XXVI.

11 For a good discussion of the institution of the *podesta* in Italy, see D. Waley, *The Italian City-Republics* (London, 1969), pp. 32–36.

12 Fanelli, *Firenze*, p. 24.

13 Cited by Fanelli, *Firenze*, pp. 25–28.

14 For an introductory note on the Guelf–Ghibelline rivalries, see Waley, *The Italian City-Republics*, p. 115 et seq.

15 Fanelli, *Firenze*, pp. 29–31.

16 Dante Alighieri, *Paradiso* (c. 1319–20), XV, 97–100.

17 For a useful introduction to the city in all of its aspects in this era see P. Antonetti, *La vita quotidiana a Firenze ai tempi di Dante* (Milan, 1983).

18 On these urban improvements see Fanelli, *Firenze*, p. 33.

19 The Prato's location is recorded today by the street of that name, terminating at the homonymous Porta al Prato.

20 In *De re aedificatoria*, Alberti devotes an entire chapter to the subject; see Leon Battista Alberti, *De re aedificatoria* (c. 1452), IV, V.

21 On the sixth circle of walls, see Fanelli, *Firenze*, pp. 35–37, and maps on pp. 26, 43, 45, 47 et seq.

22 On the city gates, see pp. 172–75.

23 A reliable contemporary authority on the new city walls is Villani, who was the senior government official in charge of the works; see Villani, *Cronica*, IX, CCLVI.

24 It remains the tallest tower in the city, followed by the campanile of the cathedral.

25 The exact date of Arnolfo's death remains unknown; although often stated to be 1302, he may have lived until 1308 or 1309, but was almost certainly deceased by 1310.

26 Alberti, *De re aedificatoria*, V, III.

27 There are numerous biographies on Dante, but see especially the *Enciclopedia Dantesca* (Rome, 1978) 6 vols. See also Antonetti, *La vita*; and G. Pampaloni, *Firenze al tempo di Dante* (Rome, 1973).

28 Fanelli, *Firenze*, p. 41; see also Davidsohn, *Storia*, vol. VII, pp. 480 et seq.

29 This work was initiated by Gualtieri di Brienne, Duke of Athens, whom the Florentines had nominated "Signore in perpetuo" in 1342. However, a popular insurrection forced him to flee the city in July of that year.

30 For general figures on the population, see Pampaloni, *Firenze*, p. XVII; see also Villani, *Cronica*, IX, CLXII, and XI, XCIV.

31 Fanelli, *Firenze*, p. 53; see also N. Rodolico, "Note stilistiche sulla popolazione fiorentina," *Archivio storico italiano* (1902), XXIX.

32 Leonardo Bruni, *Laudatio florentinae urbis*, cited by Fanelli, *Firenze*, pp. 53–54.

33 Cited by G. Brucker, *Renaissance Florence* (New York, 1969).

34 For all of the above see Fanelli, *Firenze*, pp. 55–68.

35 On the importance of the *carroccio* see Antonetti, *La vita*, p. 129; and Villani, *Cronica*, VI, LXXV.

36 Fanelli, *Firenze*, p. 59. On the role of the market in the medieval period, see especially D. Calabi, *Il mercato e la citta* (Venice, 1993); on the markets of Florence, see pp. 85–90.

37 Chief among these institutions were San Marco, the Santissima Annunziata, the Spedale of San Giovanni Battista, and Santa Maria Assunta. There were no fewer than twelve monasteries/churches and five hospitals on the northern section of the Via San Gallo alone.

38 From Villani's *Cronica*, cited by C. Hibbert, *Florence: Biography of a City* (Harmondsworth, 1993), p. 43. Villani describes the river as "regale" in *Cronica*, I, XLIII.

39 The design of the Ponte alla Carraia has been attributed to Giotto. See D. Gioseffi, *Giotto architetto* (Milan, 1963).

40 On the Ponte Vecchio, see especially J. Mesquit, "The City and the Bridge in Medieval Europe," in *Rassegna* (issue entitled "Inhabited Bridges," Bologna, December 1991,), pp. 20–25, 59–61.

41 On the Ciompi, see V. Rutenburg, *Popolo e movimenti popolari nell'Italia del 300 e 400* (Bologna, 1971).

CHAPTER 3

1 Vasari's version of Brunelleschi's speech to the syndics of the cathedral regarding the construction of the cupola in Giorgio Vasari, *Lives of the Artists* (second ed. 1568; transl. J. Foster, London, 1878), I, p. 427.

2 The bibliography on the Medici is naturally enormous; an excellent general survey is provided by J. R. Hale, *Florence and the Medici: The Pattern of Control* (London, 1977), esp. pp. 9–21. See also F. Schevill, *The Medici* (New York, 1949), pp. 56–66.

3 In 1466 Luca Pitti was involved in a further attempt to overthrow the Medici; see Hale, *Florence and the Medici*, pp. 46–48.

4 For a summary see G. Fanelli, *Firenze* (Rome and Bari, 1980), pp. 68–69.

5 On Brunelleschi's works see pp. 178–79, 206–21. For the urban context see Fanelli, *Firenze*, p. 71 et seq.

6 The best overall survey of Brunelleschi's work is still E. Battisti, *Filippo Brunelleschi* (Milan, 1976).

7 In recognition of this role, nearly all subsequent views and plans of the city place the cupola of the cathedral at the very center.

8 Battisti, *Filippo Brunelleschi*, p. 196 et seq.

9 For the patronage of Cosimo, see esp. G. Holmes, *The Florentine Enlightenment* 1400–1450 (Oxford, 1969), passim.

10 See pp. 255–67.

11 Francesco Guicciardini, *Storie fiorentine* (Bari, 1931), cited in J. B. Ross and M. M. McLaughlin, *The Portable Renaissance Reader* (London, 1968), p. 269.

12 See above, note 3.

13 On Lorenzo's political career, see Hale, *Florence and the Medici*, pp. 49–75. See also N. Rubinstein, *The Government of Florence under the Medici 1434–1494* (Oxford, 1966).

14 On the Pazzi conspiracy, see Hale, *Florence and the Medici*, pp. 66–67; Schevill, *The Medici*, pp. 117–34.

15 On the Medici bank, see R. de Roover, "The Medici Bank," *Journal of Economic History*, VI, 1 (1946). See also R. de Roover, *The Rise and Decline of the Medici Bank 1397–1494* (Harvard, 1963).

16 Books on Lorenzo's patronage of the arts are numerous. See, for example, a recent study, P. L. Rubin and A. Wright, *Renaissance Florence: the Art of the 1470s* (London, 1999), with a good bibliography.

17 In G. R. B Richards, *Florentine Merchants in the Age of the Medici* (Cambridge, Mass., 1932).

18 The "della catena" view (Kupferstickkabinett, Berlin) is attributed to Francesco di Lorenzo Rosselli, and has been dated by some to as early as c. 1472, although others have dated it to the early 1480s.

19 See Fanelli, *Firenze*, pp. 83–86.

20 See the long extract of Dei's *Laudatio*, in Fanelli, *Firenze*, pp. 82–85. Dei also wrote a letter to a Venetian correspondent in 1472, couched in much the same patriotic terms, published in J. B. Ross and M. M. McLaughlin eds., *The Portable Renaissance Reader* (Harmondsworth, 1978), pp. 165–67.

21 Benedetto Dei, *Cronica fiorentina*, in G. C. Romby, *Descrizioni e rappresentazioni della città di Firenze nel XV secolo* (Florence, 1979).

22 On the stylistic development of the palazzi, see p. 252 et seq. See also L. Ginori Lisci, *The Palazzi of Florence: Their History and Art* (Florence, 1985), trans. J. Grillo.

23 On Palazzo Pitti, see C. Conti, *Il Palazzo Pitti; la sua primitiva costruzione e successivi ingrandimenti* (Florence, 1887).

24 There is considerable information on the building of Palazzo Strozzi in R. Goldthwaite, *The Building of Renaissance Florence* (Baltimore, 1980).

25 Translated by C. E. Detmold (Boston, 1882), cited in Ross and McLaughlin, *The Portable Renaissance Reader*, p. 263.

26 On Savonarola, see D. Weinstein, *Savonarola and Florence: Prophesy and Patriotism in the Renaissance* (Princeton, 1970). On the period, see J. R. Hale, *Machiavelli and Renaissance Italy* (London, 1972).

27 On the reinstatement of the Medici, see Hale, *Florence and the Medici*, pp. 87–118.

28 On Alessandro, idem, pp. 118–27.

29 Vasari, *Lives of the Artists*, V, p. 492.

30 Giovanni dalle Bande Nere came from another branch of the clan; he was the great-grandson of Lorenzo, the brother of Cosimo, *pater patriae*.

31 On Cosimo's reign, see Hale, *Florence and the Medici*, pp. 133–43. See also C. Booth, *Cosimo I, Duke of Florence* (Cambridge, 1921).

32 Many of these works of fortification were designed and supervised by the indefatigable Baldassare Lanci, Cosimo's military architect; see also Vasari, *Lives of the Artists*, IV, p. 409.

33 See Fanelli, *Firenze*, pp. 99–107, for details of the census.

34 See also Fanelli, *Firenze*, pp. 91–99.

35 See p. 145 et seq. On Vasari, see C. Conforti, *Giorgio Vasari architetto* (Milan, 1993).

36 On Ammannati, see M. Kiene, *Bartolomeo Ammannati architetto* (Milan, 1995). On Vasari, see above note 35.

37 On the government and administration of the state in this period, see esp. E. F. Guarini, *Lo stato mediceo di Cosimo I* (Florence, 1973); on the Siena wars, see R. Cantagalli, *La Guerra di Siena* (Siena, 1962).

38 As reported by Vasari himself in *Lives of the Artists*, V, p. 553.

39 One of the most prominent of these monuments is the Colonna della Giustizia in the Piazza Santa Trinita. The monolithic granite column was given by pope Pius IV to Cosimo, who erected it in celebration of the victory over Siena. It was installed in 1565.

40 Its urban dignity was further enhanced by the statues representing the four seasons, added in 1608.

41 On the villas, see G. Gobbi, *La villa fiorentina; elementi storici e critici per una lettura* (Florence, 1980); see also C. Cresti, *Civiltà delle ville toscane* (Udine, 1992).

42 Vasari, *Lives of the Artists*, V, p. 481.

43 On the reigns of Francesco and Ferdinando I, see Hale, *Florence and the Medici*, pp. 144–65.

44 The decorative program of the studiolo reflected many of Francesco's interests; see L. Berti, *Il principe dello studiolo: Francesco I dei Medici e la fine del Rinascimento fiorentino* (Florence, 1967). The manufacture or assembly of articles in *pietra dura* is a highly specialized technique, that uses many different colors and types of marble and other sometimes semi-precious stones. It was frequently applied to table tops and cabinetry, of which there are fine examples at the Pitti. The most ambitious work ever attempted using these techniques is the Cappella dei Principi at San Lorenzo.

45 On Buontalenti, see A. Fara, *Bernardo Buontalenti* (Milan, 1995).

46 On the Cappella dei Principi, see M. Gregori ed., *Cappelle barocche a Firenze* (Milan, 1990).

47 Fanelli, *Firenze*, pp. 116–17.

48 For further analysis on Bonsignori see Fanelli, *Firenze*, pp. 122–26, with several detailed reproductions. A copy is also on public display in the Museo di Firenze com'era.

49 For a useful introduction to the lunettes of Utens, see D. Mignani, *Le ville medicee di Giusto Utens* (Florence, 1980). (The paintings are today on display in the Museo di Firenze com'era.)

50 Sir John Reresby, *Memoirs and Travels* (London, 1904), p. 80.

51 See Hale, *Florence and the Medici*, pp. 177–96, for a brief overview of this long period of decline. See also Fanelli, *Firenze*, p. 129–33.

52 On the Baroque architecture of Florence, see M. Mosco, *Itinerario di Firenze barocca* (Florence, 1974); and C. Cresti, *L'architettura del seicento a Firenze* (Rome, 1990).

CHAPTER 4

1 C. Hibbert, *Florence: the Biography of a City* (Harmondsworth, 1993), p. 216.

2 See G. Fanelli, *Firenze* (Rome and Bari, 1980), pp. 139–68, for a general survey of the Lorraine era.

3 The Arco di Trionfo was designed by Jean Nicholas Jadot, and was originally less ornate; the decorative sculptures were added in 1744–55.

4 See Fanelli, *Firenze*, p. 140, 144–55, for a selection of the numerous eighteenth-century *vedute* and maps, including that of Ferdinando Ruggieri. For the definitive catalog of these maps, see A. Mori and G. Boffito, *Firenze nelle vedute e piante* (Florence, 1926; facsimile reedition Rome, 1998).

5 See C. Hibbert, *The Grand Tour* (London, 1974). Horace Walpole and William Hazlitt were both very impressed by the city; for the latter see his "Notes of a Journey through France and Italy," in *Collected Works*, vol. 9 (London, 1904).

6 Cited in C. Hobday, *A Golden Ring: English Poets in Florence from 1373 to the Present Day* (London, 1997), p. 170.

7 See Fanelli, *Firenze*, pp. 169–82, for a summary of urban works in this period. See also A. Lensi, *Napoleone a Firenze* (Florence, 1936).

8 See V. Giusti, *Un censimento fiorentino sotto Napoleone I* (Rome, 1925).

9 See the two "before" and "after" views by V. Simoncini, reproduced here on p. 84.

10 See Fanelli, *Firenze*, pp. 196–97, for the plans showing the location of the chief civic and public works in this period. See also *Firenze e provincia* (TCI Guide, Milan, 1993), with map on p. 72.

CHAPTER 5

1 Giovanni Villani, *Cronica fiorentina* (written c. 1330; new ed. Florence, 1844–55), VII, XCIX.

2 On this original relationship, see G. Morozzi, *Santa Reparata: l'antica cattedrale fiorentina* (Florence, 1987), with plan on p. 6.

3 G. Poggi ed., *Il Bigallo* (Florence, 1905).

4 On these works, see G. Fanelli, *Firenze* (Rome and Bari, 1980), pp. 46–52.

5 Idem.

6 On the festival of San Giovanni Battista, see P. Antonetti, *La vita quotidiana a Firenze ai tempi di Dante* (Milan, 1983), pp. 156–58.

7 For a general survey of Florentine festivals, see L. Artusi and S. Gabrielli, *Le feste di Firenze* (Rome, 1991). See also P. Gori, *Le feste fiorentine attraverso i secoli* (Florence, 1990).

8 Dante Alighieri, *Paradiso* (c. 1319–20), XV, p. 134–35.

9 Among the extensive bibliography on the baptistery are G. Marchini, *Il battistero e il duomo di Firenze* (Florence, 1992); C. Pietramellara, *Battistero di San Giovanni a Firenze* (Florence, 1973); and esp. P. degli Innocenti, *Le origini del Bel San Giovanni: da Tempio di Marte a Battistero di Firenze* (Florence, 1994).

10 The first date of consecration remains unknown, but it had clearly been in use for 150 years prior to 1059.

11 See also E. W. Anthony, *Early Florentine Architecture and Decoration* (Harvard, 1927), esp. pp. 3–20.

12 For the mosaics of the baptistery, the definitive work is A. de Witt, *I mosaici del Battistero di Firenze* (Florence, 1954), 5 vols.

13 There are many works on Pisano, Ghiberti, and the three portals; see, for example, J. Beck, *Le porte del battistero di Firenze* (Florence, 1985); K. Clark et al., *The Florence Baptistery Doors* (London, 1980). See also G. Brunetti, *Ghiberti* (Florence, 1966); G. Marchini, *Ghiberti architetto* (Florence, 1978); R. Krautheimer, *Ghiberti's Bronze Doors* (Princeton, 1971).

14 Villani, *Cronica fiorentina*, IX, XII.

15 For illustrations of Giotto's drawing, see for example, J. White, *Art and Architecture in Italy 1250–1400* (Harmondsworth, 1987). See esp. D. Gioseffi, *Giotto architetto* (Milan, 1963); C. Guasti, *S Maria del Fiore: la costruzione della chiesa e del campanile secondo i documenti* (Florence, 1887); and M. Trachtenberg, *The Campanile of Florence Cathedral* (New York, 1971).

16 Work on Arnolfo's facade of the cathedral was completed only up to the level of the tops of the porches; see p. 104. However, it was clearly intended to be as rich and ornate a work as the tower.

17 See J. Pope Hennessey, *Italian Gothic Sculpture* (London and New York, 1970), esp. pp. 21–25.

18 From inscriptions discovered during the excavations in the 1970s.

19 See Morozzi, *Santa Reparata*, pp. 16–21, for detailed plans of Santa Reparata.

20 Villani, *Cronica fiorentina*, cited in C. Hibbert, *Florence: Biography of a City* (Harmondsworth, 1993), p. 48.

21 The bibliography for the cathedral is naturally very extensive, but see esp. P. Sanpaolesi and M. Bucci eds., *Duomo e Battistero di Firenze* (Florence, 1966); G. Marchini, *Il Battistero, il duomo e il museo dell' Opera del duomo di Firenze* (Florence, 1972). See also Guasti, *Santa Maria del Fiore*.

22 On Poccetti's illustration, see Pope Hennessey, *Italian Gothic Sculpture*, fig. 37.

23 On the career and works of Andrea Pisano, see also M. G. Burresi, *Andrea, Nino e Tommaso Pisani* (Milan, 1983); and Pope Hennessey, *Italian Gothic Sculpture*.

24 On this stage of the development of the plan see Guasti, *Santa Maria del Fiore*, and Morozzi, *Santa Reparata*. There is an accessible summary of the history of the construction of the present church in White, *Art and Architecture in Italy*, pp. 51–52, 495–502.

25 See White, *Art and Architecture in Italy*, p. 497.

26 On the Siena cathedral, idem, pp. 234–40.

27 Idem, p. 498.

28 Alberti, *Della pittura* (1435–36), introduction dedicated to Brunelleschi.

29 The bibliography on the cupola is very extensive, as its structure and construction have been the subject of much detailed investigation. See esp. E. Battisti, *Filippo Brunelleschi* (Milan, 1976); H. Klotz, *Filippo Brunelleschi: The Early Works and the Medieval Tradition* (New York and London, 1990); as well as the more specialized studies of L. Bartoli, esp. *Il disegno della cupola di Brunelleschi* (Florence, 1994), with a good technical bibliography; H. Saalman, *Filippo Brunelleschi: The Cupola of Santa Maria del Fiore* (London, 1980); and R. King, *Brunelleschi's Dome* (London, 2000).

30 Cited in Bartoli, *Il disegno*, p. 33, note 17. The revisions were dated 13 March 1421 and 24 January 1425 (florentine calendar).

31 There is a useful and accessible summary of the complex structural issues in R. Mainstone, "Brunelleschi's Dome," *Architectural Review* (September 1977). See also Bartoli, *Il disegno*, passim.

32 A squinch is a relieving arch that bridges the corner of a square or faceted drum, from which a dome with a circular plan can rise.

33 "Built without centering" are Alberti's famous words. In the introduction to *Della pittura*, he wrote: "facta sanza alcun ajuto di travamenti o di copia di legname."

34 On the lantern, see Bartoli, *Il disegno*, p. 59 et seq.

35 The Tower of the Winds is a small octagonal Classical temple in Athens, on the faces of which were carved depictions of the winds and a sundial.

36 See also Battisti, *Filippo Brunelleschi*.

37 Giorgio Vasari, *Lives of the Artists* (second ed. 1568; transl. J. Foster, London, 1878), I, p. 474.

38 The surviving models of the cathedral facade are illustrated in H. Millon and V. M. Lampugnani, eds., *Rinascimento: da Brunelleschi a Michelangelo* (Milan, 1994), pp. 25–31.

39 See also discussion of the modern facade of the cathedral p. 296.

CHAPTER 6

1 Dante Alighieri, *Purgatorio* (c. 1319–20), VI, 76–78, on the tragic decline of the proud traditions of Italian government and independence.

2 For a useful general introduction, see D. Waley, *The Italian City–Republics* (London, 1969). See also P. Antonetti, *La vita quotidiana a Firenze ai tempi di Dante* (Milan, 1983), esp. pp. 110–35.

3 Niccolò Machiavelli, *The Prince* (c. 1513–14), p. 48.

4 For a summary of the history of the Bargello and the contents of the present museum, see *Firenze e provincia* (TCI guides, Milan, 1993), pp. 372–83.

5 There are no good general works on the Bargello, but see J. White, *Art and Architecture in Italy 1250–1400* (Harmondsworth, 1987), pp. 59–71 for a summary of the typology.

6 Leon Battista Alberti, *De re aedificatoria* (c. 1452), V, IX, on the design of buildings for the dispensation of justice.

7 The original medieval fabric is not well served by publications, although for some discussion of Brunelleschi's transformations see H. Klotz, *Filippo Brunelleschi: The Early Works and the Medieval Tradition* (New York and London, 1990), pp. 67–75, and E. Battisti, *Filippo Brunelleschi* (Milan, 1976), p. 69 et seq.

8 Charles Dickens, *Pictures from Italy* (1844; new ed. London, 1973), p. 239.

9 The Roman and early Christian eras are well illustrated by models, plans and artefacts in the Museo di Firenze com'era.

10 On the general urban history of this district, see pp. 36, 38–40.

11 G. Fanelli, *Firenze* (Rome and Bari, 1980), chapter 4.

12 Fanelli, *Firenze*, p. 42.

13 The loggia is poorly served by secondary sources, but for contemporary records of its construction, see for example R. Goldthwaite, *The Building of Renaissance Florence* (Baltimore, 1980), pp. 282, 356, 369.

14 Cited by C. Hibbert, *Florence: Biography of a City* (Harmondsworth, 1993), p. 163. Several contemporary paintings that show the death of Savonarola are in the Museo di Firenze com'era.

15 Hibbert, *Florence*, p. 226 et seq.

16 Giovanni Villani, *Cronica fiorentina* (written c. 1330; new ed. Florence, 1844–55), IX, XXVI et seq.

17 The bibliography for the Palazzo Vecchio includes A. Lensi, *Palazzo Vecchio* (Rome and Milan, 1929); see also White, *Art and Architecture*, pp. 241–43, and J. Paul, *Der Palazzo Vecchio in Florenz* (Florence, 1969).

18 See TCI *Firenze*, pp. 175, 181, 182, and 188, for key plans showing the stages of expansion of the palazzo.

19 For the later Medicean works at the palazzo, see U. Muccini, *Il salone dei cinquecento in Palazzo Vecchio* (Florence, 1990); and U. Muccini and A. Cecchi, *Le stanze del principe in Palazzo Vecchio* (Florence, 1991).

20 Vasari describes his own work in the Palazzo Vecchio in Giorgio Vasari, *Lives of the Artists* (second ed. 1568; transl. J. Foster, London, 1878), V, p. 545 et seq.

21 Decorated chiefly by Francesco Morandini and Jacopo Zucchi, to a program devised by Vasari and Vincenzo Borghini.

22 Dickens, *Pictures from Italy*, p. 240.

23 See L. H. Heydenreich and W. Lotz, *Architecture in Italy 1400 to 1600* (Harmondsworth, 1974), pp. 321–23 for a summary of the project. See also Vasari's own record in *Lives of the Artists*, V, p. 553.

24 Vasari, Ibid.

25 See TCI *Firenze*, pp. 235–36, for an overview of the chief works in the Corridoio. Many were from Cosimo's own collections.

26 On the Uffizi collections, see the definitive work L. Berti, ed., *Gli Uffizi: catalogo generale* (Florence, 1980). See also C. Caneva et al., *Gli Uffizi: guida alle collezioni e catalogo completo dei dipinti* (Florence, 1986).

27 Dickens, *Pictures from Italy*, p. 239.

28 On the authorship of Palazzo Pitti, see Heydenreich and Lotz, *Architecture*, pp. 40–41.

29 See M. Kiene, *Bartolomeo Ammannati architetto* (Milan, 1995), and C. Conti, *Palazzo Pitti* (Florence, 1887).

30 See F. Inghirami, *L'imperiale e reale Palazzo Pitti* (Fiesole, 1828).

31 For an overview of the Pitti collections, see TCI *Firenze*, pp. 470–99, and more specifically S. Padovani, *La galleria palatina* (Florence, 1990).

32 Alberti, *De re aedificatoria*, IX, IV.

33 C. Caneva, *Il giardino di Boboli* (Florence, 1982).

34 See A. Fara, *Bernardo Buontalenti* (Milan, 1995).

CHAPTER 7

1 Leon Battista Alberti, *De re aedificatoria* (c. 1452), III, I

2 The essential work on all aspects of the Florentine construction industry is R. Goldthwaite, *The Building of Renaissance Florence* (Baltimore, 1980). Much of the contents of this chapter is based on this key source.

3 For bricks and kilns see Goldthwaite, *The Building*, pp. 191–212.

4 Goldthwaite, *The Building*, pp. 216–18, 229.

5 Idem, pp. 221–29.

6 Idem, pp. 269–86.

7 Idem, pp. 256–58.

8 Idem, pp. 270–72.

9 For an introduction to the *arti* in general, see P. Antonetti, *La vita quotidiana a Firenze ai tempi di Dante* (Milan, 1983), pp. 172–82.

10 Goldthwaite, *The Building*, pp. 249–51.

11 Idem, pp. 317–31, 435–39.

12 Idem, pp. 92–93, 132 et seq.

13 Idem, pp. 373 et seq.

14 For the training of craftsmen elsewhere, see esp. A. Thomas, *The Painter's Practice in Renaissance Tuscany* (Cambridge, England, 1995).

15 Goldthwaite, *The Building*, p. 365. The term "engineer" (*inzegniere*, or other similar spellings) was used in northern Italy from as early as the end of the thirteenth century. A College of Engineers was founded in Milan in 1563.

16 The most useful recent study of architectural models and drawings is undoubtedly H. Millon and V. M. Lampugnani, eds., *Rinascimento: da Brunelleschi a Michelangelo* (Milan, 1994), passim. See also Goldthwaite, *The Building*, pp. 372–80.

17 On Brunelleschi's background, see also pp. 206–8.

18 The definitive study of Alberti's work is still F. Borsi, *Leon Battista Alberti* (Milan, 1975); but see also R. Tavernor, *On Alberti and the Art of Building* (Yale, Connecticut, and London, 1998), for a modern reappraisal of his philosophical approach. See also A. Grafton, *Leon Battista Alberti, Master Builder of the Italian Renaissance* (London, 2000).

CHAPTER 8

1 Leon Battista Alberti, *De re aedificatoria* (c. 1452), IV, IV

2 There are few useful modern works on the city's medieval defences, but see M. Borgatti, *Le mura e le torri di Firenze* (Rome, 1900).

3 For Michelangelo's works of defence for the city, see J. Ackerman, *The Architecture of Michelangelo*, vol. 1 (London, 1961), pp. 45–53.

4 J. R. Hale, *Florence and the Medici: The Pattern of Control* (London, 1977), p. 158.

CHAPTER 9

1 Leon Battista Alberti, *De re aedificatoria* (c. 1452), VIII, VI

2 See P. Antonetti, *La vita quotidiana a Firenze ai tempi di Dante* (Milan, 1983), pp. 271–73.

3 For the location of the medieval hospitals and other charitable establishments, see G. Fanelli, *Firenze* (Rome and Bari, 1980), map fig. 17, p. 49.

4 On the architecture of the Innocenti, see E. Battisti, *Filippo Brunelleschi* (Milan, 1976), pp. 46–68; and H. Klotz, *Filippo Brunelleschi: The Early Works and the Medieval Tradition* (New York and London, 1990), pp. 107–27.

5 For a history of the hospital, see G. Pampaloni, ed., *Lo spedale di Santa Maria Nuova* (Florence, 1961).

6 For a map showing the location of the guildhalls, see Fanelli, *Firenze*, p. 47, fig. 15. For a general survey of the history of the *arti*, see L. Artusi, *Le arti e i mestieri di Firenze* (Rome, 1990).

7 For a general outline of medieval city markets with some detail of the Florentine markets, see D. Calabi, *Il mercato e la citta* (Venice, 1993), esp. pp. 85–90.

8 See, for example, the famous Alinari collection of photographs; for the Mercato Vecchio, see Fanelli, *Firenze*, fig. 168.

CHAPTER 10

1 Leon Battista Alberti, *De re aedificatoria* (c. 1452), VII, III

2 For the Badia at Settimo, see C. C. Calzolari, *La storia della badia a Settimo* (Florence, 1976); for the Badia Fiorentina, see A. di Gaetano, *Della badia fiorentina* (Florence, 1951). There is also an accessible summary in *Firenze e provincia* (TCI guides, Milan, 1993), pp. 383–87.

3 The attribution to Arnolfo is now fairly widely accepted.

4 See E. W. Anthony, *Early Florentine Architecture and Decoration* (Harvard, 1927); for San Miniato, see also F. Tarani, *La basilica di San Miniato al Monte* (Florence, 1910).

5 For all of these early churches, see M. Lopez Pegna, *Le più antiche chiese fiorentine* (Florence, 1971); and the encyclopaedic survey by A. Busignani and R. Bencini, *Le chiese di Firenze* (Florence, 1972–89), 4 vols.

6 For a discussion of the urban impact of these complexes, see, for example, L. Benevolo, *Storia della città* (Rome and Bari, 1976), esp. p. 389 et seq. (on Bologna), and p. 437 et seq. (on Florence).

7 For Santa Maria Novella see U. Baldini ed., *Santa Maria Novella* (Florence, 1981); see also J. White, *Art and Architecture in Italy 1250–1400* (Harmondsworth, 1987), pp. 27–30.

8 For Santa Croce, see esp. M. Bucci, *La basilica di Santa Croce* (Florence, 1965).

9 For Arnolfo here, see V. Mariani, *Arnolfo e il gotico italiano* (Naples, 1967).

10 For Santa Trinità, see G. Marchini and E. Micheletti, eds., *La chiesa di Santa Trinità a Firenze* (Florence, 1987).

11 See C. Chiarelli and G. Leoncini, *La Certosa del Galluzzo a Firenze* (Milan, 1982).

12 For Orsanmichele, see G. Morozzi, *Il restauro di Orsanmichele* (Florence, 1967); also P. Bargellini, *Orsanmichele a Firenze* (Milan, 1969).

13 The attribution to Arnolfo was first made by Vasari.

14 For the external sculptures of Orsanmichele, see J. Pope Hennessey, *Italian Gothic Sculpture* (London and New York, 1970), esp. pp. 49, 207–8, 213, 217–18.

15 For Brunelleschi's early work see H. Klotz, *Filippo Brunelleschi: The Early Works and the Medieval Tradition* (New York and London, 1990), passim, and E. Battisti, *Filippo Brunelleschi* (Milan, 1976).

16 For the Barbadori chapel, see Klotz, *Filippo Brunelleschi*, pp. 145–47, and Battisti, *Filippo Brunelleschi*, p. 98 et seq.

17 For the Sagrestia Vecchia, see Klotz, *Filippo Brunelleschi*, p. 129 et seq., and Battisti, *Filippo Brunelleschi*, p. 79–97.

18 For San Lorenzo, see Battisti, *Filippo Brunelleschi*, p. 179 et seq. See also E. Luporini, *Brunelleschi: forma e ragione* (Milan, 1964).

19 On Santo Spirito, see Battisti, *Filippo Brunelleschi*, p. 196 et seq. See also E. Capretti, *Il complesso di Santo Spirito* (Florence, 1991); and G. Fanelli, *Brunelleschi* (Florence, 1980).

20 For further discussion of these complex issues, see also R. Wittkower, *Architectural Principles in the Age of Humanism* (London, 1988), esp. p. 18 et seq. See also R. Tavernor, *On Alberti and the Art of Building* (New Haven and London, 1998).

21 Alberti, *De re aedificatoria*, VIII, IV.

22 Wittkower, *Architectural Principles*, p. 22 et seq.

23 Battisti, *Filippo Brunelleschi*, p. 222 et seq.

24 Ibid. But for the radically different view that the chapel is not the work of Brunelleschi, but instead by Michelozzo, see M. Trachtenberg, "Perché la Cappella dei Pazzi non è di Brunelleschi," *Casabella* (June, 1996).

25 The bibliography on Santa Maria degli Angeli is not extensive, but see Battisti, *Filippo Brunelleschi*, pp. 248–56.

26 Giorgio Vasari, *Lives of the Artists* (second ed. 1568; transl. J. Foster, London, 1878), I, p. 414. Vasari's eulogy, which opens his biography of Brunelleschi, was to be followed by many others in a similar vein. Among Brunelleschi's near-contemporaries, Alberti was almost as flattering.

27 The best works on Michelozzo are O. Morisani, *Michelozzo architetto* (Turin, 1951); and M. Ferrara and F. Quinterio, *Michelozzo di Bartolomeo* (Florence, 1984).

28 Ferrara and Quinterio, *Michelozzo*, p. 185 et seq.

29 Idem, p. 213 et seq. and Morisani, *Michelozzo*, p. 59.

30 For Alberti's role in this complex saga, see Tavernor, *On Alberti*, pp. 147–58.

31 For Alberti and the Rucellai, see Tavernor, *On Alberti*, pp. 79–124; and F. Borsi, *Leon Battista Alberti* (Milan, 1975), pp. 59–126.

32 For the facade of Santa Maria Novella, see Wittkower, *Architectural Principles*, pp. 47–51; Tavernor, *On Alberti*, pp. 99–105; Borsi, *Alberti*, pp. 75–105.

33 See Borsi, *Alberti*, p. 84 for a detailed analysis of these proportions.

34 Borsi, *Alberti*, pp. 105–25, with many illustrations; also Tavernor, *On Alberti*, pp. 106–19.

35 Ferrara and Quinterio, *Michelozzo*, p. 385.

36 For Santa Maria delle Carceri, see esp. G. Corti and P. Marselli, *La chiesa di Santa Maria della Carceri in Prato* (Florence, 1982).

37 For Sangallo generally, see G. Marchini, *Giuliano da Sangallo* (Florence, 1942); more recent is S. Borsi, *Giuliano da Sangallo: I disegni di architettura e dell'antico* (Rome, 1985).

38 See note 22 above; see also G. Morollo, C. Acidini, and L. Marchetti, *L'Architettura di Lorenzo il Magnifico* (Milan, 1992).

39 There are several excellent works on Michelangelo as architect; still particularly valuable are J. Ackerman, *The Architecture of Michelangelo* (London, 1961), and A. Nova, *Michelangelo architetto* (Milan, 1984); also G. C. Argan and B. Contardi, *Michelangelo architetto* (Milan, 1990); and P. Portoghesi and B. Zevi, eds., *Michelangelo architetto* (Turin, 1964).

40 For the facade of San Lorenzo, see Ackerman, *Michelangelo*, vol. 1, pp. 11–20, with considerable further detail in vol. 2, pp. 3–17. Michelangelo's model is illustrated in H. Millon and V. M. Lampugnani, eds., *Rinascimento: da Brunelleschi a Michelangelo* (Milan, 1994), p. 47.

41 For the Sagrestia Nuova see Ackerman, *Michelangelo*, vol. 1, pp. 21–32; see also Nova, *Michelangelo*, p. 37 et seq.

42 For the tomb sculptures, see esp. L. Berti, *Michelangelo: le tombe medicee* (Florence, 1965).

43 For the Biblioteca Laurenziana, see Ackerman, *Michelangelo*, vol. 1, pp. 33–44, vol. 2 pp. 33–42; see also Nova, *Michelangelo*, p. 97 et seq.

44 See A. Fara, *Bernardo Buontalenti* (Milan, 1995), p. 243 et seq.

45 On the Cappella dei Principi, see C. Cresti, *L'Architettura del seicento a Firenze* (Rome, 1990), p. 42 et seq.

46 For a more detailed study of the *cappella*, particularly the *pietra dura* decorations, see U. Baldini, A. M. Giusti and A. Pampaloni Martelli, *La Cappella dei Principi e le pietre dure a Firenze* (Milan, 1979).

47 See Cresti, *L'Architettura*, p. 54 et seq.

48 Idem, p. 35 et seq.

49 Cresti, *L'Architettura*, p. 212.

50 Idem, p. 217. See also M. Mosco, *Itinerari di Firenze barocca* (Florence, 1974).

51 Cresti, *L'Architettura*, p. 180. See also Busignani and Bencini, *Le chiese di Firenze*, vol. 3, p. 199 et seq.

CHAPTER 11

1 Leon Battista Alberti, *De re aedificatoria* (c. 1452), V, XIV

2 The most prominent surviving towers are illustrated in L. Capellini et al, *Guida di Firenze:*

architettura (Florence, 1988), pp. 31–37. The best study of the typology, from the social as well as the physical aspect, is L. Macci and V. Orgera, *Architettura e civiltà delle torri: torri e famiglie nella Firenze medievale* (Florence, 1994).

3 See G. Fanelli, *Firenze* (Rome and Bari, 1980), fig. 18 and appendix 11; the figure shows the location of approximately 150 of the more important recorded towers.

4 For the cottages of the poor, see P. Antonetti, *La vita quotidiana a Firenze ai tempi di Dante* (Milan, 1983), p. 33 et seq. See also R. Goldthwaite, *The Building of Renaissance Florence* (Baltimore, 1980), passim.

5 The essential survey for all aspects of the domestic interior is P. Thornton, *The Italian Renaissance Interior 1400 to 1600* (London, 1991), with many illustrations. For floor, wall, and ceiling finishes see pp. 33–66; for discussion of the planning and functions of individual rooms see part 3; particularly useful are the floor plans of Palazzo Strozzi and Palazzo Medici, pp. 305, 307.

6 For the Rucellai loggia, see F. Borsi, *Leon Battista Alberti* (Milan, 1975), pp. 75–79, and R. Tavernor, *On Alberti and the Art of Building* (New Haven and London, 1998), pp. 119–24.

CHAPTER 12

1 Leon Battista Alberti, *De re aedificatoria* (c. 1452), IX, II.

2 The most useful general surveys on the Florentine palazzi are L. Ginori Lisci, *I palazzi di Firenze nella storia e nell'arte* (Florence, 1972), 2 vols; M. Bucci and R. Bencini, *I palazzi di Firenze* (Florence, 1973), 3 vols; and A. Busignani and R. Bencini, *I palazzi di Firenze* (Florence, 1974).

3 Ginori Lisci, *I palazzi di Firenze*, p. 683 et seq.

4 For Palazzo Spini Feroni, idem, p. 127.

5 For Palazzo Davanzati, Idem, p. 163. See also G. Carocci, *Palazzo Davanzati: ricordi storici* (Florence, 1910).

6 Giovanni Rucellai, *Il zibaldone quaresimale* (begun c. 1457).

7 The attribution to Brunelleschi is by no means universally accepted.

8 For Palazzo Medici Riccardi, in the Via Larga, the bibliography is extensive, but see Bucci and Bencini, *I palazzi di Firenze*, vol. 1, p. 7 et seq.; M. Ferrara and F. Quinterio, *Michelozzo di Bartolomeo* (Florence, 1984); and esp. G. Cherubini and G. Fanelli eds., *Il Palazzo Medici Riccardi di Firenze* (Florence, 1990).

9 For Palazzo Rucellai see R. Tavernor, *On Alberti and the Art of Building* (New Haven and London, 1998), p. 79 et seq, with a valuable analysis of the design of the facade. See also F. Borsi, *Leon Battista Alberti* (Milan, 1975), p. 59 et seq.

10 On Rossellino and the Pienza project, see esp. C. R. Mack, *Pienza: The Creation of a Renaissance City* (Ithaca, New York, and London, 1987).

11 For some recent comments on the attribution of the Rucellai loggia, see Tavernor, *On Alberti*, p. 119 et seq.

12 See G. Marchini, *Giuliano da Maiano* (Florence, 1959); and Bucci and Bencini, *I palazzi di Firenze*, vol. 1 (on the quartiere di Santa Croce), p. 75.

13 On Palazzo Antinori, see Bucci and Bencini, *I palazzi di Firenze*, vol. 2 (on the quartiere di Santa Maria Novella), p. 55 et seq. Attributions have also been made to Giuliano da Sangallo.

14 On Luca Pitti and his palace, see Bucci and Bencini, *I palazzi di Firenze*, vol. 3 (on the quartiere di Santo Spirito).

15 For Palazzo Gondi, see A. Tonnesmann, *Der Palazzo Gondi in Florenz* (Worms, Germany, 1983).

16 The model of Palazzo Strozzi is also illustrated in H. Millon and V. M. Lampugnani, eds., *Rinascimento: da Brunelleschi a Michelangelo* (Milan, 1994), pp. 72–73. For much documentary evidence on the construction of the palazzo see R. Goldthwaite, *The Building of Renaissance Florence* (Baltimore, 1980), passim. See also G. Pampaloni, *Palazzo Strozzi* (Florence, 1982).

17 For the social and cultural aspects of the use of the Renaissance palazzo, see esp. Goldthwaite, *The Building*; and P. Thornton, *The Italian Renaissance Interior 1400 to 1600* (London, 1991), passim.

18 This is a pattern that can also be seen in other Italian cities, particularly Venice.

19 See Goldthwaite, *The Building*, p. 105.

20 See Thornton, *The Italian Renaissance Interior*, passim.

21 Giovanni Boccaccio, *The Decameron* (c. 1350), p. 64.

22 Alberti, *De re aedificatoria*, V, XIV.

23 The Medici estates were all carefully depicted by Giusto Utens in 1599 in the paintings that were commissioned by Ferdinando I to decorate the family villa at Artimino. The fourteen lunettes are all now displayed in the Museo di Firenze com'era.

24 For a useful general introduction on Careggi, see D. Mignani, *Le ville medicee di Giusto Utens* (Florence, 1980); see also G. Contorni, *La villa medicea di Careggi* (Florence, 1992).

25 For Poggio a Caiano, see Mignani, *Le ville medicee*, pp. 55–57; and S. Bardazzi and E. Castellani, *La villa medicea di Poggio a Caiano* (Prato, 1981), 2 vols.

26 The influence of Poggio was profound, and is especially clear in Palladio's villas in the Veneto in the latter part of the sixteenth century.

27 For Castello, see A. Fara, *Bernardo Buontalenti* (Milan, 1995), p. 217 et seq.

28 For Pratolino, see Fara, *Buontalenti*, and also Mignani, *Le ville medicee*, pp. 35, 73–77.

29 For the gardens at Pratolino, see esp. I. Zangheri, *Pratolino, il giardino delle meraviglie* (Florence, 1987), 2 vols.

30 For Artimino, see Fara, *Buontalenti*, p. 255 et seq.

31 For Poggio Imperiale, see C. da Prato, *La real villa del Poggio Imperiale* (Florence, 1895).

32 Cited by U. Procacci in *La casa Buonarroti a Firenze* (Florence, 1965), p. 6.

33 Bucci and Bencini, *I palazzi di Firenze*, vol. 3, p. 121 et seq.

34 Idem, p. 97 et seq.

35 See esp. L. Frommel, S. Ray, and M. Tafuri, *Raffaello architetto* (Milan, 1984).

36 Bucci and Bencini, *I palazzi di Firenze*, vol. 2, p. 41 et seq.

37 Idem, vol. 1, p. 53 et seq.

38 See esp. M. Fossi, *Bartolomeo Ammannati, architetto* (Naples, 1957), and also M. Kiene, *Bartolomeo Ammannati architetto* (Milan, 1995).

39 See, for example, book 4, chapter 6, fn. 30 and 31 in the first English edition published by James Leoni (London, 1611).

40 See Fara, *Buontalenti*.

41 Bucci and Bencini, *I palazzi*, vol. 3, p. 99 et seq.

42 Idem, vol. 1, p. 81 et seq.

43 For Palazzo Corsini al Parione, see esp. C. Cresti, *L'Architettura del seicento a Firenze* (Rome, 1990).

44 See L. Ginori Lisci, *I palazzi di Firenze nella storia e nell'arte* (Florence, 1972), p. 519 et seq.

45 For the Casino della Livia, see Cresti, *L'Architettura*, p. 156; on the Palazzina Reale, idem, p. 181 et seq.

CHAPTER 13

1 Theodosia Garrow Trollope, *Social Aspects of the Italian Revolution* (London, 1861).

2 The best general summary of this period is still G. Fanelli, *Firenze* (Rome and Bari, 1980), esp. chapter 10.

3 Idem, pp. 191–92.

4 On Florence as capital of unified Italy, see F. Borsi, *La capitale a Firenze e l'opera di Giuseppe Poggi* (Florence, 1970). See also G. Spadolini, *Firenze* capitale (Florence, 1979).

5 For plans showing the chief urban interventions of the Poggi era, see *Firenze e provincia* (TCI guides, Milan, 1993), pp. 72–73. On Poggi's works, see Borsi, *La capitale a Firenze*.

6 For photographs of the walls in the process of demolition, see Fanelli, *Firenze*, p. 205.

7 See also the "before" and "after" photographs in Fanelli, *Firenze*, pp. 206–7.

8 The Museo di Firenze com'era contains a fascinating detailed model of the district of the Mercato Vecchio prior to the clearances.

9 G. Carocci, *Il Mercato Vecchio di Firenze* (Florence, 1884). See also G. Carocci, *Il ghetto di Firenze* (Florence, 1886). For plans of the Mercato Vecchio before and after the demolitions see Fanelli, *Firenze*, pp. 213, 214.

10 For all of this period see Fanelli, *Firenze*, chapter 12.

11 TCI *Firenze*, p. 34. See also M. Zoppi, *Firenze e l'urbanistica: la ricerca del Piano* (Florence, 1982).

CHAPTER 14

1 Vitruvius, *Ten Books of Architecture* (First century BC), chapter 1 on the education of the architect.

2 See above, chapter 13, note 4.

3 See esp. O. Raggi, *La chiesa di Santa Croce e la sua facciata* (Florence, 1863).

4 For the saga of the cathedral facade, see L. del Moro, *La facciata di Santa Maria del Fiore* (Florence, 1888).

5 See esp. S. Fei, *Firenze 1881–1898: la grande operazione urbanistica* (Rome, 1977).

6 For this period, see C. Cresti, *Firenze 1896–1915: la stagione del Liberty* (Florence, 1978).

7 P. Desideri et al., *Pier Luigi Nervi* (Bologna, 1979).

8 For the Santa Maria Novella station, see C. Cresti, *Architettura e fascismo* (Florence, 1986); see also F. Bandini, *La stazione di Santa Maria Novella* (Florence, 1987). The station is not a particularly "fascist" work in the popular sense of the term.

9 For the bridges see the L. Capellini et al, *Guida di Firenze: architettura* (Florence, 1988), pp. 224, 236, 243.

10 A. Belluzzi and C. Conforti, *Giovanni Michelucci: catalogo delle opere* (Milan, 1986).

11 For all of the above, see Capellini, *Guida di Firenze*, p. 225 et seq.

Biographical Notes

ALBERTI, LEON BATTISTA (1404 – 1472)
Born in Genoa of an exiled Florentine noble family, Alberti studied at the universities of Padua and Bologna, and visited Rome in 1432 in a posting attached to the Holy See. In 1434 he wrote the first systematic study of the Classical Roman orders of architecture, and first visited Florence that same year. Alberti was a prolific theorist and writer. His treatise on painting, *Della pittura* (which was dedicated to Brunelleschi, whose work he greatly admired) codified for the first time the laws of perspective. His built work in Florence was almost exclusively the result of the patronage of Giovanni Rucellai, his patron and friend; for Rucellai Alberti designed the family palazzo (in about 1460) in which the three classical orders were used, superimposed, for the first time in the city. He also designed the family chapel at San Pancrazio (1467) and completed the upper part of the facade of Santa Maria Novella (1458–70), again under Rucellai's patronage. Alberti's later projects took him away from Florence, chiefly to Mantua and Rimini, as well as many further visits to Rome, where he continued his research on the classical orders. His many influential writings include a short treatise on sculpture, and *De re aedificatoria*, his famous treatise on architecture written in the 1440s but finally published in 1452. The treatise was enormously influential, the first comprehensive theoretical and practical handbook to architectural design since Vitruvius.

AMMANNATI, BARTOLOMMEO (1511 – 1592)
Educated in Florence and then Venice, where he collaborated with Sansovino on the Biblioteca Marciana, Ammannati worked in Rome in the 1550s, and after 1555 chiefly in Florence again, where he became known as a sculptor and architect. In both fields he was influenced by Michelangelo, whose work he completed at the Biblioteca Laurenziana and the Sagrestia Nuova at San Lorenzo. His best known sculptural work in Florence is the Neptune Fountain in the Piazza della Signoria. Ammannati spent several years modernizing Palazzo Pitti for Cosimo I and his wife Eleonora of Toledo, including the imposing rear cortile and the terraces of the Boboli gardens. He designed several palaces in Florence including that of the Grifoni, Giugni, and Ramirez, as well as the new Ponte Santa Trinità that replaced the one lost in the floods of 1558.

ARNOLFO DI CAMBIO (1245 – c1302)
Born near Siena, Arnolfo was active mostly as a sculptor in Rome in the 1280s and 1290s. His architectural output is more elusive, although today he is generally credited with the initial design of the new cathedral of Santa Maria del Fiore in Florence, where he is also recorded as the capomaestro in 1294. The overall plan of the great church, including the octagonal crossing, was established by Arnolfo (although the nave was later extended); he also began the facade, which was only completed in its lower orders; it was dismantled in 1587. Many other attributions to him have been made in this period, including the design of the final circuit of the city walls, the original loggia of Orsanmichele, the Palazzo Vecchio, the modernization of the Badia Fiorentina (1284–1310), and the great Franciscan church of Santa Croce (begun in 1294). These last two are the only buildings generally accepted as his work, while the remainder are still speculative. The chief features of Arnolfo's style are clear, precise structural forms, usually planar, and with minimal decoration; the austere, noble discipline of the interior at Santa Croce is very characteristic.

BACCIO D'AGNOLO (1462 – 1543)
He collaborated with Cronaca and Sangallo on the great hall in the Palazzo Vecchio and was later the capomaestro at the cathedral from 1508 to 1515. His architectural work is classical and refined, as exemplified by the campanili of San Miniato and Santo Spirito. He also designed the Palazzo Bartolini Salimbeni in the Piazza Santa Trinità, a highly original interpretation "alla Romana," with bold aedicules for the windows and a powerful cornice.

BRUNELLESCHI, FILIPPO (1377 – 1446)
Arguably the greatest of Florence's architects and one of the most influential figures in the history of European Renaissance architecture, Brunelleschi did not receive a classical humanist education, but first learned practical skills as a goldsmith and sculptor. He had a gift for the acquisition of knowledge in many different fields, among which was a profound interest in the classical heritage; his knowledge also extended to the study of mathematics and engineering. He is first recorded in the workshop of Florence's cathedral in 1409, and in 1418 presented his first proposal for the completion of the cupola. In 1423 he was given responsibility for the immense task, which was only finally completed in 1434 (followed by the construction of the lantern after 1436). The cupola represents Brunelleschi's finest technical achievement, although his prolific output in the city included the early Ospedale degli Innocenti (1421–24) and the beginning of the reconstruction of San Lorenzo (from 1423). The Innocenti was the first attempt to create a new, rationally planned public square in Italy since the classical era; but the piazza itself was only completed long after his death. The Sagrestia Vecchia at San Lorenzo is an early synthesis of some his preoccupations with volumes and proportions, as well as the establishment of a clear visual language for the component elements of structure. The two great churches of San Lorenzo and Santo Spirito both represent mature examples of his application of precise ratios and modules to every element of the construction, together with a rigorously ordered classical language; their influence was to be profound. The Pazzi chapel at Santa Croce marks a further development of the smaller-scale volumetric study of the Sagrestia Vecchia, and both were to be highly influential in the development of centralized church plans. Upon his death, Brunelleschi's fame and reputation were probably unique in the history of the development of an individual body of work by a single architect.

BUONTALENTI, BERNARDO (1536 – 1608)
A student of Ammannati, Buontalenti was one of the most prolific and characteristic architects of the later cinquecento. He was court architect to the Medici for many years, and was also responsible for the design of pageants and other events. Buontalenti was the Medici architect for the completion of the Uffizi, and for the remodeling of the family villa at Pratolino, which included the extensive redesign of the gardens with Mannerist grottoes and fountains. He submitted several designs for the completion of the facade of the cathedral, and for that of Santa Trinità, and designed many works of fortification for the Tuscan state, as well as the Belvedere fort in Florence. His architecture is inventive and Mannerist in style.

CACCINI, GIOVANNI BATTISTA (1556 – 1612)
A pupil of Dosio, Caccini worked as both a sculptor and architect in Florence. Among his sculptures are two of the four seasons that decorate the Ponte Santa Trinità, *Estate* (summer) and *Autunno* (autumn), as well as a number in the Boboli gardens, which are in the manner of Giambologna. His architectural works include the choir and baldacchino of Santo Spirito, the main portico of the Santissima Annunziata and the entrance portal of the Palazzo Nonfinito. In all of these works we see a powerful, Baroque style, strongly modeled and energetically detailed.

CRONACA (SIMONE DEL POLLAIUOLO) (1457 – 1508)
An architect of the generation that succeeded Brunelleschi, Cronaca's oeuvre remains rather elusive and varied. He completed the cupola of Giuliano da Sangallo's sacristy at Santo Spirito, as well as the richly decorated barrel-vaulted vestibule. At Palazzo Strozzi he completed the upper facade including the magnificent cornice, but his most important work is probably San Salvatore al Monte, where, inside the single aisleless nave, superimposed classical orders were used in a church for the first time in Florence. Palazzo Dei, later Guadagni, from about 1503, set a precedent in its austerely simple facade that was followed by many others in the cinquecento.

DONATELLO (c1386 – 1466)
Master of sculpture in marble and bronze, Donatello was one of the greatest Italian Renaissance artists. His genius emerged in sculptures such as *St. George*, made for the exterior niches of Orsanmichele in about 1415, and found its full force with later works such as *Habakkuk* for the campanile, where, in a revival of classical influence, the human personnality is shown with a new conviction, in striking contrast to medieval art.

FERRI, ANTONIO (1651 – 1716)
A late Baroque architect, Ferri was responsible for several notable interiors, among them the stair of honor and the great hall in the imposing Palazzo Corsini al Parione. In 1698 he worked for the same family at their villa at Castello. His most prominent Florentine work is San Frediano in Cestello, begun in 1680; the tall nave is generously lit, and the church's characteristic cupola, built in 1698, dominates the western Oltrarno.

FOGGINI, GIOVANNI BATTISTA (1652 – 1725)
He worked under Nigetti for a time at the Capella dei Principi, and after 1685 designed the large northern extension to the Palazzo Medici on the Via Larga for the Riccardi family. The facade faithfully follows Michelozzo's original design, but the interior contains sumptuous new apartments and staircases. Also active as a sculptor, his works include figures for the Corsini chapel at the Carmini and parts of the high altar at Santa Maria Maddalena dei Pazzi. His most notable church project is the remodeled San Giorgio alla Costa (1705), a rare but delightful Florentine Rococo interior.

GHIBERTI, LORENZO (c1378 – 1455)
Important early Renaissance sculptor, Ghiberti's doors for the baptistery in Florence from 1425–52, named the "Gates of Paradise," are considered one of the masterpieces of Italian art in the Quattrocento. Ghiberti's other works inculde three bronze statues for Orsanmichele and the reliefs for Siena cathedral. He also wrote treatises on art history and theory.

GIOTTO DI BONDONE (c1267 – 1337)
Often referred to as the "father of Florentine painting," Giotto is primarily known as a painter rather than as an architect. He was trained under Cimabue, and his earliest known fresco cycles are those in the upper church at Assisi. Later cycles include that of San Francesco, again at Assisi, those at the Scrovegni or Arena chapel at Padua, and the Peruzzi chapel at Santa Croce in Florence. Giotto's sole major work of architecture is the campanile of the cathedral in Florence, which he designed and begun in 1334; the upper orders were completed by others, with significant variation from his original design, but the overall concept was retained, and the tower is generally regarded as the most beautiful campanile in Italy. He was also chief master for the cathedral works for the two years prior to his death in 1337.

MAIANO, GIULIANO DA (1432 – 1490)
Initially best known as a skilled craftsman in intarsio (for example the doorway to the Sala dell'Udienza in the Palazzo Vecchio), Giuliano later worked as an architect in Florence and many other Tuscan cities. In Florence his work includes the Palazzo dello Strozzino, the external cladding of the drum of Brunelleschi's cupola at the cathedral, and the palaces of the Pazzi (begun 1458), and Bon, later Antinori (1465). Palazzo Pazzi established a pattern for the elegant, disciplined facades later also developed by Cronaca, while the Antinori facade remains one of the most highly refined, but with a minimalist severity that fuses earlier gothic typologies with a new classical discipline.

MEDICI, COSIMO I DE' (1519 – 1574)
He succeeded Alessandro de' Medici as duke of Tuscany in 1537, and in 1569 received the title of grand duke, which the Medici were to carry until the end of the dynasty in the early eighteenth century. During his long period of power Cosimo transformed the city into a highly personalized hereditary duchy. Cosimo patronized the arts extensively; many of the works commissioned were intended principally to reinforce his own status and image as the supreme head of state. Among the artists he patronized were Vasari, Giambologna, and Ammannati. Cosimo was also responsible for the profoundly significant relocation of the hub of Florentine government: he modernized the Palazzo Vecchio and constructed the Uffizi and the Corridoio Vasariano. He also established the court at Palazzo Pitti, which he expanded considerably in size to make it one of the largest palaces in Italy.

MEDICI, COSIMO "IL VECCHIO" DE' (1389 – 1464)
The unwritten ruler of Florence from 1434 to 1464, he is generally recognized as the founder of the dynasty that ruled the city nearly uninterruptedly for three centuries. After a year in exile in Venice following a coup by the Albizi and Strozzi families, Cosimo returned to Florence, and, although he held no official title, his power and influence ensured that the Medici clan effectively ruled the city's institutions of government for the next thirty years. Cosimo's wealth originated in banking, and the Medici bank continued to flourish during his reign. He was also a skilled politician and diplomat, responsible in large part for the Peace of Lodi, which established peace in northern Italy for twenty-five years. Cosimo was a highly educated and enlightened patron of the arts, who provided the city with much-needed stability; even though his rule replaced an earlier communal form of government he was widely popular, and after his death was given the honorific title of *pater patriae* (father of the nation) by the Florentines themselves. Cosimo patronized such artists and architects as Ghiberti, Donatello, Brunelleschi, and Michelozzo.

MEDICI, LORENZO "IL MAGNIFICO" DE' (1449 – 1492)
Lorenzo was the grandson of Cosimo, *pater patriae*, and in 1469 succeeded the short reign of his father Piero as de facto ruler of the city. Lorenzo's character made him an uneven ruler, creative and intellectual rather than a skilled diplomat. His power was challenged by the Pazzi, a rival dynasty, and he barely survived an assassination attempt, which killed his brother. Although he was less financially astute, and the family's banking fortune suffered, he inherited the cultural enlightenment of his grandfather, and patronized many of the city's finest craftsmen and artists, most notably the young Michelangelo, but also Andrea del Verrocchio, Sandro Botticelli, Giuliano da Sangallo.

MICHELANGELO BUONARROTTI (1475 – 1564)
One of the most outstandingly gifted and creative masters of the later High Renaissance, Michelangelo was active and prolific in many fields: as a sculptor, painter, poet, and architect. He was for three years apprentice to Domenico Ghirlandajo (1488–91), but also studied classical sculpture under the patronage of the Medici. He was adopted, "almost as a son" in his own words, by Lorenzo de' Medici at the palace in the Via Larga, where he met many distinguished humanists and artists, and was particularly influenced by Poliziano. In 1494 he fled Florence after the death of Lorenzo, to Bologna and then to Rome. From 1496 to 1506 he was intensively active in Rome, where he returned again in 1508 to paint the frescoes of the Sistine chapel. His important period in Florence began in 1516. His first project, the new facade for San Lorenzo, was abandoned by his patron, Pope Leo X, but he was commissioned to build the Sagrestia Nuova and the Biblioteca Laurenziana at San Lorenzo, both for the Medici. In 1529 he was made procurator general for the defense of the city, and reinforced Florence's fortifications, particularly at San Miniato. In 1534 Michelangelo left Florence once more permanently for Rome, where he worked on many further projects, including the Last Judgement in the Sistine Chapel, the replanning of the Campidoglio, the Porta Pia, Palazzo Farnese, and the conversion of the baths of Diocletian into the church of Santa Maria degli Angeli.

MICHELOZZO DI BARTOLOMMEO (1396 – 1472)
One of the three outstanding architects of the early Florentine Renaissance, Michelozzo's career is often overshadowed by those of his mentor, Brunelleschi, and his slightly younger contemporary, Alberti. He trained with Ghiberti and for many years was the family architect of the Medici, for whom most of his chief works were undertaken. These included the extensive modernization and extension of the convent of San Marco, including its elegantly refined library, and the church and conventual buildings at the Santissima Annunziata. Both evince considerable spatial skills and the adoption of a clear vocabulary of classical detailing. Perhaps his most important work, though, was the new Medici family palace on the Via Larga. This massive and imposing work established a new scale and treatment to the Florentine palazzo that was to form the basis of the development of the typology for the next century. Michelozzo also modernized the two Medici villas at Cafaggiolo and Careggi, where older fortified farmhouses were given new facilities while still retaining much of their medieval appearance. In many senses Michelozzo's work naturally continues that of Brunelleschi, although his more traditional roots are still detectable.

MICHELUCCI, GIOVANNI (1891 – 1990)
An outstanding figure of twentieth century Tuscan architecture, Michelucci's extremely long career embraced several distinct stylistic phases, among them the more mainstream modernism of public works in the 1950s and 1960s and, by contrast, the highly sculptural form of San Giovanni Battista, the famous Autostrada church of 1961. His first major project, with a group of collaborators, was the new railway station of Santa Maria Novella (1933–35) which remains one of the most remarkable works of the era in Italy. His later, postwar works include the Cassa di Risparmio, the Post Office building on Via Pietrapiana, and reconstruction around the southern bridgehead of the Ponte Vecchio.

NERVI, PIER LUIGI (1891 – 1979)
The most outstanding Italian architect-engineer of the twentieth century, Nervi's remarkable skill lay in his fusion of projects of large-scale structural engineering — which he had studied — with his highly creative sensitivity of a natural and self-taught architect. His approach reached its maturity in a series of projects in which the spatial and dynamic qualities of reinforced concrete reached new heights. One of his earlier works was the Stadio Comunale, the sports stadium in Florence, built in 1930–32, which was followed by the exhibition hall Turin in 1948, and the two stadia built in Rome for the 1960 Olympic games, the Palazzo and Palazzetto dello Sport. The latter was arguably the most refined, elegant sports stadium built in Europe until the work of Renzo Piano at Bari 35 years later, which was clearly inspired by Nervi's earlier example.

NIGETTI, MATTEO (1560 – 1649)
A major figure in Florentine architecture of the later Renaissance and Mannerist period, Nigetti was collaborator and follower of Buontalenti. His Mannerist work is characterized by the eclecticism typical of the later works patronized by the Medici court. The Cappella dei Principi, the opulent Medici mausoleum begun in 1604, was completed up to the cupola by 1625; Nigetti was assisted and then succeeded in the long program to completion by Foggini and Ruggieri. It remains the most grandiose of the Medici commissions, whose uniquely rich internal decoration in *pietra dura* marked the apogee of this particular technique. Nigetti's other outstanding work is the church of Santi Michele e Gaetano, but he completed only the transepts and the choir; the nave and facade were completed by Gherardo Silvani. The whole building is a fairly rare, outstanding example of exuberant later Florentine Baroque. At Ognissanti Nigetti added the facade in 1637 to Bartolomeo Pettirossi's slightly earlier church, another lively and original composition on the north bank of the Arno.

PARIGI, ALFONSO (1606 – 1656) **AND GIULIO** (1571 – 1635)
The Parigi were a Florentine family of architects and engravers, the most prominent of whom were Giulio and Alfonso the Younger. Giulio's chief works were the enlargement of the Medici villa at Poggio Imperiale in 1622–24, the first stage of the reconstruction of the Arcispedale di Santa Maria Nuova after 1612, and the enlargement of Palazzo Pitti in 1618, which was continued after 1640 by Alfonso. The chief works of Alfonso included the expansion of the vast Palazzo Corsini al Parione and the church of San Giovannino degli Scolopi, where he added the vaulted ceiling and completed the facade begun earlier by Ammannati, including the paired columns.

POGGI, GIUSEPPE (1811 – 1901)
An architect, engineer, and urban designer, Poggi was responsible for the most radical and extensive works to the fabric of Florence since the era of the Medici. In 1865 he presented to the Comune his development plan for the city, which included the demolition of the medieval walls to form a series of grand boulevards with major intersections and new piazze at the city gates. The plan also provided for a new railway station, a Campo di Marte (military training ground), and new roads on the southern hills, the Viale dei Colli, as well as the Piazzale Michelangelo. New residential quarters were also laid out at Piagentina and Savonarola. Poggi's buildings include Palazzo Calcagnini and Villa Favard, as well as large apartment blocks at the Piazza Beccaria and Piazza della Libertà. Many of Poggi's buildings are in a refined neoclassical style, owing much to the Florentine tradition; they contributed considerably to the new scale of the city in the era following Unification.

RAPHAEL (RAFFAELLO SANZIO) (1483 – 1520)
Primarily known as a painter, Raphael was born in Urbino, and first visited Florence in 1504. He was in Rome from 1508, where his magnificent frescoes for popes Julius II and Leo X secured his fame and reputation. His output thereafter was prolific, and in 1514 he was appointed chief architect at St Peter's following the death of Bramante. In Florence his architectural oeuvre was limited to two projects, one partially executed, while the other was not. Palazzo Pandolfini commissioned by Pope Leo X was built in 1515–20, but never completed. The palazzo is perhaps the finest in the "alla romana" style in the city, with powerfully modeled fenestration and a strongly projecting cornice. The design of the palace strongly influenced later architects such as Gherardo Silvani. Raphael's design for the facade of San Lorenzo, again under the patronage of Leo X, one of several in a limited competition, did not find favor with the pope, as it was too purely architectonic. Instead a richer, more complex proposal from Michelangelo was preferred, which was itself later abandoned.

RUCELLAI, GIOVANNI (1403 – 1481)
Member of an outstanding Florentine dynasty of merchants and bankers, Giovanni was a remarkable patron of the arts, arguably the most important in the city after Lorenzo de' Medici. His patronage of architecture and, above all, his support of Alberti started in 1444, when the architect began a long program of reconstruction of the family palazzo on the Via della Vigna Nuova, the famous facade of which was designed in about 1453. In 1448 work began on the Rucellai chapel at the family church of San Pancrazio, which incorporated the Holy Sepulchre monument, again by Alberti. This was followed by the construction of the loggia opposite his palace. Giovanni employed Alberti once again to complete the facade of Santa Maria Novella, begun in about 1458 and completed in 1470. He also amassed a fine collection of paintings, among which were works by Paolo Uccello and Filippo Lippi.

RUGGIERI, FERDINANDO (1691 – 1741)
A late Baroque architect, Ruggieri's work included the final completion of the Cappella dei Principi, including the external cladding of the chapel in pietra forte and white marble, and the windows of the cupola; he was also largely responsible for the execution of the imposing Palazzo Capponi to an initial design by Carlo Fontana. Ruggieri designed two important church projects, the facade of the church of the Filippini in 1715 (which became part of the complex known as San Firenze), and the reconstruction of Santa Felicità, after 1736. The rather monumental facade of the former is greatly enlived by sculptures by Gioacchino Fortini. Santa Felicità had a unique function as the Medici family's own chapel, and as rebuilt by Ruggieri has a stately imposing interior, with pronounced vertical emphasis.

SANGALLO, ANTONIO, "IL VECCHIO" (1455 – 1534) **AND GIULIANO** (1445 – 1516)
Giuliano and his younger brother Antonio were the most important members of this "clan" of architects, the third significant member being Antonio the Younger (1483–1546), nephew of the first two. Giuliano is a very important figure in the generations that followed Alberti. Strongly influenced by Brunelleschi, one of his early works was the cloister of Santa Maria Maddalena de' Pazzi, followed by the sacristy at Santo Spirito, begun in 1488, the latter a highly refined exercise in the manner of Brunelleschi, with an octagonal plan and detailing in *pietra serena*. Palazzo Gondi evinces a robust facade style following the principles established by Michelozzo for the Medici, while his 1490 model for the vast, imposing Palazzo Strozzi took these principles to further heights of imposing massing and monumental grandeur; Palazzo Strozzi represents the Renaissance Florentine palace at its most mature, most rigorously and rationally designed. The palace was later completed by Cronaca. Giuliano's most important works outside the city were the Medici villa at Poggio a Caiano and the church of Santa Maria delle Carceri at Prato. Both were, in very different ways, highly influential buildings; the villa became a prototype for many that followed and the church at Prato was influential in propagating the principles of centralized church planning after Alberti's precepts. Antonio collaborated with Giuliano on many projects, and built the famous Loggia dei Serviti which reflects Brunelleschi's Ospedale degli Innocenti in the Piazza della Signoria. Much of his oeuvre centered on works of fortification, at Castel Sant' Angelo in Rome, at Livorno and elsewhere. After 1518 he established himself at Montepulciano, where his later work is located. Most of the work of their nephew Antonio the Younger is in Rome, where he assisted Bramante, and was one of the chief masters at St. Peters.

SAVONAROLA, GIROLAMO (1452 – 1498)
A Dominican friar based at the San Marco monastery in Florence, Savonarola attacked the power and corruption of the city and its politician in his sermons. With the expulsion of the Medici from Florence in 1494, he became the spokesman for a large number of disaffected citizens, and attempted to set up a model Christian republic. Although he held no formal office or title, Savonarola effectively took control of the city, imposing rigid moral codes and instigating campaigns against luxury and venality. The establishment of the Council of Five Hundred led to the rapid construction of the great hall to house the council in the Palazzo Vecchio. He incurred the enmity of Rome, however, by denouncing the corruption of the papacy, and was excommunicated by Pope Alexander VI in 1497. He was then tried in Florence and, found guilty of sedition and heresy, was hanged and then burned in the Piazza della Signoria on 23 May 1498.

SILVANI, GHERARDO (1579 – 1675) **AND PIER FRANCESCO** (1620 – 1685)
Gherardo and his son Pier Francesco were the most prominent architects in Florence in the seventeenth century. Gherardo's work, largely in a late Mannerist style, includes the facade of the church of Santi Michele e Gaetano, whose rational and disciplined screen is greatly enlivened by the more Baroque sculptures of Balthasar Permoser. Gherardo is associated with a number of palazzi in the city, including Palazzo Strozzi del Poeta (1626), and Palazzo Castelli Fenzi (1634), both simply but powerfully modeled examples of the "alla romana" style. His son Pier Francesco developed the great sprawling Palazzo Corsini on the Lungarno, with its unusual U-shaped plan, while his ecclesiastical masterpiece is the richly ornate Baroque Corsini chapel at the Carmini. His new church of San Frediano in Cestello was less successful, and was demolished in 1679 to make way for a new project by Giulio Cerruti. Pier Francesco also designed the Filippini church, which was to form part of the San Firenze complex.

VASARI, GIORGIO (1511 – 1574)
Vasari was the archetypal polymath of the sixteenth century, equally active and prolific in many different fields, as architect, painter, and indefatigable chronicler of the *Lives of the Artists*. His reputation was initially established as a painter, with a style based on the early Mannerism of Michelangelo and Raphael. His first period of success was in Rome, under the patronage of the Farnese, and the first edition of his famous *Vite de' piu eccellenti architetti, scultori e pittori* (the *Lives of the Artists*) was published in 1550, the year he returned to Florence. Vasari became closely associated with Cosimo I, for whom he planned the Uffizi and the Corridoio Vasariano, thus fundamentally transforming the physical form of the heart of Florence. He was also responsible for a long series of modernizations within the Palazzo Vecchio, notably the great Salone dei Cinquecento, where he was responsible for the complete narrative cycles of paintings on the walls and the ceiling, the two suites of private apartments, and the study of Francesco I. He also planned great spectacles in the piazza, and was the founder of the Accademia del Disegno in 1561. In 1568 the second, considerably expanded edition of the *Vite* was published, incorporating biographies of Vasari's contemporaries; despite some vagaries and attributions that are no longer held, it has remained constantly in print and is still a fundamental source today.

Key to map locations

CHURCHES

1 Badia Fiorentina
2 Battistero di San Giovanni (baptistery)
3 Carmini
4 Orsanmichele
5 San Firenze
6 San Frediano in Cestello
7 San Giorgio alla Costa
8 San Giovannino degli Scolopi
9 San Jacopo Sopr'Arno
10 San Lorenzo
11 San Marco
12 San Miniato al Monte
13 San Niccolò Sopr'Arno
14 San Salvatore al Vescovo
15 Santa Croce
16 Santa Felicità
17 Santa Maria degli Angeli
18 Santa Maria del Fiore (cathedral)
19 Santa Maria Maddalena de'Pazzi
20 Santa Maria Maggiore
21 Santa Maria Novella
22 Santa Trinità
23 Santi Apostoli
24 Santi Michele e Gaetano
25 Santissima Annunziata
26 Santo Spirito
27 Santo Stefano al Ponte

PALACES

28 Palazzo Acciaiuoli
29 Palazzo Antinori
30 Palazzo dell'Arte della Lana
31 Palazzo del Bargello
32 Palazzo Bartolini Salimbeni
33 Palazzo della Borsa
34 Palazzo Capponi
35 Palazzo Corsini al Parione
36 Palazzo Davanzati
37 Palazzo Gianfigliazzi
38 Palazzo dei Giudici
39 Palazzo Gondi
40 Palazzo Grifoni
41 Palazzo Guadagni
42 Palazzo Medici Riccardi
43 Palazzo delle Missioni
44 Palazzo Mozzi
45 Palazzo Nonfinito
46 Palazzo Pandolfini
47 Palazzo di Parte Guelfa
48 Palazzo Pazzi
49 Palazzo Pitti
50 Palazzo Rucellai
51 Palazzo Spini Feroni
52 Palazzo Strozzi
53 Palazzo Strozzi del Poeta
54 Palazzo Strozzino
55 Palazzo Uguccioni
56 Palazzo Vecchio (Palazzo dei Priori)

OTHER BUILDINGS

57 Arcispedale di Santa Maria Nuova
58 Arco di Trionfo
59 Biblioteca Laurenziana
60 Campanile
61 Casa di Bianca Cappello
62 Corridoio Vasariano
63 Forte Belvedere
64 Fortezza da Basso
65 Giardino di Boboli
66 Loggia di Bigallo
67 Loggia del Pesce
68 Loggia Rucellai
69 Loggia di San Paolo
70 Loggia della Signoria (dei Lanzi)
71 Mercato Nuovo
72 Mercato di San Lorenzo
73 Ospedale di Bonifacio (former)
74 Ospedale di San Giovanni di Dio
75 Ospedale degli Innocenti
76 Parco delle Cascine
77 Piazza Beccaria
78 Piazza d'Azeglio
79 Piazza dell'Indipendenza
80 Piazza della Repubblica
81 Piazza della Signoria
82 Ponte alla Carraia
83 Ponte alle Grazie
84 Ponte San Niccolò
85 Ponte Santa Trinità
86 Ponte Vecchio
87 Porta Faenza
88 Porta al Prato
89 Porta Romana
90 Porta San Frediano
91 Porta San Gallo
92 Porta San Niccolò
93 Porta alla Zecca
94 Roman amphitheater (site of)
95 Torre degli Alberti
96 Torre della Castagna
97 Torre dei Corbizi (or Donati)
98 Torre della Pagliazza
99 Uffizi
100 Villa Favard

Glossary of Terms

ARTE
Florentine trade or craft guild. The *arti* were divided into two or three categories at different periods, the *arti maggiori* being the most senior group, and which eventually came to control almost all political power in the city.

BADIA
Abbey, usually of the Dominican or Benedictine orders

BASILICA
Originally, in Roman times, a large hall for the assembly of the population to vote; later, the term was adopted to describe Romanesque churches that had a similar form: a long, colonnaded nave, with two side aisles, and a chancel which was often raised on steps, and with an apsidal (radiused) east end.

BIFORA
A two-light window, widely used on the facades of Renaissance Florentine palazzi.

BRACCIO, pl. BRACCIA
The Florentine unit of length, equivalent to just under 2 feet, or 58.4 cm.

BORGO, pl. BORGHI
Generally refers to a suburb of a city, a district usually just outside the city's defensive walls.

BUGNATO
Rusticated stonework, used extensively on the facades of Florentine palazzi from the later medieval era through to the Renaissance.

CAMPANILE
Bell-tower, usually a freestanding structure detached from the church which it serves.

CAPOMAESTRO
The chief master of a building project, who superintends and coordinates the work of the individual trade masters.

CARRARA
City near the northern coastline of Tuscany, famous for the very high quality of its white marble. The stone was the most highly regarded of all Italian marbles for sculpture, and was used by Michelangelo and most of the leading sculptors of the Renaissance.

CASTELLO
In Italian, a castle; here refers to a small borgo two miles northwest of the city of Florence, where the Medici owned a villa.

CERTOSA
A Carthusian monastery (in English, usually charterhouse); specifically here refers to the Certosa at Galluzzo a few miles southwest of Florence.

CIVITAS
The Renaissance concept of civilized urban living, a subject of widespread debate in the early quattrocento, and one of the key issues in the works of Alberti, who discussed at length the qualities that should be associated with the design of cities.

COMUNE
In Italy, the *comuni* were a large number of independent and self-governing city states, which flourished during the medieval era. By the fourteenth century, most of the *comuni* had been suppressed, and were subjected to the rule of individual dynastic families.

CONTADO
The immediate rural surroundings of a major city, on which it is usually dependent for its protection, and which, in turn, provides the city with much of its agricultural products, for example flour, wine, olives, and fruit and vegetables.

CORTILE
Usually describes the enclosed central courtyard of a palazzo or other major building.

DUOMO
The cathedral, or the seat of the bishop.

FIORINO
The Florentine gold coin, which became a widely accepted currency over much of Europe as a result of its exceptional fineness, and due to the strength and stability of the Florentine economy; it is very similar in value and general appearance to the Venetian ducat.

GONFALONIERE
A title widely used in late medieval Italy; traditionally it meant a standard-bearer, but by extension was the title often given to a city's chief magistrate.

GUELFS AND GHIBELLINES
The two principal rival political factions of medieval Florence. The Guelfs supported the papacy and the interests of the merchant classes, whereas the Ghibellines were supporters of the German Roman Emperor and his claims for ascendency over the papacy and Italian cities; the Ghibellines tended to favor the old aristocracy rather than the merchant class. This factionalism was rife in Florence in the later thirteenth century, and the Guelfs achieved the peak of their influence in 1266 when they took the city and the Ghibellines were exiled.

LOGGIA, pl. LOGGE
A covered space which could fulfill a number of different functions; some logge (for example that of the Rucellai) were built by noble families as meeting places for members of the clan; others (the Loggia del Pesce, the Mercato Nuovo) served market functions; still others (the Loggia dei Lanzi) were built as public spaces for civic or other occasions.

LUNETTE
A high-level window, often semicircular in shape, and placed above another larger window or doorway.

LUNGARNO
The term generally used for the streets or quays along the banks of the river Arno. Similar terms are used in other Italian cities, for example the Lungotevere in Rome.

MUGELLO
A district of Tuscany north of Florence, centered on the valley of the river Sieve. The Medici clan had its origins in the Mugello.

ORTO
An orchard or market garden; hence the name Orsanmichele, a corruption of San Michele in Orto.

OLTRARNO
Literally "on the other side of the Arno." The district of Florence on the south bank of the Arno, which remained less extensively developed, and with a smaller population than the north bank.

PENDENTIVE
The saillike surface which provides the transition between a square base and a faceted or circular cupola which rises above it.

PIANO NOBILE
The principal story of accommodation, usually of a private palazzo; this is almost always the first story above the ground.

PIETRA DURA
Literally "hard stone"; in Florence the term is used particularly for works of applied art (especially furniture), which are clad with small pieces of precious and semi-precious stones or rare marbles, often to intricate designs. The Ufficio delle Pietre Dure was established at the Uffizi by Ferdinando de' Medici in 1588 to provide for workshops specialising in this craft, the most extensive use of which was in the interior decoration of the Cappella dei Principi. The workshops still flourish today.

PIETRA FORTE
Literally "strong stone"; a biscuit-coloured limestone which was quarried extensively in the environs of Florence, particularly in Monte Oliveto and the former Boboli garden district. The stone is, in fact, relatively soft, and although widely used on many of the city's famous monuments, has suffered considerable degradation from atmospheric pollution.

PIETRA SERENA
The second famous building stone of the city is a type of macigno, a fairly soft, blue-grey calcareous sandstone, most of the quarries for which are to the east and northeast of the city, particularly around Fiesole and Settignano. It is well suited to internal use, and can be carved in detail as a result of its fine, even grain. It was widely used by Brunelleschi and Michelozzo.

PODESTÀ
Title given to the chief magistrate of Florence and other cities; he was usually a foreigner, with an often brief term of office, whose appointment was intended to render impartial justice, free from internal pressures and interests.

PRATO
City to the northwest of Florence, famous for centuries for the production of wool cloth and other fabrics. It also produced a highly regarded green marble, which was used on a number of the city's finest monuments.

PRIORE
Title given to the elected heads of Florence's *arti*; later the title was transferred to denote members of the ruling "cabinet" of the city's government.

QUARTIERE, pl. QUARTIERI
In Florence, one of the four administrative districts of the city. These were altered from time to time, although for much of its history, there were three quartieri on the north side of the Arno, and one on the south side, the Oltrarno.

RUSTICATION
Stonework in which the stone surface is often left very roughly carved was a widespread feature of Florentine palazzi, particularly in the early Renaissance. Rustication was also often refined such that each storey was given a slightly different treatment, with the coarsest face to the basement storey, and the most refined treatment on the top story. Palazzo Gondi is a fine example of this approach. See also Bugnato.

SGRAFFITO
A technique of wall decoration whereby a surface is decorated with one color of plaster, which is then covered by a second layer of a contrasting color, usually black on white, or the reverse. Parts of the outer layer are removed to reveal the other color beneath, thus forming rich and complex decorative patterns. The technique was widely used in Florence, but many examples have been lost; among the few that survive is the notable house of Bianca Cappello on the Via Maggio.

SPORTO, pl. SPORTI
Overhanging jetty of the upper stories of a building, built to provide additional space in the house. Attempts were made to outlaw the practice in Florence as it increased the danger of spread of fire, and made the streets below the jetties extremely dark. Among the prominent surviving examples is the Palazzo dell'Antella in the Piazza Santa Croce, which is also covered with sgraffito decoration.

STEMMA, pl. STEMMI
A coat of arms or other heraldic device; in Florence usually applies to the noble clans or the arti.

TORRE
In Italy, a tower; in Florence the term refers to the tall, fortified towers of the influential families during the medieval era, which were attached to their houses, and were resorted to in times of urban strife.

VIA, VIALE
Via is the general Italian term for a street; a viale is a broad street, i.e. a boulevard or avenue.

VILLA
The narrow, original definition is of a house, usually fairly substantial, in the countryside, often with a farm or other lands attached to it; the villa was used by the wealthier citizens of the city as a place to which to escape for the villeggiatura during the hottest months of the summer. The land of the villa also often provided products for the family's city palazzo, for example wine, olive oil, and fruit.

VILLEGGIATURA
The practice of wealthy Florentines of moving from the city during the heat of summer to their country estates, which generally consisted of a villa surrounded by gardens and working farmland.

ZECCA
A mint, producing coinage.

Bibliography

1 PRIMARY SOURCES

ALBERTI, L B *Della pittura* (written 1436). Engl. ed., trs. C. Grayson, *On Painting* (London, 1991).

ALBERTI, L B *De statua* (written c. 1464; 1st ed. C. Bartoli, Florence, 1568; new ed. M. Collareta, Livorno, 1998).

ALBERTI, L B *De re aedificatoria* (written c. 1452; 1st ed. Florence, 1485). 1st Engl. ed., G. Leoni, *The Ten Books of Architecture* (London, 1755); new Engl. ed., J. Rykwert, N. Leach, and R. Tavernor, eds. and trs., *On the Art of Building in Ten Books* (London and Cambridge, Mass., 1988).

BALDUCCI PEGOLOTTI, F *La pratica della mercatura* (written c. 1310–1340). Engl. ed. A. Evans, Cambridge, Mass., 1936).

BOCCACCIO, G *Il decamerone* (written c. 1350). Engl. ed., trs. G. H. McWilliam, *The Decameron* (Harmonsdworth, 1972).

CENNINI, C *Il libro dell'arte* (written 1370). Engl. ed. trs. D. V. Thompson, *The Craftsman's Handbook* (New York, 1960).

DANTE ALIGHIERI *La divina commedia* (written c. 1304–21; ed. R. Fornaciari, Florence, 1904; numerous other eds) .

DANTE ALIGHIERI *La vita nuova* (written 1292–95; ed. M. Scherillo, Milan, 1911; numerous other eds).

FILARETE (ANTONIO AVERLINO) *Trattato di architettura* (written 1461–64). Engl. ed. trs. J. R. Spencer, *Treatise on Architecture* (New Haven and London, 1965).

GHIBERTI, L *I commentari* (written c. 1447; ed. O. Morinsani, Naples, 1947).

MANETTI, A *Filippo Brunelleschi* (written c. 1450; Stuttgart, 1887).

MACHIAVELLI, N *Il principe* (written c. 1513–14; ed. G. Lisio: Florence 1899). Engl. ed. trs. G. Bull, *The Prince* (Harmondsworth, 1961).

PETRARCH, F *Le rime* (ed. S. A. Nulli, Milan, 1956).

VASARI, G *Le vite de' piu eccellenti architetti, scultori e pittori*, 2 Vols (1st ed. Florence, 1550; sec. ed. 1568). Engl. ed., trs. J. Foster, *Lives of the Most Eminent Painters, Sculptors, and Architects* (London, 1878). Also referred to as *Lives of the Artists*.

VILLANI, G *Cronica fiorentina*, 9 books (written c. 1330; new ed. Florence 1844–55); English ed., trs. R. E. Selfe & P. H. Wicksteed, *Chronicles* (London, 1906).

2 GENERAL HISTORIES, POLITICAL AND SOCIAL

ADY, C M *Lorenzo de' Medici and Renaissance Italy* (London, 1960).

ANTONETTI, P *La vita quotidiana a Firenze ai tempi di Dante* (Milan, 1979).

BRION, M *The Medici* (London, 1980).

DAVIDSOHN, R *Geschichte von Florenz*, 8 Vols (Berlin, 1896–1927).

GUTKIND, C S *Cosimo de' Medici, Pater Patriae* (Oxford, 1938).

HALE, J R *Florence and the Medici: The Pattern of Control* (London, 1977).

HALE, J R *The Civilisation of Europe in the Renaissance* (London, 1993).

HOLMES, G *The Florentine Enlightenment 1400–1450* (London and Oxford, 1969).

LARNER, J *Culture and Society in Italy 1190–1420* (London, 1971).

LOPEZ, R S AND I W RAYMOND *Medieval Trade in the Mediterranean World* (New York, 1955).

RUBINSTEIN, N *The Government of Florence under the Medici* (Oxford, 1966).

SCHEVILL, F *Medieval and Renaissance Florence* (London, 1961).

SCHEVILL, F *The Medici* (New York, 1949).

VILLARI, P *The Life of Savonarola* (London, 1896).

VILLARI, P *The Life of Machiavelli* (London, 1892).

WALEY, D *The Italian City–Republics* (London and New York, 1969).

3 ARCHITECTURE AND THE ARTS: GENERAL WORKS AND SURVEYS

ARGAN, G C *L'architettura italiano nel duecento e trecento* (Florence, 1937).

BERENSON, B *Italian Painters of the Renaissance* (Oxford, 1930).

HAY, D ed. *The Age of the Renaissance* (London and New York, 1986).

PAOLETTI, J T AND G M RADKE *Art in Renaissance Italy* (London, 1997).

POPE HENNESSEY, J *Italian Gothic Sculpture* (London, 1955).

POPE HENNESSEY, J *Italian Renaissance Sculpture* (London, 1958).

VENTURI, A *Storia dell'arte italiana*, 18 Vols (Milan, 1901–40).

WHITE, J *Art and Architecture in Italy 1250–1400* (Harmondsworth, 1966).

4 MONOGRAPHS AND SPECIALIST STUDIES

ACKERMAN, J S *The Architecture of Michelangelo*, 2 Vols (London, 1961).

ANGELINI, A *Piero della Francesca* (Florence, 1987).

ANTHONY, E W *Early Florentine Architecture and Decoration* (Harvard, 1927).

ARGAN, G C *Botticelli* (Geneva, 1989).

BALDINI, U ed., *Santa Maria Novella: la basilica, il convento, i chiostri monumentali* (Florence, 1981).

BARDAZZI, S AND E CASTELLANI *La villa medicea di Poggio a Caiano*, 2 Vols (Prato, 1981).

BARGILLI, E *La cattedrale di Fiesole* (Florence, 1883).

BAROCCHI, P *Il Rosso Fiorentino* (Gismondi, 1950).

BAROCCHI, P *Vasari pittore* (Milan, 1964).

BARTOLI, L *Il disegno della cupola del Brunelleschi* (Florence, 1994).

BATTISTI, E *Cimabue* (New York, 1967).

BATTISTI, E *Filippo Brunelleschi* (Milan, 1976).

BATTISTI, E *Giotto* (Geneva, 1990).

BELLANDI, S *La chiesa di Santo Spirito di Firenze* (Florence, 1921).

BENNET, R AND D WILKINS *Donatello* (Oxford, 1984).

BERTI, C *Palazzo Davanzati* (Florence, 1958).

BORGATTI, M *Le mura e le torri di Firenze* (Rome, 1900).

BORSI, F *La capitale a Firenze e l'opera di Giuseppe Poggi* (Florence, 1970).

BORSI, F *Firenze del cinquecento* (Rome, 1974).

BORSI, F *Leon Battista Alberti* (Milan, 1975).

BORSI, S *Giuliano da Sangallo* (Rome, 1985).

BUCCI, M *La basilica di Santa Croce* (Florence, 1965).

BUCCI, M AND R BENCINI *Palazzi di Firenze*, 4 Vols (Florence, 1973).

BUSIGNANI, A *Pollaiuolo* (Florence, 1969).

BUSIGNANI, A AND R BENCINI *Chiese di Firenze*, 4 Vols (Florence, 1972–82).

BUTTERFIELD, A *The Sculptures of Andrea del Verrocchio* (New Haven, 1997).

CARROCCI, G *Firenze scomparsa* (Florence, 1898).

CARROCCI, G *Il Mercato Vecchio di Firenze* (Florence, 1884).

CARROCCI, G *Palazzo Davanzati: ricordi storici* (Florence, 1910).

CARROCCI, G *La villa medicea di Careggi: memorie e ricordi* (Florence, 1888).

CASAZZA, O *The Brancacci Chapel Frescoes* (London, 1992).

CASAZZA, O *Masaccio* (Florence, 1990).

CASSARINO, E *La villa medicea di Artimino* (Florence, 1990).

CAVALLUCCI, C J *Santa Maria del Fiore: storia documentata* (Florence, 1881).

CHERUBINI, G AND G FANELLI eds, *Il Palazzo Medici Riccardi di Firenze* (Florence, 1990).

CONFORTI, C *Giorgio Vasari architetto* (Milan, 1993).

CONTI, C *Il Palazzo Pitti, la sua primitiva costruzione e successivi ingrandimenti* (Florence, 1887).

CRESTI, C *L'architettura del Seicento a Firenze* (Rome, 1990).

DETTI, E *Firenze scomparsa* (Florence, 1970).

DEZZI BARDESCHI, M *La facciata di Santa Maria Novella* (Pisa, 1969).

FANELLI, G *Firenze (Le citta nella storia d'Italia)* (Bari and Rome, 1980).

FANELLI, G *Brunelleschi* (Florence, 1980).

FARA, A *Bernardo Buontalenti* (Milan, 1995).

FERRARA, M AND F QUINTERIO *Michelozzo di Bartolomeo* (Florence, 1984).

FOSSI, G *Filippo Lippi* (Florence, 1989).

GADOL, J *Leon Battista Alberti* (Chicago, 1969).

GNUDI, C *Giotto* (Milan, 1959).

GOLDTHWAITE, R *The Building of Renaissance Florence* (Baltimore, 1980).

GORI MONTANELLI, L *Brunelleschi e Michelozzo* (Florence, 1957).

GUASTI, G *Santa Maria del Fiore: la costruzione della chiesa e del campanile* (Florence, 1887).

HOLMES, G *The Florentine Enlightenment 1400–1450* (Oxford, 1969).

HORSTER, M *Andrea del Castagno* (Oxford, 1980).

DEGLI INNOCENTI, P *Le origini del Bel San Giovanni* (Florence, 1994).

JANSON, H W *The Sculpture of Donatello* (Princeton, 1957).

KIENE, M *Bartolomeo Ammannati architetto* (Milan, 1995).

KLOTZ, H *Filippo Brunelleschi: The Early Works and the Medieval Tradition* (New York, 1990).

KRAUTHEIMER, R *Lorenzo Ghiberti* (Princeton, 1970).

LENSI, A *Palazzo Vecchio* (Milan and Rome, 1929).

LENSI ORLANDI, G *Le ville di Firenze di qua d'Arno e di la d'Arno*, 2 Vols (Florence, 1978).

LUPORINI, E *Brunelleschi: forma e ragione* (Milan, 1964).

MACCI, L AND V ORGERA *Architettura e civilta delle torri: torri e famiglie nella Firenze medievale* (Florence, 1994).

MARIANI, V *Arnolfo di Cambio* (Rome, 1943).

MARCHINI, G *Il Battistero e il duomo di Firenze* (Florence, 1972).

MARCHINI, G *Giuliano da Sangallo* (Florence, 1942).

MIGNANI, D *Le ville medicee di Giusto Utens* (Florence, 1980).

MILANESI, G ed. *Le opere di Giorgio Vasari*, 4 Vols (Florence, 1878–85).

MONTI, R *Andrea del Sarto* (Milan, 1965).

MORGAN, C H *The Life of Michelangelo* (New York and London, 1981).

MORISANI, O *Michelozzo architetto* (Turin, 1951).

DEL MORO, L *La facciata di Santa Maria del Fiore* (Florence, 1888).

MOSCO, M *Itinerari di Firenze barocca* (Florence, 1974).

PAATZ, E AND W *Die Kirchen von Florenz*, 6 Vols (Frankfurt, 1952–55).

PASSERINI, L *Del pretorio di Firenze* (Florence, 1865).

PIETRAMELLARA, C *Il battistero di San Giovanni a Firenze* (Florence, 1973).

PIETRAMELLARA, C *Santa Maria del Fiore a Firenze: I tre progetti* (Florence, 1984).

POGGI, G *Il duomo di Firenze* (Berlin, 1909).

POGGI, G *Or San Michele* (Florence, 1895).

POGGI, G *Il Bigallo* (Florence, 1905).

POGGI, G *Sui lavori per l'ingrandimento di Firenze 1864–77* (Florence, 1882).

PONENTE, N *Raphael* (Geneva, 1990).

POPE HENNESSEY, J *Luca della Robbia* (Oxford, 1980).

PORTOGHESI, P AND B ZEVI eds, *Michelangelo architetto* (Turin, 1964).

PREVITALI, G *Giotto e la sua bottega* (Milan, 1974).

ROCCHI, G ed, *Santa Maria del Fiore: rilievi, documenti, indagini strumentali, interpretazioni: il corpo basilicale* (Milan, 1988).

ROCCHI, G ed, *Santa Maria del Fiore: piazza, battistero, campanile: rilievi, documenti, indagini strumentali, interpretazioni* (Florence, 1996).

ROSSI, P A *Le cupole di Brunelleschi* (Bologna, 1982).

SAALMAN, H *The Bigallo* (New York, 1969).

SAALMAN, H *The Church of Santa Trinità in Florence* (New York, 1966).

SANPAOLESI, P *Brunelleschi* (Milan, 1962).

SANPAOLESI, P *La cupola di Brunelleschi* (Florence, 1965).

SANPAOLESI, P *La cupola di Santa Maria del Fiore: il progetto, la costruzione* (Florence, 1977).

SCIALLA, G C *Ville medicee* (Novara, 1982).

SINDONA, E *L'Opera completa di Cimabue* (Milan, 1975).

VON STEGMANN, C AND H VON GEYMULLER *Die Architektur der Renaissance in Toscana*, 11 Vols (Munich, 1885–1908).

TARANI, F *La basilica di San Miniato al Monte* (Florence, 1910).

TAVERNER, R *On Alberti and the Art of Building* (New Haven and London, 1988).

UCCELLI, G B *Della badia fiorentina* (Florence, 1858).

WHITE, J *Duccio* (London, 1979).

ZANGHERI, L *Pratolino, il giardino delle meraviglie*, 2 Vols (Florence, 1987).

ZANGHERI, L *Ville della provincia di Firenze: la città* (Milan, 1989).

Index

PHOTOGRAPHIC CREDITS
(l = left, r = right, t = top, b = bottom, c = center)

ALINARI
27, 289 (b)

ARCHIVIO COMMUNALE, Firenze
85

NICOLÒ ORSI BATTAGLINI
2–3, 15, 17 (t), 24 (r), 26, 28–29, 30 (r), 33, 35, 40, 42, 54, 56, 58, 59, 63, 69, 70 (r), 72, 73, 80 (t & b), 82, 83, 90, 93 (b), 95, 96 (r), 97, 100 (r), 105 (t & b), 109, 110, 112 (lt, lb & r), 113 (bl), 118 (c), 119, 134, 168 (b), 173 (b), 174 (t), 188 (l), 189, 223 (tl & tr), 239, 241 (l), 270, 271 (b), 272, 273, 284–85, 293 (l & r), 294, 295 (l & r), 298 (l & r), 299, 300–301, 302, 303

BIBLIOTECA NAZIONALE, Firenze Ms.Magl.XXV 551 fol. 29r
16

BIBLIOTHEQUE NATIONALE DE PARIS, Lat. 4802 Prolemy, folio 132v.
57

© MARIO CIAMPI
4–5, 18–19, 20, 22, 24 (l), 31, 32, 38 (r), 39, 53, 55, 68 (l), 76, 79, 86–87, 88, 89, 92, 93 (t), 106, 115, 116–17, 123, 124 (l), 125 (b), 127, 131, 140 (l & r), 141, 142, 143 (l), 145, 148, 154, 155, 177, 183, 191, 197 (br), 198–99, 200 (t), 201, 207, 225, 229, 234 (r), 235, 240, 242 (l & r), 247, 249, 253l, 256 (b), 258, 261, 262 (t), 263, 265 (l), 268 (r), 274 (r), 279, 280–81, 282, 283, 286, 287, 296, 297 (t & b)

REPRODUCED BY PERMISSION OF THE PROVOST AND FELLOWS OF ETON COLLEGE
171

DAVID FINN
70 (l)

FOTOTECA UNIONE, Roma
113 (tl)

RICHARD GOY
14, 21, 30 (l), 34, 36 (t), 37, 43, 50 (l), 60 (l & r), 68 (r), 74, 101, 107, 129 (r), 132 (r), 150 (r), 156, 157, 158, 159, 173 (t), 178, 179 (t), 181 (t), 205 (l), 260 (tl), 264, 265 (tr), 277 (l), 292

INDEX, Firenze
62, 125 (t), 137, 150 (l) / photo Cantarelli 146, 192 (tl), 224 (l), 246 (l), 253 (r), 275, 276, 277 (r), 278 / photo Perugi 233, 271 (t) / photo Summerfield 49 / photo Tosi 12–13, 197 (bl), 205 (r), 254

ISTITUTO DI STORIA DELL'ARCHITETTURA E RESTAURO, UNIVERSITY DI FIRENZE
126, 208 (b)

© KÖNEMANN VERLAGSGESELLSCHAFT, PHOTO ACHIM BEDNORZ, Cologne
96 (l), 99, 108, 114 (tr), 160–61, 168 (t), 193, 197 (t), 227

MUSEO DELL'OPERA DEL DUOMO, Siena
100 (l)

MUSEO NAZIONALE, Firenze
232

MUSEUM OF FINE ARTS, Boston
46

THE NATIONAL GALLERY, London
52 (b), 118 (t)

PHAIDON ARCHIVE
61, 67, 84 (l & r), 98, 102 (l & r), 111, 120 (t, cl & br), 121 (t & b), 130, 132 (l), 136, 165, 166, 179 (b), 186, 188 (r), 192 (tr), 203 (l & r), 208 (b), 210 (l & r), 219, 221, 223 (b), 228, 230, 232, 241 (r), 246 (br), 260 (tr), 268 (bl) / A. Blunt, *Festschrift* 147 (r) / G. Fanelli, *Le citta nella storia d'Italia 77* / L. da Ginori Lisci, *I Palazzi di Firenze nella storia e nell'arte* (Firenze, 1972) 260 (b) / A.H.V Grandjean de Montigny, *Architecture toscane ou palais, maisons et autres edifices de la Toscane* 36 (b), 104 (b), 139 147 (l), 151, 152, 153, 192 (bl), 194, 209, 214, 215, 218, 224 (r), 256 (tl & tr), 265 (rb) / W&E Paatz, *Die Kirchen von Florenz* 200 (cr)

© ANTONIO QUATTRONE
38 (l), 41, 44 (t & b), 52 (t), 71, 91, 133, 143 (r), 168 (c), 182, 184–85, 190, 245 (l), 259, 260 (b), 289 (tr)

RABATTI & DOMINGIE PHOTOGRAPHY
25, 51, 65, 104 (t), 128, 167, 175, 211, 212–13

RIBA PHOTOGRAPHS COLLECTION / G. Fanelli *Firenze: architettura e città*, vol 2 (1973)
50 (r), 124 (r), 129 (l), 181 (b), 192 (br), 195, 202, 204 (t & b), 255 (r), 262 (b), 274 (l)

RIBA PHOTOGRAPHS COLLECTION / Florenz Deutsche Kunstverlag, (1983)
139 (b)

RIBA PHOTOGRAPHS COLLECTION / F. Ruggieri, *Edifici di Firenze . . .* (1755) vol ii:
234 (tl & bl), vol iii: 174 (b), vol iv: 236 (l & r)

SCALA
17 (cl), 66, 208 (t), 217, 231, 244, 245 (r), 246 (tr), 255 (l), 268 (tl)

SOPRINTENDENZA AI BENI ARTISTICI E STORICI, Florence
170

UFFIZI, Gabinetto Disegni e Stampe, 248 A.r
113 (tr)

Phaidon Press Limited
Regent's Wharf
All Saints Street
London N1 9PA

Phaidon Press Inc.
180 Varick Street
New York, NY 10014

www.phaidon.com

First published 2002

ISBN 0 7148 3911 6

A CIP catalogue record for this book is available from the British Library.

Printed in China

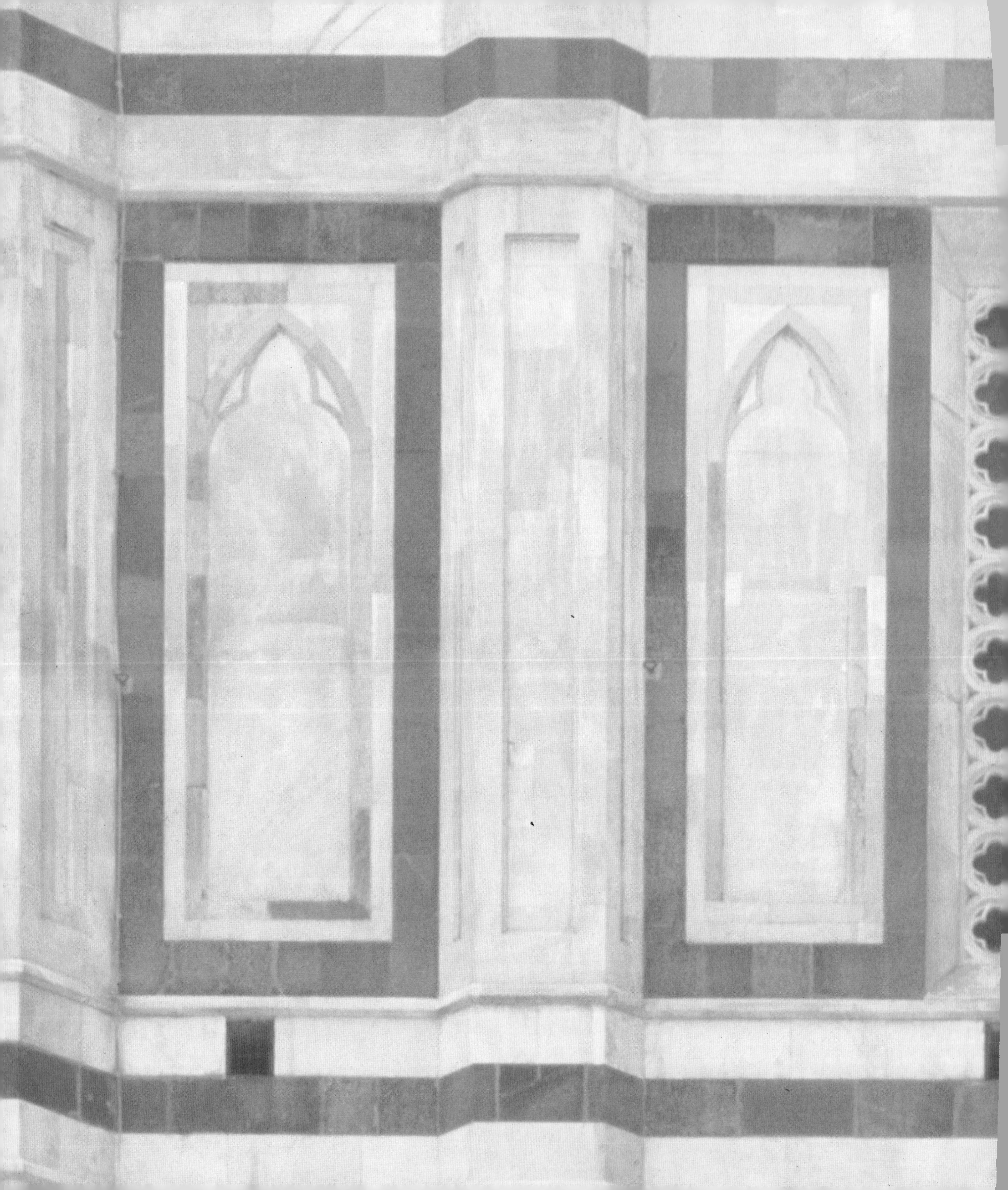